Carolin Gebauer
Making Time

Narratologia

Contributions to Narrative Theory

Edited by
Fotis Jannidis, Matías Martínez, John Pier,
Wolf Schmid (executive editor)

Editorial Board
Catherine Emmott, Monika Fludernik, José Ángel García Landa, Inke Gunia,
Peter Hühn, Manfred Jahn, Markus Kuhn, Uri Margolin, Jan Christoph Meister,
Ansgar Nünning, Marie-Laure Ryan, Jean-Marie Schaeffer, Michael Scheffel,
Sabine Schlickers

Volume 77

Carolin Gebauer

Making Time

World Construction in the Present-Tense Novel

DE GRUYTER

ISBN 978-3-11-128024-0
e-ISBN (PDF) 978-3-11-070813-4
e-ISBN (EPUB) 978-3-11-070819-6
ISSN 1612-8427

Library of Congress Control Number: 2021931845

Bibliographic information published by the Deutsche Nationalbibliothek
The Deutsche Nationalbibliothek lists this publication in the Deutsche Nationalbibliografie;
detailed bibliographic data are available on the Internet at http://dnb.dnb.de.

© 2022 Walter de Gruyter GmbH, Berlin/Boston
This volume is text- and page-identical with the hardback published in 2021.
Printing and binding: CPI books GmbH, Leck

www.degruyter.com

For my grandmother

Acknowledgments

This book is the revised version of a Ph.D. thesis I submitted to the Faculty of Humanities of the University of Wuppertal in November 2019. The defense took place in February 2020.

I am indebted in the first place to my supervisor Roy Sommer, who supported my studies and doctoral thesis in the best possible way, enabling me to write this book in a stimulating and cooperative environment. For countless inspiring conversations, crucial advice, tireless patience, and unwavering motivation and encouragement, as well as critical and constructive feedback, I am profoundly grateful. I also owe a large debt of gratitude to Ansgar Nünning, the external reviewer of my thesis. His work has always been a great inspiration for my own thinking and writing and I am deeply grateful for his invaluable feedback on this book and the generosity with which he has supported my academic work. During my doctoral studies, I was fortunate to have profited at many levels from the staff of the University of Wuppertal's Center for Narrative Research, and I would especially like to thank Birgit Spengler, Sandra Heinen, and Katharina Rennhak for valuable comments and fruitful discussions of my research project. I must also thank the editors of *DIEGESIS* for accepting me into the journal's executive team from its inception, and for enabling me to establish many contacts within the narratological world. To the editors of *Narratologia*, especially Matías Martínez and Wolf Schmid, I am indebted for including my book in their renowned series, and I wish to thank Myrto Aspioti, Stella Diedrich, and Elisabeth Stanciu at De Gruyter's for their support and assistance in preparing the manuscript for publication.

At various stages of my book's development I have been able to present my work for discussion at conferences of the International Society for the Study of Narrative and the European Narratology Network, at the Summer Course in Narrative Studies at Aarhus University, at the Frankfurt Memory Studies Platform, and at several workshops co-organized by Wuppertal's Center for Narrative Research and the Graduate Schools "Factual and Fictional Narration" at the University of Freiburg and "Practices of Literature" at the University of Münster. To all of these organizations I am grateful for their support. For their helpful feedback and stimulating conversations I am especially grateful to Jan Alber, Dorothee Birke, Marco Caracciolo, Maria Dorr, Astrid Erll, Dominique Hipp, Stefan Iversen, Erin James, Elizabeth King, Karin Kukkonen, Susan S. Lanser, Marlene Marcussen, Lena Mattheis, Brian J. McAllister, Jarmila Mildorf, Elizabeth Nixon, Nancy Pedri, Brian Richardson, David Rodriguez, and Sean A. Yeager. My special thanks go to Monika Fludernik and James Phelan for their reading recommendations and motivating feedback on my first ideas on the functional potential of present-tense narration, which encouraged me to keep looking for further uses of the fictional present in contemporary narrative fiction. I would also like to thank Irmtraud Huber, whose inspiring study on present-tense narration in contemporary narrative fiction provided a great starting point for my own reflections. To Jan Alber and James Phelan I am, moreover, indebted for granting me the ISSN Graduate Student International Travel Award 2018, and I gratefully acknowledge the financial support of the German Academic Exchange Service that enabled me to attend various conferences abroad.

I am likewise grateful for the many programs and initiatives at my home university run by the Center for Graduate Studies and the former Ph.D. network *International promovieren in Wuppertal*, which created a welcoming and supportive environment for Ph.D. students. I had the opportunity to discuss the progress of my project on a regular basis with my fellow participants in the doctoral colloquium at the Department of English and American Studies and the members of the interdisciplinary narrative research working group "AG Erzählforschung" – the inspiring discussions that evolved in this environment were always highly appreciated. Besides Janine Hauthal, who followed my research with the greatest interest and friendly advice, I have many close colleagues to thank for their support, especially during the final stage of my project, most of all Luisa Banki, Martin Dreher, Meike Dreiner, Lea Espinoza Garrido, Julian Hanebeck, Bettina Hofmann, Nicholas Hurford, Tobias Keith, Monika Kieslich, Svenja Kneer, Tobias Korte, Wolf Christoph Seifert, Katharina Thome, Marie Vent, Julia Wewior, and Antonius Weixler. To Joseph Swann, who read the final version of my manuscript, I am especially indebted for his proofreading and copy editing skills. Any remaining mistakes and typos in this book are my own.

Last but not least, my deepest thanks are due to my friends – Nicole, Svenja, Linda, Cathy and Dave, Maria and Ryan, Ulf and Bojana – and my family. My wonderful nieces and nephews always knew how to make me forget the amount of work still to be done and to enjoy the here and now with them. My gratitude for the overwhelming support of my sisters Nicolé and Kerstin during times of personal crisis is impossible to put into words. However, I owe my largest debt of gratitude to my parents Inge and Karl-Heinz Gebauer, without whose encouragement and reassurance I would have never had the emotional strength that was required to accomplish the demanding – and sometimes quite stressful – task of writing this book.

Carolin Gebauer
Wuppertal, December 2020

Contents

List of Figures and Tables —— XV

Abbreviations of Titles —— XVII

1 Introduction —— 1
1.1 Present-Tense Usage in Contemporary Narrative Fiction: A New Debate —— 1
1.2 Theoretical Preliminaries: The Relation between Present-Tense Narration, Time, and Narrative Worldmaking —— 8
1.3 Beyond the 'Grammatical' Fallacy: Key Arguments and Structure of this Book —— 11

Part I: Mapping the Research Field on Present-Tense Narration

2 Linguistic, Narratological, and Philosophical Considerations on Tense Usage in Narrative Fiction —— 21
2.1 The Beginnings of a Theoretical Engagement with Fictional Tense Usage: Käte Hamburger's Thoughts on the Epic Preterite and Their Consequences for Present-Tense Narration —— 21
2.2 Diachronic Approaches to Present-Tense Narration: The Evolution of the Present Tense as a Genuine Tense of Narration —— 25
2.3 Synchronic Approaches to Present-Tense Narration: Investigating the Present Tense from an Interdisciplinary Perspective —— 29
2.3.1 Linguistic Approaches: Present-Tense Usage as a Disqualifier of Narrative —— 30
2.3.2 Narratological Approaches: The Structuralist Understanding of Narrative and the Problematic Case of Present-Tense Narration —— 35
2.3.2.1 Conceptual Problems of Fictional Present-Tense Usage: Implications of Simultaneous Narration for the Narratological Paradigm —— 37
2.3.2.2 Alternatives to Simultaneous Narration: Attempts at 'Naturalizing' the Fictional Present Tense —— 40
2.3.3 Philosophical Approaches: On the Irrelevance of a Tensed Understanding of Time in Narrative Fiction —— 45

Part II: A Narratological Model of Present-Tense Usage in Narrative Fiction

3   The 'Grammatical' Fallacy, or: Why We Need a Descriptive and Analytical Model of Present-Tense Narration —— 53

4   The Formal-Structural Dimension of Fictional (Present-)Tense Usage: Textual Distribution and Narrative Orchestration —— 64
4.1   Formal Criteria for Determining the Distribution of Tense Usage in Narrative Fiction: Variety, Scope, and Prominence —— 64
4.2   Structural Criteria for Analyzing the Orchestration of Tense Usage in Narrative Fiction: Tense Alternation and Foregrounding of Tense —— 68

5   The Functional Dimension of Fictional Present-Tense Usage: Uses and Functions of Present-Tense Narration —— 81
5.1   Encoding the Here-and-Now: Present-Tense Narration and Narrative Worldmaking —— 81
5.2   The Referential Function —— 86
5.3   The Immersive Function —— 94
5.4   The Metareferential Function —— 98
5.5   The Communicative Function —— 106
5.6   The Synchronizing Function —— 110
5.7   The Thematic Function —— 119
5.8   The Rhetorical Function —— 121
5.9   The Transmodal Function —— 128
5.10   Modeling the Process of Worldmaking in Present-Tense Narration, or: The Functional Matrix of Fictional Present-Tense Usage —— 136

6   The Syntactic Dimension of Fictional Present-Tense Usage: Correlations between (Different Kinds of) Present-Tense Narration and Other Narrative Strategies and/or Phenomena —— 140
6.1   The Multifunctionality of Fictional Present-Tense Usage —— 140
6.2   The Functional Interplay of Present-Tense Narration with Other Narrative Strategies and/or Phenomena —— 142

Part III: Uses and Functions of Present-Tense Narration in Contemporary Narrative Fiction

7   **Narrative of Reformation: The Revision of History and Narrative Form in Hilary Mantel's *Wolf Hall* (2003) and *Bring Up the Bodies* (2012) —— 151**

7.1   The Revisionist Character of Mantel's Tudor Narratives: Turning a Historical Villain into a Fictional Hero —— 151

7.2   Creating a Likeable Character: The Empathic Impact of Mantel's Referential Use of the Fictional Present —— 158

7.3   Foresight Instead of Hindsight: Representing History as Future Turning Points —— 164

7.4   Witnessing History in the Making: Spatial Non-Contextualization, Associative Storytelling, and the Immersive Potential of Mantel's Present-Tense Usage —— 168

8   **Narrative of Punishment: Experientiality, Immersion, and the Representation of Narrative Space in Margaret Atwood's *Oryx and Crake* (2003) —— 173**

8.1   Encountering Unknown Worlds to Come: Anthropocene Fiction as a Model for Reality —— 173

8.2   Before and After the Apocalypse: Temporalizing Atwood's Heterogeneous Use of Fictional Tense —— 180

8.3   Posthuman Space, Episodic Plot Structure, and the Thematic and Descriptive Functions of the Fictional Present —— 182

8.4   Dynamic Descriptions and the Immersive Function of Present-Tense Narration —— 190

9   **Narrative of Reminiscence: Intercultural Understanding and Narrative Empathy in Nadeem Aslam's *Maps for Lost Lovers* (2004) —— 194**

9.1   Nurturing the Intercultural Mind: The Empathic Potential of Intercultural Narratives —— 194

9.2   Addressing an Out-Group Readership: Tense-Switching and the Communicative Situation of Aslam's Novel —— 199

9.3   Foregrounding Narrative Space: The Topochronic Dynamics of Aslam's Narrative —— 205

9.4   Narrative Immediacy and Hyper-Analepsis as Means of Strategic Empathizing —— 213

10	**Narrative of Deception: Narrative Progression, Suspense, and Surprise in Don Winslow's *The Power of the Dog* (2005) — 218**
10.1	About Drug Lords, DEA Agents, and Webs of Deception — 218
10.2	Spatial Disorientation, Narrative Sequentiality, and Temporal Immersion: Winslow's Chronotopic Present-Tense Narration — 221
10.3	Leading the Reader Up the Garden Path: Covert Omniscient Narration and Orchestrated Multiperspectivity — 228
10.4	Creating Suspense and Surprise: The Narrative Dynamics of the Thriller — 235
11	**Narrative of Emergence: Metanarration, Intertextuality, and the Disclosure of Worldmaking in Ian McEwan's *Nutshell* (2016) — 240**
11.1	First Contact with a Narrating Fetus — 240
11.2	Framing the Narrative Scenario: Metareferential Present-Tense Narration as a Means to Naturalize McEwan's Antimimetic Narrator — 242
11.3	Delayed Exposition, Emerging Plot, and Narratorial Inferences: Combining Synchronizing, Thematic, and Descriptive Uses of the Fictional Present — 248
11.4	The Play with Generic Conventions: McEwan's Intertextual References to the Detective Novel — 251
12	**Narrative of Emancipation: Character-Centered Illusion, Cognitive Dissonance, and Narrative Unreliability in Emma Donoghue's *Room* (2010) — 257**
12.1	'Strange' Narrators, Cognitive Dissonance, and Character-Centered Illusion — 257
12.2	Exploring "Room": Jack's Strange Perception of the World and the Dominant Use of Thematic Present-Tense Narration — 261
12.3	Taking Jack's Perspective: Immersive Present-Tense Usage, Unreliable Narration, and Suspense — 266
12.4	Adapting to "Outer Space": Descriptions, Explanations, and the Transmodal Function of the Fictional Present — 271

13	Narrative of Life: Orality, Narrative Authority, and the (Broken) Illusion of Immediacy in Irvine Welsh's *Skagboys* (2012) and *Dead Men's Trousers* (2018) —— 276
13.1	Narrative Expansion and the Representation of Time: Some Preliminary Thoughts on the Temporal Structure of Prequels, Coquels, and Sequels —— 276
13.2	A Different Kind of Narrative Illusion: The Communicative Function of Present-Tense Narration, Small Stories, and Narrative (In)Coherence —— 280
13.3	Oral Storytelling vs. Written Narrative: The Nexus between Fictional Tense Usage and Narrative Authority —— 289
13.4	The Broken Illusion of Narrative Immediacy: Why the Concept of 'Telling to the Moment' Is Not Always Successful —— 292
14	Concluding Remarks, or: The Future of Research on Present-Tense Narration —— 301
14.1	What This Book Has to Offer... —— 301
14.2	... What Else Could Be in Store... —— 306
14.3	... and What the Present-Tense Novel Can Tell Us about Contemporary Culture —— 310

Works Cited —— 319

Author Index —— 361

Subject Index —— 367

List of Figures and Tables

Figures

Figure 1: A Model for the Process of Worldmaking in Present-Tense Narration —— 137
Figure 2: The Process of Worldmaking in Different Present-Tense Novels
    – Sample Novel A —— 138
Figure 3: The Process of Worldmaking in Different Present-Tense Novels
    – Sample Novel B —— 138
Figure 4: The Process of Worldmaking in Different Present-Tense Novels
    – Sample Novel C —— 139
Figure 5: The Process of Worldmaking in Different Present-Tense Novels
    – Sample Novel D —— 139

Tables

Table 1: Distribution of Fictional Tense in Ali Smith's *Hotel World* (2002 [2001]) —— 77
Table 2: Formal and Structural Categories for Analyzing Fictional Tense Usage —— 80
Table 3: Correlations of Present-Tense Narration with Other Narrative Strategies
    and/or Phenomena —— 142
Table 4: Analytical Categories for Describing the Correlation between Present-Tense
    Narration and Other Narrative Strategies —— 148
Table 5: Distribution of the Various Narrators in Welsh's *Skagboys* (2012) —— 280

Abbreviations of Titles

AA	Walter Abish, *Alphabetical Africa*
BB	A. L. Kennedy, *The Blue Book*
BC	David Mitchell, *The Bone Clocks*
BUB	Hilary Mantel, *Bring Up the Bodies*
CI	Mark Haddon, *The Curious Incident of the Dog in the Night-Time*
DC	Charles Dickens, *David Copperfield*
DMT	Irvine Welsh, *Dead Men's Trousers*
HF	Nick Hornby, *High Fidelity*
HT	Margaret Atwood, *The Handmaid's Tale*
J	Alain Robbe-Grillet, *Jealousy*
MD	Herman Melville, *Moby-Dick; or, The Whale*
MLL	Nadeem Aslam, *Maps for Lost Lovers*
N	Ian McEwan, *Nutshell*
NM	Halle Butler, *The New Me*
OC	Margaret Atwood, *Oryx and Crake*
OS	Richard Powers, *The Overstory*
P	Samuel Richardson, *Pamela; or, Virtue Rewarded*
PA	James Joyce, *A Portrait of the Artist as a Young Man*
PD	Don Winslow, *The Power of the Dog*
"*PT*"	Hilary Mantel, "The Present Tense"
R	Emma Donoghue, *Room*
RC	Daniel Defoe, *Robinson Crusoe*
S	Henry Fielding, *Shamela*
SB	Irvine Welsh, *Skagboys*
ST	Zadie Smith, *Swing Time*
SV	Don Winslow, *Savages*
T	Nick McDonell, *Twelve*
TJ	Henry Fielding, *Tom Jones: The History of a Foundling*
TND	Corey Mesler, *Talk: A Novel in Dialogue*
TS	Laurence Sterne, *The Life and Opinions of Tristram Shandy, Gentleman*
VF	William Makepeace Thackeray, *Vanity Fair: A Novel Without a Hero*
WH	Hilary Mantel, *Wolf Hall*
WN	Italo Calvino, *If on a Winter's Night a Traveler*

The abbreviations refer to the editions listed in the bibliography.

1 Introduction

Since histories must be in the past, then the more past the better, it would seem, for them in their character as histories, and for him, the teller of them, rounding wizard of times gone by.

– Thomas Mann, "Foreword"
to *The Magic Mountain*

1.1 Present-Tense Usage in Contemporary Narrative Fiction: A New Debate

Kazunari Miyahara opens his 2009 article "Why Now, Why Then?: Present-Tense Narration in Contemporary British and Commonwealth Novels" with a quiz: enumerating six novels by Anne Enright, DBC Pierre, J. M. Coetzee, Graham Swift, Penelope Lively, and Keri Hulme, he asks what they have in common. The answer he is looking for is not that these six narratives, published between 1984 and 2003, have all won the Booker Prize, but that they are all "narrated basically in the present tense" (Miyahara 2009, 241). After revealing this, Miyahara goes on to name further present-tense novels published within the same time span, each of which pertains to a different genre. These include a fictional autobiography by Margaret Atwood, a mystery novel by Deborah Moggach, a prose-poem by Jacqueline Wilson, a picture book for children by Paul McCartney and Philip Ardagh, and a techno-thriller by Paul J. McAuley.

In retrospect, one can say that Miyahara observed the beginning of a new aesthetic trend. Today, more than ten years later, one could easily substitute more recent narratives for those in his enumeration and propose the conundrum again. What do the following novels have in common: Margaret Atwood's speculative narrative *The Heart Goes Last* (2016 [2015]), Avni Doshi's *Burnt Sugar* (2020), a novel about dementia and the relationship between mother and daughter, *Infinite Detail* (2019), Tim Maughan's debut novel which was declared *The Guardian*'s best science fiction and fantasy book of 2019 (cf. Roberts 2019, n.p.), E. L. James's bestselling erotic romance trilogy – *Fifty Shades of Grey* (2012 [2011]b), *Fifty Shades Darker* (2012 [2011]a), and *Fifty Shades Freed* (2012); Christina Dalcher's *Vox* (2018), a dystopian novel about the suppression of women's right to speak and use language in a futuristic America; the internationally bestselling thriller *Gone Girl* (2012) by Gillian Flynn; *Autumn* (2016), *Winter* (2017), *Spring* (2019), and *Summer* (2020), Ali Smith's "Seasonal Quartet" dealing with current sociopolitical issues such as Brexit, the European refugee crisis, climate change activism, or the COVID-19 pandemic; Louise O'Neill's *Asking for It* (2016 [2015]), an Irish narrative about rape; Rachel Seiffert's *The Dark Room* (2002 [2001]), a historical novel about the German nazi regime; *The Light of Day* (2018 [2003]), a mysterious detective novel by Graham Swift; Suzanne Collins's young adult trilogy – *The Hunger Games* (2011 [2008]), *Catching Fire* (2011 [2009]), and *Mockingjay* (2011 [2010]); Joanne Ramos's *The Farm* (2019), a novel about commercial surrogacy; Meredith Russo's GLBTQ novel *Birthday: A Love Story Eighteen Years in the Making* (2019); and Richard Powers's *The Overstory* (2018), winner of the 2019 Pulitzer Prize for Fiction? In 2020, one could continue this list at length, while the answer to Miyahara's question remains the same: all these contemporary novels share the aesthetic feature of being written, either entirely or at least largely, in the present tense. In other words, they all defy a notion of narrative which Thomas Mann still took for granted when he wrote the foreword to his modern classic *Der Zauberberg* [*The Magic Mountain*] in 1924 – namely that stories ought to be told with the benefit of hindsight and therefore in the past tense.[1]

The evident popularity of present-tense narration among contemporary novelists has given rise to a new debate about narrative aesthetics. Both authors and critics have recently been arguing as to whether narrative fiction should be written in the past or present tense, advocating their disparate positions across various channels of public discourse. In her short story "The Present Tense," published in the *London Review of Books* in January 2016, Hilary Mantel, for example, has her first-person narrator, a female high school teacher, ask her students, "[W]hat makes a good story?" (19). Mantel's narrative closely reproduces the classroom discussion, during which the teacher and her students jointly compile a list of features the teacher had in mind when asking the question: "Suspense. Characters we care about. A cracking pace. Not too much description. Touch of humour. Smart dialogue. A twist in the ending." ("PT," 19) What is interesting about this list is that far more of its items relate to the design than to the content of a narrative. According to Mantel's high school teacher, a good story defines itself not so much by its plot as by the way it presents its plot to the reader.

---

1 In the German original of Mann's quotation in the epigraph, the aspect of tense becomes even more explicit, as Mann actually describes the teller of stories as a "rounding wizard of the imperfect tense" rather than "of times gone by": "[...] denn Geschichten müssen vergangen sein, und je vergangener, könnte man sagen, desto besser für sie in ihrer Eigenschaft als Geschichten und für den Erzähler, den raunenden Beschwörer des Imperfekts." (Mann 1990 [1924], 9)

But there is one central narrative strategy the high school teacher has forgotten to include in her list: the use of tense. Not only does the title of the story, "The Present Tense," draw readers' attention to the fact that the narrative is written in the present tense, but the narrator even stages this specific choice of tense as a means to render her story more interesting for the narratee. Thus, when she pauses the account of her classroom discussion in order to describe the interior of the school building (a former boarding school), she is almost apologetic about having to temporarily switch to the past tense: "Each classroom . . . and here I should be drifting towards the past tense, but stay with me, if you will . . ." ("PT," 19) Taken together, the title of Mantel's short story and the narrator's metanarrative comment on tense usage imply a certain authorial predilection for the present tense. Indeed, readers who are familiar with Mantel's fiction will know that she frequently employs present-tense narration. In her most recent award-nominated and award-winning novels *Wolf Hall* (2010 [2009]), *Bring Up the Bodies* (2013 [2012]), and *The Mirror & the Light* (2020), the present tense even features as the dominant tense of narration.

The present tense is, however, not everyone's cup of tea. Dorte Hansen, the 21-year-old narrator of Helle Helle's novel *This Should Be Written in the Present Tense* (2014 [2011]), goes so far as to report current events in the past tense, admitting to the reader that she "hated the narrative present" (57). Although this may sound exaggerated, many readers may well share Dorte's strong aversion. When the Man Booker Prize jury announced the 2010 competition finalists, they received harsh criticism for shortlisting three novels written largely in the present tense: Tom McCarthy's *C* (2010), Emma Donoghue's *Room* (2010), and Damon Galgut's *In a Strange Room* (2010).[2] As the previous year's winner of Britain's most coveted literary prize, Mantel's *Wolf Hall*, was also written entirely in the present tense, literary critics were evidently tired of this new trend. They did not hesitate to express their indignation publicly: The present tense suddenly became a topic of widespread discussion in the review pages of newspapers, with most articles lamenting rather than praising it.[3]

The leading voices in this debate were the British authors Philip Hensher and Philip Pullman. Their criticism of the increasing use of the present tense in contemporary narrative fiction is summarized in an article published in *The*

---

[2] Irmtraud Huber (2016, 1–2) refers to the public debate surrounding the final nominees for the Man Booker Prize 2010 in the introduction to her monograph on present-tense narration in contemporary fiction. In his study on the notion of the present, *What is the Present?* (2018), Michael North likewise discusses this debate (cf. 130–131).
[3] Cf. e.g. Hensher 2010, Lea 2010, Miller 2010, Mullan 2010, Pullman 2010, and Roberts 2010.

Telegraph (cf. Roberts 2010): while Hensher is cited as saying the present tense sprawled across the English novel "like Japanese knotweed,"[4] Pullman apparently called it "a silly affectation" that "does nothing but annoy" (Roberts 2010, n.p.).[5] The dismissive stance of the two authors seems to reiterate a critique of present-tense narration from over 30 years ago. In the article "A Failing Grade for the Present Tense," published in *The New York Times* in 1987, William H. Gass had already voiced his disapproval of the growing tendency among novelists to deploy the present as the dominant tense of narration, comparing it to a rampant literary disease:

> What was once a rather rare disease has become an epidemic. In conjunction with the first person, in collusion with the declarative mode, in company with stammery elisions and verbal reticence – each often illnesses in their own right – it [i.e. the present tense] has become that major social and artistic malaise called minimalism, itself a misnomer. (Gass 1987, n.p.)[6]

All these examples suggest that, almost a century after Mann's emphatic assertion that stories "must be in the past," present-tense narration has become a major issue for contemporary authors and literary critics. Indeed, we face an unprecedented boom in narratives whose tense defies the conventions of traditional literary storytelling. After all, novelists long confined themselves to using the present tense merely as a rhetorical device that served to highlight specific narrative events within an otherwise past-tense context (this specific use of the present tense is traditionally referred to as the *historical present*), but they have now started to test the potential of that tense as a consistent and dominant tense of narration.[7] While in the 1950s the present tense was still considered an

---

4 For Hensher's complete statement on the present tense, cf. Hensher 2010.
5 In his personal statement in *The Guardian*, published a week after the article in *The Telegraph*, Pullman (2010, n.p.) repeated his criticism of the present tense, albeit in weakened form: "What I did say, in an email to the Telegraph journalist who asked me about it, was that the use of the present tense in fiction had been getting more and more common, and I didn't like it."
6 Interestingly enough, Gass additionally claims that present-tense narration is most commonly used by women writers (cf. 1987, n.p.). It is only a coincidence that most of the present-tense novels I have enumerated at the beginning of this Introduction were also written by female writers. However, the present study contains more novels by male than by female authors, which suggests that Gass's contention is no longer valid today.
7 In her article "Chronology, Time, Tense and Experientiality in Narrative" (2003a), Monika Fludernik distinguishes three different types of present-tense usage in narrative texts: (1) the deictic use of the present tense, which points to the communicative situation between the narrator and his or her narratee, (2) the intermittent use of the present tense, which is also

unusual characteristic of the French *nouveau roman*, it qualifies today as a common narrative feature that is no longer restricted to experimental fiction. We encounter it in various genres, ranging from the historical novel to science fiction, from romance to thriller, from young adult fiction to children's books. Bestsellers like Suzanne Collins's *Hunger Games* series (2008–2010), Paula Hawkins's *The Girl on the Train* (2015), or E. L. James's *Fifty Shades of Grey* trilogy (2010–2011) are written in the present tense; and present-tense narration can also be found in critically acclaimed literary fiction, as more and more novelists – J. M. Coetzee, Margaret Atwood, and Ian McEwan, to name only three – have started to deploy it in their work as well.

Further evidence for the continuing growth of the corpus of present-tense narrative can be found in the longlists and shortlists for literary awards. The 2019 Booker shortlist again contained two novels written largely in the present tense – Lucy Ellmann's *Ducks, Newburyport* (2019) and Bernadine Evaristo's *Girl, Woman, Other* (2019) – as well as two that combine past and present tenses: Margaret Atwood's *The Testaments* (2019), which uses the present tense in an otherwise past-tense account whenever one of the three first-person narrators reflects upon her act of sharing her personal experiences with a potential future reader, and Chigozie Obioma's *An Orchestra of Minorities* (2019), which is mostly written in the past tense, but with almost all its twenty-six chapters opening in the present tense. A year later, present-tense narrative even dominated the Booker longlist. Consisting of 13 novels in total, the "Booker Dozen" of 2020 featured six present-tense novels – Tsitsi Dangarembga's *This Mournable Body* (2018), Avni Doshi's *Burnt Sugar* (2020), Gabriel Krauze's *Who They Was* (2020), Hilary Mantel's *The Mirror & the Light* (2020), Maaza Mengiste's *The Shadow King* (2019), and C Pam Zhang's *How Much of These Hills Is Gold* (2020) – as well as Colum McCann's *Apeirogon* (2020), which occasionally deploys the intermittent present tense in a predominantly past-tense discourse, and Anne Tyler's *Redhead By the Side of the Road* (2020), in which the local use of the present-tense both at the beginning and the end of the novel frames an otherwise past-tense narrative.[8] The phenomenon of present-tense narration thus features even more prominently among recent nominees for the Booker Prize than it did in the shortlist of 2010, which sparked the controversial debate among novelists and

---

known as the historical present tense, and (3) the consistent use of the present tense, which spans entire novels or at least longer passages of text (cf. Fludernik 2003a, 124). Although I am primarily concerned here with Fludernik's third type of present-tense usage, the consistent use of the present tense, the other two types will also be discussed where necessary.

8 The 2020 Booker shortlist was announced shortly after completion of this Introduction.

literary critics ten years ago. What is more, the fact that the 2019 jury decided to award the prize to two novels which make considerable use of the present tense – Atwood's *The Testaments* and Evaristo's *Girl, Woman, Other* – suggests that present-tense narration has also gained increasing popularity among literary critics.[9]

Needless to say, the new trend has not gone unnoticed by literary scholars. In her monograph *Present-Tense Narration in Contemporary Fiction: A Narratological Overview* (2016), Irmtraud Huber reviews more than 40 English novels published between 2000 and 2015 that make extensive use of the present tense.[10] Interestingly enough, this development is not restricted to the Anglophone literary landscape. Jürgen H. Petersen (1992; 1993, 24) notices a similar phenomenon in contemporary German narrative fiction,[11] and Armen Avanessian and Anke Hennig (2015 [2012]) discuss not only English and German, but also French and Russian examples in their book-length study of the subject.[12] In light of this, it is fair to say that the current increase in present-tense narration in narrative fiction constitutes a far-reaching literary trend affecting many national literatures of the Western world.

Furthermore, the examples of Mantel's and Helle's narratives as well as the Man Booker Prize debate show that the present tense seems to polarize both authors and readers. Some love it (e.g. Mantel), others hate it (e.g. Helle's narrator, Hensher, Pullman, and Gass); and yet some readers simply ignore it, either because they do not care or because they fail to notice in which tense a narrative is written. "[T]he narrative present," Monika Fludernik (1996, 256) accordingly holds, "is both a rather unknown oddity and a technique of unremarked-upon familiarity." This paradoxical situation may also be the reason why, in

---

9 Since its initiation in 1969, this was only the third time that the Booker Prize has been jointly awarded to two authors; the previous joint-winners were Nadine Gordimer and Stanley Middleton in 1974 and Michael Ondaatje and Barry Unsworth in 1992 (cf. the announcement of the winners of the Booker Prize 2019 on *The Booker Prizes* homepage on October 14, 2019: https://thebookerprizes.com/resources/media/pressreleases/margaret-atwood-and-bernardine-evaristo-are-joint-winners-2019-booker, accessed August 31, 2020).
10 As Huber (2016, 3) chose her examples mainly from the longlists of the Man Booker Prize between 2000 and 2014, she primarily discusses British and Commonwealth fiction.
11 More specifically, he states that the card file underlying his study of the modern German novel, *Der deutsche Roman der Moderne* (1991), comprises 75 novels completely written in the present tense and more than 150 novels that combine past and present tenses (cf. Petersen 1992, 71). However, Petersen gives no concrete indication of the total number of novels he has examined.
12 The original German version of Avanessian and Hennig's *Präsens: Poetik eines Tempus* was published in 2012; I quote here from the English translation, published in 2015.

comparison with other grammatical categories such as 'person' (e.g. first-person narrative vs. second- and third-person narrative) or 'number' (e.g. 'I'-narration vs. 'we'-narration), the present tense has not yet received widespread attention within narrative theory. Although narratologists have already dedicated several articles or book chapters to it,[13] comprehensive studies of the phenomenon are still quite rare,[14] with the result that little of the narrative potential of the present tense has yet been accounted for in a systematic manner.

However, the growing popularity of the present tense among contemporary authors, as well as the continuing discussion of this new tendency in various media,[15] gives rise to the assumption that the phenomenon will continue to attract a wider interest in the field of literary studies, and especially in narrative studies.[16] The present book takes a first step in this direction. As the controversial reactions toward present-tense narration demonstrates, the fictional present tense is an interesting phenomenon that deserves further investigation. Building upon the valuable work of its precursors, the study will seek, then, to provide a narrative theory of present-tense narration in fiction that does justice to the particularities of this specific tense by examining it from various perspec-

---

13 Cf. e.g. Avanessian 2013; Avanessian and Hennig 2015; Cohn 1993; 1999, Ch. 6; Damsteegt 2005; DelConte 2007; D'hoker 2019; Fludernik 1996, Ch. 6.3.1; 2003a; Hansen 2008; Miyahara 2009; Ohme 2018; Petersen 1992; and Phelan 1994. Cf. also the contributions in Avanessian and Hennig's (2013b) collected volume on the present-tense novel.
14 To my knowledge, there are only four monographs on present-tense usage in narrative fiction, namely Avanessian and Hennig 2015 [2012], Casparis 1975, Damsteegt 2004, and Huber 2016. Although Theo Damsteegt's work focuses primarily on present-tense usage in Modern Hindi fiction, it nevertheless provides interesting insights into the phenomenon that can also be applied to other Indo-European languages, including Germanic languages such as English.
15 Since the debate concerning the shortlist for the Man Booker Prize 2010, the present tense has repeatedly occupied the mind of literary critics (cf. e.g. Baker 2011, Chee 2015, and Lea 2015). Besides, present-tense narration has paved its way into guidebooks on creative writing. In *On Writing Fiction: Rethinking Conventional Wisdom About the Craft* (2011), for example, creative writing professor David Jauss weighs up the advantages and disadvantages of present-tense narration (cf. Ch. 4).
16 In fact, we can already find first indications of such a development. For example, in the introduction to her monograph on present-tense narration, published in 2016, Huber observes that "[o]nly a few among the reviewers of Hilary Mantel's *Wolf Hall* (2009) and *Bring Up the Bodies* (2012) [...] have so far found her use of present-tense narration worth much comment" (2). Four years later the situation has drastically changed. I have consulted altogether 32 secondary texts on Mantel's Tudor novels, and half of these discuss, or at least mention, her unconventional use of the present tense in her historical fictions (see Chapter 4.1.1).

tives of (post-)classical narratology, including structuralist, cognitive, linguistic, and rhetorical narratology.[17]

1.2 Theoretical Preliminaries: The Relation between Present-Tense Narration, Time, and Narrative Worldmaking

From the heterogeneous reactions toward (the rise of) present-tense usage in fiction outlined above, we can draw an important conclusion. Notwithstanding the failure of some readers to notice the tense in which a narrative is written, tense usage must actually do something to a narrative text – otherwise, usage of the present tense would not polarize readers to such an extent. One may, therefore, postulate that fictional storytelling works differently in different tenses, past, present, and future; in which case an author's choice of tense will strongly influence his or her fictions. More specifically, I would argue that present-tense narration operates differently than past-tense narration with regard to the form and structure of a narrative, as well as its content. This means not only that the narrative design of present-tense narratives differs from that of past-tense narratives, but also – as Irmtraud Huber (2016, 109) rightly maintains – that present-tense narratives may allow for different stories to be told than do past-tense narratives.[18]

This leads me directly to the title of this book: *Making Time: World Construction in the Present-Tense Novel*. The main title is admittedly a little provocative, as it alludes to the stance on present-tense narration currently prevailing in the field of narrative research – something I shall challenge in this study. As I will show in Chapter 2.3.2, narratological studies on present-tense narration have so far usually associated tense usage with the aspect of time or temporality. The reason for this is that the traditional model of narrative, established mainly by Gérard Genette (1980 [1972]; 1988 [1983]) and Franz K. Stanzel (1995 [1979]), construes tense usage in narrative fiction as an indicator of the temporal relation between the narrative events and the act of narration. Within the narrato-

---

[17] For a detailed discussion of the different approaches within postclassical narratology, cf. Alber and Fludernik 2010, Nünning 2003, Nünning and Nünning 2002, and Sommer 2012. The term "linguistic narratology" stems from Fludernik (2012, 76), who uses it to designate approaches within narratology that draw primarily on linguistics to analyze narrative fiction.
[18] This study will only juxtapose present-tense with past-tense narratives, not with future-tense narratives, because, from a narratological perspective, past-tense narratives are the default case (see Chapter 2.3.2). Both present- and future-tense narratives represent deviations from this norm.

1.2 Theoretical Preliminaries: Present-Tense Narration, Time, Narrative Worldmaking

logical paradigm, then, the present tense is most often equated with a specific type of narration which simulates the practices of real-time reporting and which has become known by the terms *simultaneous narration* (cf. Genette 1980 [1972], 218–219) or *concurrent narration* (cf. Margolin 1999, 150–153). This means that present-tense narrative is frequently associated with a synchronicity between the narrative events and the account of these events: a synchronicity that manifests itself primarily in the fact that the act of narration takes up as much time as do the narrative events themselves.[19]

For two good reasons, my study endeavors to break with this tradition. First, we ought to accept that tense usage works differently in narrative fiction than it does in everyday conversation. As Dorrit Cohn contends in the "Preface" to her seminal monograph *The Distinction of Fiction* (1999), "fictional narrative is unique in its potential for crafting a self-enclosed universe ruled by formal patterns that are ruled out in all other orders of discourse" (vii). Concurring with Cohn's view on the distinctive nature of fictional discourse, I maintain that this contention specifically applies to tense usage. I particularly ground this hypothesis in Suzanne Fleischman's (1990, 1991a) work on the nexus between tense and narrativity, in which she notes "that the relationships between time and tense in narrative are not the same as those obtaining in ordinary language" (1990, 3). Although I do not fully agree with the argument she derives from this assertion (I will further elaborate on Fleischman's theory in Chapter 2.3.1), I here nevertheless adopt the premise of her studies, which I believe to be absolutely correct. Hence, I will proceed from the assumption that, in fiction, tense usage in general and present-tense narration in particular need not necessarily be related to the aspect of temporality. For, as Fludernik (2003a, 121; italics in the original) rightly observes, "[n]o natural relationship between the choice of grammatical *tense* in narratives and underlying temporal relations obtains."[20]

Secondly, we should not forget that the construction of narrative time as an integral part of narrative worldmaking (cf. Goodman 1978; Herman 2002, 2009a, 2009b) works independently from tense usage. Drawing on David Herman's (2002) argument on narrative temporalities in his renowned *Story Logic: Prob-*

---

19 A prime example of such synchronicity is real-time reporting of the kind that takes place in the live coverage of sports such as football games or baseball matches.
20 Mark Currie (2009, 354) likewise holds that, in narrative fiction, "there can be no straightforward or precise relation between the tense of a verb and the time to which it refers, and [that] the severing of this relationship makes it as possible to live the present in a mode of envisaged retrospect as to experience events tensed as past as a kind of present."

lems and Possibilities of Narrative (cf. Ch. 6), I would maintain that the representation of narrative time always involves various narrative strategies, or – to borrow Herman's term – "textual cues," which invite readers "to assign to events in the storyworld [i.e. their mental models of the fictional world] a place (relative to one another) in time" (211). According to Herman, these textual cues above all include the temporal categories of 'order,' 'duration,' and 'frequency,' as identified by Genette (1980 [1972], Ch. 1–3). Since none of these categories relates to tense usage, we can infer that the process of making narrative time does not hinge on the choice of tense. Temporal relations between narrative events can be expressed in any narrative, irrespective of whether it is written in the past, present, or future tense. We can thus find anachronies (e.g. analepses and prolepses), instances of narrative pause, scene, summary, or ellipsis, as well as singulative, repeating, or iterative narration in past-, present-, and future-tense narratives alike.[21]

In view of these observations, I contend – against many previous narratological studies of the phenomenon – that the present tense, as used in fiction, does not constitute a purely temporal category. Since the first publication of Genette's "Discours du récit" in 1972,[22] narrative theorists have reduced the use of the present tense to simultaneous narration, even though, as we have seen, tense usage does not necessarily have anything to do with the construction of time in narrative fiction. How can this dilemma be resolved? I propose that we move away from the idea that the present tense represents nothing but a verbal category and assume instead that, in fictional texts, its contribution to the process of narrative worldmaking may be greater and more various than has so far been believed. I will therefore argue here that present-tense narration qualifies as a complex narrative phenomenon that should be treated as a fully-fledged narrative strategy rather than just a temporal or linguistic category. I will show that, in narrative fiction, the present tense can achieve many more effects than it does in ordinary discourse: its narrative potential far exceeds merely pointing to the temporal relation between the narrated story and the act of narration. Moreover, that it fulfills such a wide range of different functions makes of present-tense narration a many-faceted strategy that can be effectively used in

---

21 Further evidence for this claim is the fact that the process of narrative world building also works in a tenseless language like Burmese (cf. Comrie 1985, Ch. 2.5), Chinese (cf. Lin 2012, 671–682; Smith 2008, 234–235), or several standardized varieties of Malay such as Indonesian (cf. Pipit 2019, 202), Thai (cf. Smith 2008, 239), and Vietnamese (cf. Bui 2019).
22 I here reference the 2007 edition of Genette's study, *Discours du récit: essai de méthode*, which brings together two separate essays: his "Discours du récit," first published in 1972, and "Nouveau discours du récit," first published in 1983.

numerous genres of contemporary narrative fiction, including literary as well as popular fiction.

However, it is difficult to grasp such a modified understanding of present-tense narration in terms of a paradigm of narrative grounded only in the analogy between fictional and factual discourse. A prime task of this book is to devise a narratological model of present-tense narration that provides sufficient analytical categories for us to identify and adequately describe the particular features of present-tense usage in narrative fiction. Having said this, I would once more like to stress that the aim of the study is not to develop a "tense-based theory of narrative" (Currie 2007, 150) or "tense narratology" (Currie 2013, 3) for present-tense narration – that is, a theory that allows us to describe the "tense structure" (Currie 2013, 1) according to which present-tense narratives operate.[23] While the analysis of the temporal structure of present-tense narratives is, of course, also part of my endeavor, such a restricted focus on the aspect of temporality would not do justice to the complexity of the phenomenon of present-tense narration. Rather, my project sets out to design a narrative model that extends and enhances the traditional narratological paradigm, including both its temporal and non-temporal components, so that it is adapted to the analysis of the various ways of worldmaking that become effective in the contemporary present-tense novel.

1.3 Beyond the 'Grammatical' Fallacy: Key Arguments and Structure of this Book

To realize this undertaking, I will proceed in three consecutive steps, each of which will constitute a separate main part of this book. Part I maps the research field on present-tense narrative by presenting a survey of previous research on fictional tense usage in general and present-tense narration in particular. To my knowledge, the first study to address the question of the role of tense usage in narrative fiction is Käte Hamburger's *Logik der Dichtung* [*The Logic of Litera-*

---

[23] According to Currie (2013, 1; italics in the original), the traditional past-tense narrative, for example, "operates according to a tense structure quite different from the one we normally assume for it. This tense structure is the future perfect, the tense that refers to something that lies ahead and yet which is already complete, not what *will happen*, but what *will have happened*." As will become obvious in the course of this study, present-tense narratives can – but need not necessarily – exhibit a different tense structure, namely that of the future simple, the tense that relates to something that lies ahead and is by no means complete, something that *will happen*.

ture], first published in 1957. According to Hamburger, the intermittent use of the present tense in past-tense narratives loses its significance, as its presentifying function is already fulfilled by what she refers to as the "epic preterite," that is, the narrative use of the past tense which serves to designate not so much the past as the present of the narrative events. Although Hamburger focuses exclusively on the historical present, ignoring the phenomenon of consistent or (as I will call it here) global present-tense narration, her argument on fictional tense usage is nevertheless central to my work. The reason for this is that her seminal monograph prompted many humanities scholars, including linguists, literary scholars, and philosophers, to further examine the use of tense in narrative fiction. The second chapter of this book will introduce studies which either deal explicitly with the present tense or adduce arguments on fictional tense usage in general that can be fruitfully applied to the phenomenon of present-tense narration.

More specifically, I will argue in Chapter 2 that previous research on fictional (present-)tense usage divides into two broader approaches, diachronic and synchronic. The former comprise linguistic as well as narratological studies that trace the historical evolution of the present tense as a narrative and fictional tense on par with the traditional past tense. The latter can be subdivided into three separate groups that belong to the disciplines of linguistics, narratology, and philosophy. As I will demonstrate, each of these groups construes fictional (present-)tense usage differently. While linguistic studies conceive of the present tense as a distinctive feature of non-narrative or non-fictional discourse, narratological studies do not question the narrative status of the present tense, but rather tackle the logical problem that present-tense narration violates an understanding of narrative grounded in the common belief that narration is only possible in retrospect (see Mann's quotation in the epigraph to this Introduction). Finally, the philosophical approaches in question suggest that tense usage becomes irrelevant in narrative fiction, contending that our understanding of fictional time is on principle untensed or tenseless.

Part II introduces a narratological model of present-tense tense usage in narrative fiction. On the basis of the observations in Chapter 2, I will argue that synchronic approaches proceed from different premises when engaging with present-tense narration. Although their arguments differ substantially, linguistic and philosophical approaches both imply that, in fictional contexts, tense usage functions differently than it does in ordinary discourse. Yet they fail to specify the implications such a role may entail for a narratological understanding of narrative. Narratological approaches, on the other hand, postulate that tense usage always works in the same manner, regardless of whether it is used

1.3 Beyond the 'Grammatical' Fallacy: Key Arguments and Structure of this Book — 13

in fictional or factual discourse. Against this background, Chapter 3 argues that the narratological paradigm of narrative fiction rests on what I shall refer to as *the 'grammatical' fallacy*, that is, the erroneous belief that fictional tense usage in general and present-tense narration in particular can be explained solely with recourse to the grammatical rules applying to ordinary language usage. The result of this fallacy is the conceptualization of tense as a deictic category which points to the temporal relation between the narrative events and the act of narrating these events. This, in turn, has often led to the incorrect equation of present-tense narration with simultaneous narration.

I propose to move beyond this 'grammatical' fallacy by integrating linguistic and philosophical insights on fictional tense usage into the narratological paradigm. By introducing the distinction between *grammatical tense* and *fictional tense*, I will adopt the linguistic and philosophical position that tense usage operates differently in factual and fictional discourses. Starting from this modified conceptualization of fictional tense usage, I will devise, in Chapters 4 to 6, a narratological model of fictional tense usage which allows us to better describe and adequately analyze the various dimensions of present-tense narration: its *formal-structural, functional*, and *syntactic dimensions*. The tripartite structure of this model accompanies and expresses an increase in its present-tense specificity from the formal-structural to the syntactic dimension. That is to say, the categories and concepts I shall introduce in the formal-structural part of this model hold for any fictional tense, be it the past, the present, or the future, whereas the categories I shall present in the syntactic part have been developed exclusively for the analysis of present-tense narration. The functional part of my model sits between these two poles, identifying functions of fictional tense usage that are either confined to present-tense narrative or may be relevant for all types of narrative, whether past-, present-, or future-tense.

The first part of my narratological model of (present-)tense usage – Chapter 4 – relates to the *formal-structural dimension*. Here, I will introduce three formal and two structural criteria that will allow me to propose 14 analytical categories with which to examine fictional tense usage in general. The formal criteria include (1) variety of tense usage, (2) frequency and scope of tense usage, and (3) prominence of tense usage. They will enable me to differentiate between *homogeneous* and *heterogeneous tense usage*, between *global* and *local tense usage*, and between *central* and *peripheral tense usage*, respectively. The structural criteria comprise (1) tense alternation and (2) the foregrounding of tense. Depending on whether tense alternation operates according to a specific pattern or not, I will distinguish between *tense-switching* and *tense-mixing*; with respect to tense-switching, I will, moreover, distinguish between *temporaliza-*

tion and *detemporalization*, that is, between tense shifts that are related to time and those that are not related to time. When it comes to the foregrounding of tense usage, I will present four different kinds of foregrounding: (1) *alternate foregrounding*, (2) *typographical foregrounding*, (3) *paratextual foregrounding*, and (4) *metanarrative foregrounding*.

The second part of my model, which scrutinizes the *functional dimension* of fictional tense – Chapter 5 – will introduce a matrix of fictional tense usage designed specifically to describe the textual and cognitive functions of present-tense narration. By discussing various ways in which present-tense narration may contribute to the process of narrative worldmaking, I will identify eight different potential functions of present-tense usage in narrative fiction: (1) the *referential function*, (2) the *immersive function*, (3) the *meta-referential function*, (4) the *communicative function*, (5) the *synchronizing function*, (6) the *thematic function*, (7) the *rhetorical function*, and (8) the *transmodal function*. As I will demonstrate, one half of these functions (including the referential, metareferential, thematic, and transmodal functions) may also apply to other fictional tenses such as the past or the future tense, whereas the other half (comprising the immersive, communicative, synchronizing, and rhetorical functions) is applicable exclusively to the fictional present. Furthermore, I will show that these eight functions of present-tense narration are not mutually exclusive, but could theoretically all be employed within one and the same narrative.

Finally, the third part of my model, which concerns the *syntactic dimension* of present-tense narration – Chapter 6 – will provide ten analytical categories that describe not only combinations of different uses of the fictional present, but also the correlation between present-tense narration and other narrative strategies and/or phenomena. I will develop these categories by means of the following criteria of differentiation: (1) type of correlation, (2) hierarchical relation between the correlating functions or strategies, and (3) frequency and scope of the correlating functions or strategies. With regard to the first criterion I will identify two different phenomena that can be investigated: the *multifunctionality* of present-tense narration (i.e. as involving several or all of the functions of fictional present-tense usage introduced in the second part of my narrative model) and the *functional interplay* of present-tense narration with other narrative strategies and/or phenomena. I will differentiate, in view of the multifunctionality of present-tense narration, between *dominant* and *recessive functions* (criterion 2) on the one hand, and between *recurring* and *non-recurring functions* (criterion 3) on the other. With respect to the functional interplay of present-tense narration with other narrative strategies and/or phenomena I will distinguish between *main* and *ancillary strategies* (criterion 2), as well as between *fixed* and *variable correlations* (criterion 3).

In Chapters 7 to 13, which together form the longest, third part of this book, I will deploy this tripartite narratological model to explore empirically how the present tense is used in contemporary narrative fiction. Consecutive chapters will analyze and interpret nine present-tense novels: Hilary Mantel's *Wolf Hall* (2010 [2009]) and *Bring Up the Bodies* (2013 [2012]), Margaret Atwood's *Oryx and Crake* (2004 [2003]), Nadeem Aslam's *Maps for Lost Lovers* (2006 [2004]), Don Winslow's *The Power of the Dog* (2006 [2005]), Ian McEwan's *Nutshell* (2016), Emma Donoghue's *Room* (2010), and Irvine Welsh's *Skagboys* (2012a) and *Dead Men's Trousers* (2018). The selected novels represent a wide range of genres, from the historical novel (Mantel), through the thriller (Winslow), to experimental fiction (McEwan); all of them were published in the twenty-first century (the earliest novel in my corpus being Atwood's *Oryx and Crake*, first published in 2003).[24] By including both genre fiction and literary fictions in my model interpretations, I will seek to present a comprehensive, albeit not exhaustive, picture of how the phenomenon of present-tense narration is deployed in various genres of narrative fiction.

My readings of the nine novels mentioned above pursue three different objectives. First, I will seek to show how the use of the fictional present can influence textual as well as cognitive processes of narrative world building: To what extent do these effects of tense choice have a specific bearing on textual as well as cognitive models of narrative storyworlds as a whole? To what extent do the textual as well as cognitive models of storyworlds evoked by present-tense narratives differ from those generated by past-tense narratives? In other words: by analyzing these nine narratives, I will try to highlight the particularities of present-tense as opposed to past-tense narration and spell out to what extent the worldmaking power of the present-tense novel performs differently than that of the more traditional past-tense narrative. In doing so, I will alternate between the analysis of formal features of fictional tense usage and the interpretation of textual as well as cognitive functions of both present- and past-tense narration. My readings of the nine novels in my corpus will consequently differ

---

24 Here I follow the lead of Silke Horstkotte and Leonhard Herrmann's (2013) anthology on contemporary German fiction as well as Irmtraud Huber's (2016) monograph on present-tense narration in contemporary English fiction: both of these studies take the millennium as a benchmark that demarcates contemporary narrative from earlier fiction. In contrast to Huber, however, I do not restrict my corpus to British and Commonwealth fiction, but also include American and Canadian fiction.

in the degree to which they accentuate the diverging processes of analysis and interpretation.

Analyzing the use of the present tense in various generic contexts will enable me, moreover, to illustrate not only the ubiquity, but also the aesthetic versatility of present-tense narration in contemporary narrative fiction. This second aspect arises from the observation that the fictional present tense may contribute to the distinctive features of specific narrative genres such as the intercultural novel or the thriller. As my readings of Aslam's and Winslow's novels will demonstrate, in the former case, the present tense may engage with the genre's project of fostering intercultural understanding by means of evoking narrative empathy, whereas in the latter case the present tense may serve to enhance the genre's main goal of producing other readerly effects such as narrative suspense and urgency. We will see that the present tense operates similarly in the other genres, too, which is why it seems reasonable to assume that fictional tense, just like any other narrative strategy, correlates with the generic properties of a specific work.

However, I would like to emphasize that the various uses of the fictional present tense I will identify in my model interpretations only serve to highlight specific generic features; they should not be conceived of as generic features as such. That is to say, the functions of present-tense narration I will discuss in, for instance, my reading of Mantel's fictions need not necessarily apply to other historical novels written in the present tense; conversely, they may well be encountered in other genres like, say, the climate change novel or experimental narrative. To put this more generally: my readings of different present-tense novels in Part III of this study do not imply that the functions of present-tense narration identified in a specific narrative are always the same for the genre to which that narrative pertains; nor do my model interpretations imply a fixed correlation between the form of a specific narrative and its use of the present tense. That the present study does not primarily seek to make a contribution to genre theory also accounts for the fact that generic aspects feature to varying degrees in my reading of the novels in my corpus.

This leads me to the third and final main goal of my model interpretations. Arguing that present-tense narration usually acts in accordance with the unique characteristics of different narrative genres – or more precisely the specific narrative strategies these genres deploy to create their storyworlds – I will have to resort to a number of narratological concepts and categories not directly related to fictional tense usage, and therefore not discussed in connection with the narratological model I will introduce in Part II of this study. Having said that, an important criterion for the selection of the sample novels to be discussed in

1.3 Beyond the 'Grammatical' Fallacy: Key Arguments and Structure of this Book — 17

Part III was not only the variety of their distinctive generic qualities, but also the richness of the various narrative strategies they make use of. My corpus accordingly ties in with a series of narratological approaches that address narrative phenomena such as prospective narrative and turning points (Mantel's novels), experientiality (Atwood's novel), immersion (Mantel's and Atwood's novels), narrative empathy and cognitive dissonance (Mantel's, Aslam's, and Donoghue's novels), suspense and surprise (Winslow's novel), narrative authority (Welsh's novels), intertextuality (McEwan's novel), 'unnatural' narrative (McEwan's novel), unreliable narration (Donoghue's novel), and conversational narrative (Welsh's novels). As a result, despite the fact that present-tense narration as such constitutes an inherently formal as well as aesthetic element of narrative, Part III of this book will seek to yoke the textual (i.e. formal and structural) with the contextual interests of narratology, in the hope of rendering my model of present-tense narration compatible with formal and contextual narratologies alike.[25]

Finally, Chapter 14 will provide a conclusion and outlook, discussing the outreach and scope of the narratological model of fictional (present-)tense usage developed in Part II of this study. This will involve not only summarizing the narratological implications of the model interpretations in Part III, but also identifying five different lenses through which narrative theorists and literary scholars may seek to further investigate the phenomenon of present-tense narration. These include the perspectives of genre theory, and historical, contextualist, and transmedial narratology, as well as an interdisciplinary point of view involving the fields of linguistics, philosophy, digital humanities, and empirical literary studies. In a final discussion of possible reasons for the current surge in present-tense narrative that integrates various perspectives from literary, cultural, and media theory, as well as sociology, I will propose some hypotheses about potential insights deriving from this new aesthetic trend with regard to the human experience of time in contemporary culture. After this outline of further avenues of research and discussion related to the fictional present tense, the study will close with a plea for reconsideration of the common belief that storytelling is only possible in retrospect, or – to borrow Mann's formulation – that any narrative "must be in the past."

---

25 I here resort to Roy Sommer's (2012, 152–154) distinction between formal and contextual narratologies as the different main approaches of postclassical narratology. While the former include both synchronic approaches and diachronic approaches, each of which is characterized by a structuralist bias, the latter include, among others, (trans-)generic narratologies, feminist, ethnic, (cross-)cultural, and postcolonial narratologies, and rhetorical narratologies, as well as cognitive and affective narratologies.

Part I: **Mapping the Research Field on Present-Tense Narration**

2 Linguistic, Narratological, and Philosophical Considerations on Tense Usage in Narrative Fiction

2.1 The Beginnings of a Theoretical Engagement with Fictional Tense Usage: Käte Hamburger's Thoughts on the Epic Preterite and Their Consequences for Present-Tense Narration

Theoretical engagements with tense usage in narrative fiction look back on a long tradition, which has its beginnings in the 1950s. The German literary scholar and philosopher Käte Hamburger was the first to draw attention to this narrative phenomenon. In *Die Logik der Dichtung*, first published in 1957, she sets out to establish a linguistic theory of literature that describes the language of literature in relation to the general system of language.[1] With this end in mind, she investigates the three main genres of literature (i.e. narrative fiction, drama, and poetry); the third chapter of her study, which is dedicated to narrative, deals in large part with the closely related aspects of tense usage, deixis, and style. Up to today, Hamburger's work has been widely received not only in German literary studies,[2] but also in an international context: the second, revised edition of her monograph, which was published in 1968, was translated into English in 1973 under the title *The Logic of Literature*.[3]

Hamburger's programmatic study provides important insights into the use of tense in narrative fiction. Within the framework of her theory of literature, she introduces a specific use of the past tense, the epic preterite, which she

---

[1] I will include in this literature survey studies that deal with fictional tense usage in German, English, and Romance languages, especially French. From a linguistic perspective, this may at first seem a little problematic since each of these languages has a different tense system consisting not only of verb tenses, which are similar in the respective languages, but also of verb aspects, which differ from language to language. For the purpose of this project, however, these differences can be set aside, as I will focus primarily on the use of verb tense and generally overlook that of aspect in narrative fiction.
[2] A concise overview of the outreach and critique of Hamburger's work within the field of German literary studies can be found in Vogt 2014 [2006], 21–41.
[3] Here and in the following, I will, where possible, quote from the English translations of French and German sources and comment in footnotes on any deviation from the original. In case no authoritative English translation is available, I will quote from the original (i.e. French or German) sources and provide a free translation of the respective text passages.

construes as a distinctive feature of narrative fiction written in the third person (cf. Hamburger 1973 [1968], 64–81).⁴ The epic preterite, Hamburger argues, distinguishes itself from uses of the past tense in ordinary discourse in that it "loses its grammatical function of designating what is past" (1973 [1968], 66). To illustrate this, she cites several examples from English and German classics, including Johann Wolfgang von Goethe's *Wilhelm Meisters Lehrjahre* [*Wilhelm Meister's Apprenticeship*] (2004 [1795/1796]) and Virginia Woolf's *Mrs. Dalloway* (1996 [1925]); her most famous case in point is a quote from Alice Berend's *Die Bräutigame der Babette Bomberling* [*Babette Bomberling's Bridegrooms*] (2019 [1915]): "Tomorrow was Christmas Eve" (*Morgen war Weihnachtsabend*) (66). In any "real speaking situation" (Hamburger 1973 [1986], 71), this sentence would be considered ungrammatical since it combines the past tense ("was") with a deictic future adverb ("tomorrow") – in ordinary discourse we would usually say "It was Christmas Eve *the next day*." In third-person narrative fiction, however, this combination is unproblematic, as it immediately identifies the quote "as a sentence occurring in a novel" (Hamburger 1973 [1986], 72–73). Hamburger consequently concludes that the epic preterite must have been "relieve[d] [...] of its temporal meaning of referring to the past" (1973 [1986], 74).⁵

This atemporal quality is due to a shift of the deictic center of the text. In third-person narratives, Hamburger contends, "the originary point occupied by the I (the experience- or statement-I), i.e., the *Origo* of the system of temporal and spatial coordinates which coincides or is identical with the Here and Now" (1973 [1968], 67; italics in the original), is replaced by "fictive I-Origines, i.e., reference or orientational systems which epistemologically, and hence temporally, have nothing to do with a real I who experiences fiction in any way—in

---

4 Hamburger (1973 [1968], 313) excludes first-person narratives from the scope of narrative fiction, as she believes that they ought to be conceived of as instances of what she refers to as a "feigned reality statement" (*fingierte Wirklichkeitsaussage*), that is, a statement which is not simply "not real," as is the case with 'genuine' fiction, but rather "something pretended, imitated, something inauthentic and non-genuine."
5 Jochen Vogt (2014 [2006], 35n20) reminds us that Roland Barthes makes a similar assertion in *Writing Degree Zero* (1968 [1953]): "Obsolete in spoken French, the preterite, which is the cornerstone of Narration, always signifies the presence of Art; it is a part of a ritual of Letters. Its function is no longer that of a tense." (30) We should note, however, that the English translation of Barthes's statement is not precise enough: in the French original, Barthes (1972 [1953], 27) speaks of a specific form of the past tense, namely the *passé simple*, which is exclusively used in literary language. The *passé simple* is thus the only form of the French past tenses which is "[o]bsolete in spoken French," according to Barthes; the *passé composé* (the compound past), the *imparfait* (the imperfect), and the *plus-que-parfait* (the past perfect), by contrast, are certainly used in oral discourse (cf. Barthes 1972 [1953], 27).

other words with the author or the reader" (1973 [1968], 73–74). More specifically, this means that the story transmitted to the reader is not presented from the perspective of the narrator (i.e. the narrative agent who usually reveals himself or herself in the use of the first-person pronoun *I*); rather, the center of consciousness underlying the narrative belongs to one or several fictive characters that only come into existence via the narrative discourse (i.e. the narrative agents readers encounter in the text as third parties). It is this shift from a real I-*origo* to one or several fictive I-*origines* that deprives the epic preterite of its grammatical function of referring to the past: the epic preterite no longer designates the past of the speaker, but relates to the characters' present, which is why it can also be combined with deictic temporal adverbs which, in ordinary discourse, can only be used with present or future tenses (e.g. *now*, *today*, or – to reiterate the example from Berend's novel – *tomorrow*).

The specific characteristics of the epic preterite also influence the ways in which past-tense narratives deploy the present tense (cf. Hamburger 1973 [1968], 98–110). Hamburger accordingly stresses that

> [f]ictionalization, action presented as the Here and Now of the fictive persons, *nullifies the temporal meaning of the tense* in which a piece of narrative literature is narrated: the preteritive meaning of the grammatical past tense, as well as the present meaning of the historical present (1973 [1968], 98; italics in the original).

The reason for this, she explains, is that the use of the historical present, that is, the intermittent shift to the present tense within an otherwise past-tense context, is almost always analyzed in relation to the past. As a consequence, the historical present is often believed either to fulfill the function of rendering the narrative events more immediate than does the epic preterite – an effect which Hamburger calls "presentification" (*Vergegenwärtigung*) (1973 [1968], 99) – or of depicting selected events in a more vivid manner within a past-tense discourse – an effect which she labels "dramatic visualization" (*dramatische Veranschaulichung*) (1973 [1968], 102).

However, according to Hamburger, these functions which are traditionally attributed to the historical present only hold within the context of historical documents, that is, factual narratives in which the preterite still displays the grammatical feature of referring to events that have happened in the past. In epic fiction, by contrast, the preterite loses its grammatical, and thus also its temporal quality, so that the effects of presentification and visualization become superfluous:

> In historical statement the present tense is different from the past, which here has the function of portraying past-ness. In the epos, in the novel, on the other hand, it is no dif-

ferent from the past tense; that is, it is not functionally different. Since here the preterite does not infringe upon the experience of the fictive Here and Now, it need not be replaced by a tense which in a differently structured context, namely that of the reality statement, eventually can have such a fictionalizing effect, an effect which here would not equally well be produced by the past tense itself. Thus, without exception, in every fictional context where the historical present appears, we can replace it with the preterite without noticing any change in our experience of fiction. (Hamburger 1973 [1968], 107)

In Hamburger's understanding, then, the historical present serves no function within narrative fiction which could not also be performed by the epic preterite, and hence turns out to be dispensable.[6]

With respect to the present-tense novel, Hamburger's considerations concerning present-tense usage are problematic. Apart from the fact that she limits her argument to third-person narratives, thus excluding first-person narratives altogether,[7] she additionally reduces present-tense narration to the historical present, where it is a foregrounding device within past-tense narratives. As other literary scholars have pointed out, however, the present tense loses this rhetorical function as soon as an entire narrative is written in the present tense (cf. e.g. Cohn 1999, 99; Fludernik 1992b, 89), which means that Hamburger's argument does not hold at all for the present-tense novel. Admittedly, Hamburger wrote her text at a time when present-tense narratives were rare: according to Franz K. Stanzel (1981b), the trend toward a consistent use of present-tense narration in narrative fiction only started in the 1960s.[8] It is, then, fair to

---

6 Ann Banfield, who radicalizes Hamburger's theory in *Unspeakable Sentences: Narration and Representation in the Language of Fiction* (1982), goes so far as to claim that narratives which foreground the mode of represented speech or thought (i.e. the type of third-person narrative Hamburger has in mind here) "[do] not normally allow the present tense at all" (98).
7 As a matter of fact, Hamburger has been criticized for making the use of the epic preterite conditional on the use of third-person pronouns in narrative texts. Monika Fludernik (2003a, 122–123; 2008 [2005]b, 611) and Franz K. Stanzel (1959, 3–6), for example, argue that this specific use of the past tense hinges not so much on the grammatical category of person as on the question whether the mode of narration or that of focalization prevails in a narrative text. W. J. M. Bronzwaer (1970, 41–62) carries Stanzel's critique of Hamburger to extremes, maintaining that the use of the epic preterite is not even limited to narrative fiction, but instead qualifies as a distinctive feature of free indirect style, which can be deployed in both fictional and nonfictional (written) discourse.
8 Needless to say, we can also find scattered instances of present-tense narrative before that time. Christiane Rohde (1993) and Ruoxing Tang (1997) have investigated the use of the present tense in the German ballad of the late eighteenth and early nineteenth centuries. Although the ballad represents a "generic [hybrid]" (Nünning and Schwanecke 2013, 117) between poetry and narrative that is not included in the corpus of this study, it must nevertheless be acknowledged as a literary text that makes use of present-tense narration. In his article "The Historical

say that Hamburger's early approaches to fictional tense usage do justice neither to the ubiquity and scope nor to the diversity and versatility of present-tense narration in the twenty-first century novel.

Although Hamburger's discussion of the fictional present tense seems outdated in view of recent trends in narrative fiction, her deliberations on fictional tense usage in general and the epic preterite in particular have inspired many linguists and literary scholars to further scrutinize the ways in which narrative texts deploy tense. Since the initial publication of *Die Logik der Dichtung* in 1957 a lot of research has been done on tense usage in narrative fiction, and the boom of the present-tense novel in contemporary fiction is producing more and more studies that deal specifically with the phenomenon of present-tense narration.

Very broadly, existing research on fictional present-tense usage can be divided into diachronic and synchronic approaches. While the former strive to reconstruct the historical development of present-tense narration since the beginnings of literary storytelling, the latter focus primarily on the particularities of present-tense narration, describing it from the different, yet complementary, perspectives of linguistics, narratology, and philosophy. Chapter 2.2–2.3 will outline the positions of these two broad approaches, first introducing their premises and main arguments and then discussing their merits and shortcomings for the project of devising a narratological model of present-tense narration.

2.2 Diachronic Approaches to Present-Tense Narration: The Evolution of the Present Tense as a Genuine Tense of Narration

The central objective of diachronic approaches to present-tense narration is to provide a historical survey of how the present tense, which used to occur only in intermittent passages of narrative fiction, has evolved into a genuine tense of

---

Present in Narrative Literature, Particularly in Modern German Fiction," published in 1946, John R. Frey, moreover, identifies some dozen narratives published during the 1920s and the 1930s that were written entirely in the present tense. Yet these few narratives remain an exception: most of the examples Frey discusses make use of what I will later refer to as *heterogeneous tense usage* (see Chapter 4.1), that is, they deploy both the past and present tense. Against this background one could also construe the increasing interest in the present tense since the 1960s as a response to the *nouveau roman* of the previous decade, which was also very fond of the present tense (cf. Miyahara 2009, 242; Petersen 2010, 55).

narration which nowadays can span an entire novel. There are two competing narratives here, one from the camp of narratologists and one from that of linguists. A closer look at these alternatives, however, reveals that they do not really exclude each other, but proceed from different premises: the narratological version focuses primarily on the aspects of fictionality and narrativity, whereas the linguistic account highlights the aspect of mediality.

The narratological perspective on the evolution of present-tense narration was first proposed by the German scholars Armen Avanessian and Anke Hennig, who, in a series of book chapters and articles, traced the emergence of the genre of the present-tense novel.[9] The central argument of their historical review is that, since the beginning of the twentieth century, the present tense has developed from a "tense of the factual" (*Tempus des Faktischen*) (Avanessian and Hennig 2015 [2012], 15) to a fictional as well as narrative tense. Avanessian and Hennig relate this functional shift in present-tense usage to two successive changes within the genre of narrative fiction. Initially, they argue, the modernist novel departed from "the narratological dogma of retrospectivity," that is, "[t]he assumption that there is an orderly interplay in which the prospective course of the *fabula* is retrospectively recovered by the *sujet*," with the result that "[f]*abula* and *sujet* are paradoxically synchronous" (Avanessian and Hennig 2015 [2012], 16; italics in the original). In the second stage narrative fiction freed itself from the constraints of the epic preterite, whose presentifying function tend "to block the experience of the past as such" (Avanessian and Hennig 2015 [2012], 16), so that the present-tense novel was eventually able "to narrate the past by analyzing the processes by means of which the reader constructs the course of a *fabula* from a *sujet* at hand" (Avanessian and Hennig 2015 [2012], 17; italics in the original).

Avanessian and Hennig's historical survey has a transnational perspective, as they take their examples not only from German, but also from English, French, and Russian literature. The German anglicist Irmtraud Huber has recently adapted their ideas to an exclusively Anglophone context. In the second chapter of her monograph *Present-Tense Narration in Contemporary Fiction: A Narratological Overview* (2016), Huber traces the historical development of present-tense usage in English fiction. Since the rise of the novel during the eighteenth century, she contends, English narrative fiction has been characterized by a tendency toward "believable and realistic narrative situations," preferring "the use of the past tense" (Huber 2016, 6): "After all, in real life, we cannot

---

9 Cf. Avanessian and Hennig 2013a, 246–249; 2013c; 2015; 2015 [2012], Ch. 1; cf. also Avanessian 2013, 363–365.

experience and narrate both at the same time. It is only ever possible to tell of events that happened to us in retrospect, since we need time and leisure to narrate them or write them down." (Huber 2016, 6) The present tense, by contrast, is mainly – albeit not exclusively – associated with simultaneity. Its extensive use has therefore long been avoided in realist writing and instead been reserved for experimental, (post-)modernist texts which either foreground the discourse mode of description or point toward other genres (i.e. drama and poetry) (cf. Huber 2016, 6–13).

Drawing extensively on Avanessian and Hennig, Huber delineates how, over the course of literary history, the present tense has succeeded in casting off these associations with other (non-narrative) discourse modes or genres. By the end of the twentieth century, the present had transcended its previous status as a "non-narrative and non-fictional" tense and had turned into a "tense of narration proper" (Huber 2016, 13), which now serves as a new "signpost of fictionality" (Huber 2016, 14). With reference to this process of aesthetic emancipation, Huber argues that contemporary present-tense narratives are no longer interested in propounding plausible narrative scenarios. The genre of the present-tense novel rather "highlights its own status as fiction, as a self-justifying discourse which no longer seeks to imitate non-fictional forms of communication" (Huber 2016, 20).

A linguistic version of the history of the present tense has been put forward by Benjamin Meisnitzer. Published in 2016, his monograph *Das Präsens als Erzähltempus im Roman: Eine gedruckte Antwort auf den Film* seeks to shed light on how the present tense is deployed in the dominant narrative genres of various periods, ranging from ancient historiography and the heroic epics of the Middle Ages to the postmodern narrative texts of the second half of the twentieth century and contemporary narrative fiction. In this extensive historical overview, Meisnitzer focuses primarily on Romance and Germanic languages, including Portuguese, Spanish, French, German, and English; in one of his chapters he additionally broaches the tempus system of Russian.

Meisnitzer's project follows the hypothesis that the historical development of present-tense narration can be divided into three stages each of which establishes a different use of the present tense: (1) the aspectual or aoristic present (*aspektuelles oder aoristisches Präsens*) often found in Latin historiographic texts as well as in epic poems of the Middle Ages (cf. 2016, Ch. 6);[10] (2) the histor-

---

[10] On a related note, cf. also Monika Fludernik's article "The Historical Present Tense in English Literature: An Oral Pattern and Its Literary Adaptation" (1992b), in which she applies a sociolinguistic model, which she originally devised for the analysis of the use of the historical

ical present or – as Meisnitzer prefers to call it – "perspectival present" (*vergangenheitsaktualisierendes oder perspektivisches Präsens*), which serves to foreground specific narrative events within a past-tense narrative (cf. 2016, Ch. 7.1-7.2); and (3) the narrative present (*narratives Präsens*), that is, the increasing use of the present as a dominant tense of narration during the twentieth century (cf. 2016, Ch. 7.3-7.5). According to Meisnitzer, the transition from phase 1 to phase 2 – the replacement of the aoristic with the perspectival present – is a consequence of the evolution of modern Romance languages from Vulgar Latin, i.e. the various dialects of Latin spoken during the classical period of the Roman Empire. These developments brought about a shift within the verbal system from the predominantly aspectual of Classical Latin to the predominantly temporal of the Romance languages (cf. Meisnitzer 2016, 227).

The transition from phase 2 to phase 3 – i.e. the emergence of the narrative present tense – on the other hand, does not stem from yet another change within the verbal system of these languages, but is due rather to pragmatic changes resulting from a shift in conventional discourse norms (cf. Meisnitzer 2016, Ch. 9.2). This shift, Meisnitzer argues, was largely owing to the invention of film toward the end of the nineteenth century. Thanks to its specific properties, this new medium managed to present narrative events as if they were happening now, in the very moment of representation. Meisnitzer consequently reads the increase in present-tense narration during the nineteenth century as a response to these developments: by negating the temporal distance between the actual occurrence of the narrative events and the act of reporting these events, the narrative present succeeds in creating an impression of immediacy which moves the medium of written narrative closer to that of film (cf. Meisnitzer 2016, 242–252).

As these alternative versions of the historical development of the present into a genuine tense of narration reveal, narratologists and linguists alike seek causes for the recent boom in present-tense narrative. Avanessian and Hennig,

---

present tense in conversational storytelling (cf. Fludernik 1991, 1992a), to medieval English narrative. She then utilizes the findings of her analysis to compare the use of the historical present tense in medieval literature and later narrative fiction, starting from the nineteenth century. In doing so, Fludernik proceeds from the assumption "that one can find precisely the same oral pattern in medieval English narrative and in English literature up until the eighteenth century," which saw the rise of narrative fiction by giving birth to the novel as an independent genre (1992b, 77). After that, she argues, the structure and make-up of narrative changed considerably, with the result that the historical present tense which we nowadays know especially from the context of the nineteenth-century realist novel constitutes a narrative phenomenon completely different from the historical present of medieval narrative.

as well as Huber, tie the contemporary popularity of present-tense narration to a shift within the narrative paradigm; yet both parties construe this shift in different ways. According to Avanessian and Hennig, it marks a new understanding of the temporal relation between story and narrative discourse, whereas, in Huber's view, it represents the transition from a predominantly mimetic framework to one which also allows for clearly anti-realistic narrative scenarios. To put it differently: while Avanessian and Hennig see the rise of the present-tense novel as a sign of a reconceptualization of the temporal structure of narrative, Huber views it as a violation of the conventional narrative form resulting from an increased openness toward literary experimentation. Meisnitzer, on the other hand, conceives of the modern present-tense narrative as a direct response to the medium of film.

Despite these differences between the narratological and linguistic versions of the history of the present tense, both approaches understand the current trend toward present-tense narration as an attempt to break with a longstanding literary tradition – namely that stories are told in retrospect. As we will see in Chapter 5.2, this convention is an important touchstone against which literary scholars, especially narratologists, evaluate the particularities of present-tense narration.

2.3 Synchronic Approaches to Present-Tense Narration: Investigating the Present Tense from an Interdisciplinary Perspective

While diachronic approaches to present-tense narration form a heterogeneous group that traces the development of the phenomenon from various linguistic and narratological angles, synchronic approaches are variously situated in either linguistics, narratology, or philosophy, with each discipline construing fictional tense usage in a different way. While linguistic studies tend to take tense usage as a criterion for distinguishing different modes of communication (i.e. fictionality vs. factuality) and discourse (i.e. narrative vs. commentary or discursive speech) (see Chapter 2.3.1), narrative theorists prefer to regard it as a characteristic of the 'voice' of a text (cf. Genette 1980 [1972], Ch. 5), i.e. a linguistic feature relating to the temporal distance between the story and the narrative discourse that conveys the story to the reader (see Chapter 2.3.2). Compared with these disciplinary traditions, philosophical approaches take a more radical stance, claiming that in narrative fiction tense usage has no particular significance at all (see Chapter 2.3.3).

2.3.1 Linguistic Approaches: Present-Tense Usage as a Disqualifier of Narrative

Generally speaking, one can say that linguistic approaches to present-tense narration tie in with Käte Hamburger's discussion of tense in *The Logic of Literature*, as they postulate that narrative fiction works by its own grammatical rules, which differ from those of ordinary usage.[11] The study which remains closest to Hamburger's theory is Harald Weinrich's *Tempus: Besprochene und erzählte Welt*, first published in 1964.[12] Seizing on Hamburger's conceptualization of the epic preterite as a marker of fictionality, Weinrich (2001 [1964], Ch. I.5) holds that every tense potentially indicates a specific text type. In a rather unconvincing manner, given the current rise of the present-tense novel, he divides German tenses into two groups.[13] One contains all those tenses which, according to Weinrich, qualify as linguistic signs of commentary or discursive texts (*besprechende Tempora*), namely the present (*Präsens*), the present perfect (*Perfekt*), the simple future (*Futur*), and the future perfect (*Futur II*); the other comprises all remaining tenses of German which, in Weinrich's system, signal narrative (*erzählende Tempora*), namely the preterite (*Präteritum*), the past perfect (*Plusquamperfekt*), the conditional I (*Konditional*), and the conditional II (*Konditional II*). This dichotomy, Weinrich explains, is particularly relevant for the relationship between author and reader of a specific text (cf. 2001 [1964], II.2). Discursive tenses such as the present suggest a high degree of relevance for both writer and addressee,[14] thus demanding the reader's enhanced attention, whereas narrative tenses expose a text's narrative quality and indicate to the reader that he or she can perceive the text in a more relaxed manner.[15]

---

11 I would like to stress that the literature survey presented in this chapter only focuses on linguistic studies which deal with present-tense narration in narrative fiction; as a consequence, work on present-tense usage in non-fictional narrative discourse (cf. e.g. Altshuler 2016; Becker and Stude 2017, Ch. 3.3; and Zint 2001) cannot be discussed here.
12 For an abridged English version of Weinrich's theory, cf. Weinrich 1970.
13 Although Weinrich makes this distinction with reference to German, his study, which actually focuses primarily on Romance languages, also contains English examples.
14 Since there is no authoritative translation of Weinrich's terms *besprechende Tempora* and *erzählende Tempora* (the English essay that gives a condensed overview of his theory only paraphrases these categories), I here resort to Monika Fludernik's (2012, 81) translation of Weinrich's *besprechende Tempora* as 'discursive tenses.' However, rather than using her translation of *erzählende Tempora* as 'narrating tenses,' I prefer the term *narrative tenses*.
15 Interestingly enough, Weinrich's elaborations concerning the speech attitude expressed by different tenses echo a previous claim by Roland Barthes (1968 [1953], 32; italics in the original): "The narrative past is [...] a part of a security system for Belles-Lettres. Being the image of

While Weinrich's theory is mainly inspired by Hamburger's work, it also builds on a model of the French verbal system proposed by Émile Benveniste in his *Problems in General Linguistics* (1971 [1966]).[16] Like Weinrich, Benveniste proceeds from the assumption that the French temporal system splits into two separate, yet largely complementary realms, namely those of *histoire* and *discours* (cf. 1971 [1966], Ch. 19).[17] According to Benveniste, the realm of *histoire* is confined to writing, particularly historical writing, and is therefore characterized by linguistic restrictions concerning the grammatical categories of person and tense. That is to say, an historical account is always formulated in the third person and can only resort to one of the following three tense forms: the aorist (*aoriste*) or preterite (*passé simple*), the imperfect (*imparfait*), and the past perfect (*plus-que-parfait*). The realm of *discours*, by contrast, is comparatively free

---

an order, it is one of those numerous formal pacts made between the writer and society for the justification of the former and the serenity of the latter. The preterite [i.e. the *passé simple*] *signifies* a creation: that is, it proclaims and imposes it. Even from the depth of the most somber realism, it has a reassuring effect because, thanks to it, the verb expresses a closed, well-defined, substantival act, the Novel has a name, it escapes the terror of an expression without laws: reality becomes slighter and more familiar, it fits within a style, it does not outrun language. […] On the contrary, when the Narrative is rejected in favour of other literary genres, or when, within the narration, the preterite is replaced by less ornamental forms, fresher, more full-blooded and nearer to speech (the present tense or the present perfect), Literature becomes the receptacle of existence in all its density and no longer of its meaning alone. The acts it recounts are still separated from History, but no longer from people."

16 As Carl Vetters (1996, 165n2) reminds us, Benveniste's article was originally published in 1959, five years before Weinrich's monograph, and reprinted in the essay collection *Problèmes de linguistique générale* in 1966.

17 In the original, Benveniste speaks of "plans d'énonciation différents" (1966, 238), which actually translates as "different planes of utterance" (1971 [1966], 206). However, I prefer Fludernik's (1993b, 46) free translation of Benveniste's original formulation as "separate realms." But I retain his original terms of *histoire* and *discours* rather than their standard English translations, 'history' and 'discourse.' The reason for this is that the English term *history* also denotes historiography, a meaning not contained in the same way in Benveniste's original word choice. Even though Benveniste uses historiography as his main example when discussing the realm of *histoire*, the term refers to "the narration of past events" in general, which means that it can also apply to narrative fiction (1971 [1966], 206). I therefore think that *histoire* would be better translated in this context as 'story.' This, however, would lead to the problem that, in a narratological work, the terms *story* and *discourse* already have a fixed denotation, as they refer to the intradiegetic and extradiegetic communicative levels of narrative texts. On a related note, cf. also Fludernik 2012, 81; italics in the original: "The confusion about *discours* and discourse […] suggests that a translation into English of Benveniste's *discours* as discourse is misleading. *Histoire* and *discours* do not have a one-to-one relation to the story/discourse dichotomy."

of linguistic constraints. Implying the presence of a speaker and an addressee, it can use both first- and third-person pronouns; and it can deploy almost every verbal tense form except the aorist, which in French is a distinctive feature of written language. Having said that, Benveniste identifies three tense forms which preferably occur in *discours*, namely those banned from *histoire*: the present (*présent*), the present perfect (*parfait*), and the future (*future*) (cf. Benveniste 1971 [1966], 242–243).

In *The Fictions of Language and the Languages of Fiction* (1993b), Monika Fludernik juxtaposes Weinrich's and Benveniste's theories of tense. She argues that Weinrich's model "improves upon Benveniste" as it considers not only "the *textual* function of the temporal system," but also "the *contextual* implications of choice of tense" (Fludernik 1993b, 51; italics in the original). Besides, she warns that Benveniste's approach might be too language-specific, as he exclusively concentrates on the French temporal system (cf. Fludernik 1993b, 46).[18] Despite these admittedly important differences, however, both theories have in common that they ascribe the present tense to that type of text (Weinrich) or discourse mode (Benveniste) which, in the context of each dichotomy, either must (Weinrich) or at least may (Benveniste) be regarded as non-narrative.[19] In Weinrich's case, we can even go so far as to argue that his distinction between narrative and discursive texts additionally alludes to the distinction between the fictional and non-fictional. This becomes most obvious in his analysis of tense usage in fairy tales (cf. Weinrich 2001 [1964], 64–67). In his opinion, it is no coincidence that almost every German fairy tale starts with the formulation "Es war einmal..." and closes with the sentence "Und wenn sie nicht gestorben sind, so leben sie noch heute." While reading (or listening to) a fairy tale, the past tense of the first sentence invites us to become immersed in the narrated world, a world which clearly differs from our reality, whereas the shift to the present tense in the final sentence indicates that we have to return to the real world as the narrative comes to an end.[20] In Weinrich's theory, then, the past

---

18 Indeed, Benveniste's clarifications concerning the *passé simple* cannot be adapted to Germanic languages such as English or German: these languages contain no grammatical tense forms exclusively used in literary writing.
19 As Fludernik (1993b, 46) clarifies, Benveniste's category of *discours* comprises all possible forms of everday conversation, which may – but do not necessarily have to – qualify as instances of (conversational) storytelling.
20 Interestingly enough, Weinrich's argument does not hold for English fairy tales as both standardized formulations – "Once upon a time there was/were..." and "And they lived happily ever after" – are written in the past tense.

2.3 Synchronic Approaches to Present-Tense Narration — 33

tense can – but need not necessarily – serve as a signal of fictionality;[21] the present tense, however, can never fulfill such a fictionalizing function.

Another linguist who links choice of tense to a specific genre is Suzanne Fleischman. In her 1990 monograph *Tense and Narrativity: From Medieval Performance to Modern Fiction*, she construes narrative as a marked variety of language usage which subverts the grammatical conventions of everyday communicative language. She maintains that, in this marked context, it is the use of the past tense that represents the standard case (rather than the use of the present tense, which constitutes the unmarked case in ordinary discourse).[22] Starting from this hypothesis, Fleischman sets out to examine four different narrative genres from four different periods of European literature, all of which use the present as a dominant tense of narration (cf. 1990, Ch. 8): the French epic poem, the Hispanic ballad or historical romance, English monologue fiction in the tradition of Virginia Woolf, and the French *nouveau roman*. By thus juxtaposing medieval orature or – as she, herself, calls it – "preliterate fiction" (Fleischman 1990, 308) with (post-)modernist (written) fiction, Fleischman shows that each of these different types of narrative may deploy the present tense in completely different ways and to completely different ends. Yet she also highlights that the examples of present-tense storytelling she surveys "all involve a measure of dechronologization and a shrinking of specifically narrative elements," which, in turn, "opens the way, on the one hand, for performed stories to approach actual dramatic performance, and, on the other, for the discourse of reflections and perceptions to approach lyricism" (Fleischman 1990, 309). Diverse as they may be, Fleischman's examples thus all seem to share the same motivation for using the present tense – namely its inherent metalinguistic function which "identif[ies] the discourse as something other than narrative" (1990, 308). Based on these observations, Fleischman eventually draws the conclusion that "[a]ll genres which choose the PR [i.e. present tense] as the basic tense for reporting information work in some way against the narrative norm" and therefore ought to be regarded as being "consciously or unconsciously antinarrative" (1990, 11; small capital letters in the original).

Although Fleischman's argumentation differs considerably from Weinrich's and Benveniste's theories, her theory is based on the same premise. In fact, all of the linguistic approaches I have presented in this chapter proceed from the

---

21 Cf. also Vetters (1996, 171), who stresses that Weinrich's dichtotomy of discursive vs. narrative tenses as such does not posit a distinction between fictional and non-fictional texts.
22 An abridged outline of the argument of Fleischman's book can be found in Fleischman 1991a.

assumption that the present constitutes a tense that is on principle precluded from narrative. For Benveniste, the present tense cannot occur in written narrative at all, meaning, reciprocally, that as soon as a text makes use of this specific tense, it can no longer be regarded as an instance of narrative fiction. Weinrich and Fleischman, on the other hand, do not deny the fact that the present tense can also occur in narrative texts. Nonetheless, they both argue, albeit on different grounds, that any narrative text which makes use of the present tense automatically forfeits its narrativity by approaching either discursive speech (Weinrich) or the genres of drama and poetry (Fleischman).

Considering the recent boom in present-tense narration, these linguistic approaches to tense usage in narrative fiction call for some critique. In disapproving Weinrich's and Benveniste's theories regarding the German and French tense systems, Carl Vetters (1996, Ch. 3.3) already demonstrated that verbal tense does not qualify as a useful criterion for distinguishing between different text types or discourse modes such as commentary and narrative. I would merely add that none of the linguistic approaches described above (including that put forward by Fleischman) do justice to the ubiquity of present-tense narration in contemporary narrative fiction.[23] Were we to apply these approaches to the numerous recent novels that are written entirely, or at least largely, in the present tense, we would have to conclude that none of these texts qualify as instances of narrative. From a narratological standpoint, however, the opposite is true: none of them forfeit their narrativity or "narrativeness" (Abbott 2014, 587), for the simple reason that tense choice is not a defining criterion of narrative.

---

[23] For a related argument, cf. Jürgen H. Petersen's (1993) repeated critique of Weinrich's theory: "[V]or allem die Ausbreitung des Präsens als Darbietungstempus [in narrative texts] hat inzwischen ein Ausmaß erreicht, welches Weinrichs Tempussystem ebenso außer Kraft setzt wie das von Käte Hamburger" (24) ["[E]specially the proliferation of the present as a tense of presentation [in narrative texts] has, in the meantime, reached a level that overrules Weinrich's tense system in the same manner as it does Hamburger's" (my translation)]; and "[Weinrichs] strikte Definition des Präsens als eines besprechenden Tempus, das auf keinen und in keinem Fall als erzählendes Tempus vorkommt und vorkommen darf, ist durch die epische Praxis in der Moderne ganz einfach überspült und falsifiziert worden" (175) ["[Weinrich's] strict definition of the present as a discursive tense that under no circumstances does or can occur as a narrative tense has simply been washed away and falsified by the epic practice of modernity" (my translation)]. James Phelan (1994, 224) criticizes Fleischman's theory in a similar fashion: "Fleischman's position is well-argued, provocative, and, I think, inadequate. It is inadequate because it does not take sufficient account of actual narrative practice, the way in which many recent narrative artists have experimented with the homodiegetic simultaneous present." Although Phelan only speaks of the homodiegetic present, I believe that we can extend his argument to include heterodiegetic present-tense narratives.

Against this background, then, linguistic approaches to present-tense narration seem of limited use for narrative theorists. Nevertheless, we will see that the main premise underlying these linguistic approaches – namely that tense seems to fulfill different functions in narrative fiction than it does in ordinary discourse – continues to serve as a good starting point for a narrative poetics of present-tense narration.

2.3.2 Narratological Approaches: The Structuralist Understanding of Narrative and the Problematic Case of Present-Tense Narration

While most linguistic approaches to tense usage think of narrative fiction as operating differently from other (non-fictional) discourse modes, narratological approaches see an analogy between fictional and factual narration. Starting from the premise that the former works in a similar way to the latter, the classical narratological paradigm, based on the structuralist theories of Gérard Genette (1980 [1972], 1988 [1983]) and Franz K. Stanzel (1955, 1995 [1979]), conceives of narrative texts as presenting a fictive communicative situation. More specifically, it presupposes the existence of an anthropomorphic narrative instance, the narrator, addressing a fictive narratee to tell of events he or she has either witnessed or experienced. Structuralist approaches to narrative thus differentiate between two ontologically distinct communicative levels of narrative texts, which Seymour Chatman (1978) labels "story" and "discourse."[24] Narrative discourse, on the one hand, represents the level of narrative transmission on which the narrator performs the act of narration, addressing his or her fictive interlocutor. The story, on the other hand, features the narrative's actual content, constituting that narrative plane where the fictive characters interact and the narrative events unfold.

The narratological paradigm of narrative, moreover, postulates that the events which constitute a story must logically precede the act of narration. Shlomith Rimmon-Kenan (2002 [1983], 90) notices that "[c]ommon sense tells us that events may be narrated only after they happen," which may be one of the reasons why, according to Robert Scholes (1980, 209), "[i]t is a formal feature of narrative texts – a part of their grammar – that the events are always presented in the past tense, as having already happened." Dorrit Cohn (1999, 96), as one

---

[24] Genette (1980 [1972], 227–231) distinguishes intradiegetic and extradiegetic levels of narrative communication. However, since in English the terms *story* and *discourse* are more common, I will deploy Chatman's terminology in this book.

among many others, emphatically affirms these observations: "Life tells us that we cannot tell it while we live it or live it while we tell it. Live now, tell later."[25]

The strong conviction that telling a story is only possible in retrospect even forms part of what Suzanne Fleischman (1990, 263) calls our "narrative norm," that is, "a set of shared conventions and assumptions about what constitutes a well-formed story." For one of the most important tenets of this norm is that "narratives refer to specific experiences that occurred in some past world (real or imagined) and are accordingly reported in a tense of the PAST." (Fleischman 1990, 263; small capital letters in the original)[26] Referring to Fleischman's argument, James Phelan (1994, 226–227) concludes that, from a mimetic point of view, it seems an unwritten law that, for any account of a sequence of events to be regarded as an instance of stable narrative, it has to exhibit a double temporal structure: the present of the narrator vs. the past of the narrated events. In other words: there must always be a temporal distance between the two narrative planes of story and discourse.

The notion that "mimesis controls the occasion of narration" (Phelan 1994, 227) influences both rhetorical and structuralist concepts of present-tense usage in narrative fiction. As we shall see in the next chapter, many narratological studies equate present-tense narration with the mode of simultaneous (or concurrent) narration (cf. Genette 1980 [1972], 218–219; Margolin 1999, 150–153), which means that they construe present-tense usage as an indication of a lack of temporal distance between the narrative events and the act of reporting these events. Such an interpretation of present-tense narration gives rise to a problem which Armen Avanessian and Anke Hennig (2015 [2012], 3) have called the "aporia of synchrony" (*Gleichzeitigkeitsaporie*), namely the logical impossibility of "contemporaneously experiencing and telling [a] story." I will argue that narratological research on present-tense usage responds to this aporetic situation in two different ways: it either accepts the non-mimetic character of simultaneous narration, investigating how the use of the present tense defies not only the traditional narrative model but also narratological concepts and categories

---

[25] Similar statements can be found, for instance, in Brandt 1997, xi; Chatman 1978, 82; Cummins 1998, 113; Fleischman 1998, 1320; Harvey 2006, 71–72 and 73; Margolin 1999, 143; Nemoianu 2014, 106; and Zipfel 2001, 159.

[26] According to Fleischman, the other three tenets of the narrative norm are: "(b) that while narratives contain both sequentially ordered events and non-sequential collateral material, it is the events that define narration; (c) that the default order of the *sjuzhet* in narratives is iconic to the chronology of events in the *fabula* they model; and (d) that narratives are informed by a point of view that assigns meaning to their contents in conformity with a governing ideology, normally that of the narrator" (1990, 263).

(see Chapter 2.3.2.1), or it looks for ways to conceptualize present-tense narration differently from simultaneous narration by seeking alternative readings of this specific usage (see Chapter 2.3.2.2).

2.3.2.1 Conceptual Problems of Fictional Present-Tense Usage: Implications of Simultaneous Narration for the Narratological Paradigm

In the revised version of his *Dictionary of Narratology* (2003 [1987]), Gerald Prince defines tense as "[t]he set of temporal relations [...] between the situations and events recounted and their recounting" (98). Prince's definition shows that, in classical narratology, this verbal category refers to the temporal relation between the two distinct narrative levels of story and discourse, thus constituting a phenomenon which relates to the narratological category of 'voice' (cf. Genette 1980 [1972], Ch. 5). This conceptualization of the use of tense as a means to indicate the time of narrating can be traced back to Gérard Genette, who, in *Narrative Discourse* (1980 [1972]), holds that a narrator always needs to be located in time:

> I can very well tell a story without specifying the place where it happens, and whether this place is more or less distant from the place where I am telling it; nevertheless, it is almost impossible for me not to locate the story in time with respect to my narrating act, since I must necessarily tell the story in a present, past, or future tense. (Genette 1980 [1972], 215)

The quotation reveals that, according to Genette, the temporal situatedness of a narrator clearly depends on the tense in which the narrative is written. On the basis of tense choice, then, he distinguishes four different types of narration which help us to identify a narrator's temporal "position relative to the story" (Genette 1980 [1972], 216): (1) subsequent or past-tense narration, (2) prior or future-tense narration, (3) simultaneous or present-tense narration, and (4) interpolated narration, which is a conflation of subsequent (i.e. past-tense) and simultaneous (i.e. present-tense) narration (cf. Genette 1980 [1972], 217–223).[27]

---

[27] Genette's distinction of the four different types of narration has been adopted in many introductions to narrative theory (cf. e.g. Fludernik 2009, 51; Jahn 2017, N5.1.4; Lahn 2016, 104–107; Martínez and Scheffel 2009 [1999], Ch. 3.a); Rimmon-Kenan 2002 [1983], 90–91; Thomas 2016, 48), albeit sometimes in a new terminology. Rimmon-Kenan (2002 [1983], 90–91), for instance, renames Genette's four categories (1) ulterior narration, (2) anterior narration, (3) simultaneous narration, and (4) intercalated narration. Since her terms represent mere synonyms rather than redefinitions of Genette's categories, I will use them here interchangeably with Genette's terminology. A special case is Prince's (1982, 27) adaptation of Genette's

Genette's correlation of tense usage with the narrator's temporal position in relation to the story has strongly shaped narratologists' understanding of present-tense narration. This manifests itself in the plethora of narratological studies that equate the phenomenon with simultaneous narration.[28] The first study in this tradition is Dorrit Cohn's article "'I doze and wake': The Deviance of Simultaneous Narration."[29] Following Genette's lead, Cohn investigates how simultaneous present-tense narration violates the traditional narrative model when used in first-person narratives.[30] Given that first-person present-tense narration challenges the conventional belief that storytelling is only possible in hindsight, Cohn discusses two reading strategies, the historical present and the interior monologue, that strive to reconcile this unconventional form with the law of retrospection. While the former conceives of the present tense "as a metaphorical 'as if' present that stands in for the past tense" (Cohn 1999, 102), the latter regards it "as the normal tense of silently expressive self-communion, a language that emerges in a fictional mind without aiming at communicative narration or narrative communication" (Cohn 1999, 103).

As Cohn explains, both these resolutions seek to normalize first-person present-tense narration by having recourse to different conventions of fictional realism:

---

typology, as he only identifies three categories in this context: (1) posterior, (2) anterior, and (3) simultaneous narration. Besides, Prince is the only narratologist mentioned here who makes explicit that these different types of narration do not actually hinge on fictional tense usage, contending "that the tenses used in narrating a series of events do not necessarily correspond to the time of the narrated in relation to that of the narration" (1982, 28).

28 Cf. e.g. Bode 2005, 120–122; 2013, 12–16; Brandt 1997; Cohn 1993, 1999; DelConte 2007; D'hoker 2013, 2019; Farner 2014, 194–195; Hansen 2008; Jahn 2017, N3.3.11; Lahn 2016, 83; Marsden 2004, 107; Nielsen 2011, 59–65; Phelan 1994; 2013a, 179–183; Philipowski 2018; Richardson 2002a, 53; 2019, 117; Rimmon-Kenan 2002 [1983], 91; and Ryan 1993.

29 Cohn's article was first published in 1993 and only later reprinted as the sixth chapter of her monograph *The Distinction of Fiction* (1999). I here quote the 1999 version of her text.

30 Cohn (1999, 98) concentrates exclusively on first-person present-tense narratives because she believes "that there is an essential distinction between the functioning of tenses" in third- and first-person narrative situations: "The departure from the tensual norm (whether local or global) in *third*-person novels does not affect their temporal structure in essential ways; for, to the degree that the past tense creates the experiential present of fictional minds, it becomes semantically (i.e. temporally) moot, hence indifferently replaceable by the present tense. In *first*-person novels, by contrast, the past tense of narration ineluctably refers to the speaker's own past – to a time that is necessarily understood as anterior to the present moment in which the discourse is uttered." (Cohn 1999, 98; italics in the original)

The historical present resolution calls on the norms of formal mimeticism that the realist tradition ties to *first*-person fictional narration: the imitation of an autobiographical discourse where the narrating self refers to the past life of an experiencing self. The interior monologue resolution calls on the norms of verisimilar psychological presentation that mark the tradition of *third*-person realist fiction: the transparency of fictional characters that grants inside views into their consciousness. (Cohn 1999, 104; italics in the original)

Cohn, for her part, holds the view that first-person present-tense narration defies both of these conventions:

Its innovation, to state it bluntly, is to emancipate first-person fictional narration from the dictates of formal mimetics, granting it the same degree (though not the same kind) of discursive freedom that we take for granted in third-person fiction: the license to tell a story in an idiom that corresponds to no manner of real-world, natural discourse. (Cohn 1999, 104–105)

According to Cohn, then, first-person present-tense narration cannot be explained with the help of common narratological concepts (i.e. the historical present tense or interior monologue) and is therefore incompatible with the classical narrative model.[31]

While Cohn is predominantly interested in the non-mimetic character of fictional present-tense usage, Monika Fludernik (1996) focuses on the formal and structural characteristics of present-tense narration. Discussing the linguistic properties of the present tense, she points out that this specific tense "substitutes for *all* tenses except the present perfect and the future, which belong to the present-tense system" (Fludernik 1996, 254; italics in the original). Consequently, the present tense can assume all functions that are traditionally served by the preterite in the context of past-tense narration. As Fludernik argues, this "loss of the deictic distinction between present-tense *nows* and past-tense *thens*," in turn, causes "the loss of even more crucial narratological distinctions" (1996, 254; italics in the original). These are, on the one hand, the distinction of the separate narrative planes (i.e. story vs. discourse) – as the narrator's comments and evaluations of the narrative events can no longer be linguistically distinguished from reportative narrative (cf. also Baroni 2017, 120, 126) – on the other the differentiation between the narrative modes of narration and "direct speech (interior monologue) or 'shifted' forms of present-tense free indirect discourse" (Fludernik 1996, 254; cf. also Farner 2014, 198–199). Hence, Fluder-

---

31 In this respect, Irmtraud Huber's (2016) contention that contemporary present-tense narration has emancipated itself from a realist understanding of retrospective narrative ties in perfectly with Cohn's argument (see Chapter 2.2).

nik eventually concludes that present-tense narration "radically blurs the line between external and internal events" as represented in narrative texts (1996, 254; cf. also D'hoker 2019, 186).

Based on these particularities of present-tense narration – that is, its challenge of mimesis as well as its violation of the traditional narratological paradigm of narrative – narrative theorists have investigated the potential effects of fictional present-tense usage on readers. More specifically, previous research on present-tense narration has frequently linked the phenomenon to a non-teleological form of narration which is free of any (retrospective) reflection on the part of the narrator,[32] and some studies have even interpreted fictional present-tense usage as a textual feature of unreliable narration (cf. Hansen 2008, Ohme 2018). However, if we consider the diversity of the contemporary present-tense novel, such a generalizing reading of the present tense is not always satisfactory. There may, of course, be some novels that do combine the present tense with other narrative strategies in order to create the impression of simultaneous narration, thus increasing the illusion of narrative immediacy or causing readers to doubt the narrator's trustworthiness. Yet the majority of contemporary narratives deploy the present tense to other ends. As James Phelan (1994, 228) reminds us, "mimesis is not a product of faithful imitation of the real (whatever that is) but rather a set of conventions for representing what we provisionally and temporarily agree to be the real." Many studies of present-tense narration seem to concur with this position, offering alternative readings which abandon the notion that the use of the fictional present tense qualifies as a distinctive feature of simultaneous narration.

2.3.2.2 Alternatives to Simultaneous Narration: Attempts at 'Naturalizing' the Fictional Present Tense

In her recent monograph on present-tense usage in contemporary narrative fiction, Irmtraud Huber (2016) not only traces the diachronic development of present-tense narration (see Chapter 2.2), but also distinguishes different uses of the present tense in the twenty-first-century English novel. In addition to simultaneous present-tense narration, she identifies three further types, the narrative deictic, the retrospective, and interior monologue. Huber's first type, the narra-

---

32 Cf. e.g. Bode 2005, 120–122; 2013, 15–16; Brandt 1997, xii; Farner 2014, 196; Margolin 1999, 151–153; and Phelan 1994, 179–183. Christian Paul Casparis (1975, Ch. 1.4.3) similarly argues that present-tense novels usually qualify as what he calls a "novel of non sequiturs," that is, novels that "[present] a sequence of action before recognition of consequence and causality" (67).

tive deictic, is identical with Monika Fludernik's (2003a) category of deictic present-tense usage. Since Fludernik subsumes under this category all narrative passages in which the present tense refers to the communicative situation between fictive narrator and narratee, Huber regards it as "the often least conspicuous and most traditional" manifestation of present-tense narration (2016, 23).[33]

Retrospective present-tense narration, Huber's second category, is modeled on Armen Avanessian and Anke Hennig's (2015 [2012], 58–88) notion of an "asynchronous present" or else "the present tense of the past." If used for retrospective narration, Huber explains, the present tense points from the here-and-now of the narrative's discourse to a past moment of the diegesis (cf. 2016, 39–40). Although noting that this second type of present-tense usage is closely related to the familiar concept of the historical present, she nevertheless draws a distinction between the two usages. Unlike the conventional historical present, which occurs intermittently within past-tense narrations, the retrospective present is used consistently throughout an entire narrative discourse, with the result that it no longer "serves to mark narrative peaks or moments of transition" in an otherwise past-tense context (Huber 2016, 39). Like the historical present, however, retrospective present-tense narration does not violate the temporal distance between the enunciation and the enunciated, irrespective of the narrative situation in which it occurs (cf. Huber 2016, 54).[34]

Like narrative deictic and retrospective narration, Huber's third category of present-tense usages that differ from simultaneous present-tense narration,

---

[33] A similar hypothesis underlies Marcel Vuillaume's *Grammaire temporelle des récits* (1990), which suggests that, in traditional past-tense narratives, the past tense normally refers to the story of a narrative (*la fiction principale*), whereas the intermittent use of the present tense generally serves to designate the narrator's discourse (*la fiction secondaire*) (cf. Ch. III.2.1.2).

[34] As well as Avanessian and Hennig and Huber, other narrative theorists have also made a case for retrospective present-tense narration. For example, Seymour Chatman (1978, 83) maintains that, even in present-tense narratives, the "story-time is still usually the past"; Marie-Laure Ryan (1993, 138) claims that "present-tense fiction is actually a disguised form of retrospective narration"; and Fludernik (1996, 252) argues that "[p]resent-tense narrative, in so far as it operates in a standard teleological fashion, attempts to square the circle, performing the blatantly impossible: it narrates 'as if' in the preterite, but does so in the present tense." Anne Waldron Neumann's (1990) perceptive reading of J. M. Coetzee's *Waiting for the Barbarians* (1980) similarly demonstrates that present-tense narration does not automatically imply synchronicity between story and narration, and in his analysis of Rick Moody's short story "The Grid" (1998 [1995]), Rüdiger Heinze (2013, 124–125) also contends that "there is a narrator who looks back at events as they happened in the past but chooses to tell them using the present tense" (125).

interior monologue, also circumvents the logical improbability of a narrative situation in which story and discourse levels temporally coincide. Interior monologue can be encountered in what Huber refers to as "narrative[s] without a narratee" (2016, 55), that is, narratives which focus on the internal state(s) of one or several characters. In lieu of "indicat[ing] a narrative situation for which there would be neither time nor location or addressee," such narratives pretend "to reflect the current thoughts of the protagonist" (Huber 2016, 55).[35] By obscuring the act of narration proper, interior monologue thus avoids problems that might be caused by a seeming simultaneity between experience and its narrative mediation.[36]

Despite Huber's main argument that contemporary narrative fiction has freed itself from a "mimetic bias favour[ing] believable and realistic narrative situations" (2016, 6; see also Chapter 2.2), each of the three new types of present-tense narration she introduces still enables readers to resolve logical problems arising from present-tense usage by resorting to an understanding of (retrospective) storytelling that is modeled on reality. This is, however, not the only option. In his article "Erzählen im Präsens: Die Korrektur herrschender Tempus-Theorien durch die poetische Praxis in der Moderne" (1992), Jürgen H. Petersen discards the realistic model of retrospective narration. Revisiting linguistic ideas of fictional tense usage, specifically those advanced by Harald

---

35 Huber's view that present-tense narration can generate a "narrative without a narratee" is substantiated by Matt DelConte's (2007) contention that the absence of a narratee is a distinctive feature of present-tense narration. He therefore introduces the concept of the absentee narratee, that is, "the illusion (maintained by both narrator and author) that someone within the story world is listening to the narrative even though the narrative structure does not accommodate that someone" (DelConte 2007, 433).

36 Just as Huber's category of retrospective present-tense narration is inspired by Avanessian and Hennig's reflections on an asynchronous use of the present tense, so too her understanding of interior monologue resonates with previous research on present-tense narration. The argument that the present tense may function as a distinctive feature of consistent internal focalization can already be found in prior work by Dorrit Cohn (1968; 1978, 186–216, 223–232, 264–265; 1999, 107) and Theo Damsteegt (2004, 2005). It is important to note, however, that Damsteegt introduces a new category for representing a character's consciousness in first-person narrative which he terms "Internal Focalization of Awareness (IFA)." This specific strategy, he explains, implies that the narrative events "are reported by the I-as-narrator but are focalized, in the sense of being mentally perceived, by the I-as-character," so that "[t]he present-tense action reports [...] indicate an awareness on the character's part of his or her actions at the very moment they are being performed" (Damsteegt 2005, 42). What is more, the category of IFA substantiates my claim from Footnote 14 in the Introduction – namely that, although Damsteegt investigates present-tense usage in Modern Hindi narratives, his work nevertheless provides valuable insights that can also be applied to English fiction.

Weinrich (see Chapter 2.3.1) and Käte Hamburger (see Chapter 2.1), he introduces a distinction between three different uses of the present tense in narrative fiction that differs markedly from Huber's proposal: (1) the discursive or reflexive present (*besprechendes oder reflektierendes Präsens*), (2) the fictionalizing present (*Fiktions-Präsens*), and (3) the epic or fictional present (*episches* or *fiktionales Präsens*).

The first category, the discursive present, can be found in what Petersen labels the 'essayistic novel' (*Essay-Roman*), that is, a novel which refrains from narrating events that are happening within a fictive storyworld in favor of describing and reflecting upon this specific world. Petersen's reflexive present tense thus complies with Weinrich's juxtaposition of discursive and narrative texts. His second type, the fictionalizing present, represents a specific use of the present tense which explicitly stages the narrated material as pure fiction, that is, as contrived and invented by the narrator. In contrast to the reflexive present, the fictionalizing present does not negate the discourse mode of narration, but rather foregrounds it.[37] Thus, while Petersen's first category of present-tense usage still seems to confirm Weinrich's distinction between discursive and narrative tenses, his second category clearly contradicts it.[38] Finally, Petersen's third category, the epic present, can be understood as a timeless tense that constitutes a hermetic fictional space. That is to say, it can be thought of as the counterpart to Hamburger's epic preterite, the only difference being that Petersen's epic present tense is not confined to third-person narratives, but may also occur in first-person texts.[39]

The crucial difference between Huber's and Petersen's typologies lies in their understanding of fictional tense usage. Huber conceives of tense as a deictic category that designates the temporal relation between narrative events and the act of narrating these events; in her typology, the various uses of present-tense narration are consequently always linked to the narrator's temporal position in relation to the story. Petersen, on the other hand – in resorting to the linguistic argument that tense usage functions not so much as a temporal category but as a generic feature helping us to distinguish different text types (i.e.

---

[37] Cf. Petersen 1992, 79: "Das Fiktions-Präsens stellt eine besondere Art des erzählenden Präsens dar und besitzt daher einen eindeutig epischen Charakter." ["As a special form of the narrative present, the fictionalizing present has a distinctly epic character." (My translation)]

[38] In light of this, one can think of Petersen's fictionalizing present as a precursor of Avanessian and Hennig's (2015 [2012], Ch. 3) "imaginary present" (*imaginäres Präsens*), i.e. a present tense that expresses "a *textual imaginary*" (141; italics in the original).

[39] The reason for this is that Petersen (1992, 80) does not agree with the unique status of a 'feigned' statement which Hamburger attributes to homodiegetic narrative texts.

discursive vs. narrative texts) – sees the present tense as what Fludernik (1996, 252) calls an "adeictic tense," that is, a specific use of tense that has been "deprived of its deictic significance."

Different as Huber's and Petersen's typologies may be, they both exhibit shortcomings in their treatment of present-tense narration. As I have argued elsewhere (cf. Gebauer 2017, 103), Huber's study displays an idiosyncratic use of the concept of interior monologue, which she does not distinguish from less immediate and more coherent modes of thought representation such as psycho-narration or narrated monologue (cf. Cohn 1978, Ch. 1 and Ch. 3).[40] But what is even more important in the context of this project is that her categories are still too closely modeled on the structuralist paradigm of narrative, which relates tense usage to time (see Chapter 2.3.2.1). Petersen, on the other hand, links specific uses of the present tense to specific narrative forms. More particularly, he claims that his first type of present-tense narration, the reflexive narrative present, is a distinctive feature of the essayistic novel. However, as my examples will show, the modes of description, as well as commentary – and thus the use of the descriptive as well as the discursive present – may also prevail in other literary genres such as the *nouveau roman*.[41] Nonetheless, Petersen makes a valid point in adopting the linguistic view that, in the context of narrative fiction, tense usage does not fulfill any temporal function.[42] As I will show in Part II and particularly Chapter 5, this insight is a useful starting point for an adequate description of the various uses of the present tense in narrative fiction.

---

[40] I will discuss Huber's category of interior monologue in greater detail in my reading of Emma Donoghue's novel *Room* (see Chapter 12.2).
[41] Interestingly enough, Petersen (1992, 68–71) discusses the *nouveau roman* in his critique of Hamburger's theory, where he characterizes Alain Robbe-Grillet's use of the present tense in *La Jalousie [Jealousy]* (2012 [1957]) as an instance of narration rather than description: "Bei Robbe-Grillet hingegen begegnet ein [sic] erzählendes Präsens, was sich daran zeigt, daß die Rezeption einer Passage im Präsens im Wesentlichen mit der einer Passage im Präteritum identisch ist." (Petersen 1992, 69) ["In Robbe-Grillet, by contrast, we find a narrative present, as indicated by the fact that the reception of a passage written in the present tense is basically identical with that of a passage written in the past tense." My translation)] Although such a "substitution test" (Casparis 1975, 36) may be a useful strategy for the purpose of scrutinizing possible functions of the present tense, it does not help us determine whether a text passage qualifies as narrative or descriptive. In this respect, I find Petersen's argument less than convincing.
[42] Cf. Petersen 1992, 88: "Denn da das Präsens ebenso als Fiktions- wie als fiktionales, d. i. episches Präsens fungieren kann [...], büßen die Tempora natürlicherweise die mit ihnen bisher verknüpften Eigenschaften ein." ["For, since the present can function as both a fictionalizing and fictional, i.e. epic, present (...), tenses naturally forfeit those characteristics which have usually been associated with them." (My translation)]

However, before we can carry this notion further by discussing its consequences for the narratological framework, we must first turn to various philosophical approaches. These offer yet another perspective on fictional tense usage.

2.3.3 Philosophical Approaches: On the Irrelevance of a Tensed Understanding of Time in Narrative Fiction

Philosophical approaches to tense usage in narrative fiction differ considerably from linguistic and narratological approaches in that they do not investigate the formal and structural implications of this verbal category. Proceeding from the assumption that "narrative is the principal way in which our species organizes its understanding of time" (Abbott 2008 [2002], 3), they construe tense rather as a conceptual means that helps us to better explain our experience of time both in real life and in fiction. The most relevant study in this context is probably Paul Ricœur's *Temps et récit* [*Time and Narrative*] (1983–1985). In the second volume of his seminal work, *La configuration dans le récit de fiction* (1984), he combines linguistic and narratological approaches to fictional tense usage, integrating them into a tripartite model of the human experience of time in narrative. The model posits three different stages of mimesis (*mimèsis*): mimesis I or preconfiguration (*préconfiguration*), mimesis II or configuration (*configuration*), and mimesis III or reconfiguration (*reconfiguration*).[43] Criticizing Harald Weinrich for utilizing verbal tense as a criterion for distinguishing discursive and narrative text types (cf. Ricœur 1985 [1984], 66–77),[44] Ricœur argues that one cannot completely detach tense usage from the notion of time. For, autonomous as the temporal system of a language may be in relation to time – as exhibited in the common denominations of different tense forms – it never entirely breaks with our experience of real time (cf. Ricœur 1985 [1984], 73–74). Ricœur grounds this argument on his conception of the very nature of mimesis II: given that the configuration of time in narrative fiction functions as an intermediary between mimesis I and mimesis III, it only defies the grammatical denominations of our experience of real time, that is, our tensed understanding

---

[43] Ricœur (1984 [1983], Ch. 3) thus conceptualizes our experience of time in narrative as a hermeneutic circle in which our perception of the configuration of narrative time (mimesis II) is not only grounded on our preconception of time as we experience it in the real world (mimesis I), but also has the capacity to influence this understanding of real time in new ways (mimesis III).

[44] For a critique of Weinrich's model, see Chapter 2.3.1.

of past, present, and future (preconfiguration), in order to reinvent this time with grammatical resources that are much more diverse (reconfiguration) (cf. Ricœur 1985 [1984], 76).

On the basis of this assumption, Ricœur goes on to challenge Käte Hamburger's notion of the atemporal quality of past-tense usage in narrative fiction (cf. Ricœur 1985 [1984], 88–99).[45] Taking recourse to the structuralist paradigm of narrative fiction, which posits a relation between the fictional present tense and the narrator, he contends that even the epic preterite retains its function of designating the past. This is because the use of the past tense in narrative fiction refers to narrative events that take place at a moment in time which may constitute the characters' *hic et nunc*, but which is nevertheless postulated as preceding the narrator's present.[46] Ricœur's approach accordingly aligns with the narratological view that tense usage often serves to foreground the double temporal structure of narrative texts in that the present tense refers to the narrative discourse, i.e. the moment in which the narrator tells the story (think of Fludernik's and Huber's category of the deictic present outlined in Chapter 2.3.2.2), and the past tense to the story, i.e. the narrative events that happen in the world evoked by the narrator's account.

While Ricœur's hermeneutic understanding of fictional tense usage is still closely related to both linguistic and narratological theories, recent philosophical studies on tense in narrative fiction approach the topic from a completely different angle. In their 2016 monograph *Time in Fiction*, Craig Bourne and Emily Caddick Bourne explore the phenomenon of fictional time through the lens of analytic philosophy, thus aligning themselves with the tradition of a metaphysics of fiction. Bourne and Caddick Bourne's study is divided into four different parts, the first of which is entirely dedicated to the topic of tense in fiction. Unlike Ricœur, the authors use the term *tense* in a metaphysical (rather than a

---

[45] For an outline of Hamburger's theory, see Chapter 2.1.
[46] Cf. Ricœur 1985 [1984], 98–99; italics in the original: "One answer comes to mind. Could we not say that the preterite preserves its grammatical form and its privilege because the present of narration is understood by the reader as *posterior* to the narrated story, hence that the told story is the *past of the narrative voice*? Is not every told story in the past for the voice that tells it? Whence the artifices employed by writers of other ages, who pretended to have found the diary of their hero in a chest or in an attic, or to have heard the story from a traveler. Such an artifice was intended to simulate, in the latter case, the signification of the past for memory, and in the former, its signification for historiography. When the novelist casts these artifices aside, there still remains the past of the narrative voice, which is neither that of memory nor that of historiography but that which results from the relation of the posteriority of the narrative voice in relation to the story it tells."

linguistic) sense, investigating not so much the phenomenon of tense usage in narrative fiction as the conceptualization of the temporal ordering of the events presented in these texts.[47] Having said that, their insightful findings on our understanding of fictional time raise some important issues for tense usage in narrative fiction.

The starting point for Bourne and Caddick Bourne's engagement with tense in fiction is J. Ellis McTaggart's distinction between a tensed and an untensed or tenseless understanding of time. First introduced in his essay "The Unreality of Time" (1908), McTaggart's distinction (aka the distinction between the A-theory and B-theory of time) describes two ways in which we can order events in time. The A-series implies that the present exists, that the past did exist, and that the future will come to exist; events can consequently be ordered in terms of whether they are past, present, or future – they are tensed. The B-Series, on the other hand, dispenses with the notion of a perpetual existence of the present, so that events are no longer thought of as being past, present, or future, but rather as being 'earlier than,' 'later than,' or 'simultaneous with' each other – they are untensed or tenseless. McTaggart, moreover, states that, in order for events to exist in time, they have to be ordered in relation to an A-series as well as a B-series.

Previous applications of McTaggart's theory to fictional time have demonstrated that, even though "we can order [...] fictional events as earlier or later than one another, it is not appropriate to attempt to locate them using tenses" (Bourne and Caddick Bourne 2016, 33).[48] The reason for this, Bourne and Caddick Bourne explain, is that "the mechanism for *deciding* which time is present [...] requires location in the time series" (2016, 35; italics in the original), which, however, is impossible, given that we cannot be physically located in a fictional world. As a consequence, we can neither "identify any fictional event as pres-

---

[47] In this regard, Bourne and Caddick Bourne's study comes very close to Mark Currie's (2007, 2013) work on narrative temporality, which uses tense as a metaphor to better describe the complex temporal structures underlying fictional narrative texts.

[48] Bourne and Caddick Bourne draw on the preliminary work by Gregory Currie (1992; 1995, Ch. 7; 1998; 1999, 53–57) and Robin Le Poidevin (1988; 2007, Ch. 8), who have both discussed the implications of McTaggart's theory for our understanding of time in fiction. It is important to note, though, that Currie and Le Poidevin adduce a different argument from that of McTaggart, who also links his considerations as to the A-theory and B-theory to fictional time. In the second part of his two-volume study *The Nature of Existence* (1927a/1927b), McTaggart contends that, although fictional events are not really located in time at all because they are non-existent, they are usually imagined as if they did exist in time, which, in turn, means that they are also imagined in both the A-series and the B-series (cf. McTaggart 1927b, 16–17).

ent" nor "earlier fictional events as past or later ones as future" (Bourne and Caddick Bourne 2016, 33). Prior studies have concluded from this insight that fictional time series should be conceived as B-series rather than A-series. Bourne and Caddick Bourne depart from this prevalent view, observing "that most fictions leave it *indefinite* whether their time series is an A-series or a B-series" (2016, 38; italics in the original). That is not to say, though, that these fictions do not represent events as an A-series (e.g. as being located in a fictional past, present, or future) because, as these authors warn us, we must "not confuse our not being in a position to identify a fictional present with there being no fictional present" (Bourne and Caddick Bourne 2016, 41).

What does this mean for tense usage in narrative fiction? If we follow the lead of the narratological approach and construe fictional tense usage – in analogy to tense usage in ordinary discourse – as the temporal relation between the narrator's report of narrative events and the actual occurrence of those events, Bourne and Caddick Bourne's argument implies that this temporal relation between discourse and story becomes indeterminable. For, if we cannot identify any moment that is depicted in the narrative as the present of the fictional storyworld, there is no way for us to make out the temporal positioning of the narrator in relation to this fictional present. As a result, any tense form (e.g. the present, past, or future tense) loses its deictic anchoring.[49] This, in turn, implies that we cannot possibly decide whether the narrator tells of the narrative events in retrospect, in anticipation, or simultaneously with their occurrence. To put it in a nutshell: the moment we can no longer discern a fictional present in a narrative text, the use of tense becomes irrelevant, because the text then lacks any point of reference against which the temporal relations of before and after can be measured.

The problem I see in this conceptualization of fictional time lies in the fact that Bourne and Caddick Bourne exclude the reception of narrative fiction from their theoretical considerations.[50] As Mark Currie, in *About Time: Narrative,*

---

[49] I will provide a more detailed discussion of the phenomenon of deixis in connection with fictional tense usage in Chapter 5.2.
[50] Admittedly, the authors briefly broach the ability of readers to imaginatively transport themselves to a specific moment within fictional worlds (cf. Bourne and Caddick Bourne 2016, 36–37), yet they soon dismiss this option as a possible solution to the metaphysical problem of fictional time series: "Thus, in the absence of a compelling rival mechanism for locating oneself at a particular fictional time, we are inclined to agree with Currie and Le Poidevin that it does not make sense to judge, of any *particular* fictional event, whether it is past, present, or future; or, equivalently, to pick out some fictional events as *the* fictionally present ones." (Bourne and Caddick Bourne 2016, 37; italics in the original)

Fiction and the Philosophy of Time (2007), argues, the act of reading narrative fiction also offers a model of time:

> The reading of a novel [...] involves the passage of events from a world of future possibilities into the actuality of the reader's present, and onwards into the reader's memory. Read in the right order, therefore, the novel is asymmetrical in the same way that time is, since the present of the reading becomes a kind of gateway through which words, descriptions and events pass in their transition from the realm of possibility into the realm of actuality. The experience of reading, thus described, corresponds to a tensed conception of time and represents the egocentric, or subjective, pole in the relation of the reading subject to the textual object. (Currie 2007, 16; cf. also Currie 2009, 365)

The metaphor of the gateway that Currie introduces in this quotation helps us to dispose of the difficulties analytic philosophers such as Bourne and Caddick Bourne have in determining the present of fictional texts. According to Currie, it is the present of the reading which constitutes the fictional present, as this moment functions as a temporal gate through which each narrative event has to move as a specific narrative is read from beginning to end. During this process of reading, the narrative events pass from a state of future possibility in the realm of fiction the reader does not yet know about, via the state of being actual events in the fictional universe in which the reader is currently immersed, to the state of being past events in a storyworld that continues to exist in the reader's memory. By thus construing the fictional present not as a static, but rather as a flexible point in a time series that hinges on the moment of reading, Currie enables us to unequivocally identify the experience of reading narrative fiction as an A-series or – as he himself formulates it – "as a tensed conception of time."[51]

However, even if we adopt Currie's understanding of fictional time, this does not change the fact that, seen from the perspective of analytic philosophy, the use of verbal tense is insignificant for the temporal structure of narrative texts. During his own engagement with McTaggart's theory and its application to narrative fiction, Currie stressed that the process of reading a novel is tensed in two respects: "it is tensed not only in relation to the reader's historical now, but also the now into which the reader is interpellated [sic] by the fiction, ir-

---

[51] In *Time and the Novel* (1972), A. A. Mendilow proposes a similar argument: "There is as a rule one point of time in the story which serves as the point of reference. From this point the fictive present may be considered as beginning. In other words, the reader if he is engrossed in his reading translates all that happens from this moment of time onwards into an imaginative present of his own and yields to the illusion that he is himself participating in the action or situation, or at least is witnessing it as happening, not merely as having happened." (Mendilow 1972, 96–97)

respective of history." (Currie 2007, 149) Viewed in this light, the fictional present is always constituted by that moment in fictional time the reader is currently reading about. This moment always and invariably forms the fictional 'now,' regardless of whether a narrative is written in the past tense or the present.[52]

By thus separating the temporal structure of narrative from tense usage, the philosophical argument enables us to challenge the central premise of most narratological approaches to present-tense narration, namely that fictional tense usage usually indicates the moment of narration. This does not mean, however, that, in the context of narrative fiction, tense loses its significance altogether. As Christian Paul Casparis (1975, 33) justifiably claims, "[t]he difference in tense usage reflects no temporal difference, it reflects different ways of perceiving, interpreting, and relating particular events." The following chapter will discuss the consequences of a modified understanding of fictional tense usage for a narratological model of present-tense narration.

---

[52] On a related note, cf. also Mendilow 1972, 97: "Verbally, all may be equally past; psychologically, once the point of reference [for the fictional present] has been established, each event presented in its time-order constitutes a point in the past series considered as a now, and whatever is out of sequence in relation to that series of points is considered as relatively past or future."

Part II: **A Narratological Model of Present-Tense Usage in Narrative Fiction**

3 The 'Grammatical' Fallacy, or: Why We Need a Descriptive and Analytical Model of Present-Tense Narration

As the preceding survey of cross-disciplinary approaches to present-tense usage in narrative fiction has shown, narrative theory is in need of a descriptive and analytical model of present-tense narration that is differentiated enough to do justice not only to the ubiquity, but also to the diversity of present-tense usage in the contemporary novel. This research lacuna primarily stems from the way in which previous work on the fictional present has conceived of this specific narrative tense. Most narratological approaches I have discussed in Chapter 2 reveal what I shall henceforth designate as *the 'grammatical' fallacy*: Proceeding from the premise that the fictional present tense represents a linguistic or textual feature of narrative texts comparable to tense use in ordinary discourse, these approaches assume that it represents a grammatical category which, by definition, refers to the temporal relation between the act of narration and the narrated events. Thus it always expresses some kind of temporal property. What these approaches largely ignore, however, is that, more often than not, tense usage operates differently in fictional from the way it does in non-fictional discourse.

Linguistic and philosophical approaches both recognize this difference; yet the conclusions they draw from this insight defeat narratological purposes. Instead of maintaining that the use of the present tense is excluded from the discourse mode of narrative (the linguistic position) or insinuating that tense usage does not matter in narrative, as time is tenseless in fictional texts (the philosophical position), it would be more promising to inquire into the formal, structural, and functional implications of both linguistic and philosophical approaches for a narratological model of present-tense narration. How, for example, does the fact that the present tense is usually associated with (non-narrative) discursive speech influence today's new practices of storytelling? Does the process of narration work differently in present- from the way it does in past-tense narratives? What are the textual functions of present-tense usage in narrative fiction and what are its cognitive effects? For, even if it is true that tense does not serve any temporal purpose in narrative fiction, as both linguistic and philosophical approaches suggest, this does not automatically mean that it does not fulfill any function at all. How, then, does the present tense influence the process of narrative worldmaking, and how exactly – if at all – does it contribute to the representation of time in narrative fiction? This chapter will address these and related questions by integrating some of the linguistic and philosophical considerations on (present-)tense usage that were presented in the previous chapter into a narratological model of present-tense narration. To do this, however, we first need to overcome the 'grammatical' fallacy underlying the classical narratological paradigm.

Interestingly, although we can think of the 'grammatical' fallacy as a (mis-)interpretation of the present tense inspired by linguistic insights into tense usage in everyday communication and non-literary written discourse, the feature seems more prominent in narratological than in linguistic contexts. That is to say, the majority of narratological studies dealing with present-tense narration try to explain the phenomenon in terms of common grammatical rules, which is also the reason why I have called the fallacy '*grammatical.*' But I would like to emphasize at this point that the term '*grammatical' fallacy* is not intended to mean that the present tense should not be regarded as a grammatical category. What I would like to express by this term is rather that, if used in narrative fiction, the present tense – or, in fact, any tense – may serve so many purposes that exceed the deictic function of expressing the temporal relation between the speaker and the content of their utterance that it no longer seems sufficient to describe the phenomenon of fictional tense usage solely with reference to grammar. I in no way dispute the grammatical status of tense as a verbal category as such. In order to indicate this qualification, I put the adjective *grammatical* in inverted commas.

Most narratologists acknowledge that present-tense narration is not limited to the function of referring to a specific here-and-now; yet they all link the use of the present tense to the aspect of temporality, thus abiding by the rules of (present-)tense usage stated in grammar books. In her chapter on "The Deviance of Simultaneous Narration" in *The Distinction of Fiction* (1999), Dorrit Cohn argues, for example, that "the present is the most pluri-significant of all tenses" (106), adding that, when "[u]sed as a global fictional tense," it "can potentially bring into play all these meanings and more, fusing and confusing, consuming and subsuming them to create a grammatically homologous field of unparalleled semantic tension, instability, flexibility, and ambiguity" (107). A similar argument can be found in Monika Fludernik's chapter on "The Narrative Present" in *Towards a 'Natural' Narratology* (1996), where she stresses that "the present tense manifests a pronounced multi-functionality" (254), which is why it can be deployed as a substitute for all tenses except those belonging to the present-tense system.[1] In the most recent monograph on *Present-Tense Narration in Contemporary Literature* (2016), Irmtraud Huber follows her precursors in claiming that "the present tense has today come to fulfil all the functions of past-tense narrations" (17). The reason for this, she argues, is that this specific tense can evoke different narrative scenarios (i.e. narrative deictic narration, retrospective narration, interior monologue, and simultaneous narration), each of which exhibits a different temporal distance between the narrative events and the narrator's act of relating these events (e.g. in the first two scenarios this temporal distance is rather large, whereas in the second two scenarios, it is rather small) (cf. Huber 2016, 18–19; see also Chapter 2.3.2.2). Huber therefore concludes that "contemporary present-tense narration is highly heterogeneous" (2016, 17).

Constantly reiterated in narratological work on present-tense narration, the 'multifunctionality argument' invites comparison with another verbal category that has been excessively discussed by narratologists, namely that of person. Thanks to its pluri-significance, the fictional present tense may remind us of those ambiguous personal pronouns that are used in the context of second-person narration or homodiegetic plural narration. In the first case, the second-person pronoun singular *you* can, for example, refer to the implied reader, the flesh-and-blood reader, a generic 'you,' or – in the form of a first-person pronoun in disguise – even to the autodiegetic narrator of a fictional narrative;[2] in the second case, the first-person pronoun plural *we* can, for instance, relate to a specific group of characters the narrator feels he or she belongs to, a specific social community within the storyworld that exhibits a collective identity, or the collective between the narrator and the fictive narratee(s).[3] When used in narrative fiction, the actual meaning of the personal pronouns *you* and *we* thus always depends on the narrative context in which these pronouns occur (cf. Bekhta 2017a, 108; Mildorf 2016, 146–147).

---

1 In a later article, however, Fludernik (2003a, 121) notes that the choice of tense in narrative fiction is not responsible for the underlying temporal structure of these texts (see also Chapter 1).
2 For the various "typolog[ies] of address" (Iliopoulou 2019, 18) in second-person narratives, cf. e.g. Bonheim 1983; Capecci 1989; Fludernik 1993a; 1994; 2011, 105–113; Herman 1994; Iliopoulou 2019, Ch. 1; Korte 1987; Margolin 1994; Parker 2018; Reitan 2011; Richardson 1991; 2006, Ch. 2; and Schofield 1996.
3 A systematic discussion of the possible meanings of the pronoun *we* in narrative fiction is provided, among others, in Bekhta 2017a; 2017b; 2020, Ch. 2; Fludernik 2011, 114–117; Gallotti and Lyne 2019; Marcus 2008, 2009; Margolin 1996, 2000, 2001; and Richardson 2006, Ch. 3; 2009.

I would argue that the same applies to the present tense: if we want to make sense of the use of this specific verbal category in narrative fiction, we have to take into account the entire narrative context in which it occurs. It is clearly not a coincidence that Fludernik opens her discussion of present-tense narration in *Towards a 'Natural' Narratology* (1996) with a detailed analysis of Judith Small's short story "Body of Work" (cf. 249–251). This three-page present-tense narrative was first published in *The New Yorker* on July 8, 1991. Fludernik examines it very thoroughly, going through the text paragraph by paragraph. In so doing, she shows that Small deploys the fictional present tense in various ways to achieve different textual as well as readerly effects within her story: As Fludernik demonstrates, Small's use of the fictional present generates the illusion of narrative immediacy, creates the impression of interior monologue, simulates the mode of filmic description, and evokes familiar patterns of oral narrative (cf. 1996, 250). Fludernik's analysis of tense usage in "Body of Work" illustrates perfectly that the function of the fictional present can vary not only from narrative to narrative, but even within a single narrative. As a consequence, it is not sufficient to analyze occasional instances of present-tense narration that have been taken out of their narrative context: we must always have to consider the narrative as a whole.

It follows that an adequate analysis of present-tense narration does not allow of any variant of either form-to-function mapping or function-to-form mapping.[4] We jump to the wrong conclusion if we regard the use of the present tense as a distinctive feature of simultaneous narration suggesting a synchronicity between the narrative events and the act of narrating these events (form-to-function mapping). Chapter 5 will explain that the present tense contributes very little to the evocation of such a narrative scenario (see 5.6 below). The same chapter will also demonstrate that to connect only one specific narrative function with present-tense narration (function-to-form mapping) is likewise premature: present-tense usage can, in fact, serve a wide range of purposes in narrative fiction. Although readers are generally quick to ascribe to the fictional present tense a sense of immediacy and urgency, it would be wrong to assume that this is a default function of present-tense narration.

The reason for this is what psychonarratologists refer to as "confounding" (Bortolussi and Dixon 2003, 51–55): a process that takes place during reader reception of narrative strategies. Marisa Bortolussi and Peter Dixon argue that whenever a specific textual feature and a specific readerly response covary, or

---

4 For a discussion of the distinction between form-to-function mapping and function-to-form mapping, cf. Jacobs and Jucker 1995.

co-occur, "there are three possible causal explanations: The first variable [i.e. the textual feature] can cause the second [i.e. the readerly response], the second variable can cause the first, or some other, third, variable may cause both of these" (2003, 52).[5] With respect to the phenomenon of present-tense narration, this means that if we observe the textual feature of fictional present-tense usage as covarying with the reader's feeling of accessing the narrative events in the very moment that they are happening, we readily draw the conclusion that present-tense narration generates narrative immediacy and urgency. According to Bortolussi and Dixon's argument, however, we must not ignore the possibility that there could also be a third "confounding variable" (2003, 52) causing both of the other two variables by (a) requiring that a narrative be written in the present tense and (b) separately evoking the impression of narrative immediacy and urgency.

In fact, the possibility that the covariation between fictional present-tense usage and readers' hypotheses about the function of this specific tense is actually caused by a third variable is highly plausible. As my readings of various present-tense novels in Part III will show, it is never the present tense alone that brings about a specific textual or readerly effect, but always its combination with other narrative strategies such as the representation of time and space, narrative pace, narrative voice, and focalization (for a complete list of narrative strategies with which the present tense can correlate, see Chapter 6).[6] Thus the

---

5 Bortolussi and Dixon (2003, 51–59) introduce the concept of confounding in the context of textual experiments designed to investigate the causes for specific reader responses to narrative texts. Starting from the premise that "particular reader constructions [are] caused by particular features of the text," the authors contend that "the best technique for assessing such causation is to conduct *textual experiments*, in which particular features of a text are identified and manipulated by the researcher" (Bortolussi and Dixon 2003, 51; italics in the original). More specifically, they explain that, "[i]n a properly designed textual experiment, several versions of a text are created that are identical except for the single, manipulated feature," and conclude that "[e]xperiments of this sort have a special relationship to causal explanations and, as a consequence, should be used whenever possible to evaluate hypotheses concerning the connection between features and constructions" (Bortolussi and Dixon 2003, 51). In the context of these textual experiments, the confounding variable represents a third variable that interferes with the covariation between a specific textual strategy and a specific readerly response – that is, it compromises any possible interpretation of the textual strategy as the cause of the readerly response.
6 This ties in with Jarmila Mildorf's (2016) argument with respect to the use of personal pronouns in narrative fiction. Exploring the relationship between second-person narration and readerly involvement, she maintains that "it is not so much the second-person pronoun alone but its occurrence in and its interplay with a given discourse context that need to be taken into consideration" (Mildorf 2016, 146). The reason she suggests for this is that "the indexical pro-

potential functions of present-tense narration always depend on the narrative context in which the tense is used, which is why any attempts at form-to-function mapping or function-to-form mapping inevitably fail to do justice to the complexity of this narrative phenomenon.[7]

Admittedly, the 'multifunctionality argument' still prevalent in work on present-tense narration acknowledges the grammatical complexity of the fictional present and hence emphasizes the temporal heterogeneity of this specific tense. However, this argument overlooks the multi-faceted effects of present-tense narration; these exceed the temporal scope of the present tense as expounded in grammar books. In her work on the nexus between tense and narrativity, Suzanne Fleischman (1990, 1991a) – as we have seen in Chapter 1 – contends that the relationships between tense and time in narrative fiction do not reflect those of ordinary language. With Fleischman I would argue that, when used in narrative fiction, the present tense no longer functions as a simple grammatical category, but rather serves as a fully-fledged narrative strategy. It can generate various textual as well as readerly effects which are by no means necessarily restricted to the representation of the temporal relation between the act of narration and the narrative events.

A general objection to this discussion is related to my claim in the Introduction that readers may not even notice that a novel is written in the present tense. Indeed, it is true that many readers are oblivious to a narrative's specific tense use. For example, whenever I ask my students in which tense the last novel they read was written, the majority of them cannot remember whether it was the past or the present. This may be partly due to the fact that I mostly teach freshmen or second-year students who have not yet developed a profound analytical interest in narrative form. However, I get similar responses when asking some of my colleagues whether they prefer present- or past-tense narratives: even literary scholars with a narratologically trained eye sometimes overlook the tense in which a narrative is written – or at least they forget it as soon as they have finished reading the text (cf. also Harrison 1995, 80). For authors, on the other hand, the choice of tense is a deliberate and strategic decision. The reason for this is that both the past and present tenses facilitate or impede specific ways of

---

noun *you* does not operate in a discursive vacuum," but is instead always affected by "other linguistic features" (Mildorf 2016, 146; italics in the original).

7 On a related note, cf. also Vera and Ansgar Nünning (2000b, 31), who argue that there is no one-to-one correlation between narrative forms and functions. See also Meir Sternberg (1982, 148; italics in the original), who, following the "Proteus Principle," observes that "in different contexts [...] the same form may fulfill different functions *and* different forms the same function."

storytelling.[8] From the perspective of narrative design, it makes a great difference whether a text is written in the past or the present tense.

Using the analogy of the grammatical category of person will again help me clarify my argument. Since the onset of discourse-oriented narratology,[9] the traditional paradigm of narrative considers the category of person as a central feature for analyzing the phenomenon that Gérard Genette (1980 [1972], Ch. 5) first referred to as "voice." Here, Genette's binary opposition between homodiegetic and heterodiegetic narrators is seminal (cf. 1980 [1927], 227–231) – even though not every narratologist takes up Genette's terminology.[10] In Franz K. Stanzel's (1986 [1979], xvi) typological circle, the opposition between first- and third-person reference similarly forms one of the three constitutive elements that define a specific narrative situation.[11]

Both Genette's and Stanzel's theories enable us to see that, even though the distinction between homodiegetic (or first-person) narration and heterodiegetic (or third-person) narration is also based on the single grammatical category of person, it has decisive implications for the narrative perspective of a specific text. While only those narratives in which the narrator appears as a first-person speaker can confront readers with an overt narrator whose presence enables them to enter into the narrative illusion of being told a story (cf. Nünning 2000, 69; 2001b, 27),[12] it is only in third-person narratives that the narrator can recede

---

8 This is also reflected in recent writer's guides that present the fictional present as one of the careful choices an author has to make during his or her craft of fiction course. In *Steering the Craft* (1998), Ursula K. Le Guin states that "[n]arrative tense [...] [is] something prose writers need to think about, to be conscious of, so they can choose the tense appropriate to the effect they want" (70). And, in her opinion, the past and present tenses are not mutually interchangeable; rather, "[t]here are times the present tense is the right one, and there are times the past tense is the right one" (Le Guin 1998, 75). David Jauss shares Le Guin's attitude toward fictional tense usage. In the fourth chapter of *On Writing Fiction: Rethinking Conventional Wisdom About the Craft* (2011), the creative writing professor enumerates seven advantages and ten disadvantages of fictional present-tense usage that may help writers make that choice. Moreover, any spontaneous, non-systematic Google search for the items *fictional present, narrative present, present-tense fiction* and the like reveals numerous writing blogs or discussion forums on creative writing that also deal with the question of whether to use the past or present tense when writing fiction.
9 For a distinction between discourse-oriented and story-oriented narratology, cf. Neumann and Nünning 2008, 18–19.
10 James Phelan (2005), for example, prefers the term *character narration* over that of *homodiegetic narration*.
11 The other two constitutive elements are perspective and mode (cf. Stanzel 1986 [1979], xvi).
12 A more detailed discussion of Nünning's concept of narrative illusion (*Erzählillusion*) or mimesis of narration (*Mimesis des Erzählens*) will be provided in Chapter 5.4.

so much into the background (covert narrator) that readers get the impression of having immediate access to the character's thoughts, emotions, and experiences.[13] Of course, these are only the most obvious differences between homodiegetic and heterodiegetic narratives; yet they suffice to illustrate that an author's decision in favor of either a homodiegetic or a heterodiegetic narrator entails not only the choice of a specific personal pronoun, but defines an entire narrative scenario. The significance of the personal pronoun in narrative texts far surpasses its grammatical function, and every literary scholar, especially every narratologist, seems to accept this without any caveat.

I believe that the same ought to apply to tense usage in narrative fiction. We tend to attach little importance to fictional tense usage because we believe that it is only a simple grammatical category. This impression is reinforced by the fact that we rarely notice the tense in which the novels we read are written (unless we force ourselves to pay attention to it, for example when performing a close reading or a narratological analysis), and if we do, we quickly forget it once we have put the book aside. However, if we accept Roy Sommer's (2020a) contention that we remember not the content or formal make-up of the narratives we read, but rather the cognitive and emotional experience of reading these texts,[14] the same will probably hold for a narrative's use of personal pronouns. Do we remember whether the last novel we read was a first-person or a third-person narrative? I doubt that my students would answer this question with "yes," unless the last novel they read featured a conspicuous speaking agent such as the unreliable narrator Humbert Humbert in Vladimir Nabokov's *Lolita* (2006 [1955]) or Mark Haddon's autistic child narrator in *The Curious Incident of the Dog in the Night-Time* (2004 [2003]). But they would probably remember whether they could engage with the protagonist of the story, sharing his or her thoughts and feelings, or whether they perceived the storyworld from an internal or an external point of view. However, our recollections of the sense of strategic narrative empathy (*sensu* Keen 2007) or spatiotemporal immersion (*sensu* Ryan 2015 [2001], 93–99) do not help us to remember the narrative situation, for such reading experiences can be evoked by homodiegetic and hetero-

---

13 For a distinction of the terms *overt narrator* and *covert narrator*, cf. Chatman 1978, Ch. 5.
14 Cf. Sommer 2020a, 94; italics in the original: "Being immersed in fictional worlds, readers activate all sorts of knowledge and memory systems, most of them short-term, some meant to last. Most likely, though, what we remember is not the narrative design of a novel, its structure, form, or style (unless these are explicitly foregrounded), or even the content, which can be captured in a plot summary, but first and foremost the reading experience itself. We will retain fond memories of a novel long after we have forgotten all the details, the 'existents' (as narratologists call the nitty-gritty of storytelling): characters, names, settings, events."

diegetic narratives alike (cf. Nünning 2014, 177–220). In Sommer's hypothesis, then, we also forget about the grammatical category of person in narrative texts. Yet narratology rightly gives great importance to this grammatical feature of narrative voice. Why, therefore, should we not also proceed similarly with fictional tense usage?

In light of the parallels between the grammatical categories of tense and person, I would argue that the distinction between past- and present-tense narration can be construed as analogical to the distinction between homodiegetic (first-person) narration and heterodiegetic (third-person) narration. That is to say, an author's choice of a specific tense is of similar significance for the narrative design of a specific text as the decision for or against a specific personal pronoun. Against this background I propose the key distinction between *grammatical tense* and *fictional tense*: Grammatical tense is the linguistic category that enables us to indicate in ordinary communication whether we are referring to past, present, or future. Fictional tense is the narrative device that helps authors to bring about specific textual as well as readerly effects in narrative fiction. When used as a fictional narrative strategy, tense can express a temporal relation between the narrative events and the act of narration. Yet it does not necessarily do this, and may fulfill various other (non-temporal) functions instead. Fictional tenses (i.e. the fictional past, present, and future) therefore ought to be set apart from any notions of diegetic time: i.e. of the temporal dimension of the storyworlds evoked in narrative fiction (the diegetic past, present, and future).[15]

This redefinition of fictional tense as a proper narratological category also changes our understanding of the phenomenon of present-tense narration. As soon as we start to conceive of the fictional present tense as a complex, multi-

---

15 I would like to stress that, although I construe fictional tense as a narrative strategy which is not necessarily related to the aspect of time, my intention is not to endorse an "atemporal view" (Zucchi 2001, 322–324) by any suggestion that fictional tenses never "express temporal relations," that is, that "they [never] indicate anteriority, posteriority or coincidence with the time of utterance" (Zucchi 2001, 322). I would, rather, emphasize that a temporal interpretation of fictional tense usage is only one of many possible options; for, in the context of narrative fiction, tense can fulfill numerous other functions which do not contribute to the construction of narrative time. In light of this, my conceptualization of the fictional present tense should not be confused with Dorrit Cohn's (1999, 106) understanding of the fictional present as a specific use of the present tense in homodiegetic narratives which "dislocat[es] the narrated text from a temporally fixed point of origin, much as Hamburger's interpretation of the past tense in third-person fiction detaches it from the obligatory retrospection it signifies in nonfictional discourse."

functional narrative strategy, we realize that, to describe this narrative phenomenon adequately, we need to identify descriptive and analytical instruments that go beyond grammatical and temporal categories. This is exactly what this study strives to do.

In the remaining chapters of the theoretical part of this book (Part II), I shall present a narratological model of present-tense narration that provides categories and concepts for an accurate description and analysis of the forms and functions of present-tense usage in narrative fiction. The model has been designed in such a way that it enables us to recognize and address the complexity of fictional tense usage in general as well as the characteristic features of fictional present-tense usage in particular. More specifically, my descriptive and analytical model of present-tense narration will allow us to

1. systematically describe formal as well as structural aspects of fictional (present-)tense usage by means of clearly defined concepts and differentiated categories (see Chapter 4);
2. identify different functions of present-tense narration in narrative fiction (see Chapter 5);
3. characterize the ways in which these functions interact with each other or correlate with different narrative strategies and/or phenomena by identifying and providing useful categories to systematically describe such aspects (see Chapter 6).

As this list shows, the descriptive and analytical instruments I shall here introduce can be subdivided into three different groups, each of which relates to a different dimension of (present-)tense usage in narrative fiction: the *formal-structural* (group 1), the *functional* (group 2), and the *syntactic dimensions* (group 3).[16]

---

16 The three-dimensional structure of my narratological model of present-tense narration is inspired by Vera and Ansgar Nünning's (2000b, 20–26) conceptualization of narrative multiperspectivity, which is grounded in literary theory. If we want to describe and analyze the phenomenon of multiperspectivity in narrative texts systematically, the authors argue, we should take eight different dimensions into consideration: (1) the formal or discourse-oriented dimension, (2) the semantic dimension, (3) the syntactic dimension, (4) the pragmatic dimension, (5) the functional dimension, (6) the referential and cultural dimension, (7) the normative and ideological dimension, and (8) the diachronic dimension. Since multiperspectivity, however, differs as a narrative phenomenon from tense usage (the latter exclusively qualifies as a formal device, whereas the former involves both the 'how' of narrative transmission and the 'what' of narrative content), I here only adopt those dimensions which relate to the discourse (rather than the content) level of narrative texts.

In covering three different dimensions of fictional present-tense usage, my narratological model exhibits a gradual increase in specificity to the effect that the particularities of present-tense narration become successively more important as the argumentation proceeds. The formal and structural component of the model investigates the distribution and narrative staging of present-tense narration within a narrative text. Since the categories and concepts I will identify in this context are not restricted to the use of the present tense, they can equally be applied to other fictional tenses such as the past or the future tense. The functional component of the model, then, is largely confined to the phenomenon of present-tense narration: By addressing the possible textual and readerly effects of present-tense narration, I distinguish eight functions of fictional tense usage which primarily concern the fictional present, with a few exceptions which can also become effective in past- or future-tense narration (I will explicitly indicate these exceptions in Chapter 5.1). Finally, the syntactic component of my model examines how the tense-specific functions differentiated in Chapter 5 may interact with each other and how the fictional present can correlate with other narrative techniques. In the context of this third dimension, the focus of interest lies exclusively on the present tense; other fictional tenses are set aside.

Taken together, then, all three components of my narratological model of present-tense narration provide a well-stocked tool box that facilitates a precise and differentiated description of the formal and structural dimension of fictional tense usage in general as well as the functional and syntactic dimensions of fictional present tense usage in particular. More importantly, in addition to its combination of broad and narrow categories – that is, categories which hold for all fictional tenses and those which only apply to the fictional present – the model's tripartite structure allows us to explore the multifacetedness of fictional present-tense usage from both a text-centered and a reception-oriented perspective. In the model interpretations that form the second part of this thesis I shall then illustrate how my narratological model of present-tense narration can be used in practice by employing my descriptive tools and analytical instruments to reveal the narrative design of a selection of present-tense novels from various genres.

4 The Formal-Structural Dimension of Fictional (Present-)Tense Usage: Textual Distribution and Narrative Orchestration

When analyzing tense usage in narrative fiction, we first need to examine its formal and structural dimensions. This entails two factors: the distribution of tense within a narrative text and the ways in which the text orchestrates its use of tense. In what tense is a specific narrative written? Does it employ more than one tense form? If so, do the tense shifts follow a regular pattern? Does a narrative foreground its specific use of fictional tense, so that readers consciously notice it, or does the text rather treat it in a subtle way, so that readers tend to overlook it?

If we want to understand how exactly fictional tense forms operate within a specific text, we first need to consider such formal and structural aspects. An analysis of fictional tense usage that does justice to the complexity and multifacetedness of this narrative technique always requires that we take a thorough look at the phenomenon – close reading is certainly the method of choice here.[1] In the following two subsections of this chapter, I will present three formal and two structural criteria that may help us to better describe and more adequately analyze tense usage in narrative fiction.

4.1 Formal Criteria for Determining the Distribution of Tense Usage in Narrative Fiction: Variety, Scope, and Prominence

The first formal aspect to examine is the *variety of fictional tense usage*. In this respect, it is useful to distinguish between the two categories of *homogenous* and *heterogeneous usage*. Homogeneous tense usage prevails in those narratives which deploy only one specific tense form as their tense of narration, whereas heterogeneous tense usage applies to narratives which employ two or more different tense forms. While traditional past-tense narrative may commonly feature only the preterite as its tense of narration – think, for example, of James Joyce's *A Portrait of the Artist as a Young Man* (2000 [1914–1915]), Oscar

---

[1] For a detailed description of the methodology of narratological textual analysis, cf. Sommer 2010 and 2020b.

Wilde's *The Picture of Dorian Gray* (1994 [1891]), or Virginia Woolf's *Mrs. Dalloway* (1996 [1925])² – homogeneous tense usage in the present-tense novel is extremely rare. To my knowledge, the only present-tense novel that exhibits homogeneous tense usage is *The Unnamable* (2010 [1953]) – apart from Samuel Beckett's experimental play with the genre of the novel, I have not yet encountered any book-length narrative that deploys the fictional present as its only tense of narration.

This may be attributed to the dual temporal structure of the genre, more precisely its division into story and discourse (cf. Chatman 1990, 9; Herman 2009a, 92–97), which facilitates not only a chronological, but also a non-chronological representation of the narrative events (cf. Sternberg 1990; Wittenberg 2018).³ As a matter of fact, every novel, whether written in the past or present tense, has its moments of analepsis or prolepsis, at least if it is of a reasonable length (cf. Nelles 2016, 413). In past-tense narratives, such anachronies are usually rendered in a tense form which also belongs to the past-tense system, with the result that paralepses normally feature the past perfect and prolepses some future-in-the-past form (e.g. a construction with 'would' or 'was going to'). Present-tense narratives, by contrast, build in this context on tense variation, to the extent that anachronies are most often expressed in the past (analepsis) or future tense (prolepsis). Present-tense novels therefore frequently contain passages in which the tense of narration intermittently switches from the present to either the preterite or the future.⁴

Past-tense narratives may also feature instances of tense shift; yet these shifts usually occur in different contexts. For example, past-tense narratives that exhibit an overt narrator usually make use of the present tense in order to

---

2 It is not by chance that all the examples I name here qualify as instances of Stanzel's (1955, Ch. IV) figural narrative situation. The reason for this is that the figural narrative situation is the only typical narrative situation in which the narrator recedes so much into the background that he or she is no longer graspable in the text. Stanzel's other two narrative situations, the first-person and the authorial narrative situations, both feature an overt narrator who explicitly appears in the text. Both of these narrative situations thus stage the distinction between the narrative planes of story and discourse which, as I will further explain below, is usually indicated by the use of different tense forms.

3 A detailed discussion of the double temporality of narrative and its implications for the classical narratological paradigm is given in Chapter 5.4.

4 There are also novels which deviate from these standard patterns. In *How Novels Work* (2006), John Mullan discusses the example of John le Carré's past-tense narrative *The Constant Gardener* (2018 [2001]), which indicates instances of analepsis by means of a shift from past to present tense. Le Carré uses the past tense for the narrative action and the present tense for the protagonist's memories (cf. Mullan 2006, 74–76).

refer to the communicative situation between the narrator and the narratee on the discourse level, thus contrasting the narrator's present with the characters' past (cf. Fludernik 1993b, 47–51, 198–199).[5] Monika Fludernik (2003a, 123) first referred to this specific use of the fictional present as its "deictic use," and this term has been adopted by other literary scholars working on present-tense narration (cf. Huber 2016, Ch. 3).[6] The example of the deictic use of the fictional present indicates that the variety of tense usage in past-tense narratives results not so much from the non-chronological depiction of the narrative events – as is the case in the context of present-tense narration – as from the temporal distance between the occurrence of the narrative events and the narrator's act of reporting these events.

The fact that both present- and past-tense narratives are often characterized by heterogeneous tense usage gives rise to the question of the *frequency and scope of the use of a specific tense* within a narrative. Again, two categories can be distinguished with the help of this quantitative criterion: *global* and *local tense usage*.[7] Global tense usage refers to the prominent use of a specific tense throughout an entire text. In fact, it is the global use of a specific fictional tense that allows us to speak of 'past-,' 'present-,' or 'future-tense narratives' in the first place. While one could cite numerous examples of global past- and present-tense narratives – e.g. almost all the novels I will discuss in Part III qualify as instances of global use of the fictional present[8] – this is much more difficult for future-tense narratives. Nevertheless, one example comes to mind: Christine Brook-Rose's *Amalgamemnon* (1984). Local tense usage, on the other hand, relates to other tenses occurring within a narrative that features the global use

---

[5] Marcel Vuillaume (1990, Ch. III.2.1.2) likewise argues that, in traditional past-tense narratives, the use of the present tense usually refers to the narrator's discourse, whereas the past tense designates the story. Andreas Ohme (2018, 103) makes the same point when discussing the temporal relation between story and discourse levels of a narrative text: "Bezieht sich der Erzähler auf das von ihm vermittelte Geschehen, so verwendet er das Präteritum, bezieht er sich hingegen auf den Vermittlungsvorgang, so benutzt er das Präsens." ["When the narrator refers to the events he is communicating, he uses the preterite; however, when he refers to the act of communication, he uses the present tense." (My translation)]

[6] For a more detailed discussion of Fludernik's understanding of the deictic use of the fictional present, see Chapter 5.2.

[7] I here borrow my terminology from Dorrit Cohn (1999, 102), who uses the expressions *global use of the present* and *local use of the present* to distinguish between narratives that are entirely written in the present tense and past-tense narratives that only deploy the present tense intermittently.

[8] The sole exception is Margaret Atwood's *Oryx and Crake* (2004 [2003]), which is partly written in the present tense and partly in the past tense (see Chapter 8).

of a different tense. If, for example, a present-tense novel partly deploys past and future tenses (e.g. in connection with flashbacks and flashforwards), then the bulk of this narrative is written in the present tense (global present-tense usage), whereas the past and future tenses only occur locally within the text (local past- and future-tense usage).

Another qualitative criterion similarly connected to the category of heterogeneous tense usage is the *prominence of a specific tense* within a narrative. In this context, one can differentiate between *central* and *peripheral tense usage*. If I illustrate these binary opposites here on the example of the fictional present, this is due only to my interest in present-tense narration. At this stage of my narratological model this does not imply that the categories in question do not also apply to past- and future-tense narration. Quite the contrary: as with all the other categories I introduce in this section, the distinction between central and peripheral tense usage holds for all common fictional tenses – the past, the present, and the future.

We can speak of a central use of the fictional present if this specific tense plays a more prominent role than all the other tenses used in a text. When Hilary Mantel's historical novels *Wolf Hall* (2010 [2009]), *Bring Up the Bodies* (2013 [2012]), and *The Mirror & the Light* (2020) for instance, deploy the present tense to help readers immerse themselves in the complex and unsettling intrigues of the court of King Henry VIII in sixteenth-century London, this specific tense fulfills a much more salient function than do the other tenses Mantel occasionally employs in her narratives. For it is only the present tense which allows readers to transport themselves right onto the narrative scene, allowing them to feel as if they were contemporaries of the protagonist Thomas Cromwell, Chief Minister of the King.[9] The example, moreover, demonstrates that the central use of a fictional tense is closely linked to its global use: only if a tense dominates a narrative can it perform a superior function in relation to the other tenses occurring in the text.

Conversely, peripheral present-tense usage can be found exclusively in narratives which feature the fictional present as a local tense of narration. A perfect example in this context is, again, what Fludernik (2003a, 124) identifies as "the deictic use of the present tense" – that is, the occurrence of the present tense in a past-tense narrative where it refers to the here-and-now of the narrator on the discourse level (rather than to the here-and-now of the characters on the story level). As will be discussed in greater detail in Chapter 5.4, such a peripheral use of the fictional present is sometimes combined with metanarrative comments in

---

[9] I will provide an analysis and interpretation of Mantel's first two Tudor novels in Chapter 7.

which narrators of past-tense narratives reflect upon their activity of storytelling. By either heightening the authenticity of the act of narration, or drawing readers' attention to the constructed nature of the narrative (cf. Nünning 2001a, 147–148), these metanarrative comments may achieve various effects to which the use of the present tense certainly contributes. However, as long as the narrative does not qualify as an instance of metafiction which, as such, continually reminds readers of its artificial status,[10] these present-tense reflections on the part of the narrator usually constitute only a small part of the novel. In this case, the referential function of the past tense clearly outweighs the metareferential function of the present tense.[11]

4.2 Structural Criteria for Analyzing the Orchestration of Tense Usage in Narrative Fiction: Tense Alternation and Foregrounding of Tense

While the criteria I have presented so far (i.e. variety, frequency and scope, and prominence) all relate to the formal level of fictional tense usage, the remaining two criteria I will discuss in this section are concerned with the structural level of this narrative device. The first of these structural criteria addresses the question of *tense alternation*.[12] If a narrative exhibits heterogeneous tense usage, it

---

10 For a more thorough definition of metafiction, cf. Macrae 2019, Ch. 1.1; Neumann and Nünning 2014, 344–345; Nünning 2001a, 128–133; 2004a, 16; and Wolf 1993, 2001.

11 I provide a detailed discussion of the different functions of fictional present-tense usage in Chapter 5.

12 Few narratological studies explore the phenomenon of fictional tense alternation. So far, tense variation, especially the shift between past and present tense, has been extensively discussed in connection with oral (including conversational) storytelling (cf. e.g. Banfield 1982, 165–167; Chafe 1994, 207–210; Fleischman 1990, 199–203; Fludernik 1991; Harvey 1986; Johnstone 1978; Labelle 1987; Levey 2006; Rodríguez Louro and Ritz 2014; Schiffrin 1978, 1981; Wolfson 1978, 1979, 1981, 1982), as well as the telling of folk tales (cf. Leith 1995a, 1995b). In the context of narrative fiction, however, tense alternation has been investigated predominantly with respect to the phenomenon of the historical present – that is, the intermittent use of the present tense within a past-tense narrative. In his book *Tense Without Time: The Present Tense in Narration* (1975), Christian Paul Casparis provides a comprehensive overview of research on the historical present in narrative fiction until 1975. Interestingly enough, more recent studies on the historical present primarily investigate its usage in medieval English and German literature, particularly focusing on genres which mark the transition from oral to written literature such as courtly love-songs, ballads, and the so-called Spielmann epic (cf. e.g. Fleischman 1986; 1990, Ch. 3.7–3.8; 203–205; Fludernik 1992a, 1992b; Philipowski 2018; Zeman 2010, Ch. 7.2–7.3, 8.1). Few studies deal with tense alternation in twentieth-century and contemporary narrative

4.2 Structural Criteria for Analyzing the Orchestration of Tense Usage in Fiction — 69

necessarily makes use of tense shifts. Depending on whether these shifts follow a discernible pattern, one can distinguish between *regular* and *irregular forms* of tense alternation: I shall henceforth refer to these as *tense-switching* and *tense-mixing* respectively. With regard to tense-switching, one can, moreover, differentiate between the subforms of *temporalization* and *detemporalization* – that is, between instances of tense-switching motivated by the temporal or deictic meaning of different tense forms, and instances motivated by some non-grammatical, and thus atemporal significance of tense.

We can speak of temporalization whenever a narrative deploys different tense forms in order to refer to different time frames within the fictive universe. This is, for example, the default case in any typical first-person past-tense narrative which deploys the strategy of tense-switching to "[foreground] [...] the deictic distance between the act of narration and the story level" (Fludernik 1996, 262). In this context, the present tense refers to the here-and-now of the narrating 'I' and the past tense to the here-and-now of the experiencing 'I,'[13] as the following excerpt from the "Prologue" to Zadie Smith's homodiegetic novel *Swing Time* (2016) perfectly demonstrates:

> I <u>looked</u> at my phone, it <u>was</u> sitting on the counter in airplane mode. I <u>had been</u> offline for seventy-two hours and **can remember feeling** that this should be counted among the great examples of personal stoicism and moral endurance of our times. (*ST*, 1–2; my emphasis)

In the present-tense novel, by contrast, such time-tense relation is somewhat different: here, the opposition between past and present tenses does not necessarily express the temporal distance between the story and the act of narration. Instead, the present tense points to the present situation of the protagonist "in reference to the plot level" (Fludernik 1996, 262) (i.e. irrespective of whether this character is also the narrator of the narrative or not),[14] while the past tense relates to his or her reminiscences of past events and experiences. As a result, temporalization occurs not only in Graham Swift's detective novel *The Light of Day* (2018 [2003]), in which the first-person narrator George Webb, a former policeman who is now a private detective, remembers a case that happened two

---

fiction (cf. e.g. Fleischman 1990, 285–295; Fludernik 1996, Ch. 6.3.4; 2002, 26–32; Njubina and Schischkowa 1990; Osselton 1982; Ruin 1983; Viola 1988; Zeman 2018, 252–253).
13 For the distinction between the narrating and experiencing 'I,' cf. Stanzel 1972 [1964], 31–39.
14 For a more comprehensive discussion of the referential potential of the fictional present, see Chapter 5.2.

years earlier, but also in Margaret Atwood's post-apocalyptic novel *Oryx and Crake* (2004 [2003]), in which an anonymous heterodiegetic narrator tells the fate of Snowman, the seemingly last human survivor within a posthuman world who constantly yearns for his former pre-apocalyptic life.[15]

Detemporalization, on the other hand, occurs in narratives which use the strategy of tense-switching not so much for a temporal purpose as to some other effect which does not hinge on the linguistic definition of tense as a grammatical category. Probably the most popular example in this connection is the historical present: this intermittent use of the present tense in a predominantly past-tense narrative generally serves to foreground a specific narrative scene by making it more lively and immediate.[16] But tense-switching can also fulfill a thematic function. In the English translation of Haruki Murakami's *Hard-Boiled Wonderland and the End of the World* (2003 [1985]), the opposition between past and present tenses is used to refer to the two different plots, each of which is set in one of the first-person narrative's main settings: passages written in the past tense deal with narrative events that take place in Hard-Boiled Wonderland (i.e. a futuristic Tokyo), whereas passages written in the present tense relate to the events that occur at the End of the World (i.e. a fantastic and surreal parallel universe).[17] Han Kang's *The Vegetarian* (2015 [2007]) similarly features a regular shift pattern between past and present tenses. Unlike Murakami's text, however, Kang's narrative juxtaposes past- and present-tense narration not in order to separate different narrative threads, but merely to set the fictional reality apart from the dreams of the female protagonist Yeong-hye. Tense-switching in *The Vegetarian* thus bears similarities to a temporary shift from the mode of narration to that of interior monologue in traditional past-tense narratives (cf. Fludernik 1996, 262). Finally, authors may utilize tense-switching as a structural

---

15 I will provide a fuller reading of Atwood's novel in Chapter 8.
16 Cf. e.g. Abbott 2008 [2005], 341; Cohn 1999, 98–99; Fleischman 1990, 75; Fludernik 2003a, 124; Schlenker 2004, 281, 297–298; and Zeman 2018, 252–253.
17 In the Japanese original, both storylines are distinguished not via tense alternation, but through a shift between different variants of the first-person pronoun singular. Murakami's homodiegetic narrator hence employs the more formal *watashi* to refer to himself in the plot which is set in Hard-Boiled Wonderland and the more intimate *boku* to point to his self in the plot which is set at the End of the World (cf. Rubin 2003, 117). According to Jay Rubin (2003, 217), "[t]he words 'Watashi' and 'Boku' give very different impressions in Japanese, such that the Japanese reader can open the book at any point and know immediately which narrative is spread out on the page." Unlike Japanese, the English language does not have different variants for the first-person pronoun singular, which is why Alfred Birnbaum "translat[ed] the 'End of the World' sections into the present tense" in order to "[make] a distinction between the two narrators' worlds that is natural in English" (Rubin 2003, 117).

device. In Zadie Smith's *NW* (2013 [2012]), for instance, the opposition between past and present tenses is used as one of several strategies to distinguish between the different perspectives of the four protagonists Leah, Felix, Natalie, and Nathan, who successively serve as the main focalizers of the narrative.

These examples of temporalization and detemporalization suggest that tense-switching represents the standard case of tense alternation in narrative fiction. Tense-mixing, by contrast, is much rarer. Since tense-mixing does not follow any discernible – let alone regular – pattern, I will here refrain from attempting to systematize it any further. Instead, I would like to illustrate the phenomenon with the example of Walter Abish's *Alphabetical Africa*. Published in 1974, this postmodern literary text represents a linguistic experiment. The narrative consists of 52 chapters, each of which is headed with a letter from the alphabet. The first chapter, which is headed "A," only contains words beginning with the letter *a*. In the second chapter, chapter "B," all words begin with either the letter *a* or *b*. The third chapter with the headline "C" adds words which start with *c*, and so on. Abish's text follows this aesthetic principle until chapter 26 (i.e. chapter "Z") which finally has all letters of the alphabet at its disposal. The 26 letters are still available in the next chapter, which is also headed "Z." Starting from this point of the narrative, the pattern unfolds backwards. This means that the subsequent chapters do not gain, but lose another letter, so that the novel's final chapter, once more headed "A," again exclusively contains words beginning with the letter *a*.

Not only does Abish's language game restrict the novel's development of a storyworld (a coherent plot can only be detected in the middle chapters in which sufficient letters are available), it also influences the way in which the narrative deploys verbal tense. In the first chapter "T," the protagonist, who also serves as the first-person narrator of the novel, flies to Tanzania in order to celebrate with its people the anniversary of its Queen's arrival. The following scene depicts how the narrator disembarks from the airplane:

> A ragged guard of honor <u>greeted</u> me as I <u>stepped</u> off the plane. I <u>had been detained</u> in Nairobi, and <u>arrived</u> three days late. The guard of honor <u>had been standing</u> at attention round the clock for three days (that's how I run things over here, <u>said</u> Quat) and <u>kept</u> collapsing from fatigue and sunstroke. Queen Quat nimbly <u>stepped</u> over their bodies, coming toward me with outstretched hands. All of Tanzania **is** privy to our embrace. The moment her familiar perfume <u>tickled</u> my nose I <u>started</u> to sneeze. Dear boy, <u>said</u> Quat. Quat **doesn't look** a day older. Her face **breaks** into a lovely smile. Everyone around her **is** relieved. She has quite a temper, <u>explained</u> Tiutu. I too **feel** relieved, sensing that I had nothing to fear, despite my malicious books, my malicious insinuations. (*AA*, 52; my emphasis)

The first part of the scene is written in the past tense. At first sight, the reader is thus led to believe that the narrator tells of the events in retrospect. Toward the end of the paragraph, however, the narrative starts to switch back and forth between past and present tense (see my emphasis). Yet the text offers no plausible explanation for these shifts: the sudden shift from fictional past to fictional present can neither be interpreted as the use of the classical historical present to highlight a specific event, nor can it be naturalized as a so-called gnomic present expressing facts or states of affairs.[18] Since conventional readings of this abrupt tense shift do not apply here, Abish's tense use must have other reasons. Considering the arbitrariness of the shifts, we can assume that it serves a meta-referential purpose, reminding us that the novel is first and foremost a deconstructive linguistic game which allows the referential character of language to fade into the background.[19]

The second structural criterion relevant for a thorough analysis of fictional tense usage involves the question of *foregrounding*. This concept has its origins in linguistics, more precisely its subbranch of stylistics.[20] Willie van Peer (2007, 99) defines foregrounding as "a theory about the form of literature, about language, the raw material out of which literature is made," which, by also taking "readers' reactions to such form" into consideration, "link[s] it to the functions of literary texts more generally." Foregrounding is interested on the one hand in the degree to which literary texts deviate from ordinary language usage; on the other hand, it investigates the readerly effects that can be brought about by such deviation (cf. van Peer et al. 2007, 197). To put it in a nutshell: "[t]he term 'foregrounding' refers to how deviations from some background norm of expectations enter the attentional foreground, producing cognitive 'deautomatisation.'" (Sinding 2008 [2005], 180)

Having said that, how can the concept of foregrounding serve as a structural criterion for analyzing fictional tense usage? As already observed, many readers are oblivious to tense usage in narrative fiction. Yet this changes as soon as a narrative foregrounds its specific use of fictional tense: once a text accentuates the ways in which it deploys one or several tense forms, the strat-

---

18 For a discussion of the notion of the gnomic present, cf. Harvey 2006, 77; Stanzel 1995 [1979], 145–146; and Steinberg 1971, Ch. II.I.1.d).
19 Hanna Meretoja (2014, 61) provides a further example of tense-mixing in arguing that most of the novels by Alain Robbe-Grillet "[shift] tense without apparent motivation."
20 According to Willie van Peer (2007, 99), the study of this phenomenon goes back as far as Greek Antiquity; however, it was only in 1916 and 1917 that it was turned into a proper theory by the Russian Formalists, and it has since continued reappearing on the research agenda of stylistic scholars.

egy attracts readers' attention and requires an act of interpretation; one has to make sense of it. We can conceptualize such cognitive processing of fictional tense usage with reference to Monika Fludernik's (1996, Ch. 1.2.3) concept of narrativization, a strategy that helps readers to naturalize texts by having recourse to narrative schemata.[21] Fludernik argues that during the process of narrativization, readers deploy frames which are grounded in their real-world experience as well as their literary knowledge in order to grasp possible textual oddities they encounter while reading narrative texts.[22]

In the remaining part of this chapter I will introduce different strategies with which a narrative text may foreground fictional tense and hence invite readers to naturalize its use. In Chapter 5, I will then focus on the process of narrativization by discussing the functional dimension of fictional present-tense usage. If, as I shall argue, the possible functions of present-tense narration are not textual givens but readers' hypotheses about the meaning of this tense in narrative texts, such hypotheses might also be conceived as reading strategies that help readers narrativize or naturalize present-tense narration.

Narrative fiction may use different strategies to draw readers' attention to its use of tense. Since these strategies may affect different aspects of a narrative text, I will here identify four different ways in which fictional tense usage can be foregrounded: (a) *alternate foregrounding*, (b) *typographical foregrounding*,

---

21 Fludernik's concept of narrativization is inspired by what Jonathan Culler (1975, Ch. 7) refers to as "naturalization." According to Culler, "the fundamental paradox of literature" lies within the fact that we are so fascinated with literary texts because they contrast strongly with how we communicate in everyday life (1975, 134): "[their] formal and fictional qualities bespeak a strangeness, a power, an organization, a permanence which is foreign to ordinary speech" (Culler 1975, 134), with the result that they somehow elude our comprehension. Culler therefore argues that, if we want to make sense of the language used in literature, we have to turn it into a kind of communication we are able to understand – that is, we have "to reduce its strangeness" by falling back "upon supplementary conventions which enable [literature], as we say, to speak to us" (1975, 134). In other words, we rely on interpretive patterns which are already familiar to us in order to explain textual elements that strike us as strange or unaccountable (cf. Alber 2009, 81).

22 In linguistics, the concept of narrativization or naturalization is known as *refamiliarization*, a process David S. Miall and Don Kuiken (1994, 394) define as a reconsideration or reevaluation of "the textual context in order to discern, delimit, or develop the novel meanings suggested by the foregrounded passage." The only difference between the linguistic and the literary concept lies in the greater emphasis Miall and Kuiken put on the emotional aspect of refamiliarization: "[I]n general, such reconsideration of the text surrounding foregrounded features will be guided by the feelings that have been evoked in response to those features. [...] [T]he feelings accentuated while reading foregrounded passages sensitize the reader to other passages having similar affective connotations." (Miall and Kuiken 1994, 395)

(c) *paratextual foregrounding*, and (d) *metanarrative foregrounding*. Each of these categories can apply to all fictional tense forms (i.e. the fictional past, present, and future). Moreover, despite being discussed in separate subsections, these foregrounding strategies are not mutually exclusive but can be combined in a single narrative context.

(a) Alternate Foregrounding
Alternate foregrounding always highlights fictional tense usage by means of a juxtaposition of at least two different tense forms. To be more precise, it usually takes the form of one of the variations of tense alternation discussed earlier in this chapter, namely tense-switching or tense-mixing. For instance, readers probably notice the shift in tense when David Copperfield, the first-person narrator of Charles Dickens's eponymous novel (1994 [1849-1850]), relates the events of his mother's funeral:

> If the funeral had been yesterday, I could not recollect it better. The very air of the best parlour, when I went in at the door, the bright condition of the fire, the shining of the wine in the decanters, the patterns of the glasses and plates, the faint sweet smell of cake, the odour of Miss Murdstone's dress, and our black clothes. Mr. Chillip **is** in the room, and **comes** to speak to me.
> "And how is Master David?" he **says**, kindly.
> I **cannot** tell him very well. I **give** him my hand, which he **holds** in his.
> [...] And now the bell **begins** to sound, and Mr. Omer and another **come** to make us ready. As Peggotty was wont to tell me, long ago, the followers of my father to the same grave were made ready in the same room.
> There **are** Mr. Murdstone, our neighbour Mr. Grayper, Mr. Chillip, and I. When we **go** out to the door, the bearers and their load **are** in the garden; and they **move** before us down the path, and past the elms, and through the gate and into the churchyard, where I have so often heard the birds sing on a summer morning.
> We **stand** around the grave. The day seems different to me from every other day, and the light not of the same colour—of a sadder colour. [...] (*DC*, 116–117; my emphasis)

The passage is representative of Dickens's frequent use of the historical present in his work.[23] By making his autodiegetic narrator intermittently switch from

---

23 Cf. e.g. Beckwith and Reed 2002; Carlisle 1971; Mullan 2018; and Pettitt 2013. According to Casparis (1975, 62), Dickens qualifies as the first English author "to use the Present [sic] tense in a structured manner on a large scale." A similar argument is put forward by John Mullan (2018, 149), who even characterizes Dickens's novels as pioneer work with regard to fictional tense usage: "In his use of the historic present Dickens was perhaps influenced by a book he much admired, Carlyle's *History of the French Revolution*, which dramatised each key episode in present-tense narration. But the portioning out of tenses – the sharp dividedness of the

4.2 Structural Criteria for Analyzing the Orchestration of Tense Usage in Fiction — 75

past to present tense, the author renders the scene more intense and vivid for the reader,[24] emphasizing rhetorically that this sad moment in David's life overshadows all other memories of his past. Thus, before switching back to the past tense, the narrator states that "[e]vents of later date have floated from [him] to the shore where all forgotten things will reappear, but this stands like a high rock in the ocean" (*DC*, 117).

An even more drastic instance of alternate foregrounding can be found in the sixth chapter of Margaret Atwood's *The Handmaid's Tale* (1986 [1985]). In this chapter of the novel, the autodiegetic narrator Offred tells her readers for the first time about the Wall in the theocratical state of Gilead, the former United States of America. The government uses this remnant of pre-Gileadean times as a platform on which to exhibit the victims of the religiously motivated public executions, which are ironically referred to as "Salvagings." After being killed or "salvaged," Offred explains to the reader, the sinners are hanged on hooks that "have been set into the brickwork of the Wall, for this purpose" (*HT*, 42). When Offred passes the Wall and sees six men in white coats hanging there, she infers that today's victims must have been doctors or scientists and that, consequently, none of these men can be her former husband Luke: "Luke wasn't a doctor. Isn't." (*HT*, 43)

The juxtaposition between past and present tenses in Offred's statement catches the eye, calling for explanation. Before talking about Luke, Offred informs us that, to her, "[t]hese bodies hanging on the Wall are time travellers, anachronisms. They've come here from the past." (*HT*, 43) The same holds for her family: Even though she has to think a lot of her husband and their daughter Hannah, Offred has not seen her family for a very long time and does not even know what happened to them after the three of them were caught during their attempt to flee to Canada. Against this background, Offred's formulation "Luke wasn't a doctor" suggests that she already thinks – at least unconsciously – that her husband is dead by now. However, the fact that she corrects the past into the present tense demonstrates that she is still hoping that, against all

---

narrative – is something new. It is enough to make you think that Dickens was foreseeing the narrative trickery of literary fiction at the end of the twentieth and beginning of the twenty-first century. The formal division of a book into alternating sections in different tenses became something of a feature of novels in the 1980s and 1990s."

24 Dorrit Cohn (1978, 198–199) consequently reads this passage as an example of what she calls the "'evocative' present," that is, a use of the present tense which, "though it must logically refer to a past experience, momentarily creates an illusory ('as if') coincidence of two time-levels, literally 'evoking' the narrated moment at the moment of narration" (198).

odds, he might be alive after all. Atwood effectively deploys the shift from the past to the present tense to highlight Offred's feelings in this specific situation.

(b) Typographical Foregrounding
Typographical foregrounding draws readers' attention to fictional tense usage by a change in font or typeface. It is usually combined with alternate foregrounding, to the extent that instances of tense alternation co-occur with typographic deviation to reinforce the effect of tense-switching or tense-mixing. Haruki Murakami's *Hard-Boiled Wonderland and the End of the World* (2003 [1985]) – already mentioned in connection with detemporalization – serves as a perfect example of such a combination. In the German translation of the Japanese novel (cf. Murakami 2007 [1985]), the two settings, Hard-Boiled Wonderland and the End of the World, are not only distinguished by a regular switching between the past and present tense, but also by a different typographical layout: while the past-tense chapters referring to Hard-Boiled Wonderland make use of a sans-serif typeface, the present-tense chapters relating to the End of the World deploy a serif font. Although these repeated changes in the text's layout are primarily supposed to indicate the spatiotemporal shifts between the narrative's distinct settings, they additionally serve to emphasize the change in narrative style which is mainly brought about by the text's strategy of tense-switching.[25]

(c) Paratextual Foregrounding
In addition to tense shifts or typographic deviation, paratextual information can also serve as a foregrounding strategy for fictional tense usage. Ali Smith's *Hotel World* (2002 [2001]), for example, consists of the following chapters: (1) "past," (2) "present historic," (3) "future conditional," (4) "perfect," (5) "future in the past," and (6) "present." Since these chapter headings designate a specific grammatical tense, one might assume that each chapter is written in the tense stated as its title. However, this assumption soon turns out to be false: the entire novel is narrated in either the present or the preterite. The novel's distribution

---

[25] It should be noted, though, that this typographic gimmick is a decision made not by Murakami himself, but by the publisher. In the English translation of the novel (Vintage Books 2003), the repeated shifts in setting are typographically marked only in the chapter headings (those that refer to the End of the World are italicized, whereas those that point to Hard-Boiled Wonderland are not). Apart from this, the entire novel is printed in the same font.

of fictional tense usage throughout the different chapters is summarized in the following table:

Table 1: Distribution of Fictional Tense in Ali Smith's *Hotel World* (2002 [2001])

Chapter Number	Chapter Title	Fictional Tense Used
1	past	present tense
2	present historic	present tense
3	future conditional	past tense
4	perfect	past tense
5	future in the past	present tense & past tense
6	present	present tense

As Table 1 demonstrates, the titles of the different chapters in *Hotel World* seldom coincide with their respective use of tense: only in Chapters 2 and 6, titled "present historic" and "present" respectively, does the narrative actually deploy the present tense. The incongruence between the chapter headings and the actual tense use already becomes obvious in the first chapter, which is called "past" but is written in the present tense. Considering this, the paratext of *Hotel World* clearly functions as a means to foreground Smith's use of fictional tense in this specific novel. That is to say, the chapter headings compel readers to pay attention to the aspect of fictional tense, irrespective of whether they match the choice of tense in the respective chapters or not. The irregular tense pattern of the novel moreover ensures that the effect of foregrounding is maintained until the end of the novel: the tense of the next chapter remains a constant surprise.

(d) Metanarrative Foregrounding
Finally, metanarrative foregrounding emphasizes a narrative's use of a tense via its narrative environment. Rather than deploying textual (e.g. tense shifts and/or typographic deviation) or paratextual features (e.g. chapter headings) to accentuate fictional tense usage, this specific kind of foregrounding relies on metanarrative comments to draw readers' attention to a narrative's tense use. The following passage from Henry Fielding's *Shamela* (1999 [1741]), which stages a parodic near-rape of the protagonist by her later secret lover Parson Williams, serves as a perfect illustration in this connection:

> Mrs *Jervis* and I are just in Bed, and the Door unlocked; if my Master should come — Odsbobs! I hear him just coming in at the Door. **You see I write in the present Tense, as Parson *Williams* says.** Well, he is in Bed between us, we both shamming a Sleep, he steals his Hand into my Bosom, which I, as if in my Sleep, press close to me with mine, and then pretend to awake. — I no sooner see him, but I scream out to Mrs *Jervis*, she feigns likewise but just to come to herself; we both begin, she to becall, and I to bescratch very liberally. After having made a pretty free Use of my Fingers, without any great Regard to the Parts I attack'd, I counterfeit a Swoon. Mrs *Jervis* then cries out, O, Sir, what have you done, you have murthered poor *Pamela*: she is gone, she is gone. — (S, 18; italics in the original; my emphasis)

Fielding here clearly mocks the writing style of his contemporary Samuel Richardson by revealing the logical weaknesses of the concept of 'writing to the moment,' which Richardson established as the most important distinctive feature of the epistolary novel of the eighteenth century (cf. Ball 1971, 24).[26] Not only does the text suggest that Shamela writes to her mother about the attempted rape while Parson Williams is still trying to molest her – this scenario alone is already highly unrealistic – but it also implies that her perpetrator is reading the letter along over her shoulder, commenting on her writing style (see my emphasis). Yet the passage not only functions as an amusing parody of the genre of the epistolary novel in general and Richardson's *Pamela; or, Virtue Rewarded* (2003 [1740]) in particular; as Irmtraud Huber (2016, 6) observes, it also serves to expose the temporal structure of the traditional first-person narrative, in which the narrator usually tells her experiences in retrospect:

> Even while Fielding is making fun of this style of writing, he nevertheless eventually recuperates the mimetic narrative situation by marking Shamela's usage of the present tense as a conscious rhetorical move, and the narrative soon returns to the more conventional past tense. (Huber 2016, 6)

Fielding's use of the present tense in this passage is foregrounded, then, not so much as an interim deviation from the novel's global fictional tense (the conventional simple past) but through Shamela's explicitly stressing it.

* * *

Table 2 below (see page 80) provides a concluding overview of the formal and structural categories introduced in this chapter. As indicated in the left-hand column, the first three criteria of differentiation (variety, frequency and scope,

---

26 I will discuss Richardson's concept in greater detail in Chapter 13.4.

and prominence) refer to the formal dimension of fictional tense usage, whereas the last two criteria (tense alternation and foregrounding of tense) relate to its structural dimension. The table also contains some visual markers: The bidirectional arrows in the first three rows indicate that the binary categories to their left and right should be conceived not as clear-cut opposites, but as the extreme ends of a scale. We can thus distinguish between different degrees of homogeneous (or heterogeneous), global (or local), as well as central (or peripheral) tense usage, which means that there might also be narratives that position themselves in the gray area between those poles. The horizontal line below the category of tense-switching in the row relating to tense alternation indicates that temporalization and detemporalization are different forms of tense-switching. The 'not equal to' icon between tense-switching and tense-mixing is to be read in conjunction with the structural categories in the last two rows: While tense-switching and tense-mixing clearly exclude each other (tense alternation either does or does not follow a specific pattern), the forms of tense-switching, as well as the categories that describe different types of foregrounding, are not mutually exclusive, but may complement one another. That is to say, a novel can combine temporalization and detemporalization just as it can integrate the various kinds of foregrounding.

Although I do not claim that the schematic overview of Table 2 is exhaustive – further formal and structural criteria for distinguishing different forms of fictional tense usage might well be identified – I nevertheless believe that the categories presented in this chapter will enrich any narratological investigation of present-tense narration. There are two reasons for this: These categories not only allow classification of narrative texts according to their tense usage (i.e. heterogeneous vs. homogeneous tense usage, tense alternation vs. no tense alternation, foregrounding vs. no foregrounding of fictional tense), they also provide a differentiated framework for a precise description of the textual distribution as well as narrative orchestration of such usage. The benefit of such an analytical framework is twofold: On the one hand, these terminological distinctions facilitate a more accurate analysis of fictional tense usage; on the other, such heuristic analytical categories provide a narratological basis that enables us not only to address the systematic differences of different fictional tense forms, but also to explore more thoroughly the functional as well as syntactic dimensions of the use of a specific fictional tense. The remaining chapters of the theoretical part of this book will be devoted to such an exploration with respect to present-tense narration.

Table 2: Formal and Structural Categories for Analyzing Fictional Tense Usage

	Criterion for Differentiation	Analytical Categories			
Formal	*variety of tense usage*	homogenous tense usage	⟷		heterogeneous tense usage
	frequency and scope of tense usage	global tense usage	⟷		local tense usage
	prominence of tense usage	central tense usage	⟷		peripheral tense usage
Structural	*tense alternation*	tense-switching		≠	tense-mixing
		temporalization	detemporalization		
	foregrounding of tense usage	alternate foregrounding	typographical foregrounding	paratextual foregrounding	metanarrative foregrounding

5 The Functional Dimension of Fictional Present-Tense Usage: Uses and Functions of Present-Tense Narration

5.1 Encoding the Here-and-Now: Present-Tense Narration and Narrative Worldmaking

As I have already argued in Chapter 3, the fictional present constitutes a complex narrative strategy that can fulfill a wide range of different functions in narrative texts. To systematically describe these functions, I will draw on the aspect of narrative worldmaking. In his study *Ways of Worldmaking* (1978), the philosopher Nelson Goodman investigates how symbols and symbol systems can be involved in making worlds and argues that the question of style plays a central role in this process:

> Although most literary works say something, they usually do other things, too; and some of the ways they do some of these things are aspects of style. Moreover, the what of one sort of doing may be part of the how of another. Indeed, even where the only function in question is saying, we shall have to recognize that some notable features of style are features of the matter rather than the manner of the saying. In more ways than one, subject is involved in style. (Goodman 1978, 23)

According to Goodman, style determines the ways in which symbol systems can create worlds while simultaneously depending on the make-up of these worlds. "For sometimes," he explains, "style *is* a matter of subject," meaning both "that subject may influence style" and "that some differences in style consist entirely of differences in what is said" (Goodman 1978, 25; italics in the original). Goodman therefore concludes that "[s]tyle comprises certain characteristic features both of what is said and of how it is said, both of subject and of wording, both of content and of form" (1978, 27). Against this background, fictional present-tense usage can be conceived as a narrative strategy which, by bringing about a specific style of narration, not only contributes to the various ways in which narrative worlds can be created, but is also – at least to some degree – indicative of the nature of these worlds. However, before being able to discuss how exactly the fictional present participates in the creation of narrative worlds, I first need to clarify some terminological as well as methodological issues.

When discussing the process of narrative worldmaking from a narratological perspective, one of the most important concepts is that of the storyworld. The term *storyworlds* originates from the field of cognitive narratology, where it refers to readers' notions about the worlds that are evoked by any kind of narrative, be it fictional or non-fictional. David Herman, who first introduced the term in *Story Logic: Problems and Possibilities of Narrative* (2002), defines storyworlds as "mental models of who did what to and with whom, when, where, why, and in what fashion in the world to which recipients relocate—or make a deictic shift [...]—as they work to comprehend a narrative" (5).[1] His definition suggests that mental representations of textual worlds play a fundamental role in the process of narrative understanding. "[S]tory recipients, whether readers, viewers, or listeners," Herman argues, "work to interpret narratives by reconstructing the mental representations that have in turn guided their production" (2002, 1). That is to say, readers try to imagine "storyworlds on the basis of textual cues and the inferences that [these cues] make possible" (Herman 2002, 6). By thus conceptualizing narrative sense-making as the cognitive activity of "[m]apping words (or other kinds of semiotic cues) onto worlds" (Herman 2009a, 105), Herman emphasizes the power of narrative to create possible or even alternative worlds: if narrative artifacts such as texts, films, computer games, and the like enable their recipients to form mental representations of imaginary worlds, these artifacts must, reciprocally, "provide blueprints for the creation and modification of such mentally configured storyworlds" (Herman 2009b, 73).

Although I fully agree with Herman's argument concerning the process of narrative sense-making, I nevertheless believe that his blueprint metaphor is a little misleading: the concept of blueprint – originally a photographic copying method – is simply too mechanistic to do full justice to individual readings of narratives. Since the metaphor of the blueprint suggests that the mental construction of storyworlds depends exclusively on textual cues – the underlying idea of the copying method is that a specific textual feature always triggers the same invariable cognitive response within readers – it seems to promote the practice of form-to-function mapping (cf. Jacobs and Jucker 1995). To avoid such an unintended effect, I would therefore replace Herman's conceptualization of the narrative text as a blueprint with a new metaphor from the field of music: sheet music. Construing narrative texts as sheet music seems more appropriate to me, as this metaphor retains all the features of narrative worldmaking Her-

---

[1] Herman's (2002, 5) understanding of storyworlds is inspired by the linguistic concept of the discourse model, which "can be defined as a global mental representation enabling interlocutors to draw inferences about items and occurrences either explicitly or implicitly included in a discourse." For a further discussion of the linguistic prototype of Herman's concept, cf. e.g. Emmott 1997, Green 1996 [1989], Grosz and Sidner 1986, McKoon et al. 1993, and Webber 1979.

man introduces, while additionally acknowledging the flexibility of this cognitive process depending on the individual: as every pianist may play, say, Beethoven's "Rondo A Capriccio Op. 129" in a distinct manner, so may every reader interpret a narrative differently.[2]

In narrative fiction, the use of the present tense as the dominant or global tense of narration serves as an important textual cue that figures into the process of worldmaking. I have already spelled out in Chapter 3 that, although some readers do not consciously take note of – or even care for – the tense in which a narrative is written, the question of tense choice always requires a deliberate decision on the part of the author, as it influences the various ways in which a story can be told. Given that authors thus deploy a specific fictional tense every bit as knowingly as they use any other narrative strategy, fictional tense constitutes an integral part of the textual 'scores' which help readers to form mental models of the narrative 'compositions' of fictional worlds.

With this in mind, I shall argue in this chapter that the present tense may fulfill various functions when used in narrative fiction. These functions can be divided into eight different kinds: (1) *referential*, (2) *immersive*, (3) *metareferential*, (4) *communicative*, (5) *synchronizing*, (6) *thematic*, (7) *rhetorical*, and (8) *transmodal*. While one half of the functions I distinguish here (the referential, metareferential, thematic, and transmodal functions) may also apply to other fictional tenses such as the past and future tenses, the other half (the immersive, communicative, synchronizing, and rhetorical functions) pertains exclusively to the fictional present. Before exploring the potential functions of present-tense narration further, however, I first need to clarify what exactly I mean when using the term *functions* in this study. To do so, I will draw on Roy Sommer's (2000) understanding of the "potential impact" (*Wirkungspotential*) of literary texts.[3]

According to Sommer, the potential impact of a text represents the sum of all possible hypotheses readers make about the potential effects of its design. Every literary text contains specific narrative strategies which structure and organize its content in a particular way, thus contributing to the text's overall

---

[2] I would like to thank Roy Sommer for bringing the slight inaccuracy of Herman's metaphor to my attention and for helping me to devise this new metaphor.

[3] Apart from the potential impact of a text, Sommer (2000) identifies two further phenomena that literary scholars traditionally subsume under the term *function*, namely the "desired impact" (*Wirkungsabsicht*) of a literary text (i.e. the author's intention) and its "historical impact" (*historische Wirkung*) – its reception by contemporary readers. Whenever I here use the term *function*, I will exclusively refer to a text's potential effects, neglecting the remaining significances Sommer distinguishes.

meaning. When interpreting literary texts, Sommer argues, readers make assumptions about the potential effects of the narrative strategies they encounter in these texts (cf. Sommer 2000, 328–329). Narrative strategies, therefore, influence the reading process, but they cannot ensure that all readers perceive the same text in a similar manner. Readers' claims about the potential effects of narrative strategies must, then, be regarded as hypotheses about a text's specific impact which can vary in each individual case:

> Der Funktionsbegriff bezieht sich hier daher auf Annahmen über die Relationierung der Textelemente durch Leserinnen und Leser, die jeweils einen Teilbereich des Wirkungspotentials, d.h. der Gesamtheit der denkbaren Lesarten oder der virtuellen Gesamtstruktur des Textes, aktualisieren bzw. realisieren. (Sommer 2000, 330)
>
> [Thus the concept of function refers here to readers' assumptions about the relationship between textual elements: Each of these assumptions updates or realizes a partial aspect of a text's potential impact, that is, the entirety of its imaginable readings, of its virtual overall structure. (My translation)]

As Sommer suggests, a text can never unfold its potential effects all at once. Since every reader interprets a text differently, individual readings of the same text emphasize only a subset of its overall potential impact:

> Erst im Leseprozeß wird in Abhängigkeit von den spezifischen Voraussetzungen der Leser ein bestimmter Teil des Wirkungspotentials realisiert und in einer Lesart konkretisiert, während andere Möglichkeiten der Interpretation verworfen werden. (Sommer 2000, 330–331)
>
> [It is only during the process of reading that, depending on readers' specific predispositions, a certain aspect of a text's potential impact is realized and concretized in the form of a specific reading while other possible interpretations are rejected. (My translation)]

What does this mean for the possible functions of present-tense narration? Sommer's notion of the potential impact of fictional texts enables the different functions of the present tense discussed in this chapter to be conceived as hypotheses about how the present tense can contribute to the process of narrative worldmaking. More specifically, the eight uses of the fictional present distinguished above describe the diverse ways in which this specific tense can shape the 'scores' – to reiterate my musical metaphor – of the narrative 'composition' of fictional worlds. As these hypotheses involve assumptions about how the present tense interacts with other narrative techniques and devices, such as the narrative perspective, narrative pace, representation of time and space, representation of character consciousness, use of specific discourse modes, and linguistic style, they can be primarily understood as textual functions which influ-

5.1 Encoding the Here-and-Now: Present-Tense Narration and Narrative Worldmaking — 85

ence the process of world-building predominantly on a textual level, where they yield particular narrative effects.

Yet storyworlds involve not only textual representations of possible worlds and their potential narrative effects, but also the mental models which readers form on the basis of these depictions. This chapter, therefore, will also turn to the cognitive component of Herman's concept, investigating how readers can potentially integrate fictional present-tense usage into mental representations of the worlds evoked by narrative fiction.

A word on my conceptualization of the reader is important here. Drawing on Umberto Eco's (1979, 11) concept of the model reader, I conceive of the reader as a textual strategy, that is, "a textually established set of felicity conditions [...] to be met in order to have a macro-speech act (such as a text is) fully actualized." Thus, whenever I use the term *reader* in this book, I refer not so much to physical readers who actually read the narratives I am discussing, but rather to Eco's understanding of the model reader as a notion that can be devised from these texts. When I refer explicitly to physical readers in the real world, I use the term *flesh-and-blood readers*.

Combining both text-centered and context-oriented narratological approaches,[4] the dual perspective of this chapter allows me both to explore how present-tense narration encodes notions of the here-and-now in narrative texts, and to demonstrate how readers make sense of such encodings. Accordingly, the functions of present-tense narration introduced in the following pages must be construed not only as assumptions about the purely textual effects of an author's use of the fictional present, but also as hypotheses about strategies with which readers can naturalize the peculiarities and oddities of the fictional present on the basis of these assumptions.[5]

---

[4] The distinction between text-centered and context-oriented narratological approaches was first introduced by Ansgar Nünning (2003). While text-centered approaches (e.g. 'classical,' i.e. structuralist, narratology) mainly focus on the static product of narrative texts by examining its distinctive features and specific properties, context-oriented ('postclassical') approaches (e.g. cognitive, feminist, postcolonial, transgeneric, and transmedial narratology) are principally interested in the open and dynamic processes of the reception and evaluation of narrative fiction (cf. Nünning 2003, 243). For the distinction between classical and postclassical approaches within the field of narrative theory, cf. also Alber and Fludernik 2010, Herman 1999, Nünning and Nünning 2002, and Sommer 2012.

[5] The concept of naturalization or narrativization is explained in greater detail in Chapter 4.2 above.

5.2 The Referential Function

In linguistics, fictional tense has often been defined as a deictic category.[6] This first raises questions about the deictic center from which the referential quality of the present tense can be determined. In his pioneering monograph *Sprachtheorie: Die Darstellungsfunktion der Sprache* (1965 [1934]), Karl Bühler maintained that the phenomenon of deixis operates within the "deictic field of language" (*Zeigfeld der Sprache*), that is, that sphere of human language usage which enables us to perform the act of pointing by exclusively linguistic means (cf. Ch. II). Bühler compares the deictic field of language with a coordinate system which includes a temporal and a spatial axis and positions the speaker of an utterance at its zero point where these axes intersect. By thus establishing the speaker's location within time and space as the I-here-now-origo of the deictic field,[7] Bühler posits the speaker of an utterance as the point of reference on the basis of which we make sense of deictic expressions. Conversely, the basic deictics *now*, *here*, and *I* constantly refer to the origin of a specific speech act (cf. Bühler 1965 [1934], 102).

Indeed, due to "the inherent 'egocentricity' of deictic expressions" (Semino 2011, 418) in everyday communication, we usually tend to assume that the deictic center of an utterance is its enunciator: "The *I*," Keith Green (1995, 19; italics in the original) notes, "is at the zero-point of the spatiotemporal coordinates of the deictic context. Language is a drama-event in which the first person takes the principal role." Narrative fiction, however, is characterized by a more complex deictic structure than conversational discourse. As Gisa Rauh (1985b) argues, fictional narratives may posit several deictic fields:

> Es ist [...] zu beobachten, daß in fiktionalen Erzähltexten verschiedene Orientierungszentren gesetzt werden können, an denen deiktische Ausdrücke jeweils orientiert sind. Da ist zum einen das Orientierungszentrum des Erzählers, da sind zum anderen Orientierungszentren von Figuren. (Rauh 1985b, 70)[8]

---

6 For linguistic studies which regard tense as a relational rather than purely semantic category, cf. e.g. Fuchs 1991; Green 1996 [1989], 20–21; Janssen 1996; Kleiber 1993; Leiss 1992, Markus 1977; Meisnitzer 2016, Ch. 4.2.1; Nemoianu 2014, 103–104; Rauh 1982, 1983a, 1984, 1985a, 1988; Schopf 1991; Tatishvili 2011; Vetters 1993; and Zeman 2010, Ch. 3.1.1; 2018.
7 Apart from *origo*, the center of a deictic field is also often referred to as *deictic center* or *zero point*. I will here use these synonyms interchangeably.
8 In her monograph *Linguistische Beschreibung deiktischer Komplexität in narrativen Texten* (1978), Rauh differentiates between two types of text: those which display only one deictic field (cf. Ch. 3.2.1) and those which feature several deictic fields (cf. Ch. 3.2.2). Fictional texts belong

[In fictional narrative texts, different deictic centers can be observed toward which deictic expressions are oriented. On the one hand, there is the deictic center of the narrator; on the other hand, there are the deictic centers of the characters. (My translation)]

According to Rauh (1978, 141), a fictional narrative can be divided into a "'dominant' deictic field" (*'dominantes' Zeigfeld*) which is oriented toward the narrator (i.e. I-here-now origo of the narrator) and one or several "'embedded' deictic field(s)" (*'eingebettete/s' Zeigfeld/er*) which relate(s) to one or several character(s) (i.e. I-here-now origines of the characters). The text accordingly contains a personal deixis, which always refers to the narrator of the text (irrespective of whether he or she qualifies as homo- or heterodiegetic), as well as spatial and temporal deixes, which can either refer to the narrator or the characters.

What is special about this complex deictic structure is that fictional narrative texts can display interferences between their dominant and embedded deictic fields. Proceeding from the observation that narrative passages may simultaneously point to the deictic center of the narrator and that of a different character, Rauh (1978, 139–145) contends that fictional narratives can reveal a so-called double perspective (*doppelte Perspektive*). Käte Hamburger's (1973 [1968], 64–81) category of the epic preterite serves to illustrate this claim. Rauh (1985b, 71) argues that in narrative texts written in the epic preterite, the deictic center for tense usage is the fictive I-origo of the narrator, whereas the point of reference for temporal adverbs is the fictive I-origo of a character. In Hamburger's often quoted example, "Tomorrow was Christmas" (see Chapter 2.1), then, the simple past form of the verb *be* refers to the deictic field of the narrator, who tells the story in retrospect; the temporal adverb *tomorrow*, on the other hand, relates to the I-here-now origo of the character, who experiences the events as they happen within the diegetic world (cf. Rauh 1985b, 71).[9]

---

to the second type because they could possibly exhibit a here-and-now for every single situation their narrative agents might find themselves in: "Somit gilt, daß die Anzahl von Zeigfeldern in fiktionalen Texten nicht auf eine Summe begrenzt ist, die sich aus der Anzahl der erzählten Figuren plus dem Erzähler zusammensetzt, sondern, daß die Anzahl der Zeigfelder sehr viel höher sein kann. Jede erzählte Figur kann, wie wir es am Beispiel des Ich-Erzählers als Figur demonstriert haben, im Zentrum zahlreicher Zeigfelder stehen." (Rauh 1978, 135) ["Thus, the number of deictic fields in fictional texts is not restricted to a certain sum which is the result of the number of narrated characters plus the narrator, but the number of deictic fields can be much higher. Every narrated character can, as we have demonstrated with reference to the example of the first-person narrator as a character, be the center of numerous deictic fields." (My translation)]
9 Cf. also Armen Avanessian and Anke Hennig (2015 [2012], 133) as well as Sonja Zeman (2018, 248–249), who likewise argue that Hamburger's sample sentence of the epic preterite features a

Although Hamburger regards the epic preterite as a distinctive feature of heterodiegetic (or third-person) narratives, Rauh's considerations demonstrate that such a double perspective can also be found in first-person narratives. Discussing a brief excerpt from the third chapter of Herman Melville's *Moby-Dick; or, The Whale* (2002 [1851]), she explains that, in the context of homodiegetic narration, the duality arises not so much from the interference of the I-here-now origo of the narrator and the I-here-now origines of the characters as from a shift in perspective from the point of view of the narrator as narrator to that of the narrator as character (cf. Rauh 1978, 142–144). The passage in question from Melville's novel begins as follows:

> But there was no time for shuddering, for now the savage went about something that completely fascinated my attention, and convinced me that he must indeed be a heathen. Going to his heavy grego, or wrapall, or dreadnaught, which he had previously hung on a chair, he fumbled in the pockets, and produced at length a curious little deformed image with a hunch on its back, and exactly the color of a three days' old Congo baby. Remembering the embalmed head, at first I almost thought that this black manikin was a real baby preserved in some similar manner. But seeing that it was not at all limber, and that it glistened a good deal like polished ebony, I concluded that it must be nothing but a wooden idol, which indeed it proved to be. For now the savage goes up to the empty fire-place, and removing the papered fire-board, sets up this little hunchbacked image, like a tenpin, between the andirons. The chimney jambs and all the bricks inside were very sooty, so that I thought this fire-place made a very appropriate little shrine or chapel for his Congo idol. (*MD*, 35)

According to Rauh, the excerpt recounts a past experience of Melville's first-person narrator. In doing so, it features an interesting shift in perspective from Ishmael, the narrator to Ishmael, the character, and back again. More specifically, Rauh argues that, when Ishmael says in the first sentence that "there was no time for shuddering, for now the savage went about something that completely fascinated [his] attention," the past tense takes Ishmael, the narrator as its deictic center, whereas the temporal adverb *now* already prepares a change in the point of view from which the narrative events are presented. This shift in perspective, Rauh continues, is completed in the second but last sentence: "For now the savage goes up to the empty fire-place, and removing the papered fire-board, sets up this little hunchbacked image [...]." Here, it is not only the temporal adverb *now* that refers to the I-here-now origo of Ishmael, the character, but also the verbs which are inflected in the present tense. Rauh further shows

---

split between temporal and personal deixis. For a more detailed discussion of the deictic quality of the epic preterite, cf. Rauh 1983b, 40–47.

that, eventually, the last sentence again features the single perspective of Ishmael, the narrator, indicated by a shift back to the past tense: "The chimney jambs and all the bricks inside were very sooty, so that I thought this fire-place made a very appropriate little shrine or chapel for his Congo idol." Taking all these examples into consideration, one can conclude that Rauh's analysis of the excerpt from *Moby-Dick* perfectly serves to substantiate, from a linguistic perspective, Franz K. Stanzel's (1972 [1964], 31–39) differentiation between the narrating and the experiencing 'I' in the typical first-person narrative situation.[10]

Rauh's analysis of the deictic complexity of narrative fiction enables the referential function of present-tense narration to be described more precisely. As her reading of the extract from *Moby-Dick* illustrates, it is not only the deictic center of temporal expressions that can be dislocated from the fictive I-origo of the narrator, as is the case in heterodiegetic narratives written in the epic preterite; the deictic center of verbal tense usage can similarly be dissociated from the speaker's here-and-now. When deployed referentially, the present tense refers to a specific place and point in time within the confines of the narrative universe, that is, a specific *hic et nunc* within the storyworld. But this timespace does not necessarily have to constitute the here-and-now of the narrator; it can also represent the here-and-now of one or several character(s).[11] Whether narrator or characters serve as the point of reference eventually hinges on a text's communicative situation and narrative perspective.[12]

---

10 Even if Rauh (1978) does not explicitly refer to Stanzel in her discussion of Melville's novel, one can nevertheless assume that she was familiar with his work, as she quotes his theory elsewhere in her study (cf. Ch. 1.3).

11 On a related note, cf. also Avanessian and Hennig (2013d, 7–9), who argue that a deictic use of the present tense in narrative fiction can refer to different narrative agents, such as the narrator, the (fictive) narratee, and the characters.

12 This contention is inspired by Stanzel's (1955, Ch. I; 1959, 3–6) argument that readers' temporal orientation within fictive worlds depends to a large extent on the narrative situation of the texts evoking these worlds. A similar contention can be found in Zeman (2018, 247): "Die Perspektivierungsleistung von Tempus basiert [...] auf einem komplexen deiktischen Prozess, in dem nicht nur eine temporale Perspektivierung der Ereigniszeit in Relation zur Sprechzeit erfolgt, sondern gleichzeitig auch eine reflexive Situierung der Sprecher-Origo. Auf diese Weise ist Tempus als deiktische Kategorie eng mit erzähltheoretischen Fragen nach dem Sprecher bzw. Erzähler verknüpft." ["The perspectivizing performance of tense is based on a complex deictic process which offers not only a temporal perspective on the time of the events in relation to the time of speaking, but also a reflexive location of the speaker's origo. Tense as a deictic category is thus closely linked to narratological questions concerning the speaker or the narrator." (My translation)]

According to Monika Fludernik (2008 [2005]b, 611), Franz K. Stanzel's (1981a; 1995 [1979], Ch. 6) teller/reflector opposition represents the most useful dichotomy for determining the referential significance of fictional tense usage. The teller mode, she explains, prevails exclusively in first-person narratives. For only in these texts "is the current speaker a deictic entity with existential properties" which "are grounded in the first-person narrator's role as a personalized teller figure and its necessary embodiment" (Fludernik 1996, 252). Yet it is important to stress that the term *first-person narrative* may include not only the classical first-person singular narrative, but also the less common first-person plural narrative.[13] Third-person narratives, by contrast, "need not foreground the presence of a personalized narrator figure" (Fludernik 1996, 252–253), with the result that, in these texts, "the deictic opposition between the act of enunciation and the related events is [...] much muted" (Fludernik 1996, 253). As Fludernik clarifies, however, the reflector mode is not restricted to third-person narratives, but also occurs in "first-person texts with reduced enunciational activity" (1996, 253). On the basis of the distinction between teller- and reflector-mode narratives, one can conclude, referring back to Rauh, that narrators can serve as the reference point for fictional present-tense usage only in texts which foreground the teller mode. In narratives that give priority to the reflector mode, the deictic center for the present tense must lie with the characters.[14]

When deployed in teller-mode narratives, the present tense can thus serve the purpose of pointing to the communicative situation between the fictive narrator and the fictive narratee.[15] As mentioned before (see Chapter 4), Fludernik

---

13 This is an important note because most recent studies treat so-called we-narratives as an independent narrative form which is different from so-called I-narratives (cf. Bekhta 2017a, 2017b, 2020).

14 Proceeding from an egocentric view of temporal deixis, Fludernik herself draws a different conclusion from the teller/reflector dichotomy: As reflector-mode narratives feature a narrator, who is either not graspable for the reader or whose function as a storyteller recedes to a large extent into the background, she argues that any fictional tense used in these texts ought to be regarded "as an adeictic tense" which, given that it is devoid of any deictic anchoring point, "would typically not be aligned with a speaking subject" (Fludernik 1996, 252; cf. also Fludernik 2003b, 123; 2008 [2005]a, 593; 2008 [2005]b, 612) Following this line of thought would lead to the suggestion that the present tense could never fulfill a referential function in reflector-mode narratives. This, again, would mean that the referential function of the fictional present could only point to the here-and-now of the narrator, thus excluding the I-here-now-origines of the characters.

15 As a matter of fact, this seems to be the most conventional use of the fictional present that can be encountered in almost every past-tense narrative featuring a first-person or authorial narrative situation.

(2003a, 124) calls this specific function of present-tense narration "the deictic use of the present tense"; her explanation of the term is misleading, though, as it suggests that the fictional present can only fulfill a referential function if it "refer[s] to the narrators and/or reader's here-and-now." More often than not, temporal references to a narrative's discourse level restrict themselves to brief remarks on the part of the narrator commenting on the act of narration. When the first-person narrator of Daniel Defoe's *Robinson Crusoe* (2001 [1719]), for example, tries to recollect his feelings when he was, for the second time, caught in a thunderstorm at sea, the present tense clearly refers to the moment of narration and hence evokes the here-and-now of Robinson as the narrating 'I':

> But if I **can** express at this distance the thoughts I had about me at that time, I was in tenfold more horror of mind upon account of my former convictions, and the having returned from them to the resolutions I had wickedly taken at first, than I was at death it self; and these added to the terror of the storm, put me into such a condition, that I **can** by no words describe it. (*RC*, 11–12; my emphasis)

Irmtraud Huber (2016, Ch. 3), however, demonstrates that in contemporary Anglophone literature, narratorial insertions often stretch over extensive passages, developing a plot of their own. This is, for instance, the case in Colm Tóibín's *The Testament of Mary* (2012), a retelling of the life of Jesus from the first-person perspective of his mother. As the novel integrates a subplot on the discourse level which addresses Mary's current situation, it not only serves as a retrospective account of the life of Jesus from Mary's point of view, but also relays the narrator's own, still unfolding story (cf. Huber 2016, 25–26).[16]

While in narratorial comments the present tense usually refers to the narrator, its deixis clings to the narratee whenever the narrator turns to his or her interlocutor. A textbook example of such a scenario is the very beginning of Italo Calvino's *If on a Winter's Night a Traveler* (1998 [1979]), in which the narrator encourages his readers to become immersed in the storyworld they are going to read about in the novel:[17] "You are about to begin reading Italo Calvino's new

---

16 Elene Tatishvili (2011) observes a similar trend with respect to short narratives. Homodiegetic present-tense narratives, she argues, "may include reports of past events and have a secondary temporal nucleus. However, the narrated past is not drastically separated from the narrator's 'now' and the overall integrated temporal structure of the narrative is not affected. In fact, it is the 'narrating I' or the situation taking place in his/ her present that carries the emphasis, while the past episodes have an illustrative function." (Tatishvili 2011, 19)

17 In line with Susan S. Lanser's (1995) insistence that narrators are always gendered, I will assign either the male or the female third-person pronoun singular whenever referring to the narrator of a specific narrative text.

novel, *If on a winter's night a traveler*. Relax. Concentrate. Dispel every other thought. Let the world around you fade." (*WN*, 3) The use of both the second-person pronoun and the imperative mode leaves no doubt that the speaker here addresses his intended audience, so that the present tense of the first sentence must relate to the deictic center of the narratee (and not that of the narrator). Like narrators' commentaries on the narrative act, instances of direct reader's address can be limited to short apostrophes or, in the case of second-person texts such as Calvino's novel, A. L. Kennedy's *The Blue Book* (2012 [2011]), and Caroline Kepnes' *You* (2015 [2014]) even extend over an entire narrative.[18]

Unlike their counterparts, reflector-mode narratives do not showcase an explicit narrative scenario, so that the present tense can take neither the fictive narrator nor his or her fictive interlocutor as its spatiotemporal deictic anchor. In such cases, the present tense should be conceived "as the normal tense of silently expressive self-communion, a language that emerges in a fictional mind without aiming at communicative narration or narrative communication" (Cohn 1999, 103). Instead of relating to a *hic et nunc* on the text's discourse level, the fictional present thus refers to a here-and-now located in the consciousness of a specific character. Reflectoral first-person narratives usually evoke mental timespaces of this kind by means of an interior monologue (cf. Cohn 1999, 103–104), which is why Huber (2016, 55) calls them "narrative[s] without a narratee." That is to say, even though these texts exhibit an explicit speaking subject, this narrative agent should be conceived as a character within the diegesis rather than as the narrator on the discourse level.[19] Heterodiegetic narratives, on the other hand, are not confined to a specific mode for presenting consciousness, and may consequently generate mental timespaces by resorting to any means of internal focalization.[20]

---

18 It should be noted, however, that this only holds for the small number of second-person narratives in which the second-person pronoun clearly refers to the implied reader and hence must not be interpreted as either a general 'you' or a substitute for the first-person pronoun. Fludernik's (1993a, 222) and Brian Richardson's (1991, 314) interpretation of the second-person pronoun in Jay McInerney's *Bright Lights, Big City* (2006 [1984]) as an 'I in disguise' for one would serve as a counterexample in which the fictional present refers not to the narratee, but the narrator-protagonist of the novel. A more recent case in point is Tsitsi Dangarembga's *This Mournable Body* (2020).
19 Using Stanzel's (1972 [1964], 31–39) distinction between an experiencing and a narrating version of the narrative instance speaking in the first-person narrative situation, one could also say that these texts prioritize the experiencing over the narrating 'I.'
20 For the narrative construction of characters' minds in fictional texts, cf. e.g. Cohn 1978; Herman 2002, 330; 2009a, Ch. 6; 2012; and Palmer 2004; as well as the contributions in Herman 2011.

Having discussed the deictic potential of present-tense usage, I can now turn to the question of how the deictic quality of the fictional present influences the process of narrative worldmaking. David Herman (2002) explains that,

> [i]n trying to make sense of a narrative, interpreters attempt to reconstruct not just what happened—who did what to or with whom, for how long, how often and in what order—but also the surrounding context or environment embedding existents, their attributes, and the actions and events in which they are more or less centrally involved (13–14).

The referential use of the fictional present clearly has the potential to relate to all of the three dimensions of storyworlds that Herman (2009a, 128–132) distinguishes – the WHAT, WHERE, and WHEN dimensions – as it helps to shape the spatiotemporal profile of fictional worlds by mapping narrative events onto specific spatiotemporal coordinates. These coordinates, in turn, constitute the deictic center of the here-and-now represented in a specific narrative. Against this backdrop, I submit that the referential dimension of fictional present-tense usage may offer readers spatiotemporal orientation within the textual world. As my readings of several present-tense novels in Part III will demonstrate,[21] storyworlds evoked by present-tense narration can often, on a temporal level, be divided into the past and the present of the characters and/or the narrator. In most cases, each of these time frames is assigned a different fictional tense: while the present tense indicates the present of the storyworld, the preterite signals its past. In view of this, I would suggest that, as soon as the narratives have established such tense shifts, readers see through this pattern of temporalizing tense-switching (see Chapter 4.2). Fictional tense in these texts may then function as a temporal marker, giving readers a sense of orientation with regard to the spatiotemporal structure of the storyworld.[22]

---

21 See especially Chapters 8, 9, and 12.
22 In this connection, cf. also Jürgen H. Petersen (1993, 27, 89), who considers the juxtaposition of past and present tenses an essential requirement for referential tense usage in narrative fiction: "[N]ur, wenn das Präsens als Darbietungstempus Verwendung findet, kann das ursprünglich zeitlose epische Präteritum überhaupt eine Zeitfunktion erhalten, da es sonst keinen Zeit-Maßstab besitzt." (23) ["Only if the present is used as the tense of presentation can the epic preterite, being originally atemporal, gain a temporal function; otherwise, it lacks any temporal criterion." (My translation)]

5.3 The Immersive Function

Not only can the present tense offer readers spatiotemporal orientation during the activity of worldmaking by outlining concrete timespaces of fictional worlds, it can also serve as an immersive device that helps readers to mentally experience these timespaces. This immersive function can be better described, however, once one understands how readers can engage with the imaginary worlds they read about in fictional narratives. Deictic shift theory, a subbranch of cognitive science (cf. Galbraith 1995, Segal 1995, Zubin and Hewitt 1995), postulates that, in Erwin M. Segal's (1995, 14) words, "[r]eaders and writers of narratives sometimes imagine themselves to be in a world that is not literally present. They interpret narrative text as if they were experiencing it from a position within the world of the narrative." This cognitive act of immersion (cf. Ryan 2015 [2001]) – aka transportation (cf. Gerrig 1993, Green 2010, Green and Brock 2000, 2002), or narrative absorption (cf. the contributions in Hakemulder et al. 2017) – is brought about by a deictic shift consisting in the (mental) relocation of the readers' perspective (which is per se anchored in reality) to "a cognitive stance within the world of the narrative" (Segal 1995, 15). To put this differently: during the process of reading narrative fiction, readers can "shift their deictic center from the real-world situation to an image of themselves at a location within the story world" (Segal 1995, 15). Being part of the mental model which readers construct on the basis of the textual world, this new location represents "a particular time and place within the fictional world, or even within the subjective space of a fictional character" (Segal 1995, 15).

According to Marie-Laure Ryan (2015 [2001], 98–99), narrative immersion involves two different types of deictic shift which she refers to as the "logical act of recentering" and the "imaginative act of recentering." The logical act of recentering, she argues, "sends the reader from the real world to the nonactual possible world created by the text" (Ryan 2015 [2001], 98), whereas the imaginative one "relocates the reader from the periphery to the heart of the storyworld and from the time of narration to the time of the narrated" (Ryan 2015 [2001], 99). Conceiving the logical act of recentering as a "constitutive gesture of fictionality" (Ryan 2015 [2001], 98), Ryan contends that every fictional narrative can encourage readers to project themselves into the storyworld evoked by the text and to maintain this cognitive stance throughout the process of reading. The imaginative act of recentering, on the other hand, requires greater effort on the part of recipients because it demands a deictic shift to the narrative's setting at the particular moment in time when the narrative events are supposed to be happening. As Ryan points out, "[t]his experience of being transported onto the narrative scene is so intense and demanding on the imagination that it cannot be sustained for a very long time" (2015 [2001], 99). She therefore concludes that "an important aspect of narrative art consists [...] of varying the distance" between the narrated events and the point of view from which these events are presented, "just as a sophisticated movie will vary the focal length of the camera lens" (Ryan 2015 [2001], 99).

The fictional present tense can serve to reduce such distance in so far as it enables readers to project themselves into the here-and-now of the narrative. Ryan rightly contends that, being "the tense of presence, the present is inherently more immersive than the past" (2015 [2001], 97). The reason for this, she explains, is that the use of the present tense often purports a synchronicity "between the occurrence of the events and the speech act of their report" (Ryan 2015 [2001], 97), even though present-tense narration by definition does not necessarily imply such co-occurrence between story and narration.[23] By creating the impression of simultaneous narration, the present tense suggests that the narrative events are still unfolding and that, accordingly, the eventual outcome of the plot is not yet clear. Readers are thus led to believe that they learn about the narrative events as they are happening, which causes them to experience these events from a cognitive stance that is located in the here-and-now of the events rather than in the here-and-now of the retrospective act of telling about these events (Ryan 2015 [2001], 97).[24]

But why is this so? Why is present-tense narration so readily associated with the notion of simultaneity, and why does this connotation enhance the sense of narrative immersion for readers? According to Ryan's (1991, Ch. 3) principle of minimal departure – an interpretive rule she establishes to describe how readers may reconstruct textual universes during the process of reading – "we reconstrue the central world of a textual universe in the same way we recon-

---

23 For a more detailed discussion of the relationship between present-tense narration and simultaneous narration, see Chapter 5.6.
24 Ryan's hypothesis that the present tense facilitates immersion has been proven in a textual experiment designed by Andrea Macrae (2016) to investigate how personal and temporal deixis influence "readers' perspective-taking within imaginative conceptualisations of a fictional narrative scene" (64). The results of Macrae's experiment suggest that readers are "more likely to conceptually identify with the view-point of the narrator-character or character focaliser" – i.e. they are more likely to take on a perspective from within the storyworld represented in a specific narrative – "if the narration is in the present tense than if the narration is in the past tense" (Macrae 2016, 71–72). Macrae's empirical study thus corroborates the findings of earlier empirical research conducted by Erwin M. Segal et al. (1997), who also found out that fictional tense played a role in story interpretation, but could not yet specify this role (cf. also Macrae 2016, 66).

strue the alternate possible worlds of nonfactual statements: as conforming as far as possible to our representation of AW" (51), that is, the actual world which forms the center of our system of reality. When we construct mental models of the worlds evoked in fictional narratives, we "project upon these worlds everything we know about reality," making no adjustments except for those dictated by the texts (Ryan 1991, 51). With respect to present-tense narration, this means that readers tend to interpret the use of the fictional present just as they would that of the grammatical present in everyday communication, as a deictic category referring to a specific here-and-now.

Combined with the principle of minimal departure, the rules governing the processes of recentering provide a plausible explanation as to why the present tense can facilitate immersion into storyworlds. As David Herman (2002, 15) explains, readers rely on deictic shifts to grasp the underlying logic of the fictional worlds they read about: "[M]aking sense of narrative requires relocating to the space-time coordinates organizing perception and interpretation of possible worlds more or less distinct from the world that tellers and interpreters of stories treat as actual." (Herman 2002, 15) Readers, therefore, shift their real I-origo to either the fictive I-origo of the narrator (in teller-mode narratives) or to that of the character serving as internal focalizer (in reflector-mode narratives). Thanks to this act of recentering, they experience the storyworld from the center of consciousness that functions as the point of reference for the fictional present, and consequently tend to assume that this specific tense refers to their shifted here-and-now. However, since in reflector-mode narratives this here-and-now always coincides with the narrative scene, readers get the impression that they are experiencing the events while they are actually happening. Yet the same effect can also arise in passages of teller-mode narratives which do not focus on the communicative situation between narrators and narratees, but instead foreground the experiencing versions of their narrating agents,[25] or – as the following example will illustrate – in second-person narratives that explicitly address an implied reader.

A. L. Kennedy's *The Blue Book* (2012 [2011]) represents such a second-person text in which the pronoun *you* clearly refers to the (implied) reader. The novel starts with a direct reader's address – "But here this is, the book you're reading"

---

25 This is, for instance, the case in the example Ryan (2015 [2001], 97–98) discusses in her account of the relation between fictional present-tense usage and immersion. Taking a present-tense scene from Marguerite Duras's first-person past-tense novel *L'Amant* (1984), she analyzes the use of the historical present which, in homodiegetic narratives, is traditionally deployed to mark a temporary change in perspective from the narrating to the experiencing 'I.'

(*BB*, 1) – and continues to elaborate on the relationship between the fictive reader and the book they are currently holding in their hands. The way in which reader and book seem to connect with each other resembles the intimate relationship between two lovers: while the reader gives all his or her attention to the book as if it were a lover he or she was about to kiss, the book feels flattered by the reader's devotion and reciprocates his or her attention by helping the reader to imagine a story (cf. *BB*, 1). Since Kennedy chooses the present tense to compare the fictive book and its fictive reader with a love-couple, her narrative encourages its flesh-and-blood readers to identify themselves with the implied reader and to similarly engage with the novel they are reading.

Having put readers in a receptive mood, the covert narrator proceeds to herald them to the spatiotemporal setting of the narrative and its characters:

> And this is when it [i.e. the book] needs to introduce you to the boy.
> This boy.
> This boy, he is deep in the summer of 1974 and by himself and cutting up sharp from a curve in the road and climbing a haphazard, wriggling style and next he is over and on to the meadow, his purpose already set.
> No, not a *meadow*: only scrub grass and some nettles, their greens faded by a long, demanding summer and pale dust.
> So it's simply a field, then – not quite who [sic] it was in its spring.
> A field with an almost teenager live [sic] inside it. (*BB*, 1–2; italics in the original)

In addition to introducing readers to the first character in the novel, the passage invites them, by the way in which it depicts the boy's spatiotemporal setting, to project themselves into the specific timespace of the narrative. It not only situates the boy on a field in the midsummer of 1974, but also anticipates readers' possible attempts at orientating themselves within the storyworld: First, they learn that the boy is running along a street and across a meadow; next, the narrator revises his account, correcting himself that it is not really a meadow, but rather a field that has been parched by the heat of the summer sun. He, the narrator, seems to apply the principle of minimal departure here: As the term *meadow* will evoke the image of high green grass and colorful flowers, he decides to describe the field in greater detail, so that readers get a more precise idea of the setting. The novel's use of the present tense intensifies this effect, causing readers to feel not only that they are experiencing the fictional world themselves, but also that they are actually witnessing the genesis of this world. In thus combining present-tense narration with a detailed description of the spatiotemporal setting, Kennedy's narrative heightens the sense of immersion for readers and animates them to shift their I-origo to a cognitive stance located at the heart of the narrative scene.

However, as Ryan (2015 [2001]) notes (and as I have already mentioned above), readers cannot long sustain the imaginative act of recentering: "if the present enjoys an immersive edge over the past, this edge becomes considerably duller when the present invades the whole text and becomes the standard narrative tense" (98). Readers will get used to consistent present-tense narration, with the result that the fictional present tense eventually loses its quality as an immersive means that stands in stark contrast to the use of a less immediate and less urgent past tense: "Continuous presence becomes habit, habit leads to invisibility, and invisibility is as good as absence." (Ryan 2015 [2001], 98) Consequently, the immersive use of the fictional present preserves its intensity only if it is constantly contrasted with past-tense narration. For only then will it encourage readers to repeatedly perform an act of imaginative recentering.[26]

5.4 The Metareferential Function

While the referential and immersive functions of present-tense narration emphasize the mimetic dimension of storyworlds, thus heightening the sense of aesthetic illusion for readers,[27] the metareferential function of the fictional present foregrounds the synthetic dimension, by drawing readers' attention to the fact that the narratives which yield these storyworlds are artificial constructs.[28] Previous research on metareference has proposed a number of categories that help to classify the various metareferential strategies occurring in narrative

---

26 Cf. also Ryan 2015 [2001], 98: "For immersion to retain its intensity, it needs a contrast of narrative modes, a constantly renegotiated distance from the narrative scene, a profile made of peaks and valleys."
27 For a discussion of the concept of aesthetic illusion, cf. Wolf 1993, 2004, 2014.
28 I borrow the terms *mimetic* and *synthetic* from James Phelan and Peter J. Rabinowitz (2012, 7), who argue that readers "develop interests and responses of three broad kinds, each related to a particular component of the narrative: mimetic, thematic, and synthetic." The authors define these different kinds of readerly interest in narratives as follows: "Responses to the mimetic component involve readers' interests in the characters as possible people and in the narrative world as like our own, that is, hypothetically or conceptually possible and still compatible with the laws and limitations that govern the extratextual world. [...] Responses to the thematic component involve readers' interests in the ideational function of the characters and in the cultural, ideological, philosophical, or ethical issues being addressed by the narrative. Responses to the synthetic component involve an audience's interest in and attention to the characters and to the larger narrative as artificial constructs, interests that link up with our aesthetic judgments." (Phelan and Rabinowitz 2012, 7)

fiction.²⁹ To systematically describe the metareferential potential of present-tense narration, I will here draw on Werner Wolf's (2009) distinction between *fictio*-metareference and *fictum*-metareference. While the first term denotes that type of metareference which "implies a statement on, and elicits the idea of, mediality and the ontological artefact status of the work in question," the second relates to "the truth-value of the work under discussion or its 'fictionality' in the conventional sense" by foregrounding the work's relation to reality (Wolf 2009, 41). Wolf's dichotomy corresponds with Birgit Neumann and Ansgar Nünning's (2014, 344) differentiation between the concepts of metanarration and metafiction: "metanarration," they argue, "refers to the narrator's reflections on the act or process of narration," whereas "metafiction concerns comments on the fictionality and/or constructedness of the narrative" (Neumann and Nünning 2014, 344).³⁰ In light of this distinction, I would argue that fictional present-tense usage serves a metareferential function if, and only if, it either highlights the narrative act evoked by a specific text or lays emphasis on the narrative's inventedness – i.e. the fact that the narrative does not reveal any reference point that is linguistically anchored in reality.

---

29 Cf. e.g. Fludernik 2003b; Macrae 2019; Nünning 2001a, 2001b; Scheffel 1997; and Wolf 2001. The term *metareference* itself has been theorized by Werner Wolf (2007b, 2009). His typology of different forms of reference in literature and other media is the most comprehensive account of metareference to date. Wolf distinguishes four types of reference: (1) heteroreference, (2) self-reference, (3) self-reflection, and (4) metareference. In the case of heteroreference, a specific work, genre, medium, or artefact refers to entities or states of affairs which exist outside of its semiotic system, meaning that its referents are situated either within our real world or within some imaginary reality (cf. Wolf 2007b, 31). Self-reference, on the other hand, relates to all forms of intra-systemic reference, more precisely those instances of reference which manifest themselves either in elements of a specific semiotic system pointing to themselves (or even to the system in its entirety), or in elements of that system that have recourse to other similar, or even identical elements belonging to the very same system (cf. Wolf 2007b, 31). According to Wolf, instances of self-reference do not necessarily cause recipients to reflect upon the structural design of a specific work or the properties of its semiotic system (cf. Wolf 2007b, 33); consequently, the work's heteroreference comes to the fore again (cf. Wolf 2001, 70). The recipients' recognition of the nature of self-referential elements, however, constitutes the distinctive quality of self-reflection. For instances of self-reflection encourage recipients to think about the constructedness of a specific work by noticeably drawing their attention to other elements of that semiotic system (cf. Wolf 2007b, 33). Finally, in the case of metareference, the self-reflexive potential of narrative strategies is so strong that it clearly outweighs their heteroreferential function, with the result that the latter is correspondingly restricted or almost nonexistent (cf. Wolf 2001, 70).
30 For a further discussion of both terms, cf. also Fludernik 2003b, 10–15 and Nünning 2001a, 128–133; 2004a.

More specifically, the present tense can accentuate the act of narration and thus the aspect of narrative mediacy by drawing the reader's attention to the double temporal structure of narrative texts. As Seymour Chatman (1990, 9) explains: "Narrative entails movement through time not only 'externally' (the duration of the presentation of the novel, film, play) but also 'internally' (the duration of the sequence of events that constitute the plot)." It is exactly this "doubly temporal logic" (Chatman 1990, 9) which divides a narrative into the two narrative planes of story and discourse. While the act of narration on the discourse level operates on a purely chronological basis, the temporal logic on the story level

> entails the additional principle of causality (event *a* causes *b*, *b* causes *c*, and so on) or, more weakly, what might be called 'contingency' (*a* does not directly cause *b*, nor does *b* cause *c*, but they all work together to evoke a certain situation or state of affairs *x*) (Chatman 1990, 9; italics in the original).

The distinction between story and discourse traditionally manifests itself in a temporal distance between the two narrative planes, meaning that the narrator recounts the events happening within the storyworld in hindsight. However, present-tense narration can also foreground a narrative's double temporality, if it stresses the narrator's retrospective perspective on the narrated events. This is, for example, the case at the beginning of Charles Dickens's *David Copperfield* (1994 [1849–1850]), where the narrator opens his autobiographical account with the following comment on his act of narration:

> Whether I shall turn out to be the hero of my own life, or whether that station will be held by anybody else, these pages must show. To begin my life with the beginning of my life, I **record** that I <u>was</u> born (as I <u>have been informed</u> and **believe**) on a Friday, at twelve o'clock at night. It <u>was</u> remarked that the clock <u>began</u> to strike, and I <u>began</u> to cry, simultaneously. (*DC*, 13; my emphasis)

In the first sentence of the quotation, written in the future tense, the narrator announces that he is about to relate his own life story. After thus establishing the communicative channel between narrator and narratee, Dickens's text changes from a prospective perspective oriented toward David's imminent act of storytelling to a retrospective perspective oriented toward the protagonist's former life. In this moment of hindsight, the narrative juxtaposes the present with the past tense to keep the narrator's discourse separate from the narrative's story (see my emphasis): The present tense refers to the here-and-now of the narrating version of David, who is communicating with the fictive reader, while the past tense points to a former version of his self that experienced or was at least informed about the events his narrating self is now telling. Thanks to the recurring shifts between present and past tenses, the second sentence of the excerpt calls readers' attention to the temporal relation between story and discourse, the consequence being that the fictional present makes them aware of the fact that Dickens's autodiegetic narrator looks back on his former life, recalling experiences from his past.[31]

As the example from Dickens's novel demonstrates: for the fictional present to fulfill a *fictio*-metareferential function, a narrative has to meet three criteria. First, it has to occur in the context of a metanarrative comment, that is, a statement on the part of the narrator in which he or she reflects upon, explains, evaluates, or thematizes his or her act of storytelling (cf. Nünning 2001a; 2001b, 32–37). This already leads to the second criterion, namely that the narrative has to evoke what Ansgar Nünning (2000, 2001b) calls "narrative illusion" (*Erzählillusion*), that is, it has to create an explicit communicative scenario in which a fictive narrator addresses a fictive addressee, telling a story either about himself or herself (if he or she is a homodiegetic narrator) or about some other character (if he or she is a heterodiegetic narrator). Since such a "mimesis of narration" (*Mimesis des Erzählens*) can only occur in narratives which feature an overt narrator (cf. Nünning 2001b, 29), the *fictio*-metareferential function is restricted to teller-mode narratives. Finally, the narrative has to make use of both present and past tenses. For only if there is an opposition between these tenses can the present tense unequivocally refer to the discourse level of a narrative, hence setting the narrator's here-and-now apart from the past tense (which relates to the story level). In other words, the present tense lacks such deictic clarity in narratives written entirely in the present because, in such cases, fictional tense usage does not allow readers to distinguish between the time frame in which the narrated events take place and the time frame in which the narrator tells of these events (cf. Fludernik 1996, 254; see also Chapter 2.3.2.1).

However, this does not mean that the fictional present always serves a metareferential purpose as soon as it occurs in a narrative which switches between past and present tenses. Heterogeneous tense usage (see Chapter 4.1) will yield a metareferential use of the fictional present only if the other two criteria

---

[31] According to Irmtraud Huber (2016, 8), first-person narration features such use of the fictional present very frequently. In this specific type of narrative, she argues, "it is not unusual for the narrating *I* to discuss his or her own story, to provide the reader with some idea of the moment and circumstances of narration and to comment on the situation of the experiencing *I*. The present tense is thus set against the past tense in order to mark the temporal distance that separates the narrated time from the time of narration." (Huber 2016, 8; italics in the original)

are also fulfilled – that the fictional present occurs in the context of a metanarrative comment (first criterion) which contributes to the text's evocation of a narrative illusion (second criterion). Nonetheless, I would emphasize that, however necessary, these criteria are not sufficient. Consider the following example from the sixth chapter of the first volume of Laurence Sterne's *The Life and Opinions of Tristram Shandy, Gentleman* (2003 [1759–1767]):

> In the beginning of the last chapter, I <u>inform'd</u> you exactly *when* I was born;—but I <u>did not inform</u> you, *how*. *No*; that particular <u>was reserved</u> entirely for a chapter by itself;—besides, Sir, as you and I **are** in a manner perfect strangers to each other, it <u>would not have been</u> proper to have let you into too many circumstances relating to myself at once.—You **must have** a little patience. (*TS*, 11; italics in the original; my emphasis)

Given that Sterne's first-person narrator directly addresses his narratee, there is no doubt that this quotation creates the impression of narrative illusion or mimesis of narration, thus meeting the second criterion. Since Tristram here overtly comments on his act of narration, the passage also qualifies as an instance of metanarration, which means that the first criterion is fulfilled as well.

Yet we can see in this excerpt that, even if a metanarrative passage features an alternation between past and present tenses, these tense shifts need not necessarily refer to the temporal distance between the narrated events and the act of reporting these events. Tristram here clearly uses both tenses to refer to the discourse level: while the past tense relates to his previous act of storytelling (he admits that he has withheld some information from his narratee), the present tense points to the current relation between narrator and narratee (Tristram clarifies that both of them "are in a manner perfect strangers to each other").[32] The example thus serves to illustrate that the sufficient criterion for the fictional present to fulfill a metareferential function is not only that the narrative features a shift between past and present tenses, but that this shift foregrounds the temporal distance between story and narration.

Highlighting instances of metanarration, the *fictio*-metareferential function of the fictional present bears a striking resemblance to its deictic usage as discussed in Chapter 5.2. As per Monika Fludernik (2003a, 124), the deictic use of the present tense "covers the narrator's communications with the reader/narratee and comprises authorial commentary, gnomic and proverbial statements and addresses to the narratee." Based on this definition, Irmtraud Huber (2016, 8) further argues that the deictic present-tense usage "marks a pause in the course of narrative events, a metafictional moment in which the reader is

---

[32] One could also say that both tenses fulfill a referential function here (see also Chapter 9.2).

reminded of the moment of reading, or in which the narrator muses about the writing process and/or the reception of his or her work." Huber's interpretation of Fludernik's category clearly suggests that the fictional present always serves a metareferential purpose when used as a deictic means.

In my view, though, the deictic use of the fictional present should not be confused with its metareferential use. The reason for this is that the present tense can be utilized in narratives to refer to the here-and-now of either the narrator or the narratee without necessarily causing any metareferential effect. I have already discussed the example from *Tristram Shandy*, in which the fictional present does not serve a metareferential purpose because the text uses both present and past tenses to relate to the discourse level of the narrative. However, the fictional present, if it is contrasted with the past tense in order to highlight the temporal distance between the narrative events and the act of narration, may also lack any metareferential potential.

When Robert Fleming, the homodiegetic narrator of Nick Hornby's *High Fidelity* (1995), for instance, records the moment in which he had his first intimate experience with a girl, the novel features a shift between present and past tenses:

> I **can't remember** now how she <u>did</u> this. I **don't think** I <u>was</u> even aware of it at the time, because halfway through our first kiss, my first kiss, I **can recall** feeling utterly bewildered, totally unable to explain how Alison Ashworth and I <u>had become</u> so intimate. (*HF*, 3; my emphasis)

While the present tense here clearly refers to the current situation of the narrator, the past tenses relate to his teenage self (see my emphasis). Hornby juxtaposes the tenses in order to distinguish between the narrating and experiencing versions of his protagonist, but still the excerpt does not qualify as an explicit metanarrative comment: Robert only mentions that he remembers a certain experience from his former life; unlike Dickens's and Sterne's narrators, David and Tristram, however, he does not thematize his narrative act, so that readers are not necessarily induced to reflect upon the process of narration itself. Even though Hornby's tense use foregrounds the temporal distance between story and narration, the present tense in the given example fulfills not so much a metareferential as a referential function.[33]

---

33 Drawing on Nünning's (2001a, 137–138) typology of different forms of metanarration, one could, of course, read this passage from Hornby's novel as an instance of implicit metanarration. According to Nünning, all narratorial utterances which relate to the communicative level of narrative transmission can be regarded as metanarrative comments of some sort:

Against this backdrop, then, I would contend that Fludernik's category of deictic present-tense usage can fulfill either a metareferential or a referential function, depending on the narrative context in which it occurs: When the fictional present is deployed in metanarrative comments where it is set against the past, thus stressing the dual temporality of the narrative text, it serves as a metareferential strategy; however, in cases which do not qualify as instances of metanarration, the referential function of the present tense dominates. Nevertheless, I would also stress that the transition between the metareferential and referential functions of a deictic fictional present is fluid, because the process of metaization that lies at the heart of any metanarrative strategy always emerges from the interaction between the narrative text and its readers.[34] For only if readers recognize the metareferential potential of narratorial comments can a narrative cause its recipients to become aware of its mediality; and only if they notice a text's mediality can they appreciate the metareferential potential of fictional present-tense usage.

When the fictional present fulfills a *fictum*-metareferential function, on the other hand, it foregrounds not so much the process of narration and the dual temporality of narrative texts as the fact that the storyworlds evoked by these

---

"'Metanarrativ' in einem weiteren Sinne sind daher alle vermittlungsbezogenen Funktionen von Erzählinstanzen, d.h. Erzähleräußerungen mit primärem Bezug zum Erzählvorgang bzw. zur Kommunikationssituation auf der Ebene der erzählerischen Vermittlung." (Nünning 2001a, 132) ["Thus, all functions of narrative instances which relate to narrative mediation, that is, all utterances on the part of the narrator which primarily refer to the act of narration or the communicative situation on the plane of narrative transmission, qualify as 'metanarrative' in a broader sense." (My translation)] This certainly also holds for the example from *High Fidelity*. However, it is important to note that the (rather low) metareferential potential of this passage resides not so much in Hornby's use of tense as in the narrator's choice of verbs which refer to his mental activities (i.e. *remember, think, recall*). Not every metanarrative comment derives its metareferential potential from tense alternation, just as not every tense alternation is a sign for a metareferential use of the fictional present.

34 Wolf (2011, v–vi) defines the process of metaization as "the movement from a first cognitive, referential or communicative level to a higher one on which first-level phenomena self-reflexively become objects of reflection, reference and communication in their own right." The insertion of a second, higher logical level from which the object level of a medium or artifact can be reflected upon evokes what Wolf calls "meta-awareness," that is, "the at least passive or latent knowledge that a given phenomenon is not 'reality' as such but something thought, felt or represented by someone else, in short that this is a phenomenon or a 'reality' processed through a medium" (Wolf 2009, 27). By thus rendering a work's "*mediality or representationality [...] an object of more or less active awareness*" (28; italics in the original), metaization techniques "activate[] a certain *cognitive frame* in the recipient's mind" which causes its heteroreferentiality to fade into the background (Wolf 2009, 27; italics in original).

texts represent a product of their narrators' imagination. Jürgen H. Petersen (1992, 73–79; 1993, 28–30) maintains that present-tense narration can emphasize the fictional status of narrative storyworlds, signaling to the reader that the narrated events are pure fiction. He designates this specific present-tense use the "fictionalizing present" (*Fiktions-Präsens*),[35] whereas Armen Avanessian and Anke Henning (2015 [2012], Ch. 3) prefer the term "imaginary present" (*imaginäres Präsens*). A representative example of the *fictum*-metareferential function of present-tense narration can be found in Margaret Atwood's *The Handmaid's Tale* (1986 [1985]): After readers have learned from the first-person narrator Offred what happened to her best friend Moira when she fled from the Red Centre (the place where the Republic of Gilead instructs fertile women to become submissive and obedient baby producers), Offred concedes that she has just made everything up. "This is just a reconstruction," she admits, and continues: "All of it is a reconstruction. It's a reconstruction now, in my head, as I lie flat on my single bed rehearsing what I should or shouldn't have said, what I should or shouldn't have done, how I should have played it. If I ever get out of here –" (*HT*, 144) Since there is no doubt that the present tense refers to the story which the narrator has just told her narratee, Offred's avowal makes plain that she tells the narrated events not as they have actually happened, but as she imagines them to have taken place.

Not only does Atwood's narrator distort the reality of the fictional world, however, she also invents the narrative scenario in which she relates her fate as a handmaid. This becomes most obvious when she directly addresses the fictive reader: "By telling you anything at all, I'm at least believing in you, I believe you're there, I believe you into being. Because I'm telling you this story I will your existence. I tell, therefore you are." (*HT*, 279) Offred's statement reveals that she does not know who her interlocutor is or whether there is anybody at all to whom she is addressing her narrative account. As the "Historical Notes" at the end of the novel indicate, Offred must be recording her story on tape without actually knowing if someone will ever find these recordings and listen to them (cf. *HT*, 311–324). With its many *verba cogitandi* and *volendi* (see the repetition of *believe* and the occurrence of *will*, respectively), each of which is inflected in the present tense, her apostrophe of a hypothetical reader reveals that her interlocutor is nothing but an imaginary construct. The fictional present emphasizes that she is not telling her story to a narratee who actually exists in the storyworld, but to a mental projection. These examples from *The Hand-*

---

35 I provide a more detailed discussion of Petersen's category of the fictionalizing present in Chapter 2.3.2.2.

maid's Tale demonstrate that the fictional present tense can function as a metareferential signal of fictionality if it identifies the story of a specific narrative and/or the narrative act which produces this story as (an) imaginary construct(s).[36]

5.5 The Communicative Function

A close relation of the *fictio*-metareferential function, the communicative function of present-tense narration foregrounds the aspect of narrative that David Herman (2009a, 37) calls "situatedness": the fact that "[n]arrative is a mode of representation that is situated in – must be interpreted in light of – a specific discourse context or occasion for telling" (Herman 2009a, 37). More specifically, in its communicative use, the fictional present simulates a scenario of oral storytelling, enhancing readers' impression that they are literally being told a story by the 'voice' speaking in the text (cf. D'hoker 2019, 182–183, 185). The communicative function of the fictional present is consequently linked to the concept of narrative illusion discussed in the previous chapter. It primarily occurs, then, in first-person or second-person narratives (i.e. 'I'- or 'we'-narratives vs. 'you'-narratives) which create the illusion of an anthropomorphic narrative agent by including narratorial comments and/or reader's address in the narrative discourse. Nonetheless, the fictional present can also achieve a communicative effect in third-person narratives with an overt narrator – i.e. in third-person texts which, in Stanzel's (1986 [1979], xvi) typological circle, are located at the intersection between figural and authorial narrative situations. In other words, a mimesis of oral narration can emerge in all present-tense narratives in which the teller mode outweighs the reflector mode.

The communicative function of present-tense narration is grounded in a specific oral use of the present tense: the conversational historical present.[37] First coined by Nessa Wolfson in *CHP: The Conversational Historical Present in American English Narrative* (1982), the term denotes the use of the present tense in conversational storytelling, where it typically marks narrative turns and emphasizes the tellability of events.[38] A perfect illustration can be found in "UFO or

---

[36] For a further discussion of the metareferential potential of Atwood's use of the present tense in *The Handmaid's Tale*, cf. Gebauer 2020, 29–30.
[37] For a discussion of the concept of oral narrative or conversational narrative, cf. Fludernik 2014a, Gülich 2020, Mildorf 2018, and Norrick 2000, 2007.
[38] Cf. e.g. Fludernik 1991, 1992a; Quasthoff 1980, Ch. 5; Schiffrin 1978, 1981; and Wolfson 1978, 1979, 1981, 1982.

the Devil" (2002), a conversational narrative that Herman discusses in the article "Storytelling and the Sciences of Mind" (2007) and throughout his monograph *Basic Elements of Narrative* (2009a). Titled by Herman himself, the narrative is an extract from a tape-recorded interview conducted by two white women fieldworkers in the course of a research project on the dialects spoken in western North Carolina with an anonymous 41-year-old African American woman from Texana, North Carolina, whom Herman, in his transcription of the interview, calls Monica (cf. Herman 2009a, 166). In this interview, Herman explains, Monica recalls a frightening experience from her childhood when she and her friend were "pursued menacingly by a large, glowing, orange ball that Monica characterizes [...] in the interview as '[a] UFO or the devil'" (Herman 2009a, 10). Since Monica's report of this exciting moment in her life displays a high degree of tellability, it does not come as a surprise that she tells the entire story in the conversational historical present.[39]

Although the notion of tellability was originally "developed in conversational storytelling analysis," it has meanwhile "proved extensible to all kinds of narrative, referring to features that make a story worth telling, its 'noteworthiness'" (Baroni 2014, 836). However, conversational narratives and fictional narratives attribute different significance to the concept. In the context of conversational storytelling, the question whether a story is worth telling or not always plays a central role and is "often negotiated and progressively co-constructed through discursive interaction" (Baroni 2014, 836)[40] – something that does not hold for narrative fiction. Due to the unidirectional communication between author and flesh-and-blood reader that underlies any narrative text, authors and their audiences do not so much negotiate as agree upon the question of tellability. We can assume that every author considers his or her narrative tellable and that every reader who reads the text from beginning to end probably concurs. Nonetheless, the question of a story's tellability is also relevant for narrative fiction, where individual readers have individual preferences and are intrigued by different texts. In fictional narratives, the concept of tellability is thus closely linked to the notion of narrative interest, that is, the question why readers are attracted to specific stories and what it is that makes narrative texts appealing to them (cf. Herman and Vervaeck 2009).

---

39 A full transcription of Monica's narrative can be found in Herman (2007, 310–311; 2009a, 166–172). Ohio State University Press furthermore provides an audio file containing a recording of the story that can be accessed via the following URL: https://ohiostatepress.org/journals/Narrative/herman-audio.htm (accessed August 31, 2020).
40 Cf. also Norrick 2000, 105–107; 2004; 2005; 2007, 134–136.

Despite the fact that narrative fiction does not generally negotiate the notion of tellability to the same extent as conversational narratives, some fictional narratives draw on the conventions of conversational storytelling, including the conversational historical present, in order to simulate the impression of orality. Here is an example from Halle Butler's *The New Me* (2019):

> I enter the showroom, they**'re** playing Coldplay, and I say "Morning!"
> Karen, the senior receptionist, and technically my supervisor, smiles at me like I can**'t** tell that she**'s** faking, and says "Hi, Maddie" and I say "Hi!" but that**'s** not my name. It**'s** Millie, not Maddie. I want to go up to her and prostrate myself on her desk, my ribs activating her shitty gold stapler, the one I know she loves so much, over and over, by thrashing, spending staples all over her desk, while I explain to her the difference between Mildred and Madison. <u>I want to press my nose into her keyboard and tell her that my parents both went to grad school, I was raised correctly and in a good home, and it**'s** an insult to my mother, the professor, to imply that she named me Madison after the mermaid from fucking *Splash*, when I was named after my great-great-grandmother, a *suffragette*, you fucking thankless cunt, and in this fantasy, I become insensible and start crying, deep from the gut, which is**n't** much of a fantasy, as far as fun and variety are concerned.</u>
> I smile at Karen again, leave the front desk, and walk through the showroom, past the re-created, tasteless living spaces, to my station in the back offices. (*NM*, 7; italics in the original; my emphasis)

In this scene, the first-person narrator Millie, a bitter and frustrated thirty-year-old woman who feels stagnant in her life, reports how her supervisor at work calls her by the wrong name. The excerpt shows several characteristics which, taken together, create the illusion of orality: not only does the text feature many short forms (see my emphasis), which is quite unusual in written discourse, it also reveals an interesting pattern of punctuation, stringing together several main and subordinate clauses with commas in lieu of periods (see especially the fifth and longest sentence, underlined in the quotation above).[41] In addition to this, the passage contains expletives ("shitty" and "you fucking thankless cunt") which strengthen the impression that the narrator's account is intended to represent an instance of spoken (rather than written) discourse.

---

[41] To be more precise, the sentence could be divided into at least three different sentences, each of which would then still contain one or several subordinate clauses: (1) "I want to press my nose into her keyboard and tell her that my parents both went to grad school, [that] I was raised correctly and in a good home"; (2) "[I]t's an insult to my mother, the professor, to imply that she named me Madison after the mermaid from fucking *Splash*, when I was named after my great-great-grandmother, a *suffragette*, you fucking thankless cunt"; (3) "[I]n this fantasy, I become insensible and start crying, deep from the gut, which isn't much of a fantasy, as far as fun and variety are concerned."

One might object to this analysis that, since Millie is talking about her feelings here, the passage could also be read as an instance of what Dorrit Cohn (1978, 161–165) refers to as a "self-quoted monologue," and that such an interpretation would be incompatible with an illusion of conversational storytelling. However, I find such a reading unconvincing for the following two reasons: First, Millie most of the time refers to her boss Karen with the third-person pronoun *she* instead of the second-person pronoun *you* (if this was really a direct quotation of her thoughts, she would probably address Karen directly throughout the entire paragraph, just as she does when insulting her as a "fucking thankless cunt"). Secondly, she explicitly points out that all of this is only happening in her imagination ("in this fantasy") – a meta-perspective which would not have been provided in an interior monologue. With that said, I would rather consider the excerpt as an instance of what Cohn designates as "self-narrated monologue" (1978, 166–172). Such an interpretation of the scene is perfectly consistent with the illusion of oral narration: The excerpt gives readers the feeling that Millie wants to immediately share with them her acute displeasure at the fact that Kate cannot remember her real name, and in doing so, she talks herself into a comical state of anger during which she imagines behaving like a defiant child.

The pattern of conversational present-tense usage exemplified in Butler's novel looks back on a tradition originating in the oral performance of narrative folklore during the Middle Ages. As various studies on European medieval folk tales demonstrate, these early narratives often feature passages that resemble today's oral pattern of present-tense usage.[42] However, neither the conversational historical present nor the historical present of medieval oral literature should be confused with the classic historical present encountered in nineteenth-century realist fiction (cf. Fludernik 1992b, 77; Quasthoff 1980, 225–226). While the former constitute a narrative strategy that foregrounds narrative events by stressing their reportability, the latter – deployed to excess, for instance, by Charles Dickens[43] – represents a rhetorical device that serves to make a narrative scene present for readers by "render[ing] [it] more vivid and heighten[ing] its affective impact" (Huber 2016, 9).[44]

---

[42] For a discussion of present-tense usage in medieval narrative, cf. Fludernik 1992b, for English; Fleischman 1986, for French; Fleischman 1990, Ch. 8.1–8.2, for French and Spanish; and Zeman 2010, Ch. 7.2, for German.

[43] Dickens's use of the historical present is discussed in Beckwith and Reed 2002, especially 306–313; Huber 2016, 9; and Pettitt 2013, especially 121–126.

[44] In this light, the classic historical present tense fulfills not so much a communicative as a referential and immersive function.

Thanks to its simulated orality, the communicative use of the fictional present is also often combined with an imitation of vernacular speech (cf. D'hoker 2019, 182–183). The presentation of non-standard linguistic varieties – a narrative technique also known as *literary dialect*[45] – can be found in various narrative genres spanning different literary periods. Examples include – but are not limited to – the work of American realist and regionalist writers, with Mark Twain leading the way (cf. Hurm 2003), and subcultural popular narratives written in the style of Irvine Welsh's '*Trainspotting*' series (see Chapter 13, especially Chapter 13.2), as well as postcolonial and intercultural novels such as Samuel Selvon's *The Lonely Londoners* (2006 [1956]) or Marlon James's *A Brief History of Seven Killings* (2014) (cf. Gymnich 2007, Ch. IV.2; Reichl 2002, Ch. IV.4.3). In these novels all largely written in non-standard varieties of English, the present tense not only foregrounds the oral character of the narrative, but also accentuates its vernacular language.

5.6 The Synchronizing Function

Positioning itself at the intersection of the referential and metareferential functions (see Chapters 5.2 and 5.4), the synchronizing function of present-tense narration becomes effective as soon as narratives make use of simultaneous or concurrent narration (cf. Genette 1980 [1972], 218–219; Margolin 1999, 150–153), more specifically, as soon as they present the narrative events at the moment they are happening within the storyworld.[46] Since the present is the only fictional tense that can express such a lack of temporal distance between story and discourse,[47] present-tense narration is often equated with simultaneous or concurrent narration. However, this chapter will show that in most cases such an

---

45 The term *literary dialect* traces back to Sumner Ives (1971 [1950], 146), who defines the concept as "an author's attempt to represent in writing a speech that is restricted regionally, socially, or both."
46 According to Uri Margolin (2014, 784), "it is necessary to distinguish between authentic and apparent concurrent narration." While the former consists in reporting narrative events literally as they happen, the latter "involves a deictic shift in that the events being ostensibly reported in real time as they unfold are in fact past or future to the speaker's temporal position" (Margolin 2014, 784). This chapter deals with the relationship between fictional present-tense usage and authentic concurrent narration.
47 While the past tense usually creates the impression that the narrator relates the events in hindsight, the future tense generally suggests a prospective narrative perspective (cf. e.g. Fludernik 2009, 100; Genette 1980 [1972], 216–217; Jahn 2017, N5.1.4; Lahn 2016, 106; Rimmon-Kenan 2002 [1983], 90–91).

equation proves erroneous, based as it is on what I have termed *the 'grammatical' fallacy* (see Chapter 5.1) – that is, the assumption that tense operates in exactly the same way in fictional texts as does grammatical tense in everyday communication. The impression of synchronicity between narrated events and the act of reporting these events depends, I shall argue, not merely on the use of the fictional present, but on an interplay between present-tense narration and other narrative strategies.

Interestingly enough, narrative research often associates fictional present-tense usage with the notion of simultaneity. Gérard Genette (1980 [1972], 217) clearly links the two modes, defining simultaneous narration as "narrative in the present contemporaneous with the action."[48] Dorrit Cohn corroborates the hypothesis that fictional present-tense usage is connected with a particular shaping of the genre's double-layered temporality when she discusses first-person present-tense narratives in a 1993 article, as well as in the sixth chapter of *The Distinction of Fiction* (1999), both of which bear the subtitle "The Deviance of Simultaneous Narration." Nor are Genette and Cohn the only narratologists who equate these two modes: ever since present-tense narration first attracted attention, many narratological studies have treated the phenomenon in connection with concurrent narration.[49]

However, as the diversity of present-tense novels in contemporary literature reveals, fictional present-tense usage is by no means restricted to simultaneous narration. More recent studies have therefore started to question the equation of the two modes. Armen Avanessian and Anke Hennig, for instance, argue that over the course of time the fictional present has evolved into what they call an "asynchronous present," relating to states of affairs that actually lie in the past.[50] "The asynchronous present tense," they contend, "brings to light an anterior moment in the present of fiction and a non-contemporaneous moment

---

48 Even in the revision of his narrative theory, *Narrative Discourse Revisited* (1988 [1983]), Genette still equates "narrating conducted entirely in the present" with "wholly simultaneous narrating" (82).
49 Cf. e.g. Bode 2005, 120–122; 2013, Ch. 1.4; Brandt 1997; DelConte 2007; D'hoker 2013, 2019; Farner 2014, 194–195; Hansen 2008; Jahn 2017, N3.3.11 and N5.1.4; Lahn 2016, 83 and 105; Marsden 2004, 107; Nielsen 2011, 59–65; Phelan 1994; 2013a, 179–183; Philipowski 2018; Richardson 2002a, 53; 2019, 117; Rimmon-Kenan 2002 [1983], 91; and Ryan 1993; see also Chapter 2.3.2.1.
50 Cf. Avanessian and Hennig 2013a; 2013c, 160–178; 2015; 2015 [2012], 58–88; cf. also Avanessian 2013.

in narrative retrospection" (Avanessian and Hennig 2015 [2012], 224).[51] Recognizing that "[n]umerous contemporary novels use present-tense narration in a retrospective sense," Irmtraud Huber (2016, 39) similarly identifies a present-tense usage that brings about instances of the more traditional form of subsequent or ulterior narration (see also Chapter 2.3.2.2).[52]

The same reasoning applies to the relationship between the use of the fictional present and prior or anterior narration. Despite claiming that present-tense usage actually represents a distinctive feature of simultaneous narration, Genette, in *Narrative Discourse: An Essay in Method* (1980 [1972]), acknowledges that prior narration may also employ the present tense. He thus defines this specific type of narration as "predictive narrative, generally in the future tense, but not prohibited from being conjugated in the present" (Genette 1980 [1972], 217). In her own introduction to narrative theory, *Narrative Fiction: Contemporary Poetics* (2002 [1983]) – whose second edition was published thirty-one years after Genette's original monograph – Shlomith Rimmon-Kenan echoes his definition, almost verbatim: "It [i.e. anterior narration] is a kind of predictive narration, generally using the future tense, but sometimes the present." (Rimmon-Kenan 2002 [1983], 91) Although research on present-tense narration has not yet made a serious case for its provision of a prospective narrative perspective, Genette's and Rimmon-Kenan's conceptualizations of prior or anterior narration both show that such a scenario is conceivable.

Given that the use of the present tense thus represents a necessary, but not sufficient criterion for simultaneous narration,[53] I would argue that present-tense narration can fulfill a synchronizing function only in those narratives which diminish the temporal distance between story and narration to such a

---

[51] For a further discussion of Avanessian and Hennig's notion of the asynchronous present, cf. also North 2018, 126–128.
[52] In addition to Avanessian and Hennig and Huber, Elene Tatishvili (2011, 11) and Frank Zipfel (2001, Ch. 4.5.2) also maintain that present-tense narratives can yield both simultaneous and retrospective narration. Dietrich Weber (1998, 46) even holds that present-tense narratives with a retrospective perspective are more common than those whose simultaneous narration resembles a life report or an instance of teichoscopy: "In der Praxis geschehensdarstellender Texte in der Literatur dürfte man es meist mit dem letzteren Fall zu tun haben: mit Präsenserzählungen. Die Struktur der Live-Reportage oder Teichoskopie ist kaum tragfähig für ganze Texte." ["In practice, literary texts that represent occurrences most commonly fall under the latter category: present-tense narratives. The structure of the life report or teichoscopy is hardly viable for complete texts." (My translation)]
[53] Cf. also Margolin 1999, 150: "[T]here is no full overlap between grammatical and semantic features, so it is only a subset of present-tense literary narratives that can be meaningfully recuperated as creating the illusion of concurrent narration."

degree that the occurrence of the narrated events and the speech act of their account actually appear synchronous. But how do we recognize concurrent narration if we can no longer rely on the present tense as its distinctive feature? According to Huber (2016, 40), the retrospective use of the present tense "can often only be distinguished from simultaneous narration within the narrative context, for example, by moments of hindsight and narrative distance indicating a retrospective point of view." I would argue that the same holds true for the prospective use of the present tense. We consequently have sufficient grounds to interpret a narrative's present tense use as an instance of prior or anterior narration if the narrative displays analogous moments of foresight which, in turn, suggest a prospective point of view. Conversely, this means that, whenever a narrative lacks any such moments of either foresight or hindsight, we can assume a synchronicity between the occurrence of its narrative events and the act of narration.

As I have demonstrated elsewhere (cf. Gebauer 2018), the temporal relation between a narrative's story and its discourse depends on the interaction of a specific tense use with other narrative strategies and linguistic features. These include, among others, the narrative situation, dominant discourse mode (i.e. narration vs. focalization), duration of the narrative act in relation to the duration of the narrated story, and mode(s) of representing speech or consciousness deployed in the narrative, as well as the text's linguistic register.[54] A representative passage from David Mitchell's *The Bone Clocks* (2015 [2014]) aptly illustrates how the fictional present can act in unison with other narrative strategies to evoke synchronicity between story and narration. The scene depicts the protagonist, fifteen-year old Holly Sykes, quarrelling with her mother after she has spent the previous evening with her boyfriend, returning home two hours later than her parents had actually permitted:

> I pour some milk over my Weetabix and take it to the table. Mam clangs the lid onto the pan and comes over. 'Right. What have you got to say for yourself?'
> 'Good morning to you too, Mam. Another hot day.'
> 'What have you got to *say* for yourself, young lady?'
> If in doubt, act innocent. ''Bout what exactly?'
> Her eyes go all snaky. 'What time did you get home?'
> 'Okay, okay, so I was a bit late, *sorry*.'
> 'Two hours isn't "a bit late". Where were you?'

---

[54] On a related note, cf. also Zipfel (2001, 162–163), who similarly argues that the retrospective character of present-tense narratives may be indicated by means of other linguistic features or reflective comments on the part of the narrator.

I munch my Weetabix. 'Stella's. Lost track of time.'
'Well, that's peculiar, now, it really is. At ten o'clock *I* phoned Stella's mam to find out where the hell you were, and guess what? You'd left before eight. So who's the liar here, Holly? You or her?'
Shit. 'After leaving Stella's, I went for a walk.'
'And where did your walk take you to?'
I sharpen each word. 'Along the river, all right?'
'Upstream or downstream, was it, this little walk?'
I let a silence go by. 'What *diff*rence does it make?'
There's some cartoon explosions on the telly. Mam tells my sister, 'Turn that thing off and shut the door behind you, Sharon.'
'That's not fair! Holly's the one getting told off.'
'*Now*, Sharon. And you too, Jacko, I want—' But Jacko's already vanished. When Sharon's left, Mam takes up the attack again: 'All alone, were you, on your "walk"?'
Why this nasty feeling she's setting me up? 'Yeah.'
'How far d'you get on your "walk", then, all alone?'
'What – you want miles or kilometres?'
'Well, perhaps your little walk took you up Peacock Street, to a certain someone called Vincent Costello?' The kitchen sort of swirls, and through the window, on the Essex shore of the river, a tiny stick-man's lifting his bike off the ferry. 'Lost for words all of a sudden? Let me jog your memory: ten o'clock last night, closing the blinds, front window, wearing a T-shirt and not a lot else.' (*BC*, 4–5; italics in the original)

The argument is presented from Holly's perspective, and she also serves as the homodiegetic narrator in this passage.[55] In addition to the fact that Holly uses the present tense, her narrative discourse features two other main characteristics indicative of simultaneous narration: it deploys scenic narration and creates the illusion of narrative immediacy.

The term *scene* (cf. Genette 1980 [1972], 94), which is also known as isochrony (cf. Fludernik 2009, 33), relates to Genette's (1980 [1972], Ch. 2) temporal category of duration and describes a narrative scenario in which the time of narrating and the narrated time coincide.[56] Mitchell's text generates this specific narrative tempo by rendering the conversation between Holly and her mother exclusively in direct speech. Besides, it largely mutes the voice of the

---

55 The novel contains altogether four different first-person narrators: the first and the last parts are narrated by Holly, whereas the three middle parts are told by different characters who come into contact with Holly at various points of her life.
56 For an explanation of the distinction between the time of narrating (*Erzählzeit*) and the narrated time (*erzählte Zeit*), cf. Müller 1968 [1947]; 2011 [1947], 75–83. An alternative to Günther Müller's dichotomy, which is more frequently deployed in Anglophone narratological discourse, is Seymour Chatman's (1978, 62) differentiation between discourse time and story time. I will here use Müller's and Chatman's terminology interchangeably.

narrating 'I,' except for very few intermissions in which Holly describes the facial expression of her mother ("Her eyes go all snaky") or explains what is going on in the kitchen (e.g. she informs us that "[t]here's some cartoon explosions on television" or that her brother is no longer in the room).

While the concept of scene constitutes a narratological category specifying a text's narrative pace, the concept of narrative immediacy refers not so much to a narrative strategy as to an effect. The excerpt from *The Bone Clocks* achieves this specific effect by giving us immediate and unfiltered access to Holly's thoughts ("If in doubt, act innocent," "Shit"), thus suggesting that she is experiencing the argument with her mother in the very moment that she tells about it (otherwise, she would have had time to reflect upon the situation and would have reacted less impulsively). This impression is, moreover, reinforced by the fact that Holly does not inform us that she does not know what to say when her mother asks her if she met Vincent the night before. From her mother's next question ("Lost for words all of a sudden?"), we can infer that Holly must be searching for the right answer in this situation; yet she does not explicitly communicate her hesitation to the reader, with the result that her narrative discourse indicates this pause only with a brief description of what she sees when looking out of the kitchen window. By combining the present tense with a version of homodiegetic, scenic narration which integrates the modes of description, direct speech, and direct thought to create an illusion of narrative immediacy, Mitchell's novel here reduces the temporal distance between story and narration to such an extent that readers get the impression that Holly tells the events as she is currently experiencing them.

Needless to say, Mitchell cannot maintain synchronicity between story and discourse throughout his entire novel, which comprises over 600 pages. Holly's narrative account accordingly soon accelerates, summarizing the narrative events: "I only cry a bit, and it's shocked crying, not boo-hoo crying, and when I'm done I go to the mirror. My eyes're a bit puffy, but a bit of eye-liner soon sorts that out . . . Dab of lippy, bit of blusher . . . Sorted." (*BC*, 6–7) Judging from the brevity of this quotation, it is safe to say that it takes us less time to read this paragraph than it takes Holly to stop crying and adjust her makeup. As the narrating time is shorter than the narrated time, the narrative here features retrospective (rather than simultaneous) narration.

Given that simultaneous narration actually represents a rare phenomenon that cannot be sustained easily over longer stretches of narrative,[57] there may

---

[57] Marie-Laure Ryan (1993) even maintains that simultaneous narration can only be found in non-fictional narratives, more specifically in instances of real-time narration which we encoun-

well be only a limited number of possible correlations between present-tense usage and other narrative techniques which, taken together, negate the temporal distance between story and narration. Hence, the synchronizing function may rate among those functions of fictional present-tense usage which occur less frequently and less extensively than one might actually expect.[58]

A further problem with regard to Genette's traditional definition is that it makes simultaneous narration conditional on the speech act that produces the narrative.[59] His definition implies that, strictly speaking, simultaneous narration can only occur in teller-mode narratives as they disclose the act of narration; reflector-mode narratives, by contrast, obscure the level of narrative transmission, with the result that it is impossible to determine the temporal relation between story and discourse levels in these texts. However, the concept of simultaneous narration also becomes relevant to reflector-mode narratives as soon as we start focusing not only on narrators, but also on focalizers; for the latter, just as the former, have a specific temporal stance towards narrative events, either experiencing these events as currently happening within the storyworld or remembering or anticipating their occurrence.

A scene from Nick McDonell's *Twelve* (2003 [2002]) can serve to clarify this point. After having an accident while ice-skating, Andrew has to stay for observation in hospital, where he has to share a room with another teenager, Sean, who has been involved in a car accident. When Sean's girlfriend Sara comes to visit him, Andrew cannot take his eyes off her:

> Sara gives Andrew the once-over as she comes in, then looks at Sean's IV and kisses him on the forehead.

---

ter, for example, in sport broadcasts or news reports (for a similar argument, cf. also Weber [1998, 45–46]). However, Elinor Ochs and Lisa Capps (2001, 162) argue that not even such accounts of events "occurring in the instantaneous present" are genuine examples of concurrent narration. The reason for this, they explain, is that "[t]he action takes place immediately before a speaker encodes it, but is treated as happening at the moment of telling" (Ochs and Capps 2001, 162).

58 This impression is confirmed by the numerous examples Huber discusses in her monograph on *Present-Tense Narration in Contemporary Literature* (2016): Even though she examines 42 novels that deploy the fictional present as their dominant tense of narration, she only regards twelve of them as creating plausible scenarios of simultaneous narration.

59 Genette (1980 [1972], 216–223) originally discusses the phenomenon of simultaneous narration – along with the other types of narration he distinguishes in this context (i.e. subsequent, prior, and interpolated narration) – in his chapter on narrative 'voice': the category he introduces to subsume all possible traces a narrative instance "has left" or "is considered to have left [...] in the narrative discourse it is considered to have produced" (214).

"Ohh, how are you? How's your arm?"
"I don't know."
Andrew is watching and listening from the other bed. He is pretending to be half asleep as he takes in Sara's beauty. She is wearing tight jeans and has her hair in a ponytail. Andrew is horny.
"Where are your parents?" she asks Sean.
"Came and went."
"So what do the doctors say?"
"I don't even know."
"You must be on pretty heavy drugs, huh?"
"Yeah."
"Can I have some?"
"No, those are for when I go home." Sean sounds suddenly angry.
"It was a joke," she says.
Andrew laughs, and Sara turns to him but can't seem to decide whether to smile or scowl. She does both. Sean drifts off.
"Sorry. I'm Andrew."
"Sara." (*T*, 56)

McDonell's novel is told by an anonymous heterodiegetic narrator who offers readers an alternating insight into the minds of the various characters. In this excerpt, it is Andrew who serves as the focalizer. We learn that he is attracted to Sara and that he "[pretends] to be half asleep" in order to be able to observe her; moreover, we can see that he speculates about her thoughts because she "can't seem to decide" whether she should "smile or scowl" at him.

Apart from their different narrative situations, the excerpts from *Twelve* and *The Bone Clocks* have many similarities. Like Mitchell's text, McDonell's deploys the present tense, scenic narration, and direct speech to evoke the illusion of immediacy, thus suggesting simultaneity between the narrative events and their representation. The only difference is that in the example from *Twelve* this lack of temporal distance stems not so much from the narrator as from the focalizer. In other words, it is not the homodiegetic narrator who reports the events while they are happening, but Andrew who perceives these events from a stance within the here-and-now of the storyworld. In fact the given scene from *Twelve* features what Luc Herman and Bart Vervaeck (2005 [2001], 76), resorting to Rimmon-Kenan's (2002 [1983], 79–80) temporal facets of focalization, call "synchronic focalization."[60]

---

[60] I deliberately quote Herman and Vervaeck in this context because I consider their understanding of Rimmon-Kenan's concept more fitting for my purpose. Rimmon-Kenan explicitly hinges the concept of synchronic focalization on the existence of an internal focalizer, which, in her terminology, means a character-focalizer: "[...] internal focalization is synchronous with

Having said that, simultaneous narration is, I think, best conceived as a phenomenon depending on what Uri Margolin (1999, 166) refers to as a "mediating consciousness" – that is, the center of consciousness constituting the point of view from which the narrative events are presented. Simultaneous narration negates the temporal distance between the narrative planes of story and discourse by implying that narrative events are represented, or rather *presented*, as they are happening.[61] The act of concurrent presentation, then, can be attributed either to an overt narrator or a focalizing character, both of whom may equally serve as the center of consciousness from which the narrative events are perceived. This modified definition of simultaneous narration as an act of simultaneous *presentation* that can involve either the mode of narration or that of focalization provides a more adequate description of the synchronizing function of the fictional present: By negating any temporal distance between story and discourse, present-tense narration can suggest that the narrative events and their depiction happen simultaneously, irrespective of whether narrator or focalizer functions as mediating consciousness. With this in mind, I suggest that the term *simultaneous* or *concurrent narration* be reserved to instances of simultaneous presentation found in teller-mode narratives and the term *simultaneous* or *concurrent focalization* to instances of simultaneous presentation encoun-

---

the information regulated by the focalizer. In other words, an external focalizer [that is, a narrator-focalizer] has at his disposal all the temporal dimensions of the story (past, present and future), whereas an internal focalizer is limited to the 'present' of the characters." (Rimmon-Kenan 2002 [1983], 79–80) Herman and Vervaeck's definition, on the other hand, allows for a combination of synchronic focalization with external or narrator-focalizers and thus also includes reflector-mode narratives written in the first person: "[...] perception can take place simultaneously with the events, in which case there is synchronic focalization." (Herman and Vervaeck 2005 [2001], 76)

61 I here draw on a definition of narrative by Ryan (2005b) – who, in turn, resorts to H. Porter Abbott's (2008 [2002], 13) definition – as "the representation of an event or a series of events." What Ryan finds useful about Abbott's very basic definition is that, "despite its lack of precision, [...] it relies on the medium-free concept of representation. It tells us that narrative is a signifier of a variable nature—the representation—that calls to mind a meaning—or signified— of a fixed nature, the 'event or series of events'" (Ryan 2005b, 4). Still, Ryan also modifies Abbott's definition, and this seems to me crucial when it comes to redefining the phenomenon of simultaneous narration. More specifically, she proposes "to make the prefix *re* of representation optional, in order to accommodate two kinds of texts: narratives that represent events from a retrospective point of view—events that are already 'in the book' of history; and narratives that present events as they occur, as is the case with live broadcasts, computer games, and perhaps even drama and movies" (Ryan 2005b, 4). It is exactly this latter kind of narrative that is brought about by what I will here call *simultaneous presentation*.

tered in reflector-mode narratives; the term *simultaneous* or *concurrent presentation* holds for both cases.[62]

5.7 The Thematic Function

Closely linked to the synchronizing function of the fictional present is its thematic function, an aspect which belies the widespread opinion that because of the "aporia of synchrony" (Avanessian and Hennig 2015 [2012], 3; see also Chapter 2.3.2) associated with it – i.e. the logical impossibility of experiencing the world and simultaneously recounting this experience – present-tense narration qualifies as an instance of what, in narratological discourse, has become known as 'unnatural' or antimimetic narration.[63] Thanks to the qualities of the grammatical present (the present tense we make use of in ordinary conversation), the fictional present usually evokes within readers the notion of simultaneity. Because the former designates actions that are happening in the present, we take for granted that the latter likewise signals that the act of narration is taking place at the same moment as the narrative events. Due to this grammatical overlap, present-tense narration is often thought to create a scenario of simultaneous or concurrent narration – a logical impossibility.[64]

So far, narrative research has mainly devoted itself to discussing the nonmimetic characteristics of present-tense narration in connection with homodiegetic narratives,[65] with the result that few studies have investigated the nonmimetic potential of present-tense narration in heterodiegetic narratives (cf. Ryan 1993; Ohme 2018). But Gérard Genette's (1980 [1972], 227–231) distinction between homodiegetic and heterodiegetic narration is not helpful in this context, as the question of the implausibility, or even impossibility, of present-tense narration can arise in any narrative text that features an overt narrator,

---

[62] It should be noted that this understanding of simultaneous focalization bears no relation to Rimmon-Kenan's (2002 [1983], 78) homonymous term which refers to "a panoramic view [...] of things 'happening' in different places."
[63] For a discussion of the various definitions of 'unnatural' or antimimetic narrative, cf. e.g. Alber et al. 2010, 2012, 2013; Alber and Heinze 2011; and Richardson 2012a, 20; 2012b, 2015, Ch. 1; 2016, 389–391.
[64] Cf. e.g. Bode 2005, 120–122; 2013, Ch. 1.4; Brandt 1997; Cohn 1993, 1999; DelConte 2007; D'hoker 2013; Farner 2014, 194–195; Hansen 2008; Jahn 2017, N3.3.11; Lahn 2016, 83; Marsden 2004, 107; Nielsen 2011, 59–65; Phelan 1994; 2013a, 179–183; Philipowski 2018; Richardson 2002a, 53; 2019, 117; Rimmon-Kenan 2002 [1983], 91; and Ryan 1993; see also Chapter 2.3.2.
[65] Cf. Cohn 1993, 1999; DelConte 2007; D'hoker 2013, 2019; Hansen 2008; Nielsen 2011; and Phelan 1994; 2013a, 179–183.

irrespective of whether this agent is involved in the story or not. Nevertheless, the two narrative types pose different problems with regard to the present tense's negation of dual temporality in narrative discourse. Armen Avanessian and Anke Hennig (2015 [2012], 40) argue that, "while the first-person narrator of a present-tense text has no time in which she could report on her synchronous experiences" (for how could she possibly manage to live and tell at the same time?), "the third-person narrator has no place from which he could narrate the experiences of a character" (because where exactly in the storyworld should this narrative agent be located without the other characters noticing him?). In light of these considerations, it seems more accurate to draw on Franz K. Stanzel's (1981a; 1995 [1979], Ch. 6) distinction between teller-mode and reflector-mode narratives when it comes to discussing the (non-)mimetic dimension of present-tense narration; for (as I have argued in Chapter 5.4) only teller-mode narratives can create a mimesis of narration (cf. Nünning 2000, 2001b); only in these narratives, therefore, can the use of the present tense violate such a mimetic illusion.

The thematic use of the fictional present, however, circumvents this problem, as it creates a narrative scenario in which simultaneous narration is possible without leading to an aporetic moment in the synchronicity between narrative events and the reporting of these events. After all, thematic present-tense narration occurs exclusively in narratives in which "presence" and/or "contemporaneity" constitute(s) (the) story's central theme(s). Creating the illusion of narrative immediacy and concurrent narration, the thematic function of the fictional present foregrounds these themes and renders them obvious to readers; hence its unmistakable resemblance to the synchronizing function of present-tense narration. Moreover, it not only draws on the most distinctive characteristics of the synchronizing function, but, like its close relative, it also integrates aspects of the referential and metareferential functions.

Some examples from contemporary literature may serve to illustrate these aspects. Maud, the 82-year-old first-person narrator of Emma Healey's *Elizabeth Is Missing* (2014), suffers from Alzheimer's disease, which is slowly but surely eradicating the memories of her past. Christine, the forty-seven-year-old homodiegetic narrator of S. J. Watson's *Before I Go to Sleep* (2011), had an accident at the age of twenty-nine, and her serious head injuries have since led to post-traumatic amnesia. As a result, she wakes every morning wondering about the identity of the unknown woman staring at her in the mirror. Simon, the character narrator of Anna Smaill's *The Chimes* (2015), lives in a surreal, dystopian London where reminiscences are prohibited and memory loss is universal. To ensure this collective state of mind, the population of the city is ruled by an immense musical instrument, the Cadrillon, a brainwashing device that extinguishes human memory within 24 hours by means of an omnipresent and gradually intensifying tinnitus.

Since these three novels all suggest that their protagonists are either incapable of (Maud and Christine) or prevented from (Simon) recollecting their past, the fictional present appears to be the sole logical choice of tense which enables them to relate their experiences convincingly. In the context of Healey's, Watson's, and Smaill's narratives, then, the use of the present tense does not violate our common understanding of retrospective storytelling, because the character-narrators do not seem to have any past of which they could tell (to be more precise, they do not remember their past). Instead, the present tense renders the discourse of the individual first-person narrators more authentic.[66]

Before turning to the next function of present-tense narration, I should make a few concluding remarks on my choice of examples in this section. With a view to supporting my argument that the thematic function of the present tense counters the widely held assumption that the fictional present brings about 'unnatural' narrative scenarios, I have discussed only first-person narratives here; and *Elizabeth Is Missing*, *Before I Go to Sleep*, and *The Chimes* seem appropriate because they each feature an overt narrator who gives rise to a mimesis of narration (my selection criterion is, then, not so much the first-person narrative situation as the fact that all these texts qualify as teller-mode narratives). The selection of texts does not in the least imply that the thematic function of the fictional present cannot be found in third-person narratives. Evidence to the contrary can be seen in Irmtraud Huber's (2016, 48–51) reading of *C* (2010), which convincingly interprets Tom McCarthy's use of the present tense, among other things, as a linguistic means to highlight one of the novel's central themes, "the development of wireless communication" (Huber 2016, 50).[67]

5.8 The Rhetorical Function

The preceding functions of present-tense narration all influence readers in their act of forming mental representations of fictional worlds. More specifically, this means that, in the context of these uses of present-tense narration, readers con-

---

[66] For a detailed discussion of the concept of authentic narration (*authentisches Erzählen*), cf. Weixler 2012, 17–21.
[67] For further examples of different thematic uses of present-tense narration, cf. also Harvey 2006, 87–92.

sciously or unconsciously incorporate the fictional present in the mental models they construct of the worlds they read about in narrative fiction, for example because this tense draws their attention, or even transports them to a specific here-and-now within the storyworld (referential and immersive functions), evokes a specific narrative scenario (metareferential, communicative, and synchronizing functions), or highlights a central theme in the narrative (thematic function). The rhetorical function affects the process of world building by more subtle means, manipulating readers' narrative experience (cf. Phelan 2007) by imperceptibly guiding their interests in the spatiotemporal configurations of the textual world in question. In his essay "Forms of Time and of the Chronotope in the Novel," Mikhail M. Bakhtin argues (2014 [1981]) that literary texts produce unified "chronotopes" whose temporal and spatial characteristics are inseparably interwoven.[68] Given that storyworlds always have both a spatial and a temporal dimension, Bakhtin's notion of timespaces is, from the perspective of narrative worldmaking, incontestable. As this chapter will show, however, fictional present-tense usage can destabilize the balance between the spatial and temporal components of the chronotope. Since such an effect relates to narratives in their entirety rather than to isolated passages, it is necessary to investigate the progression of present-tense narratives – i.e. the possible ways in which they unfold over time.[69]

The concept of narrative progression comes from the field of rhetorical narratology where it features prominently in the work of James Phelan.[70] According to Phelan (2002, 211), the term *progression* "refers to narrative as a dynamic event, one that must move, in both its telling and its reception, through time." In exploring narrative progression, he argues, we investigate "how authors generate, sustain, develop, and resolve readers' interests in narrative" (Phelan 2002, 211). Such narrative dynamics, Phelan continues, are "given shape and direction by the way in which an author introduces, complicates, and resolves

---

[68] With this concept Bakhtin seeks to account for the fact that all spatial elements of a fictional world represented in literary texts inevitably contain a temporal component and vice versa. In other words, narrative space and narrative time are mutually dependent – a relationship that manifests itself in a complex interplay: the abstract and intangible notion of time becomes visible through spatial concretization within the chronotope; conversely, temporalization turns the empty and static concept of space into a dynamic momentum (cf. Frank 2015, 160).
[69] Following Michael C. Frank's (2015, 168) suggestion of conceiving Bakhtin's notion of the chronotope as a flexible "concept in progress" which can be easily integrated into new contexts, I here reconceptualize it as a narratological category that can be applied to identify the spatiotemporal dynamics of a specific narrative.
[70] Cf. Phelan 1981, 2005, 2007, 2013b, 2017, and especially 1989, 1996.

(or fails to resolve) certain instabilities which are the developing focus of the authorial audience's interest in [...] narrative[s]" (2002, 211). Phelan distinguishes two major kinds of unstable relation, which he calls "instabilities" and "tensions." Instabilities occur on the story level of narrative texts, where they constitute conflicts "between characters" which are "created by situations, and complicated and resolved through actions" (Phelan 2002, 211). Tensions, by contrast, evolve on the discourse level, and represent "instabilities—of value, belief, opinion, knowledge, expectation—between authors and/or narrators, on the one hand, and the authorial audience on the other" (Phelan 2002, 211). Although some narratives "progress primarily through the introduction and complication of instabilities" and others "progress primarily through tensions," Phelan stresses that the two kinds of unstable relation are not mutually exclusive, meaning that there are also narratives which progress by displaying both instabilities and tensions (2002, 211).[71]

Phelan's notion of tensions between narrators and (implied) readers – especially those relating to knowledge and expectation – appears to be most relevant in the context of present-tense narration. That is not to say that present-tense novels cannot also progress through instabilities; yet I believe that the tensions arising between narrators and readers in present-tense narratives operate differently from those in past-tense narratives. My assumption is based on the observation that the present-tense novel exhibits more complex spatio-temporal configurations than the traditional past-tense novel. As already outlined in the discussion of the synchronizing function of fictional present-tense usage (see Chapter 5.6), present-tense narration can create a narrative scenario that is logically impossible, the consistent use of the present tense suggesting that the narrative events are presented while they are happening – irrespective of whether this is actually the case or not. By insinuating synchronicity between story and narration, present-tense narrative leads readers to believe that they

---

[71] Embodying "the movement of a narrative from beginning to end and the principles governing that movement" (Phelan 1996, 219), Phelan's concept of narrative progression presents the rhetorical equivalent of David Herman's (2009a, 75) notion of event sequencing, which posits that "[n]arrative representations cue interpreters to draw inferences about a structured time-course of particularized events." Although Phelan's and Herman's concepts refer to the same phenomenon, they examine it from different angles: Phelan focuses on the perspective of the (implied) author, asking how narratives manage, by means of specific textual strategies, to prompt readers to perceive their temporal unfolding in particular ways. Herman, on the other hand, concentrates not so much on the production of narratives as on their reception, investigating how narrative representations allow readers to gather information that enables them to mentally reconstruct the temporal unfolding of the narrated events.

are dealing with an instance of simultaneous or concurrent narration, thus heightening their feeling that the narrator cannot offer them a comprehensive picture of the storyworld evoked by the text.

However, Bakhtin's concept of the chronotope allows further exploration of the dynamics of present-tense narrative. The lack of temporal distance between story and narrative discourse complicates the timespace of the present-tense novel: since the act of narration and the narrated events no longer seem to be separated in time, readers conceive of the narrator's discourse as a communicative act that is closely intertwined with the spatiotemporal circumstances of the diegetic world. The chronotope of the present-tense narrative, then, involves not only the storyworld, but also the narrative act itself. As a result, present-tense narratives facilitate a specific type of narrative progression which, I believe, is not to be found in past-tense narratives. The reason for this is that the use of the present tense controls readers' experience of the spatiotemporal storyworlds in that it highlights either narrative space or narrative time. I therefore propose a distinction between two kinds of spatiotemporal configurations encountered in present-tense narrative: the chronotope and the topochrone.

Drawing on Bakhtin's (2014 [1981], 250) claim that chronotopes "are the organizing centers for the fundamental narrative events of the novel,"[72] I conceptualize chronotopic configurations of present-tense narrative as timespaces which foreground the concept of time while largely neglecting that of space. In more concrete terms, this means that, in present-tense novels which exhibit such chronotopes, progression is determined by the concept of time rather than space. To achieve such an effect, chronotopic present-tense narratives employ a specific way of storytelling: in lieu of describing the spatiotemporal setting in detail, they reduce this information to a minimum by either briefly specifying the place and time of the narrative events in the narrative discourse or restricting these indications to the paratext. Since chronotopic present-tense narratives, moreover, emphasize narrative sequentiality, they resort not so much to

---

72 In addition to its "narrative, plot-generating significance" (Bemong and Borghart 2010, 6), Bakhtin (2014 [1981], 250–251) identifies three further meanings of the chronotope, pointing out that chronotopes can exhibit representational importance, that they can serve as the basis for differentiating generic types, and that they can even possess a semantic meaning (cf. also Bemong and Borghart 2010, 5–6). Indeed, Bakhtin has often been criticized for never providing a clear definition of the chronotope (cf. e.g. Bemong and Borghart 2010, 5; Frank 2015, 160; Ladin 1999, 213; Scholz 1998, 143–145), a lack of both analytical and systematic precision that has led to very different interpretations of the concept in literary and cultural studies (cf. Bemong and Borghart 2010, 5–8).

the mode of telling as to that of showing.⁷³ As a consequence, they largely refrain from presenting their characters' consciousness and instead stress the mode of external focalization; the pace of narration in these texts is correspondingly fast.

The relative importance of time and space is reversed in the topochronic present-tense novel. In a 2003 essay on "Russo-Soviet Topoi," Mikhail Epstein uses the Bakhtinian concept of the chronotope to examine Soviet civilization, discovering a pattern which he terms "topochrone":

> [...] *chronos* is consistently displaced and swallowed up by *topos*. Chronos tends toward zero, toward the suddenness of miracle, toward the instantaneousness of revolutionary or eschatological transformation. Topos, correspondingly, tends toward infinity, striving to encompass an enormous land mass and even the earth itself. (Epstein 2003, 277; italics in the original)⁷⁴

Adopting Epstein's notion of the topochrone, I suggest that topochronic configurations of present-tense narration give priority to the concept of space over that of time. In the topochronic present-tense novel, then, the setting is more important for narrative progression than the coherent representation of events, and the narrative accordingly focuses on the depiction of space and the characters' emotional responses to it. The progression of topochronic present-tense narratives, however, like that of chronotopic present-tense narratives, is brought about by a specific form of storytelling. Featuring numerous passages of detailed descriptions of the spatiotemporal setting, which are often closely tied to the representation of the consciousness of one or several character(s), the former consequently exhibit a slow pace of narration. By combining the depiction of narrative space with internal focalization, topochronic present-tense narratives frequently create spatiotemporal settings which have a metaphorical and sometimes even emotional significance and thus contribute to the central themes of these narratives.⁷⁵

---

73 For the distinction between the modes of telling and showing, cf. Lubbock 1965 [1921], 59–76.
74 Even though Epstein does not mention the term *topochrone* explicitly in his essay, he introduces the term in his entry on "Russo-Soviet topoi," which is actually the beginning of his essay, on his academic website *IntelNet*: http://www.emory.edu/INTELNET/ar_topo.html (accessed August 31, 2020).
75 For considerations of the symbolic meaning of narrative space, cf. e.g. Ryan 2014, 805–806 and Lotman 1977 [1971], 217–231; an informative description of the concept of emotional space can be found in Ryan et al. 2016, 39–43. Contemporary work on the concept of 'sense of place' in narrative, moreover, adduces the argument that narrative space can assume a pronounced

Owing to its specific spatiotemporal structure, the topochrone challenges the understanding of narrative as a dynamic event that moves, in its telling, through time (Phelan). The notion of narrative progression always entails a certain degree of narrative linearity, for it suggests that the events presented in a narrative text can be projected onto a linear continuum. As a consequence, we usually believe that any narrative universe – at least mimetic ones in which fictional time seems to play by the same rules as 'real' clock time – consists of the different temporal states of past, present, and future. The reason for this assumption is that narrative texts normally contain various forms of anachronies such as analepses (flashbacks) and prolepses (flashforwards), which enable readers to construct a mental timeline on which they can arrange the narrated events.[76]

Topochronic present-tense narratives, however, engage in "a 'polychronic' style of narration" (Herman 2002, 212) which orders events in such an indeterminate way that it impedes any concrete temporal localization of narrative events and hence yields what David Herman designates as "fuzzy temporality" (2002, 212–220).[77] Drawing mainly on associative representations of characters' consciousness reminiscent of the modernist novel (cf. Stevenson 2008 [2005], 317–318), topochronic present-tense narration seems to generate a simultaneity of non-simultaneous events, as it blends the present of the storyworld with its past and/or future by constantly integrating flashbacks and/or flashforwards into its subjective depictions of narrative space. As a result, readers may find "it difficult or even impossible to assign narrated events a fixed or even fixable position along a timeline in the storyworld" (Herman 2002, 212).

Against this backdrop, the classical narratological concepts of analepsis and prolepsis no longer allow an adequate description of temporal representations in topochronic present-tense narratives. In fact, the topochrone of the

---

experiential quality for both fictional characters and flesh-and-blood readers: cf. Caracciolo 2013 and Easterlin 2012.

76 William Nelles (2016) even goes so far as to claim that literary narrative never forgoes an – at least to some degree – anachronic mode of storytelling, inasmuch as narratives of any length always include passages of analepsis and/or prolepsis. For an extensive discussion of the concept of narrative anachrony, cf. the chapter on "Order" in Gérard Genette's *Narrative Discourse: An Essay in Method* (1980 [1972], Ch. 1).

77 Cindy Weinstein (2015, 5) has even coined a term for those narratives which stage such "a breakdown in temporal logic": "Tempo(e)rality is the term I use to describe novels whose hold on sequence is wobbly. To put it simply, what happens first, what happens second, what is before and what is after is often difficult to discern, and, as a consequence, tense, particularly the past tense, loses its position as a temporal anchor." (Weinstein 2015, 4)

present-tense novel facilitates a form of narration which I shall refer to as *circumleptic narration*. The adjective *circumleptic* derives from the noun *circumlepsis* which I here introduce as a complement to the concepts of prolepsis and analepsis. While Gérard Genette's (1980 [1972], 48–79) conceptual pair designates narrative anachronies which qualify as either pure flashbacks or pure flashforwards, I construe instances of circumlepsis as narrative anachronies that consist in a constant oscillation between different temporal states. Instances of circumlepsis may comprise the entire scope of the temporal continuum of a fictional storyworld by constantly skipping back and forth between past, present, and future; in such cases, I suggest speaking of instances of *comprehensive* or *timeless circumlepsis*, as they integrate both flashbacks and flashforwards. Yet circumlepses may also restrict themselves to confusing the states of past and present or present and future;[78] for such instances I propose the terms *hyper-analepsis* and *hyper-prolepsis*, respectively, to stress their overall analeptic or proleptic quality.[79]

Despite their distinctive differences, my concepts of the chronotope and topochrone also have some similarities. Following Bakhtin's contention that representations of time and space are always closely connected in narrative fiction, I would emphasize that both chronotope and topochrone only embody different relations of dominance with respect to spatiotemporal representations without excluding either the aspect of time or that of space. Hence, although one constituent of the Bakhtinian chronotope is always dominant in my own conceptions of the chronotope and topochrone, both chronotopic and topochronic present-tense narratives invariably point to a link between *chronos* (time) and *topos* (space). For each emphatic kind of spatiotemporal configuration bears within it the negative of its counterpart. Yet such extensive foregrounding of either time or space is only possible because the use of the fictional present raises certain readerly expectations: By feigning synchronicity between story and narration – the rhetorical function of present-tense narration here resembling the thematic in that both draw on the synchronizing function – the rhetorical use of the present tense allows readers to sense that the narrative they are currently reading will not enable them to get an entire picture of the

---

[78] An example of a present-tense novel which confounds the diegetic past and present in this way is Guy Burt's *A Clock Without Hands* (2005 [1999]), previously published as *The Dandelion Clock* (cf. Birke 2008, Ch. V.1).

[79] I am grateful to Roy Sommer, who generously shared his ideas concerning the phenomenon of hyper-prolepsis with me and thus encouraged me to further think about temporal representations in topochronic present-tense narratives.

fictional world presented in the text, so that gaps in the spatiotemporal continuum of that world may no longer disturb them.

In closing this section, I must explain why I have not illustrated the rhetorical use of the fictional present with concrete examples. As my outline of the chronotope/topochrone divide has clarified, the rhetorical function of the present tense affects the phenomenon of narrative progression, which, in turn, concerns a narrative in its entirety. The wide-ranging scope of the rhetorical function of present-tense narration thus warrants a comprehensive analysis of individual narratives. The claim that a narrative evokes either a chronotope or topochrone, requires analysis of the way in which the narrative depicts both its setting and its plot; analyzing a single scene without its narrative context would lead to confusion as to how narratives unfold in time. So I have refrained here from discussing isolated passages from present-tense novels and refer instead to my readings of Nadeem Aslam's *Maps for Lost Lovers* (in Chapter 9) and Don Winslow's *The Power of the Dog* (in Chapter 10), where the concepts of the chronotope and topochrone will be further examined.

5.9 The Transmodal Function

While the communicative function of fictional present-tense usage introduced in Chapter 5.5 evokes within readers the impression of oral storytelling (rather than written narrative), the transmodal use of the fictional present elicits a different discourse mode from that of narrative. Seymour Chatman (1990, Ch. 1) distinguishes three major text types: narrative, description, and argument; David Herman (2008; 2009a, 79–100) similarly differentiates between narrative, description, and explanation. As Chatman explains, diverging text types do not necessarily exclude each other, but may also "operate *at each other's service*" (1990, 10; italics in the original). A novel, for example, can feature not only narrative, but also description, argument, and explanation without forfeiting its narrativity. Similarly, descriptive, argumentative or explanatory texts do not automatically lose their descriptive, argumentative, or explanatory quality as soon as they contain passages featuring characteristics of other text types. Drawing on Helmut Bonheim (1986), one can, therefore, conceptualize descriptive, argumentative, and explanatory passages occurring in narrative texts as "narrative modes" rather than text types – that is, as different discourse modes (i.e. description, argument, and explanation) appearing in the text type of narrative.[80] Bonheim, however, identifies four different narrative modes – description, speech, report, and comment – which diverge somewhat from Chatman's and Herman's classifications. Combining both typologies will, then, provide us with a spectrum of seven different discourse modes encountered in narrative texts: narrative, report, description, argument, explanation, comment, and speech.

With recourse to Werner Wolf (2007a, 18–21), we can, moreover, conceive of these diverging discourse modes as different "semiotic macro-modes" or cognitive "macro-frames." Wolf argues that discourse modes represent mental constructs which are "aimed at regulating specific forms of organizing signs in various genres and media for specific purposes" and which are therefore easily "recognized owing to certain typical functions and other features" (Wolf 2007a, 8).[81] In light of Wolf's definition, the transmodal function of present-tense narration becomes operative whenever the present tense serves to underline the fact that the discourse of a narrative resorts to a manner of representation typically associated with a discourse mode other than narrative or report. That is to say, the transmodal use of the fictional present creates the impression that the 'voice' speaking in a narrative text does not narrate (narrative mode) or report (reporting mode) a story, but instead describes (descriptive mode), argues for (argumentative mode), explains (explanatory mode), comments on (commentary mode), or enacts (i.e. speech mode) the content of the story. Accordingly, readers are led to believe that they encounter the storyworld presented in the narrative not so much because the text tells them about it (narrative and reporting mode) as because it describes (descriptive mode), explains (argumentative, explanatory, and commentary modes), or shows it to them (speech mode).

Since the transmodal use of the fictional present consists in foregrounding representation strategies typically encountered in discourse modes other than narrative or report, it always functions according to the same principle, which I shall, therefore, illustrate here primarily with reference to description, taking

---

80 In analogy to Bonheim's 'narrative' modes, one could also speak of 'descriptive,' 'argumentative,' and 'explanatory' modes to denote discourse types typically used in descriptive, argumentative, and explanatory texts.
81 Wolf's definition of cognitive macro-frames very much resembles Herman's (2009a, 76) conceptualization of discourse modes "both as cognitive activities and as forms of communication, that is, text types embedded within interactional, social, institutional, and other contexts for communicative practice" (cf. also Herman 2008, 438). The only difference between their approaches is that Wolf discusses the concept exclusively in the context of literature and other media, whereas Herman's argument incorporates all types of communication – fictional, nonfictional, monomedial, or multimedial.

this to also cover the modes of argument, explanation, comment, and speech. Moreover, apart from narrative itself, description is the mode that, to date, has gained most attention within the field of narrative theory.[82] Although the genre of the novel has incorporated descriptive passages ever since its inception in the eighteenth century, it is especially in the genre of the *nouveau roman* – the French experimental 'New Novel' of the 1950s and 1960s – that the discourse mode of description gained great popularity. Hence, the *nouveau roman* perfectly lends itself to exemplifying the descriptive present[83] – i.e. the transmodal use of the present tense evoking the discourse mode of description.

Comprising works by writers such as Michel Butor, Alain Robbe-Grillet, Claude Simon, and Nathalie Sarraute, the New Novel promoted a way of writing which, for that time, was innovative and unconventional. According to Gerald Prince (2008 [2005], 398), the genre rejected, among other things, "the methods of the realist novel and its descendants," and thus dismissed "essentialist psychology, linear chronology, mechanistic chains of cause and effect, [and] conventional novelistic props like character and plot." Robbe-Grillet, for instance, repudiates the principles of narrative realism by paying particular "attention to the surface of things," with the result that his writing seems to "[transform] the nature and function of description" in narrative texts (Prince 2008 [2005], 398). Consider the following passage from his novel *Jealousy* (2008 [1959]), in which a jealous husband observes his wife while she is brushing her hair:

> The brush descends the length of the loose hair with a faint noise something between the sound of a breath and a crackle. No sooner has it reached the bottom than it quickly rises again towards the head, where the whole surface of its bristles sinks in before gliding down over the black mass again. The brush is a bone-coloured oval whose short handle disappears almost entirely in the hand firmly gripping it.
>   Half of the hair hangs down the back, the other hand pulls the other half over the shoulder. The head leans to the right, offering the hair more readily to the brush. Each time the latter lands at the top of its cycle behind the nape of the neck, the head leans further to the right, then rises again with an effort, while the right hand, holding the brush, moves away in the opposite direction. The left hand, which loosely confines the hair between the wrist, the palm and the fingers, releases it for a second, and then closes on it again, gathering the strands together with a firm, mechanical gesture, while the brush continues its course to the extreme tips of the hair. The sound which gradually varies from one end to the other is at this point nothing more than a dry, faint crackling, whose last sputters occur once the brush, leaving the longest hair, is already moving up the ascend-

---

82 For narratological studies on description, cf. e.g. Bal 1981; Fludernik 2014b; Genette 1969, 56–61; Hamon 1982, 1993 [1981]; Lopes 1995; Mosher 1991; Nünning 2007; Ronen 1997; Wagner 2018, Ch. 1; and Wolf 2007a.
83 For a further discussion of the descriptive present, cf. Zeman 2018, 251–252.

ing part of the cycle, describing a swift curve in the air which brings it above the neck, where the hair lies flat on the back of the head and reveals the white streak of a parting. (*J*, 33–34)

Suzanne Fleischman (1990, 299) rightly points out that "[i]n a conventional narrative this entire passage might be reduced to a single narrative or restrictive clause: 'She brushed/was brushing her hair.'" Robbe-Grillet chooses to depict the situation in detail: Imitating a film sequence in slow motion, the quotation adopts the perspective of the jealous husband, whose gaze zooms in on the head and upper body of his wife to "[scrutinize] the movements […] of her body parts and hairbrush as the brush moves through her hair, as if independent of a controlling agent" (Fleischman 1990, 298). Thanks to the minute description of each brush stroke, narrative time comes virtually to a halt. Robbe-Grillet's use of the present "obliterate[s] the perception of passing time" (Fleischman 1990, 298): "The conceptualization of time as a continuum stretching backward (and conceivably forward) from the Speaker's [sic] present is no longer appropriate; there is only the here-and-now of the text" (Fleischman 1990, 298). Since passages like the 'hairbrush scene' abound in Robbe-Grillet's text (cf. Fleischman 1990, 299), *Jealousy* seems to generate an extensive pause: the narrative action (i.e. the representation of narrative events) stands still, even though the act of narration (i.e. the present-tense description of objects, characters, and setting) continues.[84] Rather than producing "a dynamic linear pattern of events," the novel "represent[s] a totality, a static whole resembling a picture" (Fleischman 1990, 298) and accordingly challenges the dual temporality traditionally assumed to underlie narrative texts (see Chapter 5.4).

The excerpt from *Jealousy*, however, is a more obvious example of present-tense description than will be often encountered in narrative fiction. Generally, narrative texts drawing on the discourse mode of description do so in a more subtle way. Consider the following, significantly shortened passage from Richard Powers's *The Overstory* (2018) which traces the lifespan of a group of chestnut trees planted by the character Jørgen Hoel from the six chestnuts he collected on the evening when he proposed to his wife Vi Powys (cf. *OS* 5–6):

One of the six chestnuts fails to sprout. But Jørgen Hoel keeps the surviving seedlings alive. […] At the end of the first season, his fields are full and the best of his seedlings stands over two feet tall.

---

[84] On a related note, cf. Torsten Pflugmacher's (2008 [2005], 101) definition of description as "a text-type which identifies the properties of places, objects, or persons. Classical narratology defines description as a narrative pause interrupting the presentation of the chain of events."

In four more years, **the Hoels have three children** and the hint of a chestnut grove. The sprigs come up spindly, their brown stems lined with lenticels. The lush, scalloped, saw-toothed, spiny leaves dwarf the twigs they bud from. [...]

The years unfold both fat and lean. [...] The trees thicken like enchanted things. [...] Fissures in their bark swirl like barber poles as the trunks twist upward. In the wind the branches flicker between dark and paler green. The globes of leaves sweep out, seeking ever more sun. [...] By the time **war comes again** to the infant country, the five trunks have surpassed the one who planted them.

The pitiless winter of '62 **tries to take another baby**. It settles for one of the trees. The oldest child, John, destroys another, the summer after. [...]

The draft arrives in '63. The young and single men go first. Jørgen Hoel, at thirty-three, with a wife, small children, and a few hundred acres, gets deferred. [...]

One more spring, and the three remaining trees burst out in cream-colored flowers. The blooms smell acrid, gamy, sour, like old shoes or rank undergarments. Then comes a thimbleful of sweet nuts. [...]

"There will be bushels," Jørgen says. [...] "We can sell the extra, in town."

"Christmas presents for the neighbors," Vi decides. **But it's the neighbors who must keep the Hoels alive, in that year's brutal drought**. One more chestnut dies of thirst in a season when not even the future can be spared a drop of water.

Years pass. The brown trunks start to gray. Lightning in a parched fall, with so few prairie targets tall enough to bother with, hits one of the remaining chestnut pair. Wood [...] goes up in flames. [...]

The sole remaining chestnut goes on flowering. But its blooms have no more blossoms to answer them. No mates exist for countless miles around, and a chestnut, though both male and female, will not serve itself. (*OS*, 7–9; my emphasis)

This long excerpt is a perfect example of what Harold F. Mosher (1991, 427), with reference to Meir Sternberg's (1981, 76) concept of pseudo-description,[85] refers to as "narratized description" – that is, a passage of description disguised as narration. The narrator's present-tense discourse here clearly qualifies as a description, for it primarily delineates the development of the chestnut trees over a stretch of several years: the chestnuts sprout, the trees grow, leaves bud and blossoms burst from twigs. Instead of presenting a series of events, the text confines itself to depicting the different states of the trees over the course of time. Yet Powers manages to camouflage the descriptive quality of his text by combining this sketch of the life span of several plants with a synopsis of some key events that happen within the storyworld while the trees are growing through the years. Readers learn that Jørgen and his wife have three children,

---

[85] More specifically, Sternberg (1981, 76) differentiates between "pseudo-description, where the sequence of spatial representation turns into a sequence of spatial clues and anchors for a developing action, and pure description (pseudo-action included), where the spatial sequence does not even coincide with a sequence of chronological landmarks."

that one of them becomes seriously ill in the winter of '62, that Jørgen is called up to fight in '63, and that some years later the Hoels suffer a harvest shortage as a result of a drought (see my emphasis). In short, the text provides a very rough and selective overview of Jørgen's family life. Powers's present-tense passage consequently has the reverse effect from Robbe-Grillet's: in lieu of creating an extensive pause, Powers's descriptions accelerate the narrative pace, effectuating a summary of the narrative events.

Although it is not necessary to examine the other discourse modes in depth here – as I have explained above, the transmodal use of the fictional present always follows the same pattern – a few further examples may aptly demonstrate how narrative fiction deploys the transmodal use of the fictional present in connection with different discourse modes. In *The Course of Love* (2016), Alain de Botton makes use of the argumentative present. The novel traces the love story of a couple, Rabih and Kirsten, from their first encounter and the moment they fall in love via their happy marriage to the deep problems they have to overcome during their relationship. The love story is told in chronological order through the voice of a covert heterodiegetic narrator. Every few pages, however, de Botton intermits his narrator's present-tense account of the development of the couple's relationship to insert philosophical arguments on the concept of love, which are also written in the present tense. By thus constantly switching between narrative and argumentative modes, the novel partly reads more like an essay than a narrative text.

An example of the transmodal use of the present tense eliciting the discourse mode of explanation can be found in Mark Haddon's *The Curious Incident of the Dog in the Night-Time* (2004 [2003]). The novel is told by Christopher Boone, a teenager with Asperger's Syndrome, a developmental disorder that manifests itself in a proclivity for lists, patterns, and the truth, which is also reflected in his narrative discourse. For instance, in Chapter 19, which is actually the eighth chapter of the novel, Christopher informs us that he gives prime numbers (instead of cardinal numbers) to the chapters of his narrative because he likes this type of natural numbers. He then goes on to explain "how you work out what prime numbers are" (*CI*, 14):

> First, you write down all the positive whole numbers in the world.
> [...]
> Then you take away all the numbers that are multiples of 2. Then you take away all the numbers that are multiples of 3. Then you take away all the numbers that are multiples of 4 and 5 and 6 and 7 and so on. The numbers that are left are the prime numbers. (*CI*, 14)

It is no coincidence that the narrator here switches to the present tense (most of his narrative is told in the past tense), as the gnomic present is the tense normally used for definitions or explanations.

However, the explanatory function of the fictional present is often more subtle than in the Haddon example, where it occurs in an explicit definition. It can also be employed, for example, in metanarrative passages of teller-mode narratives, irrespective of whether these texts feature a global use of the past or the present tense. At the beginning of the past-tense novel *Tom Jones: The History of a Foundling* (1973 [1749]), Henry Fielding's authorial narrator explicates the entertaining function of literature by drawing a comparison between the activities of reading a novel and going to a restaurant. Unlike the rest of the novel, this comparison is written in the present tense:

> An Author ought to consider himself, not as a Gentleman who gives a private or eleemosynary Treat, but rather as one who keeps a public Ordinary, at which all Persons are welcome for their Money. In the former Case, it is well known, that the Entertainer provides what Fare he pleases; and tho' this should be very indifferent, and utterly disagreeable to the Taste of his Company, they must not find any Fault; nay, on the contrary, Good-Breeding forces them outwardly to approve and to commend whatever is set before them. Now the contrary of this happens to the Master of an Ordinary. Men who pay for what they eat, will insist on gratifying their Palates, however nice and even whimsical these may prove; and if every Thing is not agreeable to their Taste, will challenge a Right to censure, to abuse, and to d——n their Dinner without Controul. (*TJ*, 25)

Closely connected with the explanatory mode of the present tense is the commentary mode, which also frequently appears in first-person or authorial narrative situations – that is, past- or present-tense narratives which exhibit an overt narrator. In "Before the Curtain," the preface to William Makepeace Thackeray's past-tense novel *Vanity Fair: A Novel Without a Hero* (1994 [1847–1948]), the authorial narrator comments on the scene which the "Manager of the Performance" witnesses when "look[ing] into the Fair" (xv):

> A man with a reflective turn of mind, walking through an exhibition of this sort, will not be oppressed, I take it, by his own or other people's hilarity. **An episode of humour or kindness touches and amuses him here and there**;—a pretty child looking at a gingerbread stall; a pretty girl blushing whilst her lover talks to her and chooses her fairing; poor Tom Fool, yonder behind the waggon, mumbling his bone with the honest family which lives by his tumbling;—**but the general impression is one more melancholy than mirthful**. (*VF*, xv; my emphasis)

The authorial narrator uses two different discourse modes in this short passage: on the one hand, he depicts the scene by describing what the different characters are doing (a child looks at a gingerbread stall, while a young man flatters his girlfriend), on the other hand, he comments on the atmosphere which is created by this sight (see my emphasis). Since almost the entire paragraph is written in the present tense (only the first sentence uses the future tense), the text here combines two different transmodal uses of the fictional present: the descriptive present and the present as associated with commentary.

Finally, Cory Mesler's *Talk: A Novel in Dialogue* (2002) is a telling example of the transmodal use of the fictional present simulating the mode of speech. *Talk* is a collection of random everyday conversations between the protagonist Jim, a metropolitan bookstore owner, with various other characters. The following excerpt reproduces parts of a conversation between Jim and his wife:

—So this guy **comes** in today and he**'s** got a handful of books to sell.
—Did you remember to call Stacey about doing our tax return?
—Am I telling a story here?
—Sorry, go ahead.
—This guy **comes** in—
—I got that part, he's selling books.
—Right. And he **pulls** out, you know, and Almanac from 1983, a, I don't know, a Reader's Digest Condensed with like and Irving Wallace and a Peter Benchley in it, a couple of mass markets **look** like they've been read by a couple dozen school kids and an old Latin textbook. Ok?
—So you told him his tastes were abysmal and sent him packing.
—Thanks. No, I kindly told him he didn't have anything we needed but we appreciated him thinking of us.
—Of course you said that.
—Are you being unnecessarily downputting tonight?
—Downputting? Is that a verb?
—Never mind.
—Oh, finish the anecdote. I'm sorry.
—So he **gets** indignant, right? He **says**, your sign says you buy books.
—Ha. I guess he thought he had you there.
—Right. And I allowed as to how we don't buy everything, but he**'s** pissed and he **goes** out the door muttering and cursing and grumbling how he'll take his business elsewhere. I felt like chasing him down and pressing him about how much business he's done with us in the past. I mean I'd never seen this joker before but he**'s** suddenly irate with me and leveraging me with a threat never to bring me his musty refuse ever again. I was a might steamed.
—Of course you were. Tell me again why you love retail.
—I know. But, of course, I don't love retail. I just love selling books.
—I know. (*TND*, 111–112; my emphasis)

The quotation shows that Mesler's text is exclusively written in dialogue, dispensing not only with narrative mediation, but even with any paratext that might provide readers with a context for these conversations. The excerpt neither names the characters who are currently talking to each other, nor specifies where and when the conversation takes place. Mesler's text just presents the characters' utterances, so that readers have to infer everything else from what they are saying to each other. What is most interesting in the context of this chapter, however, is that Jim uses the conversational historical present (cf. Wolfson 1978, 1979, 1982; see also Chapter 5.5) when telling his wife about the customer who came into his shop wanting to sell him a book (see my emphasis). Mesler's adherence to the conventions of conversational storytelling convincingly imitates oral speech, rendering the dialogues in his novel authentic.

5.10 Modeling the Process of Worldmaking in Present-Tense Narration, or: The Functional Matrix of Fictional Present-Tense Usage

Although this chapter set out to define the different functions of fictional present-tense usage as clearly and distinctly as possible, I would emphasize that a clear-cut distinction is not in every case possible. The eight functions of fictional present-tense usage introduced here do not represent fixed types, recognizable on the basis of set criteria, which perform uniformly in every narrative in which they occur in the manner of form-to-function mapping. They constitute dynamic modes of present-tense narration which operate differently depending on their specific narrative context. Because of their flexibility, the different functions of the fictional present may sometimes even overlap, which is why in many instances of fictional present-tense usage it might be difficult to distinguish between, say, the referential and the metareferential functions or the communicative and transmodal functions when these evoke the discourse mode of speech. Furthermore, the preceding chapters have also demonstrated that an individual function may draw on one or several other functions, as is especially the case with the thematic and rhetorical functions. Chapters 5.7 and 5.8 have shown that these uses of the fictional present both resort to the synchronizing function of present-tense narration, unfolding their own potential under the premise that the fictional present feigns concurrent narration. The list of functions of fictional present-tense usage provided in this chapter should, then, be regarded as a heuristic for the description and analysis of the various nuances of present-tense narration. In conclusion, I accordingly propose a set of models illustrating how the different functions of present-tense narration contribute heuristically to narrative worldmaking.

5.10 The Functional Matrix of Fictional Present-Tense Usage

A useful conceptual framework for understanding the process of worldmaking in the context of present-tense narration is the transformation matrix, that is, a rectangular array of numbers, symbols, or expressions arranged in rows and columns. In mathematics, more specifically in linear algebra, the transformation matrix serves to describe a linear transformation between two finite-dimensional vector spaces. Using the framework of the transformation matrix as an analogy, one can model the process of world building in the present-tense novel as follows:

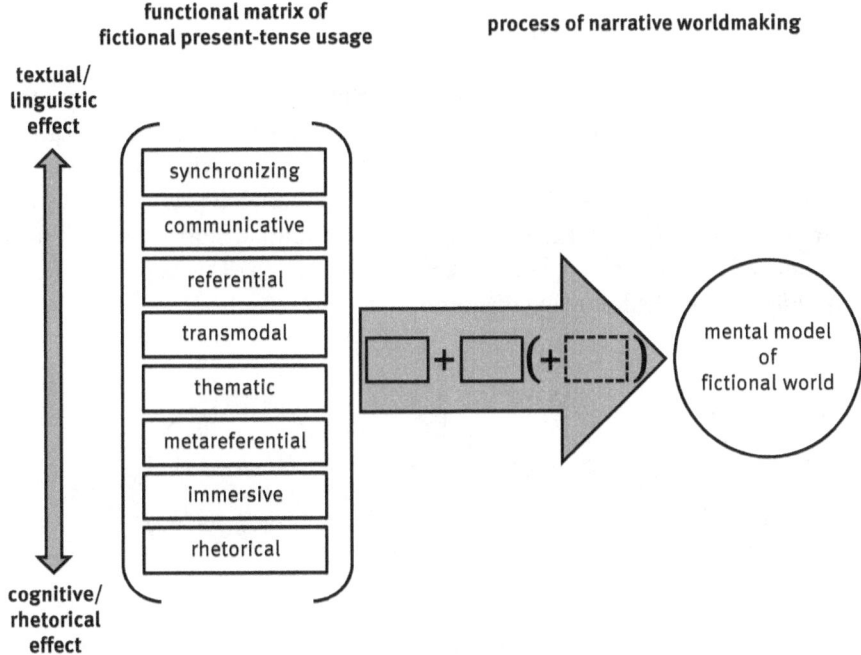

Figure 1: A Model for the Process of Worldmaking in Present-Tense Narration

Figure 1 depicts the functions of fictional present-tense usage as a matrix that influences the process of narrative worldmaking. Just as the numerical values in a mathematical transformation matrix map specific points onto a straight line within a finite-dimensional vector space, so the entries in the functional matrix of fictional present-tense usage map specific textual features and/or cognitive particularities of the fictional present onto the mental representations of the fictional worlds evoked by narrative texts. The different functions included in the matrix are arranged on a vertical scale between the end poles "textual/linguistic effect" and "cognitive/rhetorical effect." While the functions positioned closer to the "textual/linguistic" pole mainly emphasize the textual effects of present-tense narration, the functions closer to the "cognitive/rhetorical" end primarily stress its cognitive impact on readers. However, even though the hierarchical order within the matrix (which is due only to representational restrictions) suggests a strictly linear arrangement of the functions along the scale, this order must not be conceived as fixed, but rather as subject to fluctuation. A specific transmodal use of the fictional present, for instance, can generate a stronger textual effect than a particular referential use; similarly, a particular metareferential use of present-tense narration can have a greater cognitive impact than a particular rhetorical use.

Furthermore, it is important to note that the model in Figure 1 visualizes the prototype of the functional matrix of fictional present-tense usage which encompasses all potential effects of present-tense narration. That is to say, the transformation matrix differs for individual novels, because every novel works differently – meaning that it not only represents a unique storyworld, but also resorts to individual strategies of narrative worldmaking. This aspect of diversity is illustrated in the following diagram:

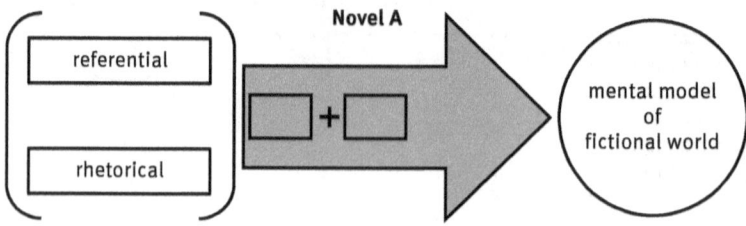

Figure 2: The Process of Worldmaking in Different Present-Tense Novels – Sample Novel A

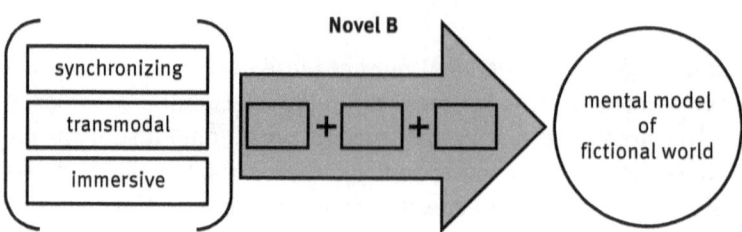

Figure 3: The Process of Worldmaking in Different Present-Tense Novels – Sample Novel B

5.10 The Functional Matrix of Fictional Present-Tense Usage — 139

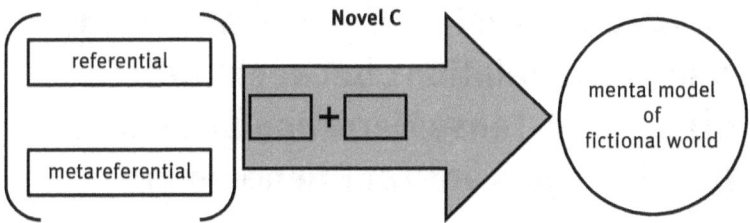

Figure 4: The Process of Worldmaking in Different Present-Tense Novels – Sample Novel C

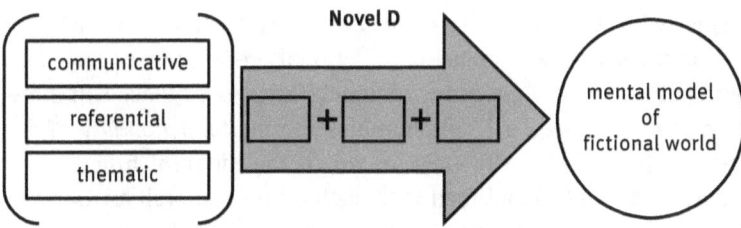

Figure 5: The Process of Worldmaking in Different Present-Tense Novels – Sample Novel D

The four figures above present four hypothetical novels A, B, C, and D, all of which draw on different uses of the fictional present and therefore also exhibit a functional matrix for their specific present-tense usage. In addition, Figures 2 to 5 show that one and the same novel can feature several functions of fictional present-tense usage at the same time. One can even assume that a single novel exhibits all eight functions of fictional present-tense usage, thus approaching the prototype matrix represented in Figure 1 (see page 137). Hypothetically, such a scenario is conceivable, however unlikely it is to occur. A similarly rare case would be a novel that features only one particular use of the fictional present. As indicated by the symbols in the arrow in Figure 1 (i.e. the three regular rectangles one of which is put in parentheses), present-tense novels usually combine at least two different uses of the fictional present. The following chapter will focus more closely on the correlation between different uses of present-tense narration, as well as the interplay of the fictional present with other narrative strategies, by investigating the syntactic dimension of present-tense usage.

6 The Syntactic Dimension of Fictional Present-Tense Usage: Correlations between (Different Kinds of) Present-Tense Narration and Other Narrative Strategies and/or Phenomena

The preceding chapter has shown something of the complexity of present-tense narration. The discussion of its different functions has, moreover, demonstrated that the fictional present as such does not perform a specific narrative function, but that the use of the present tense invariably correlates with a series of other narrative strategies without which its specific effects could not be achieved. The present chapter on the syntactic dimension of fictional present-tense usage sets out to explore the different configurations in which the present tense can interact with other narrative strategies.[1] This includes the *multifunctionality* of fictional present-tense usage – i.e. the ways in which the different functions of present-tense narration can be combined with each other[2] – as well as the *functional interplay* of present-tense narration with other narrative techniques. These will be discussed separately in two subsections of this chapter.

6.1 The Multifunctionality of Fictional Present-Tense Usage

I have argued in Chapter 5.10 that, theoretically speaking, the eight functions of present-tense narration distinguished in the functional matrix of fictional present-tense usage (see Figure 1 on page 137) could all become effective within one and the same narrative. However, I have not yet proposed any analytical categories to describe how these different functions might correlate with each other. Here I will make up for this neglect by discussing two criteria for differentiating such categories.

When analyzing the multifunctionality of fictional present-tense usage, we can first investigate the *hierarchical relation* between the different functions of

---

[1] As stated in Footnote 16 of Chapter 3, I borrow the notion of the syntactic dimension from Vera and Ansgar Nünning (2000b, 21–22), who, in their discussion of the narrative phenomenon of multiperspectivity, use it as an umbrella term to describe the relationing of the individual perspectives within a multiperspective text. In the context of my narrative model of present-tense narration, then, the syntactic dimension identifies the relationing of various narrative strategies as they interact with each other to achieve a specific narrative effect.
[2] For a discussion of multifunctional present-tense usage in short fiction, cf. D'hoker 2019.

this tense, and here we can differentiate *dominant* from *recessive functions*. In biology, the adjectives *dominant* and *recessive* refer to the Mendelian inheritance patterns of specific genetic traits which show that a dominant allele, or variant form of a given gene, is more likely to prevail against a recessive one when passed on from parent to offspring. Using these terms as an analogy for describing the hierarchical relation between different functions of present-tense narration within a specific narrative, I suggest that *dominant* refers to the functions which play the most important role within the text and are therefore more salient and probably also more easily detectable in a narratological analysis, while *recessive* relates to those uses within the same narrative which are less relevant and consequently less prominent. In a multifunctional present-tense narration scenario, the dominant functions will outweigh their recessive counterparts. Since this hierarchical relation can only be determined across an entire text, I will here refrain from giving a concrete example and instead postpone such an illustration to my reading of Emma Donoghue's *Room* in Chapter 12.

A second criterion of differentiation is the *frequency of occurrence* of a specific function. We can here distinguish *recurring* from *non-recurring functions*. Recurring functions, on the one hand, represent those uses of the fictional present which become effective throughout the entire narrative and together form a regular functional pattern. This is the case, for instance, in Shari Lapena's *The Couple Next Door* (2017 [2016]), which regularly switches between a synchronizing use of the fictional present that creates the impression of narrative immediacy and a form of referential present-tense narration that grants readers an insight into the minds of the various characters.

Non-recurring functions, on the other hand, constitute uses of the present tense which occur solely at a specific point within a narrative. Drawing on Gérard Genette's (1980 [1972], 194–198) concept of alterations, we can think of these functions as "a momentary infraction of the code which governs [a coherent] context without thereby calling into question the existence of the code" (195).[3] A perfect example of a non-recurring function can be found in a scene from Ian McEwan's *Nutshell* where the unborn first-person narrator deploys the "imaginary present tense" (Avanessian and Hennig 2015 [2012], Ch. 3; see also

---

3 Genette (1980 [1972], 195) introduced the term *alterations* – which originally stems from the field of classical music, where it refers to "a momentary change in tonality, or even a recurrent dissonance" – to describe temporary changes in focalization which give either "less information than is necessary in principle" (paralipsis) or "more than is authorized in principle in the code of focalization governing [a narrative]" (paralepsis). His definition of alterations as "isolated infractions" of the "dominant mode" or "grammar" of the text can be well transferred to the phenomenon of present-tense narration.

Chapter 5.4) in order to make up a conversation between his father and his uncle at which his mother is not present, so that the narrator cannot overhear it (cf. McEwan 2016, 35–38). As I will show in Chapter 11, this form of *fictum*-metareferential present-tense narration is not typical of McEwan's novel, which overall uses *fictio*-metareferential narration, but should be conceived as an intermittent violation of the regular pattern of present-tense narration discernible in that text.

6.2 The Functional Interplay of Present-Tense Narration with Other Narrative Strategies and/or Phenomena

Given that the fictional present generally acts together with other narrative strategies to fulfill a specific textual function or achieve a specific readerly effect, the next step is to explore the ways in which this tense correlates with other narrative strategies. This involves identification of different correlations between present-tense narration and other narrative techniques and/or phenomena, a variety of which are listed in Table 3. Each item in this list (left-hand column) is accompanied by a series of key questions bearing on the specificities of the given correlation (right-hand column); illustrations of most of these points will be provided in Part III.

Table 3: Correlations of Present-Tense Narration with Other Narrative Strategies and/or Phenomena

Representation of time	How does the fictional present interact with narratological categories that relate to narrative time such as order (cf. Genette 1980 [1972], Ch. 1), duration (cf. Genette 1980 [1972], Ch. 2), or frequency (cf. Genette 1980 [1972], Ch. 3)? What is the relation between present-tense narration and chronological and/or anachronic ways of storytelling? How does the fictional present influence narrative pace? Does it affect how often an event that happens in the story is presented on the discourse level?
Representation of space	How does present-tense narration contribute to the construction of narrative space? To what degree can the fictional present facilitate depictions of the narrative setting? How can the present tense help readers to create "cognitive maps" of the storyworld evoked by a specific narrative (Ryan 2003; Ryan et al. 2016, Ch. 4)? To what extent can present-tense narration yield a "sense of place" for readers (Caracciolo 2013; Easterlin 2012, 111–151)?
Narrative distance	What kind of temporal relation between story and narration does the present tense express (cf. Genette 1980 [1972], 216–223; Margolin 1999; Rimmon-Kenan 2002 [1983], 90–92; Prince 1982, 27–29)? Does it serve to create

Narrative distance (continued)	temporal distance between the narrative events and the act of narrating these events: i.e. does it generate the impression of retrospective or prospective narration, or create an illusion of immediacy by evoking a scenario of simultaneous narration? However, the concept of narrative distance is not restricted to the narrator's temporal position in relation to the narrative events, but may also "[refer] to the narrator's degree of involvement in the story she tells" (Abbott 2008 [2002], 74). Seen from this angle, it may be worth investigating how the use of the fictional present correlates with the narrator's personal involvement in the events depicted in the narrative (cf. Clement 1991).
Narrative voice	How does the present tense affect the narratological category of 'voice' (cf. Genette 1980 [1972], Ch. 5)?[4] How does present-tense narration correlate with different types of narrators (homodiegetic vs. heterodiegetic [cf. Genette 1980 (1972), 243–252]) and typical narrative situations (cf. Stanzel 1986 [1979])? How does the fictional present interact with more experimental narrative voices such as those recognizable in second-person narration and 'we'-narratives (cf. Damsteegt 2004, Ch. 9; DelConte 2013/2014; Fludernik 1995, 109; Gebauer 2020, 22–26; Parker 2011/2012, 173; Reitan 2011, 162–166; Richardson 1994)?
Narrative illusion	How can present-tense narration evoke a "narrative illusion" (*Erzählillusion*) or "mimesis of narration" (*Mimesis des Erzählens*) (Nünning 2000; 2001b)? To what extent does its use characterize "authentic narration" (*authentisches Erzählen*) (Weixler 2012, 17–21) or serve as a strategy of authentication (cf. Martínez 2004, 15–16; 2020, 524–526)?
Metanarration	How does the fictional present interact with the phenomenon of metanarration and its various subforms (cf. Fludernik 2003b; Neumann and Nünning 2014; Nünning 2001a, 2004a)? How can it contribute to the evocation of *fictio*- or *fictum*-metareference (cf. Wolf 2009)?
Narrative levels	On what narrative plane does fictional present-tense usage become effective? Does it affect the discourse or story level of a narrative text (cf. Chatman 1978)? To what degree does it facilitate instances of metalepsis (cf. Genette 1980 [1972], 234–237)? How does it interact with different types of narrative transgression such as figurative and ontological metalepsis (cf. Hanebeck 2017, Ch. 2.2.4)?
Focalization	How does the fictional present relate to the narratological category of focalization (cf. Genette 1980 [1972], 185–198)? How does it correlate with the various subtypes of focalization such as Genette's (1980 [1972], 189–194) tripartite distinction between internal, external, and zero-focalization or Mieke Bal's (1985 [1980], 102–106) binary opposition between internal and external focalization? To what extent does it influence ways of representing

---

4 Christian Paul Casparis (1975, 36), for example, claims "that tense and 'person' are in some way interdependent and [that] their combination has certain distinguishable effects on the meaning of an utterance and perhaps even on narrative technique."

Focalization (continued)	consciousness in narrative fiction (cf. Cohn 1978 as well as the contributions in Herman 2011), particularly strategies like interior monologue (cf. Cohn 1978, Ch. 5–6; 1993; 1999, Ch. 6; Damsteegt 2004, Ch. 8; Fleischman 1991b) or free indirect discourse (cf. Bronzwaer 1970, Ch. III; Fludernik 1993b, Ch. 3.4.2–3.4.3)?
Multi-perspectivity	How does present-tense narration correlate with the narrative phenomenon of multiperspectivity? To what degree does it foster different types of multiperspectivity such as multiperspective narration, focalization, or structure (cf. Nünning and Nünning 2000a, 43–46)?
Narrative authority	How does the present tense help narrative texts generate narrative authority (cf. Dawson 2009, 149–157; 2013, 54–61; Lanser 1992)? In what narrative contexts does it raise or undermine a narrator's authority? To what degree does it differ from other fictional tenses with respect to its function as a narrative means that gives authority to the 'voice' speaking in a narrative text?
Unreliable narration	How do the fictional present and unreliable narration correlate with each other? Does the present tense qualify as a textual feature of narrative unreliability (cf. Hansen 2008, Ohme 2018)? What type of narrative unreliability and/or untrustworthiness can be evoked by the use of the fictional present (cf. Jacke 2018, 2020, Nünning 2015, Pettersson 2015, Vogt 2015, 2018, Zerweck 2019)?
Antimimetic/ 'unnatural' narration	To what degree does present-tense narration qualify as an example of 'unnatural' or antimimetic narration (cf. Alber et al. 2010, Richardson 2012a)? Do present-tense narratives violate the mimetic code of narration (cf. Nielsen 2011, 59–65; Phelan 2013a, 179–183)?
Intertextuality	To what extent do the fictional present and instances of intertextuality interact with each other?[5] Does the present tense, for example, facilitate or impede distinctive features of narrative subgenres such as the historical novel or thriller? Does it evoke other literary genres such as poetry, drama, or film script?[6]

---

5 I here use the concept of intertextuality as an umbrella term which subsumes not only those instances of intertextuality in which a specific text explicitly (or implicitly) refers to another text – Ulrich Broich (1985, 48–52) designates this type of intertextuality as "reference to an individual text" (*Einzeltextreferenz*) – but also those in which a text refers to a different genre by drawing on stylistic and/or representational strategies typical of that genre – Manfred Pfister (1985b) labels this second type of intertextuality "system reference" (*Systemreferenz*). For a further discussion of the distinction between these types of intertextuality, cf. also Pfister 1985a, 17–19.

6 Recent work by Jonathan Culler provides a comprehensive investigation of the various functions of the present tense in poetry (cf. Culler 2014a, 166–176; 2014b; 2015, 283–295); further texts dealing with the use of the present tense in this genre are Harvey 2006, 77–78; Langer 1953, 260–275; and Wright 1974. A discussion of present-tense usage in drama can be found in Korthals 2003, Ch.V.6 and Muny 2008, 77–78.

6.2 The Functional Interplay of the Present Tense with Other Narrative Strategies — 145

Intermediality	How do present-tense narration and the phenomenon of intermediality correlate (cf. Rajewsky 2002, 2005)? More specifically, how does the fictional present interact with intermedial strategies such as media combination (cf. Rajewksy 2002, 15–16; 2005, 51–52) or intermedial references (cf. Rajewsky 2002, 16–17; 2005, 52–53)?
Orality vs. literacy	How is the phenomenon of present-tense narration connected with the concepts of orality and literacy (cf. Fleischman 1990, 1991a; Meisnitzer 2016, 215–236)? Under what narrative circumstances does it evoke the impression of conversational storytelling (cf. Fleischman 1990, 306–308; 1991a, 91–92) or (historical) oral narrative (cf. Zeman 2010) rather than that of written narrative?
Fictionality vs. factuality	To what degree does present-tense usage function as a signpost of fictionality (cf. Cohn 1990; 1999, Ch. 7)?[7] In what narrative contexts does the present tense qualify as a "fictionalizing narrative strategy" (*fiktionalisierendes Erzählverfahren*) (Klein and Martínez 2009, 4; cf. also Nielsen 2010, 290–291) or indicate a "factual mode of narration" (*faktualer Modus von erzählender Rede*) (cf. Klein and Martínez 2009, 2)?

The list above contains the correlations I have most frequently encountered in (contemporary) present-tense novels and which I consider most characteristic of present-tense narration. Hence the selection is a result of the convergence of intuitive and abstract, systematic knowledge at the core of narrative theory (cf. Sommer 2017). It goes without saying that it is not exhaustive and may be supplemented by further narrative strategies.

In order to analyze and describe concrete correlations between present-tense narration and other narrative techniques in a systematic manner, we again need adequate analytical categories. Drawing on the same criteria of differentiation as in the previous section on the multifunctionality of present-tense narration (see Chapter 6.1), we can describe the hierarchical relation between the narrative strategies involved in a specific correlation and determine their scope. So far as the *hierarchichal relation* is concerned, we can distinguish between *main* and *ancillary strategies*. Main strategies are the driving narrative forces that bring about a specific effect (and without which this effect cannot be achieved). Ancillary strategies, on the other hand, merely reinforce an effect created by other narrative techniques; the effect could also be maintained if the ancillary strategies were not used in the text at all.

---

[7] For a more recent discussion of the nature of signposts of fictionality, cf. Dawson 2015, 85–87 and Nielsen et al. 2015a, 106–107; 2015b, 66–67.

The hierarchical relation between correlating narrative strategies can be best explained with reference to two different instances of present-tense narration. As I argued in Chapter 5.5, the phenomenon of simultaneous (or concurrent) narration hinges on a combination of the fictional present with other strategies that generate a narrative scenario. Taken together, all the components of this combination evoke synchronicity between the narrative events and the act of representing these events. Within this correlation, the present tense clearly qualifies as a main strategy, for it is the only fictional tense which automatically triggers within readers the cognitive frame of simultaneity. Even if the same narrative strategies might also generate "isochrony" (Fludernik 2009, 33) between story and discourse when used in a past-tense narrative, they would still not create the impression that the narrative events and the narration of those events took place at the same time.

The hierarchical relation between the fictional present and other narrative techniques seems to be reversed if the present tense correlates with the phenomenon of intertextuality. As examples like Margaret Atwood's *Hag-Seed: The Tempest Retold* (2016), which contains two longer episodes that evoke the notion of a play script (cf. *HS*, 3–5, 210–212), and Don Winslow's *Savages* (2011 [2010]), which includes several passages resembling a film script,[8] demonstrate, the present tense is not among the most important strategies to which narrative texts may resort when imitating other literary genres. What seems more crucial here is their formal and structural make-up: Not only are the respective passages written in dialogue, but they also make use of stage directions or scene descriptions typical of the mimicked genres. In these texts, then, the fictional present fulfills not so much a main as an ancillary function, serving merely to accentuate the play with generic conventions already established by other (para-)textual features.

With regard to the *scope of correlating strategies*, I would propose a distinction between *fixed* and *variable correlations*. One can speak of a 'fixed correlation' of present-tense narration with other narrative techniques if this extends over the entire narrative, with the fictional present always interacting in the same way with the given strategies, as is the case in Margaret Atwood's *Oryx and Crake*, which I will discuss in Chapter 8. Variable correlations, by contrast, arise as soon as the fictional present interacts with different narrative strategies in disparate ways within one and the same narrative. Relevant examples can be found in Nadeem Aslam's *Maps for Lost Lovers* or Irvine Welsh's *Skagboys*, in

---

8 Cf. *SV*, 14, 57, 85–87, 108, 175–178, 229–230, 241–242, 287–288.

6.2 The Functional Interplay of the Present Tense with Other Narrative Strategies — 147

which the correlations depend on the narrative contexts where they occur (see Chapters 9 and 13).

* * *

The table on the next page provides a synoptic overview of the syntactic categories introduced in this chapter. The left-hand column of Table 4 identifies the criteria for distinguishing different analytical categories for an adequate description of the ways in which the fictional present may correlate with other narrative strategies. The division of these categories into two different columns (middle and right-hand columns) depends on whether a specific form of present-tense narration is combined with (an)other use(s) of the present tense (multifunctionality) or whether the fictional present interacts with (an)other narrative technique(s) (functional interplay). Like Table 2 (see Chapter 4.2), Table 4 also shows, through the use of bidirectional arrows, that the binary categories describing the hierarchical relation between correlating functions or strategies, as well as the frequency and scope of such collocations, should again be understood as the extreme ends of a scale (rather than polar opposites). Hence all the boundaries concerned – between dominant and recessive, and recurring and non-recurring functions, as well as between main and ancillary strategies, and fixed and variable correlations – are fluid.

To conclude, I would once more emphasize that the list of analytical categories for describing the syntactic dimension of fictional present-tense usage (see the middle and right-hand columns in Table 4) is not exhaustive, nor are the respective sums of the categories for analyzing the formal-structural dimension of fictional tense usage, nor again the functions of present-tense narration introduced in the previous two chapters. Likewise, I would stress that the syntactic categories identified above should also be conceived as heuristic categories allowing for a systematic description and analysis of the correlation of the fictional present with other narrative strategies. Taken together, the three different layers of the analytical model of present-tense narration presented here (i.e. the formal-structural, functional, and syntactic dimensions) provide a well-equipped tool-box for analyzing and interpreting the fictional present in a manner which, as I hope and believe, does sufficient justice to the particularities of this narrative phenomenon. In the remaining part of this book, I will illustrate the heuristic potential of these categories for exploring the narrative design of the contemporary present-tense novel.

Table 4: Analytical Categories for Describing the Correlation between Present-Tense Narration and Other Narrative Strategies

Criterion for Differentiation	Analytical Categories	
type of correlation	multifunctionality of present-tense narration involving several or all of the following functions: – referential function – immersive function – metareferential function – communicative function – synchronizing function – thematic function – rhetorical function – transmodal function	functional interplay of present-tense narration with other narrative strategies and/or phenomena such as: – representation of time – representation of space – narrative distance – narrative voice – narrative illusion – metanarration – narrative levels – focalization – multiperspectivity – narrative authority – unreliable narration – antimimetic/'unnatural' narration – intertextuality – intermediality – orality vs. literacy – fictionality vs. factuality
hierarchical relation between correlating functions or strategies	dominant functions ⟷ recessive functions	main strategies ⟷ ancillary strategies
frequency and scope of correlating functions or strategies	recurring functions ⟷ non-recurring functions	fixed correlations ⟷ variable correlations

Part III: Uses and Functions of Present-Tense Narration in Contemporary Narrative Fiction

7 Narrative of Reformation: The Revision of History and Narrative Form in Hilary Mantel's *Wolf Hall* (2003) and *Bring Up the Bodies* (2012)

7.1 The Revisionist Character of Mantel's Tudor Narratives: Turning a Historical Villain into a Fictional Hero

Most readers – literary scholars included – appear oblivious to fictional tense usage: if they notice the present tense at all, they usually do not consider it particularly important. Of course there are personal preferences, as the recent controversy surrounding the present-tense novel reveals (see Chapter 1). Yet such strong sentiments are the exception rather than the rule: while some critics prefer the past tense, the default in narrative fiction, others quite like present-tense narration. Most tend to ignore it, however, as my survey of research on the novels discussed here will show: although all nine contemporary narratives that form the corpus of this study are, at least in most part, written in the fictional present, secondary literature on these novels has so far largely neglected the aspect of tense usage.

Having said this, one notable exception is work on Hilary Mantel's novels *Wolf Hall* and *Bring Up the Bodies*, published in 2009 and 2012. At the time of writing,[1] the present tense features in 16 of the 27 articles and five reviews which – according to the MLA International Bibliography – have been published on these texts.[2] A possible explanation for the unusual interest in present-tense narration in this instance is that Mantel's narratives belong to the genre of historical fiction, which is generally associated with retrospection. Since historical novels are considered to represent events that happened in the past, we expect these narratives to be written in the past tense.

Mantel's unconventional use of the present tense matches the overall revisionist character of *Wolf Hall* and *Bring Up the Bodies*. Following Marion Gymnich (2018), I classify Mantel's Tudor narratives as examples of a type of histori-

---

[1] This chapter was completed in 2019, which is also the reason why it does not take *The Mirror & the Light* into consideration (the third and final installment of Mantel's Tudor trilogy was only published in March 2020).
[2] Cf. Arias 2014, 23, 28–29; Brosch 2017, 2018; Funk 2018, 97; Geçikli 2013, 94; Greenblatt 2009, 24; Gymnich 2018, 82; Huber 2016, 76–79; Johnston 2017, 543, 548; Kim 2018, 8; Lehtimäki 2011, 51, 54; O'Connor 2018, 30; Rosenberg 2017, 168; Sandberg 2017, 58; Tayler 2009, n.p.; and Wilson 2015, 155.

cal fiction which Ansgar Nünning calls the "revisionist historical novel" – i.e. as narrative texts which rewrite history in an unconventional manner, reinterpreting traditional historiography and finding new ways of representing historical events (cf. Nünning 1995a, Ch. 3.3.3; 1997, 221–223; 2004b, 361–363). Drawing on previous research on *Wolf Hall* and *Bring Up the Bodies*, I contend in the first place that both novels "exoticise" (Arias 2014) the reign of Henry VIII, taking an unusual stance on the developments that in historical discourse have become known as the English or Henrician Reformation (cf. Kim 2018, 2n3, 3; O'Connor 2018, 28) or Tudor Revolution (cf. Elton 1953).[3] Possibly inspired by the work of Geoffrey R. Elton, who, in his book *The Tudor Revolution in Government: A Study of Administrative Changes in the Reign of Henry VIII* (1953), argues that Thomas Cromwell, the King's chief minister, was the mastermind behind England's modernization during Henry's reign, Mantel makes Cromwell the protagonist of her fictional work on the Tudor dynasty.[4]

Based on these insights, I would argue secondly that *Wolf Hall* and *Bring Up the Bodies* yield a 'narrative of reformation' which not only consists in the revision of our view of the religious and political changes that took place in England under Henry VIII, but which also challenges generic conventions in replacing the traditional retrospective perspective – a distinctive feature of revisionist historical fiction – with a prospective perspective. To achieve these effects, both novels combine the formal features of present-tense usage, covert narration, and internal focalization. By depicting the narrative events predominantly from Cromwell's point of view, Mantel's narratives enable readers to perceive these events like contemporaries and hence succeed in giving a new account of Henry's rule and its impact on sixteenth-century Britain.

Before developing this argument, we first need to clarify the term *revisionist historical fiction*. In the first volume of his comprehensive two-volume study of

---

[3] While the terms 'English' or 'Henrician Reformation' refer only to the religious changes in Henry's reign, the term 'Tudor Revolution' relates to all the political reforms of this period.

[4] Cf. Wessendorf 2018, 232: "Mantel's novels were influenced by the writings of the [...] British historian Geoffrey Rudolph Elton, who rejected the longstanding notion of Cromwell as the hatchet man and willing tool of Henry VIII and considered him instead a driving force behind what he called, not uncontestedly, the 'Tudor Revolution' of the 1530s. According to Elton, Cromwell's achievements included the following reforms: 'The creation of a national Church under a layman as supreme head, the insertion into the system of a sovereign law-making Parliament, the consolidation of diverse members of the commonwealth into a unitary state, and indeed the recasting of the central administration which replaced government by the king by government under the king—all these ... characterise the age of Thomas Cromwell and make it an age of change sufficient to permit thoughts of revolution.'"

the historical novel (cf. Nünning 1995a, 1995b), Nünning defines the revisionist historical novel as a type of historical fiction that critically engages with history and the cultural heritage (1995a, 268).[5] Such narratives, he argues, question conventional patterns of meaning, emphasize the opposition between past and present, and transgress both thematic and formal boundaries distinctive of the traditional historical novel. Nünning's definition of revisionist historical fiction is based on Brian McHale's (1987, 90) understanding of the postmodern historical novel as doubly revisionist:

> First, it revises the *content* of the historical record, reinterpreting the historical record, often demystifying or debunking the orthodox version of the past. Secondly, it revises, indeed transforms, the conventions and norms of historical fiction itself. (McHale 1987, 90; italics in the original)

Taking up McHale's argument, Nünning (1995a, 268) stresses that revisionist historical novels challenge outdated traditions by defamiliarizing not only the traditional themes of historical fiction but also the conventional forms in which these are presented. Furthermore, he points out that the term *revisionist historical fiction* establishes an implicit connection between innovative trends within the genre and historiographic tendencies that seek to replace canonical traditions with alternative constructions and representations.

Starting from these premises, Nünning identifies three areas in which the revisionist historical novel differs from more traditional forms like the documentary or realist historical novel. First, it deals predominantly with topics that allow of a critical stance toward outdated thought patterns concerning the past, revealing an altered understanding of history. Secondly, it exploits the privileges of fiction *vis-à-vis* historiographic discourse to a much greater extent than do more traditional types of historical narrative. Thirdly, these texts draw heavily on representations of the past, fictional or otherwise, inspired by new perspectives on history, memory, time, and historical knowledge (cf. Nünning 1995a, 268–269). Nünning accordingly summarizes the key features of revisionist historical fiction as follows:

---

5 Nünning (1995a) distinguishes five types of historical fiction that can be arranged on a continuum between heteroreferentiality and autoreferentiality. While documentary and realist historical fictions focus predominantly on the representation of historical events on the story level, metahistorical and historiographic metafictions exhibit a high degree of metafictional reflection on questions relating to historical theory on the discourse level (cf. Nünning 1995a, 257). The revisionist historical novel sits between these poles, integrating both heteroreferential and autoreferential strategies to a more or less equal degree (cf. Nünning 1995a, 271–272).

Als 'revisionistische historische Romane' werden [...] demnach solche literarischen Erzähltexte bezeichnet, die der Gattung neue Themenbereiche erschließen, in denen eine kritische Erzählweise [...] dominiert, die experimentelle Erzählverfahren zur Geschichtsdarstellung verwenden und Parallelen zu den vielfältigen historiographischen Neuerungen dieses Jahrhunderts aufweisen, die ebenfalls als 'revisionistisch' bezeichnet werden und zu einer Erweiterung des Gegenstandsbereichs sowie zu einer verstärkten methodischen Selbstreflexion geführt haben. (Nünning 1995a, 269)[6]

[We may thus label 'revisionist historical novels' those literary narrative texts that allow the genre to explore new subjects, that are characterized by a dominantly critical narrative style, that use experimental narrative strategies to depict history, and that show parallels to the various historiographic innovations of this century which are likewise referred to as 'revisionist' and that have led to a broadening of the scope of historiography as well as to an increasingly methodological self-reflection. (My translation)]

In my reading of *Wolf Hall* and *Bring Up the Bodies* as instances of the revisionist historical novel, I will first focus on Mantel's thematic revisions of the Henrician Reformation and Tudor Revolution and then go on to discuss the experimental narrative techniques she deploys in order to present this revised history to her readers. One of the most important strategies she resorts to is the global use of present-tense narration.[7]

According to Nünning, the revisionist historical novel often seeks to rewrite history in a different manner from that of traditional historiography. This usually manifests itself in the structure of narrative transmission, for, more often than not, revisionist historical narratives depict historical events from the perspective of suppressed or marginalized social groups or characters who have been

---

[6] More recently, the subgenre which Nünning calls "the revisionist historical novel" has been renamed the "'neo-historical' novel" (Rousselot 2014, 2). In her introduction to a collected volume on contemporary neo-historical fiction, Elodie Rousselot (2014) argues that the neo-historical novel "consciously re-interprets, rediscovers and revises key aspects of the period it returns to" (2) by striving not only to re-imagine history on a thematic level (cf. 4), but also to "create new forms" of representation (3). Although Rousselot does not seem to know of Nünning's typology of historical fiction (at least none of his publications on this topic, not even the English ones, appear in the bibliography of her article), her description of the neo-historical novel largely conforms with Nünning's proposal.

[7] On that score, cf. also Nünning (1995a, 273), who describes the global use of the fictional present in Malcolm Bradbury's *The History Man* (2012 [1975]) as a decisive formal feature allowing the work to be constructed as a revisionist historical novel. Kazunari Miyahara (2009, 246) adduces a similar argument in characterizing the fictional present as an effective strategy enabling novelists to write "histories from below." The reason for this, he explains, is that the present tense diminishes the "authoritative, authorized, and authoritarian" tone usually associated with historical narratives written in the past tense (Miyahara 2009, 245–246).

construed as the losers of history (cf. Nünning 1995a, 271). Mantel's novels *Wolf Hall* and *Bring Up the Bodies* produce such a "history from below" (Nünning 1997, 221) in that they present the events of the Henrician Reformation and Tudor Revolution from Thomas Cromwell's point of view.⁸ I will discuss the narrative perspective of Mantel's novels in greater detail below (Chapter 7.3 and 7.4); here I will emphasize only that the historical Thomas Cromwell belonged to a social group within Tudor society that has been generally neglected by historiography: the son of an artisan blacksmith, Cromwell belonged to the yeomanry, whose members did not have any direct access to the life of the court. It is all the more surprising that he managed to climb the social ladder and eventually became one of the King of England's closest counselors. However, his humble origins might be one of the reasons why he has largely "remained in obscurity in historical records" (Arias 2014, 22). Mantel's novels clearly break with this tradition: Inspired by Elton's revisionist historical records, which argue that Cromwell was, in fact, the most important manipulator of Henry VIII's politics, *Wolf Hall* and *Bring Up the Bodies* put the blacksmith's son at the heart of their story, shedding light on this otherwise rather obscure historical personage.⁹

As previous research on Mantel's Tudor novels has shown, the few historical records that actually do focus on Cromwell depict him as "a villain in the history of England" (Lehtimäki 2011, 48), "a self-serving, power-hungry, and money-grabbing opportunist" (Wessendorf 2018, 233), "a soulless political operator" and "monster of destruction" (Kim 2018, 4) – in short: a man "who was widely hated in his lifetime" (Brosch 2017, 166), for his "reputation [...] made his contemporaries fear him" (LaCroix 2017, 66). Indeed, Stephen Greenblatt (2009, 22) concludes that, "[t]here was nothing remotely glamorous or romantic in his person."¹⁰

---

8 According to Gymnich (2018, 76), "[i]t is largely due to the choice of focalizer that Mantel's novels can be categorized as revisionist historical fiction" because the figural narrative situation allows the author to reimagine history "from the point of view of a political 'insider' whose narrative is very much informed by his own interests and goals."
9 Cf. Arias 2014, 23: "As Mantel has posited in an interview, she noticed the obscurity of Cromwell's position in history, due to the fact that no one had addressed his story [...], and it was her 'desire to commune with the dead and gain wisdom, make atonement, or restore what had been believed lost' [...], thus offering an arresting portrait of this cunning politician." And Mantel's pioneering idea has been successful: since the publication of her Tudor novels in 2009 and 2012, historians and biographers have shown increasing interest in Thomas Cromwell (cf. e.g. Borman 2014, Everett 2015, Loades 2013, MacCulloch 2018).
10 According to the historian Paul van Dyke (1904, 696), the sinister portrayal of Cromwell derives from his contemporary, Reginald Pole, cardinal and archbishop of Canterbury, who "denounced [Cromwell] as a false counselor who helped the descent of a once innocent and

This view of Cromwell is reflected in literature and art. In Robert Bolt's play *A Man for All Seasons* (1990 [1960]), for example, Henry describes his adviser as a "jackal[] with sharp teeth" (55);[11] and the most famous portrait of Cromwell by Hans Holbein (dated c. 1532–1534), shows an unequivocally forbidding man. The awe-inspiring appeal of Holbein's presentation of Cromwell is even mentioned in *Wolf Hall*. When Mantel's Holbein gives his finished portrait to his client, the fictive Cromwell notices that "Hans has made his skin smooth as the skin of a courtesan, but the motion he has captured, that folding of the fingers, is as sure as that of a slaughterman's when he picks up the killing knife" (*WH*, 525). Holbein's portrait makes Cromwell understand why others are intimidated by his outward appearance: now he himself can see that he "look[s] like a murderer" (*WH*, 527; cf. also *BUB*, 8).

However, Mantel only seizes on the traditional, negative representation of Cromwell in order to write against it. As Renate Brosch (2018, 67) observes, Cromwell's realization that he looks like a murderer, as well as his son's immediate confirmation – "Did you not know?" (*WH*, 527) – "may come as a shock to readers, because thus far they have been largely screened from any negative judgement of Cromwell's character by his positive self-appraisal." Mantel's representation "renders the historical story of Thomas Cromwell in the Tudor court in a new, unfamiliar light" (Lehtimäki 2011, 48), portraying him as a "fascinating hero" (Arias 2014, 19; cf. also Gymnich 2018, 76). Her Cromwell defies any characterization as an evil villain, displaying numerous admirable character traits that evoke the reader's sympathy. According to Brosch (2018, 60) these include "intercultural competence (he is fluent in many languages), financial and legal genius, psychological insight, physical courage, wit and last but not least a greater interest in others than himself." This fictive Cromwell

> stands for secular scepticism and pragmatic relativism instead of moral principles, for intercultural connections instead of faith in an essential national identity. In terms of world picture, he belongs to the new inquisitive, open-minded and scientifically informed men of his time. Cromwell is something of a cosmopolitan *avant la lettre*, with his knowledge gathered in travels outside England and among people of all walks of life. His interest in new ideas, such as those of Copernicus and Machiavelli, reflects the exploding

---

pious king into tyranny, crime, and irreligion by flattering evil passions for his own gain." The vision of Cromwell as evil, unscrupulous, and vicious has been preserved through the centuries (cf. e.g. Cobbett 1994 [1824–1827] as well as Merriman 1968 [1902]), and can still be encountered today (cf. Hutchinson 2007).

[11] In this context, cf. also Andrew James Johnston (2017, 539), who argues that "Cromwell [...] has featured in a great many novels, though rarely as the central protagonist and hardly ever as a character winning the readers' sympathies."

knowledge systems and the increasing sense of uncertainty in the early modern world, registered in frequent, slightly fantastic references to the shifting nature of reality, this 'quaking world' where 'nothing ... seems steady' and where the ground is shifting under the feet [...]. (Brosch 2018, 60; italics in the original)[12]

The unconventionality of Mantel's presentation is reinforced by the fact that she reverses the roles traditionally attributed to Cromwell and another important historical figure of the time – Thomas More.[13] In historiography as well as fictional adaptations of the Tudor dynasty,[14] More has usually been depicted as a man of principle who was executed by the cunning Cromwell for adhering unwaveringly to his Catholic faith (cf. Arias 2014, 30; Wessendorf 2018, 242). Mantel's *Wolf Hall*, however, reinterprets both historical personages. Her Cromwell, Brosch (2017) argues,

> seeks reconciliation between religious extremists, whereas her More seeks absolute conformity. Mantel's Cromwell is not vengeful: when he interviews More in the Tower, he wants to give him an opportunity to save his life, as we find out from his inner deliberations which Mantel invented contrary to historical evidence [...]. Mantel's More is vain, arrogant and unrelenting. In attempting to extinguish both Tyndale and his influence, he holds torturing heretics or tricking them into a confession to be a 'blessed' act. (167)

By reimagining More, "the saintly martyr of common imagination" as a "vicious, ruthless, hideous figure" (de Groot 2016, 24), the diametrical opposite to her ethical and humane Cromwell, Mantel presents readers with two equally unusual profiles. Stylizing Cromwell as a "character whose reputation has been marred by history" (Arias 2014, 23; cf. also de Groot 2016, 24),[15] her defamiliarized character constellation is entirely in line with the generic conventions of the revisionist historical novel.

---

[12] For a detailed analysis of Mantel's positive depiction of Cromwell, cf. also Rosenberg 2017, 160–165.
[13] According to Jerome de Groot (2016, 24), Mantel's depiction of the character of Thomas More even represents "one of the most revisionist things" about her novel *Wolf Hall* (cf. also Gymnich 2018, 76).
[14] The most prominent examples are Bolt's play as well as the popular TV series *The Tudors* (2007–2010), created and written by Michael Hirst (cf. Lehtimäki 2011, 65n59).
[15] Cf. Nünning 1995a, 271: "Außerdem tragen Figurendarstellung und -konstellation in revisionistischen Geschichtsfiktionen dazu bei, Figuren als Opfer historischer Prozesse und Ereignisse erscheinen zu lassen." ["Besides, the representation of characters and character constellations in revisionist historical fictions contribute to make characters appear as victims of historical processes and events." (My translation)]

However, it would be impossible for Mantel's revisionist narratives to deviate so strongly from the historical biography of Thomas Cromwell if they did not also experiment with the traditional form of the historical novel. In the remaining sections of this chapter, I will, then, explore the innovative narrative strategies Mantel uses in order to render her version of Cromwell's life authentic. As I will show, it is primarily the combination of internal focalization and present-tense narration that allows Mantel her unconventional retelling of the rise of Thomas Cromwell in the turbulent reign of Henry VIII.

7.2 Creating a Likeable Character: The Empathic Impact of Mantel's Referential Use of the Fictional Present

The secondary literature on *Wolf Hall* and *Bring Up the Bodies* stresses that Mantel presents the narrative events continually and exclusively from the perspective of her protagonist Thomas Cromwell.[16] In principle, this is not wrong, yet all of these studies ignore that, although exhibiting a predominantly figural narrative situation in which Cromwell serves as the reflector figure (*sensu* Stanzel), both novels also feature several passages in which the narrative perspective oscillates between modes of heterodiegetic narration with an overt and a covert narrator. The first passage of this kind can be found very early in *Wolf Hall*, following the novel's opening scene, in which Thomas Cromwell is almost beaten to death by his father Walter. After the incident, he flees to his sister Kat's house. When Kat's husband, Morgan Williams, arrives home from work and sees Kat attending to Thomas, who is disfigured by his injuries, he offers Thomas some money and advises him to "take to the road" (*WH*, 10) in order to get away from his brutal father. The conversation between Kat, Morgan, and Thomas, during which they discuss Morgan's plan, is interrupted by the following paragraph:

> He doesn't know [how he will pay Morgan back]. Breathing is difficult, but that doesn't mean anything, it's only because of the clotting inside his nose. It doesn't seem to be broken; he touches it, speculatively, and Kat says, careful, this is a clean apron. She's smiling a pained smile, she doesn't want him to go, and yet she's not going to contradict Morgan Williams, is she? The Williamses **are** big people, in Putney, in Wimbledon. Morgan **dotes** on her; he **reminds** her she's got girls to do the baking and mind the brewing, why doesn't she sit upstairs sewing like a lady, and praying for his success when he goes off to

---

16 Cf. Brosch 2017, 168; 2018, 57, 62; Funk 2018, 97; Gymnich 2018, 76–77; Huber 2016, 77; Rosenberg 2017, 168; and Wilson 2015, 155.

7.2 The Empathic Impact of Mantel's Referential Use of the Fictional Present — 159

London to do a few deals in his town coat? Twice a day she could sweep through the Pegasus in a good dress and set in order anything that's wrong: that's his idea. And though as far as <u>he **can** see</u> she works as hard as ever she did when she was a child, <u>he **can** see</u> how she might like it, that Morgan would exhort her to sit down and be a lady. (*WH*, 10; my emphasis)

The first three sentences of this excerpt qualify as what Dorrit Cohn (1978, Ch. 3) refers to as "narrated monologue." More specifically, the narrative here gives us an insight into Thomas Cromwell's mind without giving up the distinction between focalizer and narrator: Even though we learn Thomas's thoughts at this moment, the use of the third-person pronoun indicates that we are still 'hearing the voice' of the covert narrator, who conceals himself behind Thomas's consciousness. This changes in the fourth sentence, where the narrative suddenly informs us about the thoughts of all the characters involved in the scene. We learn that Kat does not want her brother to leave and that Morgan would actually prefer his cherished wife not to do any housework but to behave "like a lady." Yet Thomas believes that his sister would not like this, for she has been working hard ever since she was a girl.

From a purely formal perspective, there is no objection that Thomas Cromwell serves as the only focalizer in the entire paragraph. In fact, the repetition of the formulation "he can see" in the last sentence even suggests that he is making assumptions about his sister's attitude toward Morgan on the basis of her behavior (see my emphasis). However, if we consider the narrative context of this passage, another interpretation becomes possible: Since Thomas has just been beaten up by his father, he is probably suffering from severe pain. As a consequence, it is highly unlikely that he is reading his sister's mind in this particular situation, or even reflecting about the relationship between her and his brother-in-law. The statement "The Williamses are big people" might therefore signal a shift from covert to overt heterodiegetic narration: the second part of the quotation no longer renders Thomas's thoughts, but instead qualifies as a narratorial comment introducing the characters Kat and Morgan as well as their social background to the reader.

We encounter here a shift from the mono-perspectival mode, with Thomas Cromwell as the internal focalizer, to the multi-perspectival mode of zero-focalization which presents the thoughts of every character involved in the scene.[17] This momentary change in the novel's narrative perspective can be

---

[17] I here use Genette's (1980 [1972], 185–194) terminology of focalization. If we were to apply Rimmon-Kenan's (2002 [1983], 75–78) terminology in this context, we would speak of a shift from internal to external focalization, i.e. from a character- to a narrator-focalizer.

correlated with a shift in Mantel's use of the fictional present: While, in the first three sentences, the present tense fulfills a referential function, pointing to Thomas's thoughts and perceptions, the remaining sentences in the paragraph mostly feature an explanatory present which serves primarily as a strategy of characterization, enlarging on the characters' background as well as their relationships with one another (see my emphasis).

Drawing an analogy with Greek drama, Siobhan O'Connor (2018, 31) argues that, in those passages of Mantel's *Wolf Hall* which are "detached from Cromwell's perspective, the narrative voice takes on the mantle of Chorus," that is, a traditional device to provide contextual information on the setting, plot, and characters of a specific scene which cannot be acted out on stage. I would argue that in both of Mantel's Tudor novels the narrator best performs such a "choric function" (O'Connor 2018, 31) when he informs readers about the historical context of the narrative events. The following excerpt is a representative example of such an instance:

> Even as the court is sitting, King François in Italy is losing a battle. Pope Clement is preparing to sign a new treaty with the Emperor, Queen Katherine's nephew. He [i.e. Cromwell] doesn't know this when he says, 'This is a bad day's work. If we want Europe to laugh at us, they've every reason now. (*WH*, 147)

The quotation perfectly demonstrates that the present-tense explanations concerning the intentions of both the King of France and the Pope can indeed not represent Cromwell's thoughts (for, as the text indicates, he does not yet know about these developments), but should rather be construed as the result of the narrator's omniscience and omnipresence.[18]

As narratorial comments in *Wolf Hall* and *Bring Up the Bodies* are usually very short, they may be easily overlooked by inattentive readers. One of the most salient of such comments can be found in *Bring Up the Bodies*:

---

[18] A further indication of these qualities can be found in brief moments of prolepsis in which the narrator gives us an insight into the storyworld's future. Consider the following examples: "He [i.e. Cromwell] will never tell the cardinal about Mary Boleyn, though the impulse will arise" (*WH*, 135); "Later, he [i.e. Cromwell] will remember that night towards the end of December when he found the cardinal listening to music. He will run it through his mind, twice and over again" (*WH*, 168); "But the winter king, less occupied, will begin to think about his conscience. He will begin to think about his pride. He will begin to prepare the prizes for those who can deliver him results" (*WH*, 252); and "He [i.e. Cromwell] is moving too fast to make much of her [i.e. Jane Rochford's] last sentence; though, as he will admit later, the detail will affix itself and adhere to certain sentences of his own, not yet formed" (*BUB*, 114).

> Thomas Cromwell is now about fifty years old. He has a labourer's body, stocky, useful, running to fat. He has black hair, greying now, and because of his pale impermeable skin, which seems designed to resist rain as well as sun, people sneer that his father was an Irishman, though really he was a brewer and a blacksmith at Putney, a shearsman too, a man with a finger in every pie, a scrapper and brawler, a drunk and a bully, a man often hauled before the justices for punching someone, for cheating someone. How the son of such a man has achieved his present eminence is a question all Europe asks. [...] He was out of the realm from boyhood, a hired soldier, a wool trader, a banker. No one knows where he has been and who he has met, and he is in no hurry to tell them. He never spares himself in the king's service, he knows his worth and merits and makes sure of his reward [...]. Every day Master Secretary deals with grandees who, if they could, would destroy him with one vindictive swipe, as if he were a fly. Knowing this, he is distinguished by his courtesy, his calmness and his indefatigable attention to England's business. He is not in the habit of explaining himself. He is not in the habit of discussing successes. But whenever good fortune has called on him, he has been there, planted on the threshold, ready to fling open the door to her timid scratch on the wood. (*BUB*, 6–7)

The narrative here visibly chooses the perspective of the heterodiegetic narrator who provides a detailed characterization of the protagonist, not only describing Cromwell's outward appearance, personality, and dealings with his enemies, but informing readers that people around Europe are wondering how the lowborn son of a brewer and blacksmith could become the closest adviser to the English King. Given that this present-tense description of Cromwell's character appears at the beginning of *Bring Up the Bodies*, we can construe it as the novel's exposition, which may serve two different purposes, depending on whether readers have also read *Wolf Hall* or not: In the latter case, the passage simply functions as an introduction of the protagonist, whereas in the former it qualifies as an instance of internal analepsis, providing a condensed summary of the plot of *Wolf Hall*.[19] Taken together, then, all these examples show that those parts of Mantel's novels which feature an overt narrator usually correlate with a transmodal use of present-tense narration: either the explanatory or the descriptive present. The reason for this is that the novel's narratorial voice manifests itself primarily through explanations concerning the characters' social background (first example) or the historical context of the narrative events (sec-

---

19 According to Genette (1980 [1972], 49), internal analepsis designates a flashback that refers to a point in time covered by the narrative, whereas external analepsis relates to events that occurred before the onset of the narrative. Despite its reference to events that happened before the beginning of *Bring Up the Bodies*, I would, however, define the exposition of this novel as an instance of internal analepsis: in the larger context of Mantel's Tudor novels, the flashback still refers to events presented in *Wolf Hall*.

ond example), or through descriptions characterizing the protagonist (third example).

Apart from occasional narratorial intrusions, however, the events depicted in both *Wolf Hall* and *Bring Up the Bodies* are consistently presented from Cromwell's point of view. More specifically, Mantel invites her readers to perceive the storyworld from the protagonist's perspective by combining a strategy which Renate Brosch (2017, 170; 2018, 63) designates as "obscure" deixis with the technique of present-tense narration. Especially in *Wolf Hall*, she avoids mentioning Cromwell's name whenever he serves as the focalizer, exclusively deploying the pronoun *he* to refer to his character. Creating an authentic effect of experientiality in Monika Fludernik's (1996) sense,[20] this strategy is perfectly in line with the mode of internal focalization: From a mimetic perspective, Cromwell would probably never think of himself as Cromwell, but rather in the first person 'I,' which would then, in a figural narrative perspective, translate into the third-person pronoun *he*. Yet such fuzzy or – to again borrow Brosch's formulation – "obscure" deixis may easily confuse readers. The reason for this is that Mantel's extensive use of the third-person pronoun violates the English grammatical rule that, as an anaphoric expression, a personal pronoun always "requires a referential noun in the near vicinity in order to be identifiable" (Brosch 2017, 170).[21] What is more, numerous other characters in both novels share the protagonist's given name Thomas, so the reader's state of confusion about the identity of the characters "is sometimes maintained even in cases where Christian names, rather than pronouns, are used" (Johnston 2017, 544).[22]

Mantel's referential use of present-tense narration, on the other hand, strengthens the effect of internal focalization by rendering Cromwell's experiences more immediate. Since the fictional present points to the here-and-now of the focalizer's consciousness rather than to the here-and-now of the narrator, readers get the impression that they have direct access to Cromwell's perceptions. We not only perceive the storyworld from his point of view, but also share his experiences of the narrative events as they are happening. The present tense

---

20 A more detailed discussion of Fludernik's concept is provided in Chapter 8.1.
21 For a similar argument, cf. also Brosch 2018, 63; Gymnich 2018, 76; and Wilson 2015, 156.
22 Since countless commentators, especially on the internet, complained about these ambiguities in *Wolf Hall* (cf. Brosch 2017, 170; 2018, 63), Andrew James Johnston (2017, 544) assumes that Mantel decided to make her second novel more reader-friendly in this respect: "Indeed, the issue of the pronouns is one of the relatively few features in which the two novels do differ, since criticism of her unidentifiable pronouns led Mantel to introduce, in *Bring Up the Bodies*, a higher frequency of personal names into narrative situations where the pronoun 'he' [as well as the name Thomas] might otherwise not have provided sufficient clarity: 'he, Cromwell...'"

suggests a lack of hindsight, and this absence of temporal distance to the narrative events, in turn, implies that the heterodiegetic narrator, who actually has a comprehensive overview of the plot, recedes completely into the background. This direct and immediate insight into Cromwell's mind "evokes the experience of following the events through [his] eyes" (Nünning 2014, 190), which lends authenticity to the novels' figural narrative situation. Brosch (2018) felicitously summarizes the effect of Mantel's referential use of the fictional present in the following terms:

> For a historical novel especially, the present tense is still somewhat unusual. To *Wolf Hall*'s experiential approach it is brilliantly appropriate, because it creates a sense of momentariness that seems natural and genuine for an experiencing mind. (Brosch 2018, 65)[23]

Interestingly enough, however – as previous research on Mantel's Tudor novels has repeatedly observed – although both narratives present the events from Cromwell's perspective, they nevertheless do not unveil the protagonist's thoughts, feelings, and emotions to the reader.[24] "While Cromwell is the reflector of the figural narrative," Irmtraud Huber (2016) notes,

> in Genette's terms the focalisation of his narrative cannot be defined as either clearly internal or clearly external. It is internal insofar as we are exclusively presented with Cromwell's point of view; it is external insofar as Cromwell's thoughts, motives, emotions and even his past remain largely hidden from the reader in spite of the fact that the narrative perspective repeatedly merges entirely with that of the protagonist (77).

Brosch (2018, 66) convincingly links this paradox to Cromwell's figured personality. Mantel's protagonist, she maintains, "is not given to acts of pure self-expression or self-examination but is interested mainly in the observation and awareness of others; he is constantly engaged in reading and judging other minds" (Brosch 2018, 66; cf. also Brosch 2017, 176).

Although we can find more than sufficient textual evidence in Mantel's work to substantiate Huber's and Brosch's contentions, I do not find their arguments wholly convincing. A reading attentive to Cromwell's mental and emotional state will reveal that the novel does indeed contain some passages that shed light on his thoughts and feelings. For example, readers learn a lot about

---

23 On a related note, cf. also Wolfgang Funk (2018) and Leigh Wilson (2015), who both read Mantel's idiosyncratic narrative perspective (i.e. the combination of ambiguous deixis and the fictional present) as a means to create new – to borrow Wilson's term – "reality effects."
24 Cf. Brosch 2017, 176; 2018, 65–66; Gymnich 2018, 77; Huber 2016, 77; Johnston 2017, 543; Lehtimäki 2011, 54; and Wessendorf 2018, 232.

Cromwell's affection for his family: The narrative informs us that, after his beloved wife Liz dies from the sweating sickness, he avoids sleep for weeks because he dreads the thought of waking up in the morning having "to learn the lack of her all over again" (*WH*, 106). On the occasion of the death of his two daughters caused by the same illness only a few years later, the narrative, moreover, discloses to us that he has been very proud of his eldest daughter Anne, who was learning Greek, and that "[i]t has always seemed impossible to him that some act of his [...], some unthinking thing that he and Liz did, on some unmemorable night," gave life to his enchanting youngest daughter Grace (*WH*, 152).

And Cromwell's thoughts and feelings present him not only as a loving and caring father and spouse, but also as a devoted and loyal adviser. Readers learn that Cromwell still holds to his former master, Cardinal Wolsey, even after he has fallen into disfavor with the King: "If he [i.e. Cromwell] were to give himself a piece of advice for Christmas, he'd say, leave the cardinal now or you'll be out on the streets again with the three-card trick. But he only gives advice to those who are likely to take it." (*WH*, 170) At a later point in *Wolf Hall*, we learn that "he admires Henry more and more" (*WH*, 436) and that he shares feelings of both joy and sorrow with his new master, the King (cf. *WH*, 485, 513).

By granting us these scattered glimpses into the protagonist's mental and emotional state, Mantel's novels present us with a figure with whom we can empathize. Since Cromwell shows many feelings we can readily relate to – he suffers when his wife and daughters die, he is loyal to his master Wolsey, and he admires his King – we have difficulties squaring Mantel's depiction with the negative image of the historical Cromwell presented in historiography and other fictional representations of his person. In other words, we cannot imagine that the man we read of in *Wolf Hall* and *Bring Up the Bodies* is the cold-blooded, unscrupulous, and vengeful tyrant of common account. Mantel's portrait acts decisively against this notion, presenting a man who is loved by his contemporaries – "He is a good friend and master; this is said of him everywhere" (*WH*, 585) – and who refuses accusations of malintent in an enviably unimpressed manner: "He doesn't want revenge," *Wolf Hall* puts it, "just clarification" (*WH*, 432).

7.3 Foresight Instead of Hindsight: Representing History as Future Turning Points

Mantel, then, paints a positive picture of Cromwell by allowing readers to get access to his mind. However, the 'true secret of success' for her defamiliarized depiction is probably that her novels lack historical hindsight. Almost consistently written in a referential present that points to the here-and-now of her figure's consciousness, Mantel's novels conceal Cromwell's unfortunate fate from their readers (the historical Thomas Cromwell was beheaded in 1540). Perceiving the narrative events predominantly from the protagonist's perspective, readers witness Cromwell's rise without anticipating his downfall. For Cromwell himself cannot know that he will soon follow Cardinal Wolsey, Thomas More, and Anne Boleyn to the block – that he, too, will fall from grace and go down in history as one of the most unfortunate of the King's advisers (cf. Brosch 2018, 63).[25]

Returning to Ansgar Nünning's definition of the revisionist historical novel, we can, therefore, argue that Mantel's referential use of present-tense narration is central to her innovative account of Tudor history. According to Nünning (1995a, 283), revisionist historical fiction makes the rewriting of history the principle of narrative representation. In this light, the present tense in *Wolf Hall* and *Bring Up the Bodies* contributes to Mantel's rewriting of the past inasmuch as it reverses the conventional temporal structure of historical fiction. Most revisionist historical narratives present the narrative events they tell of in retrospect – in other words, there is a temporal distance between the occurrence of the events and the act of representing these events. Mantel's use of the present tense, however, negates the impression of what in narratology is known as "subsequent" or "retrospective" narration (Genette 1980 [1972], 220–223; Margolin 1999, 146–150), replacing it with its diametrical opposite – "prior," "anterior," or "prospective" narration (Genette 1980 [1972], 219–220; Rimmon-Kenan 2002 [1983], 91; Margolin 1999, 153–159).[26]

Since the referential function of the present tense implies that readers come to know of the narrative events in the very moment that Cromwell himself ex-

---

[25] Cf. also Greenblatt 2009, 22–23: "[T]hroughout the novel, Mantel invites us to forgo easy irony and to suspend our awareness of what is going to come to pass. To be sure, she offers aficionados of the period quiet pleasures: when Holbein complains that he has to complete a portrait of the French ambassador de Dinteville, we know that he is at work on his magnificent painting *The Ambassadors*; when Thomas Wyatt discloses his erotic obsession with Anne Boleyn, we know that his private notebooks are full of the love poems for which he is now celebrated; when we glimpse the unctuous musician Mark Smeaton hovering around the court, we know that he will eventually be accused of adultery with Anne and executed along with her other alleged lovers. But none of this latent knowledge actually matters. The triumph of the historical novel, in Mantel's vision, is to reach a point of ignorance."
[26] I have discussed the differences between retrospective and prospective narration in greater detail in Chapters 2.3.2.1 and 5.6.

periences these events, both of Mantel's narratives forfeit any notion of hindsight. In lieu of evaluating and reflecting upon events that happened in the past, Cromwell observes and analyzes the status quo of the storyworld, which helps him to see his chances for a successful future: "There is a world beyond this black world. There is a world of the possible. A world where Anne can be queen is a world where Cromwell can be Cromwell. He sees it; then he doesn't. The moment is fleeting. But insight cannot be taken back." (*WH*, 205) Even though this passage focuses more on the protagonist's present than the future, it reveals that Cromwell is always forward-thinking (cf. LaCroix 2017, 66): every political step he takes, every new law he drafts, every sentence he says to the King, as well as every service he does to Anne – in fact, everything he does is ultimately designed to ensure his own success.

The unusual temporal perspective of Mantel's Tudor novels also has an influence on the event structure of these narratives. In a close reading of a passage from Kazuo Ishiguro's *The Remains of the Day* (1989), Ansgar Nünning (2012b, 33–36) shows that revisionist narrative reconstructions of the past depend on the depiction of events regarded by the narrator as turning points: "occurrences which are accredited with a high degree of relevance, importance and the potential to change the direction of the plot" (Nünning 2012b, 40). Turning points, Nünning contends, must not be "understood as something given or natural" (2012b, 39); rather, they should be conceived "as something that is made or constructed by an observer or storyteller, who wants to highlight particular episodes" for a specific reason (2012b, 39). Strictly speaking, we can even think of them as "non-event[s]" because "the very moment that marks the turning point does not constitute a particularly eventful incident in itself, but it has usually been preceded by one or several important events" (Nünning 2012b, 44). Nünning explains that turning points are constructed in a process of 'narrativization' that "impose[s] a temporal order on our amorphous and, more often than not, chaotic flow of experience," so that we can better come to terms with these experiences (2012b, 39). Functioning as a sense-making device which involves the processes of "selection, deletion, abstraction and prioritisation" (Nünning 2012b, 40), turning points can only be identified in retrospect, with the benefit of hindsight (cf. Nünning 2012b, 35–36).

At first glance, this implies that, due to their lack of a retrospective perspective, *Wolf Hall* and *Bring Up the Bodies* do not feature any turning points. Because Mantel's present-tense account presents the narrative events from the point of view of Cromwell who is only just experiencing these events, her novels cannot possibly give readers any clue as to whether these events will really turn out to be decisive either in the protagonist's life or in wider history. However, we have to reconsider this position as soon as we take the "prospective quality of turning points" (Sommer 2019, 313) into account. Roy Sommer (2019, 313) reminds us that "[i]n real life we tend to mark not only past events, but also future happenings as turning points, anticipating an event's significance and discussing its possible consequence(s) before things actually happen." Some future events are even "so eagerly anticipated that we imagine them as 'hyper-events' that will change everything" (Sommer 2019, 313).

If we read Mantel's novels through Sommer's lens, we will uncover yet another skill of Mantel's protagonist. Although Cromwell cannot foresee the future, he has the rare gift of correctly anticipating the consequences of events. After the Cardinal's downfall, for instance, Cromwell soon realizes that he will "come down with him" (*WH*, 149) unless he takes his destiny into his own hands. This is the moment when he begins striving to win the King's favor, starting with a private conversation during which he impresses Henry with his pragmatism as well as rational sincerity and candor (cf. *WH*, 180–184). Another example concerns not so much Cromwell's personal career as the future of the entire country: When he drafts a new legislation in the King's interest, "[h]e hesitates, his quill hovering," as he writes the sentence "This realm of England is an Empire" (*WH*, 426). He is, it seems, sensible to the fact that he is "mak[ing] momentous history at the desk" (Kim 2018, 25): Historians often regard the Ecclesiastical Appeals Act of 1532 as the key legal foundation of the English (or Henrician) Reformation, which marks the beginning of "England's destiny as a sovereign independent state" (Kim 2018, 25).[27] It is this ability to foresee the potential of present acts for future turning points that makes Cromwell an intellectual as well as moral hero of Mantel's first two Tudor novels.[28]

---

27 Markus Wessendorf (2018, 242) enumerates further historical turning points that the fictive Cromwell recognizes: "Mantel's Cromwell, within the context of the 1530s, identifies these turning points as a major power shift from theologically legitimized rulers to secular trade and banking, a newly discovered potential of using legislation and accounting as instruments for political change, and the realization that people can be empowered through vernacular translations of the Bible and a strengthening of parliamentarianism."
28 Against this background, it seems all the more ironic that Cromwell does not foresee, or at least cannot prevent his own downfall, even though Anne Boleyn already anticipates it: "You must study your advantage, Master Secretary. Those who are made can be unmade." (*BUB*, 133)

7.4 Witnessing History in the Making: Spatial Non-Contextualization, Associative Storytelling, and the Immersive Potential of Mantel's Present-Tense Usage

So far I have mainly focused on how Mantel's referential use of the fictional present fosters the portrait of a protagonist who represents a hero of his time. This is not, however, the only function the present tense fulfills in Mantel's novels; the remaining part of this chapter will focus on the immersive potential of present-tense usage in *Wolf Hall* and *Bring Up the Bodies*. Mantel herself writes in an article for *The Guardian*:

> The basic decision about the book was taken seconds before I began writing. 'So now get up': the person on the ground was Cromwell and the camera was behind his eyes.
> The events were happening now, in the present tense, unfolding as I watched, and what followed would be filtered through the main character's sensibility. (Mantel 2012, n.p.)

Mantel's statement shows that, together with her internal focalization on the protagonist, her use of the fictional present is intended to help readers project themselves into Cromwell's mind, so that they witness the narrative events from his position within the here-and-now of the storyworld. There is another dimension to this, however: The immersive effect of the present tense does not just result from its correlation with the figural narrative situation; it is also and especially due to two further strategies I will here refer to as *spatial non-contextualization* and *associative storytelling*.

First, *spatial non-contextualization*: Mantel's novels carefully avoid "describing the physical world of Cromwell" (Wilson 2015, 155). More traditional documentary or realist historical novels contain, more often than not, precise and detailed depictions of the narrative setting (cf. Nünning 1995a, 261, 263). *Wolf Hall* and *Bring Up the Bodies*, by contrast, provide spatial descriptions only where Cromwell actually reflects on his environment. During his first appointment with Anne Boleyn at York Place (Cardinal Wolsey's residence before his decline), for example, Cromwell notices a tapestry on the wall: "Look, there are Solomon and Sheba, unrolled again, back on the wall. There is a draught; Sheba eddies towards him, rosy, round, and he acknowledges her: Anselma, lady made of wool, I thought I'd never see you again." (*WH*, 199) There are three reasons why Mantel provides this comparatively detailed delineation of the tapestry in Anne's room: First, Cromwell remembers that the same tapestry was there before, when the cardinal was still living there (cf. *WH*, 21), but was taken down on the King's orders after Wolsey's banishment from court (cf. *WH*, 49).

7.4 Witnessing History in the Making: The Immersive Potential of the Present Tense — 169

Secondly, the representation of Sheba on the tapestry reminds him of a woman, Anselma, whom he once loved when he lived in Antwerp (cf. *WH*, 23). Thirdly, later in the novel, Henry will notice that Cromwell is fascinated by the woman on the tapestry and will give him this artwork as a gift (cf. *WH*, 348). It is only because the tapestry of King Solomon and the Queen of Sheba has an important meaning to Cromwell that it deserves a more detailed description in *Wolf Hall*.[29]

The strategy of spatial non-contextualization creates for readers the impression of unmediated access to Cromwell's mind, and thus the storyworld as he experiences it. Mantel's use of the present tense contributes to this effect by excluding any retrospective perspective on the narrative events. More traditional (realist) historical novels typically display an overt narrator who fulfills the function of a historian (cf. Nünning 1995a, 264) and would likely seek to provide their readers with a vivid picture of sixteenth-century England. Mantel's novels, on the other hand, mostly conceal their heterodiegetic narrator, who has a more distanced view of the storyworld than the protagonist. Because of this seeming lack of hindsight, *Wolf Hall* and *Bring Up the Bodies* offer little, if any, spatial orientation to their readers.

The second term, *associative storytelling*, relates to Cromwell's mind-style. In *Linguistics and the Novel* (1977), Roger Fowler defines the phenomenon of mind-style as "any distinctive linguistic presentation of an individual mental self" (103), which expresses itself in different discourse structures. According to Fowler,

> [a] mind-style may analyse a character's mental life more or less radically; may be concerned with relatively superficial or relatively fundamental aspects of the mind; may seek to dramatize the order and structure of conscious thoughts, or just present the topics on which a character reflects, or display preoccupations, prejudices, perspectives and values which strongly bias a character's world-view but of which s/he may be quite unaware. (1977, 103)

In Mantel's Tudor novels, Cromwell's mind-style manifests itself in the fact that both narratives frequently jump from one narrative scene to the next without providing any transitions that might signal these shifts to the reader. A few paragraphs from *Wolf Hall* illustrate the point:

> When the summer plague comes back, he says to Mercy and Johane, shall we send the children out?
> [...]

---

[29] For an extensive discussion of the paintings mentioned in *Wolf Hall*, cf. Szymański 2014.

> Mercy says, can anyone outrun it? They take comfort from a belief that since the infection killed so many last year, it won't be so violent this year; which he does not think is necessarily true, and he thinks they seem to be endowing this plague with a human or at least bestial intelligence: the wolf comes down on the sheepfold, but not on the nights when the men with dogs are waiting for him. Unless they think the plague is more than bestial or human – that it is God behind it – God, up to his old tricks. When he hears the bad news from Italy, about Clement's new treaty with the Emperor, Wolsey bows his head and says, 'My Master is capricious.' He doesn't mean the king.
>
> On the last day of July, Cardinal Campeggio adjourns the legatine court. It is, he says, the Roman holidays. News comes that the Duke of Suffolk, the king's great friend, has hammered the table before Wolsey, and threatened him to his face. They all know the court will never sit again. They all know the cardinal has failed. (*WH*, 148–149)

The first two paragraphs of this excerpt revolve around Cromwell's household: readers learn that, after Cromwell's wife has already succumbed to the sweating sickness, he considers sending his children out of the city when the plague strikes again. The second paragraph exhibits an interesting change in subject: while the first part of the paragraph still renders Cromwell's thoughts on the sweating sickness, the last two sentences suddenly deal with the most recent political developments, preparing the theme of the next paragraph, which focuses on Cardinal Wolsey's downfall. The second paragraph thus presents readers with a shift from Cromwell's domestic to his political life. This shift, however, is nowhere indicated in the text, not even with a line break. As such associative jumps occur quite frequently, Rosario Arias (2014, 25) concludes that "[t]he personal and political episodes are interspersed in the novel in such a way that there cannot be any distinction between them."

Again, it is the immersive function of the present tense that reinforces the associative style of Mantel's narrative discourse. By foreclosing any sense of hindsight, the present tense deprives her account of Cromwell's life of any temporal distance which would allow for a teleological depiction of the narrative events. As Renate Brosch (2018) observes of *Wolf Hall* (and the same holds for *Bring Up the Bodies*),

> the present tense implies discontinuity; it could be called a narrative tense of less authority. By giving us the past in present tense, *Wolf Hall* immerses us in uncertainty, suggesting that we cannot yet know which detail or marginal person will become important. The unordered, associative impressions of lived experience align the reader with the focalizing Cromwell since both share the task of having to discover significance and coherence in a seemingly chaotic world. (65)

This impression of a shared experience between Mantel's readers and the focalizer in her novels is foregrounded even more sharply in the passages which use

7.4 Witnessing History in the Making: The Immersive Potential of the Present Tense — 171

the first-person plural pronoun *we* to explicitly include readers in Cromwell's experience of the fictional Tudor world:

> Stephen Gardiner! Coming in as he's [i.e. Cromwell] going out, striding towards the king's chamber, a folio under one arm, the other flailing the air. Gardiner, Bishop of Winchester: blowing up like a thunderstorm, when for once **we** have a fine day.
>
> [...]
>
> At court you might expect him. Anticipate him. But here? While **we** are still hunting through the countryside and (notionally) taking **our** ease? 'This is a pleasure, my lord bishop,' he says. 'It does my heart good to see you looking so well. The court will progress to Winchester shortly, and I did not think to enjoy your company before that.' (*BUB*, 37; my emphasis)

While the first occurrence of the first-person plural pronoun in this excerpt could still be read as an exclusive 'we' that does not include the reader, the second occurrence leaves no doubt that it is an inclusive 'we' that also addresses Mantel's readers and hence invites them to share Cromwell's experience of "hunting through the countryside and (notionally) taking our ease." Although passages of this kind are rare in *Wolf Hall*, they occur fairly frequently in *Bring Up the Bodies*.

The examples given above demonstrate that, in combination with the strategies of spatial non-contextualization and associative storytelling, Mantel's immersive use of the present tense can be construed as an instance of what Armen Avanessian and Anke Hennig (2015 [2012], 224) refer to as the "asynchronous present tense": a type of retrospective present-tense narration that identifies a narrative event as taking place in the present of the fictive storyworld although it must, from a narrative standpoint, clearly lie in the past (cf. Avanessian and Hennig 2015 [2012], 224; see also Chapter 5.6). According to Avanessian and Hennig, the asynchronous present tense should consequently be understood as a counterpart to Käte Hamburger's (1968 [1957]) epic preterite:

> The asynchronous present tense [...] operates the inverse of the presentifying function of the epic past tense, where presentification constitutes a fictional (contemporaneously past) present. Asynchrony, in contrast, constitutes a fictional (non-contemporaneously present) past. (Avanessian and Hennig 2015 [2012], 65)

With regard to Mantel's novels this means that her use of the present tense invites readers to project themselves into Cromwell's mind, from where they can perceive the narrative events in the very moment they unfold. Thanks to this immersive effect, Mantel's readers are enabled to experience the past as the present, as history in the making so to speak. Against this backdrop, one can conclude with Andrew James Johnston (2017, 548) that it is indeed Mantel's use of present-tense narration which renders her revisionist account of the Henrician Reformation and the Tudor Revolution so authentic. Her fictional present makes us "realise that the past we are being told about is not some general story-past, but an actual former present, a past once very much alive and inescapable to those who experienced it first-hand" (Johnston 2017, 548), as did Thomas Cromwell, the unfortunate counselor of King Henry VIII.

8 Narrative of Punishment: Experientiality, Immersion, and the Representation of Narrative Space in Margaret Atwood's *Oryx and Crake* (2003)

8.1 Encountering Unknown Worlds to Come: Anthropocene Fiction as a Model for Reality

The age of the Anthropocene, the geological epoch in which carbon-burning activities of humans are believed to be permanently damaging planet Earth, is characterized by a growing awareness of the possible consequences of such change. This concern is being increasingly dealt with in climate-change or "Anthropocene" (Trexler 2015) fiction, the narrative genre that stages the imminence and/or possible results of ecological cataclysms.[1] The primary objective of these novels is to raise readers' awareness of the environmental ramifications of the emission of CO_2 and other greenhouse gases, thus awakening or strengthening their "ecological thought" (Morton 2010) and behavior.[2]

To achieve this aim, Anthropocene narratives may create different kinds of storyworlds. Sylvia Mayer (2014) conceives of climate change novels as specific instances of risk narratives, which can be divided into two different types: the narrative of catastrophe and the narrative of anticipation. While the former portray a disastrous future scenario in which climate change has already culminated in a "global climate collapse" (Mayer 2014, 23), the latter represent a storyworld in which natural disasters (as a consequence of global warming)

---

1 In their survey article "Climate Change in Literature and Literary Criticism," Adam Trexler and Adeline Johns-Putra (2011, 186) state that "[t]he past two decades have seen an increasing amount of fiction dealing with this issue [i.e. anthropogenic climate change], and a particular explosion in the numbers of such novels in the past 10 years." They substantiate their claim by providing a historical overview of climate change novels which pertain to both genre fiction and literary fiction (cf. Trexler and Johns-Putra 2011, 186–188). Trexler further examines a considerable number of climate change novels in his monograph *Anthropocene Fictions: The Novel in a Time of Climate Change* (2015).
2 Timothy Morton (2010, 7) defines ecological thought as "the thinking of interconnectedness": "The ecological thought is a thought about ecology, but it's also a thinking that is ecological. Thinking the ecological thought is part of an ecological project. The ecological thought doesn't just occur 'in the mind.' It's a practice and a process of becoming fully aware of how human beings are connected with other beings—animal, vegetable, or mineral." (Morton 2010, 7)

have not yet happened, but are nevertheless realistically conceivable. Both types of risk narrative proceed from "the awareness of possible catastrophe as a point of reference" (Mayer 2014, 26), yet they differ in perspective. Narratives of catastrophe address the consequences of climate change in retrospect by evaluating imaginable environmental disasters that have actually occurred within the storyworld. Narratives of anticipation, on the other hand, merely foreshadow potential natural catastrophes that may or may not happen in the future of their diegetic universe.[3]

Setting out to analyze and interpret Margaret Atwood's climate change novel *Oryx and Crake*, this chapter will concentrate on the former type of Anthropocene fiction, the narrative of catastrophe, which I shall henceforth also refer to as *post-apocalyptic climate change* or *post-apocalyptic Anthropocene fiction*. First published in 2003, *Oryx and Crake* is the first installment in Atwood's internationally celebrated *MaddAddam* trilogy, which further comprises the two volumes *The Year of the Flood* and *MaddAddam*, published in 2009 and 2013.[4] The novel is set in a future world in which the consequences of anthropogenic climate change have already caused serious damage to planet Earth. Readers are confronted with the particular spatial circumstances of Atwood's fictional world right at the onset of the novel:

> Snowman wakes before dawn. He lies unmoving, listening to the tide coming in, wave after wave sloshing over the various barricades, wish-wash, wish-wash, the rhythm of heartbeat. He would so like to believe he is still asleep.
> On the eastern horizon there's a greyish haze, lit now with a rosy, deadly glow. Strange how that colour still seems tender. The offshore towers stand out in dark silhouette against it, rising improbably out of the pink and pale blue of the lagoon. The shrieks of the birds that nest out there and the distant ocean grinding against the ersatz reefs of rusted car parts and jumbled bricks and assorted rubble sound almost like holiday traffic. (OC, 3)

---

[3] With recourse to Ansgar Nünning's (2012a, 65–71) concise differentiation between the concepts of crisis and catastrophe, one could also say that narratives of anticipation qualify as crisis narratives. The reason for this is that they revolve around "a special kind of event, or perhaps rather non-event, since they – according to their etymology – mark precisely the critical turning point at which a decision about the further progress of the incident has to be made amongst a number of possibilities" (Nünning 2012a, 67). Hence in these narratives the catastrophe could still be prevented if all parties involved in the crisis (i.e. the characters in these narratives) made the right decisions and acted accordingly.

[4] This chapter is concerned only with *Oryx and Crake*, the first volume of Atwood's *MaddAddam* trilogy. The two sequels exhibit a different narrative structure, so my argument in this chapter holds neither for *The Year of the Flood* nor for *MaddAddam*.

The opening paragraphs of Atwood's narrative evidently describe an inundated cityscape. We learn that ocean waves are sloshing over barricades, towers rising out of the water, as well as rusted car parts, jumbled bricks, and assorted rubble which form some kind of ersatz reef. In depicting this setting, the narrative already creates a gloom-laden atmosphere. Accordingly, we are informed that the first light of dawn produces "a rosy, deadly glow" against which "[t]he offshore towers stand out in dark silhouette," that the birds are shrieking (instead of singing), and that the protagonist would like to believe he was still sleeping, possibly because he wishes this was all a bad dream.

Atwood's use of the fictional present intensifies this effect for different reasons. On the one hand, the tense creates a sense of immediacy by inviting readers to mentally project themselves directly onto the narrative scene. We get the feeling of being located in the here-and-now of the storyworld, lying next to Snowman, looking at the "pink and pale blue of the lagoon" whose surface seems to cover a new Atlantis. On the other hand, Atwood's choice of the present tense "hints at a traumatic past event yet withholds the context that would allow the reader to understand what has happened, or is still happening, or what it all means" (Snyder 2011, 477). In short, the present-tense description transports us to some post-apocalyptic world which, although being largely "unreadable," seems so "uncanny" that probably none of us would ever want to be at this place (Snyder 2011, 477).

The beginning of Atwood's novel illustrates some highly interesting features of post-apocalyptic climate change narratives from the perspective of narrative worldmaking, inasmuch as they produce, in the fashion of thought experiments, "models for the world" (McHale 2011). Drawing on the generic features of dystopian fiction (cf. Mayer 2014, 26), they evoke storyworlds which do not resemble reality.[5] According to a frequently quoted definition by Lyman Tower Sargent (1994, 9), the genre of dystopia represents "a non-existent society described in considerable detail and normally located in time and space that the author intended a contemporaneous reader to view as considerably worse than the society in which that reader lived." Narratives of climatic catastrophe carry this dystopian notion to extremes, not only presenting undesirable social mod-

---

[5] Brian McHale (2011) conceives of literature as a modeling system which may fulfill the two different functions of modeling *of* and modeling *for* reality. If literature creates a model *of* reality, it imitates reality as it already exists, whereas in yielding a model *for* reality it contrives an innovative draft of a possible, as yet non-existent, reality. As McHale points out, it is exactly the latter function which applies to the genre of science fiction, and I would extend his argument to include other related narrative genres such as speculative fiction (cf. Atwood 2011, 1–11), post-apocalyptic fiction, and climate-change fiction.

els, but also creating settings in which the world familiar to contemporary readers has come to an end; thus in Atwood's novel, a great flood seems to have caused an entire city to sink into the sea. Qualifying as instances of post-apocalyptic dystopia,[6] narratives of catastrophe portray a doomsday scenario which "involves the breakdown of social, economic, political, and cultural structures" (Mayer 2014, 26). These post-apocalyptic circumstances, in turn, bring about a form of life that is "marked by dramatic experiences of displacement, toxic pollution, and species extinction" (Mayer 2014, 26). The latter aspect also applies to *Oryx and Crake*, for, as I will argue below, Snowman seems to be the last human survivor in Atwood's storyworld (see Chapter 8.2).

Moreover, as Antonia Mehnert (2014, 61) contends, post-apocalyptic Anthropocene novels generate "riskscapes [...] in which territorial distinctions decline in importance and socio-cultural practices are disembedded from place." From these natural catastrophes, there is no safe haven: Faced with the imminent danger of natural cataclysm, people turn into nomads, traveling from one place to another to escape the forces of nature. This also applies to Atwood's protagonist, who wanders aimlessly in the post-apocalyptic world of *Oryx and Crake* (see Chapter 8.3). In Mehnert's view, such increased mobility eventually robs fixed places of any cultural meaning (cf. 2014, 63). She accordingly holds that the narrative settings of climate change novels no longer serve as "anthropological places," that is, spaces which "[provide] cultural identity and memory" (Tomlinson 1999, 109), but instead become extreme manifestations of what the anthropologist Marc Augé (2008 [1992], 63) identifies as "non-places," that is, "space[s] which cannot be defined as relational, or historical, or concerned with identity."[7] My reading of *Oryx and Crake* will demonstrate that Atwood's storyworld represents exactly such a 'non-place.'

---

[6] For a more detailed definition of this dystopian subgenre as well as a brief outline of its diachronic development, cf. Chang 2011, 4–6 and Hollm 2015, 379–384, respectively.

[7] Strikingly, these descriptions of post-apocalyptic Anthropocene fiction focus primarily on thematic aspects of these narratives, ignoring structural aspects and techniques of storytelling. The majority of previous studies of Anthropocene fiction also seem unaware of narratological concepts and terminology. Thus Mayer (2014) uses the term *scenario* to refer to what, in narratological terms, would translate as storyworlds, while Mehnert (2014) refers to "people" and "places," where narratologists would, in order to highlight the constructedness of textual entities and mental representations, speak rather of characters and settings. The lack of a narratological and cognitive perspective may result from the overridingly ideological goals of most studies of climate change fiction: Rather than construing post-apocalyptic novels as an artistic construct, they view them as a contribution to the critical discourse on climate change (cf. Mayer 2014, 36). Astrid Bracke (2018) consequently argues that contemporary literary fictions help shape the climate change discourse taking place in postmillennial societies. It seems

Taken together, these distinctive features of the narrative of catastrophe foreground the world-creating power of Anthropocene fiction, whose post-apocalyptic storyworlds confront us with spaces that largely exceed our real-life experience and, in some cases, even our imagination. Opening *Oryx and Crake*, we may find it difficult to think in Snowman's terms, for we cannot imagine what it must be like to live in a world that has become uninhabitable for the human species. Yet, we can readily bridge these imaginative gaps once we are willing to engage with Atwood's thought experiment. Drawing on Erin James's *The Storyworld Accord: Econarratology and Postcolonial Narratives* (2015), I will argue that the very ability of narrative fiction to create unfamiliar imaginary spaces forms the cornerstone for the endeavor of Anthropocene fiction to enhance its readers' ecological sensibilities. According to James, the reception of such texts can foster readers' "awareness and understanding for different environmental imaginations and experiences" (2015, xv), which, in turn, I would add, constitute a fundamental prerequisite for ecological thinking.

Although James's project deals principally with postcolonial narratives, her concept of econarratology can be perfectly transferred to the genre of Anthropocene fiction. James sees econarratology as a mode of reading which "pair[s] ecocriticism's interest in the relationship between literature and the physical environment with narratology's focus on the literary structures and devices by which writers compose narratives" (2015, xv). Within this theoretical framework, reading – or, indeed, any type of narrative reception – can be conceived as "a virtual form of environmental experience, in which interpreters of narratives access mental models of material contexts they otherwise would not know" (James 2015, xi–xii). Conversely, this implies that narrative texts can "offer readers the textual cues they require to transport themselves to an alternative space and time" (James 2015, xii), enabling them "to simulate and live in environments they would otherwise be denied and experience those environments from an alternative perspective" (James 2015, 24).

As James notes herself, recognizing the potential of narrative fiction to facilitate imaginative environmental experiences lays the groundwork for a fruitful dialogue between ecocriticism and literary theory, specifically narratology:

---

to me, however, that we are currently witnessing a shift in perspective, as the number of narratological studies that investigate the narrative form and constructed nature of Anthropocene fictions has considerably increased over the past few years (cf. e.g. Caracciolo 2018, 2019, Meifert-Menhard 2020, and Weik von Mossner 2017, as well as the contributions in Chihaia et al. 2020 and in James and Morel 2020, here especially in Part III).

> Econarratological readings of narrative storyworlds, via their analysis of the textual cues that aid the immersion of readers into subjective spaces, times, and experiences, help us appreciate the fact that aesthetic transformations of the real really do stand to reshape individual and collective environmental imaginations. That reshaping is an essential role that literature can play in protecting the earth. (James 2015, 39)

These lines already suggest the relevance of James's argument – namely "that reading narratives can help bridge imaginative gaps" (2015, 3) between diverging environmental imaginations and thus encourage readers to try on the subjective environmental experience of others (cf. 2015, 2) – not only to postcolonial discourses, but also to interdisciplinary discussions concerning "the global nature of the modern environmental crisis" (2015, 39). Proceeding from her statement, I would maintain that the environmental imaginations presented in post-apocalyptic Anthropocene fiction can enhance readers' ecological awareness by allowing them to mentally explore the experience of post-apocalyptic spaces which, though non-existent, are nonetheless conceivable in light of the current state of climate change.

But how exactly does this work? How can narratives permit readers to experience spaces they do not (yet) know from real life? The concept of experientiality serves as a useful tool to answer this question. Monika Fludernik first introduced the concept in *Towards a 'Natural' Narratology* (1996), where she defined it as the "quasi-mimetic evocation of 'real-life experience'" (12).[8] According to Fludernik, experientiality constitutes the core of any natural form of storytelling, which is why she hinges the distinct quality of being narrative on the representation of experientiality or some kind of anthropomorphic consciousness (cf. 1996, 26–28): "I here argue that *narrativity is a function of narrative texts and centres on experientiality of an anthropomorphic nature.*" (Fludernik 1996, 26; italics in the original) Fludernik's definition of narrativity, then, postulates that "there can […] be narratives without plot, but [that] there cannot be any narratives without a human (anthropomorphic) experiencer of some sort at some narrative level" (1996, 13).

If a narrative does not exhibit an explicit first-person speaker who can take on the role of such an experiencing narrative agent, "the locus of experientiality becomes the reader who 'naturalizes' or 'narrativizes' the text" (Culler 2018, 244).[9] Fludernik's model offers different kinds of narrativization which help

---

[8] For a more recent discussion of experientiality in which Fludernik comments on the reception and revision of her concept over the twenty years following the publication of *Towards a 'Natural' Narratology*, cf. Fludernik 2018, 337–344.

[9] I have already elaborated on Fludernik's concept of narrativization in Chapter 4.2.

readers to make sense of narrative texts. In this model, Jonathan Culler (2018, 244) concludes, "[c]ognitive frames and concepts enable readers to process stories":

> When readers confront texts, they cast about for ways of recuperating them as narratives by applying the macro-frame of narrativity. They attempt to recognize what they find in terms of the real-world script of *telling*, the schema of perception (*viewing*), or access to their own narrativizable experience (*experiencing*). Then at another level they adopt the cognitive parameters of various types of stories and elements of naturally occurring storytelling situations. (Culler 2018, 244; italics in the original)[10]

In his contributions to a theory of experientiality, Marco Caracciolo takes up Fludernik's concept and develops it in a new direction.[11] Unlike Fludernik, he understands experientiality not as a defining criterion of narrativity, but as a narrative phenomenon that emerges in the interaction between narrative texts and their readers (cf. Caracciolo 2014, 47). He accordingly recommends that "we should think of experientiality as a kind of network that involves, minimally, the recipient of a narrative, his or her experiential background, and the expressive strategies adopted by the author" (Caracciolo 2014, 49) and concludes: "At the root of experientiality is, then, the tension between the textual design and the recipient's experiential background" (Caracciolo 2014, 49). Accordingly, the process of receiving narrative fiction can not only reveal unfamiliar "imaginative contents" to readers, but also feature "experiential qualities" (Caracciolo 2014, 5) that deviate from their "experiential background" (Caracciolo 2014, 4). He identifies two psychological mechanisms involved in this process:

> [T]he first is the triggering of memories of past experiences—experiential traces, as they are known in the psycholinguistic literature. The second is mental simulation, which allows readers to put together past experiential traces in novel ways, therefore sustaining their first-person involvement with both fictional characters and the spatial dimension of storyworlds. (Caracciolo 2014, 5)

The reception of fiction consists, then, of a "two-way movement" (Caracciolo 2014, 5) between narrative texts and readers' experiential backgrounds: narratives can simulate experiences readers recognize from real life, but can also "bring about a restructuring of each reader's experiential background by generating new 'story-driven' experiences" (Caracciolo 2014, 5), and it is precisely

---

10 For a more detailed synopsis of Fludernik's model, cf. also Fludernik 2003c and 2010b.
11 I here quote from Caracciolo's monograph, *The Experientiality of Narrative: An Enactivist Approach* (2014); a shortened version of his theory can be found in Caracciolo 2012.

this psychological mechanism of mental simulation that becomes effective in post-apocalyptic Anthropocene fiction.

Narratives of catastrophe like Atwood's *Oryx and Crake* offer readers "new 'story-driven' experiences" of post-apocalyptic spaces they have never inhabited in real life. In the following section I will have recourse to the notion of *qualia* – a term which philosophers of mind use to refer to "the sense of what it's like for someone or something to have a particular experience" (Herman 2009a, 144) – to investigate how Atwood's post-apocalyptic novel enables readers to imaginatively experience and even mentally inhabit a planet Earth that has been irreversibly damaged by human action. The particularity of Atwood's novel, I will argue, lies in its 'narrative of punishment,' which envisions a perpetual state of suffering reminiscent of hell. *Oryx and Crake* evokes a posthuman storyworld that functions as a metaphorical prison for the protagonist, the last human survivor, who serves a maximum sentence for the environmental misdeeds committed by his species. The effect is achieved by a forceful interplay of narrative techniques including the representation of a *posthuman space*, event sequencing, and internal focalization, as well as the use of the present tense. Focusing on the narrative design of *Oryx and Crake*, my reading contrasts with previous approaches, which dealt predominantly with thematic aspects of Atwood's narrative.[12]

8.2 Before and After the Apocalypse: Temporalizing Atwood's Heterogeneous Use of Fictional Tense

The first volume of Atwood's *MaddAddam* trilogy is set in a future world defined by the disastrous consequences of anthropogenic climate change, as well as genetic and bioengineering. Combining the voice of a covert third-person narrator with the fixed internal perspective of the protagonist, the narrative recounts the fate of Snowman (formerly known as Jimmy), who seems to be the last human survivor of a viral plague. Before the onset of the novel, Snowman's friend Crake has invented and spread a lethal, highly infectious virus, initiating a global pandemic. Crake has secretly vaccinated Snowman, however, making

---

[12] For example, a lot of research has been done on the novel's central themes of "biotechnology" (cf. e.g. Arias 2011, Boller 2014, Bosco 2010, Hengen 2010, Kozioł 2018, Mohr 2015, Stein 2010), "posthumanity" or "the extinction of humankind" (cf. e.g. Arias 2011; Boller 2018; Ciobanu 2014; Demerjian 2018; Després 2015, 152–154; Grace 2012; Jennings 2019; Korte 2008b, 2008c; Mosca 2013), and "the end of the world" (cf. e.g. Bahrawi 2013, Bowen 2017).

him immune because he has chosen him to take care of the Crakers, a group of immortal, but simple-minded humanoid mutants whom he has created in his laboratory to succeed humanity. After the apocalypse, Snowman, in accordance with his friend's wishes, guides Crake's 'children' from the laboratory to a safe, open place, where they settle.

Atwood's narrative is characterized by a "doubled time scheme" (Snyder 2011, 475–477) covering both the protagonist's post-apocalyptic present in the plague's aftermath and his pre-apocalyptic past before its outburst, the latter dimension being reconstructed through extensive analepses which periodically interrupt the principal narrative account.[13] The time levels are distinguished linguistically as well as temporally with different verbal tenses, the parts set in the storyworld's present using the present tense, while the parts relating to the past are written in the past tense (cf. Korte 2008a, 23).

Atwood here resorts to what I have called alternate foregrounding of fictional tense usage (see Chapter 4.2), a strategy to which she draws readers' attention juxtaposing past and present tenses in the different temporal settings of her novel. Functioning as a deictic means to linguistically separate the post-apocalyptic from the pre-apocalyptic setting, this tense-switching (see Chapter 4.2) enhances readers' spatiotemporal orientation within the novel's diegetic universe – an effect already established in the first section of the second chapter ("Bonfire")[14] – enabling them to rapidly temporalize Atwood's use of tense.[15] Starting from the first flashback, which begins with the sentence "Once upon a time, Snowman wasn't Snowman" (*OC*, 15), readers will recognize that the present tense denotes the present of the story, while the past tense of the analepses points to the pre-apocalyptic storyworld.[16]

Thus the pre-apocalyptic and post-apocalyptic storyworlds of *Oryx and Crake* differ not only with regard to their spatial design (the post-apocalyptic world bears little resemblance to the pre-apocalyptic world), but also in the

---

13 Atwood reverts here to a narrative pattern we encounter in other (post-apocalyptic) narratives. Cormac McCarthy's *The Road* (2007 [2006]), for example, features a post-apocalyptic plot interwoven with a large number of flashbacks depicting the storyworld before the cataclysm. Colson Whitehead's *Zone One* (2012 [2011]), as well as the Francis Lawrence 2007 film adaptation of Richard Matheson's classic *I Am Legend* (2010 [1954]), are further cases in point. However, neither of these narratives envisions the aftermath of natural disasters, imagining instead the consequences of a zombie apocalypse.
14 The novel is divided into 15 main chapters designated with numerals (1, 2, 3, etc.). Each of these chapters is subdivided into a varying number of subchapters bearing proper titles.
15 I have provided a definition of the term *temporalization* in Chapter 4.2.
16 I will discuss the first flashback in the novel in greater detail below (see Chapter 8.3).

ways in which the novel presents these settings to its readers. I have detailed these differences elsewhere (cf. Gebauer forthcoming). Here, I shall focus exclusively on Atwood's present-tense narrative, arguing that, in addition to fulfilling a referential function, her use of the fictional present has a substantial impact on the process of worldmaking in *Oryx and Crake*, adding to the post-apocalyptic atmosphere of the text conveying an embodied imaginative experience of the narrative setting and with it an idea of what it might be like to live in a world struck by a global environmental catastrophe.

8.3 Posthuman Space, Episodic Plot Structure, and the Thematic and Descriptive Functions of the Fictional Present

The post-apocalyptic world inhabited by Snowman and the Crakers does not resemble the world he knew in his former life. Cities, towns, and gated communities have turned into abandoned, desolate spaces, and the entire Earth has become a tropical planet with no seasons. Yet far from offering idyllic beach holiday scenery the novel depicts a nightmarish space which constantly challenges human existence. Atwood's post-apocalyptic storyworld can best be described as what I have elsewhere designated as a *posthuman space* (cf. Gebauer forthcoming).

This metaphor becomes effective at various levels of the post-apocalyptic storyworld of *Oryx and Crake*. Not only does Snowman's new environment confront the protagonist with regular attacks by wild animals such as genetically manipulated boars ("pigoons") and dogs ("wolvogs"), but his surroundings themselves pose a threat: the "evil rays" (*OC*, 37) of the "punishing sun" (*OC*, 6) burn his skin, "[t]he forest blots up his voice" (*OC*, 169), and the heat turns his brain to "melted cheese" (*OC*, 283). Nature is personified as a deadly enemy against which the human species stands no chance of survival: Snowman sees himself as "the last *Homo sapiens* – a white illusion of a man, here today, gone tomorrow, so easily shoved over, left to melt in the sun, getting thinner and thinner until he liquefies and trickles away altogether" (*OC*, 224; italics in the original).

As well as impacting the human body, the posthuman space in *Oryx and Crake* destroys material aspects of human culture. The "semi-flooded townhouses" of "minnow city" (*OC*, 148) suggest a prior deluge which has inundated entire building complexes, while the uncontrolled proliferation of vegetation has started to eliminate the last remnants of human civilization:

> The buildings that didn't burn or explode [during the riots immediately following the apocalypse] are still standing, though the botany **is thrusting** itself through every crack. Given time it **will fissure** the asphalt, **topple** the walls, **push** aside the roofs. Some kind of vine is growing everywhere, **draping** the windowsills, **climbing in** through the broken windows and up the bars and grillwork. Soon this district will be a thick tangle of vegetation. (*OC*, 221–222; my emphasis)

In figurative language, Atwood visualizes the threat of botany in general and vines in particular, with *thrust*, *fissure*, *topple*, *push*, *drape*, and *climb* personifying vegetation as a vital power that ineluctably erases "all visible traces of human habitation" (*OC*, 222).

In this post-apocalyptic storyworld the loss of human culture is represented by an absence of clock time. Whenever Snowman looks at his watch, it shows him the "blank face" of "zero hour" (*OC*, 3). Atwood's use of the present tense emphasizes that in this world the concept of human time has lost its meaning. Unlike the more conventional preterite, the present tense does not create the impression of narrative hindsight which would suggest that the post-apocalyptic condition might be temporary. The present tense evokes a state of endlessness. Readers will understand that Snowman's situation is hopeless: no matter how hard he tries, he cannot escape the desolation. And, what is worse, there is no end in sight to his suffering.[17]

Atwood's post-apocalyptic novel creates an 'anti-narrative' that diminishes the spatial and temporal components of narrative worldmaking. This can be best explained with recourse to Jurij M. Lotman's semantics of narrative space. In *The Structure of the Artistic Text* (1977 [1971]), Lotman sees narrative texts as containing two distinct subspaces which are not only topologically distinct (e.g. top-bottom, right-left, inside-outside), but also semantically polar (e.g. good-evil, familiar-strange, natural-artificial). The semantic topology of worlds represented in literature concretizes in specific topographical opposites (e.g. town/safety-forest/danger, mountain/repose-valley/stress, heaven/good-hell/evil) (cf. Lotman 1977 [1971], 218–229). And these subspaces are separated by a boundary that constitutes the key topological feature of narrative: "The boundary divides the entire space of the [narrative] text into two mutually non-intersecting subspaces" (Lotman 1977 [1971], 229), each of which exhibits a completely different internal structure.[18]

---

[17] A similar argument can be found in Snyder 2011, 472: "As we soon come to understand, he [i.e. Snowman] is marooned in time, cast away between a human past and a post-human future, cut off from the past yet unable to move beyond it."
[18] For a more detailed discussion of Lotman's theory, see also Gebauer forthcoming.

Lotman's theory posits that every narrative contains at least one symbolic boundary which divides its world into two subspaces. But in *Oryx and Crake* the spatial expansion of nature dissolves any such symbolic boundaries. Here water floods entire cities and whole districts are overgrown with plant life. In the unrelieved present of Atwood's storyworld, the omnipresence of nature threatens to collapse the distinction between the symbolic subspaces underlying the structure of the narrative: The distinction between wilderness and civilization is on the verge of vanishing, the former absorbing the latter, and the semantic difference usually associated with these opposites – the opposition between nature and culture – is about to lose its significance. Atwood's posthuman space stages an ecocritical understanding of the nature-culture relationship, where concepts like Timothy Morton's (2010, 28–38) "mesh" or Donna Haraway's (2003) "natureculture" can lay stress on the interconnectedness between nature and humanity, while Jane Bennett's (2010, vii) notion of "vibrant matter" questions our "habit of parsing the world into dull matter (it, things) and vibrant life (us, beings)."

The only spatial opposition which still seems valid in Snowman's world is the topological distinction of 'up' vs. 'down.' He sleeps on a tree because the wild animals most dangerous to him cannot intrude on these arboreal roosts. And during his "pilfering excursions" (*OC*, 45) through the wilderness in search of food, he climbs up ruins of compound walls or buildings to avoid sudden attacks by pigoons or wolvogs. Yet this conceptual opposition does not create different symbolic subspaces, as it cannot be associated with concrete fictional places that divide Atwood's storyworld into two parts. 'Up' does not correlate with a specific space: it can mean 'on a tree,' 'on the upper level of a building,' or 'on top of a wall'; nor is Snowman always safe when he is 'up,' for neither jungle canopies nor the remnants of former infrastructures can protect him from environmental perils like thunderstorms and lightning. In the post-apocalyptic world of *Oryx and Crake*, even the most essential boundary between human shelter and wilderness is at risk.

And the spatial structure of Atwood's text influences the novel's "narrative dynamics," its "movement [...] from its opening to its end" (Richardson 2002b, 1).[19] Lotman (1977 [1971], 240) considers the existence of two symbolically charged spaces separated by a boundary as a structural prerequisite of any plot, any narrative storyline. At the heart of each plot, he argues, lies its "smallest

---

19 According to Brian Richardson (2002b, 2), this movement "includes the beginnings of both the story and the text, the temporality of the telling, the movement and shaping of the plot, and the functions of the ending."

indivisible unit" (Lotman 1977 [1971], 232), an event which he qualifies as "the shifting of a persona across the borders of a semantic field" (Lotman 1977 [1971], 233). He construes narrative texts, then, as plotted texts (cf. Lotman 1977 [1971], 233) that feature at least one mobile character, the so-called hero-agent (cf. Lotman 1977 [1971], 240), who moves across the different semantic spaces established by these texts, crossing the boundary separating their subspaces (cf. Lotman 1977 [1971], 238). However, given that Atwood's storyworld undermines the symbolic subspaces of civilization and wilderness, the act of crossing the boundary between these two spaces becomes meaningless. Lotman would probably conclude that the spatial structure of *Oryx and Crake* rules out a proper plot.

Indeed, the part of the storyline that unfolds after the apocalypse is quite basic: Refusing to starve to death, Snowman goes on a quest for food which leads him back to the headquarters of the RejoovenEsense Compound, where Crake had planned and launched his viral assault. Snowman's trip back to "the center of the catastrophe and the site of his own traumatic memories" (Howells 2006, 170), ironically referred to as *Paradice*, is made up of brief episodic elements that can be summarized as follows:

- *Episode 1:* Upon his arrival at the compound, Snowman first comes across an abandoned house in which he searches for food (cf. *OC*, 227–233).
- *Episode 2:* Setting off again after searching the house, Snowman is surprised by a twister, from which he takes shelter in a former checkpoint building, where he also spends the night (cf. *OC*, 234–238).
- *Episode 3:* Next morning, when he wants to continue his journey to *Paradice*, he is chased by pigoons and again takes refuge in the tower of the checkpoint building, where he finally finds some food and beverages (cf. *OC*, 265–274).
- *Episode 4:* After spending another night in the checkpoint building, he resumes his journey on top of the rampart surrounding the compound, where he is caught in a thunderstorm (cf. *OC*, 275–280, 283–284, 307).
- *Episode 5:* He eventually arrives in *Paradice*, where he searches for nourishment and attends to a cut under his foot which he has sustained during his trip (cf. *OC*, 333–338).

This synopsis shows that Atwood's novel features a "tour structure" (Ryan et al. 2016, 31–32), one of the oldest forms of narrative familiar from genres such as the epic narrative, the medieval romance, or the picaresque novel. As the story follows Snowman's expedition through the post-apocalyptic wilderness, it is the temporal course of his journey (rather than causality) that determines the narrative's unfolding: the different episodes are arranged in a chronological order; they are not causally connected, so it makes no difference in which order they occur. In other words they are randomly interchangeable – except for the first and last episodes, which logically mark the beginning and end of the trip.

Atwood's novel, therefore, defies the notion that narratives are designed around a particular temporal-causal logic. In line with definitions of narrative that emphasize plot,[20] narrative texts, according to Werner Wolf (2007a, 24), usually feature "motivated actions" that fulfill the following criteria: (1) they "involve anthropomorphic agents"; (2) they "are interrelated not only by chronology but also by causality and teleology"; and (3) they "lead to, or are consequences of, conscious acts or decisions, frequently as results of conflicts" (Wolf 2007a, 24). The events of Snowman's quest meet only the first criterion, as Snowman is an anthropomorphic agent who actively decides what to do. However, since he moves within a post-apocalyptic environment in which human agency is restricted, he can no longer influence the impact of his actions. For, due to the lack of symbolic spaces in the post-apocalyptic storyworld, there are no longer any socio-cultural structures which might allow him to anticipate the consequences of his deeds and to manipulate his nonhuman adversaries: he can neither protect himself from attacks by wild animals nor circumvent the forces of nature. In fact, his actions have no impact whatsoever, which means that the various events that impinge on him are neither mutually dependent, in the sense that one event causes the other, nor do they work toward a specific closure: after his excursion to *Paradice*, Snowman simply returns to the Crakers and the shelter of his familiar tree.

Strikingly, this lack of teleology is reflected by the novel in that the first and last chapters commence in exactly the same way (except for one omission at the beginning of the novel's last chapter, which I here indicate with "[...]"):

> Snowman wakes before dawn. He lies unmoving, listening to the tide coming in [...], wish-wash, wish-wash, the rhythm of heartbeat. He would so like to believe he is still asleep.

---

[20] For a comprehensive survey of narratological works that treat plot as "a key constituent of narrative," cf. Kukkonen 2014, here 715.

> On the eastern horizon there's a greyish haze, lit now with a rosy, deadly glow. Strange how that colour still seems tender. (*OC*, 371)[21]

The absence of teleological structure demonstrates that the main argument of Lotman's semantics of space – namely that narrative plot depends on spatial structure – does in fact also apply to Atwood's novel. Because the post-apocalyptic storyworld exhibits no subspaces of socio-cultural relevance, the protagonist's human deeds and actions remain insignificant in the context of his inhospitable living environment. By impeding the development of a complex plot in which events are causally linked and lead to a definable outcome, Atwood's novel defies any sense of eventfulness, essentially curtailing the tellability of Snowman's trip back to the end of the world.[22]

That the account of Snowman's journey is written in the present tense reinforces the narrative dynamics brought about by the spatial structure of Atwood's storyworld. Simulating synchronicity between the occurrence of events within Snowman's here-and-now and the discourse that conveys these happenings to the narrative audience, the present tense leads readers to believe that they know of these events through a real-time report. And the impression is intensified by the novel's dominant mode of fixed internal focalization: Since Snowman's fate is presented exclusively from his perspective without the interference of an overt narratorial voice, readers feel that they are witnessing the events through the eyes of the protagonist while they are actually taking place. It comes as no real surprise, then, that the events do not seem to pursue a specific goal, for in a world where only the present exists human time and with it human teleology no longer have any meaning.

The reduced temporal dimension of Atwood's posthuman space certainly has an impact on the events depicted in the narrative. Ansgar Nünning (2010, 195–196) reminds us that, from a narratological perspective, events are "not understood as something given or natural, but rather as something made or constructed" (196): they only come into existence through the process of narrativization during which selected moments, occurrences, and actions are "trans-

---

21 Cf. also the beginning of *Oryx and Crake*, which I quoted in Chapter 8.1; the subordinate clause missing in the last chapter reads "wave after wave sloshing over the various barricades" (*OC*, 3).
22 Peter Hühn (2014) distinguishes two types of event: type I and type II. While the former "is treated as a defining feature inherent to every kind of narrative," the latter "is integral to a particular type of narrative, providing the foundation for its *raison d'être*, or tellability" (Hühn 2014, 160; italics in the original). When using the term *eventfulness* in connection with Lotman's model in this chapter, I refer to type II events.

ferred into a limited, structured form which is enriched with meaning" (Nünning 2010, 201–202). By thus involving a complex set of procedures such as "selection, deletion, abstraction, and prioritization or 'weighting' (in the sense of Goodman [...])" (Nünning 2010, 197), the constitution of an event requires either a retrospective perspective – for example, if we try to make sense of a happening in the past (cf. Nünning 2012b) – or a prospective perspective – for instance, if we anticipate something that might happen in the future (cf. Sommer 2019).[23] However, the endless present of Atwood's posthuman world forecloses both these alternatives, with the result that Snowman's journey consists not so much of meaningful events as of trivial happenings. Atwood's use of the present tense can thus be regarded as a thematic present, a present of hopelessness, which calls the reader's attention to Snowman's desperate situation: no matter how long he waits, riding it out, there can be no hope of change, and no matter how far he travels, he does not seem to move.

Given the endless present of *Oryx and Crake*'s post-apocalyptic world, one might draw the conclusion that Atwood's use of the fictional present has a synchronizing function. With its two time frames (the periods before and after the apocalypse), however, the novel does not draw on the mode of simultaneous presentation (see Chapter 5.6): The numerous analepses that interrupt the narrative of the protagonist's hiking tour represent Snowman's memories of the time before the apocalypse (cf. Korte 2008a, 23).[24] The very first flashback in the novel illustrates this point:

> Once upon a time, Snowman wasn't Snowman. Instead he was Jimmy. He'd been a good boy then.
>
> **Jimmy's earliest complete memory** was of a huge bonfire. He must have been five, maybe six. He was wearing red rubber boots with a smiling duck's face on each toe; **he remembers that**, because after seeing the bonfire he had to walk through a pan of disinfectant in those boots. They'd said the disinfectant was poisonous and he shouldn't splash, and then he was worried that the poison would get into the eyes of the ducks and

---

23 A more detailed outline of Nünning's and Sommer's discussion of the retrospective and prospective qualities of events is provided in Chapter 7.4 in the context of turning points in Mantel's Tudor novels.

24 Coral Ann Howells (2006, 171) therefore describes Atwood's novel as "tak[ing] the form of a third-person indirect interior monologue" that "shifts between the fictive present (always in the present tense) and Snowman's memories of his own and other people's stories (always in the past tense), contextualized and written down by the other shadowy presence" of a third-person narrator.

hurt them. He'd been told the ducks were only like pictures, they weren't real and had no feelings, but he didn't quite believe it.

So let's say five and a half, **thinks Snowman**. That's about right. (*OC*, 15; my emphasis)

As the noun phrase "Jimmy's earliest complete memory" as well as the *verba credendi remember* and *think* reveal (see also my emphasis), Atwood presents the flashback as a reminiscence. The passage accordingly reads as a combination of narrated monologue or free indirect discourse (i.e. the first two paragraphs) and quoted or interior monologue (i.e. the last paragraph), both of which grant readers an insight into Jimmy's/Snowman's mind.[25]

Admittedly, the given example is a bit misleading as the second paragraph features Jimmy, that is, an earlier version of the protagonist, as the focalizer. Yet Snowman – the current version of the protagonist – serves as the center of consciousness in the framing paragraphs, so that it is fair to say that it is him (and not Jimmy) who constitutes the origin of this flashback, particularly in view of the fact that one can find several other sentences which identify Snowman as the subject of *verba credendi* referring to the analepses in the novel.[26] Considering, then, that the numerous instances of analepsis in *Oryx and Crake* qualify as recollections on the part of the older self of the protagonist located in the here-and-now of the storyworld, we can no longer construe the present-tense account of Snowman's fate as an instance of simultaneous focalization. Since the flashbacks are ontologically embedded into the narrative discourse revolving around the post-apocalyptic storyworld, they temporarily interrupt the chronological account of Snowman's trip to the end of the world, repeatedly causing the progression of these events to stagnate. Such deceleration of the story time defies the nature of concurrent presentation and can only be achieved in the context of retrospective presentation.

In this light, rather than arguing that Atwood's use of the present tense fulfills a synchronizing function (with implications for simultaneous presentation), I would conceive of it as a descriptive present. For the descriptive use of present-tense narration can account for an exclusively chronological, non-teleological depiction of events without postulating synchronicity between their occurrence and their representation. Harold F. Mosher's (1991) concept of "'descriptized' narration" clarifies this point. Mosher uses the term to designate a textual passage which appears to be descriptive yet actually qualifies as an

---

25 For the differences (and similarities) between narrated and quoted monologue, cf. Cohn 1978, Ch. 3 and Ch. 2 respectively.
26 Cf. *OC*, 23, 30, 31, 49, 59, 61, 66, 67, 68, 75, 184, 191, 218, 232, 318, 320, 323, 338, 340.

instance of narration.[27] In other words, descriptized narration is narrative masquerading as description (see also Chapter 5.9). If we read Atwood's present-tense account of Snowman's hike to *Paradice* as an example of such a text, which "disguises a [retrospective] narration as a description" (Mosher 1991, 427), we can easily accept that the plot of *Oryx and Crake* defies any sense of closure. For instances of descriptized retrospective narration simulate that the narrative events are depicted as if they were happening simultaneously with the act of representation in order to make readers believe that they were witnessing these events at the very moment of their occurrence. In reality, however, these events are related in hindsight.

8.4 Dynamic Descriptions and the Immersive Function of Present-Tense Narration

In terms of descriptized narration, Atwood's tale invites its readers to become immersed in the protagonist's environment. Snowman's 'quest' serves above all to depict the post-apocalyptic setting of Atwood's storyworld, its present-tense account containing numerous long passages of description which allow readers to form a rich mental image of the posthuman space of the novel. In accordance with the narrative's prevailing reflector mode, most of these descriptive passages are internally focalized, with Snowman as focalizer. The following examples illustrate this structure:

> *Quotation 1:*
> After an hour of walking, Snowman comes out from the former park. He picks his way farther inland, heading along the trashed pleebland boulevards and avenues and roads and streets. Wrecked solarcars are plentiful, some piled up in multi-vehicle crashes, some burnt out, some standing intact as if temporarily parked. There are trucks and vans, fuel-cell models and also the old gas or diesel kind, and ATVs. A few bicycles, a few motorcycles – not a bad choice considering the traffic mayhem that must have lasted for days. On a two-wheeled item you'd have been able to weave in and out among the larger vehicles until someone shot you or ran into you, or you fell off. (*OC*, 221)
>
> *Quotation 2:*
> The walking has become an obstacle course for Snowman: in several places he's needed to make detours. Now he's in a narrow sidestreet, choked with vines; they've festooned

---

[27] More specifically, this means that instances of descriptized narration are characterized by "formal qualities [which] are or seem to be predominantly narrative," although their "ultimate function reveals itself to be descriptive" (Mosher 1991, 427).

8.4 Dynamic Descriptions and the Immersive Function of Present-Tense Narration — 191

themselves across the street, from roof to roof. **Through the clefts in the overhead greenery** he can see a handful of vultures, circling idly in the sky. (*OC*, 223–224; my emphasis)

Quotation 3:
Up ahead, the houses thin out and vanish. There's an interval of parking lots and warehouses, then barbed wire strung between cement posts, an elaborate gate off its hinges. End of urban sprawl and pleeb city limits, beginning of Compound turfdom. (*OC*, 225)

Snowman's perception of the urban wasteland of a former city ("pleebland") is conveyed to readers by means of a strategy, known in cognitive linguistics as "route perspective" (Fludernik 2014b, 466) or "*tour* strategy" (Ryan 2003, 218; italics in the original). That is to say, the narrative enables readers to adopt Snowman's point of view by positioning themselves "within the described space [...] as a moving focal point" (Fludernik 2014b, 466). In this way the narrative offers us a virtual tour through the abandoned city, leading us from the main roads of the periphery (Quotation 1), through the narrow sidestreets of the center (Quotation 2), to the suburbs and the rural compounds beyond (Quotation 3).

This dynamic walking tour influences the ways in which we can become immersed in the novel's storyworld. Immersion is an act of imaginative mental projection into the fictive worlds evoked by such a text (cf. Ryan 2015 [2001]).[28] The strategy of the route perspective intensifies this experience, drawing on what Herman (2002, 280–282) refers to as "projective locations," i.e. representations of space which rely less on the invariant geometric properties of objects ("topological locations") than on the orientative framework of their viewer. Projective locations, Herman explains, do not provide a topological description of the textual world as a static map, but lead the reader through the mapped area, presenting the storyworld from an on-the-ground perspective internal to that world. Erin James (2015) argues that this strategy "draws readers into the locality of the text" (58), encouraging them to experience the imaginary places represented in the narrative as if "being physically *in* them" (153; italics in the original).

This certainly applies to Atwood's representation of the post-apocalyptic storyworld in *Oryx and Crake*. The linguistic make-up of the text reinforces the sense of immersion. By using the present tense as the global tense of narration, Atwood invites her readers to undertake an imaginative act of recentering that projects them right onto the narrative scene (see Chapter 5.3). The immersive effect of the fictional present is underpinned by the use of the second-person

---

28 I have provided a more detailed discussion of the phenomenon of immersion in Chapter 5.3.

pronoun at the end of Quotation 1. As James points out, such an intermittent "reference to an unspecified narratee calls out to a hypothetical 'you' that hails all readers, no matter their reading location" (2015, 57). The text thus invites us to imagine ourselves riding a motorcycle through the traffic chaos. Even if this little thought experiment relates to a point in time which lies before the storyworld's present (i.e. the period shortly after Crake's fatal viral assault when everyone tried to flee the city), it again induces us to imaginatively project ourselves into Snowman's environment.

Although the narrative depicts its setting in great detail, granting its readers a rich environmental experience, it at no point delineates the spatial structure of its storyworld. We merely learn that there are different types of vehicles on the main streets of the city, while the smaller sidestreets are empty and overgrown with vines. Moving to the suburbs, the text, moreover, induces us to imagine parking lots and warehouses as well as the remains of a barbed wire fence that once separated the city from the adjacent compound territory. However, we learn nothing about the spatial arrangement of the vehicles and buildings, nor can we say anything about the individual routes of the different streets. Atwood's depiction of the storyworld in *Oryx and Crake* is remarkably thin on topological information or geographical coordinates. If different readers were asked to draw a map of the setting, they would probably come up with completely different versions.[29]

From a cognitive perspective, this lack of map-like specificity intensifies readers' immersion in Atwood's storyworld as it foregrounds the internal perspective of the focalizer who travels through this imaginary space. Topographical specifications would impede this immediacy, as they would suggest the interference of the external, elevated view of a heterodiegetic narrator. This, in turn, would have an impact on readers' imaginative act of recentering: if Atwood's narrative featured an overt narrator speaking within the text, readers might well interpret the present tense as indicating the narrator (rather than the protagonist) as the deictic center. The present tense would then refer to the

---

[29] For a discussion of how readers use textual cues in order to construct cognitive maps of narrative settings, cf. Ryan(2003, 219–221 and Ryan et al. 2016, 62–65. As Marie-Laure Ryan points out in this context, any graphic map of a specific narrative world is "only the more or less faithful image of a cognitive map" (2003, 222), that is, a holistic representation of the world readers create in order to follow the narrative's plot. Individual cognitive maps of a particular textual world will always differ to a certain degree, for every reader imagines the same world differently on the basis of their previous (reading) experience. Still, it seems safe to assume that the deviation between different mental models of a specific diegesis will increase in direct proportion to the text's lack of specificity with regard to the topographies it projects.

8.4 Dynamic Descriptions and the Immersive Function of Present-Tense Narration

narrator's here-and-now, and the novel would no longer sustain its potential of facilitating readers' imaginative transportation to the storyworld.

Again, the text's lack of spatial orientation means that cognitive templates based on orientational metaphors (cf. Lakoff and Johnson 2003 [1980]), metaphorical blending (cf. Schneider 2012), or spatial semantics offer little help in the process of naturalizing the posthuman space depicted in this narrative (cf. Fludernik 2010a). Since *Oryx and Crake* introduces a possible world which readers cannot easily make sense of by having recourse to the principle of minimal departure (cf. Ryan 1991, Ch. 3; see also Chapter 5.3), the novel exhibits a new kind of experientiality, confronting readers with an experience of space which they do not recognize from real life. Eluding the practices with which we usually process narrative representations of space, Atwood's inhospitable storyworld has an impact that readers do not merely comprehend notionally, but experience firsthand through the act of reading.

In light of these findings, one could conclude with Brian McHale (2011) that *Oryx and Crake* functions as a sophisticated and effective thought experiment: By visualizing a post-apocalyptic world which has succumbed to the possible consequences of anthropogenic climate change, the novel gives readers an insight into what it could be like to inhabit the Earth after it has turned into a posthuman space. Thanks to Atwood's choice of the fictional present as the global tense of narration, the novel creates the impression of narrative immediacy, encouraging readers to mentally project themselves right onto the narrative scene. The narrative invites them to perceive the post-apocalyptic environment from the spatiotemporal location of the protagonist, enabling them to imaginatively experience the novel's setting. Readers are allowed to directly witness Snowman's dreadful fate: damned as one of the last human survivors on a globally warmed Earth that constantly jeopardizes his existence, he is punished for the environmental sins of his own species without having any chance to escape from this life sentence. The effect of this – to use Marco Caracciolo's (2014, 5) formulation again – "'story-driven' experience" might be twofold, not only warning readers of the imminent dangers of today's environmental crisis, but also prompting them to reflect upon and maybe even critically question their own environmental behavior. Put simply, the experience of reading *Oryx and Crake* will hopefully inspire what Timothy Morton (2010) would refer to as the "ecological thought," stimulating readers to become aware of their own ecological responsibility.

9 Narrative of Reminiscence: Intercultural Understanding and Narrative Empathy in Nadeem Aslam's *Maps for Lost Lovers* (2004)

9.1 Nurturing the Intercultural Mind: The Empathic Potential of Intercultural Narratives

> *He stands at the window and watches the Cinnabar moth that's sheltering against the pane on the other side [...] He remembers Jugnu smiling and saying the Cinnabar have been paying attention to the way Pakistani and Indian women dress: the upper body is covered with the* kameez-shirt *which is made of a fabric printed with designs [...] while the* shalwar-trousers *single out one of the main colours of the* kameez.
>
> (MLL, 227)

> *She briefly rinses each lily stem before it takes its diagonal place inside the vase [...] Their scent is strongest at night, and since there is a hedge plant back in Sohni Dharti whose buds, like the Madonna lilies, not only open in the evening's whispers but also release a perfume as hazy as them, Kaukab's affection for the lilies has increased over the years.*
>
> *Compared with England, Pakistan is a poor and humble country but she aches for it, because to be thirsty is to crave a glass of simple water and no amount of rich buttermilk will do.*
>
> (MLL, 71)

While awaiting an appointment with his affair partner, Shamas, the male protagonist of Nadeem Aslam's *Maps for Lost Lovers*, looks through the window of the Urdu bookshop which he opened in England after migrating from Pakistan. On the outside pane of the window, he detects a Cinnabar moth, the sight of which causes him to recall his dead brother Jugnu, who once compared the color of this moth to a *shalwar-kameez*, the traditional dress combination worn by Pakistani and Indian women, which is only rarely seen in his newly adopted homeland (see first quotation). Kaukab, the female protagonist of Aslam's narrative, likewise misses her home country. Putting the flowers her daughter has given her for her birthday in a vase, she is reminded by the scent of the Madonna lilies of Pakistan, and realizes how much she misses its beauty (see second quotation).[1]

The two quotes highlight a central characteristic of Aslam's novel: Combining the use of the present tense with internal focalization, *Maps for Lost Lovers*

---

[1] According to Aroosa Kanwal (2015, 159) and Catherine Pesso-Miquel (2011, 129), the Urdu expression *Sohni Dharti* means "beautiful land."

grants readers an immediate insight into the protagonists' minds. Aslam's poetic style, with its metaphors, similes, and other tropes, reveals a perception of their here-and-now in England that constantly brings back memories of the protagonists' past life in Pakistan. Yet these recollections vary in the degree to which they evoke emotions within the characters. Shamas, on the one hand, becomes only a little nostalgic when the "vibrating shades" of the Cinnabar moth's wings remind him of the clothes worn by Pakistani women; Kaukab, on the other hand, seriously yearns for her home country. By drawing an analogy between longing and thirst, the second quotation makes clear that "she aches" for Pakistan, however "poor and humble" it is. The short excerpts from *Maps for Lost Lovers* perfectly illustrate how each protagonist deals differently with their nostalgia and homesickness.

Nadeem Aslam's second novel, first published in 2004, is set in an unnamed town in present-day England referred to in the text as "Dasht-e-Tanhaii," meaning "Wilderness of Solitude" or "Desert of Loneliness" (*MLL*, 29). The story follows the protagonist Shamas, a retired social worker and one-time poet from Pakistan, and his family, including his wife Kaukab, his three children Charag, Ujala, and Mah-Jabin, and his brother Jugnu. While the older generation is immigrant, the younger generation is born and bred in England. The characters accordingly embody the different cultures represented in the novel: Shamas, his children, and his brother have adopted a Western lifestyle, drink alcohol, and dress in a European fashion, whereas his wife is a conservative Muslim whose worldview is defined by the Qu'ran. She adheres to the values and virtues she knows from her homeland and struggles to uphold a lifestyle as close as possible to that of her former life in Pakistan, praying several times a day, only wearing saris, and never leaving the house, for she cannot speak English. The central action of the novel takes place in the first year after the death of two lovers, Chanda and Shamas's brother Jugnu, both of whom were victims of an honor killing carried out prior to the onset of the novel. The murder was committed by Chanda's fanatical Muslim brothers who would not tolerate her and Jugnu's cohabitation as an unmarried couple. Attempting now to discover the truth about the lovers' deaths, and to come to terms with their different ways of mourning, the bereaved family slowly but surely breaks apart.

Both the quotations in the epigraph to this chapter and the brief synopsis of Aslam's present-tense novel reveal that *Maps for Lost Lovers* qualifies as a type of narrative which Roy Sommer (2013, 156) identifies as an "intercultural narrative," that is, a "fictional narrative that explicitly or implicitly stages intercultural encounters of characters from diverse cultural, ethnic, and religious backgrounds." In light of Sommer's conceptualization of the typical character constellation and plot pattern of intercultural narratives, the typical setting of these texts can be construed as what Marie-Louise Pratt (1992, 26) refers to as a "contact zone," or, more precisely, a "space in which peoples geographically and historically separated come into contact with each other and establish ongoing relations."[2] In *Maps for Lost Lovers*, the Pakistani diaspora in the town the immigrants call "Dasht-e-Tanhaii" represents such a contact zone. Sommer further argues that the attribute *intercultural* can also be ascribed to narratives which show "the clash of different, subculture-specific values and beliefs within a single cultural, ethnic or religious community (e.g., between first- and second-generation immigrants in a multicultural society)" (2013, 156). This, too, is the case in Aslam's novel, for Shamas and his children have a much more open and tolerant attitude toward English culture than does his wife Kaukab.[3] According to Sommer, the ways in which intercultural narratives orchestrate such cultural differences "foster intercultural understanding in the broadest sense" (2013, 156). He therefore concludes that this genre "construct[s] cultural difference in fictional worlds in order to deconstruct, or rather encourage their readers to deconstruct, it" (Sommer 2013, 156–157).

Sommer's definition reflects a contextualist approach to intercultural narrative.[4] Arguing in favor of an "intercultural narratology" that "combine[s] structuralist descriptions of textual features with cognitive insights into narrative comprehension, within an overall interpretive framework of intercultural concepts" (Sommer 2007, 62), he focuses not only on textual aspects, but also on

---

[2] Although Pratt's definition refers to encounters in an imperial context, the term can nowadays apply to any place hosting diverse cultures such as multicultural cities, airports, plane cabins, or railway carriages to name but a few examples (cf. Reichl 2002, 41).

[3] Aslam's novel consequently does not "set[] up an East vs West dichotomy in which a normative white Britishness is contrasted with a traditional South Asian identity," but instead thematizes aspects of hybridity by staging "a more specifically British-Pakistani identity" (Bhanot 2019, 206). According to David Waterman (2015, 126; cf. also 2010, 27), "[t]he contact zone of [the Pakistani] community-in-exile [therefore] becomes a zone of friction due to the differing worldviews and ways of negotiating modernity amongst its members." For a similar argument, cf. also Pesso-Miquel 2011, 128: "[Aslam's] portrayal of the Indian diaspora seems to marginalise the usual East/West oppositions, as if [the author] had aimed at turning England and Englishness into an invisible, relatively irrelevant world, to focus instead on the staging of communalist conflicts between various groups of immigrants, all vying to shape, control and inflect the diasporic experience."

[4] In this respect, Sommer's account of intercultural narrative marks itself off from other, more text-centered, definitions. Tom Kindt's (2004) explication of the term, for example, focuses exclusively on textual aspects and hence completely ignores contextualist processes such as the production and reception of intercultural narratives.

aspects of production and reception.⁵ He claims, for example, that assumptions about authorial reader constructions frequently play an essential role in the analyses of intercultural novels (cf. Sommer 2007, 73), because the audience an author has in mind when writing may well influence the narrative design of the text:

> Certainly, the author's choice of an intended audience has no direct bearing whatsoever on the actual, i.e. real, audience – whether a novel reaches intended readers is not for the author (or narratologists) to decide. It seems very likely, however, that the choice of a particular intended audience would leave its traces in the preference for certain narrative features and strategies, e.g. regarding the translatability of linguistic and cultural concepts, the functions of intertextual references or the dramaturgical design of a story. (Sommer 2007, 74)

Based on this argument, Sommer identifies different reader constructions for two subgenres of intercultural narrative: the transcultural or cosmopolitan novel and the multicultural novel. While the former "facilitate[s] a variety of reader constructions and thus offer[s] a high degree of cultural 'translatability' or compatibility with different cultural contexts and traditions," the diversity of the latter's intended audience is more restricted, as the multicultural narrative mainly strives for authenticity (Sommer 2007, 74).⁶ Addressing a Western readership to whom it introduces Pakistani culture, *Maps for Lost Lovers* can be classified as a transcultural novel (see especially Chapter 9.2).

With Sommer (2013, 155–156), one may assume that the "aesthetic experience" of reading intercultural fiction encourages readers "to develop what one might call an 'intercultural mind,' that is, a mind-set that seeks to overcome the limitations inherent in ethnocentric worldviews and works towards intercultural dialogue and understanding." In this sense, intercultural narrative in general and transcultural narrative in particular can assuredly prompt readers "whose cultural background is significantly different from that of one or several characters in the narrative" toward an "[i]ntercultural reading [experience]" entailing an emotional as well as cognitive involvement with the culture(s) represented in these texts (Sommer 2013, 157).

How, then, does Aslam's transcultural narrative in *Maps for Lost Lovers* allow us "to adopt, albeit temporarily, the other's point of view and to engage

---

5 Sommer's (2007) "defence" of an intercultural narratology is particularly directed against a series of essays co-written by Tom Kindt and Hans-Harald Müller (2003a, 2003b, 2004), who deny the usefulness of context-oriented approaches to narrative in general and to intercultural narrative theory in particular.
6 For a detailed distinction between transcultural and multicultural writing, cf. Sommer 2001.

cognitively and emotionally with his or her perspective" (Sommer 2013, 156)? How does the author's particular style of writing, which integrates present-tense narration, internal focalization, and an abundant use of tropes, contribute to this effect? To answer these questions, we first need to clarify the concept of narrative empathy.

In a series of studies developing a theory of narrative empathy, Suzanne Keen (2007, 142) construes the concept as a rhetorical strategy which helps authors to "direct an emotional transaction through a fictional work aimed at a particular audience, not necessarily including every reader who happens upon the text."[7] She proposes a model of narrative empathy that includes three strategic varieties: (1) bounded strategic empathy, (2) ambassadorial strategic empathy, and (3) broadcast strategic empathy. Bounded strategic empathy, "occurs within an in-group," meaning that it results from "experiences of mutuality" and causes readers to share certain feelings and emotions with "familiar others" (Keen 2007, 142). Readers consequently do not have any difficulties engaging cognitively as well as emotionally with the characters of a fictional narrative working toward bounded strategic empathy as long as they belong to the group forming the text's "empathetic circle" (Keen 2007, 142); conversely, if readers are outsiders to this specific group, the narrative may prevent them from feeling empathy for its characters. Ambassadorial strategic empathy, by contrast, is directed at "chosen others with the aim of cultivating their empathy for the in-group, often to a specific end" (Keen 2007, 142). This variety of strategic empathizing accordingly tries to include readers who do not belong to the in-group presented in the narrative, inviting them to adopt the in-group's overall stance and enter the empathetic circle. Finally, broadcast strategic empathy "calls upon every reader to feel with members of a group," irrespective of whether he or she belongs to the in-group or the out-group, by emphasizing characteristics common to both groups such as "common vulnerabilities and hopes" (Keen 2007, 142).

Proceeding from Keen's theory of narrative empathy, I will argue in this chapter that Aslam's novel fosters intercultural understanding and dialogue by inviting Western readers to enter the empathetic circle. In reading *Maps for Lost Lovers* as a typical example of a transcultural novel imbued with ambassadorial strategic empathy, I will investigate the various narrative strategies Aslam deploys to encourage out-group readers to adopt the in-group's stance and thus nurture what Sommer would refer to as their "intercultural mind." In this con-

---

7 Keen has further elaborated on the concept of narrative empathy in a series of articles (cf. Keen 2006, 2008, 2010).

nection, I will show how the novel's use of tense alternation, its multifunctional use of the fictional present, its narrative perspective, and its "much-noted poetic language" (Rupp 2018, 111) interact to bring about this effect.

The quotations from *Maps for Lost Lovers* at the beginning of this chapter already allude to the unique spatiotemporal structure of Aslam's novel: Since the imaginary space of Pakistan always seems to be present in the characters' here-and-now, the narrative evokes a timespace in which, despite Aslam's temporalizing tense-switching, past and present are hard to distinguish. Aslam's 'narrative of reminiscence' foregrounds the characters' memories of their past, exhibiting a specific type of narrative dynamics which I have referred to as the *topochrone* (see Chapter 5.8): a slow narration in which the representation of space outweighs that of time. Within this topochrone, narrative time functions metaphorically, as it is always attached to a detailed depiction of narrative space. Rather than presenting a coherent successive development of events, *Maps for Lost Lovers* concentrates on showing readers how the various immigrant characters with a Pakistani background experience their new environment in England and how this space causes homesickness and nostalgia, as it constantly triggers memories of their individual pasts and their home country. In Aslam's storyworld time seems to pass not so much physically as mentally, in the minds of the characters, whose thoughts still cling to their former life in Pakistan.

9.2 Addressing an Out-Group Readership: Tense-Switching and the Communicative Situation of Aslam's Novel

Before examining the topochronic structure of Aslam's present-tense narrative, we must analyze the narrative situation of *Maps for Lost Lovers*. This will indicate how the novel addresses a Western readership that represents an out-group of the empathetic circle formed by Aslam's Pakistani characters. The gradual breakup of Shamas's family after the murder of the lovers Chanda and Jugnu is conveyed to the reader through the voice of a narrator who is not involved in the story. This type of heterodiegetic narration is combined with variable internal focalization and multiperspectivity, allowing readers to access the minds of different characters.[8] Whenever the story takes place in the characters' here-

---

[8] According to Vera and Ansgar Nünning (2000a, 42; italics in the original), Aslam's novel would qualify as a multiperspective text using multiperspective focalization rather than narration: "Multiperspektivität liegt [...] nicht nur dann vor, wenn das Geschehen von mehr als

and-now, the narrative is written in the present tense. However, the narrative is interwoven with a great number of analepses, offering readers the opportunity to glimpse into moments of the characters' pasts. During such flashbacks, the narrative temporarily switches from the present to the past tense. In this respect, *Maps for Lost Lovers* closely resembles *Oryx and Crake* because Aslam, like Atwood (see Chapter 8.2), temporalizes fictional tenses, using tense-switching to provide spatiotemporal orientation within the storyworld. This, as we shall see in the next section of this chapter, is particularly relevant for the topochrone the narrative produces in relation to the female protagonist Kaukab.

At first glance, the combination of a covert heterodiegetic narrator with multiple focalizers points to a reflector-mode narrative (cf. Fludernik 1996, 252–253; see also Chapter 5.2); yet the communicative situation underlying Aslam's text suggests that *Maps for Lost Lovers* does not qualify as a typical example of figural narrative, but rather integrates features of both figural and authorial narrative (*sensu* Stanzel). Consider the following example:

> December; and today was the last day of the trial. [...] The outcome was what most people expected. [...] Though of course there were some people who thought the verdict would go the other way. Someone even floated a rumour that Chanda's parents had paid a young man to say that he and his girlfriend had bought Chanda and Jugnu's passports from them in Pakistan and had entered Britain with them. It is said that Chanda's parents had paid a substantial amount of money—the amount varies from person to person—to the young man for telling that lie to the police. But he had taken the money and disappeared, never arriving at the police station [...]. (*MLL*, 285)

Here, the novel presents us with an external perspective on the narrative events, as none of the characters could plausibly serve as the center of consciousness

---

einem extra- oder intradiegetischen Erzähler geschildert wird. Vielmehr sind neben diesem Typus des multiperspektivisch *erzählten* Textes auch solche Erzählungen multiperspektivisch, in denen die Innenweltdarstellung auf mehrere Figuren ausgedehnt wird und in denen multiple bzw. variable interne Fokalisierung (*multiple/variable focalization*) vorherrscht. Der Typus des multiperspektivisch *fokalisierten* Erzähltextes liegt dann vor, wenn mehrere Figuren alternierend als Reflektorfiguren (*sensu* Stanzel) bzw. interne Fokalisierungsinstanzen (*sensu* Genette) fungieren." ["Multiperspectivity occurs not only if the events are depicted by more than one extradiegetic or intradiegetic narrator. Rather, as well as this type of multiperspective texts *narrated* from various perspectives, there are other narratives that qualify as multiperspective texts as they extend the representation of character consciousness to several characters by making use of multiple or variable internal focalization. This type of multiperspectivity, which consists in multiperspective *focalization*, occurs in cases in which several characters alternately serve as reflector figures (*sensu* Stanzel) or internal focalizers (*sensu* Genette)." (My translation)]

9.2 Tense-Switching and the Communicative Situation of Aslam's Novel —— 201

through which the events are perceived. There are two indicators for this lack of a "character-bound focalizer" (Bal 1985 [1980], 104): First, the passage informs us about the various opinions on the trial concerning the honor killing of Chanda and Jugnu, and we learn that most members of the community of Dasht-e-Tanhaii had expected the actual outcome of the trial, whereas others had hoped for a different verdict. The sentence "It is said that Chanda's parents had paid a substantial amount of money—the amount varies from person to person—to the young man for telling that lie to the police," moreover, implies that the narrator here reproduces an opinion prevalent in the in-group, the inhabitants of Dasht-e-Tanhaii. Secondly, the passage is written in the past tense, which suggests that rather than gaining an immediate insight into the mind of any one of the characters who experiences the narrative events in the present moment, we are confronted with the perspective of a narrator who, located on the discourse level, is not involved in the narrative events and therefore has a comprehensive overview of the scene.[9]

The example also illustrates the strategy of tense-switching to which Aslam resorts in order to signal temporary shifts in narrative perspective. Unlike the shifts between the characters' individual presents and pasts, however, the tense changes here are related not to time leaps within the storyworld but to a change in focus on either the story or discourse level of the narrative text. Aslam's novel consistently combines the present tense with the internal perspective of the characters, who are located within the diegesis. Passages which refer to the present of the storyworld, but are narrated in the past tense can, therefore, be seen to offer the point of view of an extradiegetic narrator. In this sense, Aslam's tenses deploy not only temporalization (tense-switching following a pattern related to time), but also detemporalization (tense-switching following a pattern related to non-temporal aspects of narrative).[10] The aspect in question here is the distinction between the narrative's "character-bound focalizers" (Bal 1985

---

9 Another, longer passage of the novel which reveals distinctive features of an authorial narrative situation is the third last chapter "A Leaf from the Book of Fates," which relates how Chanda's brothers Barra and Chotta murder their sister and her lover Jugnu (cf. *MLL*, 343–372). Like the extract which I have analyzed in the previous paragraph, this chapter exhibits an omniscient narrator who allows readers to get alternating insights into Barra's, Chanda's, Chotta's, and Jugnu's minds as well as foreshadows specific events in order to create tension for the reader (consider, e.g., sentences like "He didn't know that he was being watched" [*MLL*, 345], or "When Jugnu knocked on Kaukab's door—soon after being awoken by the peacocks, a few hours before he died—she was not in the house, though the light was on" [*MLL*, 354]). What is more, this chapter is also entirely written in the past tense.
10 For the distinction between temporalization and detemporalization, see Chapter 4.2.

[1980], 104) on the story level and its "non-character-bound focalizer" (Bal 1985 [1980], 105), that is, its narrator-focalizer, on the discourse level.[11]

In addition to the parts in which the narrative events are presented from the narrator's external perspective, *Maps for Lost Lovers* contains further passages that are indicative of an authorial (rather than a figural) narrative situation, inasmuch as they draw attention to Aslam's intended readership and thus to the communicative scenario of the novel. Even though readers do not get any information concerning the *persona* of the anonymous narrator, this is not true of the implied narratee. The narrator's discourse clearly suggests that he is addressing a Western readership. *Maps for Lost Lovers* features several strategies which create cultural alterity by presenting Pakistan as a foreign country and Islam as a foreign religion. At the same time, in his role as a linguistic as well as cultural mediator, the narrator constantly seeks to render Muslim culture more intelligible to Western readers.

This becomes most obvious if we focus on the character of Kaukab. Taking into account that, apart from a few words, Shamas's wife does not speak English (cf. *MLL*, 98–99), it must be assumed that she speaks either Urdu or the regional language Punjabi when she talks to members of her family or to the Pakistani community of Dasht-e-Tanhaii. However, since the narrative presents these conversations in English, the dialogue has evidently been dubbed by the narrator.[12] Yet the narrator often inserts Urdu expressions into his English discourse (e.g. "*aloo bhurta*," "*turka*," "*zarda*" [*MLL*, 37], "*dahl*" [*MLL*, 40], "*dhoti*" [*MLL*, 344; italics in the original], etc.). Functioning as "ethnic markers" (Reichl 2000, 64), these linguistic elements remind readers that the culture presented by Aslam's text deviates from their own, creating a cultural distance between flesh-and-blood readers and fictional characters. The effect is emphasized by the italicization of these expressions, which marks them visually and sets them apart from the English text (cf. Reichl 2002, 79).[13]

---

11 Using Stanzel's (1995 [1979], 83–84) terminology, one could argue that Aslam here uses the strategy of detemporalization in order to indicate shifts between the narrative's various internal perspectives (*Innenperspektive*) and its external perspective (*Außenperspektive*).
12 Susanne Reichl (2002, 102) defines "dubbing" as "a technique by which the language that a character would naturally speak on the story level of the novel is replaced by the language of narration, so that the reader on the discourse level understands what this particular character says."
13 Although the Indo-Aryan languages referred to in *Maps for Lost Lovers* – Urdu and Punjabi – use Perso-Arabic script (cf. Katzner 1995 [1977], 179) and the Gurmukhi alphabet respectively (cf. Katzner 1995 [1977], 181), the words are transcribed here into the Latin alphabet. According to Reichl (2002, 79n150), this kind of transcription is a pragmatic measure to facili-

There are different ways in which the narrator enables readers to understand the meaning of these foreign-language insertions. Without explicitly translating them, he first contextualizes the words, leaving it to the reader to infer their meaning from the given context.[14] This is, for instance, the case when the narrative uses words from the semantic fields of food or clothing like *"pilau* rice," *"shami* kebab" (*MLL*, 298), or *"shalwar-kameez"* (*MLL*, 167; italics in the original). As the exact signification of these terms is not important for readers' overall understanding of the text, they function primarily as elements indicating the cultural background of the novel (cf. Gymnich 2007, 71).

Wherever the foreign-language insertions might prevent a Western readership from understanding the text, however, the narrator intervenes as a translator. In this role he not only translates the words into English, which would be considered "glossing" (Ashcroft et al. 1989, 61–64) or "[c]ushioning" (Zabus 1996, 34), but also explains the concepts behind these foreign expressions, which often have no equivalent in the readers' culture. At the very beginning of the novel, for example, readers learn that, "in the part of Pakistan that [Shamas] **is** from, there are five seasons in a year, not four [...]: *Mausam-e-Sarma, Bahar, Mausam-e-Garma, Barsat, Khizan.* Winter, Spring, Summer, Monsoon, Autumn" (*MLL*, 5; italics in the original; my emphasis). Elsewhere in the narrative, readers learn about the divorce of a female character: "He [i.e. the husband] **said** the word *talaaq* three times: I divorce thee, I divorce thee, I divorce thee." (*MLL*, 162; italics in the original; my emphasis) With this statement, the narrator firstly supplies Western readers with a literal translation of the word *talaaq* and secondly informs them that, if a man wants to divorce his wife in Islam, all he has to do is repeat a single word three times (although this, to my knowledge, is not a truth universally accepted).

What is striking about the narratorial explanations which accompany the translations of foreign words in Aslam's narrative is that they camouflage themselves by means of their choice of tense (see my emphasis in the above quotes). Embedded in the thoughts or memories of the character currently serving as focalizer, they usually deploy the tense that refers to that character's momentary state of mind. Accordingly, the narrator's introduction of the five Pakistani

---

tate the printing of English-speaking intercultural novels, as well as an attempt to narrow "the gap between the languages and, implicitly, the cultures involved."

14 According to Chantal Zabus (1996, 35), contextualization is a "method of shadowing" which "consists in surrounding the indigenous word with a halo, an area of immediate context that involves the reader in some sort of guessing game," thus allowing him or her to get at least a rough idea about the meaning of the foreign expression.

seasons is written in the present tense because it occurs in a scene in which Shamas is watching the first snow of the year (see also Chapter 9.3). The narrator's elucidation concerning a divorce in Islam, by contrast, makes use of the past tense as it is inserted into the memories of the character Suraya, who remembers how her intoxicated husband divorced her by accident. Thanks to their variable correlation in this respect, these explanations remain subtle and can easily be mistaken for the current thoughts or reminiscences of the character-focalizer. Western readers are presented with information on Muslim culture that may be new to them and, for instance, change their understanding of Islam, yet these narratorial insertions do not disturb the reading experience – the illusion of perceiving the narrative events through a specific character's consciousness.

Occasionally, however, Aslam's predominantly covert narrator makes use of his prerogative of narratorial intrusion. That is to say, he sometimes provides readers with supplementary information about Pakistani culture which exceeds the thoughts and feelings of the characters. For instance, readers are told that

> Pakistan **is** a poor country, a harsh and disastrously unjust land, its history a book full of sad stories, and life **is** a trial if not a punishment for most of the people born there: millions of its sons and daughters have managed to find footholds all around the globe in their search for livelihood and a semblance of dignity. Roaming the planet looking for solace, they've settled in small towns that **make** them feel smaller still, and in cities that **have** tall buildings and even taller loneliness. (*MLL*, 9; my emphasis)

The narrator provides these details regarding the fictive immigrants and their country of origin after recounting how Shamas accompanies his friend Kiran to her place. She has previously approached him to ask if he could help her to lift up her father, who has fallen out of bed during the night. At first glance, the use of the present tense (see my emphasis) suggests that this excerpt again qualifies as an instance of internal focalization, for we have seen that authorial passages in Aslam's novel are usually written in the past tense. A closer look, however, reveals that the extract does not feature any strategies of consciousness representation, so we must assume that it does not reflect the thoughts of either Shamas or Kiran, but qualifies as a narratorial comment.

The narrative here features what Gérard Genette (1980 [1972], 195) has called "paralepsis," that is, a temporary change in focalization which consists of "giving information that should [in principle] be left aside" in the code of variable internal focalization governing the entire narrative. We should therefore think of this intermittent shift from the dominant mode of focalization (i.e. the characters' perspectives) to that of narration (i.e. the narrator's perspective) as a rhetorical means that serves to acquaint Western readers with some background facts about Pakistan. This reading is corroborated by the observation that the passage features a transmodal rather than referential use of present-tense narration. The fictional present here no longer refers to the consciousness of one of the characters. Instead, it fulfills an explanatory function enabling the narrator to state timeless facts about the diegetic universe.[15]

What is even more important, however, is that by temporarily violating the novel's fixed correlation of narrative perspective and tense usage, Aslam's choice of the gnomic present in this situation emphasizes the phatic connection between the narrator and the novel's implied Western readership. Attentive readers may thus notice that these elaborations on Pakistan do not represent any of the characters' thoughts and, accordingly, construe them as an invitation to engage with the characters' culture: In this way, too, Aslam's use of the fictional present draws the reader into the novel's empathetic circle. Present-tense narration in *Maps for Lost Lovers* is, however, not restricted to its referential and transmodal uses. The next section of this chapter will show how Aslam's present tense also serves a rhetorical purpose, enabling the author to generate a topochrone which is of considerable importance for the novel's endeavor to facilitate intercultural understanding and dialogue.

9.3 Foregrounding Narrative Space: The Topochronic Dynamics of Aslam's Narrative

Aslam's novel exhibits the conventional spatiotemporal dynamics of intercultural narratives concerned with migration and diaspora. While England constitutes a real, physical place within the fictive storyworld, Pakistan represents an imagined space which exists only in the characters' memories, yet still "shapes their daily life" (Lemke 2008, 172). For the South-Asian immigrants, Corinna Assmann (2018, 148) argues, "reality in England is overwritten by their longing for home and a feeling of displacement." Accordingly, *Maps for Lost Lovers* features many flashbacks to the characters' home country. Triggered by their current living environment, these memories often go hand in hand with passages of description which specify the narrative setting and reveal the characters' emotional reactions to it. In reflecting the different ways in which the protago-

---

15 Following Elene Tatishvili (2011, 4), one could conceive of this instance of present-tense usage as a "suprafictional" or else "supradiegetic" present, which "suggests that the situation it renders does not belong solely to the fictional world and its temporal limits, but equally applies to the heterodiegetic narrator's [and thus also the narratee's] present."

nists Shamas and Kaukab cope with the dialectics of longing and belonging in their newly adopted country, these spatial descriptions correlate with diverging linguistic styles and patterns of tense usage. *Maps for Lost Lovers* consequently evokes different timespaces, each of which is contingent upon the character who currently serves as the focalizer.

At the beginning of the novel, readers are confronted with a timespace focalized through Shamas in a poetic description of his figure standing at the front door of his house, watching the first snow of the season fall from the sky: "Shamas stands in the open door and watches the earth, the magnet that it is, pulling snowflakes out of the sky towards itself." (*MLL*, 3) Much research on *Maps for Lost Lovers* has discussed Aslam's poetic language;[16] yet none has analyzed his use of the present tense in this context.[17] The silence about the fictional present is surprising, given that this strategy largely contributes to the defamiliarizing effect brought about by Aslam's highly metaphoric depiction of the narrative setting. The very first sentence of the novel already leads us to believe that the present tense serves a referential function: "Shamas stands in the open door." Of course, this is not wrong, for, as we have seen in the previous section of this chapter, Aslam combines the fictional present with internal focalization in order to refer to the here-and-now of the characters' consciousness: in the present tense, we get a direct insight into Shamas's mind. As we read on, however, our referential understanding of the opening scene is disturbed. The verb *watch* makes us expect a referential object: Shamas could, for example, be watching the sky, the street, the snow, the tree in front of his house, you name it. Yet the verb is followed by a metonymy, instead: Shamas watches "the earth," which can be read as a synecdoche, more specifically a *totum pro parte*, for the referential noun *ground*. Used in conjunction with this trope, the present tense functions as an ancillary narrative strategy indicative of poetry rather than narrative.[18]

The effect is reinforced by Aslam's use of the simple rather than progressive present tense, even when writing about occurrences unfolding at the moment of utterance – after all, we would usually say "Shamas is standing in the open door watching the ground." Jonathan Culler (2014b, 233) identifies such in-

---

16 Cf. e.g. Ahmed 2015, 163–165; Chambers 2011, 180–182; 2019, 84–87; Childs and Green 2013, 110–111; McCulloch 2012, 68, 99–100 and 105–106; Moore 2009, 7–8; Pataki 2014, 82–84; Pesso-Miquel 2011, 141–146; Upstone 2010, 102–103; and Weedon 2012, 34–36.
17 Although Peter Childs and James Green (2013, 110) do briefly mention Aslam's use of the present tense, they do not set it in relation to the novel's poetic language.
18 For a detailed discussion of present-tense usage in the genre of poetry, cf. Culler 2014a, 166–176; 2014b; 2015, 283–295; Harvey 2006, 77–78; Langer 1953, 260–275; and Wright 1974.

stances of the simple present as a distinctive feature of poetry: "Generally, to note *occurrences* in the present, we use the present progressive tense: *I am walking*." (Culler 2014b, 233; italics in the original) Therefore, he continues, "[w]hen we encounter the unmarked non-progressive present tense with occurrences, we know immediately that we are dealing with a poem" (Culler 2014b, 233; cf. also Culler 2014a, 166; 2015, 287–288). While not wholly accurate – Aslam's novel is a case in point that novels are also written in the simple present – Culler's statement nevertheless suggests that, in the opening scene of *Maps for Lost Lovers*, Aslam's use of the present tense is double-coded, pointing to the current state of Shamas's mind (referential function), and at the same time defamiliarizing the narrative discourse by evoking a notion of poetry (thematic function).

The rest of the opening paragraph continues in the same manner: a metaphor equates the earth with a magnet attracting precipitation, a simile compares snowflakes to "feathers sinking in water" (*MLL*, 3), the fog from the lake nearby Shamas's house is portrayed as incense in the air, and the wooden jetty becomes a xylophone (cf. *MLL*, 3). And all these tropes use the simple present, reminding readers of the lyric present they know from poems. With its highly poetic language, the opening scene of Aslam's novel creates a subjective, even idiosyncratic image of the storyworld: Although the story is actually set in an industrial town in Northern England,[19] readers get the impression of a pastoral scene in calm and peaceful countryside (cf. Chambers 2011, 180; 2019, 84–85; McCulloch 2012, 87; Rupp 2018, 111–112).

According to Claire Chambers (2011, 180; 2019, 84–85), Aslam further defamiliarizes the setting of his novel by using a considerable number of "similes and metaphors [...] deriving predominantly from the natural and domestic spheres of Pakistan" to describe the diasporic community of Dasht-e-Tanhaii (2011, 180). She illustrates her point by discussing Shamas's perception of the wintry scene as he follows Kiran to her house (cf. *MLL*, 8). Chambers argues that, even though Shamas should have become accustomed to snow after living in England for such a long time, he still experiences it as unfamiliar (cf. 2011, 180). He perceives the snow-covered landscape "as though sealed behind glass" (*MLL*, 8) and compares this strange view with imagery he knows from his home country to render the experience more familiar. In his imagination, he thus "heat[s] up the freezing terrain" (Chambers 2011, 180) by matching the dry

---

19 Claire Chambers (2019, 79) argues in this context that Aslam's "mythical Dasht-e-Tanhaii bears close resemblance to Huddersfield and Bradford" because both of "[t]hese West Yorkshire urban spaces are home to large populations of South Asian migrants, particularly from rural areas in Azad Jammu and Kashmir and the Pakistani Punjab."

leaves of the field maples with South-Asian gold jewellery, the broken wires of the telephone pole with candles, his respiration of the cold air with the speedy breath of a hummingbird, and the cracking sound of his footsteps on the frozen grass with the sound his wife produces when preparing spices for cooking.[20]

Chambers's close reading of the scene reveals that, for Shamas, England is a real, material place in the world, whereas Pakistan has transformed into an imaginary space which only exists in his mind. In the timespace of Shamas's consciousness, Aslam's correlation of poetic language and present-tense narration maps the memories of Pakistan, steeped in the hues of nostalgia and triggered by exotic tropes, onto the fictional present, signaling to readers that his home country is still relevant for Shamas. In this sense the novel "'Pakistanizes' Great Britain" (Moraru 2018, §18), its internal focalization even conveying the impression that it is actually set in Pakistan rather than England (cf. Lemke 2008, 173).

But Shamas's nostalgia does not prevent him from adapting to British culture, as becomes evident in the scene when he remembers his first sight of snow:

> Perspective tricks the eyes and makes the snowflakes falling in the far distance appear as though they are falling slower than those nearby, and he stands in the open door with an arm stretched out to receive the small light pieces on his hand. A habit as old as his arrival in this country; he has always greeted the season's first snow in this manner, the flakes losing their whiteness on the palm of his hand to become clear wafers of ice before melting to water—crystals of snow transformed into a monsoon raindrop. (*MLL*, 5)

The melting snowflakes in his hand trigger memories of his home country, reminding Shamas that, "[a]mong the innumerable other losses, to come to England was to lose a season" (*MLL*, 5), namely the monsoon. But he has developed a strategy to compensate for this loss: he catches the first snowflakes of winter to melt in his hand and remind him of monsoon rain.[21] This little habit is repre-

---

[20] The argument that Aslam's novel defamiliarizes England by "extoici[zing]" (Ilott 2015, 78) this Western country constantly reoccurs in the secondary literature on *Maps for Lost Lovers*; synonymous terms mentioned in this context are "orientalization" (Ahmed 2015, 163–164; Geçikli 2015; McCulloch 2012, 78), "Pakistanization" (Moraru 2018, §18), and "tropicalization" (Pesso-Miquel 2011, 128).

[21] According to Corinna Assmann (2018, 147), Shamas's "personal ritual [of] commemorat[ing] the monsoon season [...] ties in with the community's many ways of remembering and protecting the memory of a home that is lost." One of the immigrants' most striking practices she discusses in this context is their "renaming [of] the streets of their neighbourhood to recall place names from home" (Assmann 2018, 147).

sentative of the way in which Shamas shields himself from the emotional distress of homesickness: He creates spaces within his new home which he can associate with his old. For example, he has painted the rooms in his house in England in exactly the same colors of the rooms in his house back in Pakistan (cf. *MLL*, 6) and named his Urdu bookshop after the name of a boat he built as a teenager – *Safeena* (cf. *MLL*, 137). By bringing Pakistan to England in his mind, Shamas can accept his new home.

While Shamas is nostalgic without longing for his life in Pakistan, his wife Kaukab suffers from serious homesickness and experiences a severe "cultural trauma" that hinders her from "adapt[ing] to [her] new situation" in England (Assmann 2018, 149). The novel shows this difference by creating a new and different timespace whenever Kaukab serves as focalizer. Unlike her husband, Kaukab does not explore her newly adopted country because she believes that "there's nothing for her out there in Dasht-e-Tanhaii, to notice or be interested in. Everything is here in this house. Every beloved absence is present here" (*MLL*, 66) – words that make explicit how Kaukab stays at home primarily to avoid contact with English (more specifically white) people, and only leaves the house if it is really necessary. Within the confines of her house, she can blank out most aspects of Western culture, with the result that the building has become, for her, "[a]n oasis—albeit a haunted one—in the middle of the Desert of Loneliness" (*MLL*, 66).[22]

It comes as no surprise, then, that the scenes presented from Kaukab's perspective lack lengthy descriptions of the British setting but are rich in flashbacks to Pakistan. A representative example is the scene in which Kaukab remembers how she met Shamas for the first time (cf. *MLL*, 67). The first sentence of this flashback illustrates how Aslam's narrative distinguishes between Kaukab's present and her past by means of temporalizing tense-switching: "She [...] **watches** from the window as [Shamas] **walks** away between the twenty maples, her husband—who, all those years ago, very nearly wasn't her husband." (*MLL*, 67; my emphasis) The opening phrases, referring to Kaukab's here-and-now, are written in the present tense ("watches," "walks"), but the relative clause already introduces a memory, and the text here switches to the past tense ("wasn't"), which is then maintained throughout the paragraph. In addition to tense alternation, the spatiotemporal shift from the fictional present of England to a past moment in Pakistan is indicated in the adverbial phrases

---

22 Cf. also Assmann 2018, 152: "For Kaukab, the family home is a sanctuary in an unfamiliar, confusing world, a place where time stands still and change is prevented."

"all those years ago" (*MLL*, 67) and "on a certain monsoon Thursday" (*MLL*, 67) that occur later in the passage.

This is different when the narrative switches back from the diegetic past to the diegetic present, where we encounter Kaukab on the point of calling her grown-up son Ujala. But the doorbell rings and she opens it to a white flower deliverer. The flashback ends appropriately with a blank line, after which the narrative proceeds as follows: "She [i.e. Kaukab] **is** about to telephone Ujala's voice, but the doorbell **rings**: she **opens** the door [...] and **finds** a white man on the doorstep. He **holds** a bouquet of Madonna lilies [...]" (*MLL*, 70; my emphasis) As at the beginning of the flashback, the spatiotemporal shift is signaled by a referential use of tense, for the text has switched back to the present tense (see my emphasis). Here, however, the narrative refrains from providing any adverbial phrases that specify the spatial setting, which once more emphasizes Kaukab's disinterest in England. The timespace evoked in her perspective revokes the timespace generated in Shamas's. For Kaukab, it is not Pakistan but England that represents an imaginary space. Missing Pakistan so dreadfully, she continually thinks herself back – which naturally prevents her from becoming acquainted with the English culture and language.

Focusing predominantly on the representation of space and the characters' reaction toward their surroundings, *Maps for Lost Lovers* generates what I have referred to as the *topochrone* (see Chapter 5.8) – that is, it yields a specific form of progression which foregrounds the aspect of space over that of time. As my previous discussion of the protagonists' diverging perceptions of England and Pakistan has shown, Aslam's novel abounds in lengthy descriptions of the setting (Shamas's perspective) as well as extensive flashbacks triggered by this same space (Kaukab's perspective). Both strategies prevent the main plot from unfolding and slow down the narrative pace. Indeed, the foregrounding of space is so prominent in the novel's topochrone that a consistent and coherent presentation of its events seems to play only a tangential role.

The topochronic structure of Aslam's narrative is exemplified in a scene depicting the generational conflict in the protagonists' family. Kaukab has spent an entire day in the kitchen preparing a large dinner for her children, who visit her in the evening. During this meal, the family discusses the status of women in Pakistan, and friction arises between the disparate opinions of the group. While the children take the view that women are suppressed in their parents' home country, Kaukab strongly disagrees and defends Islam. The situation escalates into a fresh dispute in which the three children reproach their mother for her past mistakes in trying to force them (by quite radical means) to preserve a traditional Pakistani way of life. For instance, she mixed bromide into her youngest son's supper after a Muslim cleric had told her that it was a holy salt that would calm Ujala down and make him more obedient (cf. *MLL* 311–313). Similarly, she attempted to coerce her daughter into returning to her violent and abusive husband when Mah-Jabin wanted to divorce him (cf. e.g. *MLL* 99, 117–119).

Since Kaukab has actually hoped for a happy family reunion, she is hurt by her children's reproaches. Unable to endure the fraught situation any longer, she rushes to her bedroom:

> Kaukab leaves the room and hurries upstairs, wishing to be alone. She closes the door to her bedroom and locks it, getting into bed with the intention of staying there for only a while but opening the door more than an hour and a half later. She must get downstairs quickly, she tells herself as she steps onto the landing, because otherwise Mah-Jabin would start doing the washing up [...].
>
> She comes downstairs to find Shamas bringing the chairs back into the kitchen. The dining table is already in its usual place. "Have Stella and Charag gone?" she asks. He gives a nod, and when she asks him where Mah-Jabin and Ujala are he tells her that they have gone too: "They all drove away together. Mah-Jabin knocked on your door before leaving but you didn't answer." (*MLL*, 335)

If we assume that Aslam's characters represent the mimetic type modeled on the behavior of real people (cf. Phelan 1989, 2), the passage displays several inconsistencies concerning their behavior. If Kaukab only intends to remain in her room for a couple of minutes, why does she only leave it an hour and a half later? What happens in between that causes her to change her initial plan and makes her stay on her own, although she knows that the entire family is downstairs waiting for her? It seems very important to her to put things right with her children, at least this is what she tells her husband later on: "I have things to say to Mah-Jabin [...] and I have things to say to Ujala. I hadn't expected a happy farewell but at least a tender and affectionate one." (*MLL*, 335) If reconciliation with her children really matters to her, why does she not go downstairs, apologize for her behavior, and try to sort things out? And what about Mah-Jabin's knocking on the door? Does Kaukab refuse to open the door, or does she just not hear the knocking (perhaps because she has fallen asleep)?

Her husband Shamas also behaves peculiarly in this situation. He is actually a caring and sensitive man who strives for a harmonious family life and usually tries to mediate between Kaukab and the children. So the reader might have expected him to go upstairs after Mah-Jabin's unsuccessful attempt to talk to her mother to see how his wife is doing and maybe to find out why she has neither come down again nor responded to Mah-Jabin's knocking. In fact, however, Shamas does not approach his wife at all after the visitors have left the house.

And once she comes back downstairs, he does not tell her right away that *all* their children have already gone home, but waits until she explicitly asks after each of them separately. Such behavior on his part is out of character. In this respect, too, the narrative shows a lack of (causal) clarification which would render the different characters' behavior more plausible to the reader.

But again, why is this so? I suggest that the extract can easily elide essential causal explanations because it is written in the present tense. When Kaukab realizes that her children's harsh criticism of her former disciplinary measures is justified, she first starts to vindicate herself, before eventually fleeing the scene:

> "I know you all think me the worst woman in the world," Kaukab **hears herself speak**, "but I . . ." And speaking evenly she tells everyone, turning now to Charag, now to Shamas [...] that she hadn't known the salt given to her by the cleric-ji was a bromide—whatever a bromide is—and, she **sees herself reaching** into her cardigan pocket many seconds before her hand actually makes that movement: she takes out [a] letter [...] (*MLL*, 334–335; my emphasis)

Complying with the novel's regular pattern of heterogeneous tense usage, the fictional present again highlights Kaukab's consciousness. Perceived exclusively from her perspective, the narrated events generate an impression of great immediacy. Kaukab seems overwhelmed by her own actions; she no longer thinks about what she is doing, but rather lets her emotions and feelings guide her deeds. Her volatile state is indicated by formulations like "Kaukab hears herself speak" or "she sees herself reaching into her cardigan pocket." She seems no longer in control of herself, as if her mind had been detached from her body and its actions. She can only observe her behavior passively from the outside. Her distress becomes even more apparent when Shamas informs her that their children left soon after she had locked herself in her room. She does not ask her husband calmly where they have gone or when they are coming back, but "finds herself [doing so] in panic" (*MLL*, 335).

Aslam conveys Kaukab's helpless detachment from the events of this particular scene by replacing active verb forms like "she speaks," "she reaches," and "she asks" with constructions that express a distinctly passive mood on the part of their agent ("she hears herself speak [...], sees herself reaching [...], finds herself asking"). Doing so, he perfectly captures Kaukab's precipitate actions from her own perspective. Providing a direct insight into Kaukab's state of panic, this style of narrating makes readers feel they were personally present at the scene. The rhetorical use of the present tense reinforces this immediacy, feigning synchronicity between the occurrence of events and the narrative act. Yet this simultaneity is an illusion, for although the narration seems to pause for a while, the story continues as soon as Kaukab leaves the room during the argument with her children. It is exactly this divergence between discourse time and story time that creates the lack of causality between the events outlined in the previous two pages: we do not know why Kaukab is staying in her bedroom and why Shamas does not go upstairs to see how his wife is doing because the narrative here generates an ellipsis (cf. Genette 1980 [1972], 106–109), that is, a moment of anisochrony between story time and discourse time which, by "filter[ing] out" details (Fludernik 2009, 33), suggests that the narrative is actually told in retrospect.

The rhetorical present tense, however, successfully conceals the temporal distance between the narrative levels. For this reason, readers simply fail to notice the lack of causality between the events presented here, meaning that they are not really confused by the absence of explanations that would render Kaukab's and Shamas's behavior more plausible. The fictional present induces us to perceive the narrative as an instance of simultaneous narration, which is by definition characterized by a lack of hindsight, and hence also a lack of causal explanations. We are consequently willing to accept that the text temporarily stops presenting Kaukab's point of view here: even though we generally seem to get an insight into her mental state, we do not know what she is actually doing in her room that prevents her from going back downstairs. Yet this information gap does not concern readers because it abides by the rules of narrative simultaneity. By camouflaging inconsistencies in the plot, the rhetorical present tense thus tempts us not to challenge the topochronic dynamics of Aslam's novel which clearly lays more emphasis on a detailed depiction of the narrative setting than the coherent representation of events.

9.4 Narrative Immediacy and Hyper-Analepsis as Means of Strategic Empathizing

The topochronic structure of Aslam's narrative encourages readers to empathize with the characters inhabiting the storyworld. We have seen in the previous section of this chapter how the 'snow,' 'flashback,' and 'dinner' scenes afford an insight into Shamas's and Kaukab's emotional states, drawing on correlations of present-tense narration and other empathic narrative techniques that help readers to emotionally engage with the respective character. In the 'dinner scene,' for example, Aslam's text prompts us to share Kaukab's anger, fear, and disappointment when the family reunion does not turn out to be the enjoyable evening she had expected. In other words, the narrative encourages perspective taking in order to better understand and empathize with Kaukab's feelings.

Elsewhere, the novel resorts to more subtle ways of evoking empathy within readers. In *Reading Fictions, Changing Minds: The Cognitive Value of Fiction* (2014), Vera Nünning contends that

> [a]lthough most literary studies of the role of empathy in fictional works concentrate on the characters or narrators and the ways in which their emotions are represented, the whole narrative has to be taken into account. The significance of the narrative as a whole is indicated by the finding that affective sharing of the characters' thoughts and feelings does not rely on explicit references to their emotions in the text; rather, forms of empathy are evoked even if there is no mention at all of the characters' feelings. (106)

For, as she explains, "[o]vert representations explicitly describing characters' emotions may even be less important than showing characters' expressions of their feelings by, for instance, their emotional responses or their attempts to regulate their emotions" (Nünning 2014, 107). Apart from explicitly empathic narrative techniques typically associated with narrative empathy,[23] Nünning identifies a series of narrative strategies which can stimulate readers' empathic responses to narrative texts. These include, "a precise and poetic use of language and imagery," which "may not only foreground specific emotions, but also suggest possible interpretations of them" (Nünning 2014, 109), as well as the evocation of "aesthetic feelings" (Nünning 2014, 122), i.e. "readers' emotions" which are "stimulated by linguistic and narrative devices on the surface structure of literary texts, by formal features and the choice of words," or by "non-conventional metaphors and innovations of generic conventions" (Nünning 2014, 123; cf. also Nünning 2017, 40).

Precisely these subtle empathic narrative techniques become effective in the 'snow scene' and 'flashback scene' of Aslam's novel. In the 'snow scene,' Aslam chiefly deploys narrative strategies which slow down the narrative pace. In his essay "Empathy: Affect from Bearing Witness to the Emotions of Others"

---

[23] Suzanne Keen (2007), for example, focuses on two major empathic strategies: character identification and the narrative situation of a specific text (cf. 93–96, 96–99). While the second term unequivocally refers to "the nature of the mediation between author and reader, including the person of the narration, the implicit location of the narrator, the relation of the narrator to the characters, and the internal or external perspective on characters, including in some cases the style of representation of characters' consciousness" (Keen 2007, 93), the first term needs further explanation. Keen makes clear that character identification *per se* should be conceived of not as a narrative technique, but as "a consequence of reading that may be precipitated by the use of particular techniques of characterization" such as "naming, description, indirect implication of traits, reliance on types, relative flatness or roundness, depicted actions, roles in plot trajectories, quality of attributed speech, and mode of representation of consciousness" (Keen 2007, 93).

(1991), Dolf Zillmann suggests that slow-paced narratives foster narrative empathy, whereas fast-paced narratives tend to impede empathic response on the part of their audience (cf. 160–161).²⁴ Following Zillmann's hypothesis, I would contend that Aslam's strikingly slow narration heightens the empathic potential of *Maps for Lost Lovers*. By enabling us to engage minutely with its descriptive passages, the novel draws our attention to Shamas's perceptions and emotional reactions toward the storyworld.

This effect is intensified by the poetic style of the narrative, whose use of the fictional present, paired with highly metaphorical language, defamiliarizes the discourse to such an extent that a literal reading becomes almost impossible. According to David S. Miall and Don Kuiken (1994), such unusual linguistic variation, also known as foregrounding, influences the reading process in that it deautomatizes our usual perception of written texts and prolongs the time we need to read them.²⁵ Foregrounding or the process of "creating complexity of various kinds," the authors argue, "requires [more] cognitive work on the part of the reader," and they additionally suggest that "this work is initiated and in part directed by feeling" (Miall and Kuiken 1994, 392). More specifically, this means that novel linguistic features such as metaphors or similes "strike readers as interesting and capture their attention" (Miall and Kuiken 1994, 392), forcing them to slow their reading pace for "the feelings created by [these tropes] to emerge" and an "enriched perspective" on the text to arise (Miall and Kuiken 1994, 392). In the 'snow scene,' for example, Aslam's metaphors not only complicate and decelerate our reading process, they also cause us to engage more intensively with Shamas's perspective, enabling us to better relate to his idiosyncratic perception of the wintry scene.

The passages of Aslam's novel focalized through Kaukab, in turn, abound not so much in metaphoric present-tense descriptions of the storyworld as in extensive past-tense flashbacks during which she remembers special moments

---

24 Zillmann (1991, 161) rests his argument on his observation that "representations in the mass media are characteristically fast paced" and therefore prevent "affective reactions to the emotions of others [from] run[ning] their course." According to him, this is different in narrative fiction since "verbal representations tend to be paced by the teller or are self-paced by a reader so as to permit the complete unfolding of affective responses" (Zillmann 1991, 160–161). Although I agree with Zillmann's assumption that slow-paced narratives exhibit a higher affective potential than fast-paced narratives, I do not agree that narrative fiction is *per se* more apt to evoke empathy than other (multimodal) media. After all, written narratives can also opt for a fast pace of narration that curtails empathic response (a case in point is Winslow's *The Power of the Dog*, which I will discuss in Chapter 10).

25 For a more detailed discussion of the concept of foregrounding, see Chapter 4.2.

of her former life in Pakistan (e.g. how she met her husband). But these instances of analepsis also slow down the narrative pace, albeit by different means: instead of focusing on Kaukab's perception of her present country of domicile, England, they concentrate on her recollections of Pakistan, highlighting how she still clings to her old home.

The topochronic structure of Aslam's narrative generates what I have referred to as a *hyper-analepsis* (see Chapter 5.8) as it constantly switches between the characters' here-and-now (the passages written in the present tense) and memories from their pasts (the passages written in the past tense). This circumleptic structure of *Maps for Lost Lovers* helps readers to grasp how Aslam's protagonists are stuck between two countries and two temporal frameworks. The characters find themselves in a transitory state between longing and belonging, permanently struggling with their new hybrid cultural identity.[26] As Cordula Lemke (2008, 174) argues, "[t]he memories of the parents Shamas and Kaukab [...], around which the novel is structured, determine every move of their daily lives."

To conclude, my reading of *Maps for Lost Lovers* has demonstrated that Aslam's novel fosters intercultural understanding and dialogue inviting Western readers who do not share the same cultural and religious background as its Pakistani characters to gain an insight into the dilemmas faced by immigrants and thus become part of their empathetic circle. That the novel uses the fictional present as its global tense of narration contributes to this effect in various ways: First, the transmodal, more specifically explanatory use of the fictional present stresses the phatic connection between readers and the authorial narrator, who functions as a cultural mediator. Secondly, the thematic and referential uses of this tense highlight the novel's metaphoric descriptions of the narrative setting as well as that of the extensive flashbacks. Taken together, these strat-

---

[26] Nadia Butt (2008, 162) claims that "Aslam criticises immigrants of being nostalgic about the past, and this in turn hinders the process of assimilation into a new culture." A similar argument can be found in Lemke 2008, 174: "By shrouding the new place in old memories, the new location is invented just like the home country. This process of invention, however, does not only serve to create a feeling of belonging, but works as a shield against otherness. In defiance of the new culture into which Shamas and Kaukab were forced to settle, they draw boundaries and map out borders in order to protect their memories and traditions." While these contentions may be justifiable with regard to the more traditional believers in Aslam's novel (Kaukab or Chanda's brothers, who commit the honour killing), I would nevertheless object that Butt's and Lemke's statements do not apply to the numerous characters who, despite their Pakistani background, have successfully adapted to Western culture (Shamas, Shamas and Kaukab's children, as well as the couple Chanda and Jugnu).

egies produce a topochrone in which the representation of narrative space outweighs that of narrative time. Thirdly (and finally), the rhetorical use of present-tense narration elicits the impression of narrative immediacy by feigning synchronicity between the narrative events and the act of reporting these events. All in all, then, the multifunctionality of Aslam's fictional present enables readers to put on an intercultural mind (*sensu* Sommer) situated in a metaphorical here-and-now that oscillates between their own perspective and that of the fictional characters.

10 Narrative of Deception: Narrative Progression, Suspense, and Surprise in Don Winslow's *The Power of the Dog* (2005)

10.1 About Drug Lords, DEA Agents, and Webs of Deception

Adán Barrera, one of the main characters in Don Winslow's novel *The Power of the Dog*, has allowed himself to be deceived. When he received from his imprisoned uncle Tío the order to settle the deal with the Orejuela brothers, the drug trafficker thought that all he would have to do was to hand over a suitcase with five million dollars to Manuel and Gilberto, which would persuade them to join forces with the Barreras to start a war against their mutual confederate Güero Méndez. But not for nothing is Tío Barrera considered the most powerful drug lord in Mexico: his reputation as a dangerous, ruthless, and fraudulent *narcotraficante* has spread far beyond the country's borders, and this time not even Adán is spared from becoming the victim of his uncle's unscrupulous cruelty. So here he is, standing in the center of Santa Ysabel Bridge, seven hundred feet above the Río Magdalena, watching how Fabián Martínez, the Barreras' hitman, is dragging Güero's children toward him. As Adán sees the defenseless boy and girl, both panicking and crying, he slowly realizes that he is about to perform a horrible deed which he himself has not seen coming, but which his uncle has carefully planned in advance:

> Adán feels paralyzed, his feet nailed to the wood of the bridge, and he just stands there as Fabián smiles at the Orejuela brothers and says, "Don Miguel Ángel Barrera assures you that his blood flows through the veins of his nephew."
> [...] Tío's plan is, as usual, brilliant. Even in its total, crack-inspired depravity it is deadly accurate in its perception of individual human nature. This is Tío's genius—he knows that a man who would never have the weakness to set a great evil into motion doesn't have the strength to stop it once it's moving. That the hardest thing in the world isn't to refrain from committing an evil, it's to stand up and stop one.
> To put one's life in the way of a tidal wave.
> Because that is what it is, Adán thinks, his mind whirling. If I put a stop to this now it will show weakness to the Orejuelas—a weakness that will immediately or eventually prove fatal. If I show the slightest disunity with Fabián, that, too, will guarantee our [i.e. his family's] demise.
> Tío's genius—putting me in exactly this position, knowing that I have no real choice. (*PD*, 295)

How did Adán, the 'softest' member of the Barrera family, end up in this no-win situation? Tío knows his nephew very well, and can foresee that Adán will not be intimidating enough to convince the Orejuela brothers to change sides, and that it will probably need an atrocity to make them believe that he is as determined and unethical as his uncle. Indeed, when Adán first makes his offer to Manuel and Gilberto, the former of the two brothers harshly questions Adán's relentlessness: "You are very smart, but brains alone are not enough. How *tough* are you? I will tell you the truth, Adán—you look soft to me. I do not think that you are a hard enough man to do what you say you will do, what you will have to do." (*PD*, 292; italics in the original)

Correctly anticipating the Orejuelas' reaction toward Adán, Tío arranges the scenario on the Santa Ysabel Bridge; he leads Adán into an impasse which he can only escape by carrying out his uncle's plan. In order to demonstrate the strength of the Barrera clan, as well as his own toughness, he has to consent to Fabián's killing Güero's children on the spot, in plain view of the Orejuela brothers (cf. *PD*, 296); otherwise, he would show weakness, a fatal mistake, given that Tío's punishment for such behavior would certainly put his own wife and daughter in danger (cf. *PD*, 295). Adán is a puppet on a string that will move exactly in accordance with Tío's manipulations.

To reveal Adán's realization of his situation, Winslow combines a representation of Adán's thoughts with the use of the fictional present. By feigning synchronicity between the narrative events and the act of their reporting, the present tense gives readers the impression that they are given an immediate insight into Adán's mind. Not only do we learn that he "feels paralyzed, his feet nailed to the wood of the bridge," we also witness his gradually coming to an awareness of what is going on. We share his thoughts and feelings in the very moment it dawns on him that Tío has put him in a situation in which he has no choice but to obey. Winslow's text denies readers a complete overview of the scene: Even though Adán's interior monologue about Tío's genius shows that he has immediately understood what Tío wants him to do, readers cannot yet see Tío's plan. What comes might be a duel between Adán and the Orejuela brothers during which Adán will shoot one of his opponents in front of the children's eyes. What the reader does not envisage is that Adán will give Fabián the order to throw the children over the parapet of the bridge – we simply do not see this coming.

Ingenious as Tío's plan might be, however, the drug lord does not know that someone else is actually pulling the strings. In fact, Tío himself is being manipulated by the DEA agent Art Keller. Tío does not suspect that his sophisticated plan forms part of a far-reaching retaliation campaign that Art has initiated in revenge for the death of his colleague and friend Eddie Hidalgo. When Eddie is brutally murdered in an operation against Mexican drug cartels, Art swears vengeance on everyone involved, including Güero Méndez, Tío Barrera, and his nephew Adán (cf. *PD*, 248). Having tracked down and arrested Tío, he seizes the chance to play his enemies off against each other. Knowing that the drug lord devises terrible punishments for traitors, Art deceives Tío into believing that Güero is a spy for the DEA (cf. *PD*, 269). The Barrera family is adroitly engineered into retaliating against their own kind.

The scene on the Santa Ysabel Bridge is typical of the thriller *The Power of the Dog*. Published in 2005, the first installment of Winslow's *Cartel* trilogy centers on the U.S. agent Art Keller, whose mission is to put an end to the illegal drug dealing and brutal business practices of the Mexican cartels.[1] The cartels run by the Barrera family – Don Miguel Ángel, also known as Tío, and his two nephews Raúl and Adán – control the Mexican drug markets along the border to the United States. Tracing Art's connections to the Barreras over a time span of about thirty years, the novel weaves a neatly tangled web of deception spanning all levels of political and social interaction: federal law enforcement units act against the interest of the state while the state corrupts the federal law enforcement agency; DEA agents try to convict drug bosses and, reciprocally, the drug cartels attempt to ambush the DEA; allies betray friends to their enemies; families blackmail and threaten their immediate members; married men have secret mistresses, and their wives are similarly unfaithful. Yet it is not only Winslow's characters that repeatedly become the target of deception in *The Power of the Dog*; the novel constantly leads its readers astray as well. For example, although we know all along that Art has secretly incited Tío to take vengeance on Güero, we cannot foresee Adán's role in this conflict – in this regard, we are as clueless as Adán himself.

And this is typical of Winslow's novel. The author creates a 'narrative of deception' in which one false scent follows another, and readers never gain a complete overview of the novel's character constellation and the various ways in which individual figures are involved in the numerous parallel plots. This effect, I aim to show, is achieved on the one hand through the novel's chronotopic structure,[2] which speeds up the narration, and on the other through its narrative situation, which combines the voice of a mostly covert omniscient narrator with orchestrated multiperspectivity. However, neither the narrative

---

[1] As well as *The Power of the Dog* (2005), Winslows's *Cartel* trilogy comprises *The Cartel* (2016 [2015]) and *The Border* (2019). I here only discuss the first volume of the trilogy. It is fair to say, though, that for all their complexity, the textual and readerly dynamics of the later volumes work similarly to the narrative dynamics of the first volume.
[2] For a definition of the concept of chronotope, see Chapter 5.8.

progression nor the narrative perspective of *The Power of the Dog* would be possible without a third device, the use of the present tense. The interplay of these three strategies – narrative tempo, multiperspectivity, and present-tense narration – transforms Winslow's novel into a gripping page-turner infused with the dynamics of suspense and surprise.

10.2 Spatial Disorientation, Narrative Sequentiality, and Temporal Immersion: Winslow's Chronotopic Present-Tense Narration

Central to Winslow's novel is the enduring conflict between Art and the Barrera family, and *The Power of the Dog* accordingly stages several encounters between the DEA agent and the drug bosses. These showdowns always take place in remote locations which qualify as "non-places" in the sense of Marc Augé (2008 [1992], 63) – the desert, an isolated, lonely beach, or a traffic-free bridge at night (cf. *PD*, 138–147, 464–476, and 534–539, respectively).[3] As these 'non-places' do not evoke within the characters any memories of previous events, circumstances, or experiences, they serve as neutral ground on which the protagonists can act out their various fights. From the perspective of narrative design, these settings can be conceived of as semantically empty: their narrative function consists in "form[ing] the backdrop to the events and actions represented by [the] story" (Caracciolo 2013, 425).

Given that space is purely functional in *The Power of the Dog*, it comes as no surprise that in the narrative's chronotope the depiction of the setting is subordinate to the delineation of events. In fact, Winslow's novel largely refrains from depicting the spatio-temporal circumstances of the diegetic world. The "Prologue" may serve to illustrate this observation. The novel begins with a concise statement – "The baby is dead in his mother's arms" (*PD*, 3) – which throws readers right into the scene. Such establishing sentences are typical of Winslow's novel: its chapters usually begin by giving readers a single item of information taken out of its narrative context. And, since these sentences are written in the present tense, they trick readers into believing that the narrative events must occur before they can be told by the narrator. Winslow's use of the present tense camouflages the fact that the novel is actually written from a retrospective perspective and that it features a narrator who relates the events in hindsight. More on this later.

---

[3] For a definition of Augé's concept of 'non-places,' see Chapter 8.1.

Reading on, we realize that Winslow's fictional present fulfills a referential function: it points to one or other of the protagonists' consciousnesses. Thus the first statement of the "Prologue" is followed by a passage combining thought report and quoted monologue, granting us an insight into Art's mind (see the next two paragraphs in the novel). From his thoughts we gather that the woman and her child must have been killed in a major gunfight – an impression confirmed when the text describes the "hundreds of 7.62-mm shell casings [lying] on the patio's concrete floor" (*PD*, 3). We learn that the shootout has taken place on a terrace which, if we believe the paratextual information at the beginning of the "Prologue," is located in El Sauzal in the Mexican State of Baja California. While the paratext further informs us that the year is 1997, the main text points out that the majority of shell casings on the ground stem from "the favored weapon of the Mexican *narcotraficantes*" (*PD*, 3; italics in the original). We can conclude, then, that the setting is Mexico in the late 1990s where, on a terrace in El Sauzal, the drug lords have carried out a brutal massacre in which women and children have been slaughtered.

But this is all contextual information we get. We do not know where in El Sauzal the patio is located, on which day of 1997 the action takes place, or who the victims of the massacre are. This information is withheld until the last fifth of the novel when the narrative returns to the "Prologue" scene and informs us that the terrace is part of a "compound in the countryside outside Ensenada" (*PD*, 480) belonging to Fabián Martínez's uncle. On this second encounter with the scene, we eventually learn that the massacre was carried out by the Federal Police of Mexico, headed by Manuel Sánchez, a confederate of the Barrera family. Because the *Federales* erroneously believe that Fabián has murdered Raúl Barrera (it was actually Art Keller), they exact their vengeance on Fabián and his entire family (cf. *PD*, 481).

The "Prologue" is representative of the presentation of narrative space in *The Power of the Dog*, which draws heavily on the strategy I referred to in my reading of Hilary Mantel's Tudor novels (see Chapter 7.4) as *spatial non-contextualization*. Instead of detailed descriptions of the setting, Winslow's text, that is to say, contents itself with indicating the place and sometimes also the date of the narrative events in the paratext at the beginning of a new chapter. Since the settings always refer to real places, readers get a rough idea of the spatial circumstances of the story. Apart from these few references, however, Winslow's novel provides little information that might help readers to construct a coherent storyworld. The different chapters usually start *in medias res* and delve immediately into the action. If the plot requires a shift in space or time within the same chapter, this is usually indicated with a blank line.[4]

The Power of the Dog seeks to provide as little spatiotemporal information as possible, forcing readers to make inferences from the narrative context if they want to make a mental model of the fictional world. However, correct inferences are not always possible, for the novel frequently deceives the reader by only gradually revealing essential information about the narrative setting. When, for example, Adán Barrera approaches Parada because he would like the priest to arrange a peace meeting with Güero Méndez, a conversation takes place, only at the end of which readers learn that the characters are actually talking on the phone (cf. *PD*, 342–343). Before the very last sentences of the conversation – "'I will try, Adán,' [Parada] says. It won't be easy, he thinks as he hangs up." (*PD*, 343) – we would take for granted that Adán and Parada are talking to each other in person, but a closer look unveils allusions to a telephone conversation. Parada, for instance, asks Adán if he would "come to Guadalajara" (*PD*, 342), and the narrative part of the text states that Parada "hears" Adán's admission that he is a sinful person,[5] which suggests that Adán says this in a low voice and perhaps more to himself than to his interlocutor (*PD*, 343).

Given the subtlety of these hints, other interpretations are possible. Moreover, the information gap probably need not bother the reader: in the first place, it is irrelevant for the novel's plot whether Adán and Parada are talking on the phone or in person. Secondly, the passage is written in the present tense, which again serves the purpose of pointing alternately to one or other of the characters' consciousnesses. Not only do readers learn that "Adán knows that he's rung the bell [and] hit the chord that no priest can resist" (*PD*, 342) when lying to Parada that he would like to conclude peace with his rival Güero, but they also get access to the thoughts of the priest, who is struggling to weigh up the

---

4 However, if readers cannot deduce such spatiotemporal shifts from the narrative context, the novel resorts to paratextual notes. This is, for instance, the case in Chapter 9, "Days of the Dead," which is first set in San Diego in 1994 (cf. *PD*, 297), then in Mexico in 1994 (cf. *PD*, 301), and eventually switches back to San Diego (cf. *PD*, 362). Chapters in which the action frequently shifts between different settings even combine paratextual indication and empty lines. For example, Chapter 8, "Days of the Innocents," can be divided into two parts, each marked by a paratext which informs us that the events depicted in the first part of the chapter take place in Tegucigalpa, San Diego, and Guadalajara in 1992 (cf. *PD*, 234), those of the second part in Guamuchilito, Sinaloa, and Tijuana, or in Colombia in the same year (cf. *PD*, 278). Spatiotemporal shifts within these subsections are indicated with blank lines.
5 When Parada tells Adán that his "soul [...] is blacker than hell," the latter answers: "One thing at a time, Father." (*PD*, 343)

possible risks of Adán's proposition (cf. *PD*, 342). Thanks to these insights into Adán's and Parada's minds, readers do not expect a detailed description of the situation: there is no need for the text to spell the details out. The referential function of the fictional present effectively conceals the novel's strategy of spatial non-contextualization.

The lack of a detailed description of Winslow's storyworld owes much to the fact that *The Power of the Dog* focuses primarily on presentation of the narrative events. The novel contains several plotlines, all of which are in one way or another related to the blood feud between Art and the Barreras. Since this highly complex plot structure is packed with action, intrigue, and surprising twists, it requires the reader's undivided attention. Consider the following showdown scene:

> They meet just west of the middle of the bridge.
> Scachi walks ahead of the rest, comes up to Art and says, "No offense, Arthur. I need your weapon."
> Art slides his jacket back and Scachi takes his .38 and tucks it into his belt. Then he turns Art around, makes him lean against the bridge railing and frisks him. Finding nothing, he waves for the others to come ahead.
> Art watches Tío come toward him with Nora on his arm. Like he's walking her down the aisle, Art thinks.
> Hobbs lags behind.
> Tío looks at Adán's bleeding, broken face [...]
> "Take the handcuffs off him, please," Tío says.
> Art steps behind Adán, takes the cuffs off and nudges him forward.
> Hobbs looks at Art and says, "You're a man of your word, Arthur. You're a man of honor."
> Art shakes his head. "Not really, no."
> He grabs Hobbs and spins the old man in front of him as a shield, his left hand at Hobbs' neck, the other behind his head. One twist will kill him.
> Scachi pulls his gun but is afraid to shoot.
> "Put the guns down, Sal, or I'll break his fucking neck."
> [...]
> Sal lays his gun on the bridge.
> "Now mine."
> Sal lays Keller's .38 down beside his. Then **he looks up at the ridge** behind Keller and nods.
>
> **Callan sees it.**
> **He puts the crosshairs squarely on the back of Keller's head** and takes a deep breath.
> *Change your life.* (*PD*, 535–536; italics in the original; my emphasis)

10.2 Disorientation and Immersion: Chronotopic Present-Tense Narration — 225

The final showdown between Art and the Barrera clan takes place on the Cabrillo Bridge in San Diego, California by night. As is typical of the many passages in *The Power of the Dog* in which the narrative pace speeds up, the novel here temporarily switches from the mode of telling to that of showing, enabling readers to perceive the narrative action as if they were "somehow near the events of the story" (Klauk and Köppe 2014, 846) – an effect of reduced narrative distance achieved by the functional interplay of strategies such as chronological event sequencing, multiperspectivity, isochrony of story time and discourse time, paratactic syntax, and the fictional present.

Because the events suddenly start to overturn, the narrative concentrates exclusively on relaying their chronological sequence and dispenses altogether with spatial context. It explains neither where the different characters are located on the bridge, nor who is shooting at whom; the reader is left to visualize the scene. We can infer from the extract that Callan must be in an elevated position: When Sal Scachi gives him the sign to shoot at Art, "he looks up at the ridge behind Keller," so Callan must be somewhere on that ridge, a sniper external to the immediate fray. But we draw these conclusions on the basis of the characters' actions as described in the scene (see my emphasis). Apart from these hints, the excerpt provides no spatial orientation.

And as the narrative pace accelerates, the text constrains still further the representation of the characters' thoughts and feelings. While the first paragraphs still allow us to glimpse briefly into Art's and Callan's minds (see the sentences "Like he's walking her down the aisle, Art thinks," and "*Change your life*"), what comes next denies us any insight into the characters' mental states. The scene continues as follows:

> **Callan** puts the bullet square into Scachi's head.
> Sal drops from the scope's sight.
> **Tío** dives and grabs Scachi's gun.
> **Art** turns.
> **Tío** raises the gun.
> **Art** puts two shots into his chest.
> **Tío**'s hand reflexively pulls the trigger.
> The bullet goes through Hobbs' hip and into Art's leg.
> They both go down.
>
> [...]
>
> **Adán** crawls to Tío.
> He takes the gun from his uncle's hand.
> **Callan** tries to get a shot, but Nora's in the way.

> **Art** struggles to his knees, sees Adán kneeling by Tío.
> Adán's gun goes off once, twice, both bullets zinging past Art.
> […]
> **Adán** shoots again.
> Art's head snaps back, a ribbon of blood swirls in the air, and he falls back into the bridge railing, his gun dropping to the highway below.
> Adán turns his gun on Nora.
> "GET DOWN!" **Callan** yells.
> Nora drops to the ground.
>
> So does Adán. (*PD*, 536–537; my emphasis)

Given that the narrative events are suddenly coming thick and fast, there is no longer any time for reproducing thoughts or emotions without losing track of the action. Nonetheless, even though the text temporarily ceases to inform us about the characters' cognitive and emotional states, it still draws on the strategy of multiple focalization (cf. Genette 1980 [1972], 190), more precisely, alternating multiperspective focalization (cf. Nünning and Nünning 2000a, 56), presenting the events from the shifting points of view of its various characters.[6] Art, Adán, Callan, and Tío function as the alternating deictic centers of the narrative (see my emphasis in the above quotation).

The effect of accelerated narration and pure sequentiality is reinforced by the observation that story time and discourse time seem here to coincide in duration. This impression of "scene" (Genette 1980 [1972], 94) or "isochrony" (Fludernik 2009, 33) is primarily created by the linguistic make-up of the excerpt: As the plot reaches its climax, the text reduces to short main clauses, each followed by a line break. This forces us to focus on the rapid action of the showdown. The overall structure is like a film script, with the blank lines functioning as the direction "Cut to," signaling a new camera shot or angle, and the one-line sentences as the scene description.

In fact, Winslow's style of narration, which I will call *film-script narration*, recalls the action genre of Hollywood filmmaking, whose cinematic showdown scenes usually employ fast cutting to show the different characters involved in a

---

6 Strictly speaking, Vera and Ansgar Nünning (2000a, 56) use the term *alternating multiperspective narration* (*alternierendes multiperspektivisches Erzählen*) in place of alternating multiperspective focalization. However, given that they distinguish three manifestations of narrative multiperspectivity, one of which is multiperspective focalization (the other two are multiperspective narration and structure) (cf. Nünning and Nünning 2000a, 43–46), my formulation is still correct in this context.

conflict.[7] The montage technique serves to heighten the pace and stress the gravity of the situation. Simulating this filmic pattern, the rapid shifts in focalization in Winslow's account emphasize the impression that the narrative events are shown directly to the reader rather than being recounted by a narrator external to them.[8]

The use of the present tense further strengthens Winslow's film-script style of narration and its concomitant mode of showing. By feigning simultaneous narration, *The Power of the Dog* creates a sense of what Marie-Laure Ryan (2015 [2001], 99–106) calls "temporal immersion" – it makes readers feel they were inside the moment of action, immediate witnesses to its events. They "[live] the development of the action moment by moment" and share the alternating perspectives of the different characters "whose fate is being played out" (Ryan 2015 [2001], 102). We perceive the scenario as if we were part of the shooting ourselves, ducking the bullets and losing all sense of orientation. And, in this battle between life and death, we are permanently anxious to know what will happen next, who will be killed and who will survive (cf. Ryan 2015 [2001], 102).[9] In this sense the excerpt achieves what Paul Simpson (2014) has termed "narrative urgency," constantly reminding us that there is a lot at stake in the situation.

Against this backdrop, it is primarily the fictional present that generates congruence between the textual and readerly dynamics of *The Power of the Dog*. According to James Phelan and Peter J. Rabinowitz (2012, 6), "[t]extual dynamics are the internal processes by which narratives move from beginning through middle to ending," whereas "readerly dynamics are the corresponding cognitive, affective, ethical, and aesthetic responses of the audience to those textual dynamics." In Winslow's novel the two dynamics act in unison, the text's rhetorical use of the present tense manipulating the reader to focus on the progression of the plot and ignore the gaps in the setting. By evoking the mode of concurrent narration, the present tense highlights the impression of narrative urgency: Any detailed depiction of the spatiotemporal circumstances of Winslow's storyworld, or a meandering rendition of the characters' cognitive and

---

7 In cinematic terms, the concept of fast cutting denotes a film editing technique which strings together several consecutive shots of brief duration (cf. Wharton and Grant 2005, 99).
8 This film-script style of narration is a distinguishing characteristic of Winslow's work: the sequels to *The Power of the Dog*, *The Cartel* and *The Border*, feature a similar style of narration, and the author's 2010 novel *Savages* contains several passages written and formatted as a film script (cf. *PD*, 14, 57, 85–87, 108, 175–178, 229–230, 241–242, and 287–288; see also Chapter 6.2).
9 Ryan (2015 [2001], 102) calls this particular brand of narrative interest, in which the reader is raring to know the further course of events, "what suspense."

emotional states, would interfere with the novel's chronotopic structure and impede the sense of temporal immersion experienced by readers.

10.3 Leading the Reader Up the Garden Path: Covert Omniscient Narration and Orchestrated Multiperspectivity

The chronotopic structure of *The Power of the Dog*, then, unconsciously controls the reader's perception of narrative time and space, and the manipulation of the reader becomes even more relevant in the context of the novel's narrative situation. The story is told by a heterodiegetic narrator who largely recedes into the background, giving readers alternating insights into the minds of the different characters – central features of what Franz K. Stanzel (1955, Ch. IV) designated a figural narrative situation. However, in terms of Stanzel's (1986 [1979], xvi) conception of the three typical narrative situations as a typological circle, Winslow's narrator must be located toward the middle of "the so-called *authorial-figural continuum*," which constitutes a "transitional area" between the figural and authorial narrative situation (Fludernik 2009, 94; italics in the original). For, although the covert narrator is not usually evident in the text, he occasionally intrudes into the story, judging, evaluating, or commenting on the characters' behavior.

An example of this can be found in the chapter "The Lowest Bottom Shook." At the onset of this chapter, Nora wakes up in a hotel in Mexico City with her bed shaking (cf. *PD*, 179). At first, she thinks that "she might still be asleep, still dreaming" (*PD*, 180), then starts wondering whether there is something wrong with her: "Am I sick? she wonders. She does feels [sic] dizzy, nauseated, all the more so when she gets out of bed and can't walk or even stand, as the floor seems to be rolling beneath her." (*PD*, 180) When the shaking becomes more violent, with "debris falling from the higher floors" (*PD*, 180), she eventually realizes that she is experiencing an earthquake: "Then the floor seems to slide like one of those metal plates in a funhouse, but this isn't fun—it's terrifying." (*PD*, 180) Winslow's use of the present tense here is evocative of the scene on the Santa Ysabel Bridge discussed above. The fictional present fulfills a referential function, offering readers a direct insight into Nora's awakening consciousness.

Unlike in the 'bridge scene,' however, the narrator does not completely hide behind Nora's thoughts and feelings, but also comments on the narrative events, conveying more information to us than Nora can know: "She'd be more terrified if she could see outside the building. See it literally waving, see the top of the hotel bend and sway and actually smack the top of the building next door." (*PD*, 180) The narrator no longer acts here as a covert speaker who retrogresses behind the reflector figure (in this case Nora). Instead, he becomes an overt, commenting voice who reveals his influence on the narrative discourse through "hypothetical focalization" (Herman 2002, 303), speculating about what Nora might feel if she knew more than she actually does.[10] Nonetheless, readers may well miss this narratorial interference. Because *The Power of the Dog* is entirely written in the present tense, Winslow's tense use no longer sets the mode of narration apart from that of focalization,[11] with the result that readers can no longer easily distinguish between the narrator's discourse and the characters' thoughts.

Even though authorial passages of this sort are relatively subtle in Winslow's novel and may therefore go unnoticed, they nevertheless occur fairly frequently throughout the narrative. Such narratorial intrusions manifest themselves not only in seeming intrusions into a feigned figural perspective, they also reveal themselves in passages where the narrator openly shows that he knows more than any of the focalizing characters. This is the case, for example, when the narrator relates how the Barrera brothers and Güero Méndez try to ambush each other into a fake peace meeting in order to gain power over the most lucrative drug market, the Sonora *plaza*, which adjoins the American states of Texas and Arizona:

> For a whole week the Barrera forces cruise the city, night and day, searching for Güero Méndez. [...] Raúl has technicians stationed in another safe house, using the most current high-tech equipment to scan cellular calls, trying to intercept messages that might be going back and forth between Güero and his lieutenants.
> Güero's doing the same thing. [...] Both sides are playing this game, switching cell phones constantly, moving safe houses, patrolling the streets and the airwaves, trying to

---

[10] David Herman (2002, 303) defines hypothetical focalization as "the use of hypotheses, framed by the narrator or a character, about what might be or might have been seen or perceived – if only there were someone who could have adopted the requisite perspective on the situations and events at issue."
[11] In traditional past-tense narratives, these two modes of representation are usually associated with different tenses: While the past tense refers to the here-and-now of the characters on the story level (cf. Käte Hamburger's 'epic preterite' [1973 (1968), 64–81]), the present tense relates to the present of the narrator on the discourse level (cf. Fludernik's 'deictic present' [2003a, 124]). The juxtaposition of past- and present-tense narration is discussed in greater detail in Chapter 4.1 above.

> find and kill each other with some kind of advantage before Parada sets up the peace meeting, which can only be a risky shoot-out. (*PD*, 344; italics in the original)

Showing that he knows how each party is preparing for the encounter, the narrator presents himself as omniscient and omnipresent. However, such explicit passages are rare, as the narrator's authorial perspective usually vanishes in favor of the characters' limited perspectives. And, what is most important here, Winslow's use of the fictional present conceals the narrator's comprehensive perspective precisely because it feigns the impression of simultaneous narration. This, by definition, rules out any sense of narratorial omniscience and omnipresence. As a result, readers may overlook the distinctive qualities of Winslow's narrator, and not notice that he actually has a complete overview of the narrative events and already knows the outcome of the story.

Just as the chronotopic structure of *The Power of the Dog* strongly affects the textual and readerly dynamics of Winslow's text (see Chapter 10.2), so does its narrative situation, which exhibits a speaking agent who integrates features of both an omniscient overt narrator and a covert narrator who disappears into the perspectives of several reflector figures. Due to his (mostly undisclosed) omniscience, the narrator can foresee the consequences of the different characters' behaviors and actions better than the characters themselves. Still, he does not give this information away, preferring the limited perspectives of the various characters between which he switches as the novel proceeds. Thus we learn from the passage quoted above that the Barrera brothers and Güero Méndez are trying to lure each other into a trap, for each party knows something the other one doesn't. Yet both parties are oblivious to the fact that they are being manipulated by a third party also involved in the action: It is in fact Cardinal Parada who holds all the aces, but he "is holding his cards close to his chest," so that "neither Méndez nor the Barreras can find out when or where the meeting is going to be" (*PD*, 344). The narrator, of course, already knows where Parada is going to set the meeting, yet he withholds this information from his audience in order to keep up the narrative tension. But, again, the informational gap does not bother us, because the present tense makes us believe that Winslow's narrative features the mode of concurrent rather than ulterior narration.

By combining present-tense narration with covert narratorial omniscience, Winslow's text exhibits a singular perspective structure. Vera and Ansgar Nünning (2000a, 48–52) argue that the overall perspective structure of a narrative results from the interaction of its characters' individual perspectives, the narrator's perspective, and the perspective of the fictive reader or narratee. But in the

10.3 Garden-Path Effects: Covert Omniscience and Orchestrated Multiperspectivity

hierarchical structure of authorial narrative, the narrator's perspective is usually superior to all other perspectives featured in the text;[12] the perspective of the narratee hinges accordingly on the narrator, who decides what his or her fictive interlocutor should or should not know. Having said this, the authorial narrator typically flaunts his or her omniscience, so this knowledge is usually shared with the reader, with the result that readers may know more than the characters – a discrepancy that often leads to dramatic irony, when readers know more about the possible outcome and consequences of events than do the fictive characters involved in these events.[13]

With the narrative situation in *The Power of the Dog*, however, this is different. Winslow's narrator orchestrates the various perspectives of the characters in such a way that the narratee does not really have an advantage in relation to the characters. The narrator enables readers to develop an advance in knowledge by constantly choosing more than one focalizer from whose perspective he presents the narrative events; yet the state of discrepant awareness generated by this multiperspective account fails to create dramatic irony, because readers never learn enough to assess the complexity of the situation. Indeed, Winslow's narrator draws on the strategy of multiperspective narration to lead readers up the garden path.

What does this mean? In linguistics, the term *garden-path sentence* describes "a type of sentence that traps the reader in a processing failure and re-

---

12 Cf. Nünning and Nünning 2000a, 66: "Die für die auktoriale Erzählsituation charakteristische Perspektivenstruktur zeichnet sich durch eine hierarchische Relationierung der Perspektiven aus, bei der die verschiedenen Perspektiventräger auf unterschiedlichen Kommunikationsebenen situiert sind. Sie entspricht somit dem Typus des hierarchisch über- bzw. untergeordneten multiperspektivischen Erzählens. Dabei sind die Perspektiven der Figuren in die hierarchisch übergeordnete Perspektive und Erzählung des extradiegetischen Erzählers eingebettet." ["The perspective structure typical of the authorial narrative situation is characterized by a hierarchical relationing of the different perspectives, in which the different bearers of a specific perspective are situated at different communicative levels. It corresponds, therefore, with the type of multiperspective narration that is hierarchically superordinate or subordinate. In this connection, the characters' perspectives are embedded in the hierarchically superordinate perspective of the narrative and the extradiegetic narrator." (My translation)] According to Felicitas Menhard (2009, 80–81), such a hierarchy often causes readers to believe extradiegetic-heterodiegetic narrators to have more authority and thus also to be more trustworthy and reliable than intradiegetic-homodiegetic narrators or character-focalizers whose perspective is usually conceived as more subjective and in some cases even unreliable.
13 For an adaptation of the dramatic term of *dramatic irony* to the genre of narrative, cf. Booth 1974, 63–67.

quires an act of reanalysis to recuperate its actual structure and meaning" (Jahn 1999, 169). Consider Thomas G. Bever's (1970) much-cited example sentence:

> (1) The horse raced past the barn fell. (Bever 1970, 316)

At first glance, this sentence appears ungrammatical; however, having a closer look at it, one may come up with the reading

> (2) The horse that was raced past the barn fell (Bever 1970, 316),

which complies with the grammatical pattern of sentences as illustrated by

> (3) The horse sent [or ridden] past the barn fell. (Bever 1970, 316)

According to Manfred Jahn (1999), the garden-path structure can also be transferred to larger semantic units such as jokes, riddles, and even longer stories. Even though these examples are more complex than single sentences, the principle remains the same:

> One of the main preferences is to read a text for maximum cognitive payoff. If this rule is not satisfied, then no appropriate sense can be made of the input, and the data will exhibit the very oddity that psycholinguists identify as a garden-path symptom. The garden path is confirmed if the symptom goes away on conscious or unconscious reanalysis, either by switching frames or scripts, or by reshuffling the preference rules. (Jahn 1999, 178)

Put more simply, garden-path texts or stories can be conceived of as texts which, during a first reading, lead readers astray by causing them to come up with an initial misinterpretation which they will have to revise at a later stage of perception. *The Power of the Dog* represents such a text, and it is primarily Winslow's use of present-tense narration that brings about this effect.

I will illustrate this by analyzing the novel's representation of the relationship between Nora Hayden and Adán Barrera, which constitutes an important subplot fueling the antagonism between Art Keller and the Barrera clan. Adán first meets Nora at Father Parada's home, when he asks the priest to become his uncle's pastor (cf. *PD*, 264–268). They start an affair (cf. *PD*, 269), whereupon Adán soon asks Nora to become his personal and exclusive mistress (cf. *PD*, 273–278). While it is indisputable that Adán cares about Nora (otherwise he would not demand an exclusive relationship with her), readers are led to believe for a long time that Nora, too, has feelings for Adán. The narrative thus informs us that Nora "actually likes" that man and "feels a certain sort of affection for him" (*PD*, 274), and this impression is corroborated by a series of inti-

10.3 Garden-Path Effects: Covert Omniscience and Orchestrated Multiperspectivity — 233

mate scenes between the two characters in which we have no reason to assume otherwise (cf. *PD*, 397, 404, 411).

Yet, after about 140 pages, we eventually learn that Nora is just playing games with Adán (cf. *PD*, 419–420); in reality she is Art's spy and has already enabled the DEA agent to chalk up a series of victories in his combat against the Barreras: "[Nora]'s angry [...] as she looks at Art Keller. You said that with my help you would take Adán down quickly, but it's been two and a half years. Two and a half years of pretending to love Adán Barrera, of taking a man I *loathe* inside me [...]" (*PD*, 419; italics in the original) This being the first time that the novel uncovers Nora's true feelings for Adán, her interior monologue (of which I here quote only the opening lines) takes us by surprise. All the time, the narrative has made us believe that Nora reciprocated Adán's affections and, conversely, has concealed Nora's cooperation with Art.[14] It is not only Adán who is misled by Nora (and Art), but the flesh-and-blood reader, too, who is led up the garden path by the narrative.

How does Winslow's text achieve this effect? As the narrator's account of Nora's thoughts at the beginning of her affair with Adán demonstrates, she does initially feel attracted to him. Her boss cautions her to "[b]e careful" as "[t]he Barreras are dangerous" (*PD*, 275), but Nora is unimpressed by this warning:

> Maybe, **Nora thinks** now as Adán falls into a postcoital slumber. But she hasn't seen that side of Adán and **doubts** that it even exists. He's been only gentle to her, even sweet. [...] And he's unselfish, **she thinks**. He doesn't come to bed with the consumer mentality that so many johns have [...] He doesn't treat me, **she thinks**, like a vending machine. [...] Goddamn it, **she thinks**, I like the man. (*PD*, 275; my emphasis)

Although the numerous *verba credendi* in this passage clearly indicate that the narrator here reproduces Nora's thoughts (see my emphasis), readers are nevertheless tricked into believing that they have an immediate insight into Nora's mind. We learn about her affection for Adán: Since he treats her with respect, he appears different from the macho customer the prostitute is familiar with. And she is even fascinated with the weakness he openly displays toward her: "And face it, she tells herself, you're attracted to his sorrow. To the sadness he carries with such quiet dignity. You think you can ease his pain, and you like that." (*PD*, 276)

One may wonder what happens that alters this situation. What exactly causes Nora to change her opinion about Adán so drastically that she detests

---

14 Admittedly, the novel contains two scenes depicting Art's attempts to open Nora's eyes to Adán's true character (cf. *PD*, 299–301; 369–371); but these have little apparent effect.

him in the end? The answer to this question is that Adán was responsible for the killing of Father Parada. When Parada was still alive, Nora often visited him in the orphanage at Guadalajara, where he worked, and even spent several months at his place (cf. *PD*, 259). The two of them lived together like a couple, with the only limitation that they never had sexual intercourse, which was prohibited by Parada's celibacy. Even though their relationship was strictly platonic, Nora nevertheless loved the cardinal. To her, he was "the best man [she had] ever known," and all she needed in life (*PD*, 263). In fact, she had such strong feelings for him that she did not "know what [she]'d do if anything ever happened to [him]" (*PD*, 263).

So the cardinal's death inevitably scandalizes her, providing the shock that opens Nora's eyes to Adán Barrera's true identity: He evidently has two faces, the warm-hearted lover and the cold-blooded killer. When Art proves to her that Adán is Parada's murderer (cf. *PD*, 369–37), she finally resolves to change sides. Seeking revenge for Parada's murder, she allies herself with the DEA agent and becomes an insider who helps to bring down the Barreras, especially Adán. However, readers do not learn about these developments as the narrative unfolds. Only in the 'revelation scene' does Nora's interior monologue (retrospectively) disclose her true feelings for Adán. This is where the garden-path symptoms set in: after Parada's death, the narrator ceases to take on Nora's perspective until the scene comes in which she reveals her true feelings. By breaking with the continuity of representation, the narrator denies us a comprehensive insight into Nora's mind and thus withholds important information which would enable us to better follow the plot.[15] The garden-path effect is brought about by Winslow's narrator underreporting to his readers, telling us less than he actually knows and that we 'need' to know (cf. Phelan 2005, 52).[16] Robert Vogt (2015, 133; 2018, Ch. 1.4) would probably describe the narrative discourse of *The Power of the Dog* as an instance of what he identifies as "al-

---

15 In this context, cf. also Nünning and Nünning (2000a, 56), who argue that the quantitative relationing of various perspectives may have a significant impact on the reception of narrative texts.

16 James Phelan (2005, 52) construes the narrative strategy he refers to as "underreporting" as an equivalent to what Gérard Genette (1980 [1972], 195) calls "paralipsis." However, I would argue that, in the context of *The Power of the Dog*, such an equation does not hold. Winslow's narrator deploys the strategy of underreporting so frequently that it no longer fits Genette's definition of an isolated "change in focalization [...] within a coherent context" (1980 [1972], 195) – it can no longer be understood as an intermittent violation of a dominant mode of focalization, but rather constitutes the dominant mode itself.

tered unreliable narration" (*alteriert-unzuverlässiges Erzählen*) – that is, as an act of narration which intentionally leads readers astray.[17]

Again, Winslow's use of the present tense facilitates this type of reader manipulation. Just as the present tense suggests an immediacy of insight into the characters' minds and feelings, and that the narrator relays events simultaneously with their occurrence, so it incites readers to believe that the outcome of those events is still uncertain. The ostensible lack of teleology gives readers the impression that the narrator is presenting the here-and-now of the storyworld in an unfiltered manner, making the relevance (or irrelevance) of the individual events unclear:

> the closer time of action and time of telling approach each other (until they eventually coincide), the less an essential part of narrative *mediation* will have been carried out already – namely the filtering and selection of events, their accentuation and evaluation (Bode 2013, 15; italics in the original; cf. also Bode 2005, 122).

Instead, the narrator simply describes in chronological order what is currently happening within the storyworld, eschewing any use of anachronies, such as prolepsis or analepsis, which would expose his temporal privilege in both directions: hindsight as well as foresight.[18] Against this backdrop, then, readers may readily believe that Winslow's narrator does not himself know how the story is going to proceed and cannot but keep knowledge from them. Hence they may repeatedly fall for the trick, again and again allowing the narrator to lead them up the garden path.[19]

10.4 Creating Suspense and Surprise: The Narrative Dynamics of the Thriller

So far, my reading of *The Power of the Dog* has shown that Winslow's novel can be conceived of as a 'narrative of deception' which manipulates readers through

---

17 Like Phelan, Vogt (2018, 37) bases his definition on Genette's (1980 [1972], 194–198) understanding of alterations, more precisely of paralipsis (see the previous footnote).
18 Cf. also Bode 2013, 15; italics in the original: "These recorded events seem 'in the raw', they have not been processed and weighted, and they do not yet mean anything concretely and definitively because they are *only* arranged *chronologically*, in their mere sequence and order, as everything that happens 'now' [...]."
19 On a related note, cf. also Jackendoff (1987, 244–245), Jahn (1999, 190), and Perry (1979, 357), who all argue that "recalling a garden path and its error does not necessarily protect one from falling for it again" (Jahn 1999, 190).

two main narrative strategies. First, the novel evokes a chronotope which foregrounds the representation of time over that of space. With its prominent focus on the action, readers fail to notice that Winslow's narrative does not help them construct a mental model of the storyworld. Secondly, the combination of covert omniscient narration with the discontinuity in the text's multiperspectivity often creates narrative gaps, which repeatedly lead readers astray. The effects of these narrative techniques – spatial disorientation and readerly deception – arise from Winslow's rhetorical use of the present tense, which gives the impression of a concurrent presentation of the narrative events. What has not yet been discussed in this chapter is how the interplay of these strategies (chronotopic present-tense narration, 'covert' omniscient narration, and orchestrated multiperspectivity) contributes to the aspect of genre. In what follows, I shall therefore investigate the degree to which the textual and readerly dynamics of *The Power of the Dog* bear on the generic features of Winslow's text.

The Power of the Dog qualifies as a thriller which integrates characteristics of various types of crime fiction such as hard-boiled detective fiction, the *roman noir*, and the police novel.[20] For example, Art's character traits may remind readers of the typical "lone hard-boiled protagonist" (Horsley 2010, 34); the fact that he is a DEA agent "whose social values […] lead […] him deeply to question [the legal] system [he works for], and […] whose independence and intelligence distance the officer from the larger policing group of which [he] is a part" (Messent 2010, 180) are reminiscent of the police novel; and the detailed depiction of the gory murders committed by the cartels emulate "the shift of perspective from investigator to criminal" which is typical of the *roman noir* (Pepper 2010a, 59).[21]

While most of these generic characteristics relate primarily to the content of *The Power of the Dog*, Winslow's novel also exhibits a prominent design feature that involves the temporal progression of the narrative. As is typical of a thriller, the novel creates suspense – that is, it "persistently seeks to raise the stakes of the narrative, heightening or exaggerating the experience of events by transforming them into a rising curve of danger, violence or shock" (Glover 2003,

---

20 For an overview of the distinctive features of these types of crime fiction, cf. McCann 2010; Messent 2013, 34–40; Pepper 2010b; and Worthington 2011, 121–129 for hard-boiled fiction; Messent 2013, 50–59; Pepper 2010a; and Simpson 2010 for the *roman noir*; as well as Messent 2010; 2013, 41–50; and Panek 2003 for the police novel.
21 For a generic classification of *The Power of the Dog*, cf. also Andrew Pepper (2011), who construes Winslow's narrative as a "hybrid crime-espionage novel" (415) with an implicit post-9/11 theme (cf. 415–422).

10.4 Creating Suspense and Surprise: The Narrative Dynamics of the Thriller — 237

137). According to Philip Simpson (2010), the prototypical plot of the genre is structured on the

> basic principle of [...] heightened audience anxiety created when the [protagonists are] fighting a contest against what looks like overwhelming odds. Because of the need to escalate the level of suspense to a climactic resolution, the textual reliance upon sensational plot devices (or "cliffhangers") to keep intensifying the action is one of the thriller's most obvious features. The constant presence and awareness of physical danger in the narrative is the direct result of the hyper-exaggerated violence, or the threat of it. (187–188)

In *The Power of the Dog*, reader anxiety is rooted above all in the parallel plots revolving around the conflict between Art and the drug cartels. Since all these plots eventually lead to violent encounters, they usually culminate in a battle between life and death, as is the case in the 'final showdown scene' on the Cabrillo Bridge (see Chapter 10.2). But how exactly do the textual dynamics of *The Power of the Dog* influence the ways in which Winslow's story intrigues the reader, and what role does the use of the present tense play in this context?

Research on literary suspense traditionally distinguishes between three types of "narrative intrigue" (Tjupa 2014, 568–569), or narrative interest in the plot: curiosity, suspense, and surprise. In his "Typology of Detective Fiction" (2008 [1966], 229), Tzvetan Todorov introduces the terms *curiosity* and *surprise* as two different forms of reader interest prevailing in crime fiction. Curiosity, he explains, "proceeds from effect to cause: starting from a certain effect (a corpse and certain clues) we must find its cause (the culprit and his motive)" (Todorov 2008 [1966], 229). Suspense, on the other hand, moves "from cause to effect: we are first shown the causes, the initial *données* (gangsters preparing a heist), and our interest is sustained by the expectation of what will happen, that is, certain effects (corpses, crimes, fights)" (Todorov 2008 [1966], 229; italics in the original).[22] In their "structural-affect theory of stories," William F. Brewer and Edward H. Lichtenstein (1982) identify surprise as a third emotion evoked by the discourse structure of narrative texts. While curiosity and suspense result from certainty and uncertainty about the outcome of the story, surprise is generated by an unexpected event, for instance because a previous key event has been left

---

[22] According to Shlomith Rimmon-Kenan (2002 [1983], 126), curiosity is consequently oriented toward the past of the narrative, whereas suspense is oriented toward the future of the narrative. On a related note, cf. also Langer 2008, 14–15.

out in the narrative discourse (cf. also Brewer 1996, 110–114; Hoeken and van Vliet 2000, 279).[23]

Referring not only to the temporal progression of a narrative text, but also to readers' reaction toward this progression, the concept of narrative intrigue incorporates both textual and readerly dynamics. Meir Sternberg (1992, 519) argues that the three narrative effects of suspense, curiosity, and surprise each results from the "double-time pattern" of narrative – that is, its division into a level of representation (i.e. the discourse level) and a level of the represented (i.e. the story level) – and engenders specific temporal dynamics, each of which is perceived differently by readers. The effect of suspense, which Sternberg equates with the dynamics of prospection, "arises from rival scenarios about the future: from the discrepancy between what the telling lets us readers know about the happening (e.g., a conflict) at any moment and what still lies ahead, ambiguous because yet unresolved in the world" (2001, 117). In diametrical opposition to suspense is curiosity; relying on the dynamics of retrospection, it draws readers' attention to narrative gaps that still need to be filled: "knowing that we do not know, we go forward with our mind on the gapped antecedents, trying to infer (bridge, compose) them in retrospect" (Sternberg 2001, 117). Finally, surprise combines prospection and retrospection to form the dynamics of recognition: "the narrative first unobtrusively gaps or twists its chronology, then unexpectedly discloses to us our misreading and enforces a corrective rereading in late re-cognition" (Sternberg 2001, 117).[24] Thus emerging from the "interplay of the represented and the presented dynamics" of a narrative text, these narrative effects live on either the "'iconic' concordance or 'arbitrary' tension" between the chronological sequence of narrative events on the story level and the order in which these events are presented on the discourse level (Sternberg 1992, 519). While suspense usually involves concordance and temporal continuity, the other two effects, curiosity and surprise, subsist rather on tension and temporal discontinuity (cf. Sternberg 1992, 524–528).

The Power of the Dog features the narrative effects of suspense and surprise, and neglects that of curiosity. Written in the present tense, it constantly feigns synchronicity between the narrative events and the act of their reporting. The

---

23 Work on narrative suspense that draws on the tripartite distinction introduced by Brewer and Lichtenstein (1982) includes, among other texts, Baroni 2007; 2017, 73–80; Langer 2008, 20–21; Sternberg 1992, 2001; and Wenzel 2001, 26–33.

24 Mark Currie (2013, 43) modifies Sternberg's definition of surprise, explaining that this narrative factor consists in "a certain switching of forward orientation, toward what will happen, to a backward one, toward how it came about, which takes place in the activity of interpretation in response to surprise, when the 'unexpected future springs an unexplained past.'"

fictional present contributes to the pacing of the novel, strengthening the reader's sense of narrative urgency and temporal immersion. Suspense is reinforced by the fact that Winslow's chronotopic narrative mostly obscures the narrator's omniscience and orchestrates the text's multiperspectivity in such a way that readers are led to believe that the narrator, too, is confronted with the events for the first time. By simulating the impression of simultaneous narration, the fictional present emphasizes the dynamics of prospection, while retrospection loses its relevance. This, in turn, enhances the effect of recognition, or surprise, as the present tense conceals the "temporal discontinuity between the telling and the told" (Sternberg 1992, 526) which is the prerequisite for this specific narrative interest. Since readers do not assume that the narrator tells of the narrative events in retrospect, the unexpected takes them even still more by surprise. All in all, it is the effective interplay of the dynamics of suspense and surprise brought about by the fictional present that make Winslow's novel such a page-turner.

11 Narrative of Emergence: Metanarration, Intertextuality, and the Disclosure of Worldmaking in Ian McEwan's *Nutshell* (2016)

11.1 First Contact with a Narrating Fetus

"So here I am, upside down in a woman. Arms patiently crossed, waiting, waiting and wondering who I'm in, what I'm in for." (*N*, 1) This is how the first-person narrator of Ian McEwan's *Nutshell*, first published in 2016, ponders about (the sense of) his existence at the outset of the novel. However, being a fetus of nine months that still finds itself inside its mother, such thoughts are new to McEwan's narrator:

> My eyes close nostalgically when I remember how I once drifted in my translucent body bag, floated dreamily in the bubble of my thoughts through my private ocean in slow-motion somersaults [...]. That was in my careless youth. Now, fully inverted, not an inch of space to myself, [...] my thoughts as well as my head are fully engaged. I've no choice, my ear is pressed all day and night against the bloody walls. I listen [...]. (*N*, 1)

The narrator here traces the formation of his own consciousness: In his "careless youth" – the first eight months of his mother's pregnancy – his body and brain were not yet developed enough to perceive his living environment consciously and form coherent thoughts. Now, in its ninth month, the fetus has changed. The beginning of McEwan's novel marks a crucial stage in its development, the emergence of a complex, human mind.

In formal terms, the text indicates this milestone with a shift from the past to the present tense. Used in combination with the verb *remember* as well as the temporal adverbs *once* and *now*, both tenses serve as temporal markers which refer to either the first eight months of the narrator's existence (the past tense) or his current situation (the present tense). McEwan's referential tense use provides orientation for readers. By opposing the present with the past tense, the beginning of the novel makes plain that the narrative events are presented from the standpoint of the narrator's here-and-now. Given that the narrator is a fetus that has just developed its first cognitive abilities, it cannot look back on concrete moments in its previous life, but only has a few blurred memories of its pre-existence. The narrator accordingly lacks any benefit of hindsight, which, in turn, means that he can only tell of events that happen in the present. Against this backdrop, McEwan's fictional present serves a synchronizing as well as a thematic purpose. For the tense which evokes the impression of simultaneous

https://doi.org/10.1515/9783110708134-011

narration (synchronizing function) seems the only logical choice for a narrator who cannot recollect his past (thematic function).

By foregrounding the narrator's position in the storyworld of *Nutshell*, McEwan's multifunctional use of the present tense emphasizes the spatio-temporal circumstances of the act of narration. As the last two sentences in the long quotation above reveal, the narrator is listening to what is happening outside the "bloody walls" of his mother's uterus. In so doing, he becomes an immediate witness to events that unsettle him: "I'm hearing pillow talk of deadly intent and I'm terrified by what awaits me, by what might draw me in." (*N*, 1) This statement clearly alludes to the novel's plot. Inspired by William Shakespeare's revenge tragedy *Hamlet* (2006 [1604–1605/1623]),[1] *Nutshell* tells the story of the (pregnant) female character Trudy, who betrays her husband John, a poet and intellectual, by starting an affair with his strikingly banal brother Claude. While Trudy chooses to live out the passionate affair with her brother-in-law in the marital home, her husband still holds onto their marriage and tries to fight for it. John predictably soon becomes a thorn in Trudy and Claude's flesh, which is why they contrive to kill him.

As the resident of Trudy's womb, the narrator eavesdrops the lovers' conversations about their murderous plan. However, with his limited spatio-temporal perspective, he cannot catch every conversation between Trudy and Claude. Due to his lack of hindsight, he is ignorant of the early stages of his mother and uncle's plan, which they discussed while he was still too young to perceive what was going on 'outside.' And he is sometimes asleep when they talk to each other (cf. *N*, 76) or cannot acoustically understand what they say because of bad room acoustics or noisy ambient sounds (cf. *N*, 23). So he lacks important details of Trudy and Claude's intentions and must first gather enough information to connect the dots.

Previous reviews and articles on *Nutshell* have mainly discussed McEwan's intertextual references to *Hamlet*.[2] While most of these readings bring story-related aspects such as character and plot to the fore, they largely neglect the formal features that serve to evoke a narrative illusion in McEwan's novel – i.e. readers' impression that the fetus is directly addressing them in telling a story

---

[1] Although critics repeatedly stress that "*Nutshell* is a reworking of *Hamlet*" (Neill 2016, 16), McEwan (qtd. in Neill 2016, 17) himself asserts that he "didn't really intend to write a version of *Hamlet*. It just sort of crept in."
[2] Cf. e.g. Adams 2016; Aitkenhead 2016, §10; Charles 2016a, 2016b; Clanchy 2016; Dobrogoszcz 2018, Ch. 15; Enderwitz 2019; Johnson 2016; Knights 2019, 132–133; Mars-Jones 2016; Meifert-Menhard 2019, 196, 198–199, 201; Müller 2018; Neill 2016; Scholes 2016; Shang 2017; Treuer 2016; and White 2019.

(cf. Nünning 2000, 2001b).³ This chapter breaks with that trend: Avoiding any construction of *Nutshell* as an adaptation of Shakespeare's tragedy, I will focus on the novel's metanarrative potential, which mainly stems from McEwan's global use of present-tense narration. I will argue that, by exhibiting a fetal narrator still located in its mother's uterus, *Nutshell* creates a 'narrative of emergence' which lays bare the processes of narrative worldmaking. Before he can attend to action-oriented aspects of his narrative such as the introduction of the character constellation or the representation of the plot, the unborn narrator first needs to understand who he is, where he is, and what exactly his place within the storyworld is, or rather will be. In unveiling this cognitive activity on the part of the narrator, McEwan's novel generates a metanarrative which not only reflects on the conditions and practices of fictional storytelling, but also highlights the ways in which literary fiction can play with narrative as well as generic conventions.

11.2 Framing the Narrative Scenario: Metareferential Present-Tense Narration as a Means to Naturalize McEwan's Antimimetic Narrator

The narrative scenario in *Nutshell* is characterized by a paradox. The story is told from the perspective of a nine-month-old fetus whose consciousness has just come into existence. Apart from the implausibility of such a scenario, one might expect a fetal narrator, in accordance with the logic of emergence that informs McEwan's narrative, to speak or think in a markedly simple manner.⁴ However, from the very beginning, the narrator addresses his audience with consummate eloquence (cf. Charles 2016b, n.p., James 2019, 192). Consider the following example:

> Let me summon it, that moment of creation that arrived with my first concept. Long ago [...] my neural groove closed upon itself to become my spine and my many million young

---

3 An exception is Wolfgang G. Müller's (2018) reading, which also takes the narrative transmission into account when discussing the intertextual potential of McEwan's text.
4 This is due to the fact that, in literary fiction, child narrators, who are supposed to have not yet acquired the cognitive abilities of an adult, are usually characterized by simple language, including a restricted vocabulary, simplistic syntax, and grammatical errors such as overgeneralization. Examples of this literary convention are Emma Donoghue's *Room* (2010), Mark Haddon's *The Curious Incident of the Dog in the Night-Time* (2004 [2003]), and Michelle Sacks's *All the Lost Things* (2019). Donoghue's novel will be discussed below in Chapter 12.

11.2 Framing the Narrative Scenario: Metareferential Present-Tense Narration

neurons [...] spun and wove from their trailing axons the gorgeous golden fabric of my first idea, a notion so simple it partly eludes me now. Was it *me*? Too self-loving. Was it *now*? Overly dramatic. Then something antecedent to both, containing both, a single word mediated by a mental sigh or swoon of acceptance, of pure being, something like – *this*? Too precious. So, getting closer, my idea was *To be*. Or if not that, its grammatical variant, *is*. This was my aboriginal notion and here's the crux – *is*. [...] The beginning of conscious life was the end of illusion, the illusion of non-being, and the eruption of the real. The triumph of realism over magic, of *is* over *seems*. (*N*, 2–3; italics in the original)

The narrator here displays a high level of mental and stylistic sophistication. He tries to remember the "moment of [his] creation" and to portray the emergence of his consciousness. His depiction of this process is structured like an argument: he first presents several options for his very "first idea" ("Was it *me*?", "Was it *now*?", "something like – *this*?"), each of which he then rules out again ("Too self-loving.", "Overly dramatic.", "Too precious.") until he eventually comes upon his first thought as "*To be*," or rather "its grammatical variant, *is*." But it is not the verb *to be* as such that represents the essence of this inchoate notion, it is its flection in the present tense. The conjugated verb form *is* expresses "the triumph of realism," the here-and-now of existence. McEwan's use of the present tense here fulfills a non-recurring argumentative function which helps strengthen the narrator's reasoning.[5] The effect is reinforced by the italics that foreground the inflected verb in the text.

The example demonstrates that McEwan's readers have to deal with an articulate narrator with an adult intelligence, which renders the narrative scenario of *Nutshell* even more implausible. Despite his own insistence on realism, McEwan's narrator qualifies here as an instance of what some narratologists call an "unnatural voice" – i.e. a narrator who could not (physically or logically) occur in our real world.[6] However, once we have accepted the 'unnaturalness' of the speaker, we will soon observe that his narration, far from being antimimetic, appears emphatically logical and even plausible. For within the 'unnatural' confines of the narrative scenario the fetus's performance complies with our

---

[5] For the distinction between recurring and non-recurring functions in the context of multifunctional present-tense usage, see Chapter 6.1.
[6] Cf. e.g. Alber, Nielsen, and Richardson 2012, Richardson 2006 as well as the contributions in Hansen et al. 2011. Even though the different proponents of the 'unnatural' branch of narratology each tend to define 'unnatural' or – to use Brian Richardson's term – antimimetic narrative slightly differently (for an overview of the various definitions, cf. e.g. Alber et al. 2010, 2012, 2013; Alber and Heinze 2011; and Richardson 2012a, 20; 2012b; 2015, Ch. 1; 2016, 389–391), I believe that all of them would classify McEwan's novel as a prime example of 'unnatural' narration.

'natural' practices of storytelling.[7] If, in other words, the premise of an unborn narrator is accepted, a high degree of narrative illusion or mimesis of narration is possible (cf. Nünning 2000, 2001b).[8]

McEwan's fetus adheres to the restricted, subjective perspective of an anthropomorphic first-person narrator, who can only know what he has either experienced or witnessed himself or what other characters have told him (cf. Stanzel 1955, Ch. III). In *Nutshell*, this means that the narrator can only tell of events that he perceives or witnesses from within his mother's uterus, where, in order to "listen [and] learn" (*N*, 25), he incessantly "press[es] [his] ear to the wall" (*N*, 29). Without a twin, there is no one with whom he could interact inside the maternal body; as a source of knowledge he can only rely on his own perceptions. Unable to take the perspective of others, he cannot know what they might think or feel.

The sole exception in this regard is his mother, Trudy. Lying inside her womb, he perceives the physical reactions of her body related to stress, anger, sadness, or happiness, and can make inferences about her emotional state, as the following example vividly illustrates: "Trudy's anger is oceanic [...]. I know it in her altered blood as it washes through me, in the granular discomfort where cells are bothered and compressed, the platelets cracked and chipped. My heart is struggling with my mother's angry blood." (*N*, 77) Given the physical connection between fetus and mother, the narrator can share his mother's feelings.[9] Apart from this prerogative, though, his perspective is entirely confined to his own consciousness and his current, fixed position within the storyworld.

The narrator's mimetic spatiotemporal circumstances hence compensate for the fact that *Nutshell* showcases a highly unrealistic narrative scenario. Yet McEwan's text does not require its readers to look for plausible reading strat-

---

[7] I here use the term *natural* in Monika Fludernik's sense; in *Towards a 'Natural' Narratology* (1996), she defines "natural narrative" as instances of "'naturally occurring' storytelling," that is "spontaneous conversational storytelling" (13).

[8] For a detailed discussion of Nünning's concept of narrative illusion (*Erzählillusion*) or mimesis of narration (*Mimesis des Erzählens*), see Chapter 5.4.

[9] So the narrator sometimes switches between the pronouns *I* and *we*. However, since such alternations occur only when Trudy – and he within her body – move about within the marital home (think, for example, of phrases such as "Together we descend, limping, to the humid kitchen [...]" [*N*, 45], "We lean forward, she and I, me feet first [...]" [*N*, 88], "While we descend the stairs I have time to reflect [...]" [*N*, 134]), or "We hurry down to the basement [...]" [*N*, 184]), the shift between first-person singular and first-person plural pronouns does not represent a shift from an individual to a collective consciousness, nor from singular to plural homodiegetic narration (for a definition of 'we'-narrative proper, cf. Bekhta 2017a, 2017b, 2020).

egies that help to make sense of the 'unnaturalness' of the fetus narrator: he already offers such interpretative strategies himself.[10] At the beginning of the novel, for instance, he explains why he knows such a great deal about the storyworld: "How is it that I, not even young, not even born yesterday, could know so much, or know enough to be wrong about so much? I have my sources, I *listen*." (*N*, 4; italics in the original) After naming the main source of his knowledge, namely his ability to listen to the sounds of his, or rather his mother's, surroundings (cf. Müller 2018, 382–383), he continues to specify his main source of information: first, when his mother is alone, she "likes [listening to] the radio and prefers talk to music" (*N*, 4); in addition to this activity, "she likes [listening to] podcast lectures, and self-improving audio books" (*N*, 4). Secondly, when Trudy and her friend Claude meet, "they occasionally discuss the state of the world, usually in terms of lament, even as they scheme to make it worse" (*N*, 5). The narrator eventually concludes that, owing to his spatiotemporal location, he cannot help lending an ear to all these reports, talks, and conversations, whatever their source: "Lodged where I am, nothing to do but grow my body and mind, I take in everything [...]." (*N*, 5)

Whenever the narrative provides such explanations, McEwan's text draws on a use of the present tense which Roman Kuhn (2013, 217–222) calls the "iterative present" (*iteratives Präsens*), a structure in which the narrator deploys the tense in order to delineate once (and only once) a series of events that occur regularly in the storyworld. In lieu of depicting in detail a situation in which Trudy is alone or in which she is debating with Claude, he informs the reader that Trudy *usually* listens to the radio, a podcast lecture, or an audio book when on her own, or that she *occasionally* discusses problems with Claude – a generalization in which the present tense fulfills a transmodal function as a linguistic substantiation of the narrator's explications.

Not only does the narrator explain to his audience where his knowledge about the storyworld originates, he also clarifies how he can give readers information about aspects of the novel's plot which do not immediately emanate from the characters' dialogue. This becomes evident in the following description of Trudy and Claude's candlelit dinner in a restaurant:

> Here's an example both of Claude's discourse and of how I gather information. He and my mother have arranged by telephone (I hear both sides) to meet in the evening [...] – a candlelit dinner for two. How do I know about the lighting? Because when the hour comes

---

[10] For a detailed discussion of reading strategies that allow readers to naturalize 'unnatural' or antimimetic narratives, cf. Alber 2009, 2013, 2014 and Nielsen 2013.

and they are shown to their seats I hear my mother complain. The candles are lit at every table but ours.
> There follows in sequence Claude's irritated gasp, an imperious snapping of dry fingers, the kind of obsequious murmur that emanates, so I would guess, from a waiter bent at the waist, the rasp of a lighter. […] [T]hey have the weighty menus on their laps – I feel the bottom edge of Trudy's across the small of my back. Now I must listen again to Claude's set piece on menu terms […]. **He lingers on 'pan-fried'. What is *pan* but a deceitful benediction on the vulgar and unhealthy *fried*? Where else might one fry his scallops with chilli and lime juice? In an egg timer? Before moving on, he repeats some of this with a variation of emphasis. Then, his second favourite, an American import, 'steel-cut'.** […] [A] slight tilt in my vertical orientation tells me that my mother is leaning forwards to place a restraining finger on his wrist and say, sweetly, divertingly, 'Choose the wine, darling. Something splendid.' (*N*, 5–6; italics in the original; my emphasis)

In contrast to the previous observations about Trudy's and Claude's habits, the narrator here describes a series of events that take place only once in the storyworld. However, even though the fictional present refers to the here-and-now of the narrator, it does not fulfill a referential function, but should be construed as a metareferential present foregrounding the communicative situation between the fictive narrator and his implied narratee. Thus the excerpt features numerous metanarrative comments in which the narrator explicitly reflects his act of narration.[11] He introduces his depiction of the scene by pointing out that it will illustrate Claude's speech and behavior and how he can from various signs infer both the narrative setting and the actions of other characters. Throughout his further account, he anticipates his readers' likely response. Asking – and answering – the question "How do I know about the lighting?", for example, he explains how he knows Trudy and Claude are having a candlelit dinner (he hears the palaver about it), how he knows they are looking at the menu (he feels the edge of the card on his back), and how he knows that Trudy wants Claude to stop complaining about the descriptions on the menu (he feels his body tilt as she leans forward to touch Claude's hand).

I observed in the first section of this chapter (and see 11.3 below) that in order to highlight the absence of any past in McEwan's narrator, *Nutshell* largely combines a synchronizing with a thematic use of present-tense narration. The 'dinner scene,' however, offends against this pattern: here McEwan's fictional present temporarily forfeits its synchronizing character. Rather than presenting

---

[11] With recourse to Ansgar Nünning's (2001a) typology of metanarration, such narratorial comments can accordingly be best characterized as instances of "discourse-centered metanarration" (discourse-*zentrierte Metanarration*) (144).

the dinner by means of scenic narration, which would suggest isochrony between discourse time and story time (cf. Genette 1980 [1972], 94; Fludernik 2009, 33), the narrator summarizes, briefly enumerating "in sequence" the opening events of the dinner (first emphasis in the quotation). Similarly, rather than quoting Claude's complaints about the menu verbatim, he contents himself with reproducing some in free indirect discourse while summarizing the rest of Claude's objections as a brief speech report (second emphasis). Despite being written in the present tense, the passage therefore implies that the narrator is depicting the situation with at least some temporal distance; otherwise he would not be able to recount the events in such a condensed manner. This again emphasizes the metareferential character of the excerpt: The primary objective of the 'dinner scene' is not so much to advance the plot as to acquaint readers with the singular situation and exceptional conditions of the novel's narration.

Although, as the narrative proceeds, illustrations of this complexity decrease, the narrator never altogether ceases to reflect on his storytelling abilities. In fact *Nutshell* features numerous metanarrative insertions commenting on the extraordinary perspective of its fetal narrator. For instance, when he describes Trudy's outward appearance, he adds that both his father John and his uncle Claude have often commented on the beauty of her blond hair, green eyes, and small nose (cf. *N*, 7–8). And he informs readers that, just as he can guess from the denting of the mattress whether Claude is sitting or lying on the bed (cf. *N*, 111), so he can tell from ambient sounds such as street noise, the rustling of leaves, or the sound of a portable radio that Trudy is sunbathing (cf. *N*, 31). He can even sometimes (though not always) understand what Trudy's or – if Trudy stands close enough – Claude's interlocutors are saying on the telephone (cf. *N*, 45, 165).

These explanations achieve two antithetical effects. On the one hand they help readers to naturalize the novel's narrative situation by providing plausible explications of how the narrator is actually able to witness what he relates. On the other hand they keep readers aware of the antimimetic qualities of McEwan's narrator in the first place. In his study *'Strange' Narrators in Contemporary Fiction: Explorations in Readers' Engagement with Characters* (2016), Marco Caracciolo observes that first-person narrators who "elicit feelings of strangeness in the audience" (1) initially arouse readerly reactions of "puzzlement and disorientation" (65).[12] As readers continue into the novel, however, this

---

[12] Although Caracciolo's (2016) notion of 'strangeness' is applied here to an 'unnatural' or antimimetic narrative scenario, his 'strange' narrator is not synonymous with an 'unnatural' narrator. Caracciolo's concept is broader than that of narratologists advocating 'unnatural'

initial phase of "defamiliarization" is often superseded by a phase of "refamiliarization" during which they get used to the strangeness of the homodiegetic narrator (cf. Caracciolo 2016, 65). In the case of *Nutshell*, I would argue, refamiliarization is impeded by the ongoing repetition of metanarrative comments, however brief. In this way, the narrating fetus constantly reminds readers of his 'unnaturalness' and thus sustains the defamiliarizing impact of his identity. In McEwan's novel, readers are given no opportunity to grow accustomed to the 'unnatural' voice.

11.3 Delayed Exposition, Emerging Plot, and Narratorial Inferences: Combining Synchronizing, Thematic, and Descriptive Uses of the Fictional Present

The narrator's limited perspective influences the process of narrative world-making in *Nutshell*. This primarily affects the ways in which McEwan's novel introduces the triangular relationship between Trudy, John, and Claude, which constitutes the central conflict of the plot. While the narrator informs his readers in the second chapter that the poet John – Trudy's husband, who no longer lives in the marital home, but wants to get back together with her (cf. *N*, 10–19) – is his biological father, he is not fully aware of Claude's identity: "Who is this Claude, this fraud who's wormed in between my family and my hopes?" (*N*, 20) What we learn from the narrator about Claude is that he is Trudy's new lover, John's "rival" who assails the fetus's unborn body with the "piston strokes" of his penis whenever he has sexual intercourse with Trudy (*N*, 21). The narrator, moreover, informs us that Claude "[i]nherited a seven-figure sum" of money, most of which he has already spent, and that he seems to have a job, since he "leaves [Trudy's] house around ten [and] returns after six" (*N*, 24). Yet this information appears trivial, considering that the narrator does not even know Claude's surname (cf. *N*, 24). In fact, he hardly seems to know his mother's lover at all, which is why, at the outset of the novel, he fails to notice who Claude actually is, namely Trudy's brother-in-law, his father's brother, his own uncle.

As the narrator does not immediately see through the complexity of the love triangle, he has to gather further information before he can present an overview

---

narrative theory, including not only "naturally impossible narrators" or non-human narrators such as animals, but also child narrators "who suffer from neurocognitive or developmental disorders" and "narrators who are mentally disturbed due to multiple personality disorder [...] or psychopathy" (2016, 2).

of the characters involved. Only in the third chapter of *Nutshell* does the narrator, and with him the reader, discover Claude's true identity:

> I hear him say he's meeting his brother this afternoon. He's mentioned this brother before. I should have paid more attention. [...]
> **Claude says**, 'All his hopes are on this poet he's signing up.'
> Poet? Very few people in the world sign up a poet. I only know of one. His *brother*?
> **My mother says**, 'Ah yes, this woman. Forgotten her name. Writes about owls.'
> 'Owls! A hot topic is owls! But I should see him tonight.'
> **She says slowly**, 'I don't think you should. Not now.'
> 'Or he'll come round here again. I don't want him bothering you. But.'
> **My mother says**, 'Nor do I. But this has to be done my way. Slowly.'
> There's a silence. [...]
> **Finally he says**, 'If I lend my brother money it'll be good cover.'
> 'But not too much. We won't exactly be getting it back.'
> They laugh. Then Claude and his whistling make for the bathroom, my mother turns on her side and goes back to sleep, and I'm left in the dark to confront the outrageous fact and consider my stupidity. (*N*, 29–30; italics in the original; my emphasis)

While listening to/reading this particular conversation between Claude and Trudy, both the narrator and the reader experience an epiphany. For the narrator, however, this effect sets in a little earlier than it might do for the reader. The narrator already becomes suspicious when Claude tells Trudy he is planning to see his brother in the afternoon; McEwan's readers, on the other hand, must wait for the narrator's explanation that he has heard Claude mention his brother before, but has not paid closer attention. Just as the narrator now commences to listen attentively to what Claude and Trudy are saying in this particular scene, so readers will probably read the ensuing dialogue with special care. As soon as Claude reports that John is signing up a poet, the penny drops that Claude's brother and the fetus's father might actually be the same person ("His *brother*?"), and this conjecture is confirmed when Trudy and Claude mention that Claude's brother has already visited the house and bothered her. The narrator has informed his audience in the previous chapter of the novel that this is exactly what John did the day before (cf. *N*, 10–19).

Only after this revelation can the narrator "begin to comprehend [the] situation" (*N*, 33) and explain it to his narratee: "So. My mother has preferred my father's brother, cheated her husband, ruined her son. My uncle has stolen his brother's wife, deceived his nephew's father, grossly insulted his sister-in-law's son. My father by nature is defenceless [...]." (*N*, 33) Such "delayed exposition" (Tomashevsky 2002 [1965], 169) is only possible because of McEwan's use of the fictional present in the prior quotation, where the present tense fulfills both a synchronizing and a thematic function. It suggests a synchronicity between the narrative events and the act of reporting them (synchronizing aspect) that logically follows from the narrator's spatiotemporal position within the storyworld (thematic aspect): Residing in Trudy's womb, he can only record what is currently happening within earshot; everything else remains unknown to him.

The excerpt on the previous page presents this limited narratorial perspective through scenic narration where direct verbatim speech dominates. Except for the few comments which reveal that he is finally seeing through the triangular love relationship between his mother, father, and uncle, the narrator refrains from commenting the scene and contents himself with identifying the speaker of each utterance (see my emphasis). In this situation the narrator no longer has time to indulge in thoughts, but has to concentrate on what is taking place in Trudy's bedroom: If he does not listen carefully to what she and Claude are saying, he will again miss essential information, and as he has no proper memories of the time before the "primal *is*" of his "first awareness" (*N*, 8; italics in the original), he cannot resort to any background knowledge that might help him fill the gaps.

Apart from these expositional aspects, the narrator's lack of hindsight also has an impact on the development of the plot revolving around Trudy and Claude's intention to kill John. As he draws all his knowledge about the lover's plotting exclusively from listening to their conversations, he initially knows "little of their plan. Only that it excites them, lowers their voices, even when they think they're alone." (*N*, 23–24) Hence, before being able to comprehend what the near future might bring, he again has to gather sufficient information to enable him to make "reasonable inferences" (*N*, 12) about the lovers' scheme.

This becomes clear when the narrator overhears a conversation between Trudy and Claude through which he finds out that his mother and uncle are planning to murder his father (cf. *N*, 40-42). After meeting with John to lend him the money, Claude returns angrily to Trudy and urges her to realize their plan.[13] In contrast to the 'revelation scene' where we learn that John is the fetus's father, the presentation of this conversation does not exhibit synchronicity between story time and discourse time (a prerequisite for simultaneous narration). Even though the present tense still gives readers the impression that the narrator is presenting the events at the moment of their occurrence – the dialogue between Claude and Trudy is again rendered in direct speech – the text here features many more instances of narratorial discourse inserted between

---

[13] The passage analyzed here starts with the sentence "My mother too hears the difference and says, 'What happened?'" (*N*, 40) and ends with the narrator quoting Trudy's last contribution to the conversation ("Poison" [*N*, 42]).

Claude's and Trudy's words. In these passages the narrator not only speculates about the characters' movements and actions ("My guess is they're looking at each other, into each other, a long, eloquent stare" [N, 41]), but also analyzes their tone of voice (he observes that there "[i]s a whine of complain in [Claude's] voice" [N, 40], whereas Trudy's "tone is smooth [and] nicely in control" [N, 41]). Even more important, however, is his description of the reactions of Trudy's organs (cf. N, 41): her heart starts to race, beating louder, her bowels rebel, her stomach produces acid, causing heartburn – intimate details that enable readers to infer her emotional state: Trudy is scared.

While the narrator seems to interpret the signs of his mother's body correctly ("The body cannot lie [...]" [N, 41]), Claude fails to notice Trudy's state of anxiety. We can tell this from the fact that he tries to seduce her over the further course of the conversation, "[p]ush[ing] his groin into hers" (N, 41) and curling "his index finger [...] under her cut-offs" (N, 42). The narrator, for his part, realizes that his mother is not this time aroused by Claude's sexual advances, but upset about the as yet unformed plan: "[Trudy's] pulse, which had begun to settle, leaps at [Claude's] question. Not sex but danger. Her blood beats through me in thuds like distant artillery fire [...]." (N, 42) The fetus can feel that Trudy is "struggling with a choice" (N, 42), and when she finally makes her decision and "says it into her lover's mouth" as Claude kisses her again, it becomes clear to both narrator and reader what the couple are planning, namely to kill John by poison. McEwan's descriptive use of the fictional present contributes to the act of inference. Avoiding any attempt at retrospection, it conveys the feeling that the plot evolves out of the narrator's activity of spying on the characters, for their actions only turn into events of the plot if the fetus hears of their occurrence. Any detail that the narrator misses results in gaps and incoherences, impeding both the narrator's and the readers' grasp of the narrative events.

11.4 The Play with Generic Conventions: McEwan's Intertextual References to the Detective Novel

As the novel unfolds, it presents many scenes in which Claude and Trudy, overheard by the unborn fetus, discuss their plan to kill John. From every further conversation the narrator learns more about his mother and uncle's plan and can draw more detailed and accurate conclusions about their envisaged action. In this respect, *Nutshell* features a type of intertextuality known as "generic system reference" (*generische Systemreferenz*) (Pfister 1985b, 56) or "architextuality" (Genette 1997 [1982], 4–5),[14] as it plays with narrative strategies commonly associated with the genre of detective fiction.[15] Seeking clues to the (future) crime, McEwan's fetal narrator behaves like a detective investigating a murder case. Yet, although *Nutshell* seems to build on the typical scenario of the classical "whodunit" (cf. Todorov 2008 [1966], 227–229), it does so only to defamiliarize that convention. For the narrator's task consists here not in solving a case, but in anticipating a crime by guessing what the potential culprits are planning to do.

Interestingly enough, McEwan's narrator collects so much information during his 'investigation' – a process of inferential reasoning – that he eventually seems able to foresee the consequences of Claude and Trudy's deeds better than the conspirators themselves. For instance, after Claude has presented Trudy his first ideas about poisoning John during a picnic near his brother's flat in Shoreditch (cf. *N*, 57–59), the narrator exposes the weaknesses in his uncle's plan (cf. *N*, 60). By anticipating what could go wrong in Claude's contrived scenario, the narrator creates a sense of dramatic irony,[16] which, in turn, may increase reader's interest in the development of the plot. Like the fetus in Trudy's womb, we are eager to find out what will happen next: will Claude and Trudy really see their scheme through and murder John? If they do, how will they commit the deed? Will everything turn out as they planned (i.e. they will not be suspected as culprits), or will the police eventually (or quickly) find out the truth?

In *Nutshell*, then, McEwan reverses the classical temporal structure of the detective novel from retrospective to prospective. And he does so largely by using the present tense, which suggests synchronicity between the narrative

---

[14] On a related note, cf. also Baßler 2010, 56: "In der Terminologie von Broich/Pfister [...] fallen Gattungen unter den Intertextualitätstyp der 'Systemreferenz', worunter generell die Bezugnahme auf Diskurstypen verstanden wird. Genette spricht im gleichen Sinne von 'Architextualität' als Beziehung des Textes zu Textklassen, z.B. Gattungen. Es handele sich dabei in der Regel 'um eine unausgesprochene Beziehung, die bestenfalls in einem paratextuellen Hinweis auf die taxonomische Zugehörigkeit des Textes zum Ausdruck kommt.'" ["In Broich and Pfister's terminology, genres are classified as a type of intertextuality referred to as 'system reference,' i.e. reference to discourse types. Genette likewise describes 'architextuality' as the relationship of a specific text to text types such as genres. This generally 'qualifies as a tacit relationship ideally given expression in a paratextual cue pointing to the text's taxonomic classification.'" (My translation)]

[15] Cf. also James (2019, 185) and Müller (2018), who also see McEwan's novel as an instance of crime fiction.

[16] For a discussion of the concept of dramatic irony within narrative fiction, cf. Booth 1974, 63–67.

events and the act of narration: the narrator has to speculate as he speaks, in his present, as to how future events might unfold.[17] By shifting its "tense structure" (Currie 2013, 1) from present perfect (something has happened and is still relevant, for we now want to learn *how* it happened) to future (something will happen, as somebody is planning it to happen, but we do not yet know how, when, or where), McEwan's novel qualifies as a "future narrative" (Bode 2013, 1): It "preserve[s] and contain[s] what can be regarded as defining features of future time, namely that it is yet undecided, open, and multiple, and that it has not yet crystallized into actuality" (Bode 2013, 1).

According to Christoph Bode (2013), the most distinctive feature of future narratives is their nodal structure: they present at least one situation, or node, which "allow[s] for more than one continuation" (Bode 2013, 2; cf. also Meifert-Menhard 2013, 45). The nodal structure of *Nutshell* becomes most obvious toward the end of the novel when John is already dead. After the police have interrogated Claude and Trudy and searched the marital home, they inform the lovers that they will return on the following day. Doubting the convincing quality of their statements, Claude and Trudy begin to worry about a possible arrest and ponder on what to do next. As always, the narrator comments on the situation:

> Our lives are about to change. Chief Inspector Allison looms above us, a capricious, smiling god. We won't know, until it's too late, why she didn't make the arrests just then, why she's left us alone. [...] Mother and uncle must consider that any choice they make now could be just the one she has in mind for them, and she's waiting. Just as possible, this, their mysterious plan, won't have occurred to her and they could be one step ahead. One good reason to act boldly. [...] [T]heir only chance is to make the radical choice – and now. (*N*, 185)

The fetus here weighs up two possibilities: Either the chief inspector has seen through Claude and Trudy's lie, in which case they must certainly fear a custodial sentence, or she has not become suspicious, in which case there is still a chance that they might get away with murder. The synchronizing use of the

---

17 According to Tzvetan Todorov (2008 [1966], 227), the whodunit exhibits a duality, as it "contains not one but two stories: the story of the crime and the story of the investigation." The former consists of the actual crime plot and thus includes all the circumstances of the crime under investigation. This story ends before the novel begins. The latter investigation sets in at the outset of the novel and describes how the detective reconstructs the events that led to the crime (cf. Todorov 2008 [1966], 227–229). McEwan inverts this duality in having his narrator anticipate a crime that has not happened. In this respect, the fetus preconstructs (rather than reconstructs) Trudy and Claude's murder of his father, John.

fictional present emphasizes this "nodal situation"[18] (Meifert-Menhard 2013, 46): As the narrator informs us of the narrative events while they are currently happening within the storyworld, the narrative discloses his lack of a sufficiently broad retrospective view. Admittedly, he knows that John has died by taking Claude and Trudy's poisonous drink; yet this restricted hindsight does not broaden his overall perspective on the events; he cannot reliably assess the situation, which means that either option of the forking path could be realized. In fact, it is up to the reader to decide which scenario will eventually happen: the narrative ends before we find out for sure.[19]

The task of McEwan's 'detective' is not to solve a past crime, but to thwart it; or – given that, at this particular point of the novel, Claude and Trudy have already murdered John – avenge it: "My mother *is* involved in a plot, and therefore I am too, even if my role might be to foil it. Or if I, reluctant fool, come to term too late, then to avenge it." (*N*, 3; italics in the original) However, this is not so easy, for, confined in Trudy's womb, where "he is inevitably caught in the present" (Meifert-Menhard 2019, 199), the fetus cannot intervene in the plot. He explains: "These [...] figures [i.e. the characters of the novel] turn before me, playing their parts in events exactly as they were, and then as they might have been and might yet be. I've no authority to direct the action. I can only watch." (*N*, 158) All he can do is kick Trudy in order to remind her of his existence and attract her attention whenever she does something he does not want her to do

---

18 Felicitas Meifert-Menhard (2013, 46) distinguishes between "nodal points" and "nodal situations": "In structurally simple variants of the textual FN [Future Narrative], such as the CYOA-book [the Choose-Your-Own-Adventure book], it may still be feasible to speak of 'point' when referring to the offered bifurcations – it is the location at which the reader is presented with different options as to how to continue the story at the end of each chapter. This is a 'point' in the narrative on which we can (quite literally) put our finger to identify the node. However, in many FN variants of the complex kind, it becomes very difficult, if not impossible, to 'pinpoint' *the* node, as the option for choice manifests itself as an open, polyvalent situation, as an invitation to play rather than as a concretely localizable spot." Even if McEwan's narrator explicitly mentions two alternatives here, I would characterize this forking path as a nodal situation rather than a nodal point, as readers cannot really choose between the options: In lieu of reading the story from now on in different ways, they have to stick to the narrator's chronological representation of the narrative events. The same applies to the characters: Claude and Trudy can indeed make a decision about their future behavior, but this will not affect whether the police have already gotten on to them or not.

19 On a related note, Meifert-Menhard (2013, 103; italics in the original) would probably argue that McEwan once more shifts his novel "toward actual future narration by opening up the text to the potential of *imagined* continuations by the reader, who will be prompted to speculate on possible ways to settle the 'unfinished business' the text leaves behind."

11.4 The Play with Generic Conventions: Intertextual References to Detective Fiction — 255

(cf. *N*, 99, 167). When he witnesses, for instance, how Trudy makes his father drink the poisonous smoothie, the fetus "kick[s] and kick[s] against his [father's] fate" (*N*, 99).

But his attempts are in vain and he finally tires of his passivity: "After all my turns and revisions, misinterpretations, lapses of insight, attempts at self-annihilation, and sorrow in passivity, I've come to a decision. Enough. [...] Time to join in." (*N*, 192) This is the moment when the narrator decides to take action and enter the (fictional) world. "Two weeks early and fingernails so long" (*N*, 192), he scratches open the amniotic sac. Initiating his own birth, he crosses Claude and Trudy's plan, preventing them from fleeing before the police return. Given the narrator's indirect involvement in the events of McEwan's modified detective novel, we must reconsider the fetus's role. Even though he reasons like Sir Arthur Conan Doyle's Sherlock Holmes or Edgar Allan Poe's C. Auguste Dupin, we should conceive of him rather as a modern pendant to Dr. Watson, or to Dupin's anonymous companion, a passive witness who later recounts the adventures of his detective friend.[20]

This resemblance to the traditional narrator figure in detective fiction opens up a final meta-level in McEwan's narrative. By repeatedly stressing that the fetus narrator cannot intervene in the events he relates, *Nutshell* explicitly showcases the conventional position of narrators as being "situated outside of the diegesis" (Genette 1988 [1983], 85) which their act of narration generates.[21] In conventional first-person past-tense narratives this distinction between story and discourse levels – or, if we stick to Genette's terminology, intradiegetic and extradiegetic levels – is usually marked by the narrator's temporal distance to the events he or she recounts. In *Nutshell*, however, McEwan's first-person narrator only tells of events that are happening within his here-and-now – as indicated by the novel's use of the fictional present as the global tense of narration. While the lack of temporal distance between the occurrence of events and the act of their reporting tends to conceal the distinction between the level of narra-

---

20 In this regard, cf. also Todorov (2008 [1966], 228), who argues that the investigation part of the whodunit "is often told by a friend of the detective, who explicitly acknowledges that he is writing a book; the second story consists, in fact, in explaining how this very book came to be written." In the broader sense, this feature of the detective novel also applies to *Nutshell*: although McEwan's narrator does not write a book, he makes it clear throughout the entire narrative that he is telling the story of the triangular relationship between his mother Trudy, his father John, and his uncle Claude to an implied audience.

21 Cf. also Gérard Genette's earlier assertion in *Narrative Discourse: An Essay in Method* (1980 [1972]): "The narrating instance of a first narrative is [...] extradiegetic by definition, as the narrating instance of a second (metadiegetic) narrative is diegetic by definition, etc." (229)

tive transmission and that of narrative action, it is the narrator's inability to communicate with the other characters involved in the plot that finally establishes this ontological differentiation.

Viewed in this light, the narrator's attempts to intervene in the narrative events can be construed as instances of what Gérard Genette (1980 [1972], 234–237) calls "narrative metalepsis" – i.e. the transgression of the boundary between two ontologically distinct narrative planes such as the story and the discourse levels. While the fetus's kicks against the wall of his mother's womb can be understood as instances of what in narratological discourse has become known as "rhetorical metalepsis"[22] or "discourse metalepsis" (Fludernik 2003d, 388), his premature induction of his own birth is an example of what goes by the names of *narratorial* or *immersive metalepsis* (cf. Fludernik 2003d, 389; Hanebeck 2017, Ch. 2.2.4.2.1). According to Marie-Laure Ryan (2006, 207), the former type, rhetorical metalepsis, "opens a small window that allows a quick glance across levels, but the window closes after a few sentences, and the operation ends up reasserting the existence of boundaries." With his kicks, in other words, the fetus temporarily reminds Trudy of his existence without crossing the boundary between story and discourse levels.

The situation is different in the case of immersive metalepsis. As Julian Hanebeck (2017) explains, this specific type of narrative transgression

> designates the narrative phenomenon which triggers the construction of a narrator, existent, event or utterance that 'literally' moves from the domain of the signified to the domain of the signifier (or vice versa) in a negation of the logic of the act of narrative representation (94).

This is exactly what happens when McEwan's narrator decides to be born in order to "join in": he leaves the discourse level in order to enter the diegesis. Interestingly enough, however, this transgressive act or "metaleptic move" (Macrae 2019, Ch. 4.4) does not – as Hanebeck's definition would suggest – negate "the logic of the act of narrative representation," but corroborates it. As soon as the narrator has been born, and thus entered the diegesis, his narrative account stops and McEwan's 'story of emergence' ends, for logically there can be no narrative without a narrator who is – at least during most of his or her narration – located outside the diegesis (i.e. the world) of which he or she tells.

---

[22] Cf. Hanebeck 2017, Ch. 2.2.4.1.2 as well as Ryan 2004, 441–442; 2005a, 206–207; and 2006, 206–207.

12 Narrative of Emancipation: Character-Centered Illusion, Cognitive Dissonance, and Narrative Unreliability in Emma Donoghue's *Room* (2010)

12.1 'Strange' Narrators, Cognitive Dissonance, and Character-Centered Illusion

As demonstrated in the previous chapter's analysis of *Nutshell*, Ian McEwan's 'narrative of emergence' qualifies as a metanarrative in which the 'unnatural' fetal narrator constantly foregrounds his act of narration, drawing attention to the conventions of fictional storytelling. Following James Phelan's (1989) model of literary characters,[1] we can conceive of McEwan's experimental first-person narrator as one who foregrounds his synthetic component as an imaginary construct that mainly serves as a reminder of the narrative's artificiality (cf. 2). Like *Nutshell*, Emma Donoghue's *Room* features a homodiegetic narrator whose voice may cause feelings of strangeness in readers (cf. Caracciolo 2016, 1). First published in 2010, the novel revolves around a five-year-old boy, Jack, who has been brought up in an eleven-by-eleven-foot room in which he and his mother are held captive by a man whom both call by a name which is a traditional sobriquet for the devil: Old Nick. Old Nick abducted Jack's mother seven years ago, when she was nineteen, and locked her up in the shed in his backyard, where he has since regularly raped her. Jack was born in the shed and has never left it. To him, the outside world is a vague notion, an unknown realm which he and his mother designate as "Outer Space" (*R*, 9).

Confined in this environment, Jack has "severe perceptual and cognitive disabilities" (Caracciolo 2016, 56) which manifest themselves in his narrative account of his experiences. First-time readers may stumble over his language in the opening lines of Donoghue's novel:

---

[1] Phelan (1989, 2–3) distinguishes three different components of character: (1) the synthetic, (2) the mimetic, and (3) the thematic. The synthetic component highlights that characters are textual constructs imagined by an author; the mimetic component stresses their resemblance to real people; the thematic component emphasizes that they usually stand for a specific type or class of person, such as the individual of a specific society vs. the collective of this society, men vs. women, or the ordinary vs. the exceptional human.

> Today I'm five. I was four last night going to sleep in Wardrobe, but when I wake up in the dark I'm changed to five, abracadabra. Before that I was three, then two, then one, then zero. [...]
> Ma leans out of Bed to switch on Lamp, he makes everything light up *whoosh*.
> I shut my eyes just in time, then open one a crack, then both. (*R*, 3; italics in the original)

The narrative imitates the linguistic register of an underdeveloped five-year-old. Besides calling his mother "Ma" and using onomatopoeic expressions ("whoosh") and magic formulae ("abracadabra"), which is normal enough for a child of his age, Jack humanizes different pieces of furniture (cf. Dore 2017, 66–68), denoting them with proper names ("Wardrobe," "Bed," "Lamp") rather than common nouns, and giving them a specific gender (formulations like "**he** [i.e. the lamp] makes everything light up" [my emphasis]). According to Marco Caracciolo (2016, 59), this stylistic device reflects Jack's inability to "see the difference between common nouns," such as *wardrobe*, *bed*, or *lamp*, "and proper nouns since he takes both as referring to a unique token, not to a type or category of objects." Donoghue capitalizes these nouns "in order to convey the sense that, for Jack, there is only one in the world—the one in his room" (Caracciolo 2016, 59; cf. also Moss 2015, 13). The same applies to the eleven-by-eleven-foot garden shed in which Jack and his mother live. As Jack has never seen the shed from the outside, he believes that it is the only room in the world, which is why he also refers to it as "Room."[2]

The linguistic idiosyncrasies of Jack's narrative evoke what Caracciolo calls "cognitive dissonance" – that is, they elicit within readers "feelings of strangeness as they are given access to the mental life of [Donoghue's] first-person narrator" (2016, 34).[3] But Jack's narrative account can only achieve such defamiliarization because the novel is written in the present tense. For only in this tense can synchronicity be feigned between the experiencing and narrating versions of the first-person narrator, creating the impression of narrative immediacy required by Donoghue's scenario. If the narrative was written in the past tense, readers would tend to assume that an older, and possibly more mature, Jack was relating prior experiences from a retrospective perspective, in

---

2 For a more thorough (linguistic) analysis of Jack's language, cf. Dore 2017.
3 According to Caracciolo (2016, 34–35), "[d]issonance can arise in this scenario because the character calls for two conflicting (and hence dissonant) reception strategies: on the one hand, the audience is invited to temporarily 'try on' the character's perspective through narrative empathy; on the other hand, the audience resists the character's perspective because of the failure of their folk-psychological capacities (cognitive strangeness)."

which case the narrator's underdeveloped linguistic register would seem highly implausible: Once Jack escapes from his imprisonment and becomes acquainted with the world outside the eleven-by-eleven-foot room, as it in fact happens in the second part of the novel, he begins to understand the difference between common and proper nouns, and realizes that more than one wardrobe, one bed, and one lamp exist in the world; more rooms, even, than his childhood self could conceive of.[4]

However, although Jack's narrative discourse may give rise to cognitive dissonance in readers' interaction with his character, he should not be conceived as a synthetic character like McEwan's first-person narrator. In Phelan's (1989, 2) terminology, he is, in fact, considerably mimetic, resembling any small child we might know from reality. Even if he talks more like a three-year-old than a five-year-old, we can easily find an explanation for this in his limited living environment; besides we can relate his experiences to stories we have heard about abducted children in real life (cf. Caracciolo 2016, 57). Unlike *Nutshell*, Donoghue's narrative does not generate a "meta-awareness" (Wolf 2009, 27) by drawing readers' attention to the constructedness of the text and its characters, but creates a sense of "aesthetic illusion" (Wolf 2004; cf. also Wolf 1993, 2014), enabling them to perceive the narrative events from Jack's position within the storyworld, and evoking the "feeling of being recentered in [this] world as if it were (a slice of) life, a feeling that prevails in spite of the fact, and our latent awareness of it, that this impression is triggered by a 'mere' artefact" (Wolf 2004, 325).

On a related note, Caracciolo (2016, Ch. 2) argues that Donoghue's novel enables readers to develop what he refers to as a "character-centered illusion." Construed from Wolf's understanding of aesthetic illusion (cf. Caracciolo 2016, 8–9, 15), the term describes a narrative experience that grants "readers insight into a specific character's mental processes on the basis of an analogy with real minds" (Caracciolo 2016, 11), enabling them to engage with a character's consciousness as if it were real (cf. Caracciolo 2016, 17). Thus readers of Donoghue's novel are invited to share the naïve perspective of a five-year-old first-person narrator who unconditionally believes the lie his mother has told him for his own protection, namely that the world consists of the single room he lives in and that nothing much exists outside its four eleven-foot-long walls. By taking

---

4 This is also reflected in Jack's narrative discourse: After he has fled his prison, the child ceases to personify the objects he encounters in the outside world. Margherita Dore (2017, 67) accordingly observes that "Jack uses 'Blanket' [i.e. non-standard capitalization] in the shed and 'blanket' [i.e. standard small initial letter] in the hospital."

on Jack's limited point of view, readers can cope with the feeling of strangeness caused by the child narrator and "slowly adapt to the 'difference' of [his] mental processes" (Caracciolo 2016, 57).

Caracciolo's reading of *Room* forms part of a larger, phenomenological project which seeks to study readers' experiences of narrative fiction (cf. 2016, 24–29). Against this backdrop, it stands to reason that his discussion of Donoghue's novel is interested primarily in assessing reader responses rather than undertaking a formal analysis of the narrative. Caracciolo provides a quantitative analysis of online customer reviews of *Room*, which allows him to evaluate interpretation strategies readers use to make sense of Jack's narrative voice. In this context, he covers several important formal aspects of Donoghue's text, such as the novel's successive settings inside and outside Jack's prison (cf. Caracciolo 2016, 71), the narrator's idiosyncratic language (cf. Caracciolo 2016, 59), or Jack's innocent perspective (cf. Caracciolo 2016, 71–74). However, these aspects serve only to illustrate the reviews which form the main focus of his work.

This is where my reading of *Room* sets in. In the remaining part of this chapter, I will examine the narrative design of Donoghue's novel, investigating the most important textual features and narrative strategies that contribute to the sense of a character-centered illusion with respect to her narrator. Proceeding from Caracciolo's argument that Jack goes through a significant cognitive development once he escapes from his prison (cf. 2016, 71–75), I read Donoghue's text as a 'narrative of emancipation.'[5] And I aim to show that the "heightened sense of closeness" (Caracciolo 2016, 63) to Donoghue's child narrator, which Caracciolo observes and which is highlighted in many of the reviews he quotes (cf. 2016, 62, 63, 72, 73), arises largely from the novel's correlation of various narrative strategies, including linguistic style, simultaneous narration, narratorial unreliability, and, most notably, the use of the present tense. The synergy of these strategies creates the character-centered illusion that allows its narrative "audience to follow [Jack's] cognitive development" through the novel (Caracciolo 2016, 75).

---

[5] On a related note, cf. also Naomi Morgenstern's (2018, 47) interpretation of *Room* as "a weaning narrative" which tells "the story of a child's linguistic, cognitive, psychological, and ethical development" by integrating aspects of "parenting [and] primary caregiving."

12.2 Exploring "Room": Jack's Strange Perception of the World and the Dominant Use of Thematic Present-Tense Narration

In the first part of Donoghue's novel, cognitive dissonance arises primarily from the narrator's perception of the world. Marco Caracciolo (2016) explains that

> under the influence of his mother's lies, the narrator believes that he and his mother are alone in the world: beyond the walls of their cramped room there is nothing but Outer Space, and everything they see on television is fictional ('being TV' means 'being fictional' in Jack's idiolect) (72).

Jack's distorted view of the world is mirrored in the way he interacts with his living environment: Apart from the fact that he regards the shed he and his mother live in, as well as the furniture and toys in the room, as unique entities, he also seems to bond emotionally with these objects. Not only does he attribute a gender to most of them ("Wardrobe," "Table," and "Bed," for example, are female [cf. *R*, 6, 7, and 15 respectively], whereas "Door" and "Trash" are male [cf. *R*, 9 and 20 respectively]),[6] he also communicates and interacts with them. Before going to sleep in the evening, he wishes good night not only to his mother, but also to "Room," "Lamp," "Balloon," and all the other things in the shed that mean something to him (cf. e.g. *R*, 53). When he and his mother have to dispose of a plant that died from cold when Old Nick cut off the heating and current for a couple of days, Jack cries and kisses the plant's leaves before flushing them down the toilet (cf. *R*, 126).

Furthermore, he imagines that his toys are alive and can talk:

> I can make Jeep go all around Room, it's easy except at the edge of Rug, she gets curled up under his wheels. Remote is the boss, he says, "Off you go now, you slow-coach Jeep. Twice around that Table leg, lickety-split. Keep those wheels turning." Sometimes Jeep is tired, Remote turns his wheels *grrrrrrrrr*. That naughty Jeep hides in Wardrobe but Remote finds him by magic and makes him zoom back and forward crashing into the slats. (*R*, 55; italics in the original)

The quotation is taken from the scene in which Jack wakes up and finds a remote-control jeep on the table, a belated birthday present from Old Nick. While his mother is cleaning the room, Jack plays with his new toy – an unprecedented moment in his life. Nevertheless, the narrator describes it as if it were a

---

[6] For further examples, cf. Margherita Dore's (2017, 67) study, which provides a comprehensive table of Jack's personifications and the genders Jack attributes to the items concerned.

recurring event. In combination with the temporal adverb *sometimes*, Jack's use of the simple present here acquires an iterative meaning that emphasizes the descriptive mode of the passage. In light of this, the scene serves not so much to convey the singular event of Jack's first encounter with a remote-control car as to foreground his adherence to the tacit rules of children's pretend games (cf. Harris 2000, Ch. 2).

What is striking in this context is that, in Jack's game, inanimate props (his toys, as well as various articles in the room) become active playmates which, in his imagination, communicate and interact with each other.[7] Hence the defamiliarizing impact of his make-believe on readers, because children of his age usually engage in role play with toys that are – at least to some extent – anthropomorphized, like dolls, Playmobil and Lego figures, or even stuffed animals.[8] But Jack does not differentiate between anthropomorphized and non-anthropomorphized objects, for he can only play with the toys Old Nick allows him in his prison. He knows no dolls, teddy bears, or the like. Nor has he ever communicated with anyone but his mother – a lack of social interaction he compensates by talking to the inanimate objects that populate his unusual home.[9]

Not only do Jack's perceptive and cognitive disabilities impair his perception of and interaction with the narrative storyworld, they also have a bearing on how he experiences time. Even though he can read his mother's (digital) watch and is familiar with the hours of the day (he knows when it is time to have breakfast, lunch, or dinner, or that he has to go to sleep at nine o'clock in the evening), he lacks understanding of the significance of time for human experience (cf. Davies 2016, 146). This is because every day in the room unfolds in the same manner, and this fixed routine is only interrupted by a few special events that only happen on specific days of the week: for instance, Tuesday is cleaning day and on Sundays he and his mother can wish for a specific thing they need (e.g. a particular food or a new item of clothing), which Old Nick will then get for them as a "Sundaytreat" (*R*, 25). Except for these few occasions, however, time stands still in Jack and his mother's prison, and Jack is necessarily shielded from the implications of time and its progression for his own life (cf.

---

7 Cf. also Libe García Zarranz's (2017, 49) argument that "[b]y personifying the objects in Room, Jack grants them a sense of material agency, while simultaneously depicting the boundaries between the human and the nonhuman world as porous."
8 Cf. e.g. Garner and Bergen 2006, 8; Ryabkova et al. 2017, 89; and Singer 1994, 19–20.
9 Cf. also Dore's (2017, 67) contention that "Jack not only considers [the objects in the room] as unique, but he also sees them as friends and playmates in his constant need to interact with something or someone."

12.2 Exploring "Room": Jack's Strange Perception and the Thematic Present Tense — 263

Davies 2016, 148–149). Trapped in the here-and-now of the room, Jack is unfamiliar with the concepts of past and future. As his situation precludes new experiences, he can never gain new memories; for him, the passing of years means nothing but an additional candle on his birthday cake.

It seems only logical, then, that Donoghue's novel is written in the present tense. By suggesting simultaneity between Jack's experiences and his act of reporting them, the present tense foregrounds the narrator's momentary situation and highlights his atemporal perspective. And, as we have seen in the first section of this chapter, the negation of narrative retrospection goes hand in hand with Jack's idiosyncratic language: in order to uphold a sense of character-centered illusion in a past-tense retelling of his story, an older version of Jack would have to deploy a more sophisticated register, which would not so readily strike readers as odd. Against this backdrop, the present tense clearly fulfills a thematic function: it is the only tense that ties in with Jack's 'strange' narrative voice.

Of course, one might object that past-tense narratives told from a child's point of view can also employ a discourse characterized by restricted vocabulary and a simplified language style that relies on paratactic syntax – one need only think of *A Portrait of the Artist as a Young Man* (2000 [1914–1915]). At the outset of James Joyce's past-tense novel, which portrays the religious and intellectual awakening of Stephen Dedalus, the narrator also uses the linguistic register of the protagonist, who is still a toddler at this point of the story:

> Once upon a time and a very good time it was there was a moocow coming down along the road and this moocow that was coming down along the road met a nicens little boy named baby tuckoo . . .
> His father told him that story: his father looked at him through a glass: he had a hairy face.
> He was baby tuckoo. The moocow came down the road where Betty Byrne lived: she sold lemon platt. (*PA*, 3)

Joyce's narrator adopts the vocabulary of a child still at the baby-talk stage who does not yet know the right words for glasses or beard, giving readers the feeling that they have direct access to the child's mind and strengthening – as in Donoghue's *Room* – the effect of character-centered illusion. In its narrative situation, however, Joyce's novel differs radically from Donoghue's: *A Portrait of the Artist as a Young Man* is a textbook example of the figural narrative situation, with the heterodiegetic narrator receding into the background and employing the protagonist as the center of consciousness from whose perspective the narrative events are perceived (reflector figure).[10] Shlomith Rimmon-Kenan (2002 [1983]) reminds us that

> it is not Stephen's language, nor is Stephen the narrator in this passage. For one thing, a baby who still wets the bed (see the next paragraph in the novel) is incapable of formulating complete sentences like those quoted above. For another, in this passage Stephen is referred to in the third person ('he', 'him'), an unlikely procedure if he himself were the narrator of his story (although one could perhaps argue that children often do this). (74)

Taking this argument a step further, in Franz K. Stanzel's (1986 [1976], Ch. 4) terms, Joyce's novel does not feature an "identity of the realms of existence [*Identität der Seinsbereiche*] of the narrator and the fictional characters." As a consequence, Joyce can make his narrator take the perspective of Stephen as a baby while still maintaining a retrospective perspective: i.e. he can still combine Stephen's childlike linguistic register with a past-tense account of the narrative events. In the case of Donoghue's novel, this would be impossible without losing the narrator's innocent perspective: If Jack's narrative were written in the past tense, readers would assume that he was telling his story in hindsight. For in first-person narrative situations in what goes by the term *teller mode* (cf. Fludernik 2009, 35–38; 2008 [2005]b, 611) – i.e. first-person narratives that evoke narrative illusion by creating the mimesis of storytelling (cf. Nünning 2000, 2001b) – the reader invariably takes the narrator as the deictic center of referential tense usage (cf. Cohn 1999, 98; Fludernik 1996, 252; 2008 [2005]b, 611; see also Chapter 5.2).

However, while the thematic function of present-tense narration dominates in *Room*, this does not imply that the present tense fulfills no further functions, although these become effective only in parts of the novel.[11] Some of these recessive functions have already been discussed or at least alluded to in the secondary literature on Donoghue's novel. James Phelan (2011, 74), for instance, relates Jack's use of the present tense (albeit *en passant*) to the innocence of the child's voice and to his vivid and efficient way of reporting, which suggests that Phelan conceives of this tense as a characteristic of simultaneous narration.[12] Irmtraud Huber (2016, 58–59), on the other hand, reads Jack's present-tense account of his experiences in *Room* as an example of an extended interior

---

10 In his typological circle, Franz K. Stanzel (1986 [1979], xvi) positions *A Portrait of the Artist as Young Man* at the center of that part of the circle dedicated to the figural narrative situation.
11 For the distinction between dominant and recessive functions in the context of multifunctional present-tense narration, see Chapter 6.1.
12 Indeed Phelan (1994) elsewhere equates present-tense with simultaneous narration.

monologue which "purports to reflect the current thoughts of the protagonist" (55) without suggesting the traditional communicative situation between narrator and narratee. Pointing out that Jack could "hardly even imagine an audience for his story" (Huber 2016, 59), Huber excludes any narrative scenario in which he could tell his experiences to another person, and hence rules out the possibility of simultaneous narration.[13]

I have argued elsewhere (cf. Gebauer 2017, 103) that Huber's use of the concept of interior monologue is unconvincing, because she does not differentiate it from less immediate and more coherent modes of thought representation such as psycho-narration or narrated monologue (cf. Cohn 1978, Ch. 1 and Ch. 3). As she herself admits, the narratives she construes as examples of extended interior monologue "depart from the radical modernist experiments with association and fragmented thought structure to develop interior monologues that are strikingly narrative, presenting an entirely coherent line of thought and events" (Huber 2016, 56).

Despite my reservations on this score, however, I agree with Huber that, paradoxically, one can think of no mimetic interlocutor to whom Jack could tell his story. By drawing our attention to this inconsistency, Huber's reading of *Room* perfectly illustrates my argument brought forth above in Chapter 5.6 that the traditional conceptualization of simultaneous narration hinges too much on an explicit act of narrating typical only of teller-mode narratives. For, although she construes Jack's discourse as an interior monologue (and thus an instance of reflector-mode narrative), she acknowledges that "there is no gap between the narrating *I* and the experiencing *I*, between the moment of enunciation and the events of the story" (Huber 2016, 58; italics in the original). In other words, Huber excludes the option of simultaneous narration not because she discerns a lack of synchronicity between story and discourse levels in Donoghue's text, but because Jack "do[es] not address a non-existent narratee in an act of simultaneous narration" (2016, 59) – the mode of presentation seems to be the problem here, not the lack of temporal distance between the narrative planes.

In light of these observations, when it comes to analyzing present-tense use in *Room*, *simultaneous presentation*, a term I introduced in Chapter 5.6, might seem more fitting than that of *simultaneous narration*. The reasons for this are

---

[13] In a reading of a passage from Bret Easton Ellis's *Glamorama* (1999 [1998]), which also features a first-person narrator who uses the present tense (cf. 1999 [1998], 19), Henrik Skov Nielsen (2011, 59–62) similarly argues that "[n]o communicative situation seems imaginable in which a narrator will narrate these words to a narratee" because "[t]here is no context and no occasion for telling them" (60; cf. also Nielsen 2004, 140–141).

twofold: First, the concept of simultaneous *presentation* (rather than narration) circumvents the problem that the novel lacks any plausible communicative scenario in which Jack could tell his story to somebody else, as it also entails what I have termed *simultaneous focalization*. Secondly, it enables us to see that Phelan's and Huber's interpretations of Donoghue's use of the fictional present are not mutually exclusive – after all, both authors observe a synchronicity between the narrative events and the reporting of these events – but differ only in one respect: while Phelan perceives Jack as a character-narrator, thus focusing primarily on his narrating self, Huber rather construes him as the focalizer of the story, foregrounding his experiencing self. Since the present tense dissolves the distinction between story and discourse levels (see Chapter 2.3.2.1), both interpretations are equally plausible. If, in the further course of this chapter, I prefer the term *simultaneous narration* over that of *simultaneous focalization*, this is due only to my interest in Jack's role as narrator and does not imply that I categorically reject interpretations of Donoghue's novel that foreground Jack's qualities as character-focalizer.

What is problematic, however, is that previous readings of *Room* which note Donoghue's use of the present tense invariably reduce the fictional present to a specific temporal function (i.e. the referential in Huber's, and the synchronizing in Phelan's reading), thus underestimating the full potential of Jack's present-tense discourse. Yet, in narrative fiction, the present tense operates not merely as a grammatical category explicable in exclusively linguistic terms; it is at the same time a complex narrative strategy that can be used to achieve various textual functions as well as cognitive effects (see Chapter 5). I shall illustrate this in the remaining part of this chapter, by highlighting two essential recessive functions of present-tense narration in Donoghue's novel: the immersive and the transmodal. The immersive function is particularly important in the first part of the narrative, which is set exclusively in the eleven-by-eleven-foot room, whereas the transmodal function becomes more prominent in the second part, which plays in the outside world after Jack and his mother have left their prison. Following Caracciolo's contention that *Room* traces Jack's cognitive development, I will interpret the change in Donoghue's present-tense use as an effective narrative device depicting the different stages in this development.

12.3 Taking Jack's Perspective: Immersive Present-Tense Usage, Unreliable Narration, and Suspense

In *Room*, Donoghue often combines the immersive use of the present tense with features of simultaneous narration in order to create a sense of narrative im-

12.3 Taking Jack's Perspective: The Immersive Present and Unreliable Narration — 267

mediacy. This is especially apparent in the first part of the novel, which is set inside the tiny room. Jack has never seen his biological father because Jack's mother forces the boy to hide in the wardrobe during Old Nick's nightly visits. In the following passage, Jack again has to seek shelter in the wardrobe when Old Nick comes into the room in the evening:

> *Beep beep*, that's Door. Ma jumps up and makes a sound, I think she hit her head. She shuts Wardrobe tight.
> The air that comes in is freezing, I think it's a bit of Outer Space, it smells yum. Door makes his *thump* that means Old Nick's in now. I'm not sleepy anymore. I get up on my knees and look through the slats, but all I can see is Dresser and Bath and a curve of Table.
> "Looks tasty." Old Nick's voice is extra deep.
> "Oh, it's just the last of the birthday cake," says Ma.
> "Should have reminded me, I could have brought him something. What's he now, four?"
> I wait for Ma to say, but she doesn't. "Five." I whisper it.
> But she must hear me, because she comes close to Wardrobe and says "Jack" in a mad voice.
> Old Nick laughs, I didn't know he could. "It speaks."
> Why does he say *it* not *he*?
> "Want to come out of there and try on your new jeans?"
> It's not Ma he's saying that to, it's me. My chest starts to go *dung dung dung*.
> "He's nearly asleep," says Ma.
> No I'm not. I wish I didn't whisper *five* so he heard me, I wish I didn't anything. (R, 44–45; italics in the original)

The scene illustrates how the protagonist's developmental disorder influences the way in which he perceives and processes the narrative events. Donoghue achieves this effect primarily by presenting the audience with Jack's limited point of view: We are not told what Jack's mother and Old Nick are actually doing, we only know what Jack hears or sees through the slats of the wardrobe. The narrative's present tense enhances this effect by suggesting a collapse in temporal distance between story and discourse: The events are not told from the perspective of an older Jack who looks back on the situation and has an overview of the action, but relayed *in medias res* by Jack sitting in the wardrobe in a state of excitement and fear at what might happen next. The narrating and experiencing versions of Jack here coincide, conveying an impression of compelling immediacy.

One could argue that the present-tense here fulfils a synchronizing function, and accordingly construe Donoghue's present-tense use as an instance of simultaneous present-tense narration, as I have done elsewhere (cf. Gebauer 2018, 155–159). Such an interpretation is supported by the fact that the dialogue between Old Nick and his mother is presented in the dramatic mode, which means that Jack quotes literally everything that both characters say – a clear indication of synchronicity between the occurrence of events and the act of reporting them. Jack could only draw on other representative modes such as speech report or indirect speech if he had sufficient temporal, mental, and emotional distance to summarize the conversation after it had ended. Jack, however, is suddenly no longer tired when Old Nick enters the room; he whispers in order not to be heard by him and his mother, and when Old Nick addresses him directly he regrets not having remained silent. His heartbeat starts to race. He is excited, nervous, even scared.

The overt display of nerves in Jack's account that on a discourse level substantiates the impression of simultaneous narration informs readers on the story level about his emotional state. Offering a direct insight into Jack's mind, Donoghue's text enables readers to become immersed in the storyworld and to share Jack's experience: We feel as if we were sitting in the wardrobe with him, empathizing with his fear, because we are allowed to see and hear only what he sees and hears. The synchronizing effect of the present tense heightens this emotional immersion (cf. Ryan 2015 [2001], 106–114). The fear in Jack's voice would affect us less if *Room* were written in the past tense.

With regard to the functional matrix of present-tense narration introduced in Chapter 5.10 (see especially Figure 1), I would argue that Donoghue's use of the present tense can be interpreted either as a synchronizing present evoking the impression of simultaneous narration or as an immersive present helping readers to project themselves onto the narrative scene. These alternatives highlight two important aspects of the functional dimension of fictional present-tense usage: First, they indicate that the functions identified in Chapter 5 are hypotheses representing not textual givens but fruitful analytic categories in the attempt to make sense of present-tense narration as a narrative technique. Secondly, they make it clear that the interpretation of the function(s) of the fictional present – or indeed any fictional tense – is inevitably guided by narratologists' individual interest in the narrative text, which, in turn, is contingent on their intuitive as well as their abstract, systematic knowledge (cf. Sommer 2017). This implies that both interpretations of Donoghue's present-tense use presented here are valid and relevant, albeit in different contexts. In a reading that seeks to emphasize the lack of hindsight in Donoghue's narrator, the synchronizing function will predictably be prioritized over the immersive. But if the focus falls on the claustrophobic atmosphere of *Room*, the immersive function will be preferred to the synchronizing. Thus the functional matrix of present-tense narration proposed in Chapter 5.10 serves in practice to highlight different effects of present-tense narration.

In addition to helping readers to engage with Jack's cognitive and emotional states, Donoghue's present-tense use stresses the unreliability of her first-person narrator. Jack's account of the 'wardrobe scene' illustrates what Greta Olson (2003) and Robert Vogt (2015, 131–132; 2018, Ch. II.1.2) would designate respectively as "narrator fallibility" or "ironic-unreliable narration" (*ironisch-unzuverlässiges Erzählen*),[14] namely that Jack can give readers a detailed chronological account of the narrative events without understanding their implications, whereas these are obvious to the reader. Jack's fallibility and consequent unreliability is due to his limited (visual) perception: On the one hand, he cannot know what is actually going on around him, and therefore needs to infer the action from ambient noises as well as from his mother's conversation with Old Nick. On the other hand, he has not yet developed sufficient mind-reading skills to assess the other characters' behavior.[15] So he fails to recognize that Ma is scared when she hears the sound of the electronic door lock. She jumps up and hits her head only because she wants to shut the wardrobe quickly, so that Old Nick will not see Jack. Nor does the narrator realize right away that his mother tries to avoid talking about her son in the presence of Old Nick, which is why she does not correct the latter's guess that the boy is four years old.

The dramatic implications of Jack's innocent perception of the narrative events become even more obvious as the scene unfolds. When Old Nick proceeds to perform his nightly ritual of raping Jack's mother, the five-year old boy cannot grasp what is actually going on: "When Old Nick creaks Bed, I listen and count fives on my fingers, tonight it's 217 creaks. I always have to count till he makes that gaspy sound and stops." (*R*, 46) Since Old Nick always turns off the light before his act of rape, Jack cannot see what his captor is doing to his mother, and even if he could, he would probably not realize its import. Although the boy senses that something is wrong – he starts counting, which is a sign that he is stressed – he does not understand the full horror of the situation. Ben Davies (2016, 156) accordingly argues that "Jack's narrative of Ma's sexual abuse creates its effects through implication: his counting only implies that Ma is being

---

14 Note that Vogt (2018, 31) agrees with Olson's (2003) view that ironic-unreliable narrators do not necessarily have to intentionally misreport narrative events, but can also do so because they do not know any better.
15 According to Lisa Zunshine (2006, 6), the term *mind-reading* is "used by cognitive psychologists, interchangeably with 'Theory of Mind,' to describe our ability to explain people's behavior in terms of their thoughts, feelings, beliefs, and desires." For a detailed discussion of the concept cf. also Nünning 2014, 131–149.

raped; sex takes place, but Jack is only aware of the noise of the bed creaking and Old Nick's 'gaspy sound.'"[16]

Again, Donoghue's use of the present tense strengthens this impression. By suggesting synchronicity between story and discourse, the fictional present makes plain that Jack tells his story from his stance in the here-and-now of the storyworld. In Matías Martínez's (2004, 15–16; 2020, 524–526) sense, this amounts to a strategy of authentication, evoking within readers the feeling of what Antonius Weixler (2012, 17–21) calls "authentic narration" (*authentisches Erzählen*): Because of his lack of trustworthiness, we perceive Jack as a mimetic character with whom we can empathize as we would with children in real life. Jack's distorted narrative would probably seem less authentic if Donoghue had chosen the past tense as her global tense of narration. An older and cognitively more advanced Jack telling the story in retrospect would certainly have a better overall understanding of the situation.

This is where the aspect of genre comes into play. I agree with Marco Caracciolo's (2016, 60) suggestion that *Room* resembles a thriller. Thanks to its forceful interplay of immersive present-tense usage, concurrent narration, and the narrator's untrustworthiness, Donoghue's novel develops a sense of "extended dramatic irony," inviting readers to try on Jack's naïvely innocent perspective while simultaneously allowing them to "always [see] and [understand] more than the protagonist" (Huber 2016, 58).[17] The ensuing awareness gap can evoke

---

16 Margherita Dore's (2017, 69) convincing linguistic analysis of this scene substantiates such a reading: "Jack unconsciously describes the sound made by the spring of the mattress and the bed upon which Old Nick lies while he sexually abuses Ma. The verbs *creak* and *squeak* usually refer to inanimate objects that, under pressure, produce a short, high-pitched noise, with the exception of the meaning of squeak as: 'speaking in a high voice, especially because you are upset or excited'. In the context of the fictional world of *Room*, Jack's perception of the event leads him to metaphorically overextend (i.e. analogical extensions based on perceptual similarity [...]) the meaning of these verbs to an action he does not know about and does not have adequate vocabulary for. By the same token, he uses the expression 'gaspy sound' to describe Old Nick's orgasm as he cannot interpret the cause-effect correlation between gasping and sexual intercourse."

17 In this respect, cf. also James Phelan (2011, 72–74), who argues that *Room* exemplifies the interplay of various communicative channels in narrative fiction. Analyzing another 'wardrobe scene' from the novel in which Jack has to witness how Old Nick gets angry and strangles Jack's mother (cf. *R*, 60–61), Phelan demonstrates how the novel "create[s] a synergy between the author-character-audience channel and the author-narrator-audience channel to communicate something greater than the sum of what's communicated in each channel" (2011, 73). Rather than referring to the classical structuralist communication model of narrative fiction (cf. e.g. Neumann and Nünning 2008, 27), Phelan, however, proceeds from a modified version of Chatman's (1978, 151) communication model which postulates the existence of a communica-

intense feelings of suspense. Two factors are operative here: First, the novel encourages us to engage with the subjective point of view of the first-person narrator and empathize with his emotional states. Secondly, even if Jack presents the narrative events exactly as he perceives them through his trusting eyes, we are nevertheless fully aware of his and his mother's appalling situation. Not only can we anticipate possible consequences of the character's actions in specific situations (e.g. we know that Old Nick would get furious if Ma tried to defend herself against his regular sexual assaults), but we can also foresee the trauma Jack and his mother will suffer from their captivity, which is why we hope that they will escape from their prison as soon as possible. Against this backdrop, Donoghue's narrative exhibits a distinctive feature of the psychological thriller, in the form of a sort of "character study" of the protagonist, who "must confront a blend of psychological and physical danger" (Simpson 2010, 187).

12.4 Adapting to "Outer Space": Descriptions, Explanations, and the Transmodal Function of the Fictional Present

So far, I have only concentrated on the first (captivity) part of *Room*, which is set exclusively in the well-secured garden shed.[18] The second part of the narrative is set in the outside world after Jack and his mother have escaped from their captivity. Interestingly enough, the change in the novel's setting coincides with a change in genre, for at this point, Donoghue's novel moves away from the genre of the thriller toward that of psychological fiction. Readers' attention shifts from Jack's experience of the events in "Room" to the cognitive processes in which he seeks to understand his new surroundings in the external world – i.e. from the delineation of a suspenseful plot to the representation of Jack's learning processes, in which the narrative events are of less importance (cf. McNab 1998, 1057; Palmer 2008 [2005], 474–475). A key feature of this process is Jack's struggle to come to terms with the fact that everything he seemed to know about the world was an illusion based on his mother's lies. Luckily, he is still very young, so that, although overwhelmed by reality, he adapts to his new living circumstances astonishingly fast. While his mother has serious problems finding back into her old life before she was kidnapped – she even attempts suicide (cf. *R*,

---

tive channel not only between an intratextual narrator/narratee, but also between an implied author/reader (cf. Phelan 2011, 68; 2017, 26).

18 On a related note, cf. also Margarete Rubik's (2018) reading of *Room* as a "prison novel."

311–312) – Jack seems to absorb all new impressions like a sponge, and his cognitive development surges.[19]

The cognitive development manifests itself primarily in Jack's discourse. While in the first part of *Room* his narrative voice evokes the illusion of immediacy, in the second part it becomes more reflective. In the outside world, Jack develops a conventional understanding of time which involves not only the present, but also the past and future. The following passage serves to illustrate this point:

> In Outside the time's all mixed up. Ma keeps saying, "Slow down, Jack," and "Hang on," and "Finish up now," and "Hurry up, Jack," she says *Jack* a lot so I'll know it's me she's talking to not persons else. I can hardly ever guess what time it is, there's clocks but they have pointy hands, I don't know the secret and Watch isn't here with her numbers so I have to ask Ma and she gets tired of me asking. (R, 245; italics in the original)

In contrast to the previous examples, the narrative here displays a retrospective perspective. Although Jack still speaks in the present, in this instance it no longer fulfills a synchronizing function indicative of simultaneity between story and discourse. Instead, Jack's enumeration of his mother's instructions reveals that he now compares his new situation with his life in captivity: In "Room," he always knew what time it was because his mother had a digital watch which he could read; but he cannot read the analog clocks in the external world. Jack's description of his current situation shows how he tries to make sense of the outside world by resorting to the cognitive frames he acquired during captivity. While living in "Room," there was never any reason to wait for his mother, or to hurry up, or to make it to a specific appointment, which is why such behavioral scripts are completely new to him.

Jack's learning process is emphasized by the passages in which he describes his new surroundings, as when he talks about his grandparents' house:

> This house is hard to learn. The doors I'm let go in anytime are the kitchen and the living room and the fitness suite and the spare room and the basement, also outside the bedroom that's called the landing, like where airplanes would land but they don't. I can go in the bedroom unless the door's shut when I have to knock and wait. I can go in the bathroom unless it won't open, that means anybody else is in it and I have to wait. The bath and sink and toilet are green called avocado, except the seat is wood so I can sit on that. I

---

[19] Marco Caracciolo (2016, 71) observes that "the mental processes of the narrator of *Room* change considerably as he adjusts to the external world, drawing a line of demarcation between the first part of the novel—in which Jack and his mother are still set in the room—and the second part, set after their adventurous escape."

12.4 Adapting to "Outer Space": The Transmodal Function of the Fictional Present — 273

should put the seat up and down again after as a courtesy to ladies, that's Grandma. The toilet has a lid on the tank like the one that Ma hit on Old Nick. The soap is a hard ball and I have to rub and rub to make it work. Outsiders are not like us, they've got a million of things and different kinds of each thing, like all different chocolate bars and machines and shoes. Their things are all for different doing, like nailbrush and toothbrush and sweeping brush and toilet brush and clothes brush and yard brush and hairbrush. When I drop some powder called talc on the floor I sweep it up but Grandma comes in and says that's the toilet brush and she's mad I'm spreading all the germs. (R, 328–329)

The excerpt again creates cognitive dissonance for readers, inasmuch as Jack describes his grandparents' home, an ordinary detached house, as a strange, unfamiliar place that differs from his former prison. Way too big for his liking, the house confuses him: Its numerous rooms contain far too many things, causing him to draw the conclusion that people in the outside world, including his own family, are different from him and his mother ("Outsiders are not like us"). The dissonance is intensified by Jack's copious explanations, which not only spell out the functions of the different rooms and objects, but also elaborate on the new rules he has to follow in his grandparents' home.

While in the first part of the novel Donoghue combines the immersive use of the present tense with simultaneous narration in order to create an illusion of immediacy, the second part also draws on the transmodal use of the fictional present which serves to accentuate the narrator's descriptions and explications as the child reflects upon his current situation. This change in narrative mediation enables readers to participate in Jack's cognitive development: As the second part of the novel proceeds, we see him becoming acquainted with the external world, learning and understanding a little more every day.

And the more he learns, the better his perceptive and cognitive abilities adapt to his new living environment. Consequently, when Jack and his mother return to their prison a few weeks after their escape in order to say goodbye to their former life (this is Jack's wish), the boy perceives his former prison quite differently: "We step in through Door and it's all wrong. Smaller than Room and emptier and it smells weird. [...] Nothing says anything to me. 'I don't think, this is it,' I whisper to Ma. [...] 'Has it got shrunk?'" (R, 399) Jack's reaction reveals that, after even a short period, his perceptual senses and habits have already adapted to the external world, which, in turn, suggests that he will eventually cope with his new life outside "Room."[20]

---

[20] For a similar interpretation of the ending of Donoghue's novel, cf. Caracciolo 2016, 74: "Eventually, however, Jack starts getting used to this new world. Needless to say, the road

The hopeful ending may take readers by surprise. The lack of an external perspective on Jack's development may initially hinder readers from noticing his progress – an effect intensified by Donoghue's immersive use of the present tense, which heightens the illusion of narrative immediacy. Just as we seemed to be locked up together with Jack (and his mother) in "Room," hiding with the boy in the wardrobe, so now we explore the external world with him, sharing his learning and understanding. Since this development is gradual, we may not observe it right away, but have to rely on explicit moments of hindsight in which we can compare Jack's current perception of the external world with his former worldview in "Room."

We may conclude that Donoghue uses the multifunctionality of the fictional present with marked effect to portray the cognitive and emotional development her child protagonist undergoes in the course of his escape from "Room." In the first part of the novel, set inside "Room," Donoghue deploys the present tense primarily in order to evoke the impression of simultaneous narration (synchronizing function) as well as to encourage readers to try on Jack's extraordinary perspective on the storyworld (immersive function). In the second part of the novel the author still enables readers to have an immediate insight into Jack's mind, but the narrative here gains a new retrospective perspective – the direct result of Jack's rapid perceptive and cognitive development after his escape. Donoghue expresses this shift in the temporal structure of her novel by replacing the synchronizing use of the present tense with a descriptive use which postulates at least a certain degree of hindsight on the part of her narrator (transmodal function).

It is this shift in "tense structure" (Currie 2013, 1) that differentiates Donoghue's novel from McEwan's. The narrative design of *Room* is initially quite similar to that of *Nutshell* inasmuch as neither narrator – Donoghue's child and McEwan's fetus – has a (real) past and therefore an understanding of the passage of time. Consequently, the first-person narrators of *Room* and *Nutshell* consequently have no choice but to tell their stories in the present tense. However, while the situation of McEwan's narrator remains the same throughout the narrative, Jack's situation changes radically. What Donoghue's and McEwan's novels have in common is that they both use the fictional present for a thematic purpose throughout (dominant function): In *Nutshell*, this consists in a global use of the synchronizing present which serves to stress the fetus's unalterable situation in its mother's womb. In *Room*, it manifests itself in a functional shift

---

toward 'normality' is long, but the novel does end on a hopeful note about the possibility of Jack's integration into society."

from a synchronizing to a descriptive use of the present tense, which illustrates the narrator's cognitive and emotional development (recessive functions). Against this backdrop, Donoghue's 'narrative of emancipation' serves as a striking example of the multifunctionality of present-tense narration, demonstrating how the use of the fictional present can enhance the character-centered illusion of first-person narrative in more than one way.

13 Narrative of Life: Orality, Narrative Authority, and the (Broken) Illusion of Immediacy in Irvine Welsh's *Skagboys* (2012) and *Dead Men's Trousers* (2018)

13.1 Narrative Expansion and the Representation of Time: Some Preliminary Thoughts on the Temporal Structure of Prequels, Coquels, and Sequels

In her introduction to a very recent collection on narrative expansion, *Prequels, Coquels, and Sequels in Contemporary Anglophone Fiction* (2019b), Armelle Parey defines novel expansion as a process during which "the plot and characters from a finished novel are retrieved to be developed in new adventures set before, after or during the narrative time of the source text" (2019a, 1). The products of such expansion differ from popular novel series like Joanne K. Rowling's *Harry Potter* series (1997–2007), Stephenie Meyer's *Twilight* series (2005–2008), or George R.R. Martin's *A Song of Ice and Fire* series (1996–), in that they "all return to a story that is already complete, to which the author has put an end" (Parey 2019a, 5). Unlike novel series, novelistic expansions are not planned, or at least not promoted, as a series from the beginning, but announced at a point in time after the source text has been published and, in most cases, already become a bestseller. Resorting to Lubomír Doležel's (1998, 206–207) typology of postmodernist rewrites, Parey (2019a, 1) characterizes such expansions as complements to a specific source text or protoworld – that is, as narratives which "[extend] the scope of the protoworld, by filling its gaps, constructing a prehistory or posthistory, and so on," with the result that this "protoworld is put into a new co-text" (Doležel 1998, 207).[1]

While sequels, according to Parey, represent narratives "that [go] beyond the ending of a preceding and complete work" by depicting events that happen

---

1 As well as expansion, Doležel (1998, 206–207) distinguishes two further types of (postmodern) rewrites, namely transposition and displacement. The former creates a successor world that is "parallel" to the protoworld by "preserv[ing] the design and the main story of the protoworld but locat[ing] them in a different temporal or spatial setting" (Doležel 1998, 206), whereas the latter constructs a *"polemical* [antiworld]," that is, "an essentially different version of the protoworld [by] redesigning its structure and reinventing its story" (Doležel 1998, 207; italics in the original).

in the fictional universe after the period covered by the first narrative, prequels "[consist] in a narrative of events that [take] place before the events told in a previously published narrative" (Parey 2019a, 3). Hence Ben Davies (2019, 28) refers to these as "post-narrative" and "ante-narrative," respectively. Coquels, on the other hand, are set neither in the future nor the past, but in the present of the original storyworld, evoking events that occur simultaneously to those presented in the source text (cf. Davies 2019, 28); literary critics and other literary scholars accordingly also use the terms *equels* (cf. Pullman 2017, n.p.) or *parallelquels* (cf. Berninger and Thomas 2007) in this context.[2]

Parey's distinctions offer an interesting insight into the temporal dimension of what I would call *expansive worldmaking* – the fictional world building brought about by the textual collective of a source novel and its offspring. Since narrative expansions – unlike conventional novel series – do not stick to a chronological representation of successive events, they should be considered as anachronic arrangements of various periods within a specific fictional universe. Parey accordingly argues that

> [t]he positioning regarding the original story time is a key defining and structuring factor to novel expansion that breaks them [sic] into [the] different categories [of] prequels, coquels or sequels because they move backwards, sideways or forward in the time of the story (2019a, 5).

When it comes to analyzing the temporal structure of expanding storyworlds, we usually take the timespace evoked by the source text as the here-and-now of the storyworld. Proceeding from this spatiotemporal anchoring point within the fictional universe, a prequel qualifies as a retrospective narrative that provides us with an extended flashback to the characters' past, whereas the sequel can be thought of as a subsequent narrative that extends the storyworld's present into the future.[3] Thus, when read in chronological order, source narrative, pre-

---

[2] It is important to note that Parey's (2019a, 7–8) differentiation between prequels, coquels, and sequels holds for both types of novel expansion she distinguishes in her article: autographic and allographic. Autographic expansions are created by the original author; allographic expansions – aka "literary spinoffs" (Spengler 2015) – are the product of a process in which writers "return [to] and develop in one way or another a text published by another writer" (Parey 2019a, 7). I here discuss only instances of autographic expansion.

[3] Davies (2019, 33–34; italics in the original) describes the temporal logic underlying prequels and sequels as follows: "Prequels project a narrative movement *towards* their related narratives; sequels, on the other hand, can be said to move *away* from their related narrative. Where the prequel has something of a centripetal force and movement, the latter has a centrifugal one. The prequel's appeal is bound up with expectation of the already instated *to-come*; the

quel, and sequel feature a cohesive plot that runs through all these narratives; however, because a prequel is by definition published after the source novel, the events of the plot are presented in a non-chronological order. The coquel, by contrast, does not contribute to this linear sequence of events. Given that it is set in the same timespace as the original narrative, it should be conceived of as a simultaneous narrative offering a different perspective on the here-and-now of the storyworld.

But what happens if this underlying temporal logic is violated by one or several components of the expanded fictional universe? This is clearly the case with Irvine Welsh's novels that evoke the famous '*Trainspotting*' universe. First published in 1993, Welsh's debut novel *Trainspotting* is set in the Scottish capital Edinburgh during the 1980s, the heyday of Thatcherism, and traces the lives of an unruly group of young adult males from Leith: Mark Renton (also called Rent Boy or Renton), Simon Williamson (also known as Sick Boy), Daniel Murphy (also called Spud or Danny), and Francis Begbie (also known as Franco or Begbie). The four friends attempt to suppress their unpromising future prospects of a 'life on the dole' by touring pubs and night clubs, drinking alcohol, taking drugs (especially heroin or "skag"), and seducing teenage girls and adult women. To date, Welsh has expanded the subcultural storyworld of *Trainspotting* in three further novels: the sequel *Porno* (first published 2002),[4] the prequel *Skagboys* (first published 2012), and most recently *Dead Men's Trousers*

---

sequel's appeal, on the other hand, comes from the excitement of *what next?*" Richard Saint-Gelais (2011, 78; italics in the original) advances a similar argument: "La différence entre *sequels* et *prequels* est ici, me semble-t-il, particulièrement révélatrice. Certes, si l'on s'en tient à une perspective formelle, les uns et les autres paraissent simplement emprunter des directions opposées : les *sequels* prolongent le récit vers son aval, les *prequels* vers son amont. En termes de dynamique narrative cependant, il faut bien voir qu'ils n'opèrent pas de la même manière : les *sequels* profitent de la lancée d'une histoire alors que les *prequels*, pour leur part, accomplissent une opération curieuse qui va, et pas seulement dans le sens chronologique du terme, à contre-courant du récit." ["It seems to me that, in this respect, the difference between sequels and prequels is particularly revealing. Admittedly, if one adheres to a formal perspective, the fomer and the latter simply appear to work in opposite directions: while sequels extend a narrative by going downstream, prequels do so by going upstream. In terms of dynamic narrative, however, one has to understand that they do not operate in the same manner: sequels benefit from the impetus of a story, whereas prequels accomplish a peculiar task which strives, and not only in the chronological sense of the term, against the stream." (My translation)]

4 After the 2017 release of *T2 Trainspotting*, Danny Boyle's film adaptation of Welsh's *Trainspotting* and its sequel, *Porno* was published under the same title as the film (cf. http://irvinewelsh.net/books/info/?t=T2-Trainspotting, accessed August 31, 2020).

(first published 2018), which can be regarded as a second sequel to *Trainspotting* or a sequel to the sequel *Porno*.

Welsh's '*Trainspotting*' novels are written largely in the present tense. At first glance, this suggests that the narrative events are happening right now in the present of the storyworld, or, in other words, that the fictional present fulfills a referential function in these texts. As far as the temporal structure of the source novel and its sequels is concerned, this causes no conceptual problem, as *Porno* and *Dead Men's Trousers* can be construed as continuing the original plot in the storyworld's here-and-now. In the case of *Skagboys*, however, the use of the present tense causes a rupture in the temporal logic underlying the expanded '*Trainspotting*' universe. Since the events presented in *Skagboys* happen before the onset of *Trainspotting*, the prequel is actually set in the storyworld's past, not its present. If *Skagboys* reveals the backstory of the '*Trainspotting*' universe, why is it written in the present tense? Would the past tense not be more appropriate in this context?

A possible answer to these questions is that, despite first impressions, the fictional present does not fulfill a referential function in Welsh's narratives: the author deploys it for other purposes. I shall argue in this chapter that Welsh's '*Trainspotting*' novels, in particular *Skagboys* and *Dead Men's Trousers*, create a 'narrative of life' that simulates the practices of everyday storytelling. Drawing on linguistic approaches – especially narrative analysis (or inquiry) and linguistic narratology[5] – I will investigate how Welsh's novels negotiate the concepts of orality and narrative authority. I will also engage with the notion of '*telling to the moment.*' This particular focus on Welsh's tense use will allow me to show that present-tense narration plays a more important role in connection with the concepts of narrative authority and 'telling to the moment' than it actually does in Welsh's evocation of oral speech.

---

[5] According to Monika Fludernik (2012, 76), one has to distinguish between two different linguistic approaches to narrative fiction, namely linguistic narratology and literary linguistics. As she explains, "one could say that the spirit of linguistic narratology is to do a type of literary study by resorting to linguistics, while literary linguistics is conducted in the spirit of doing linguistics by looking at literary texts" (Fludernik 2012, 76).

13.2 A Different Kind of Narrative Illusion: The Communicative Function of Present-Tense Narration, Small Stories, and Narrative (In)Coherence

Like all Welsh's '*Trainspotting*' novels, *Skagboys* qualifies as a "multiple" (O'Keeffe 1996, 8) or multiperspective narrative with regard to both focalization and narration (cf. Nünning and Nünning 2000a, 42). Not only does the novel – like Nadeem Aslam's *Maps for Lost Lovers* and Don Winslow's *The Power of the Dog* (see Chapters 9 and 10) – present the different points of view of several characters or focalizers, it also features several narrators. Thirty-nine of the novel's sixty chapters are told by homodiegetic narrators who are either protagonists or minor characters like Alison, Nicksy, or Tommy. The remaining twenty-one chapters feature a heterodiegetic narrator who can, as I will show, be characterized as an authorial narrator in Susan S. Lanser's (1992, Ch. 3–7) sense or an omniscient narrator in Paul Dawson's (2009, 2013) sense. Table 5 gives an overview of the various narrators in *Skagboys* (left-hand column); it also shows the instances (middle column) and number (right-hand column) of reccurrence of these different narrative voices throughout the sixty chapters of the novel (since Welsh's chapters are not numbered, the middle column cites the headings and indicates [in parentheses] their chronological position in the novel).

Table 5: Distribution of the Various Narrators in Welsh's *Skagboys* (2012)

Narrator/ Type of Narrator	Chapters Featuring this Narrator	Sum of Chapters
Mark/ character-narrator	Prologue: Notes from Rehab Journal (Concerning Orgreave) (Chapter 1); Blackpool (Chapter 3); First Shot: Just Say 'Aye' (Chapter 6); Held Out (Chapter 9); InterRail (Chapter 11); Funeral Pyre (Chapter 13); Freedom (Chapter 16); Union Street (Chapter 20); Heavenly Dancer (Chapter 22); A Mature Student (Chapter 24); Dirty Dicks (Chapter 33); Hogmanay (Chapter 34); The High Seas (Chapter 42);	

13.2 A Different Narrative Illusion: Present Tense, Small Stories, (In)Coherence — 281

Narrator/ Type of Narrator	Chapters Featuring this Narrator	Sum of Chapters	
Mark/ character-narrator (continued)	Junk Dilemmas No. 1 (Chapter 44); Junk Dilemmas No. 2 (Chapter 47); A Safe Port (Chapter 49); Junk Dilemmas No. 3 (Chapter 50); St Monans (Peer Education) (Chapter 51); The Rehab Diaries (Chapter 53); Junk Dilemmas No. 4 (Chapter 57)	20	
Sick Boy/ character-narrator	I Did What I Did (Chapter 2); Way of the Dragon (Chapter 8); Misery Loves Bedfellows (Chapter 12); It Never Rains . . . (Chapter 18); Northern Soul Classics (Chapter 32); Towers of London (Chapter 45); Avanti (Chapter 54)	7	
Spud/ character-narrator	Love Cats (Chapter 15); House Guests (Chapter 25); Nash Stoorie Bomb (Chapter 41); Wound Botulism (Chapter 46); Chasing Brown (Chapter 55)	5	
Begbie/ character-narrator	The Art of Conversation (Chapter 36); Soft Cell (Chapter 58)	2	
Tommy/ character-narrator	Same Again (Chapter 19)	1	
Alison/ character-narrator	The Hoochie Connection (Chapter 26); Bad Circulation (Chapter 31)	2	
Nicksy/ character-narrator	Seventh Floor (Chapter 30); The Chute (Chapter 38)	2	39
anonymous/ authorial or omniscient narrator	Notes on an Epidemic 1 (Chapter 4); Too Shy (Chapter 5); Family Planning (Chapter 7); Dutch Elm (Chapter 10); Notes on an Epidemic 2 (Chapter 14); Notes on an Epidemic 3 (Chapter 17); Baltic Street (Chapter 21); Supply Side Economics (Chapter 23); Skaggirl (Chapter 27); Notes on an Epidemic 4 (Chapter 28); The Light Hurt His Eyes (Chapter 29);		

Narrator/ Type of Narrator	Chapters Featuring this Narrator	Sum of Chapters
anonymous/ authorial or omniscient narrator (continued)	Notes on an Epidemic 5 (Chapter 35); Skin and Bone (Chapter 37); Waters of Leith (Chapter 39); Sea Dogs (1. Customs and Excise, 2. Reasonable Duties, 3. Car Deck) (Chapter 40); Desertion (Chapter 43); Notes on an Epidemic 6 (Chapter 48); The Cusp (Chapter 52); In Business (Chapter 56); Notes on an Epidemic 7 (Chapter 59); Trainspotting at Gorgie Central (Chapter 60)	21

One can immediately see from Table 5 that *Skagboys* openly showcases its multiperspectivity. As the left-hand column indicates, the novel has eight different narrators; and as the heterodiegetic chapters also take the perspective of various characters, it exhibits even more focalizers not listed in this overview.[6] At a later point in this chapter I shall discuss in greater detail the multiperspective quality of Welsh's novel and its constant shifts between the modes of homodiegetic and heterodiegetic narration. For now, I will focus on the parts of the novel that display a first-person narrator, particularly the chapters told by one of the protagonists Renton, Sick Boy, Spud, or Begbie.

What probably strikes readers most about these thirty-five chapters is that they are written in a "literary dialect" (Ives 1971 [1950]; see also Chapter 5.5), a non-standard variety of English that simulates Scots.[7] Consider the following example:

> Perversity and obstinacy are integral tae the Scottish character. Since ah said 'no' tae these cunts back in Manchester, ah've been obsessed wi heroin. Ah sometimes wish ah'd said 'aye', then ah might be mair inclined tae leave it alaine. Also, it's meant tae be a good painkiller, n this back still nips, especially at night. The doatkir thinks ah'm at it, n they paracetamols are fuckin useless.

---

[6] Welsh's authorial narrator takes not only the first-person narrators as his focalizers, but also other characters who do not feature as narrating agents in the text such as Belle and Samantha Frenchard (cf. *SB*, 63–65), Russel Birch (cf. *SB*, 186–187, 505–509), Janey Anderson (cf. *SB*, 218–221), Davie Renton, Mark's father (cf. *SB*, 285–290), Billy Renton, Mark's brother (cf. *SB*, 290–292), and Lizzie, Tommy's girlfriend (cf. *SB*, 302–305).

[7] According to Dora Maček (2005, 53), *Trainspotting* is written in "very dense Scots."

> It's an open secret in oor circle that Matty, whae gets maist ay oor speed, has been skag-happy for donks. Through him ah ken that Johnny Swan, an auld fitba mate ay mine, gets good gear. Ah huvnae really hung oot wi Johnny in ages, no since we played thegither fir Porty Thistle. He wis a decent player. Ah wis shite but applied masel like fuck tae get oot ay gaun tae the boxing club wi Begbie n Tommy. (*SB*, 57)

This is the beginning of the chapter "First Shot: Just Say 'Aye,'" told by Renton. Renton uses several expressions typical of the East Central South dialect of Scots spoken in Edinburgh and Leith, the city's port and the protagonists' home.[8] For instance, he says "aye" instead of 'yes,' "ken" instead of 'know,' "mair" instead of 'more,' or "oor" instead of 'our.'[9] Furthermore, his discourse is marked by the use of eye-dialect,[10] indicative of the fact that he pronounces many English words with a Scottish accent. To name a few examples: the prepositions *and, for, of, out, to,* and *with*, become "n," "fir," "ay," "oot," "tae," and "wi," respectively; the adjective *old* becomes "auld"; the personal pronoun *I* becomes "ah"; the verb *was* becomes "wis"; and the nouns *doctor* and *football* become "doatkir" and "fitba." The quotation demonstrates how Welsh's style of writing reproduces the "Edinburgh dialect" (O'Keeffe 1996, 7) or "Leith vernacular" (Petrie 2004, 92). This becomes even more obvious when the written version of *Skagboys* is compared with the Random House audio book, read by the Scot-

---

8 Cf. the information on the East Central South dialect provided on the website of the Scots Language Centre: https://www.scotslanguage.com/articles/node/id/76/type/referance (accessed August 31, 2020).
9 All of these words are contained in the second edition of the *Concise Scots Dictionary* (2017), published by Edinburgh University Press.
10 Marion Gymnich (2007, 106; italics in the original) defines the literary strategy of eye dialect as follows: ",Eye-dialect' beruht auf der Strategie, ein Wort – abweichend von der Standardorthographie – so zu schreiben, wie es (auch) von SprecherInnen der Standardsprache ausgesprochen wird. So reflektiert etwa die Schreibung <iz> für die dritte Person Singular Präsens des Verbs *to be* die auch in der Standardsprache übliche Aussprache des Wortes *is*, suggeriert aber paradoxerweise durch die nicht-standardisierte Schreibung dennoch eine Abweichung von der Norm." ["'Eye-dialect' relies on the strategy of spelling a word – notwithstanding standard orthography – in the way in which it is pronounced (also) by speakers of the standard language. Thus, the spelling <iz> for the third person singular present tense of the verb *to be*, for example, reflects that pronunciation of the word *is* which is also common in standard language usage; paradoxically, however, the non-standardized spelling of this word nevertheless suggests a deviation from the norm." (My translation)] In the case of *Skagboys*, however, Welsh deploys this strategy to project not so much the Standard pronunciation as a Scottish pronunciation of English.

tish actor Tam Dean Burn, who himself from Leith, has a flawless local accent (cf. Welsh 2012b).[11]

However, the chapters with a homodiegetic narrator also feature various idiolects of the individual first-person narrators.[12] The following quotations reproduce four short excerpts, each narrated by one of Welsh's protagonists:

Quotation 1 (narrator = Renton):
Ma fist pulverises that beepin bastard ay a clock intae silence. Sick Boy's lyin next tae **us** oan the mattress, beanie hat on, in a deep slumber; never even heard the alarm. If **ah**'d been rimmin the fucker aw night thaire couldnae be a worse taste in **ma** mooth. **Ah** gits up n the flat's like a fuckin fridge, n **ah** pull on a jumper and some tracky bottoms and socks. [...] It's Christmas the day eftir the morn, though **ah**'m steyin doon here, savin **masel** for New Year. (*SB*, 253; my emphasis).

Quotation 2 (narrator = Sick Boy):
As **ah** hit the foot ay the Walk it starts tae pish doon; cauld, skin-stinging rain, but **I** crack a smile, stretching my bare, T-shirted arms out [...], letting the bounty of the good Lord cool my skin.
 Tae the business at hand; **ah** get up tae the Williamson rabbit hutch on the second floor of this systems-built warren that dominates the old port proper, not the shite south ay Junction Street and Duke Street, which **ah** refuse tae acknowledge as *real* Leith. — Simon ... son ... my mother pleads, but ignoring her and Louisa and Carlotta, **I** immediately go tae the parental boudoir, tae check that the vain, posturing prick has emptied the jackets and shirts fae his wardrobe. [...] My heart races as **I** pull the creaky door open. (*SB*, 22–23; italics in the original; my emphasis)

Quotation 3 (narrator = Spud):
Tolly skint, **man**, n the bread trap ay Christmas n New Year looms. [...] Begbie comes roond the gaff, n yuv nivir seen a rooster in such a foul mood, **ken?** — Spud, he goes, pushin past us intae the flat, lookin around fir Rents n Sick Boy. — Whaire the fuck ur they two cunts?
 — Dinnae ken, man, every cat jist sortay comes n goes here, ken? ah tell um. Ah'm feelin a bit shitey, jist tryin tae tidy up a bit roond the gaff, **ken?** Sortay pill ma weight a bit, **likesay**. (*SB*, 193; my emphasis)

Quotation 4 (narrator = Begbie):
Ah sais tae **fuckin** June earlier, ah goes: thank **fuck** that's January nearly ower. A **shite fuckin** month. Baw cauld n every **cunt** steyin in aw the time, Renton sneakin away back

---

11 For a further analysis of Welsh's use of non-standard language in *Trainspotting*, which is comparable to his use of vernacular in *Skagboys*, cf. also Hames 2013, 211–215; McRae 2004, 131–132; Morace 2001, 24–28; Pollner 2005; Racolta 2017, 149–150; and Riach 2005, 36.
12 Peter Childs (2005, 245) and Aaron Kelly (2005, 50) similarly maintain that Welsh uses non-standard English in *Trainspotting* to represent the characters' various dialects.

doon tae **fuckin** London wi that wee **cunt** he hud up here. Wisnae a bad wee **fucker**, but every **cunt** should stey whaire they **fuckin** well come fae, that's what ah eywis **fuckin** well say. At least Rents came back; Sick Boy nivir even **fuckin** showed up at aw. (*SB*, 278; my emphasis)

Comparing the four quotations with each other, we notice that, even though the protagonists all speak vernacular Scots, each has an individual idiolect.[13] While Renton always uses the non-standard form of first-person singular pronouns ("ah," "ma," "masel," and "us," which, in this case, stands for 'me'; see my emphasis in Quotation 1), Sick Boy constantly switches between the vernacular ("ah") and the standard ("I") variants (see my emphasis in Quotation 2). Spud's and Begbie's discourses are even more idiosyncratic than those of their friends: Spud often addresses his narratee by asking the question "ken?" ('you know?'); besides he frequently uses insertions like "man" as well as filler expressions such as "likesay" ('like I say') (see my emphasis in Quotation 3). Finally, Begbie's discourse abounds with expletives and derogatory terms, his favorites being *fuck*, *cunt*, and *shite* (see my emphasis in Quotation 4).

Staging a literary dialect which integrates both the non-standard form of Edinburgh Scots and the different characters' idiolects, the homodiegetic chapters in *Skagboys* evoke a scenario of oral speech (or, more precisely, oral narrative).[14] Bernard O'Keeffe (1996, 7) consequently argues that the narrators of

---

13 Childs (2005, 246) goes so far as to argue that their various idiolects are the central means by which readers can tell the different homodiegetic narrators apart: "Welsh takes care to identify each narrator with particular patterns of speech and expression in their use of dialect. Thus, though it is not always clear to the reader from the content or context at the outset as to who is narrating each chapter, the language is an immediate clue."
14 On a related note, cf. also Gymnich 2007, 100: "[B]ei Äußerungen einer Erzählinstanz wird durch nicht-standardsprachliche Merkmale eine Illusion von Mündlichkeit geschaffen: Als 'fingierte Mündlichkeit' [...] dient die Inszenierung regionaler und sozialer Varietäten der Sprache dazu, die Illusion authentischer mündlicher Rede hervorzurufen, ohne dabei freilich tatsächlich mündliche Rede abzubilden oder exakt nachzuahmen." ["In the context of narratorial utterances, features of non-standard language usage evoke an illusion of orality: qualifying as a characteristic of 'simulated orality,' the narrative staging of regional and social varieties serves to evoke the illusion of authentic spoken language without, of course, actually reproducing or accurately imitating spoken language." (My translation)] Gymnich here resorts to Paul Goetsch's (1985, 202; 2008 [2005], 413) concept of "feigned or pseudo-orality" [*fingierte Mündlichkeit*], which is based on the notion that, if reproduced in written discourse, oral speech is never genuine, but feigned: "Mündlichkeit in geschriebenen Texten ist nie mehr sie selbst, sondern stets fingiert und damit eine Komponente des Schreibstils und oft auch der bewußten Schreibstrategie des jeweiligen Autors." ["Orality in written texts is never itself, but

Trainspotting, who are in some cases the same character-narrators that we find in *Skagboys*, "speak, rather than write, their stories." The fact that each of the first-person narrators uses present-tense narration heightens this narrative illusion. As both narratologists and linguists argue, we often deploy the present tense in order to tell each other about our experiences in everyday communication.[15] When used in the context of such conversational narratives, the present tense usually serves as a rhetorical device that marks the reportability of a specific event or experience (see Chapter 5.5).

I would contend that Welsh's communicative use of the fictional present in the homodiegetic chapters of *Skagboys* fulfills a similar purpose as the "conversational historical present" (Wolfson 1982) that we use in conversational storytelling. The reason for this is that almost all the characters relate events and experiences that represent a crucial rupture in their lives and therefore display a high degree of tellability: Renton, for example, tells, among other things, about the death and funeral of his younger, chronically ill brother Wee Davie (cf. *SB*, 123–138), and about how he took heroin for the first time in his life (cf. *SB*, 57–62); Sick Boy relates how he started a relationship with a teenage girl, Maria, whom he seduced into taking heroin, plunging her into misery (cf. *SB*, 152–157); Spud narrates how he collapsed on the street, having contracted a dangerous infection from using a needle too often (cf. *SB*, 343–347, 369–371); and Begbie recounts how he had to 'sign on the dole,' entered the local crime scene, and eventually ended up in prison after brutally assaulting an innocent man on Leith Walk (cf. *SB*, 278–284, 511–512).

In this way Welsh's combination of literary dialect and present-tense narration creates a narrative scenario with high mimetic potential. As the homodiegetic chapters of the novel evoke the impression of conversational storytelling, readers may feel as if the narrator-characters were actually conversing with them, telling them about their experiences in the same way as they talk to anybody else in ordinary conversation. This becomes most plain in passages where direct speech is included in the narrative discourse. As far as the representation of Scots dialect and the characters' individual idiolects is concerned, these instances of direct speech do not differ much from the speakers' narrative accounts. The lack of quotation marks additionally emphasizes the mimetic illusion of conversational narrative – after all, no such punctuation marks are

---

always feigned; thus, it is a component of the style of writing and, in most cases, also of the deliberate writing strategy of the author." (My translation)]

15 Cf. e.g. Fludernik 1991, 1992a; Quasthoff 1980, Ch. 5; Schiffrin 1978, 1981; and Wolfson 1978, 1979, 1981, 1982.

available in natural speech. Considering all this, one can conclude that the chapters in *Skagboys* that feature a first-person narrator strive to imitate what Monika Fludernik (1996) calls "'natural' narratives" – instances of storytelling we could encounter in real life.

My reading of Welsh's novel as a 'narrative of life' is, moreover, grounded on the structural make-up of *Skagboys*. Renton, Sick Boy, Spud, Begbie and the minor characters do not relate their individual stories one after another; instead, each of them tells a varying number of episodes that alternate with the episodes narrated by another character or the heterodiegetic narrator (see also the middle column in Table 5). As a consequence, the novel resembles not so much a coherent narrative as a loose compilation of different sequences reminiscent of "broken narrative." Representing a firmly established "travelling concept" (Bal 2002) of "interdisciplinary studies on the role of stories of health and illness, [...] the field known as 'trauma theory' or 'trauma studies', and [...] genres like autobiography or life stories" (Nünning and Nünning 2016, 41), broken narratives qualify as instances of (non-fictional) storytelling in which people try to come to terms with the experience of illness (cf. Kirmayer 2000 as well as the contributions in Hydén and Brockmeier 2008), trauma (cf. Armstrong 2002, Sewell and Williams 2002), or other social, political, economic, or ecological crisis (cf. Nünning and Nünning 2016). Since these narratives are always associated with a drastic rupture in people's lives, they generate "stories that are often fragmented, disorganized or where the narrative text is superseded by the performance of the story" (Hyvärinen et al. 2010b, 2).

Sketching a narratological model of broken narrative, Ansgar and Vera Nünning (2016, 55) identify six salient features of this type of storytelling:

> First, [broken narratives] are characterized by a central event or kernel that revolves around a break, break-up or disruption. Secondly, this kernel entails a high degree of eventfulness. Thirdly, they display a profound lack of the various dimensions of narrative coherence, i.e. temporal, causal, and thematic. On the basis of these subtypes of coherence, three additional features can be identified, viz. temporal discontinuity and fragmentation, questioning or suspension of causality, and "abrupt discontinuities within and between topics." (Nünning and Nünning 2016, 55)

If we apply these features to *Skagboys*, we realize that Welsh's novel perfectly fits Nünning and Nünning's model. All these stories revolve around a disruption in the lives of their first-person narrator, a drastic event or experience that engenders a high degree of tellability (criteria 1 and 2). Moreover, the fragmentary, episodic structure of Welsh's novel violates any sense of temporal, causal, or thematic coherence (criterion 3 and its three subcriteria).[16]

However, in the "Afterword" to *Beyond Narrative Coherence*, a 2010 volume on broken narrative edited by Matti Hyvärinen, Lars-Christer Hydén, Marja Saarenheimo, and Maria Tamboukou, Mark Freeman (2010) observes that "nearly every chapter in this book seeks to show that, behind the *manifest* incoherence or 'a-coherence' of the narratives in question a *latent* coherence lurks" (167; italics in the original), narrative coherence being "*deferred*, 'put on hold', until some interpretive work has been carried out" (181; italics in the original). Once this task has been accomplished, "we come to see a greater measure of coherence than meets the eye" (Freeman 2010, 181). If, following Freeman's advice, we "[let] interpretation restore meaning" (Iversen 2013, 150), a reading arises that gives coherence to the various story fragments of Welsh's text. They become thirty-nine instances of what linguists refer to as "small stories," the everyday narratives we tell each other to make sense of our experiences and form our individual and collective identities.[17] And this is where the aspect of multiperspectivity becomes relevant again. By drawing on the strategies of multiperspective narration, *Skagboys* provides readers with various perspectives on the world of Edinburgh in the 1980s and a group of young working-class adults who become addicted to heroin during their attempts to cope with the miseries their lives present them with. Viewed in this light, *Skagboys* turns into a broken life narrative that traces the reasons for the protagonists' drug addiction.

---

16 The same formal make-up is evident in Welsh's *Trainspotting*. Jennifer M. Jeffers (2005, 89), for example, argues that *Trainspotting* is characterized by a "non-stable narrative rhizome structure": "Welsh amplifies the despair and hopelessness of his out-of-work Scottish characters in the 1980s by presenting their narratives rhizomatically; one might even question categorizing the text as a novel, rather than simply a collection of sketches about a group of people more-or-less from the same economically depressed working class Edinburgh suburb." (Jeffers 2005, 89) O'Keeffe (1996, 8) proposes a similar argument: "It is sometimes difficult to identify [in *Trainspotting*] who exactly is narrating and the lack of linear narrative produces a kaleidoscopic, swirling effect, drawing the reader in and out of the lives of the young junkies, psychopaths, chancers and drifters."
17 Cf. e.g. Bamberg 2007, Bamberg and Georgakopoulou 2008, and Georgakopoulou 2006, 2007.

13.3 Oral Storytelling vs. Written Narrative: The Nexus between Fictional Tense Usage and Narrative Authority

In orchestrating the multiple voices of its different narrators, *Skagboys* raises the question of narrative authority. According to Susan S. Lanser (1999),

> [n]arratologists have often noted the privileged status of narrators vis-à-vis narrated characters: because the narrator's acts literally bring the story into existence, his or her word carries greater authority than the word of a character. Structurally, this means that the narrator always stands at a level 'above' the narrated events by virtue of narrating them. (171)

Although this privilege embraces all extradiegetic narrators, whether homodiegetic or heterodiegetic, Lanser maintains that it is especially powerful in the case of the narrative voice she characterizes as "authorial" – i.e. extradiegetic, public, and potentially self-referential.[18] For readers, she explains, the authorial narrator is *per se* believed not only to transmit, but also to create the primary narrative: "[S]ince authorial narrators exist outside narrative time (indeed, 'outside' fiction) and are not 'humanized' by events, they conventionally carry an authority superior to that conferred on characters, even on narrating characters." (Lanser 1992, 16) With regard to *Skagboys*, this implies that readers probably will ascribe the highest position of authority to Welsh's heterodiegetic narrator: Due to the lack of a textually marked distinction between the (implied) author and the heterodiegetic narrator in this novel, "readers are invited to equate the [authorial] narrator with the author and the narratee with themselves" (Lanser 1992, 16).

Welsh deploys two main strategies to stabilize the hierarchical relation between heterodiegetic narrator and (homodiegetic) narrating characters. The first is his use of literary dialect. While the first-person segments of the novel are written in Scots vernacular, the twenty-one chapters told by a heterodiegetic narrator are written in Standard English (cf. Racolta 2017, 149). Marion Gymnich (2002) sees this as a traditional technique:

> Regional and social varieties of a language were apparently deemed more or less acceptable in the domain of oral communication and, thus, by analogy, in literary dialogues, but

---

[18] Although Lanser (1992, 15–16) bases her definition of an authorial voice primarily on the terminology introduced by Gérard Genette (1980 [1972]) (i.e. extradiegetic-heterodiegetic narrator), her concept additionally invokes Franz K. Stanzel's (1995 [1979]) understanding of an authorial (as opposed to figural) mode of narration.

they were [...] seen as inferior [...] forms of language that were not appropriate for the written medium. (Gymnich 2002, 66)

Thus the distribution of vernacular speech and Standard English in Welsh's novel establishes a clear distinction between the 'conversational' narratives told by the character-narrators and the 'written' narrative presented through the voice of the authorial narrator.

Welsh's second strategy for enhancing the authority of his heterodiegetic narrator (and thus at the same time for diminishing the authority of his character-narrators) is tense usage. Given that the homodiegetic narrators usually relate their experiences in the present tense, their narratives frequently evoke the impression of immediacy, as at the beginning of "Funeral Pyre," narrated by Renton (cf. *SB*, 123). Renton's present-tense account of his preparation for his little brother's funeral evinces no temporal distance between narrator and narrative events. The chapter begins *in medias res*, leaving out any background information that might contextualize the situation, and Renton also refrains from telling us what is actually happening in this scene. We learn that Renton is standing in front of the pub mirror in his kitchen trying to put on his tie; however, we have to infer this information from his thoughts ("Another erse-up wi that scabby black tie" [*SB*, 123]) and his statement that he yanks the tie off for the tenth time. Similarly, he does not tell us that Sick Boy enters the kitchen; he suddenly sees him in the mirror: "Sick Boy's at ma shoodir, providing succour. He gets the tie right first go." (*SB*, 123) This all suggests that Renton's narrating and experiencing selves coincide (cf. Stanzel 1972 [1964], 31–39) – an effect that is only possible as a result of the synchronizing fictional present. If Renton used the past tense, readers would likely assume that he was telling of his experiences in retrospect and would expect a less eliptical depiction of the situation. With hindsight, for example, Renton would probably be less concerned about not being able to tie his tie properly: i.e. he curses ("Shite!" [*SB*, 123]) – a reaction we can interpret as a sign of his emotional overload at his brother's death. The example is representative of all the chapters that feature a homodiegetic narrator.

While the accounts of Welsh's homodiegetic narrators create the impression of narrative immediacy, the heterodiegetic chapters imply a temporal distance between story and discourse. Most of the twenty-one chapters written in Standard English use the preterite as the global tense of narration,[19] suggesting that Welsh's heterodiegetic narrator has a broader temporal overview of the narrative events than the narrating characters. The chapters "Notes on an Epidemic 1–7" serve especially to present readers with the historical context of Welsh's storyworld, providing information on the Scottish Devolution Referendum of 1979 (cf. *SB*, 46), the drastic increase in unemployment after the election of Margaret Thatcher in the same year (cf. *SB*, 139), and drug-related developments in Edinburgh, ranging from the rise of heroin, which had already started at the beginning of the nineteenth century (cf. *SB*, 151), through the shutdown of the Needle Exchange in Bread Street, Tollcross by the police in the early 1980s (cf. *SB*, 230), to the first instance of HIV infection in the city (cf. *SB*, 277) and subsequent escalation in reported HIV+ cases by the Lothian Health Board (cf. *SB*, 377, 513–515). With the benefit of hindsight, the heterodiegetic narrator can express the social criticism that underlies Welsh's novel: By tracing political and social developments in the UK during the late 1970s and early 1980s, the authorial narrator establishes a connection between Thatcherism and the explosive increase in heroin addiction among young British adults during this period. This overview of the historical context of *Skagboys* infuses the discourse of Welsh's heterodiegetic narrator with an authority which Paul Dawson (2009, 153; 2013, Ch. 3) sees as that of "the literary historian." Brought about by a specific form of omniscient narration which "relies upon the authority of the historical record and the possibilities of imaginatively recovering private or occluded moments in history," it strives "to supplement the historical record" by means of the "literary imagination" (Dawson 2009, 153; 2013, 88).

Against this backdrop, one can conclude that Welsh's correlation of fictional tense and narrative perspective, as well as standard and non-standard language, serves to establish a strong hierarchical authority among the various narrative voices of *Skagboys*. By using the present tense as their global tense of narration, the vernacular accounts of the seven first-person narrators evoke the impression of spontaneous conversational storytelling, and their various small stories seem still in the making. Using Standard English and the past tense, the chapters told through the voice of Welsh's heterodiegetic narrator, by contrast, manifest themselves as written discourse and, as such, qualify as more reflective, evaluative, and teleological than the oral narratives of the characters. Welsh draws skillfully on the synchronizing function of the fictional present,

---

19 Exceptions are "Too Shy," "Baltic Street," "Skaggirl," "Waters of Leith," "Sea Dogs," "Desertion," and "Trainspotting at Gorgie Central"; these chapters are partly or even entirely written in the present tense.

combining it with the retrospective view of the preterite to attribute different degrees of authority to his narrators. Nevertheless, the narrative immediacy sought by his use of the present tense is not always successful. I will elaborate on this in the next (and final) section of this chapter.

13.4 The Broken Illusion of Narrative Immediacy: Why the Concept of 'Telling to the Moment' Is Not Always Successful

Although *Skagboys* is characterized by a varying narrative perspective, the novel contains two chapters that may strike readers as unusual: the very first chapter, "Prologue: Notes from Rehab Journal," and "The Rehab Diaries," situated toward the end of the novel. These chapters set themselves apart as diary entries from Renton's stay at St. Monan's rehabilitation clinic, whose psychotherapists recommend that clients keep a journal in order to cope better with the experience of withdrawal. The temporary switch from oral discourse to written diary is indicated by a change in typeface from standard print to a cursive script representing Renton's handwriting.[20]

What is most interesting in the present context is the question of the tense(s) Renton employs in his "Rehab Journal." The entry for Day 9 at the rehabilitation center serves to illustrate that, generally speaking, the diary exhibits what I have termed *heterogeneous tense usage* (see Chapter 4.1) – i.e. it deploys more than one tense:

> *I'm sitting here, writing this shite and wondering why – probably because there's fuck all else to do. The folders we've been issued have two sections; a diary, with one page for each of this forty-five-day programme, and appendices where there's what they refer to as a 'journal'. Skinny-Specky explained that this is for 'developing any themes from the diaries that we may want to explore further'. Apparently the diaries are for our eyes only, and we can put anything into them. The journals we can elect to read out in the forthcoming group sessions. But nobody is going to write a fucking thing (at least not anything important); there are no locks on the doors here and nothing is secure.* (SB, 419)

Here, Renton uses the full bandwidth of fictional tenses, ranging from the past through the present to the (going-to) future: the past tense refers to the recent past, the present progressive relates to the moment of writing, and the future points to the remaining thirty-five days of Renton's rehab. This temporal struc-

---

20 Here reproduced by putting direct quotes from Renton's diary in italics.

ture is reminiscent of the eighteenth-century epistolary novel. Think, for example, of the very first letter Pamela sends her parents at the beginning of the first volume of Samuel Richardson's eponymous classic:

> *My dear Father and Mother,*
> I have great trouble, and some comfort, to acquaint you with. The trouble is, that my good lady died of the illness I mentioned to you, and left us all much grieved for the loss of her; for she was a dear good lady, and kind to all us her servants. Much I feared, that as I was taken by her ladyship to wait upon her person, I should be quite destitute again, and forced to return to you and my poor mother, who have enough to do to maintain yourselves; and, as my lady's goodness had put me to write and cast accompts, and made me a little expert at my needle, and otherwise qualified above my degree, it was not every family that could have found a place that your poor Pamela was fit for: But God, whose graciousness to us we have so often experienced, put it into my good lady's heart, on her death-bed, just an hour before she expired, to recommend to my young master all her servants, one by one; and when it came to my turn to be recommended (for I was sobbing and crying at her pillow) she could only say, 'My dear son!' and so broke off a little; and then recovering, 'Remember my poor Pamela!' And those were some of her last words! O how my eyes overflow! Don't wonder to see the paper so blotted! (*P*, 43; italics in the original)

Although the tone of Pamela's letter rather differs from Renton's diary, the texts show interesting similarities. Like Renton, Pamela resorts to heterogenous tense usage, deploying the past tense to refer to an event that happened in her not too recent past (i.e. the death of her lady) and the present to point to the moment in which she is writing. Moreover, both texts reveal a strong emotional response toward the depicted events: Renton is upset that the rehab program has made him keep a diary ("I'm sitting here, writing this shite and wondering why"), while Pamela is overflowing with tears, mourning the loss of her employer. The comparison shows that the *Skagboys* journal chapters resonate with what Samuel Richardson (1986 [1753], 4) calls "writing to the moment," a form of aesthetic illusion which, according to the novelist, consists in creating the impression that the characters are writing about an event immediately after experiencing it. Composed without hindsight, their discourses display a high level of emotional involvement.[21] This is most obvious when Renton crosses out 'misspelled' words or even whole sentences:

---

21 Cf. Richardson's own formulations, quoted in Ball 1971, 24; italics in the original: "[Richardson's] letters are '... written under the immediate Impression of every Circumstance which occasioned them'; 'All of the Letters are written while the hearts of the writers must be supposed to be wholly engaged in their subjects'; '*Much more* lively and affecting ... must be the Style of those who write in the height of a *present* distress'; and 'The minute particulars of

> [Spud] kept glancing fae me tae the flair n back, as if building up to say something, then he let fly. 'You n Matty . . . ~~you~~ youse stole that Cat Protection League money! ~~Off of~~ Offay Mrs Rylance! ~~Out of the shop~~ Ootay the shoap!'
> FUCK THAT.
> '~~We certainly did. That's how we got here, for some poxy cash. When you think of the bother we had opening it.~~ 'We certainly did. That's how I wound up here, for a few fuckin bob in a gantin plastic collection boax. The bother we had openin it . . . that's what landed us in the fuckin cells! Some troll makin an example ay druggies! A poxy collection tin!' (SB, 423; emphasis in the original)

The passage shows parts of Renton's reproduction of a conversation in which he tells Spud how he ended up in the rehabilitation clinic (i.e. he was caught stealing money from an old lady in order to buy heroin, and the judge decided that he could either be sent down or participate in a withdrawal program). Writing without much thought, Renton corrects passages he feels do not render the events or utterances adequately.

Taken too literally, Richardson's notion of 'writing to the moment' can become unrealistic. A year after the publication of *Pamela*, Henry Fielding's *Shamela* (1999 [1741]) made fun of Richardson's style with a scene that explicitly ridicules the genre's endeavor to create narrative immediacy (cf. 18) – the scene in which Shamela is nearly raped by Parson Williams (discussed above in Chapter 4.2). Here Richardson's strategy is taken to extremes, suggesting that Shamela's letter informing her mother about the sexual molestation is penned while it is actually happening. At that level, Richardson's idea of 'writing to the moment' is manifestly antimimetic. Yet Richardson (as well as other eighteenth-century authors of epistolary novels) found an effective way to circumvent the problem. As narratologists have noted, the epistolary novel draws not so much on simultaneous as on "interpolated" or "intercalated narration" (Genette 1980 [1972], 217–218; Rimmon-Kenan 2002 [1983], 91), a mode which, inserted "between the moments of the action" (Genette 1980 [1972], 217), mixes retrospective and simultaneous narration:

> [T]he extreme closeness of story to narrating produces here, most often, a very subtle effect of friction (if I may call it that) between the slight temporal displacement of the narrative of events ("Here is what happened to me today") and the complete simultaneousness in the report of thoughts and feelings ("Here is what I think about it this evening"). The journal and the epistolary confidence constantly combine what in broadcasting language

events, the sentiments and conversation of the parties, are, upon this plan, exhibited with all the warmth and spirit, that the passion supposed to be predominant at the very time, could produce, and with all the distinguishing characteristics which memory can supply in a History of recent transactions.'"

is called the live and the prerecorded account, the quasi-interior monologue and the account after the event. Here, the narrator is at one and the same time still the hero and already someone else: the events of the day are already in the past, and the "point of view" may have been modified since then; the feelings of the evening or the next day are fully of the present, and here focalization through the narrator is at the same time focalization through the hero. (Genette 1980 [1972], 217–218)

From a narratological point of view, Gérard Genette's argument here may explain the temporal structure of Renton's diary entry and Pamela's letter. Even though the strategy of 'writing to the moment' reduces to a minimum the temporal distance between the experiencing and narrating versions of the first-person narrator, when it comes to a depiction of the narrative events the distinction between those two personas remains intact. Renton's diary and Pamela's letter foreground the narrative act – the moment in which the narrators are actually producing the text. But this moment of writing does not – nor is it seen to – coincide with the narrative events; these still happen before the act of narration. Renton and Pamela both use the past tense to refer to these events and the present tense to refer to the moment of writing, a conventional distribution of fictional tense traditionally used by authors in first-person narrative situations to distinguish the experiencing from the narrating 'I.'[22]

Among the numerous entries in Renton's diary, however, there are also several passages in which he writes in the present tense about events that happened to him during the day – for example the last paragraph of the diary entry for Day 6, which is otherwise completely written in the past tense:[23] "[...] *Len comes in and talks for a wee bit, mainly about music. We have a half-hearted Beefheart discussion on the merits of <u>Clear Spot</u> [...] versus <u>Trout Mask Replica</u> [...]. He tells me again aboot the guitar in the recky room.*" (*SB*, 417; emphasis in the original) The sudden shift from the past to the present tense serves here to negate even the minimal temporal distance between Renton's narrating and experiencing selves, which is usually implied in a 'writing-to-the-moment' scenario. The paragraph suggests that Len, one of the clinic staff, enters Renton's room while he is writing his diary. However, instead of pausing the writing process in order to talk to his visitor, Renton seems to write while at the same time

---

22 Cf. e.g. Fludernik 1993b, 47–51, 198–199; Ohme 2018, 103; Vuillaume 1990, Ch. III.2.1.2; see also Chapter 4.1.
23 The entries for Days 6, 13, 15, 17, 18, 19, 23, 30, 31, 32, 35, 36, 38, 39, 41, 42, 43, and 45 either partly or entirely use the present tense. The remaining chapters only use the present tense in self-reflective passages in which Renton comments on his activity of writing or ponders on his current situation in the rehabilitation center and on his drug addiction.

talking to Len. The synchronizing use of the present tense achieves an illusion-breaking effect here similar to that of Fielding's parody: By resorting to the strategy of simultaneous narration rather than intercalated narration, it creates a logically impossible writing scenario, drawing readers' attention to the fact that the concept of 'writing to the moment' is a literary convention that actually represents a highly unrealistic storytelling scenario.

The antimimetic effect of Renton's use of present-tense narration in the above scene becomes even more obvious if we compare it to the beginning of *Skagboys*. The novel opens with the chapter "Prologue: Notes from Rehab Journal" – one of the extended journal entries that Renton writes during his stay at St. Monan's. Although entirely written in the present tense, this journal entry, as Roberto del Valle Alcalá (2016, 112; my emphasis) has observed, "**retrospectively** details [Renton's] participation in the 'Battle of Orgreave' during the 1984–5 Great Miners' Strike." The use of the present tense in this entry is detemporalized, serving not so much a referential as a rhetorical or maybe even immersive purpose: Renton is not really 'writing to the moment,' here, even if he resorts to the strategy of present-tense narration to render the account of his experiences more vivid.

The examples demonstrate that Renton's "Rehab Journal" features various uses of the present tense without establishing a fixed pattern, which makes it difficult for readers to naturalize these instances. In this respect, the diary entries stand in stark contrast to the chapters in which Renton functions as a conversational storyteller. The impression of narrative immediacy brought about by the use of the fictional present seems to work better in oral discourse than in the written diary entries. Again this is a matter of the ease with which readers can naturalize that usage: In the former case, the fictional present correlates with Renton's use of vernacular Scots and idiolect, so readers can resort to the cognitive frame of conversational storytelling to make sense of the narration (as observed in Chapter 13.2, we often deploy the present tense in everyday storytelling to highlight the reportability of our experiences). In the latter case, it is almost impossible to come up with a consistent reading that holds for all Renton's diary entries, as he uses the present tense here in many different ways. And the very variety of his usage makes it seem awkward and artificial.

One might argue that, in the context of conversational narrative, the strategy of *'telling to the moment'* does not always work.[24] *Dead Men's Trousers*

---

24 The term *'telling to the moment'* ought to be understood as my adaptation of Richardson's concept of 'writing to the moment' to the context of narrative scenarios that imitate oral instead of written discourse.

(2018), for instance, has several scenes in which the synchronizing function of the present tense serves to create the illusion of immediate storytelling, but in doing so evokes highly implausible narrative scenarios. A good example in this respect is Chapter 23,[25] in which Begbie relates how he kills the Hollywood star Chuck Ponce:

> [...] Chuck called and I drove tae San Pedro, and now we're walking along the clifftops together. Although it overlooks the port, this is a private place tae talk, particularly this deserted ocean side, a sheer drop tae the grey rocks below and the incoming tide that laps them. I'm telling him how ah love the sounds ay the waves crashing, the gulls squawking. — We used to go down to Coldingham when I was a kid. It's in Scotland. Cliffs, with rocks below, like here, I tell him. — My ma always told me to keep away from the edge, I smile. — Of course, I never listened.
>
> Chuck shimmies forward, wi that big grin on his pus. — No, I'll bet you didn't, dude! I was the same! I always had to dance to the brink of that goddam cliff, and he ambles tae the verge. Shuts his eyes. Stretches out his arms. The wind whips his hair into the sky. Then he opens those peepers again and looks doon tae the rocks. — I had to do all that shit too! That's the way we're made, bro, we dance to the edge and the weeeeeeeeeeee-aaaaahhhhh—
>
> My hearty shove oan Chuck's back sends him intae that void, squeezing his voice intae a decelerating, dissolving scream. [...] — I was bullshitting ye, mate. I did listen tae my ma. You should have listened tae yours n aw. (*DMT*, 246–247)

Is this an account of manslaughter or of premeditated murder? Does Begbie lose control of his actions and spontaneously shove Chuck off the cliff or has he planned it in advance? On this depends the convincing or unconvincing quality of Welsh's 'telling to the moment' in this scene.

Begbie's depiction of the actual crime offers no textual evidence for either option. Although Begbie says at the end of the scene that he "was bullshitting [Chuck]," this does not necessarily mean that he has actually planned the deed: readers who are familiar with Begbie's character know that he is an impulsive man who often fails to control his aggressive and destructive behavior. In his narrative account leading up to the scene, however, Begbie unveils the backstory of his relation with Chuck, which makes it clear that he has a motive for planning the murder (cf. *DMT*, 245–246). Readers learn that Chuck visited Begbie when he was in prison, hoping that Begbie would work with him on his Scottish accent for a film role. During their cooperation, Chuck promised Begbie that they "[would] be brothers forever" (*DMT*, 246). Yet Begbie never heard from his alleged friend again (Chuck did not even react to Begbie's invitations to

---

[25] Unlike the chapters in *Skagboys*, the chapters in *Dead Men's Trousers* are numbered as well as having a headline.

several of his exhibitions, his wedding, and his daughter's christening). It takes Chuck all of six years to get back to Begbie, and then it is to ask him another favor: Begbie, now an artist, is to make a sculpture of Chuck's ex-wife's head. On the basis of this backstory, readers can assume that Begbie acts intentionally in pushing Chuck off the cliff – arguably an exaggerated punishment for disloyalty, but one that is typical of Begbie's violent behavior. On receiving Chuck's order he sees his chance to retaliate against his former friend. This is doubtless why he prefers to "keep they commissions confidential" (*DMT*, 246) and asks Chuck to meet in person ("Could we meet for a wee coffee?" [*DMT*, 246]).

Although Begbie's behavior as a character (experiencing 'I') seems plausible in the 'cliff scene' (he kills Chuck out of hatred), his performance as a narrator (narrating 'I') is *prima facie* incredible and even out of character. From the other '*Trainspotting*' novels we know that Begbie enjoys telling stories that push the dark boundary of tellability, presenting transgressive experiences his interlocutors might not even want to listen to.[26] Remembering him as an unchoosy and even unscrupulous storyteller, we would expect him to boast about his plan to kill Chuck and to share his gleeful anticipation of the deed with his narratee. Begbie's silence on this score renders his narrative extremely inauthentic.

Welsh here reduces the mimetic dimension of his character-narrator to enhance the narrative's progression (cf. Phelan 2005). His Begbie tells less than we might expect of this character in this situation in order to create a moment of surprise: we are startled because we have not seen the 'cliff scene' coming. But as this surprise is intended not by Begbie the narrator, but by Welsh, the author, it risks disrupting the illusion of 'telling to the moment.' Admittedly, readers may delight in the feeling of having been caught off guard, but they may equally construe the scenario as implausible: the momentary violation of the mimetic dimension of Welsh's character-narrator exposes the constructedness of the narrative.

---

[26] Neal R. Norrick (2005) sees tellability as a scale. In conversational storytelling, he claims, "tellability emerges as a product of contextual negotiation, rather than pre-existing as a quantifiable property of a story based on its content" (Norrick 2005, 325). Proceeding from this premise, he distinguishes two sides of tellability: its lower-bounding side and its upper-bounding side. "From [the] lower-bounding side," Norrick contends, "tellability requires newness, reportability, uniqueness and/or humor – or at least the prospect of conarration" (2005, 323). The upper-bounding, or – as Norrick also calls it – "dark side" of tellability relates to stories that are regarded as improper or at least inappropriate: Depending on the context of communication, such narratives are too personal, too embarrassing, too obscene, or even too dangerous to be told (cf. Norrick 2005, 323).

13.4 The Broken Illusion of Narrative Immediacy: 'Telling to the Moment' — 299

To conclude my reading of Welsh's work, I will reaffirm the claim I made in the introduction to this chapter, that since Welsh does not use the fictional present referentially in the *'Trainspotting'* novels, the use of the present tense in these narratives (including the prequel *Skagboys*) is unproblematic. Irrespective of their rank and position in the series, they all strive to create an expanded 'narrative of life.' This is achieved by the interplay of three narrative strategies: the shift between first-person and third-person (or in this case also homodiegetic and heterodiegetic) narration, the alternation between standard and non-standard language, and tense alternation. Moreover, I have shown in this chapter that Welsh's novels exhibit a fixed correlation of these three narrative techniques according to the following pattern: The combination of first-person perspective, literary dialect, and present-tense narration evokes the impression of conversational narrative, of immediate and spontaneous oral storytelling; the combination of third-person perspective, Standard English, and past-tense narration elicits the notion of written discourse, and this is associated with retrospective teleology and narrative authority. The regular juxtaposition of these constellations shows that the distribution of fictional present and preterite in Welsh's novels is detemporalized and associated with the opposition between orality and literacy and between low and high levels of narrative authority.

Furthermore, my reading of *Skagboys* and *Dead Men's Trousers* illustrates that the fictional present is not of equal importance for all the effects generated by Welsh's combinations of narrative technique. As far as the simulation of orality in the first-person chapters is concerned, the fictional present fulfills an ancillary function: Welsh's use of literary dialect is here the decisive strategy, and the impression of oral speech would be maintained if the character-narrators spoke in the vernacular even if they used the past tense.[27] In the context of narrative authority and the illusion of 'telling to the moment,' however, present-tense narration plays a crucial role. Here the fictional present functions as the main strategy for causing Welsh's readers to believe that the character-narrators relate the narrative events as they are actually experiencing them. The effect of such a synchronizing use of the fictional present is twofold: it diminishes the characters' narrative authority *vis-à-vis* the heterodiegetic narrator, who seems to have an overview of the past, present, and future of the storyworld, but it also conveys the impression of narrative immediacy. Nevertheless,

---

[27] This is corroborated by the fact that previous work on the *'Trainspotting'* novels that discusses Welsh's use of the vernacular (cf. e.g. Hames 2013, 211–215; McRae 2004, 131–132; Morace 2001, 24–28; Pollner 2005; Racolta 2017, 149–150; and Riach 2005, 36) completely ignores the equally important use of present-tense narration.

a convincing illusion of 'telling to the moment' can be hard to achieve: It seems to work better in scenarios where the conventions of oral or everyday storytelling are functionalized to frame the written narrative. In the context of oral storytelling, such an illusion is only successful if it conforms to readers' expectations regarding the narrative or genre.

14 Concluding Remarks, or: The Future of Research on Present-Tense Narration

14.1 What This Book Has to Offer...

There has been a widespread equation in previous narratological research of present-tense usage with real-time reporting and simultaneous (or concurrent) narration. I have sought in this book, in particular by introducing the concept of the 'grammatical' fallacy, to break with this tradition, and I have done so for two reasons: First, I have argued, with reference to prior work by Dorrit Cohn (1999, vii), Suzanne Fleischman (1990, 1991a), and Monika Fludernik (2003a, 121), that narrative fiction follows different linguistic and grammatical rules from those of factual discourse, and that tense usage therefore operates differently in fiction than in ordinary communication. Secondly, I have contended, with recourse to David Herman (2002, Ch. 6), that the process of making time in narrative fiction represents an integral part of narrative worldmaking – and this functions independently of the choice of tense. That is to say, temporal relations between narrative events can be expressed in any kind of fictional narrative, irrespective of whether it is written in the past, present, or future tense.

Starting from these premises, I have suggested that we reconsider fictional tense usage. Rather than construing it as a merely grammatical – and thus temporal – category, I have consistently conceived it as a fully-fledged narrative strategy which can fulfill a wide range of different functions in narrative fiction, most of which are not related to the aspect of time (*grammatical tense* vs. *fictional tense*). This fundamental reconceptualization of fictional tense usage has enabled me to devise a comprehensive narratological theory of fictional tense to describe the particularities of present-tense narration; these often stand in stark contrast to the characteristics of more traditional past-tense narration.

More specifically, I have introduced a narratological model of fictional (present-)tense usage that is composed of three parts relating to the formal-structural dimension of fictional tense usage in general, as well as to the functional and syntactic dimensions of present-tense narration in particular.[1] The first part of this model provides a number of analytical categories relating to the formal-structural dimension of fictional tense usage. These enable us to describe the following five categories of tense usage: variety (*homogeneous* vs.

---

[1] It should be kept in mind, though, that some of the functions of the fictional present I have introduced may also apply to past-tense or future-tense narratives.

heterogeneous); frequency and scope (*global* vs. *local*); prominence (*central* vs. *peripheral*); alternation (*tense-switching*, more specifically *temporalization* and *detemporalization*, vs. *tense-mixing*); and foregrounding (*alternate, typographical, paratextual*, or *metanarrative foregrounding*). The second part of the model offers a functional matrix of present-tense narration which allows us to better explore the possible textual functions and cognitive effects of the fictional present with regard to the process of narrative worldmaking. These include the *referential, immersive, metareferential, communicative, synchronizing, thematic,* and *rhetorical functions*, as well as the *transmodal function*. Finally, the third part of my model presents different categories with which to analyze either the *multifunctionality* of present-tense narration (*dominant* vs. *recessive functions* and *recurring* vs. *non-recurring functions*) or its *functional interplay* with other narrative strategies and/or phenomena (*main* vs. *ancillary strategies* and *fixed* vs. *variable correlations* of narrative strategies).

Using this narratological model of fictional (present-)tense usage, I have investigated the use of the fictional present in the twenty-first century novel, taking as examples nine different texts: Hilary Mantel's *Wolf Hall* and *Bring Up the Bodies*, Margaret Atwood's *Oryx and Crake*, Nadeem Aslam's *Maps for Lost Lovers*, Don Winslow's *The Power of the Dog*, Ian McEwan's *Nutshell*, Emma Donoghue's *Room*, and Irvine Welsh's *Skagboys* and *Dead Men's Trousers*. My readings of these contemporary novels demonstrate not only that present-tense narration can be found in many novelistic genres, but that the fictional present is a flexible and highly complex narrative strategy with various functions which often deviate from the narrative effects germane to the preterite.

My model interpretations have also shown that the fictional present never fulfills a specific function on its own, but invariably achieves its effects only in combination with other narrative strategies and/or phenomena. These include, among other aspects, the representation of time (especially Winslow's novel), the representation of space (especially Aslam's and Atwood's narratives), narrative distance (especially Mantel's and Donoghue's texts), narrative voice (all novels), focalization and multiperspectivity (especially Mantel's, Aslam's, Atwood's, and Winslow's narratives), suspense and surprise (Winslow's and Donoghue's texts), narrative immediacy and urgency (especially Atwood's, Aslam's, Winslow's, Donoghue's, and Welsh's novels), metanarration (McEwan's narrative), unreliable narration (Donoghue's text), and narrative authority (especially Welsh's novels), as well as the use of the vernacular and the concomitant evocation of orality (Welsh's narratives).

It has, moreover, been demonstrated above that the present tense may play either a vital or a supplementary role in the creation of specific narrative effects.

In McEwan's *Nutshell* and Donoghue's *Room*, for example, the authors' choice of the present tense helps create a narrative illusion which foregrounds the practices of immediate storytelling. The narrative scenarios of these texts could not be achieved without using the present tense. In Aslam's *Maps for Lost Lovers* and Winslow's *The Power of the Dog*, on the other hand, the specific timespaces which the present tense evokes (the topochrone and the chronotope respectively) certainly contribute to the ways in which these texts generate the effects of narrative empathy (*Maps for Lost Lovers*) as well as surprise and suspense (*The Power of the Dog*), but these effects could also be realized by different means in a past-tense narrative. The same applies to the use of present-tense narration in *Oryx and Crake*. Although the fictional present encourages readers of Atwood's novel to mentally project themselves into the here-and-now of the post-apocalyptic storyworld, a past-tense narrative combining different narrative strategies than those used by Atwood could also create a sense of immersion for readers.

A further aspect illustrated by my argument is that the contemporary present-tense novel usually features more than one use of the fictional present. All my model interpretations have discussed more than one function of present-tense narration, but my readings of McEwan's *Nutshell* and Donoghue's *Room* put special emphasis on the multifunctionality of that tense. As we have seen, each of these novels exhibits a thematic use of the present tense which effectively combines the first-person narrator's unusual situation with other functions of present-tense narration. McEwan's text correlates thematic present-tense narration with the global use of the synchronizing present; in Donoghue's novel, the thematic function of the fictional present consists in a functional shift from the synchronizing to the descriptive present. Accordingly, my interpretations of these two novels have shown that in *Nutshell*, McEwan's different uses of the present tense are on a mutual par, whereas in *Room*, Donoghue primarily draws on a thematic use of present-tense narration (dominant function) which is generated by a combination of the synchronizing and the descriptive present (recessive function).

In addition to the presentation of a comprehensive, albeit not exhaustive, overview of the various uses of present-tense narration in contemporary narrative fiction, my narratological model has enabled me to question and reconsider some well-established concepts and categories of the narratological paradigm. In presenting the single components of my functional matrix of present-tense narration, I have expanded the definition of simultaneous narration, introducing the category of *simultaneous presentation* which subsumes two different modes of presentation, namely *simultaneous narration* and *simultaneous focali-*

zation. In this context, I have shown that the use of the present tense qualifies as a necessary, yet not sufficient criterion a narrative has to fulfill in order to elicit the impression of simultaneous presentation. My model interpretation of *Nutshell* has, moreover, demonstrated that the mode of simultaneous narration cannot be maintained over the stretch of an entire novel, but usually alternates with intermittent episodes of retrospective and/or prospective narration. Besides this, I have integrated Mikhail M. Bakhtin's (2014 [1981]) concept of the chronotope as a narratological category into my model. This has allowed me, first, to distinguish two different types of narrative progression, the *chronotope* and the *topochrone*, which I have illustrated in my readings of *Maps for Lost Lovers* and *The Power of the Dog*. Secondly, by introducing the concept of the topochrone I have been able to reify David Herman's (2002, 212–220) vague notion of fuzzy temporality with a new terminology which more adequately describes three specific instances of anachronic narration: *circumlepsis*, *hyper-analepsis*, and *hyper-prolepsis*.

My model interpretations have likewise encouraged me to identify a number of narrative techniques or phenomena frequently encountered in contemporary narrative fiction. Thus in my analysis of Winslow's *The Power of the Dog*, I have focused on the strategy of *film-script narration*, a style of accelerated narration reminiscent of a film script. In my reading of *Skagboys* and *Dead Men's Trousers*, I have shown how Welsh reverts to Samuel Richardson's classical concept of 'writing to the moment' – or, as I have preferred to call it, '*telling to the moment*' – which has long been frowned upon after its heyday during the eighteenth century; and I have elaborated on the temporal dimension of *expansive worldmaking* by highlighting that prequels, sequels, and coquels expand the fictional universe evoked by a source text in an anachronic way. Finally, in my interpretation of Mantel's novels *Wolf Hall* and *Bring Up the Bodies*, I have deployed the term *spatial non-contextualization* to address a style of narration that denies readers' any spatial orientation within the storyworld (a phenomenon also observed in *The Power of the Dog*); and I have used the term *associative storytelling* to denote a specific form of mind-style characterized, among other things, by sudden disruptive shifts from one narrative scene to the next. This impedes readers' spatiotemporal orientation even further.

The analysis and interpretation of some of the novels in my corpus has, moreover, prompted me to engage more closely with the models of narrative established by Gérard Genette (1980 [1972]; 1988 [1983]) and Franz K. Stanzel (1986 [1979]). My reading of *Wolf Hall* and *Bring Up the Bodies*, for example, has shown that a dominant mode of internal focalization features a somewhat obscure use of deixis (cf. Brosch 2017, 170; 2018, 63) that necessarily involves some curtailing of the text's legibility. My interpretations of *Wolf Hall*, *Bring Up the Bodies*, *Maps for Lost Lovers*, and *The Power of the Dog* have illustrated that Stanzel's model of typical narrative situations – first-person, authorial, and figural narrative situations – can justifiably be conceptualized as the arc of a circle on which the margins of the three sectors attributed respectively to each of the prototype narrative situations blend into one another. For narratives do not, in practice, necessarily confine themselves to one specific narrative situation; they may combine various features of different narrative situations, as do Mantel's, Aslam's, and Winslow's novels, all of which mostly exhibit a predominantly figural narrative situation yet occasionally display indications of a more overt narratorial voice. Finally, my reading of Donoghue's *Room* has allowed me to clarify that Stanzel's distinction between the narrating and the experiencing 'I' may still be relevant in the context of a present-tense narrative which effectively uses simultaneous or concurrent narration, even though the present tense serves to negate any temporal distance between the narrative events and the act of reporting in these texts.[2]

At first glance, all these examples seem to endorse structuralist models of narrative. Yet this should not obscure the fact that this book as a whole also sheds light on the limitations of the classical narratological paradigm. My discussion of *Nutshell*, for instance, implicitly suggests that neither Genette's taxonomy of different narrator types nor Stanzel's typological circle can fully come to grips with the peculiarity and strangeness of McEwan's first-person narrator. While my reading has shown that the fetus's discourse confirms the ontological logic underlying narrative representations – that is, the conventional assumption that, during the act of narration, the narrator is "off-diegesis" (Genette 1988 [1983], 85), situated outside the world of which he or she tells – it simultaneously raises questions concerning his presence in (or should one rather say absence from?) the story. Intuitively, one would probably consider a narrating fetus as homodiegetic despite its inability to verbally communicate with the other characters involved in the story. After all, it is located in its mother's womb, which is most certainly physically present in the storyworld. By extension, then, one could say that a fetus is part of the storyworld even though it does not yet, in the usual sense of the word, inhabit it. In *Nutshell*, however, all the other characters seem to behave as if the fetus did not exist: none of its relatives ever talk about it, nor does its mother react in any way to its repeated attempts to interact, by

---

2 As we have seen, however, the majority of present-tense narratives I have discussed in this study only feign a synchronicity between story and narrative discourse because they are actually told from a retrospective perspective.

means of kicking, with the world outside the womb. In this case, the question of the (non-)identity of the realms of existence of the narrator and the characters is impossible to answer.

McEwan's novel serves perfectly to illustrate that present-tense narration not only (as narratologists have previously pointed out) defies the story/discourse distinction in narrative texts, but also challenges other categories of the structuralist model of narrative such as that of person (cf. Genette 1980 [1972], 243–252; Stanzel 1986 [1979], Ch. 4). In this respect, my study has a shared interest with the growing narratological work on second-person narration and 'we'-narrative, which similarly tests the limits of Genette's and Stanzel's theories to adequately analyze today's practices of fictional storytelling. Narrative theorists have long sought a suitable place for second-person narration in the structuralist model of narrative, examining its similarities and differences with first-person and third-person narration (cf. e.g. Fludernik 1993a, Richardson 1991), and most recently Natalya Bekhta (2017a, 2017b, 2020) has convincingly argued that 'we'-narrative – that is, narrative texts which feature a collective voice such as the Jefferson community in William Faulkner's "A Rose for Emily" (1977 [1930]) – should be treated as an independent narrative situation. I should like to believe that this book has made a similar case for present-tense narration. The differences between past-tense and present-tense narration apparent in contemporary narrative fiction are, in my view, significant enough to construe them as conventions of two distinct narrative forms. It is arguably high time to break away from our favorite classics and work toward a less restrictive model of narrative that factors in all possible shapes of the most important (grammatical) categories involved in narrative situations: tense and person.

14.2 ... What Else Could Be in Store...

Since all books must come to an end, every study is inevitably limited. However, the scope and outreach of my narratological model is not restricted to the issues I have discussed in these pages. I believe, rather, that my tripartite model offers useful analytical tools that may help both narrative theorists and literary scholars to investigate the phenomenon of present-tense narration from further angles. These may well include the perspectives of genre theory, and historical, contextualist, and transmedial narratology, as well as an interdisciplinary perspective.

So far as genre is concerned: Although I have analyzed a large number of contemporary narrative genres that make use of present-tense narration, I could not consider all possible subgenres of the present-tense novel. A central research desideratum that has not been dealt with here is the question how the fictional present is used in hybrid genres that integrate features of both fictional and factual narrative. Admittedly, the vast majority of autobiographies, memoirs, and personal histories are still written in the past tense, yet a few recent examples, like Maggie O'Farrel's *I Am, I Am, I Am: Seventeen Brushes With Death* (2017) and Patrisse Khan-Cullors and asha bandele's *When They Call You a Terrorist: A Black Lives Matter Memoir* (2017), give us reason to assume that the trend of present-tense narration is about to find its way into this semi-fictional genre as well. To what extent does the narrative design of these present-tense narratives differ from traditional autobiographies and memoirs written in the past tense? Is the fictional present used differently in these texts than in fictional narratives? And if this is the case, which functions would we need to include in the functional matrix introduced in this study so as to render this matrix adaptable for these semi-fictional present-tense narratives?

From the perspective of diachronic narratology, it would be interesting to further trace the historical development of present-tense narration. Previous studies by Armen Avanessian and Anke Hennig,[3] Irmtraud Huber (2016), and Benjamin Meisnitzer (2016) have already proposed different historical overviews, and it would certainly be fruitful to set the developments depicted in these surveys in relation to the functional matrix of present-tense narration presented here. What functions did the present tense fulfill when first used in narrative fiction and what functions have evolved only recently? How has the functional potential of present-tense narration developed over time? Do the different stages of the development of fictional present-tense usage identified by Avanessian and Hennig, Huber, and Meisnitzer correlate with the prevalence of specific functions of present-tense narration, or does the functional matrix call for another, different history of the fictional present?

An important contextual aspect of present-tense narration that requires further research is the question of its use in different national (fictional) literatures. Previous research has already observed that the increase in present-tense novels is not restricted to English and American fiction, but also affects other literary landscapes of the Western world. According to Jürgen H. Petersen (1992; 1993, 24) and Franz K. Stanzel (1981b), the fictional present constitutes an innovative feature of the modern German novel, and Avanessian and Hennig (2015 [2012]) note a similar trend in French and Russian narrative fiction. One could

---

[3] Cf. Avanessian and Hennig 2013a, 246–249; 2013c; 2015; 2015 [2012], Ch. 1; cf. also Avanessian 2013, 363–365.

take the narratological model proposed here as a starting point for a comparison of the various ways in which different national literatures deploy the present tense. How is the fictional present used in other languages than English? Do non-Anglophone literatures feature further uses of this fictional tense than those I have introduced in the functional matrix of present-tense narration? How do translations deal with fictional tense usage (cf. Lathey 2003)? Can one detect any (diverging) preferences for specific uses of present-tense narration or for specific correlations between present-tense usage and other narrative features across different countries? Where does the model of fictional present-tense usage require modification so that it also applies to those languages in which the grammatical category of aspect, which has been largely neglected in this study, plays a much more important role than it does in English (e.g. Romance and especially Slavic languages)?[4] More to the point, how does narrative worldmaking work in tenseless languages such as Chinese or Malay? What comparable narrative techniques do these texts use to evoke timespaces?

Furthermore, from a contextualist narratological point of view, it would be worth exploring the relation of the present tense to those types of literature in which the concept and identity of the author plays a central role. The significant number of female writers in the "Primary Literature"-section in the bibliography of this book – 40 of the 93 authors listed here are women – reveals that the fictional present has become a popular aesthetic feature of women's literature. It would be an interesting endeavor to (re-)investigate, through the lens of feminist narratology, the functional potential of the present tense with respect to concepts such as narrative authority (cf. Lanser 1992) or gender-inflected unreliable narration (cf. Allrath 2005). Conversely, an application of the narratological model developed in these pages to the analysis and interpretation of novels like Meredith Russo's *Birthday: A Love Story Eighteen Years in the Making* (2019) or Bernadine Evaristo's *Girl, Woman, Other* (2019) might, in tandem with concepts such as gender performativity (cf. Butler 1993, 1999 [1990]), power relations (cf. Foucault 2002 [1994]), or the 'other' and 'othering' (cf. Said 1994 [1978]), open the way to an examination of how the fictional present contributes to narrative themes like transgender, sexual orientation and sexual identity, as well as ethnicity and race.

---

4 For prior studies on present-tense narration that also take the grammatical category of aspect into consideration, cf. Coetzee 1981 and Fleischman 1990, 1991a, 1991b.

Since this book has been exclusively concerned with written, that is, monomodal narrative fiction,[5] I have ignored an essential aspect of present-tense narration: its transmedial function. If the scope of my narratological model of fictional (present-)tense usage was broadened to the point that it also included multimodal instances of narrative, we could, for example, ask how the fictional present is used in genres like picture books, graphic novels, comics, or multimodal novels.[6] A transmedial expansion of the model could, moreover, enable a comparison of the function of fictional tense in verbal and non-verbal media. Thanks to my redefinition of tense usage as a narrative strategy that is no longer bound to our grammatical understanding of tense as a verbal category such a juxtaposition will now be possible. More specifically, this means that my modified conceptualization of fictional tense as a means of narrative worldmaking is more compatible with the analytic philosophical notion of tense as a means of structuring the human understanding of time. And it becomes easier for us, as a consequence, to explore the various ways in which the concept of fictional tense operates in different media such as narrative fiction, film, computer games, or theater.[7]

This leads me to the interdisciplinary perspective on the fictional present. As I have shown in the literature survey of this study, previous research on fictional tense is mainly located in the fields of linguistics, philosophy, and literary studies, and here more particularly in narratology. Each of these disciplines takes a different perspective on the phenomenon of present-tense narration, proceeding from the diverging premises that tense usage in narrative fiction operates in the same way (narratology) or differently (linguistics) than in factual discourses or is more or less irrelevant because our perception of fictional time is tenseless (philosophy). My narratological model of (present-)tense usage in narrative fiction has aimed to consolidate these different positions by positing a

---

5 I here use the term *monomodal* in Herman's (2009a, xii) sense in order to designate "print narrative[s] with only a verbal information track." Herman differentiates such narratives from so-called multimodal narratives which exploit more semiotic channels than just the verbal information track (feature films, for example, make use of two different semiotic channels in order to transmit a story to their audience: "the filmed image-track and the audiorecorded sound-track" [2009a, xii]).

6 For a detailed description of the genre of the multimodal novel, cf. Hallet 2009, 2014, 2015, and 2018.

7 As a matter of fact, there is already some research on the subject of "tense in film" (cf. e.g. Cardwell 2000, 2003, and Currie 1992; 1995, Ch. 7; 1998), so that it would be an interesting undertaking to set these studies in relation to the model of tense usage in narrative fiction developed in this book.

difference between grammatical tense and fictional tense (linguistic position) as well as acknowledging that the latter does not necessarily have to be related to the construction of narrative time (philosophical position). I hope, therefore, that the model proposed in these pages will occasion a reinvigoration of the dialogue between the disciplines of linguistics, philosophy, and literary studies on the differences between tense usage in non-fictional discourse (i.e. grammatical tense) and in narrative fiction (i.e. fictional tense).[8]

Last but not least, digital humanities and empirical literary studies might also make a fruitful contribution to the research on fictional tense in general and present-tense narration in particular. Text annotation programs like, for example, CATMA[9] are useful tools for narratologists in the analysis of many aspects of the formal-structural dimension of fictional tense, such as instances of heterogeneous tense usage, tense alternation, or grammatical and paratextual foregrounding of tense. Empirical studies of reading, on the other hand, could take the narratological model presented in this study as a starting point to develop experiments that test readers' physical, cognitive and/or emotional reaction toward the fictional present.[10] The results of such experiments could then be compared to the potential functions and effects of present-tense narration identified in my functional matrix of present-tense narration in order to instigate an exchange between classical, hermeneutically oriented literary studies and empirical literary studies.

14.3 ... and What the Present-Tense Novel Can Tell Us about Contemporary Culture

At the end of this summary and outlook, one further question arises: Why now? Why are we witnessing such a notable increase in present-tense narrative at the beginning of the twenty-first century? In the last three pages of *Present-Tense Narration in Contemporary Fiction: A Narratological Overview* (2016), Irmtraud Huber similarly inquires about "the reasons for the widespread popularity" of the fictional present (107). If I reiterate her question here, it is not merely to replicate it, but to emphasize its relevance: Over the years that I have been

---

8 The first attempts to reestablish a dialogue between linguistics and philosophy have already been made (cf. Ludlow 1999 as well as the contributions in Jokić and Smith 2003).
9 See https://catma.de/ (accessed August 31, 2020); an exemplary CATMA-based analysis of present-tense usage is provided in Evelyn Gius's 2015 monograph on conflict narratives (cf. Ch. 8.1).
10 An example of a possible experiment can be found in Macrae 2016, 64.

working on this book I was often asked this question by different groups of people – colleagues, undergraduate students, as well as friends and family members, who had a less theoretical and more mundane view of what I was doing. In this light, I believe the sociocultural forces behind the current surge in present-tense novels should interest not only narratologists and literary scholars, but also a wider, interdisciplinary readership.

According to Huber, the increasing popularity of fictional present-tense usage is largely the result of two factors: the growing influence of creative writing programs as well as the long-term consequences of postmodernism (cf. 2016, 108–109). She holds that present-tense narration may, on the one hand, be the result of creative writing classes which "[encourage] experimentation with style" (Huber 2016, 109). On the other hand, present-tense narrative may constitute a distinctive aesthetic feature of "literature that tries to position itself in the aftermath of postmodernism" (Huber 2016, 108) reinventing the relationship between fiction and reality:

> In face of postmodernism's critique of reality and realism, present-tense narration emphasises its own fictionality by exposing its narrative situation as impossible. Thus, the texts can make realist truth-claims without ever seeming to deny their fictional status. In this way they acknowledge postmodernist insights into the construction of reality, while at the same time continuing to make the kind of truth claims which postmodernism had condemned. (Huber 2016, 108–109)

In addition to these theory-based explanations, Huber also takes some perspectives from the social sciences and media studies into consideration. Making reference to distinguished sociological work on the experience of time in modern and late-modern Western society, she first argues that "the ever-increasing speed of social change" (Huber 2016, 107) – a process which Hartmut Rosa (2003, 2010, 2013 [2005]) has termed "social acceleration" – forces us to constantly adjust to new circumstances. However, given that these rapid changes are only superficial, they do not really alter the underlying structure of our world: "In a contemporary time of constant crisis, we run ever faster on a slippery slope just to remain in the same place." (Huber 2016, 107) In a second step, Huber relates this notion of social acceleration to Helga Nowotny's (1994 [1989], Ch. 2) conception of an "extended present." Adopting Nowotny's view that we are living in an age in which constant technological progress has caused the future to draw ever closer to the present, Huber maintains that we have started to "merely react to current events and crises, without attempting to shape our future" (2016, 107–108).¹¹ This sharp focus on the present moment, she continues, is reinforced by new communication technology, with status updates in instant messaging apps or timelines on social media sites inviting us "to constantly mark and validate our present" as well as "to deliver a current report on our actions and whereabouts" (Huber 2016, 108). The result of this, Huber concludes with recourse to the media theorist Douglas Rushkoff (2013), is a so-called present shock, a state of anxiety about society's need for constant up-to-dateness that eventually leads "to a collapse of narratives" as well as "neurotic and cultural problems" (Huber 2016, 108).

Huber acknowledges the possibility "that such a widely diagnosed focus on the present" could be responsible for the recent boom in present-tense narratives (2016, 108). The use of the fictional present, she affirms, "might seem to increase the relevance of the story that is told. Even historical events are thus transposed into the present moment, because nowadays only the present counts" (Huber 2016, 108). At the same time, however, Huber clearly expresses her reservations toward such a view, as she stresses that present-tense narration is not restricted to simultaneous narration, but may also take the shape of retrospective narrative (cf. Huber 2016, 108). She additionally contends that contemporary present-tense narratives are far too coherent to be interpreted as symptoms of what Rushkoff diagnoses as "present shock." At the same time, she remarks on the "conspicuous absence" of new media and modern communication technology from the themes of the more than 40 novels she discusses in her study (Huber 2016, 108; cf. also 106–107). Besides, none of these narratives explicitly deals with topics relating either to the acceleration of contemporary Western society or the constantly changing lifestyle of the digital age (cf. Huber 2016, 106, 108). On the basis of all these observations, Huber finally claims that

---

11 In her 1997 monograph *Chronochisms: Time, Narrative, and Postmodernism*, Ursula K. Heise makes a similar point as Nowotny (cf. 23–30). "[T]he most significant changes in the last thirty years," she argues, "have taken place in transportation and communications – especially telecommunications and information technologies – sectors that have developed at a rate unprecedented in the history of Western technology, increasing services and drastically reducing prices. Innovations in these areas and, in particular, the fusion of computers and telecommunications have foregrounded mainly two temporal values: simultaneity and instantaneity." (Heise 1997, 23) Since these temporal values are, moreover, closely linked to the permanent urge for instant availability (cf. Heise 1997, 25), Heise likewise maintains that the use of new communication and information technology "immerses the individual in a 'hyper-present' of sorts, a hyper-intensified immediacy that focuses the user's attention on a rapid succession of micro-events and thereby makes it more difficult to envision even the short-term past or future" (1997, 26).

"the old medium of the novel seems to remain quite conservative in its resistance to recent technological and social changes" (2016, 108).

On the other hand, the present-tense novel can be read as a direct response to current trends such as social acceleration or the increasing digitization of contemporary culture, which is actually one of the most important driving forces behind our accelerated lives. Such a reading takes its cue from prior work on the temporality of postmodern and contemporary fiction. In a recent monograph on contemporary English and American "fictions of time," Nina Leise (2017) maintains that the genre of narrative fiction plays a central role in the discourse of the current culture of time and its challenges for Western industrialized societies. Seen in this light, it can hardly be a coincidence that the recent increase in present-tense novels set in only shortly after the beginning of the late twentieth-century processes of digitization.[12] Ursula K. Heise, in *Chronochisms: Time, Narrative, and Postmodernism* (1997), furthermore contends that narrative constitutes the

> literary genre that is most directly dependent on its deployment in and as time, and where changes in the cultural conception of temporality can therefore be expected to play themselves out most visibly and with the greatest impact on literary form (2).[13]

It may be true that the majority of contemporary present-tense novels does not make social acceleration or new communication and information technology their explicit themes, as Huber notes; however, I would argue, with reference to Heise's contention, that these texts engage with new configurations of time in the present age (e.g. the extended present) as well as with the effects of these configurations on Western society (e.g. present shock) not through their content, but rather through their narrative form.

This becomes most obvious if we take a closer look at the temporal progression of present-tense narratives. Although my analysis of *The Power of the Dog* has concentrated mainly on how the chronotopic structure of this narrative occasionally causes the text to resemble a film script, we can also draw some parallels with the dimension of storytelling in the new media environment. Given that Winslow's thriller is constantly seeking to create suspense as well as moments of surprise, the novel never takes the time to tell one of its multiple plots from beginning to end, but instead jumps from one narrative setting to the next – and hence from one consciousness to another – whenever the depiction

---

[12] According to Leise (2017, 35), the first processes of digitization started toward the end of the 1980s.
[13] A similar argument is provided in Nünning and Sommer 2002, 50–53.

of a scene runs the slightest risk of becoming boring for the reader. One could interpret this rapid style of narration as Winslow's attempt to attune literary storytelling practices to a reading habit that is strongly influenced by the ways in which we process information through the new media. Reading an online article on a tablet or smartphone, for example, makes it almost impossible to focus exclusively on the topic of the article, as numerous hyperlinks constantly tempt our attention away to other, related subjects. Social media, furthermore, condition their users to prefer short and ephemeral content that can be processed within a few minutes, or even seconds: tweets, status updates on Facebook, or Instagram stories only seem relevant and interesting until other more immediate and more urgent posts come along. It seems to me that fast-paced multiperspective present-tense novels like *The Power of the Dog* seek to adjust to the shortened attention span of contemporary readers.

Novels which use the fictional present as an important means to create the impression of simultaneous or concurrent narration may similarly evoke new media and communication technologies. In times in which instantaneous posts and minute-by-minute updates influence our understanding of storytelling, the principle of "Live now, tell later" (Cohn 1999, 96) is slowly but surely losing its validity, or so it seems. Today, many of us no longer savor the moment by consciously experiencing it; we are too busy thinking about how we could best capture it in a picture or a video snap which we will immediately share with our friends or followers. Against this backdrop, simultaneous present-tense narration can, on the one hand, be seen as proof of the increasing medialization of narrative fiction in the modern age.[14] On the other hand, it can be taken as yet another symptom of our accelerated culture: given that nowadays everything has to happen ever more quickly, we think that we do not have the time to do things one after another. As a consequence, we share occurrences in our lives at the very moment that we are actually experiencing them, because once these occurrences are over we immediately have something else to focus on. In such an overwhelming present, it seems only logical that the acts of experiencing and narrating synchronize; otherwise, we will never have the time to tell of our experiences at all.[15]

---

[14] The phenomenon of the medialization of narrative in the context of the contemporary novel has been investigated in depth in a collected volume by Nünning and Rupp (2011).

[15] It is important to note at this point that the main examples of simultaneous present-tense narration I have discussed in this book (i.e. McEwan's *Nutshell* and Donoghue's *Room*) deploy synchronizing present-tense narration for different purposes than the evocation of new storytelling formats used in social media. Still, this does not contradict my argument here because, as my functional matrix of present-tense narration, as well as the categories of multifunction-

My analysis of the topochronic structure of *Maps for Lost Lovers*, by contrast, has demonstrated that present-tense narration need not necessarily imitate the fast-moving nature of storytelling (or rather storysharing), in digital media, but that it may also qualify as a counter-movement against the constantly increasing acceleration of our lives. Unlike *The Power of the Dog*, which rushes from event to event, Aslam's present-tense narrative takes time to describe minute details of its storyworld. By foregrounding the aspect of narrative space, *Maps for Lost Lovers* creates two completely different, yet equally complex timespaces, each of which allows readers to closely engage with one of the protagonists' (either Shamas's or Kaukab's) individual worlds. More importantly, however, Aslam's use of the present tense contributes to his poetic style of writing, which decelerates readers' processing of the world depicted in his novel by defamiliarizing it. In this regard, the novel distances itself as far as possible from the reduced attention economy of contemporary digital culture: In *Maps for Lost Lovers*, the act of reading becomes a slow activity which requires readers' full attention and concentration. Topochronic present-tense narratives like Aslam's novel thus function as what Ansgar Nünning (2016, 166–171) would characterize as an indispensable literary corrective to social acceleration, digitization, and constant availability, allowing readers to (re-)develop a sense of the importance of reflection or 'mindfulness' (*Achtsamkeitstempo*) in life (cf. also Leise 2017, 199–200).

One further argument which, I think, helps explain the growing popularity of the present-tense novel (and which has not been discussed by Huber) is grounded in cultural theory. In *Our Broad Present: Time and Contemporary Culture* (2014 [2010]), Hans Ulrich Gumbrecht puts forward the hypothesis that our age is characterized by a new chronotope which has superseded the notion of "historical time," that configuration of time that emerged in the early nineteenth century (cf. also Gumbrecht 2019 [2012], Pt. 1, Ch. 4). Drawing on the lifework of the German historian Reinhart Koselleck, Gumbrecht contends that historical time is based on a specific mindset – "historical thought" or "historical consciousness" – which postulates that humankind moves through time on a linear path leading from the past through the present to the future.[16] In accordance with historical consciousness, then, we believe ourselves to have left behind the past which now constitutes the sum of our experiences, while per-

---

ality and functional interplay, emphasize, one and the same use of the fictional present may fulfill different functions in different narrative contexts.
16 It is important to note that historical thought or consciousness is a peculiarly Western concept; Eastern philosophies construe human conception of time quite differently.

ceiving the future "as an open horizon of possibilities" toward which we are making our way (Gumbrecht 2014 [2010], xiii). Located between these past experiences and future possibilities, the present qualifies as a "moment of transition" that is almost too short to be noticed (Gumbrecht 2014 [2010], 30). It is this brief present that provides the basis for human agency, as it enables the individual "to align experiences from the past with conditions of the present and the future and to select, from the possibilities the future afford[s], projects for a transformed world that [is] always new" (Gumbrecht 2014 [2010], 31).

In the early twenty-first century, however, our understanding of time has shifted from historical consciousness to "the (sometimes uncomfortable) terrain of temporal stasis and simultaneity" (Gumbrecht 2014 [2010], 31). Today, Gumbrecht argues, the future no longer "present[s] itself as a horizon of open possibilities for action," but is instead "drawing near [...] with threatening scenarios that cannot be calculated in detail" (2014 [2010], 31). As the prospects of climate change, nuclear catastrophe, or the potential impacts of overpopulation are "becoming a reality," he continues, "we seek to gain a delay, at best; but we hardly believe anymore that disaster can be averted once and for all" (Gumbrecht 2014 [2010], 31).[17] This feeling of the loss of human agency is, moreover, coupled with a cultural memory which strives to dissolve the boundary between the present and the past (cf. Gumbrecht 2014 [2010], 31). Gumbrecht therefore concludes that the present, which previously used to be an elusive moment of transition, has turned into "an ever expending presence of simultaneities" in which we are no longer capable of forgetting anything, while simultaneously not knowing "in what direction we should progress" (2014 [2010], 32).

It occurs to me that the lack of an open future represents that property of Gumbrecht's notion of the "broad present" which is most relevant to the current

---

17 In this regard, Gumbrecht's argument about the broad present shares some striking features with Nowotny's (1994 [1989]) sociological considerations on the extended present which also deplore, albeit for different reasons, a decrease in the scope of human action: "[The future] is increasingly overshadowed by the problems which are opening up in the present. The future no longer offers that projection space into which all desires, hopes and fears could be projected without many inhibitions because it seemed sufficiently remote to be able to absorb everything which had no place or was unwelcome in the present. The future [...] is drawing closer to the present. [...] The scope of action is restricted because a part of the future is already being disposed of in the present; the ecological loops of human action become loops of time which react upon the present. The invocation of the future, in the name of which political action was justified for a long time, had to be reduced and at least partly transferred to the present." (Nowotny 1994 [1989], 50)

increase in present-tense narration in contemporary fiction. I base this claim on a point he makes in the preface to *Our Broad Present*:

> That we no longer live in historical time can be seen most clearly with respect to the future. For us, the future no longer presents itself as an open horizon of possibilities; instead, it is a dimension increasingly closed to all prognoses—and which, at the same time, seems to draw near as a menace. Global warming will proceed with all the consequences that have been foreseen for quite some time; the question remains whether humanity will manage to accrue sufficient credit for a few additional years before the most catastrophic consequences of the situation arrive. (Gumbrecht 2014 [2010], xiii)

Against such a bleak backdrop, it becomes increasingly difficult for narrative fiction to present what Brian McHale (2011) would call models *for* the world because any such projection requires that there is a future. The growing doubts about the existence of such a future for Planet Earth might be another reason why so many novelists nowadays choose the fictional present over the traditional past tense. For, as this book has shown and as the growing body of speculative fiction written in the present tense indicates (cf. Gebauer 2020), the multifarious effects of present-tense narration offer various ways of articulating the alarming seriousness of the current state of the world. These include, above all, the evocation of narrative immediacy and urgency, the facilitation of spatial, temporal, and spatiotemporal immersion, and the thematization of different conceptions of time – conceptions such as Gumbrecht's idea of the broad present or Atwood's vision of an endless present that characterizes the post-apocalyptic world depicted in *Oryx and Crake*. Even more to the point, the fictional present seems to be the only narrative tense that can – but need not necessarily – facilitate a temporal perspective that as of yet contests the existence of a diegetic future.[18]

There are, then, various reasons why authors resort to the fictional present as the dominant tense of narration, all of which hinge on the purpose this tense can serve in a narrative. Future research on the cultural functions of present-tense narrative should, therefore, focus not so much on debating the (im)plausibility of different rationales behind the popularity of the fictional present among contemporary novelists as on the question how the different functions of present-tense narration interact with cultural phenomena: Which

---

18 Generally, the fictional past suggests a retrospective perspective, meaning that the events occurring in the diegetic present are related in the diegetic future with the benefit of hindsight, whereas the fictional future implies that the narrative events have not yet happened: here the diegetic present lies in the future of the speaker who predicts the events.

contemporary narrative themes correlate with typical combinations of different functions of the fictional present? To what degree does such a 'mainstream' use of the present tense differ from innovative or experimental uses integrating other functional chains? And what topics do such experiments of present-tense narration address? The exploration of these and similar questions could certainly prove insightful and rewarding for the purposes of an "applied cultural narratology" (Nünning 2004b).

* * *

I will conclude this book by returning to its epigram, a text from the preface of *The Magic Mountain* (1999 [1924]) in which Thomas Mann claims that narratives are always told in retrospect and should accordingly make use of the past tense. The diversity of the contemporary present-tense novel invites us to critically challenge this assumption, a belief that forms a central tenet of what Suzanne Fleischman (1990, 263) has referred to as our "narrative norm" – our common understanding of what makes a well-formed story. As my model interpretations have demonstrated, the fictional present can be used in order to evoke the impression of retrospective narration (as in the novels by Mantel, Atwood, Aslam, Winslow, and Welsh), simultaneous narration (as in Donoghue's narrative), or prospective narration (as in McEwan's text).

Given the functional variety of present-tense narration in the contemporary novel, we should reconsider that narrative norm – a norm which is derived from the ways in which we tell each other stories in everyday life. Dorrit Cohn (1999, 96) and the many other narratologists I have quoted to this effect are certainly right in their contention that, in real life, storytelling is only possible with the benefit of hindsight, and it may also be true that, for this reason, most fictional narratives are written in retrospect. Yet, since my corpus clearly reveals that this does not hold for every novel, the time may have come to sincerely question the "tense structure" (Currie 2013, 1) so long believed to underlie narrative fiction. Narratives do not necessarily have to "be in the past," as Mann suggests; they may also be in the present or even in the future. Most importantly, however, they may 'be' neither in the past, nor in the present, nor in the future, but in a space that knows neither 'here' nor 'now': the imagined, and imaginary, world of narrative fiction.

Works Cited

Primary Sources

Abish, Walter. 1974. *Alphabetical Africa*. New York, NY: New Directions.
Aslam, Nadeem. 2006 [2004]. *Maps for Lost Lovers*. New York, NY: Vintage International.
Atwood, Margaret. 1986 [1985]. *The Handmaid's Tale*. London: Vintage Books.
Atwood, Margaret. 2004 [2003]. *Oryx and Crake*. New York, NY: Anchor Books.
Atwood, Margaret. 2010 [2009]. *The Year of the Flood*. New York, NY: Anchor Books.
Atwood, Margaret. 2014 [2013]. *MaddAddam*. New York, NY: Anchor Books.
Atwood, Margaret. 2016. *Hag-Seed: The Tempest Retold*. London: The Hogarth Press.
Atwood, Margaret. 2016 [2015]. *The Heart Goes Last: A Novel*. New York, NY: Anchor Books.
Atwood, Margaret. 2019. *The Testaments*. London: Chatto & Windus.
Beckett, Samuel. 2010 [1953]. *The Unnamable*. London: Faber & Faber.
Berend, Alice. 2019 [1915]. *Die Bräutigame der Babette Bomberling: Roman*. Berlin: Holzinger.
Bolt, Robert. 1990 [1960]. *A Man for All Seasons: A Play in Two Acts*. New York, NY: Vintage International.
Bradbury, Malcolm. 2012 [1975]. *The History Man*. Basingstoke and Oxford: Picador.
Brooke-Rose, Christine. 1984. *Amalgamemnon*. Manchester: Carcanet.
Burt, Guy. 2005 [1999]. *A Clock Without Hands: A Novel*. New York, NY: Ballantine Books.
Butler, Halle. 2019. *The New Me: A Novel*. London: Penguin Books.
Calvino, Italo. 1998 [1979]. *If on a Winter's Night a Traveler*. Translated by William Weaver. London: Vintage Books.
Coetzee, J. M. 1980. *Waiting for the Barbarians*. London: Secker & Warburg.
Collins, Suzanne. 2011 [2008]. *The Hunger Games*. London: Scholastic.
Collins, Suzanne. 2011 [2009]. *The Hunger Games: Catching Fire*. London: Scholastic.
Collins, Suzanne. 2011 [2010]. *The Hunger Games: Mockingjay*. London: Scholastic.
Dalcher, Christina. 2018. *Vox: A Novel*. New York, NY: Berkley.
Dangarembga, Tsitsi. 2020. *This Mournable Body*. London: Faber & Faber.
De Botton, Alain. 2016. *The Course of Love: A Novel*. London et al.: Hamish Hamilton.
Defoe, Daniel. 2001 [1719]. *Robinson Crusoe*. London: Penguin Books.
Dickens, Charles. 1994 [1849–1850]. *David Copperfield*. London: Penguin Books.
Donoghue, Emma. 2010. *Room: A Novel*. Basingstoke and Oxford: Picador.
Doshi, Avni. 2020. *Burnt Sugar*. London et al.: Hamish Hamilton.
Duras, Marguerite. 1984. *L'Amant*. Paris: Les Éditions de Minuit.
Ellis, Bret Easton. 1999 [1998]. *Glamorama*. New York, NY: Alfred A. Knopf.
Ellmann, Lucy. 2019. *Ducks, Newburyport*. Norwich: Galley Beggar Press.
Evaristo, Bernadine. 2019. *Girl, Woman, Other*. London: Hamish Hamilton.
Faulkner, William. 1977 [1930]. "A Rose for Emily." In *Collected Stories of William Faulkner*, 119–130. New York, NY: Vintage Books.
Fielding, Henry. 1973 [1749]. *Tom Jones: The History of a Foundling*. Edited by Sheridan Baker. New York, NY and London: W. W. Norton & Company.
Fielding, Henry. 1999 [1742/1741]. *Joseph Andrews* and *Shamela*. Edited by Judith Hawley. London: Penguin Books.
Flynn, Gillian. 2012. *Gone Girl: A Novel*. New York, NY: Crown Publishers.

Galgut, Damon. 2010. *In a Strange Room: Three Journeys*. London: Atlantic Books.
Goethe, Johann Wolfgang von. 2004 [1795/1796]. *Wilhelm Meisters Lehrjahre: Roman*. Munich: Deutscher Taschenbuch Verlag.
Haddon, Mark. 2004 [2003]. *The Curious Incident of the Dog in the Night-Time*. London: Vintage Books.
Hawkins, Paula. 2015. *The Girl on the Train*. London: Black Swan.
Healey, Emma. 2014. *Elizabeth Is Missing*. London: Penguin Books.
Helle, Helle. 2014 [2011]. *This Should Be Written in the Present Tense*. Translated by Martin Aitken. London: Vintage Books.
Hornby, Nick. 1995. *High Fidelity*. London: Penguin Books.
Ishiguro, Kazuo. 1989. *The Remains of the Day*. London: Faber & Faber.
James, E. L. 2012. *Fifty Shades Freed*. New York, NY: Vintage Books.
James, E. L. 2012 [2011]a. *Fifty Shades Darker*. New York, NY: Vintage Books.
James, E. L. 2012 [2011]b. *Fifty Shades of Grey*. New York, NY: Vintage Books.
James, Marlon. 2014. *A Brief History of Seven Killings*. London: Oneworld Publications.
Joyce, James. 2000 [1914–1915]. *A Portrait of the Artist as a Young Man*. London: Penguin Books.
Kang, Han. 2015 [2007]. *The Vegetarian: A Novel*. Translated by Deborah Smith. London: Portobello Books.
Kennedy, A. L. 2012 [2011]. *The Blue Book*. London: Vintage Books.
Kepnes, Caroline. 2015 [2014]. *You*. London et al.: Simon & Schuster.
Khan-Cullors, Patrisse, and asha bandele. 2017. *When They Call You a Terrorist: A Black Lives Matter Memoir*. Edinburgh: Canongate Books.
Krauze, Gabriel. 2020. *Who They Was*. London: Fourth Estate.
Lapena, Shari. 2017 [2016]. *The Couple Next Door*. London: Corgi.
Le Carré, John. 2018 [2001]. *The Constant Gardener*. London: Penguin Books.
Mann, Thomas. 1990 [1924]. *Der Zauberberg*. Frankfurt a.M.: Fischer Taschenbuch Verlag.
Mann, Thomas. 1999 [1924]. *The Magic Mountain*. Translated by H.T. Lowe-Porter. London: Vintage Books.
Mantel, Hilary. 2010 [2009]. *Wolf Hall*. London: Fourth Estate.
Mantel, Hilary. 2013 [2012]. *Bring Up the Bodies*. London: Fourth Estate.
Mantel, Hilary. 2016. "The Present Tense." *The London Review of Books* 38.1, January 7: 19–20.
Mantel, Hilary. 2020. *The Mirror & the Light*. London: Fourth Estate.
Martin, George R. R. 2011 [1996]. *A Game of Thrones*. London: Harper Voyager.
Martin, George R. R. 2011 [1998]. *A Clash of Kings*. London: Harper Voyager.
Martin, George R. R. 2011 [2000]a. *A Storm of Swords 1: Steel and Snow*. London: Harper Voyager.
Martin, George R. R. 2011 [2000]b. *A Storm of Swords 2: Blood and Gold*. London: Harper Voyager.
Martin, George R. R. 2011 [2005]. *A Feast for Crows*. London: Harper Voyager.
Martin, George R. R. 2012 [2011]a. *A Dance with Dragons 1: Dreams and Dust*. London: Harper Voyager.
Martin, George R. R. 2012 [2011]b. *A Dance with Dragons 2: After the Feast*. London: Harper Voyager.
Matheson, Richard. 2010 [1954]. *I Am Legend*. London: Gollancz.
Maughan, Tim. 2019. *Infinite Detail*. New York, NY: Farrar, Straus and Giroux.
McCann, Colum. 2020. *Apeirogon: A Novel*. London et al.: Bloomsbury.

McCarthy, Cormac. 2007 [2006]. *The Road*. New York, NY: Vintage International.
McCarthy, Tom. 2010. *C*. London: Vintage Books.
McDonell, Nick. 2003 [2002]. *Twelve*. London and New York, NY: Atlantic Books.
McEwan, Ian. 2016. *Nutshell*. London: Jonathan Cape.
McInerney, Jay. 2006 [1984]. *Bright Lights, Big Cities*. London et al.: Bloomsbury.
Melville, Herman. 2002 [1851]. *Moby-Dick; or, The Whale*. Edited by Hershel Parker and Harrison Hayford. London and New York, NY: W. W. Norton & Company.
Mengiste, Maaza. 2019. *The Shadow King: A Novel*. New York, NY: W. W. Norton & Company.
Mesler, Corey. 2002. *Talk: A Novel in Dialogue*. Livingston, AL: Livingston Press.
Meyer, Stephenie. 2006 [2005]. *Twilight*. London: Atom.
Meyer, Stephenie. 2007 [2006]. *New Moon*. London: Atom.
Meyer, Stephenie. 2007. *Eclipse*. London: Atom.
Meyer, Stephenie. 2008. *Breaking Dawn*. London: Atom.
Mitchell, David. 2015 [2014]. *The Bone Clocks*. London: Sceptre.
Moody, Rick. 1998 [1995]. "The Grid." In *The Ring of Brightest Angels around Heaven: A Novella and Stories*, 29–37. London: Abacus.
Murakami, Haruki. 2003 [1985]. *Hard-Boiled Wonderland and the End of the World*. Translated by Alfred Birnbaum. London: Vintage Books.
Murakami, Haruki. 2007 [1985]. *Hard-boiled Wonderland und das Ende der Welt*. Translated by Amelie Ortmanns. Munich: btb Verlag.
Nabokov, Vladimir. 2006 [1955]. *Lolita*. London: Penguin Books.
Obioma, Chigozie. 2019. *An Orchestra of Minorities*. London: Abacus.
O'Farrel, Maggie. 2017. *I Am, I Am, I Am: Seventeen Brushes With Death*. London: Tinder Press.
O'Neill, Louise. 2016 [2015]. *Asking for It*. London: Riverrun.
Powers, Richard. 2018. *The Overstory: A Novel*. New York, NY and London: W. W. Norton & Company.
Ramos, Joanne. 2019. *The Farm*. London et al.: Bloomsbury.
Richardson, Samuel. 2003 [1740]. *Pamela; or, Virtue Rewarded*. Edited by Peter Sabor. London: Penguin Books.
Robbe-Grillet, Alain. 2008 [1959]. *Jealousy*. Translated by Richard Howard. London: Alma Classics.
Robbe-Grillet, Alain. 2012 [1957]. *La Jalousie*. Paris: Les Éditions de Minuit.
Rowling, J. K. 2014 [1997]. *Harry Potter and the Philosopher's Stone*. London et al.: Bloomsbury.
Rowling, J. K. 2014 [1998]. *Harry Potter and the Chamber of Secret*. London et al.: Bloomsbury.
Rowling, J. K. 2014 [1999]. *Harry Potter and the Prisoner of Azkaban*. London et al.: Bloomsbury.
Rowling, J. K. 2014 [2000]. *Harry Potter and the Goblet of Fire*. London et al.: Bloomsbury.
Rowling, J. K. 2014 [2003]. *Harry Potter and the Order of the Phoenix*. London et al.: Bloomsbury.
Rowling, J. K. 2014 [2005]. *Harry Potter and the Half-Blood Prince*. London et al.: Bloomsbury.
Rowling, J. K. 2014 [2007]. *Harry Potter and the Deathly Hallows*. London et al.: Bloomsbury.
Russo, Meredith. 2019. *Birthday: A Love Story Eighteen Years in the Making*. London: Usborne.
Sacks, Michelle. 2019. *All the Lost Things: A Novel*. New York, NY et al.: Little, Brown and Company.
Seiffert, Rachel. 2002 [2001]. *The Dark Room*. London: Vintage Books.
Selvon, Samuel. 2006 [1956]. *The Lonely Londoners*. London: Penguin Books.

Shakespeare, William. 2006 [1604–1605/1623]. *Hamlet*. Edited by Ann Thompson and Neil Taylor. London: Methuen Drama.
Smaill, Anna. 2015. *The Chimes*. London: Sceptre.
Small, Judith. 1991. "Body of Work." *The New Yorker*, July 8: 30–32.
Smith, Ali. 2002 [2001]. *Hotel World*. London: Penguin Books.
Smith, Ali. 2016. *Autumn*. London et al.: Hamish Hamilton.
Smith, Ali. 2017. *Winter*. London et al.: Hamish Hamilton.
Smith, Ali. 2019. *Spring*. London et al.: Hamish Hamilton.
Smith, Ali. 2020. *Summer*. London et al.: Hamish Hamilton.
Smith, Zadie. 2013 [2012]. *NW*. London: Penguin Books.
Smith, Zadie. 2016. *Swing Time*. London et al.: Hamish Hamilton.
Sterne, Laurence. 2003 [1759–1767]. *The Life and Opinions of Tristram Shandy, Gentleman*. Edited by Melvyn New and Joan New. London: Penguin Books.
Swift, Graham. 2018 [2003]. *The Light of Day*. London et al.: Scribner.
Thackeray, William Makepeace. 1994 [1847–1848]. *Vanity Fair: A Novel Without a Hero*. Edited by Peter Shillingsburg. New York, NY and London: W. W. Norton & Company.
Tóibín, Colm. 2012. *The Testament of Mary*. London et al.: Penguins Books.
Tyler, Anne. 2020. *Redhead by the Side of the Road*. London: Chatto & Windus.
Watson, S. J. 2011. *Before I Go to Sleep*. London: Black Swan.
Welsh, Irvine. 2004 [1993]. *Trainspotting*. London: Vintage Books.
Welsh, Irvine. 2012a. *Skagboys*. London: Jonathan Cape.
Welsh, Irvine. 2012b. *Skagboys*. Narrated by Tam Dean Burn. Audible. Audiobook.
Welsh, Irvine. 2013 [2002]. *Porno*. London: Vintage Books.
Welsh, Irvine. 2018. *Dead Men's Trousers*. London: Jonathan Cape.
Whitehead, Colson. 2012 [2011]. *Zone One*. London: Vintage Books.
Wilde, Oscar. 1994 [1891]. *The Picture of Dorian Gray*. London: Penguin Books.
Winslow, Don. 2006 [2005]. *The Power of the Dog*. London: Arrow Books.
Winslow, Don. 2011 [2010]. *Savages*. London: Arrow Books.
Winslow, Don. 2016 [2015]. *The Cartel: A Novel*. New York, NY: Vintage Books.
Winslow, Don. 2019. *The Border*. New York, NY: William Morrow.
Woolf, Virginia. 1996 [1925]. *Mrs. Dalloway*. London: Penguin Books.
Zhang, C Pam. 2020. *How Much of These Hills Is Gold*. London: Virago.

Secondary Sources

Abbott, H. Porter. 2008 [2002]. *The Cambridge Introduction to Narrative*. 2nd ed. Cambridge: Cambridge University Press.
Abbott, H. Porter. 2008 [2005]. "Narration." In *The Routledge Encyclopedia of Narrative Theory*, edited by David Herman, Manfred Jahn, and Marie-Laure Ryan, 2nd ed., 339–344. London and New York, NY: Routledge.
Abbott, H. Porter. 2014. "Narrativity." In *Handbook of Narratology: Volume 2*, edited by Peter Hühn, Jan Christoph Meister, John Pier, and Wolf Schmid, 2nd ed., 587–607. Berlin and Boston, MA: De Gruyter.
Adams, Tim. 2016. "*Nutshell* by Ian McEwan Review – A Tragic Hero in the Making." *The Observer*, August 30, 2016. Accessed August 31, 2020. https://www.theguardian.com/books/2016/aug/30/nutshell-ian-mcewan-review-hamlet-foetus.

Ahmed, Rehana. 2015. *Writing British Muslims: Religion, Class and Multiculturalism*. Manchester: Manchester University Press.
Aitkenhead, Decca. 2016. "Ian McEwan: 'I'm going to get such a kicking.'" *The Guardian*, August 27. Accessed August 31, 2020. https://www.theguardian.com/books/2016/aug/27/ian-mcewan-author-nutshell-going-get-kicking.
Alber, Jan. 2009. "Impossible Storyworlds – and What to Do with Them." *Storyworlds: A Journal of Narrative Studies* 1: 79–96.
Alber, Jan. 2013. "Unnatural Narratology: Developments and Perspectives." *Germanisch-Romanische Monatsschrift* 63.1: 69–84.
Alber, Jan. 2014. "Postmodernist Impossibilities, the Creation of New Cognitive Frames, and Attempts at Interpretation." In *Beyond Classical Narration: Transmedial and Unnatural Challenges*, edited by Jan Alber and Rüdiger Heinze, 261–280. Berlin and Boston, MA: De Gruyter.
Alber, Jan, and Monika Fludernik. 2010. "Introduction." In *Postclassical Narratology: Approaches and Analyses*, edited by Jan Alber and Monika Fludernik, 1–31. Columbus, OH: The Ohio State University Press.
Alber, Jan, and Rüdiger Heinze. 2011. "Introduction." In *Unnatural Narratives – Unnatural Narratology*, edited by Jan Alber and Rüdiger Heinze, 1–19. Berlin and Boston, MA: De Gruyter.
Alber, Jan, Stefan Iversen, Henrik Skov Nielsen, and Brian Richardson. 2010. "Unnatural Narratives, Unnatural Narratology: Beyond Mimetic Models." *Narrative* 18.2: 111–136.
Alber, Jan, Stefan Iversen, Henrik Skov Nielsen, and Brian Richardson. 2012. "What Is Unnatural about Unnatural Narratology? A Response to Monika Fludernik." *Narrative* 20.3: 371–382.
Alber, Jan, Stefan Iversen, Henrik Skov Nielsen, and Brian Richardson. 2013. "Introduction." In *A Poetics of Unnatural Narrative*, edited by Jan Alber, Henrik Skov Nielsen, and Brian Richardson, 1–15. Columbus, OH: The Ohio State University Press.
Alber, Jan, Henrik Skov Nielsen, and Brian Richardson. 2012. "Unnatural Voices, Minds, and Narration." In *The Routledge Companion to Experimental Literature*, edited by Joe Bray, Alison Gibbons, and Brian McHale, 351–367. London and New York, NY: Routledge.
Allrath, Gaby. 2005. *(En)Gendering Unreliable Narration: A Feminist-Narratological Theory and Analysis of Unreliability in Contemporary Women's Novels*. Trier: Wissenschaftlicher Verlag Trier.
Altshuler, Daniel. 2016. *Events, States and Times: An Essay on Narrative Discourse in English*. Berlin and Boston, MA: De Gruyter Open. Accessed August 31, 2020. https://doi.org/10.1515/9783110485912.
Arias, Rosario. 2011. "Life After Man?: Posthumanity and Genetic Engineering in Margaret Atwood's *Oryx and Crake* and Kazuo Ishiguro's *Never Let Me Go*." In *Restoring the Mystery of the Rainbow: Literature's Refraction of Science – Volume 1*, edited by Valeria Tinkler-Villani and C. C. Barfoot, 379–394. Amsterdam and New York, NY: Rodopi.
Arias, Rosario. 2014. "Exoticising the Tudors: Hilary Mantel's Re-Appropriation of the Past in *Wolf Hall* and *Bring Up the Bodies*." In *Exoticizing the Past in Contemporary Neo-Historical Fiction*, edited by Elodie Rousselot, 19–36. London: Palgrave Macmillan.
Armstrong, Judith G. 2002. "Deciphering the Broken Narrative of Trauma: Signs of Traumatic Dissociation on the Rorschach." *Rorschachiana* 25: 11–27.
Ashcroft, Bill, Gareth Griffiths, and Helen Tiffin. 1989. *The Empire Writes Back: Theory and Practice in Post-Colonial Literatures*. London and New York, NY: Routledge.

Assmann, Corinna. 2018. *Doing Family in Second-Generation British Migration Literature*. Berlin and Boston, MA: De Gruyter.
Atwood, Margaret. 2011. *In Other Worlds: SF and the Human Imagination*. London: Virago.
Augé, Marc. 2008 [1992]. *Non-Places: An Introduction to Supermodernity*. 2nd ed. London and New York, NY: Verso.
Avanessian, Armen. 2013. "(Co)Present Tense: Marcel Beyer Reads the Past." *The Germanic Review* 88: 363–374.
Avanessian, Armen, and Anke Hennig. 2012. *Präsens: Poetik eines Tempus*. Zurich: diaphanes.
Avanessian, Armen, and Anke Hennig. 2013a. "Der altermoderne Roman: Gegenwart von Geschichte und *contemporaneity* von Vergangenheit." In *Poetiken der Gegenwart: Deutschsprachige Romane nach 2000*, edited by Silke Horstkotte and Leonhard Herrmann, 245–265. Berlin and Boston, MA: De Gruyter.
Avanessian, Armen, and Anke Hennig, eds. 2013b. *Der Präsensroman*. Berlin and Boston, MA: De Gruyter.
Avanessian, Armen, and Anke Hennig. 2013c. "Die Evolution des Präsens als Romantempus." In *Der Präsensroman*, edited by Armen Avanessian and Anke Hennig, 139–180. Berlin and Boston, MA: De Gruyter.
Avanessian, Armen, and Anke Hennig. 2013d. "Einleitung." In *Der Präsensroman*, edited by Armen Avanessian and Anke Hennig, 1–24. Berlin and Boston, MA: De Gruyter.
Avanessian, Armen, and Anke Hennig. 2015. "Tempus – Fiktion – Narration: Kevin Vennemanns Erzählen im Präsens." In *Zeiten erzählen: Ansätze – Aspekte – Analysen*, edited by Antonius Weixler and Lukas Werner, 319–341. Berlin and Boston, MA: De Gruyter.
Avanessian, Armen, and Anke Hennig. 2015 [2012]. *Present Tense: A Poetics*. Translated by Nils F. Schott with Daniel Hendrickson. London et al.: Bloomsbury.
Bahrawi, Nazry. 2013. "Hope of a Hopeless World: Eco-Teleology in Margaret Atwood's *Oryx and Crake* and *The Year of the Flood*." *Green Letters: Studies in Ecocriticism* 17.3: 251–263.
Baker, Deirdre. 2011. "Present Tensions, or It's All Happening Now." *The Horn Book Magazine*, December 29, 2011. Accessed August 31, 2020. https://www.hbook.com/?detailStory=present-tensions-or-its-all-happening-now.
Bakhtin, Mikhail M. 2014 [1981]. "Forms of Time and of the Chronotope in the Novel." In *The Dialogic Imagination: Four Essays by M. M. Bakhtin*, translated by Caryl Emerson and Michael Holquist, 84–258. Austin, TX: The University of Texas Press.
Bal, Mieke. 1981. "On Meanings and Descriptions." *Studies in 20th Century Literature* 6.1: 100–148.
Bal, Mieke. 1985 [1980]. *Narratology: An Introduction to the Theory of Narrative*. Translated by Christine van Boheemen. Toronto, ON et al.: University of Toronto Press.
Bal, Mieke. 2002. *Travelling Concepts in the Humanities: A Rough Guide*. Toronto, ON et al.: University of Toronto Press.
Ball, Donald L. 1971. *Samuel Richardson's Theory of Fiction*. The Hague and Paris: Mouton.
Bamberg, Michael. 2007. "Stories: Big or Small – Why Do We Care?" In *Narrative – State of the Art*, edited by Michael Bamberg, 165–174. Amsterdam and Philadelphia, PA: John Benjamins.
Bamberg, Michael, and Alexandra Georgakopoulou. 2008. "Small Stories as a New Perspective in Narrative and Identity Analysis." *Text & Talk* 28.3: 377–396.
Banfield, Ann. 1982. *Unspeakable Sentences: Narration and Representation in the Language of Fiction*. Boston, MA et al.: Routledge & Kegan Paul.
Baroni, Raphaël. 2007. *La Tension narrative: Suspense, curiosité et surprise*. Paris: Seuil.

Baroni, Raphaël. 2014. "Tellability." In *Handbook of Narratology: Volume 2*, edited by Peter Hühn, Jan Christoph Meister, John Pier, and Wolf Schmid, 2nd ed., 836–845. Berlin and Boston, MA: De Gruyter.

Baroni, Raphaël. 2017. *Les Rouages de l'intrigue: Les outils de la narratologie postclassique pour l'analyse des textes littéraires*. Geneva: Slatkine Érudition.

Barthes, Roland. 1968 [1953]. *Writing Degree Zero*. Translated by Annette Lavers and Colin Smith. New York, NY: Hill and Wang.

Barthes, Roland. 1972 [1953]. *Le Degré zero de l'écriture* suivi de *Nouveaux essais critiques*. Paris: Éditions du Seuil.

Baßler, Moritz. 2010. "Intertextualität und Gattung." In *Handbuch Gattungstheorie*, edited by: Rüdiger Zymner, 56–58. Stuttgart and Weimar: J. B. Metzler.

Becker, Tabea, and Juliane Stude. 2017. *Erzählen*. Heidelberg: Universitätsverlag Winter.

Beckwith, Susan Lynn, and John R. Reed. 2002. "Some Uses of the Present Tense in Dickens and Collins." *Dickens Studies Annual* 32: 299–318.

Bekhta, Natalya. 2017a. "Emerging Narrative Situations: A Definition of We-Narratives Proper." In *Emerging Vectors of Narratology*, edited by Per Krogh Hansen, John Pier, Philippe Roussin, and Wolf Schmid, 101–126. Berlin and Boston, MA: De Gruyter.

Bekhta, Natalya. 2017b. "We-Narratives: The Distinctiveness of Collective Narration." *Narrative* 25.2: 164–181.

Bekhta, Natalya. 2020. *We-Narratives: Collective Storytelling in Contemporary Fiction*. Columbus, OH: The Ohio State University Press.

Bemong, Nele, and Pieter Borghart. 2010. "Bakhtin's Theory of the Literary Chronotope: Reflections, Applications, Perspectives." In *Bakhtin's Theory of the Literary Chronotope: Reflections, Applications, Perspectives*, edited by Nele Bemong, Pieter Borghart, Michel De Dobbeleer, Kristoffel Demoen, Koen De Temmerman, and Bart Keunen, 3–16. Ghent: Academia Press.

Bennett, Jane. 2010. *Vibrant Matter: A Political Ecology of Things*. Durham, NC: Duke University Press.

Benveniste, Émile. 1966. *Problèmes de linguistique générale*. Paris: Éditions Gallimard.

Benveniste, Émile. 1971 [1966]. *Problems in General Linguistics*. Translated by Mary Elizabeth Meek. Coral Gables, FL: University of Miami Press.

Berninger, Mark, and Katrin Thomas. 2007. "A Parallelquel of a Classic Text and Reification of the Fictional – the Playful Parody of *Jane Eyre* in Jasper Fforde's *The Eyre Affair*." In *A Breath of Fresh Eyre: Intertextual and Intermedial Reworkings of "Jane Eyre,"* edited by Margarete Rubik and Elke Mettinger-Schartmann, 181–196. Amsterdam and New York, NY: Rodopi.

Bever, Thomas G. 1970. "The Cognitive Basis for Linguistic Structures." In *Cognition and the Development of Language*, edited by John R. Hayes, 279–362. New York, NY et al.: John Wiley & Sons.

Bhanot, Kavita. 2019. "Love, Sex, and Desire vs. Islam in British Muslim Literature." In *The Routledge Companion to Pakistani Anglophone Writing*, edited by Aroosa Kanwal and Saiyma Aslam, 200–212. London and New York, NY: Routledge.

Birke, Dorothee. 2008. *Memory's Fragile Power: Crises of Memory, Identity and Narrative in Contemporary British Novels*. Trier: Wissenschaftlicher Verlag Trier.

Bode, Christoph. 2005. *Der Roman: Eine Einführung*. Tübingen and Basel: A. Francke.

Bode, Christoph. 2013. "The Theory and Poetics of Future Narratives: A Narrative." In: *Future Narratives: Theory, Poetics, and Media-Historical Moment*, by Christoph Bode and Rainer Dietrich, 1–108. Berlin and Boston, MA: De Gruyter.

Boller, Alessandra. 2014. "In 'Paradice'? Test-Tube Evolution within the Natural Realm in Margaret Atwood's *MaddAddam* Trilogy." *Inklings: Jahrbuch für Literatur und Ästhetik* 32: 3245–3260.

Boller, Alessandra. 2018. *Rethinking 'the Human' in Dystopian Times: Modified Bodies and the Re-/Deconstruction of Human Exceptionalism in Margaret Atwood's "MaddAddam" Trilogy and Kazuo Ishiguro's "Never Let Me Go."* Trier: Wissenschaftlicher Verlag Trier.

Bonheim, Helmut. 1983. "Narration in the Second Person." *Recherches anglaises et américaines: RANAM* 16: 69–80.

Bonheim, Helmut. 1986. *The Narrative Modes: Techniques of the Short Story*. Cambridge: D. S. Brewer.

Booth, Wayne C. 1974. *The Rhetoric of Irony*. Chicago, IL and London: The University of Chicago Press.

Borman, Tracy. 2014. *Thomas Cromwell: The Untold Story of Henry VIII's Most Faithful Servant*. London: Hodder & Stoughton.

Bortolussi, Marisa, and Peter Dixon. 2003. *Psychonarratology: Foundations for the Empirical Study of Literary Response*. Cambridge et al.: Cambridge University Press.

Bosco, Mark. 2010. "The Apocalyptic Imagination in *Oryx and Crake*." In *Margaret Atwood: "The Robber Bride," "The Blind Assassin," "Oryx and Crake,"* edited by J. Brooks Bouson, 156–171. London and New York, NY: Continuum.

Bourne, Craig, and Emily Caddick Bourne. 2016. *Time in Fiction*. Oxford: Oxford University Press.

Bowen, Deborah C. 2017. "Ecological Endings and Eschatology: Margaret Atwood's Post-Apocalyptic Fiction." *Christianity & Literature* 66.4: 691–705.

Bracke, Astrid. 2018. *Climate Crisis and the 21st-Century British Novel*. London: Bloomsbury.

Brandt, Wolfgang. 1997. "Zum Geleit: Anmerkungen zum Gegenwartserzählen." In *"Da – horch! Es summt durch Wind und Schlossen. . .": Das präsentische Erzählen in der deutschen Kunstballade der ersten Hälfte des 19. Jahrhunderts*, edited by Ruoxing Tang, xi–xviii. Münster: Lit-Verlag.

Brewer, William F. 1996. "The Nature of Narrative Suspense and the Problem of Rereading." In *Suspense: Conceptualizations, Theoretical Analyses, and Empirical Explorations*, edited by Peter Vorderer, Hans J. Wulff, and Mike Friedrichsen, 107–127. Mahwah, NJ: Lawrence Erlbaum Associates.

Brewer, William F., and Edward H. Lichtenstein 1982. "Stories Are to Entertain: A Structural-Affect Theory of Stories." *Journal of Pragmatics* 6: 473–486.

Broich, Ulrich. 1985. "Zur Einzeltextreferenz." In *Intertextualität: Formen, Funktionen, anglistische Fallstudien*, edited by Ulrich Broich and Manfred Pfister, 52–58. Tübingen: Max Niemeyer Verlag.

Bronzwaer, W. J. M. 1970. *Tense in the Novel: An Investigation of Some Potentialities of Linguistic Criticism*. Groningen: Wolters-Noordhoff Publishing.

Brosch, Renate. 2017. "Thomas Cromwell, Our Contemporary: The Poetics of Subjective Experience as Intersubjective Ethics in *Wolf Hall*." In *The Return of the Historical Novel? Thinking About Fiction and History after Historiographic Metafiction*, edited by Andrew James Johnston and Kai Wiegandt, 163–183. Heidelberg: Universitätsverlag Winter.

Brosch, Renate. 2018. "Reading Minds – *Wolf Hall*'s Revision of the Poetics of Subjectivity." In *Hilary Mantel: Contemporary Critical Perspectives*, edited by Eileen Pollard and Ginette Carpenter, 57–72. London: Bloomsbury Academic.
Bühler, Karl. 1965 [1934]. *Sprachtheorie: Die Darstellungsfunktion der Sprache*. 2nd ed. Stuttgart: Gustav Fischer Verlag.
Bui, Thuy. 2019. "Temporal Reference in Vietnamese." In *Interdisciplinary Perspectives on Vietnamese Linguistics*, edited by Nigel Duffield, Trang Phan, and Tue Thrin, 115-140. Amsterdam and Philadelphia, PA: John Benjamins.
Butler, Judith. 1993. *Bodies That Matter: On the Discursive Limits of "Sex."* New York, NY and London: Routledge.
Butler, Judith. 1999 [1990]. *Gender Trouble: Feminism and the Subversion of Identity*. New York, NY and London: Routledge.
Butt, Nadia. 2008. "Between Orthodoxy and Modernity: Mapping the Transcultural Predicaments of Pakistani Immigrants in Multi-Ethnic Britain in Nadeem Aslam's *Maps for Lost Lovers* (2004)." In *Multi-Ethnic Britain 2000+: New Perspectives in Literature, Film and the Arts*, edited by Lars Eckstein, Barbara Korte, Eva Ulrike Pirker, and Christoph Reinfandt, 153–169. Amsterdam and New York, NY: Rodopi.
Capecci, John. 1989. "Performing the Second-Person." *Text and Performance Quarterly* 1: 42–52.
Caracciolo, Marco. 2012. "Notes for a(nother) Theory of Experientiality." *JLT: Journal of Literary Theory* 6.1: 177–194.
Caracciolo, Marco. 2013. "Narrative Space and Readers' Responses to Stories: A Phenomenological Account." *Style* 47.4: 425–444.
Caracciolo, Marco. 2014. *The Experientiality of Narrative: An Enactivist Approach*. Berlin and Boston, MA: De Gruyter.
Caracciolo, Marco. 2016. *'Strange' Narrators in Contemporary Fiction: Explorations in Readers' Engagement with Characters*. Lincoln, NE and London: University of Nebraska Press.
Caracciolo, Marco. 2018. "Notes for an Econarratological Theory of Character." *Frontiers of Narrative* 4.1: 172–189.
Caracciolo, Marco. 2019. "Form, Science, and Narrative in the Anthropocene." *Narrative* 27.3: 270–289.
Cardwell, Sarah. 2000. "Present(ing) Tense: Temporality and Tense in Comparative Theories of Literature-Film Adaptation." *Scope: An Online Journal of Film and Television Studies*, July 2000. Accessed August 31, 2020. https://www.nottingham.ac.uk/scope/documents/2000/july-2000/cardwell.pdf.
Cardwell, Sarah. 2003. "About Time: Theorizing Adaptation, Temporality and Tense." *Literature / Film Quarterly* 31.2: 82–92.
Carlisle, Janice. 1971. "*Dombey and Son*: The Reader and the Present Tense." *The Journal of Narrative Technique* 1.3: 146–158.
Casparis, Christian Paul. 1975. *Tense Without Time: The Present Tense in Narration*. Bern: A. Francke Verlag.
Chafe, Wallace. 1994. *Discourse, Consciousness, and Time: The Flow and Displacement of Conscious Experience in Speaking and Writing*. Chicago, IL and London: The University of Chicago Press.
Chambers, Claire. 2011. "Recent Literary Representations of British Muslims." In *Mediating Faiths: Religion and Socio-Cultural Change in the Twenty-First Century*, edited by Michael Bailey and Guy Redden, 175–188. Farnham: Ashgate.

Chambers, Claire. 2019. *Making Sense of Contemporary British Muslim Novels*. London: Palgrave Macmillan.

Chang, Hui-chuan. 2011. "Critical Dystopia Reconsidered: Octavia Butler's *Parable* Series and Margaret Atwood's *Oryx and Crake* as Post-Apocalyptic Dystopias." *Tamkang Review* 41.2: 3–20.

Charles, Ron. 2016a. "Ian McEwan Has Hamlet Curled Up in Fetal Position." *The Washington Post*, September 14: C1 + C4. Accessed August 31, 2020. https://www.pressreader.com/usa/the-washington-post/20160914/282187945478024.

Charles, Ron. 2016b. "Ian McEwan's *Nutshell*: A Tale of Betrayal and Murder as Told by a Fetus." *The Washington Post*, September 12, 2016. Accessed August 31, 2020. https://www.washingtonpost.com/entertainment/books/ian-mcewans-nutshell-a-tale-of-betrayal-and-murder-as-told-by-a-fetus/2016/09/12/8b31ba22-7694-11e6-b786-19d0cb1ed06c_story.html.

Chatman, Seymour. 1978. *Story and Discourse: Narrative Structure in Fiction and Film*. Ithaca, NY and London: Cornell University Press.

Chatman, Seymour. 1990. *Coming to Terms: The Rhetoric of Narrative in Fiction and Film*. Ithaca, NY and London: Cornell University Press.

Chee, Alexander. 2015. "In Defense of the Present Tense: It Is Everywhere, Including Our Writing." *Literary Hub*, August 5. Accessed August 31, 2020. https://lithub.com/in-defense-of-the-present-tense/.

Chihaia, Matei, Sandra Heinen, Matías Martínez, Katharina Rennhak, Michael Scheffel, and Roy Sommer, eds. 2020. "Narrative Theory and the Anthropocene." Special issue, *DIEGESIS: Interdisciplinary Journal for Narrative Research* 9.2. Accessed December 15, 2020. https://www.diegesis.uni-wuppertal.de/index.php/diegesis/issue/view/21.

Childs, Peter. 2005. *Contemporary Novelists: British Fiction since 1970*. Basingstoke and New York, NY: Palgrave Macmillan.

Childs, Peter, and James Green. 2013. *Aesthetics and Ethics in Twenty-First Century British Novels*. London and New York, NY: Bloomsbury.

Ciobanu, Calina. 2014. "Rewriting the Human at the End of the Anthropocene in Margaret Atwood's *MaddAddam* Trilogy." *The Minnesota Review: A Journal of Creative and Critical Writing* 83: 153–162.

Clanchy, Kate. 2016. "Book of the Week: *Nutshell* by Ian McEwan Review – An Elegiac Masterpiece." *The Guardian*. August 27. Accessed August 31, 2020.
https://www.theguardian.com/books/2016/aug/27/nutshell-by-ian-mcewan-review.

Clement, Marja. 1991. "Present — Preterite: Tense and Narrative Point of View." *Linguistics in the Netherlands* 8.1: 11–20.

Cobbett, William. 1994 [1824–1827]. *A History of the Protestant Reformation*. Edited by Hugh Arnold. Kent: Fisher Press.

Coetzee, J. M. 1981. "Time, Tense and Aspect in Kafka's 'The Burrow.'" *MLN: Modern Language Notes* 96.3: 556–579.

Cohn, Dorrit. 1968. "Kafka's Eternal Present: Narrative Tense in 'Ein Landarzt' and Other First-Person Stories." *PMLA* 83.1: 144–150.

Cohn, Dorrit. 1978. *Transparent Minds: Narrative Modes for Presenting Consciousness in Fiction*. Princeton, NJ: Princeton University Press.

Cohn, Dorrit. 1990. "Signposts of Fictionality: A Narratological Perspective." *Poetics Today* 11.4: 775–804.

Cohn, Dorrit. 1993. "'I doze and wake': The Deviance of Simultaneous Narration." In *Tales and "their telling difference": Zur Theorie und Geschichte der Narrativik*, edited by Herbert Foltinek, Wolfgang Riehle, and Waldemar Zacharasiewicz, 9–23. Heidelberg: Universitätsverlag Winter.

Cohn, Dorrit. 1999. *The Distinction of Fiction*. Baltimore, MD and London: The Johns Hopkins University Press.

Comrie, Bernard. 1985. *Tense*. Cambridge et al.: Cambridge University Press.

Culler, Jonathan. 1975. *Structuralist Poetics: Structuralism, Linguistics and the Study of Literature*. London: Routledge & Kegan Paul.

Culler, Jonathan. 2014a. "The Language of Lyric." *Thinking Verse* IV.i: 160–176.

Culler, Jonathan. 2014b. "The Strange Present Tense of the English Lyric." In: *Anglistentag 2013 Konstanz: Proceedings*, edited by Silvia Mergenthal and Reingard M. Nischik, 292–238. Trier: Wissenschaftlicher Verlag Trier.

Culler, Jonathan. 2015. *Theory of the Lyric*. Cambridge, MS and London: Harvard University Press.

Culler, Jonathan. 2018. "Naturalization in 'Natural' Narratology." *Partial Answers: Journal of Literature and the History of Ideas* 16.2: 243–249.

Cummins, Sarah. 1998. "Time Will Tell: Tense in Narration." *TTR: traduction, terminologie, rédaction* 11.1: 113–136.

Currie, Gregory. 1992. "McTaggart at the Movies." *Philosophy* 67.261: 343–355.

Currie, Gregory. 1995. *Image and Mind: Film, Philosophy and Cognitive Science*. Cambridge: Cambridge University Press.

Currie, Gregory. 1998. "Tense and Egocentricity in Fiction." In *Questions of Time and Tenses*, edited by Robin Le Poidevin, 265–283. Oxford: Clarendon Press.

Currie, Gregory. 1999. "Can There Be a Literary Philosophy of Time?" In *The Arguments of Time*, edited by Jeremy Butterfield, 43–63. Oxford et al.: Oxford University Press.

Currie, Mark. 2007. *About Time: Narrative, Fiction and the Philosophy of Time*. Edinburgh: Edinburgh University Press.

Currie, Mark. 2009. "The Expansion of Tense." *Narrative* 17.3: 353–367.

Currie, Mark. 2013. *The Unexpected: Narrative Temporality and the Philosophy of Surprise*. Edinburgh: Edinburgh University Press.

Damsteegt, Theo. 2004. *The Present Tense in Modern Hindi Fiction*. Groningen: Egbert Forsten.

Damsteegt, Theo. 2005. "The Present Tense and Internal Focalization of Awareness." *Poetics Today* 26.1: 39–78.

Davies, Ben. 2016. *Sex, Time, and Space in Contemporary Fiction: Exceptional Intercourse*. Basingstoke and New York, NY: Palgrave Macmillan.

Davies, Ben. 2019. "Prequel Ontology and Temporality: The Thresholds of John Updike's *Gertrude and Claudius*." In *Prequels, Coquels and Sequels in Contemporary Anglophone Fiction*, edited by Armelle Parey, 27–39. New York, NY and London: Routledge.

Dawson, Paul. 2009. "The Return of Omniscience in Contemporary Fiction." *Narrative* 17.2: 143–161.

Dawson, Paul. 2013. *The Return of the Omniscient Narrator: Authorship and Authority in Twenty-First Century Fiction*. Columbus, OH: The Ohio State University Press.

Dawson, Paul. 2015. "Ten Theses Against Fictionality." *Narrative* 23.1: 74–100.

De Groot, Jerome. 2016. *Remaking History: The Past in Contemporary Historical Fictions*. London and New York, NY: Routledge.

Del Valle Alcalá, Roberto. 2016. *British Working-Class Fiction: Narratives of Refusal and the Struggle against Work*. London et al.: Bloomsbury.

DelConte, Matt. 2007. "A Further Study of Present Tense Narration: The Absentee Narratee and Four-Wall Present Tense in Coetzee's *Waiting for the Barbarians* and *Disgrace*." *JNT: Journal of Narrative Theory* 37.3: 427–446.

DelConte, Matt. 2013/2014. "The Influence of Narrative Tense in Second Person Narration: A Response to Joshua Parker." *Connotations* 23.1: 55–62.

Demerjian, Louisa MacKay. 2018. "'And imperfect beings cannot make perfect decisions': Future Humans in *The Time Machine* and *Oryx and Crake*." In *Future Humans in Fiction and Film*, edited by Louisa MacKay Demerjian and Karen F. Stein, 16–31. Newcastle upon Tyne: Cambridge Scholars Publishing.

Després, Elaine. 2015. "Describing (Post)Human Species: Between Cognition and Estrangement." In *The Ethics and Poetics of Alterity: New Perspectives on Genre Literature*, edited by Maylis Rospide and Sandrine Sorlin, 142–157. Newcastle upon Tyne: Cambridge Scholars Publishing.

D'hoker, Elke. 2013. "'And the Transformation Begins': Present-Tense Narration in Claire Keegan's Daughter Stories." *Contemporary Women's Writing* 7.2: 190–204.

D'hoker, Elke. 2019. "The Relevance of Narrative Theory for the Study of Short Fiction: The Case of First-Person Present-Tense Narration." In *Relevance and Narrative Research*, edited by Matei Chihaia and Katharina Rennhak, 175–188. Lanham, MD et al.: Lexington Books.

Dobrogoszcz, Tomasz. 2018. *Family and Relationships in Ian McEwan's Fiction*. Lanham, MD et al.: Lexington Books.

Doležel, Lubomír. 1998. *Heterocosmica: Fiction and Possible Worlds*. Baltimore, MD and London: The John Hopkins University Press.

Dore, Margherita. 2017. "Narrative Strategies and Mind Style in Emma Donoghue's *Room*." *Fictions: Studi sulla narratività* XVI: 61–73.

Easterlin, Nancy. 2012. *A Biocultural Approach to Literary Theory and Interpretation*. Baltimore, MD: The Johns Hopkins University Press.

Eco, Umberto. 1979. *The Role of the Reader: Explorations in the Semiotics of Texts*. London et al.: Hutchinson.

Elton, G. R. 1953. *The Tudor Revolution in Government: A Study of Administrative Changes in the Reign of Henry VIII*. Cambridge: Cambridge University Press.

Emmott, Catherine. 1997. *Narrative Comprehension: A Discourse Perspective*. Oxford and New York, NY: Oxford University Press.

Enderwitz, Anne. 2019. "*Hamlet*, the 'Two Cultures' and the Public Author: Ian McEwan's *Nutshell*." *Germanisch-Romanische Monatsschrift* 69.4: 441–456.

Epstein, Mikhail. 2003. "Russo-Soviet Topoi." In *The Landscape of Stalinism: The Art and Ideology of Soviet Space*, edited by Evgeny Dobrenko and Eric Naiman, 277–306. Seattle, WA and London: University of Washington Press.

Everett, Michael. 2015. *The Rise of Thomas Cromwell: Power and Politics in the Reign of Henry VIII*. New Haven, CT and London: Yale University Press.

Farner, Geir. 2014. *Literary Fiction: The Ways We Read Narrative Literature*. New York, NY et al.: Bloomsbury.

Fleischman, Suzanne. 1986. "Evaluation in Narrative: The Present Tense in Medieval 'Performed Stories.'" *Yale French Studies* 70: 199–251.

Fleischman, Suzanne. 1990. *Tense and Narrativity: From Medieval Performance to Modern Fiction*. Austin, TX: University of Texas Press.

Fleischman, Suzanne. 1991a. "Toward a Theory of Tense-Aspect in Narrative Discourse." In *The Function of Tense in Texts*, edited by Jadranka Gvozdanović and Theo A. J. Janssen, 75–97. Amsterdam et al.: Royal Netherlands Academy of Arts and Sciences.

Fleischman, Suzanne. 1991b. "Verb Tense and Point of View in Narrative." In *Discourse-Pragmatics and the Verb: The Evidence from Romance*, edited by Suzanne Fleischman and Linda Waugh, 26–54. London and New York, NY: Routledge.

Fleischman, Suzanne. 1998. "Tense in Narrative." In *Encyclopedia of the Novel – Volume 2: M–Z*, edited by Paul Schellinger, 1320–1321. Chicago, IL / London: Fitzroy Dearborn Publishers.

Fludernik, Monika. 1991. "The Historical Present Tense Yet Again: Tense Switching and Narrative Dynamics in Oral and Quasi-Oral Storytelling." *Text* 11.3: 365–397.

Fludernik, Monika. 1992a. "Narrative Schemata and Temporal Anchoring." *Journal of Literary Semantics* 21.2: 118–153.

Fludernik, Monika. 1992b. "The Historical Present Tense in English Literature: An Oral Pattern and its Literary Adaptation." *Language and Literature* 17: 77–107.

Fludernik, Monika. 1993a. "Second Person Fiction: Narrative *You* as Addressee and/or Protagonist." *AAA – Arbeiten aus Anglistik und Amerikanistik* 18.2: 218–247.

Fludernik, Monika. 1993b. *The Fictions of Language and the Languages of Fiction: The Linguistic Representation of Speech and Consciousness*. London and New York, NY: Routledge.

Fludernik, Monika. 1994. "Second-Person Narrative as a Test Case for Narratology: The Limits of Realism." *Style* 28.3: 445–479.

Fludernik, Monika. 1995. "Pronouns of Address and 'Odd' Third Person Forms: The Mechanics of Involvement in Fiction." In *New Essays in Deixis: Discourse, Narrative, Literature*, edited by Keith Green, 99–129. Amsterdam and Atlanta, GA: Rodopi.

Fludernik, Monika. 1996. *Towards a 'Natural' Narratology*. London and New York, NY: Routledge.

Fludernik, Monika. 2002. "Tempus und Zeitbewusstsein: Erzähltheoretische Überlegungen zur englischen Literatur." In *Zeit und Roman: Zeiterfahrung im historischen Wandel und ästhetischer Paradigmenwechsel vom sechzehnten Jahrhundert bis zur Postmoderne*, edited by Martin Middeke, 21–32. Würzburg: Königshausen & Neumann.

Fludernik, Monika. 2003a. "Chronology, Time, Tense and Experientiality in Narrative." *Language and Literature* 12.2: 117–134.

Fludernik, Monika. 2003b. "Metanarrative and Metafictional Commentary: From Metadiscursivity to Metanarration and Metafiction." *Poetica – Zeitschrift für Sprach- und Literaturwissenschaft* 35: 1–39.

Fludernik, Monika. 2003c. "Natural Narratology and Cognitive Parameters." In *Narrative Theory and the Cognitive Sciences*, edited by David Herman, 243–267. Stanford, CA: CSLI Publications.

Fludernik, Monika. 2003d. "Scene Shift, Metalepsis, and the Metaleptic Mode." *Style* 37.4: 382–400.

Fludernik, Monika. 2008 [2005]a. "Tense and Narrative." In *The Routledge Encyclopedia of Narrative Theory*, edited by David Herman, Manfred Jahn, and Marie-Laure Ryan, 2nd ed., 592–594. London and New York, NY: Routledge.

Fludernik, Monika. 2008 [2005]b. "Time in Narrative." In *The Routledge Encyclopedia of Narrative Theory*, edited by David Herman, Manfred Jahn, and Marie-Laure Ryan, 2nd ed., 608–612. London and New York, NY: Routledge.

Fludernik, Monika. 2009. *An Introduction to Narratology*. Translated by Patricia Häusler-Greenfield. London and New York, NY: Routledge.
Fludernik, Monika. 2010a. "Naturalizing the Unnatural: A View from Blending Theory." *Journal of Literary Semantics* 39: 1–27.
Fludernik, Monika. 2010b. "Towards a 'Natural' Narratology: Frames and Pedagogy – A Response to Nilli Diengott." *JLS: Journal of Literary Semantics* 39: 203–211.
Fludernik, Monika. 2011. "The Category of 'Person' in Fiction: You and We Narrative-Multiplicity and Indeterminacy of Reference." In *Current Trends in Narratology*, edited by Greta Olson, 101–135. Berlin and Boston, MA: De Gruyter.
Fludernik, Monika. 2012. "Narratology and Literary Linguistics." In *The Oxford Handbook of Tense and Aspect*, edited by Robert I. Binnick, 75–101. Oxford et al.: Oxford University Press.
Fludernik, Monika. 2014a. "Conversational Narration – Oral Narration." In *Handbook of Narratology: Volume 1*, edited by Peter Hühn, Jan Christoph Meister, John Pier, and Wolf Schmid, 2nd ed., 93–104. Berlin and Boston, MA: De Gruyter.
Fludernik, Monika. 2014b. "Description and Perspective: The Representation of Interiors." *Style* 48.4: 461–478.
Fludernik, Monika. 2018. "Response Essay: Towards a 'Natural' Narratology Twenty Years After." *Partial Answers: Journal of Literature and the History of Ideas* 16.2: 329–347.
Foucault, Michel. 2002 [1994]. *Power: Essential Works 1954–84*. Translated by Robert Hurley et al. Edited by James D. Faubion. London et al.: Penguin Books.
Fowler, Roger. 1977. *Linguistics and the Novel*. London: Methuen and Co. Ltd.
Frank, Michael C. 2015. "Chronotopoi." In *Handbuch Literatur & Raum*, edited by Jörg Dünne and Andreas Mahler, 160–169. Berlin and Boston, MA: De Gruyter.
Freeman, Mark. 2010. "Afterword: 'Even amidst' — Rethinking Narrative Coherence." In *Beyond Narrative Coherence*, edited by Matti Hyvärinen, Lars-Christer Hydén, Marja Saarenheimo, and Maria Tamboukou, 167–186. Amsterdam and Philadelphia, PA: John Benjamins.
Frey, John R. 1946. "The Historical Present in Narrative Literature, Particularly in Modern German Fiction." *The Journal of English and Germanic Philology* 45.1: 43–67.
Fuchs, Anna. 1991. "Deixis, Relevance, and Tense/Aspect." In *The Function of Tense in Texts*, edited by Jadranka Gvozdanović and Theo A. J. Janssen, 99–123. Amsterdam et al.: Royal Netherlands Academy of Arts and Sciences.
Funk, Wolfgang. 2018. "Becoming Ghost: Spectral Realism in Hilary Mantel's Fiction." In *Hilary Mantel: Contemporary Critical Perspectives*, edited by Eileen Pollard and Ginette Carpenter, 87–100. London: Bloomsbury Academic.
Galbraith, Mary. 1995. "Deictic Shift Theory and the Poetics of Involvement in Narrative." In *Deixis in Narrative: A Cognitive Science Perspective*, edited by Judith F. Duchan, Gail A. Bruder, and Lynne E. Hewitt, 19–59. Hillsdale, NJ and Hove: Lawrence Erlbaum Associates.
Gallotti, Mattia, and Raphael Lyne. 2019. "The Individual 'We' Narrator." *The British Journal of Aesthetics* 59.2: 179–195.
García Zarranz, Libe. 2017. *TransCanadian Feminist Fictions: New Cross-Border Ethics*. Montreal, QC and Kingston, ON: McGill-Queen's University Press.
Garner, Barbara P., and Doris Bergen. 2006. "Play Development from Birth to Age Four." In *Play from Birth to Twelve: Contexts, Perspectives, and Meanings*, edited by Doris Pronin Fromberg and Doris Bergen, 3–11. New York, NY and London: Routledge.

Gass, William H. 1987. "A Failing Grade for the Present Tense." *The New York Times*, October 11, 1987. Accessed August 31. https://archive.nytimes.com/www.nytimes.com/books/98/11/01/specials/gass-present.html.

Gebauer, Carolin. 2017. "A Case for the Narrative Present: Irmtraud Huber Explores the Literary Potential of Contemporary Present-Tense Narration [Review of: Irmtraud Huber: *Present-Tense Narration in Contemporary Fiction: A Narratological Overview*. London 2016]." *DIEGESIS: Interdisciplinary E-Journal for Narrative Research* 6.1: 99–104. Accessed August 31, 2020. https://nbn-resolving.de/urn:nbn:de:hbz:468-20170606-143516-3.

Gebauer, Carolin. 2018. "When Does a Narrator Speak? The Nexus between 'Voice' and Tense Usage in Narrative Fiction." In *(Un-)Gleichzeitigkeiten*, edited by Carmen Ulrich, 143–166. Munich: iudicium Verlag.

Gebauer, Carolin. 2020. "Dreading the Future: The Ethical Implications of Contemporary Speculative Fiction." *DIEGESIS: Interdisciplinary E-Journal for Narrative Research* 9.1: 20–38. Accessed August 31, 2020. https://nbn-resolving.de/urn:nbn:de:hbz:468-20200618-090700-4.

Gebauer, Carolin. Forthcoming. "Imagining Posthuman Environments after the Anthropocene: The Function of Space in Post-Apocalyptic Climate Change Fiction." In *Narrating Nonhuman Spaces: Form, Story and Experience Beyond Anthropocentrism*, edited by Marco Caracciolo, Marlene Marcussen, and David Rodriguez. London and New York, NY: Routledge.

Geçikli, Kubilay. 2013. "Tudor People Fashioning Themselves: Hypocrisy as Opposed to Authenticity in Hilary Mantel's *Wolf Hall*." *Littera* 32: 93–105.

Geçikli, Kubilay. 2015. "Orientalisation of the Occident: Nadeem Aslam's *Maps for Lost Lovers*." *Interactions: Ege Journal of British and American Studies* 24.1–2: 79–90.

Genette, Gérard. 1969. *Figures II*. Paris: Éditions du Seuil.

Genette, Gérard. 1980 [1972]. *Narrative Discourse: An Essay in Method*. Translated by Jane E. Lewin. Ithaca, NY: Cornell University Press.

Genette, Gérard. 1988 [1983]. *Narrative Discourse Revisited*. Translated by Jane E. Lewin. Ithaca, NY: Cornell University Press.

Genette, Gérard. 1997 [1982]. *Palimpsests: Literature in the Second Degree*. Translated by Channa Newman and Claude Doubinsky. Lincoln, NE and London: University of Nebraska Press.

Genette, Gérard. 2007 [1972/1983]. *Discours du récit: essai de méthode*. Paris: Seuil.

Georgakopoulou, Alexandra. 2006. *Small Stories, Interaction and Identities*. Amsterdam and Philadelphia, PA: John Benjamins.

Georgakopoulou, Alexandra. 2007. "Thinking Big with Small Stories in Narrative and Identity Analysis." In *Narrative – State of the Art*, edited by Michael Bamberg, 145–154. Amsterdam and Philadelphia, PA: John Benjamins.

Gerrig, Richard J. 1993. *Experiencing Narrative Worlds: On the Psychological Activities of Reading*. New Haven, CT and London: Westview Press.

Gius, Evelyn. 2015. *Erzählen über Konflikte: Ein Beitrag zur digitalen Narratologie*. Berlin and Boston, MA: De Gruyter.

Glover, David. 2003. "The Thriller." In *The Cambridge Companion to Crime Fiction*, edited by Martin Priestman, 135–153. Cambridge: Cambridge University Press.

Goetsch, Paul. 1985. "Fingierte Mündlichkeit in der Erzählkunst entwickelter Schriftkulturen." *Poetica* 17: 202–218.

Goetsch, Paul. 2008 [2005]. "Orality." In *Routledge Encyclopedia of Narrative Theory*, edited by David Herman, Manfred Jahn, and Marie-Laure Ryan, 413–414. London and New York, NY: Routledge.

Goodman, Nelson. 1978. *Ways of Worldmaking*. Indianapolis, IN: Hackett Publishing Company.

Grace, Daphne. 2012. "A Beast or a God? Margaret Atwood's Vision of Posthuman Consciousness." In *Consciousness, Theatre, Literature and the Arts 2011*, edited by Daniel Meyer-Dinkgräfe, 40–49. Newcastle upon Tyne: Cambridge Scholars Publishing.

Green, Georgia M. 1996 [1989]. *Pragmatics and Natural Language Understanding*. Mahwah, NJ: Lawrence Erlbaum Associates.

Green, Keith. 1995. "Deixis: A Revaluation of Concepts and Categories." In *New Essays in Deixis: Discourse, Narrative, Literature*, edited by Keith Green, 11–25. Amsterdam and Atlanta, GA: Rodopi.

Green, Melanie C. 2010. "Transportation into Narrative Worlds: The Role of Prior Knowledge and Perceived Realism." *Discourse Processes* 38.2: 247–266.

Green, Melanie C., and Timothy C. Brock. 2000. "The Role of Transportation in the Persuasiveness of Public Narratives." *Journal of Personality and Social Psychology* 79.5: 701–721.

Green, Melanie C., and Timothy C. Brock. 2002. "In the Mind's Eye: Transportation-Imagery Model of Narrative Persuasion." In *Narrative Impact: Social and Cognitive Foundations*, edited by Melanie C. Green, Jeffrey J. Strange, and Timothy C. Brock, 315–341. Mahwah, NJ and London: Lawrence Erlbaum Associates Publishers.

Greenblatt, Stephen. 2009. "How It Must Have Been." *The New York Review of Books* LVI.17, November 5–18: 22–25.

Grosz, Barbara J., and Candace L. Sidner. 1986. "Attention, Intentions, and the Structure of Discourse." *Computational Linguistics* 12.3: 175–204.

Gülich, Elisabeth. 2020. *Mündliches Erzählen: Verfahren narrative Rekonstruktion im Gespräch*. Edited by Stefan Pfänder, Carl E. Scheidt, and Elke Schumann. Berlin and Boston, MA: De Gruyter.

Gumbrecht, Hans Ulrich. 2014 [2010]. *Our Broad Present: Time and Contemporary Culture*. New York, NY: Columbia University Press.

Gumbrecht, Hans Ulrich. 2019 [2012]. *Präsenz*. 3rd ed. Berlin: Suhrkamp.

Gymnich, Marion. 2002. "Linguistics and Narratology: The Relevance of Linguistic Criteria to Postcolonial Narratology." In *Literature and Linguistics: Approaches, Models, and Applications*, edited by Marion Gymnich, Ansgar Nünning, and Vera Nünning, 61–76. Trier: Wissenschaftlicher Verlag Trier.

Gymnich, Marion. 2007. *Metasprachliche Reflexionen und sprachliche Gestaltungsmittel im englischsprachigen postkolonialen und interkulturellen Roman*. Trier: Wissenschaftlicher Verlag Trier.

Gymnich, Marion. 2018. "Fictions of (Meta-)History: Revisioning and Rewriting History in Hilary Mantel's *Wolf Hall* (2009) and *Bring Up the Bodies* (2012)." In *The British Novel in the Twenty-First Century: Cultural Concerns – Literary Developments – Model Interpretations*, edited by Vera Nünning and Ansgar Nünning, 71–86. Trier: Wissenschaftlicher Verlag Trier.

Hakemulder, Frank, Moniek M. Kuijpers, Ed S. Tan, Katalin Bálint, and Miruna M. Doicaru, eds. 2017. *Narrative Absorption*. Amsterdam and Philadelphia, PA: John Benjamins.

Hallet, Wolfgang. 2009. "The Multimodal Novel: The Integration of Modes and Media in Novelistic Narration." In *Narratology in the Age of Cross-Disciplinary Narrative Research*, edited by Sandra Heinen and Roy Sommer, 129–153. Berlin and New York, NY: De Gruyter.

Hallet, Wolfgang. 2014. "The Rise of the Multimodal Novel: Generic Change and Its Narratological Implications." In *Storyworlds Across Media: Toward a Media-Conscious Narratology*, edited by Marie-Laure Ryan and Jan-Noël Thon, 151–172. Lincoln, NE and London: University of Nebraska Press.

Hallet, Wolfgang. 2015. "Non-Verbal Semiotic Modes and Media in the Multimodal Novel." In *Handbook of Intermediality: Literature, Image, Sound, Music*, edited by Gabriele Rippl, 637–651. Berlin and Boston, MA: De Gruyter.

Hallet, Wolfgang. 2018. "Reading Multimodal Fiction: A Methodological Approach." *Anglistik: International Journal of English Studies* 29.1: 25–40.

Hamburger, Käte. 1968 [1957]. *Die Logik der Dichtung*. 2nd ed. Stuttgart: Ernst Klett.

Hamburger, Käte. 1973 [1968]. *The Logic of Literature*. 2nd ed. Translated by Marilynn J. Rose. Bloomington, IN and London: Indiana University Press.

Hames, Scott. 2013. "On Vernacular Scottishness and Its Limits: Devolution and the Spectacle of 'Voice.'" *SSL: Studies in Scottish Literature* 39: 203–224.

Hamon, Philippe. 1982. "What Is a Description?" In *French Literary Theory Today: A Reader*, edited by Tzvetan Todorov and translated by R. Carter, 147–178. Cambridge et al.: Cambridge University Press.

Hamon, Philippe. 1993 [1981]. *Du descriptive*. Paris: Hachette Supérieur.

Hanebeck, Julian. 2017. *Understanding Metalepsis: The Hermeneutics of Narrative Transgression*. Berlin and Boston, MA: De Gruyter.

Hansen, Per Krogh. 2008. "First Person, Present Tense: Authorial Presence and Unreliable Narration in Simultaneous Narration." In *Narrative Unreliability in the Twentieth-Century First-Person Novel*, edited by Elke D'hoker and Gunther Martens, 317–338. Berlin and New York, NY: De Gruyter.

Hansen, Per Krogh, Stefan Iversen, Henrik Skov Nielsen, and Rolf Reitan, eds. 2011. *Strange Voices in Narrative Fiction*. Berlin and Boston, MA: De Gruyter.

Haraway, Donna. 2003. *The Companion Species Manifesto: Dogs, People, and Significant Otherness*. Chicago, IL: Prickly Paradigm Press.

Harris, Paul L. 2000. *The Work of the Imagination*. Oxford and Malden, MA: Blackwell Publishers.

Harrison, James. 1995. "Point of View and Tense in the Novels of J. M. Coetzee." *The Journal of Commonwealth Literature* 30.1: 79–85.

Harvey, Alynn Day. 1986. "Evidence of a Tense Shift in Personal Experience Narratives." *Empirical Studies of the Arts* 4.2: 151–162.

Harvey, John. 2006. "Fiction in the Present Tense." *Textual Practice* 20.1: 71–98.

Heinze, Rüdiger. 2013. "Strange Perspectives = Strange (Narrative?) Identities?" In *Rethinking Narrative Identity: Persona and Perspective*, edited by Claudia Holler and Martin Klepper, 117–127. Amsterdam and Philadelphia, PA: John Benjamins Publishing Company.

Heise, Ursula K. 1997. *Chronoschisms: Time, Narrative, and Postmodernism*. Cambridge et al.: Cambridge University Press.

Hengen, Shannon. 2010. "Moral/Environmental Debt in *Payback* and *Oryx and Crake*." In *Margaret Atwood: "The Robber Bride," "The Blind Assassin," "Oryx and Crake,"* edited by J. Brooks Bouson, 129–140. London and New York, NY: Continuum.

Hensher, Philip. 2010. "Opinion: Philip Hensher: The Booker Judges Should Take a Stand Against the Modish Present Tense." *The Telegraph*, September 9. Accessed August 31, 2020. https://www.telegraph.co.uk/culture/books/7991553/Opinion-Philip-Hensher.html.

Herman, David. 1994. "Textual *You* and Double Deixis in Edna O'Brien's *A Pagan Place.*" *Style* 28.3: 378–410.
Herman, David. 1999. "Introduction: Narratologies." In *Narratologies: New Perspectives on Narrative Analysis*, edited by David Herman, 1–30. Columbus, OH: The Ohio State University Press.
Herman, David. 2002. *Story Logic: Problems and Possibilities of Narrative.* Lincoln, NE and London: University of Nebraska Press.
Herman, David. 2007. "Storytelling and the Sciences of Mind: Cognitive Narratology, Discursive Psychology, and Narratives in Face-to-Face Interaction." *Narrative* 15.3: 306–334.
Herman, David. 2008. "Description, Narrative, and Explanation: Text-Type Categories and the Cognitive Foundations of Discourse Competence." *Poetics Today* 29.3: 437–472.
Herman, David. 2009a. *Basic Elements of Narrative.* Malden, MA and Oxford: Wiley-Blackwell.
Herman, David. 2009b. "Narrative Ways of Worldmaking." In *Narratology in the Age of Cross-Disciplinary Narrative Research*, edited by Sandra Heinen and Roy Sommer, 71–87. Berlin and New York, NY: De Gruyter.
Herman, David, ed. 2011. *The Emergence of Mind: Representations of Consciousness in Narrative Discourse in English.* Lincoln, NE and London: University of Nebraska Press.
Herman, David. 2012. "Character." In *Narrative Theory: Core Concepts and Critical Debates*, by David Herman, James Phelan, Peter J. Rabinowitz, Brian Richardson, and Robyn Warhol, 125–131. Columbus, OH: The Ohio State University Press.
Herman, Luc, and Bart Vervaeck. 2005 [2001]. *Handbook of Narrative Analysis.* Translated by Luc Herman and Bart Vervaeck. Lincoln, NE: University of Nebraska Press.
Herman, Luc, and Bart Vervaeck. 2009. "Narrative Interest and Cultural Negotiation." *Narrative* 17.1: 111–129.
Hoeken, Hans, and Mario van Vliet. 2000. "Suspense, Curiosity, and Surprise: How Discourse Structure Influences the Affective and Cognitive Processing of a Story." *Poetics* 26: 277–286.
Hollm, Jan. 2015. "Post-Apocalyptic Dystopia: Cormac McCarthy, *The Road* (2006)." In *Dystopia, Science Fiction, Post-Apocalypse: Classics – New Tendencies – Model Interpretations*, edited by Eckart Voigts-Virschow and Alessandra Boller, 379–393. Trier: Wissenschaftlicher Verlag Trier.
Horsley, Lee. 2010. "From Sherlock Holmes to the Present." In *A Companion to Crime Fiction*, edited by Charles J. Rzepka and Lee Horsley, 28–42. Malden, MA: Wiley-Blackwell.
Horstkotte, Silke, and Leonhard Herrmann, eds. 2013. *Poetiken der Gegenwart: Deutschsprachige Romane nach 2000.* Berlin and Boston, MA: De Gruyter.
Howells, Coral Ann. 2006. "Margaret Atwood's Dystopian Visions: *The Handmaid's Tale* and *Oryx and Crake.*" In *The Cambridge Companion to Margaret Atwood*, edited by Coral Ann Howells, 161–175. Cambridge et al.: Cambridge University Press.
Huber, Irmtraud. 2016. *Present-Tense Narration in Contemporary Fiction: A Narratological Overview.* London: Palgrave Macmillan.
Hühn, Peter. 2014. "Event and Eventfulness." In *Handbook of Narratology: Volume 1*, edited by Peter Hühn, Jan Christoph Meister, John Pier, and Wolf Schmid, 2nd ed., 159–178. Berlin and Boston, MA: De Gruyter.
Hurm, Gerd. 2003. *Rewriting the Vernacular Mark Twain: The Aesthetics and Politics of Orality in Samuel Clemens's Fictions.* Trier: Wissenschaftlicher Verlag Trier.
Hutchinson, Thomas. 2007. *Thomas Cromwell: The Rise and Fall of Henry VIII's Most Notorious Minister.* London: Weidenfeld & Nicolson.

Hydén, Lars-Christer, and Jens Brockmeier, eds. 2008. *Health, Illness and Culture: Broken Narratives*. New York, NY and London: Routledge.

Hyvärinen, Matti, Lars-Christer Hydén, Marja Saarenheimo, and Maria Tamboukou, eds. 2010a. *Beyond Narrative Coherence*. Amsterdam and Philadelphia, PA: John Benjamins.

Hyvärinen, Matti, Lars-Christer Hydén, Marja Saarenheimo, and Maria Tamboukou. 2010b. "Beyond Narrative Coherence: An Introduction." In *Beyond Narrative Coherence*, edited by Matti Hyvärinen, Lars-Christer Hydén, Marja Saarenheimo, and Maria Tamboukou, 1–15. Amsterdam and Philadelphia, PA: John Benjamins.

Iliopoulou, Evgenia. 2019. *Because of You: Understanding Second-Person Storytelling*. Bielefeld: transcript.

Ilott, Sarah. 2015. *New Postcolonial British Genres: Shifting the Boundaries*. Basingstoke and New York, NY: Palgrave Macmillan.

Iversen, Stefan. 2013. "Broken or Unnatural? On the Distiction of Fiction in Non-Conventional First Person Narration." In *The Travelling Concepts of Narrative*, edited by Matti Hyvärinen, Mari Hatavara, and Lars-Christer Hydén, 141–162. Amsterdam and Philadelphia, PA: John Benjamins.

Ives, Sumner. 1971 [1950]. "A Theory of Literary Dialect." In *A Various Language: Perspectives on American Dialects*, edited by Juanita V. Williamson and Virginia M. Burke, 145–177. New York, NY et al.: Holt, Rinehart and Winston Inc.

Jacke, Janina. 2018. "Unreliability and Narrator Types: On the Application Area of 'Unreliable Narration.'" *Journal of Literary Theory* 12.1: 3–28.

Jacke, Janina. 2020. *Systematik unzuverlässigen Erzählens: Analytische Aufarbeitung und Explikation einer problematischen Kategorie*. Berlin and Boston, MA: De Gruyter.

Jackendoff, Ray. 1987. *Consciousness and the Computational Mind*. Cambridge, MA and London: The Massachusetts Institute of Technology Press.

Jacobs, Andreas, and Andreas H. Jucker. 1995. "The Historical Perspective in Pragmatics." In *Historical Pragmatics: Pragmatic Developments in the History of English*, edited by Andreas H. Jucker, 3–33. Amsterdam and Philadelphia, PA: John Benjamins Publishing Company.

Jahn, Manfred. 1999. "'Speak, friend, and enter': Garden Paths, Artificial Intelligence, and Cognitive Narratology." In *Narratologies: New Perspectives on Narrative Analysis*, edited by David Herman, 167–194. Columbus, OH: The Ohio State University Press.

Jahn, Manfred. 2017. *Narratology: A Guide to the Theory of Narrative*. English Department, University of Cologne, May 2017. Accessed August 31, 2020. https://www.uni-koeln.de/~ame02/pppn.htm.

James, David. 2019. "Narrative Artifice." In *The Cambridge Companion to Ian McEwan*, edited by Dominic Head, 181–196. Cambridge: Cambridge University Press.

James, Erin. 2015. *The Storyworld Accord: Econarratology and Postcolonial Narratives*. Lincoln, NE and London: University of Nebraska Press.

James, Erin, and Eric Morel, eds. 2020. *Environment and Narrative: New Directions in Econarratology*. Columbus, OH: The Ohio State University Press.

Janssen, Theo A. J. M. 1996. "Deictic and Anaphoric Referencing of Tense." In *Anaphores temporelles et (in-)coherence*, edited by Walter De Mulder, Liliane Tasmowski-De Ryck, and Carl Vetters, 79–107. Amsterdam and Atlanta, GA: Rodopi.

Jauss, David. 2011. *On Writing Fiction: Rethinking Conventional Wisdom About the Craft*. Cincinnati, OH: Writer's Digest Books.

Jeffers, Jennifer M. 2005. "Rhizome National Identity: 'Scatlin's Psychic Defense' in *Trainspotting*." *JNT: Journal of Narrative Theory* 35.1: 88–111.
Jennings, Hope. 2019. "Anthropocene Feminism, Companion Species, and the *MaddAddam* Trilogy." *Contemporary Women's Writing* 13.1: 16–33.
Johnson, Carla K. 2016. "Review: Ian McEwan's 'Nutshell' is 'Hamlet' in Miniature." *The Washington Times*, September 12. Accessed August 31, 2020. https://www.washingtontimes.com/news/2016/sep/12/review-ian-mcewans-nutshell-is-hamlet-in-miniature/.
Johnston, Andrew James. 2017. "Hilary Mantel, *The Thomas Cromwell Trilogy* (2009–)." In *Handbook of the English Novel of the Twentieth and Twenty-First Centuries*, edited by Christoph Reinfandt, 536–554. Berlin and Boston, MA: De Gruyter.
Johnstone, Barbara. 1987. "'He says. . . so I said': Verb Tense Alternation and Narrative Depictions of Authority in American English." *Linguistics* 25: 33–52.
Jokić, Aleksandar, and Quentin Smith, eds. 2003. *Time, Tense, and Reference*. London and Cambridge, MA: The Massachusetts Institute of Technology Press.
Kanwal, Aroosa. 2015. *Rethinking Identities in Contemporary Pakistani Fiction: Beyond 9/11*. Basingstoke and New York, NY: Palgrave Macmillan.
Katzner, Kenneth. 1995 [1977]. *The Languages of the World*. London and New York, NY: Routledge.
Keen, Suzanne. 2006. "A Theory of Narrative Empathy." *Narrative* 14.3: 207–236.
Keen, Suzanne. 2007. *Empathy and the Novel*. Oxford: Oxford University Press.
Keen, Suzanne. 2008. "Strategic Empathizing: Techniques of Bounded, Ambassadorial, and Broadcast Narrative Empathy." *Deutsche Vierteljahrsschrift für Literaturwissenschaft und Geistesgeschichte* 82.3: 477–493.
Keen, Suzanne. 2010. "Narrative Empathy." In *Toward a Cognitive Theory of Narrative Acts*, edited by Frederick Luis Aldama, 61–93. Austin, TX: University of Texas Press.
Kelly, Aaron. 2005. *Irvine Welsh*. Manchester and New York, NY: Manchester University Press.
Kim, Margaret. 2018. "'Make or Mar': History and Fiction in *Wolf Hall*." *The Wenshan Review of Literature and Culture* 12.1: 1–29.
Kindt, Tom. 2004. "Was ist 'interkulturelle Narration'? Vorschläge zur Begriffsklärung." In *Narratologie interkulturell: Entwicklungen – Theorien*, edited by Magdolna Orosz and Jörg Schönert, 131–140. Frankfurt a.M. et al.: Peter Lang.
Kindt, Tom, and Hans-Harald Müller. 2003a. "Narrative Theory and/or/as Theory of Interpretation." In *What Is Narratology? Questions and Answers Regarding the Status of a Theory*, edited by Tom Kindt and Hans-Harald Müller, 205–219. Berlin and New York, NY: De Gruyter.
Kindt, Tom, and Hans-Harald Müller. 2003b. "Narratology and Interpretation: A Rejoinder to David Darby." *Poetics Today* 24.3: 413–421.
Kindt, Tom, and Hans-Harald Müller. 2004. "Brauchen wir eine interkulturelle Narratologie? Über Nutzen und Nachteil eines 'contextualist turn' in der Erzähltheorie." In *Narratologie interkulturell: Entwicklungen – Theorien*, edited by Magdolna Orosz and Jörg Schönert, 141–148. Frankfurt a.M. et al.: Peter Lang.
Kirmayer, Laurence J. 2000. "Broken Narratives: Clinical Encounters and the Poetics of Illness Experience." In *Narrative and the Cultural Construction of Illness and Healing*, edited by Cheryl Mattingly and Linda C. Garro, 153–180. Berkeley, CA et al.: University of California Press.

Klauk, Tobias, and Tilmann Köppe. 2014. "Telling vs. Showing." In *Handbook of Narratology: Volume 2*, edited by Peter Hühn, Jan Christoph Meister, John Pier, and Wolf Schmid, 2nd ed., 846–853. Berlin and Boston, MA: De Gruyter.
Kleiber, Georges. 1993. "Lorsque l'anaphore se lie aux temps grammaticaux." In *Le Temps: De la phrase au texte*, edited by Carl Vetters, 117–166. Lille: Presses Universitaires de Lille.
Klein, Christian, and Matías Martínez. "Wirklichkeitserzählungen: Felder, Formen und Funktionen nicht-literarischen Erzählens." In *Wirklichkeitserzählungen: Felder, Formen und Funktionen nicht-literarischen Erzählens*, edited by Christian Klein and Matías Martínez, 1–13. Stuttgart and Weimar: J. B. Metzler.
Knights, Ben. 2019. "Masculinities." In *The Cambridge Companion to Ian McEwan*, edited by Dominic Head, 120–134. Cambridge: Cambridge University Press.
Korte, Barbara. 1987. "Das Du im Erzähltext: Kommunikationsorientierte Betrachtung zu einer vielgebrauchten Form." *Poetica: Zeitschrift für Sprach- und Literaturwissenschaft* 19: 169–189.
Korte, Barbara. 2008a. "Atwood, Margaret, *Oryx and Crake* (2003)." In *Novels: Part I*, edited by Susanne Peters, Klaus Stierstorfer, and Laurenz Volkmann, 21–36. Trier: Wissenschaftlicher Verlag Trier.
Korte, Barbara. 2008b. "Fundamentalism and the End: A Reading of Margaret Atwood's *Oryx and Crake* in the Context of Last Man Fiction." In *Literary Encounters of Fundamentalism: A Case Book*, edited by Klaus Stierstorfer and Annette Kern-Stähler, 151–163. Heidelberg: Universitätsverlag Winter.
Korte, Barbara. 2008c. "Women's Views of Last Men: Mary Shelley's *The Last Man* and Margaret Atwood's *Oryx and Crake*." In *Reading(s) from a Distance: European Perspectives on Canadian Women's Writing*, edited by Charlotte Sturgess and Martin Kuester, 152–165. Augsburg: Wißner Verlag.
Korthals, Holger. 2003. *Zwischen Drama und Erzählung: Ein Beitrag zur Theorie geschehensdarstellender Literatur*. Berlin: Erich Schmidt Verlag.
Kozioł, Sławomir. 2018. "Crake's Aesthetic: Genetically Modified Humans as a Form of Art in Margaret Atwood's *Oryx and Crake*." *Critique: Studies in Contemporary Fiction* 59.4: 492–508.
Kuhn, Roman. 2013. "Zweite Person Singular Präsens: Überlegungen zu *Ein Mann der schläft* von Georges Perec." In *Der Präsensroman*, edited by Armen Avanessian and Anke Hennig, 210–223. Berlin and Boston, MA: De Gruyter.
Kukkonen, Karin. 2014. "Plot." In *Handbook of Narratology: Volume 2*, edited by Peter Hühn, Jan Christoph Meister, John Pier, and Wolf Schmid, 2nd ed., 706–719. Berlin and Boston, MA: De Gruyter.
Labelle, Marie. 1987. "L'Utilisation des temps du passé dans les narrations françaises: le passé compose, l'imparfait et le présent historique." *Revue Romane* 22.1: 3–29.
LaCroix, Alison L. 2017. "A Man for All Treasons: Crimes By and Against the Tudor State in the Novels of Hilary Mantel." In *Fatal Fictions: Crime and Investigation in Law and Literature*, edited by Alison L. LaCroix, Richard H. McAdams, and Martha C. Nussbaum, 65–88. Oxford et al.: Oxford University Press.
Ladin, Jay. 1999. "Fleshing Out the Chronotope." In *Critical Essays on Mikhail Bakhtin*, edited by Caryl Emerson, 212–236. New York, NY et al.: Twayne Publishers.
Lahn, Silke. 2016. "Wer erzählt die Geschichte? – Parameter des Erzählens." In *Einführung in die Erzähltextanalyse*, edited by Silke Lahn and Jan Christoph Meister, 3rd ed., 73–111. Stuttgart: J. B. Metzler.

Lakoff, George, and Mark Johnson. 2003 [1980]. *Metaphors We Live By*. 2nd ed. Chicago, IL: University of Chicago Press.
Langer, Daniela. 2008. "Literarische Spannung/en: Spannungsformen in erzählenden Texten und Möglichkeiten ihrer Analyse." In *Zwischen Text und Leser: Studien zu Begriff, Geschichte und Funktion literarischer Spannung*, edited by Ingo Irsigler, Christoph Jürgensen, and Daniela Langer, 12–32. Munich: edition text + kritik.
Langer, Suzanne K. 1953. *Feeling and Form: A Theory of Art Developed from "Philosophy in a New Key."* London and Henley: Routledge & Kegan Paul.
Lanser, Susan S. 1992. *Fictions of Authority: Women Writers and Narrative Voice*. Ithaca, NY and London: Cornell University Press.
Lanser, Susan S. 1995. "Sexing the Narrative: Propriety, Desire, and the Engendering of Narratology." *Narrative* 3.1: 85–94.
Lanser, Susan S. 1999. "Sexing Narratology: Toward a Gendered Poetics of Narrative Voice." In *Grenzüberschreitungen: Narratologie im Kontext / Transcending Boundaries: Narratology in Context*, edited by Walter Grünzweig and Andreas Solbach, 167–183. Tübingen: Gunter Narr Verlag.
Lathey, Gillian. 2003. "Time, Narrative Intimacy and the Child: Implications of the Transition from the Present to the Past Tense in the Translation into English of Children's Texts." *Meta* XLVIII.1–2: 233–204.
Lea, Richard. 2010. "Very Now: Has Present-Tense Narration Really Taken Over Fiction?" *The Guardian*, September 14. Accessed August 31, 2020. https://www.theguardian.com/books/booksblog/2010/sep/14/present-tense-narration.
Lea, Richard. 2015. "Make It Now: The Rise of the Present Tense in Narrative Fiction." *The Guardian*, November 21, 2015. Accessed August 31, 2020. https://www.theguardian.com/books/2015/nov/21/rise-of-the-present-tense-in-fiction-hilary-mantel.
Le Guin, Ursula K. 1998. *Steering the Craft*. Portland, OR: The Eighth Mountain Press.
Lehtimäki, Markku. 2011. "Anamorphic Narrativity: Hilary Mantel's *Wolf Hall* in the Renaissance Perspective." In *The Grotesque and the Unnatural*, edited by Markku Salmela and Jarkko Toikkanen, 43–66. Amherst, NY: Cambria Press.
Leise, Nina. 2017. *Fictions of Time: Zeitvorstellungen, -erfahrungen und -reflexionen in englischen und amerikanischen Romanen der Gegenwart*. Trier: Wissenschaftlicher Verlag Trier.
Leiss, Elisabeth. 1992. *Die Verbalkategorien des Deutschen: Ein Beitrag zur Theorie der sprachlichen Kategorisierung*. Berlin and New York, NY: De Gruyter.
Leith, Richard. 1995a. "Tense Variation as a Performance Feature in a Scottish Folk Tale." *Language in Society* 24: 53–77.
Leith, Richard. 1995b. "The Use of the Historic Present Tense in Scottish Traveller Folktales." *Lore and Language: The Journal of the Centre for English Cultural Tradition and Language* 13.1: 1–31.
Lemke, Cordula. 2008. "Racism in the Diaspora: Nadeem Aslam's *Maps for Lost Lovers* (2004)." In *Multi-Ethnic Britain 2000+: New Perspectives in Literature, Film and the Arts*, edited by Lars Eckstein, Barbara Korte, Eva Ulrike Pirker, and Christoph Reinfandt, 171–183. Amsterdam and New York, NY: Rodopi.
Le Poidevin, Robin. 1988. "Time and Truth in Fiction." *British Journal of Aesthetics* 28.3: 248–258.
Le Poidevin, Robin. 2007. *The Images of Time: An Essay on Temporal Representation*. Oxford et al.: Oxford University Press.

Levey, Stephen. 2006. "Tense Variation in Preadolescent Narratives." *Journal of English Linguistics* 34.2: 126–152.
Lin, Jo-Wang. 2012. "Tenselessness." In *The Oxford Handbook of Tense and Aspect*, edited by Robert I. Binnick, 669–695. Oxford et al.: Oxford University Press.
Loades, David. 2013. *Thomas Cromwell: Servant to Henry VIII*. Gloucestershire: Amberley Publishing.
Lopes, José Manuel. 1995. *Foregrounded Description in Prose Fiction: Five Cross-Literary Studies*. Toronto, ON et al.: University of Toronto Press.
Lotman, Jurij M. 1977 [1971]. *The Structure of the Artistic Text*. Translated by Gail Lenhoff and Ronald Vroon. Ann Arbor, MI: University of Michigan Press.
Lubbock, Percy. 1965 [1921]. *The Craft of Fiction*. London: Jonathan Cape.
Ludlow, Peter. 1999. *Semantics, Tense, and Time: An Essay in the Metaphysics of Natural Language*. London and Cambridge, MA: The Massachusetts Institute of Technology Press.
MacCulloch, Diarmaid. 2018. *Thomas Cromwell: A Life*. London et al.: Allen Lane.
Maček, Dora. 2005. "Some Reflections on the Language of Contemporary Scottish Prose." *ELOPE: English Language Overseas Perspectives and Enquiries* 2.1–2: 45–56.
Macrae, Andrea. 2016. "You and I, Past and Present: Cognitive Processing of Perspective." *DIEGESIS: Interdisciplinary E-Journal for Narrative Research* 15.1. 64–80. Accessed August 31, 2020. https://nbn-resolving.de/urn:nbn:de:hbz:468-20160607-154313-6.
Macrae, Andrea. 2019. *Discourse Deixis in Metafiction: The Language of Metanarration, Metalepsis and Disnarration*. New York, NY and London: Routledge.
Mantel, Hilary. 2012. "How I Came to Write *Wolf Hall*." In: *The Guardian*, December 7. Accessed August 31, 2020. https://www.theguardian.com/books/2012/dec/07/bookclub-hilary-mantel-wolf-hall.
Marcus, Amit. 2008. "Dialogue and Authoritativeness in 'We' Fictional Narratives: A Bakhtinian Approach." *Partial Answers: Journal of Literature and the History of Ideas* 6.1: 135–161.
Marcus, Amit. 2009. "*We* Are *You*: The Plural and the Dual in 'We' Fictional Narratives." *Journal of Literary Semantics* 37.1: 1–21.
Margolin, Uri. 1994. "Narrative 'You' Revisited." *Language and Style: An International Journal* 23.4: 425–446.
Margolin, Uri. 1996. "Telling Our Story: On 'We' Literary Narratives." *Language and Literature* 5.2: 115–133.
Margolin, Uri. 1999. "Of What Is Past, Is Passing, or to Come: Temporality, Aspectuality, Modality, and the Nature of Literary Narrative." In *Narratologies: New Perspectives on Narrative Analysis*, edited by David Herman, 142–166. Columbus, OH: The Ohio State University Press.
Margolin, Uri. 2000. "Telling in the Plural: From Grammar to Ideology." *Poetics Today* 21.3: 591–618.
Margolin, Uri. 2001. "Collective Perspective, Individual Perspective, and the Speaker in Between: On 'We' Literary Narratives." In *New Perspectives on Narrative Perspective*, edited by Willie van Peer and Seymour Chatman, 241–253. Albany, NY: The State University of New York Press.
Margolin, Uri. 2014. "Simultaneity in Narrative." In *Handbook of Narratology: Volume 2*, edited by Peter Hühn, Jan Christoph Meister, John Pier, and Wolf Schmid, 2nd ed., 777–783. Berlin and Boston, MA: De Gruyter.
Markus, Manfred. 1977. *Tempus und Aspekt: Zur Funktion von Präsens, Präteritum und Perfekt im Englischen und Deutschen*. Munich: Wilhelm Fink Verlag.

Marsden, Peter H. 2004. "Zur Analyse der Zeit." In *Einführung in die Erzähltextanalyse: Kategorien, Modelle, Probleme*, edited by Peter Wenzel, 89–110. Trier: Wissenschaftlicher Verlag Trier.

Mars-Jones, Adam. 2016. "In the Body Bag [Review of Nutshell, by Ian McEwan]." *London Review of Books* 38.19, October 6: 5–9.

Martínez, Matías. 2004. "Zur Einführung: Authentizität und Medialität in künstlerischen Darstellungen des Holocaust." In *Der Holocaust und die Künste: Medialität und Authentizität von Holocaust-Darstellungen in Literatur, Film, Video, Malerei, Denkmälern, Comic und Musik*, edited by Matías Martínez, 7–21. Bielefeld: Aisthesis Verlag.

Martínez, Matías. 2020. "Authenticity in Narratology and in Literary Studies." In *Narrative Factuality: A Handbook*, edited by Monika Fludernik and Marie-Laure Ryan, 521–531. Berlin and Boston, MA: De Gruyter.

Martínez, Matías, and Michael Scheffel. 2009 [1999]. *Einführung in die Erzähltheorie*. 8th ed. Munich: Verlag C. H. Beck.

Mayer, Sylvia. 2014. "Explorations of the Controversially Real: Risk, the Climate Change Novel, and the Narrative of Anticipation." In *The Anticipation of Catastrophe: Environmental Risk in North American Literature and Culture*, edited by Sylvia Mayer and Alexa Weik von Mossner, 21–37. Heidelberg: Universitätsverlag Winter.

McCann, Sean. 2010. "The Hard-Boiled Novel." In *The Cambridge Companion to American Crime Fiction*, edited by Catherine Ross Nickerson, 42–57. Cambridge: Cambridge University Press.

McCulloch, Fiona. 2012. *Cosmopolitanism in Contemporary British Fiction: Imagined Identities*. Basingstoke and New York, NY: Palgrave Macmillan.

McHale, Brian. 1987. *Postmodernist Fiction*. New York, NY and London: Methuen.

McHale, Brian. 2011. "Model and Thought Experiments." In *Why Study Literature?*, edited by Jan Alber, Stefan Iversen, Louise Brix Jacobsen, Rikke Andersen Kraglund, Henrik Skov Nielsen, and Camilla Møhring Reestorff, 135–155. Aarhus: Aarhus University Press.

McKoon, Gail, Gregory Ward, and Rodger Ratcliff. 1993. "Morphosyntactic and Pragmatic Factors Affecting the Accessibility of Discourse Entities." *Journal of Memory and Language* 32: 56–75.

McNab, Christopher. 1998. "Psychological Novel and *Roman d'analyse*." In *Encyclopedia of the Novel – Volume 2: M – Z*, edited by Paul Schellinger, 1057–1059. Chicago, IL and London: Fitzroy Dearborn Publishers.

McRae, Leanne. 2004. "Writing and Resistance: *Trainspotting*." *In-Between: Essays & Studies in Literary Criticism* 13.2: 117–133.

McTaggart, J. Ellis. 1908. "The Unreality of Time." *Mind: A Quarterly Review of Psychology and Philosophy* 17.68: 457–474.

McTaggart, J. Ellis. 1927a. *The Nature of Existence: Volume I*. Edited by C. D. Broad. Cambridge: Cambridge University Press.

McTaggart, J. Ellis. 1927b. *The Nature of Existence: Volume II*. Edited by C. D. Broad. Cambridge: Cambridge University Press.

Mehnert, Antonia 2014. "Things We Didn't See Coming – Riskscapes in Climate Change Fiction." In *The Anticipation of Catastrophe: Environmental Risk in North American Literature and Culture*, edited by Sylvia Mayer and Alexa Weik von Mossner, 59–78. Heidelberg: Universitätsverlag Winter.

Meifert-Menhard, Felicitas. 2013. *Playing the Text, Performing the Future*. Berlin and Boston, MA: De Gruyter.

Meifert-Menhard, Felicitas. 2019. "Ian McEwan's Brexit Politics in (a) *Nutshell*." *Journal for the Study of British Cultures* 26.2: 195–206.
Meifert-Menhard, Felicitas. 2020. "A Non-Narratable Future? Narrating Climate Change in Contemporary Forms of Storytelling." *DIEGESIS: Interdisciplinary E-Journal for Narrative Research* 9.1: 52–67. Accessed August 31, 2020. https://nbn-resolving.de/urn:nbn:de:hbz:468-20200618-090755-1.
Meisnitzer, Benjamin. 2016. *Das Präsens als Erzähltempus im Roman: Eine gedruckte Antwort auf den Film*. Tübingen: Narr Francke Attempto.
Mendilow, A. A. 1972. *Time and the Novel*. New York, NY: Humanities Press.
Menhard, Felicitas. 2009. *Conflicting Reports: Multiperspektivität und unzuverlässiges Erzählen im englischsprachigen Roman seit 1800*. Trier: Wissenschaftlicher Verlag Trier.
Meretoja, Hanna. 2014. *The Narrative Turn in Fiction and Theory: The Crisis and Return of Storytelling from Robbe-Grillet to Tournier*. Basingstoke and New York, NY: Palgrave Macmillan.
Merriman, Roger Bigelow. 1968 [1902]. *Life and Letters of Thomas Cromwell – Volume I: Life, Letters to 1535*. Oxford: Clarendon Press.
Messent, Peter. 2010. "The Police Novel." In *A Companion to Crime Fiction*, edited by Charles J. Rzepka and Lee Horsley, 175–186. Malden, MA: Wiley-Blackwell.
Messent, Peter. 2013. *The Crime Fiction Handbook*. Malden, MA and Oxford: Wiley-Blackwell.
Miall, David S., and Don Kuiken. 1994. "Foregrounding, Defamiliarization and Affect: Response to Literary Studies." *Poetics* 22: 389–407.
Mildorf, Jarmila. 2016. "Reconsidering Second-Person Narration and Involvement." *Language and Literature* 25.2: 145–158.
Mildorf, Jarmila. 2018. "Mündliches Erzählen / Alltagserzählungen." In *Grundthemen der Literaturwissenschaft: Erzählen*, edited by Martin Huber and Wolf Schmid, 229–243. Berlin and Boston, MA: De Gruyter.
Miller, Laura. 2010. "The Fierce Fight over the Present Tense." *Salon*, September 22. Accessed August 31, 2020. https://www.salon.com/2010/09/22/present_tense/.
Miyahara, Kazunari. 2009. "Why Now, Why Then?: Present-Tense Narration in Contemporary British and Commonwealth Novels." *JNT: Journal of Narrative Theory* 39.2: 241–268.
Mohr, Dunja M. 2015. "Eco-Dystopia and Biotechnology: Margaret Atwood, *Oryx and Crake* (2003), *The Year of the Flood* (2009) and *MaddAddam* (2013)." In *Dystopia, Science Fiction, Post-Apocalypse: Classics – New Tendencies – Model Interpretations*, edited by Eckart Voigts-Virschow and Alessandra Boller, 283–301. Trier: Wissenschaftlicher Verlag Trier.
Moore, Lindsey. 2009. "British Muslim Identities and Spectres of Terror in Nadeem Aslam's *Maps for Lost Lovers*." *Postcolonial Text* 5.2: 1–19.
Morace, Robert A. 2001. *Trainspotting: A Reader's Guide*. New York, NY and London: Continuum.
Moraru, Christian. 2018. "Embedded with the World: Place, Displacement, and Relocation in Recent British and Postcolonial Fiction." *Études britanniques contemporaines: Revue de la Société d'études anglaises contemporaines* 55. Accessed August 31, 2020. https://journals.openedition.org/ebc/5054.
Morgenstern, Naomi. 2018. *Wild Child: Intensive Parenting and Posthumanist Ethics*. Minneapolis, MN and London: University of Minnesota Press.
Morton, Timothy. 2010. *The Ecological Thought*. Cambridge, MA and London: Harvard University Press.

Mosca, Valeria. 2013. "Crossing Human Boundaries: Apocalypse and Posthumanism in Margaret Atwood's *Oryx and Crake* and *The Year of the Flood*." *Altre Modernità* 9.5: 38–52.

Mosher, Harold F. 1991. "Toward a Poetics of 'Descriptized' Narration." *Poetics Today* 12.3: 425–445.

Moss, Laura. "'A Science of Uncertainty': Bioethics, Narrative Competence, and Turning to the 'What If' of Fiction." *SCL: Studies in Canadian Literature* 40.2: 5–24.

Mullan, John. 2006. *How Novels Work*. Oxford: Oxford University Press.

Mullan, John. 2010. "A History of the Present Tense." *The Guardian*, September 25. Accessed August 31, 2020. https://www.theguardian.com/books/2010/sep/25/author-present-tense-john-mullan.

Mullan, John. 2018. "Dickens's Tricks." *Essays in Criticism: A Quarterly Journal Founded by F. W. Bateson* 68.2: 145–166.

Müller, Günther. 1968 [1947]. "Erzählzeit und erzählte Zeit." In *Morphologische Poetik: Gesammelte Aufsätze*, written by Günther Müller and edited by Elena Müller, 269–286. Darmstadt: Wissenschaftliche Buchgesellschaft.

Müller, Günther. 2011 [1947]. "The Significance of Time in Narrative Art." In *Time: From Concept to Narrative Construct: A Reader*, edited by Jan Christoph Meister and Wilhelm Schernus, 67–83. Berlin and Boston, MA: De Gruyter.

Müller, Wolfgang G. 2018. "The Body within the Body: Ian McEwan's Creation of a New World in *Nutshell*." *Frontiers of Narrative* 4.2: 374–391.

Muny, Eike. 2008. *Erzählperspektive im Drama: Ein Beitrag zur transgenerischen Narratologie*. Munich: Iudicium Verlag.

Neill, Rosemary. 2016. "Labour of Love and Loathing: Ian McEwan on New Novel *Nutshell*, Hamlet, His Brother and the Bard." *The Australian*, August 27–28: 16–17.

Nelles, William. 2016. "Antinomic Chronology in 'Mirrorstory.'" *Style* 50.4: 409–414.

Nemoianu, Anca M. 2014. "Time, Tense, and Narrative Style: Linguistic Insights from Contemporary Narrative Discourse." *International Journal of Language and Literature* 2.3: 99–114.

Neumann, Anne Waldron. 1990. "Escaping the 'Time of History'? Present Tense and the Occasion of Narration in J. M. Coetzee's *Waiting for the Barbarians*." *The Journal of Narrative Technique* 20.1: 65–86.

Neumann, Birgit, and Ansgar Nünning. 2008. *An Introduction to the Study of Narrative*. Stuttgart: Ernst Klett Verlag.

Neumann, Birgit, and Ansgar Nünning. 2014. "Metanarration and Metafiction." In *Handbook of Narratology: Volume 1*, edited by Peter Hühn, Jan Christoph Meister, John Pier, and Wolf Schmid, 2nd ed., 344–352. Berlin and Boston, MA: De Gruyter.

Nielsen, Henrik Skov. 2004. "The Impersonal Voice in First-Person Narrative Fiction." *Narrative* 12.2: 133–150.

Nielsen, Henrik Skov. 2010. "Natural Authors, Unnatural Narration." In *Postclassical Narratology: Approaches and Analyses*, edited by Jan Alber and Monika Fludernik, 275–301. Columbus, OH: The Ohio State University Press.

Nielsen, Henrik Skov. 2011. "Fictional Voices? Strange Voices? Unnatural Voices?" In *Strange Voices in Narrative Fiction*, edited by Per Krogh Hansen, Stefan Iversen, Henrik Skov Nielsen, and Rolf Reitan, 55–82. Berlin and Boston, MA: De Gruyter.

Nielsen, Henrik Skov. 2013. "Naturalizing and Unnaturalizing Reading Strategies: Focalization Revisited." In *A Poetics of Unnatural Narrative*, edited by Jan Alber, Henrik Skov Nielsen, and Brian Richardson, 67–93. Columbus, OH: The Ohio State University Press.

Nielsen, Henrik Skov, James Phelan, and Richard Walsh. 2015a. "Fictionality as Rhetoric: A Response to Paul Dawson." *Narrative* 23.1: 101–111.
Nielsen, Henrik Skov, James Phelan, and Richard Walsh. 2015b. "Ten Theses about Fictionality." *Narrative* 23.1: 61–73.
Njubina, L. M., and L. W. Schischkowa. 1990. In *Interdisziplinäre Aspekte des Textes: Beiträge aus der Kooperation Potsdam – Leningrad*, edited by Helmut John and Christine Keßler, 110–123. Potsdam: Brandenburgische Landeshochschule.
Norrick, Neal R. 2000. *Conversational Narrative: Storytelling in Everday Talk*. Amsterdam and Philadelphia, PA: John Benjamins Publishing Company.
Norrick, Neal R. 2004. "Humor, Tellability, and Co-Narration in Conversational Storytelling." *Text* 24.1: 74–111.
Norrick, Neal R. 2005. "The Dark Side of Tellability." *Narrative Inquiry* 15.2: 323–343.
Norrick, Neal R. 2007. "Conversational Storytelling." In *The Cambridge Companion to Narrative*, edited by David Herman, 127–141. Cambridge: Cambridge University Press.
North, Michael. 2018. *What is the Present?* Princeton, NJ and Oxford: Princeton University Press.
Nowotny, Helga. 1994 [1989]. *Time: The Modern and Postmodern Experience*. Translated by Neville Plaice. Cambridge and Malden, MA: Polity Press.
Nünning, Ansgar. 1995a. *Von historischer Fiktion zu historiographischer Metafiction – Band 1: Theorie, Typologie und Poetik des historischen Romans*. Trier: Wissenschaftlicher Verlag Trier.
Nünning, Ansgar. 1995b. *Von historischer Fiktion zu historiographischer Metafiction – Band 2: Erscheinungsformen und Entwicklungstendenzen des historischen Romans in England seit 1950*. Trier: Wissenschaftlicher Verlag Trier.
Nünning, Ansgar. 1997. "Crossing Borders and Blurring Genres: Towards a Typology and Poetics of Postmodernist Historical Fiction in England since the 1960s." *European Journal of English Studies* 1.2: 217–238.
Nünning, Ansgar. 2000. "'Great Wits Jump': Die literarische Inszenierung von Erzählillusion als vernachlässigte Entwicklungslinie des englischen Romans von Laurence Sterne bis Stevie Smith." In: *Lineages of the Novel: Essays in Honour of Raimund Borgmeier*, edited by Bernhard Reitz and Eckart Voigts-Virchow, 67–92. Trier: Wissenschaftlicher Verlag Trier.
Nünning, Ansgar. 2001a. "Metanarration als Lakune der Erzähltheorie: Definition, Typologie und Grundriss einer Funktionsgeschichte metanarrativer Erzähleräußerungen." *AAA – Arbeiten aus Anglistik und Amerikanistik* 26.2: 125–164.
Nünning, Ansgar. 2001b. "Mimesis des Erzählens: Prolegomena zu einer Wirkungsästhetik, Typologie und Funktionsgeschichten des Akts des Erzählens und der Metanarration." In *Erzählen und Erzähltheorie im 20. Jahrhundert*, edited by Jörg Helbig, 13–47. Heidelberg: Universitätsverlag Winter.
Nünning, Ansgar. 2003. "Narratology or Narratologies? Taking Stock of Recent Developments, Critique and Modest Proposals for Future Usages of the Term." In *What Is Narratology? Questions and Answers Regarding the Status of a Theory*, edited by Tom Kindt and Hans-Harald Müller, 239–275. Berlin and New York, NY: De Gruyter.
Nünning, Ansgar. 2004a. "On Metanarrative: Towards a Definition, a Typology and an Outline of the Functions of Metanarrative Commentary." In *The Dynamics of Narrative Form: Studies in Anglo-American Narratology*, edited by John Pier, 11–57. Berlin and New York, NY: De Gruyter.

Nünning, Ansgar. 2004b. "Where Historiographic Metafiction and Narratology Meet: Towards an Applied Cultural Narratology." *Style* 38.3: 352–374.

Nünning, Ansgar. 2007. "Towards a Typology, Poetics and History of Description in Fiction." In *Description in Literature and Other Media*, edited by Werner Wolf and Walter Bernhart, 91–128. Amsterdam and New York, NY: Rodopi.

Nünning, Ansgar. 2010. "Making Events – Making Stories – Making Worlds: Ways of Worldmaking from a Narratological Point of View." In *Cultural Ways of Worldmaking: Media and Narratives*, edited by Vera Nünning, Ansgar Nünning, and Birgit Neumann, 191–214. Berlin and Boston, MA: De Gruyter.

Nünning, Ansgar. 2012a. "Making Crises and Catastrophes – How Metaphors and Narratives Shape Their Cultural Life." In *The Cultural Life of Catastrophes and Crises*, edited by Carsten Meiner and Kristin Veel, 59–88. Berlin and Boston, MA: De Gruyter.

Nünning, Ansgar. 2012b. "'With the Benefit of Hindsight': Features and Functions of Turning Points as a Narratological Concept and as a Way of Self-Making." In *Turning Points: Concepts and Narratives of Change in Literature and Other Media*, edited by Ansgar Nünning and Kai Marcel Sicks, 31–58. Berlin and Boston, MA: De Gruyter.

Nünning, Ansgar. 2016. "Zeit in der Erzählkunst: Literarische Repräsentationen von Multitemporalität, Achtsamkeitstempo und ... kulturellen Zeitvorstellungen." In *Zeit in den Wissenschaften*, edited by Wolfgang Kautek, Reinhard Neck, and Heinrich Schmidinger, 145–177. Vienna et al.: Böhlau Verlag.

Nünning, Ansgar, and Vera Nünning. 2002. "Von der strukturalistischen Narratologie zur postklassischen Erzähltheorie." In *Neue Ansätze in der Erzähltheorie*, edited by Ansgar Nünning and Vera Nünning, 1–33. Trier: Wissenschaftlicher Verlag Trier.

Nünning, Ansgar, and Vera Nünning. 2016. "Conceptualizing 'Broken Narratives' from a Narratological Perspective: Domains, Concepts, Features, Functions, and Suggestions for Research." In *Narrative im Bruch: Theoretische Positionen und Anwendungen*, edited by Anna Babka, Marlen Bidwell-Steiner, and Wolfgang Müller-Funk, 37–86. Vienna: V & R unipress / Vienna University Press.

Nünning, Ansgar, and Jan Rupp, eds. 2011. *Medialisierung des Erzählens im englischsprachigen Roman der Gegenwart: Theoretischer Bezugsrahmen, Genres und Modellinterpretationen*. Trier: Wissenschaftlicher Verlag Trier.

Nünning, Ansgar, and Christine Schwanecke. 2013. "Crossing Generic Borders – Blurring Generic Boundaries: Hybridization as a Catalyst for Generic Change and for the Transformation of Systems of Genres." In *The Cultural Dynamics of Generic Change in Contemporary Fiction: Theoretical Frameworks, Genres and Model Interpretations*, edited by Michael Basseler, Ansgar Nünning, and Christine Schwanecke, 115–146. Trier: Wissenschaftlicher Verlag Trier.

Nünning, Ansgar, and Roy Sommer. 2002. "Die Vertextung der Zeit: Zur narratologischen und phänomenologischen Rekonstruktion erzählerisch inszenierter Zeiterfahrungen und Zeitkonzeptionen." In *Zeit und Roman: Zeiterfahrung im historischen Wandel und ästhetischer Paradigmenwechsel vom sechzehnten Jahrhundert bis zur Postmoderne*, edited by Martin Middeke, 31–56. Würzburg: Königshausen & Neumann.

Nünning, Vera. 2014. *Reading Fictions, Changing Minds: The Cognitive Value of Fiction*. Heidelberg: Universitätsverlag Heidelberg.

Nünning, Vera. 2015. "Reconceptualising Fictional (Un)Reliability and (Un)Trustworthiness from a Multidisciplinary Perspective: Categories, Typology and Functions." In *Unreliable Narra-

tion and Trustworthiness: Intermedial and Interdisciplinary Perspectives, edited by Vera Nünning, 83–108. Berlin and Boston, MA: De Gruyter.

Nünning, Vera. 2017. "The Affective Value of Fiction: Presenting and Evoking Emotions." In *Writing Emotions: Theoretical Concepts and Selective Case Studies in Literature*, edited by Ingeborg Jandl, Susanne Knaller, Sabine Schönfeller, and Gudrun Tockner, 29–54. Bielefeld: transcript.

Nünning, Vera, and Ansgar Nünning. 2000a. "Multiperspektivität aus narratologischer Sicht: Erzähltheoretische Grundlagen und Kategorien zur Analyse der Perspektivenstruktur narrativer Texte." In *Multiperspektivisches Erzählen: Zur Theorie und Geschichte der Perspektivenstruktur im englischen Roman des 18. bis 20. Jahrhunderts*, edited by Vera Nünning and Ansgar Nünning, 39–77. Trier: Wissenschaftlicher Verlag Trier.

Nünning, Vera, and Ansgar Nünning. 2000b. "Von 'der' Erzählperspektive zur Perspektivenstruktur narrativer Texte: Überlegungen zur Definition, Konzeptualisierung und Untersuchbarkeit von Multiperspektivität." In *Multiperspektivisches Erzählen: Zur Theorie und Geschichte der Perspektivenstruktur im englischen Roman des 18. bis 20. Jahrhunderts*, edited by Vera Nünning and Ansgar Nünning, 3–38. Trier: Wissenschaftlicher Verlag Trier.

Ochs, Elinor, and Lisa Capps. 2001. *Living Narrative: Creating Lives in Everyday Storytelling*. Cambridge, MA and London: Harvard University Press:

O'Connor, Siobhan. 2018. "History, Nation and Self: *Wolf Hall* and the Machinery of Memory." In *Hilary Mantel: Contemporary Critical Perspectives*, edited by Eileen Pollard and Ginette Carpenter, 27–40. London: Bloomsbury Academic.

Ohme, Andreas. 2018. "Der heterodigetische Präsensroman – ein Fall von *unreliable narration*?" *JLT: Journal of Literary Theory* 12.1: 93–112.

O'Keeffe, Bernard. 1996. "The Language of *Trainspotting*." *The English Review* 7.2: 6–8.

Olson, Greta. 2003. "Reconsidering Unreliability: Fallible and Untrustworthy Narrators." *Narrative* 11.1: 93–109.

Osselton, N. E. 1982. "On the Use of the Perfect in Present-Tense Narrative." *English Studies* 63: 63–69.

Palmer, Alan. 2004. *Fictional Minds*. Lincoln, NE and London: University of Nebraska Press.

Palmer, Alan. 2008 [2005]. "Psychological Novel." In *The Routledge Encyclopedia of Narrative Theory*, edited by David Herman, Manfred Jahn, and Marie-Laure Ryan, 2nd ed., 474–475. London and New York, NY: Routledge.

Panek, Leroy L. 2003. "Post-War American Police Fiction." In *The Cambridge Companion to Crime Fiction*, edited by Martin Priestman, 155–171. Cambridge: Cambridge University Press.

Parey, Armelle. 2019a. "Introduction: Narrative Expansions – The Story so Far. . ." In *Prequels, Coquels and Sequels in Contemporary Anglophone Fiction*, edited by Armelle Parey, 1–24. New York, NY and London: Routledge.

Parey, Armelle, ed. 2019b. *Prequels, Coquels and Sequels in Contemporary Anglophone Fiction*. New York, NY and London: Routledge.

Parker, Joshua. 2011/2012. "In Their Own Words: On Writing in Second Person." *Connotations* 21.2–3: 165–176.

Parker, Joshua. 2018. "Placements and Functions of Brief Second-Person Passages in Fiction." In *Pronouns in Literature: Positions and Perspectives in Language*, edited by Alison Gibbons and Andrea Macrae, 97–112. London: Palgrave Macmillan.

Pataki, Éva. 2014. "'This Dasht-e-Tanhaii called the planet Earth': The Metamorphosis of Space and Identity in Nadeem Aslam's *Maps for Lost Lovers*." *Hungarian Journal of English and American Studies* 20.2: 79–100.

Pepper, Andrew. 2010a. "The American Roman Noir." In *The Cambridge Companion to American Crime Fiction*, edited by Catherine Ross Nickerson, 58–71. Cambridge: Cambridge University Press.

Pepper, Andrew. 2010b. "The 'Hard-Boiled' Genre." In *A Companion to Crime Fiction*, edited by Charles J. Rzepka and Lee Horsley, 140–151. Malden, MA: Wiley-Blackwell.

Pepper, Andrew. 2011. "Policing the Globe: State Sovereignty and the International in the Post-9/11 Crime Novel." *MFS: Modern Fiction Studies* 57.3: 403–424.

Perry, Menakhem. 1979. "Literary Dynamics: How the Order of a Text Creates Its Meanings [With and Analysis of Faulkner's 'A Rose for Emily']." *Poetics Today* 1/2: 35–64, 311–361.

Pesso-Miquel, Catherine. 2011. "Unseen Cities: Representations of the Diasporic Experience in Nadeem Aslam's *Maps for Lost Lovers*." In *India and the Diasporic Imagination / L'Inde et l'imagiantion diasporique*, edited by Rita Christian and Judith Misrahi-Barak, 127–147. Montpellier: Presses universitaires de la Méditerranée.

Petersen, Jürgen H. 1991. *Der deutsche Roman der Moderne: Grundlegung – Typologie – Entwicklung*. Stuttgart: J. B. Metzlersche Verlagsbuchhandlung.

Petersen, Jürgen H. 1992. "Erzählen im Präsens: Die Korrektur herrschender Tempus-Theorien durch die poetische Praxis in der Moderne." *Euphorion: Zeitschrift für Literaturgeschichte* 68: 65–89.

Petersen, Jürgen H. 1993. *Erzählsysteme: Eine Poetik epischer Texte*. Stuttgart and Weimar: J. B. Metzler.

Petersen, Jürgen H. 2010. *Die Erzählformen: Er, Ich, Du und andere Varianten*. Berlin: Erich Schmidt Verlag.

Petrie, Duncan. 2004. *Contemporary Scottish Fictions: Film, Television and the Novel*. Edinburgh: Edinburgh University Press.

Pettersson, Bo. 2015. "Kinds of Unreliability in Fiction: Narratorial, Focal, Expositional and Combined." In *Unreliable Narration and Trustworthiness: Intermedial and Interdisciplinary Perspectives*, edited by Vera Nünning, 109–129. Berlin and Boston, MA: De Gruyter.

Pettitt, Clare. 2013. "Dickens and the Form of the Historical Present." In *Dickens's Style*, edited by Daniel Tyler, 110–136. Cambridge: Cambridge University Press.

Pfister, Manfred. 1985a. "Konzepte der Intertextualität." In *Intertextualität: Formen, Funktionen, anglistische Fallstudien*, edited by Ulrich Broich and Manfred Pfister, 1–30. Tübingen: Max Niemeyer Verlag.

Pfister, Manfred. 1985b. "Zur Systemreferenz." In *Intertextualität: Formen, Funktionen, anglistische Fallstudien*, edited by Ulrich Broich and Manfred Pfister, 52–58. Tübingen: Max Niemeyer Verlag.

Pflugmacher, Torsten. 2008 [2005]. "Description." In *The Routledge Encyclopedia of Narrative Theory*, edited by David Herman, Manfred Jahn, and Marie-Laure Ryan, 2nd ed., 101–102. London and New York, NY: Routledge.

Phelan, James. 1981. *Worlds from Words: A Theory of Language in Fiction*. Chicago, IL and London: The University of Chicago Press.

Phelan, James. 1989. *Reading People, Reading Plots: Character, Progression, and the Interpretation of Narrative*. Chicago, IL and London: The University of Chicago Press.

Phelan, James. 1994. "Present Tense Narration, Mimesis, the Narrative Norm, and the Positioning of the Readers in *Waiting for the Barbarians*." In *Understanding Narrative*, edited by

James Phelan and Peter J. Rabinowitz, 222–245. Columbus, OH: The Ohio State University Press.
Phelan, James. 1996. *Narrative as Rhetoric: Technique, Audiences, Ethics, Ideology*. Columbus, OH: The Ohio State University Press.
Phelan, James. 2002. "Narrative Progression." In *Narrative Dynamics: Essays on Time, Plot, Closure, and Frames*, edited by Brian Richardson, 211–216. Columbus, OH: The Ohio State University Press.
Phelan, James. 2005. *Living to Tell about It: A Rhetoric and Ethics of Character Narration*. Ithaca, NY and London: Cornell University Press.
Phelan, James. 2007. *Experiencing Fiction: Judgments, Progressions, and the Rhetorical Theory of Narrative*. Columbus, OH: The Ohio State University Press.
Phelan, James. 2011. "Rhetoric, Ethics, and Narrative Communication: Or, from Story and Discourse to Authors, Resources, and Audiences." *Soundings: An Interdisciplinary Journal* 94.1/2: 55–75.
Phelan, James. 2013a. "Implausibilities, Crossovers, and Impossibilities: A Rhetorical Approach to Breaks in the Code of Mimetic Character Narration." In *A Poetics of Unnatural Narrative*, edited by Jan Alber, Henrik Skov Nielsen, and Brian Richardson, 167–184. Columbus, OH: The Ohio State University Press.
Phelan, James. 2013b. *Reading the American Novel 1920–2010*. Malden, MA and Oxford: Wiley-Blackwell.
Phelan, James. 2017. *Somebody Telling Somebody Else: A Rhetorical Poetics of Narrative*. Columbus, OH: The Ohio State University Press.
Phelan, James, and Peter J. Rabinowitz. 2012. "Narrative as Rhetoric." In *Narrative Theory: Core Concepts and Critical Debates*, by David Herman, James Phelan, Peter J. Rabinowitz, Brian Richardson, and Robyn Warhol, 3–8. Columbus, OH: The Ohio State University Press.
Philipowski, Katharina. 2018. "Die deiktische Poetik des Präsens, oder: Wie das 'jetzt' ein 'hier' erschafft." In *Narratologie und mittelalterliches Erzählen: Autor, Erzähler, Perspektive, Zeit und Raum*, edited by Eva von Contzen and Florian Kragl, 165–192. Berlin and Boston, MA: De Gruyter.
Pipit, Mayang. 2019. "The Expression of English Linguistic Time through Simple Past Tense by Indonesian Learners." *Advances in Social Sciences, Education and Humanities Research* 254: 202–205.
Pollner, Clausdirk. 2005. "Scots 1 : English 0 – and Drugs Galore: Varieties and Registers in Irvine Welsh's *Trainspotting*." In *Anglo-American Awareness: Arpeggios in Aesthetics*, edited by Gisela Hermann-Brennecke and Wolf Kindermann, 193–202. Münster: Lit-Verlag.
Pratt, Mary Louise. 1992. *Imperial Eyes: Travel Writing and Transculturation*. London and New York, NY: Routledge.
Prince, Gerald. 1982. *Narratology: The Form and Functioning of Narrative*. Berlin et al.: Mouton Publishers.
Prince, Gerald. 2003 [1987]. *Dictionary of Narratology*. 2nd ed. Lincoln, NE and London: University of Nebraska Press.
Prince, Gerald. 2008 [2005]. "Nouveau Roman." In *The Routledge Encyclopedia of Narrative Theory*, edited by David Herman, Manfred Jahn, and Marie-Laure Ryan, 2nd ed., 398. London and New York, NY: Routledge.
Pullman, Philip. 2010. "Philip Pullman Pulls Time on the Present Tense." *The Guardian*, September 18. Accessed August 31, 2020. https://www.theguardian.com/global/2010/sep/18/philip-pullman-author-present-tense.

Pullman, Philip. 2017. "News & Articles: The Book of Dust." *Philip Pullman*, 15 February. Accessed August 31, 2020. https://www.philip-pullman.com/newsitem?newsItemID=21.

Quasthoff, Uta. 1980. *Erzählen in Gesprächen: Linguitische Untersuchungen zu Strukturen und Funktionen am Beispiel einer Kommunikationsform des Alltags*. Tübingen: Gunter Narr Verlag.

Racolta, Remus. 2017. *Alienation and Hybridity: Patterns of Estrangement in the British Novel since the 1950s*. Ph.D. diss., University of Wuppertal. Accessed August 31, 2020. https://nbn-resolving.de/urn/resolver.pl?urn=urn%3Anbn%3Ade%3Ahbz%3A468-20180711-092740-9.

Rajewsky, Irina O. 2002. *Intermedialität*. Tübingen and Basel: A. Francke Verlag.

Rajewsky, Irina O. 2005. "Intermediality, Intertextuality, and Remediation: A Literary Perspective on Intermediality." *Intermédialités / Intermediality* 6: 43–64.

Rauh, Gisa. 1978. *Linguistische Beschreibung deiktischer Komplexität in narrativen Texten*. Tübingen: TBL Verlag Gunter Narr.

Rauh, Gisa. 1982. "Über die deiktische Funktion des epischen Präteritum: Die Reintegration einer scheinbaren Sonderform in ihren theoretischen Kontext, Teil I." *Indogermanische Forschungen* 87: 22–55.

Rauh, Gisa. 1983a. "Tenses as Deictic Categories: An Analysis of English and German Tenses." In *Essays on Deixis*, edited by Gisa Rauh, 229–275. Tübingen: Gunter Narr Verlag.

Rauh, Gisa. 1983b. "Über die deiktische Funktion des epischen Präteritum: Die Reintegration einer scheinbaren Sonderform in ihren theoretischen Kontext, Teil II." *Indogermanische Forschungen* 88: 33–53.

Rauh, Gisa. 1984. "Tempora als deiktische Kategorien: Eine Analyse der Tempora im Englischen und Deutschen, Teil I." *Indogermanische Forschungen* 89: 1–25.

Rauh, Gisa. 1985a. "Tempora als deiktische Kategorien: Eine Analyse der Tempora im Englischen und Deutschen, Teil II." *Indogermanische Forschungen* 90: 1–38.

Rauh, Gisa. 1985b. "Tempus und Erzähltheorie." In *Tempus, Zeit und Text*, edited by Werner Hüllen and Rainer Schulze, 63–81. Heidelberg: Universitätsverlag Winter.

Rauh, Gisa. 1988. "Temporale Deixis." In *Temporalsemantik: Beiträge zur Linguistik der Zeitreferenz*, edited by Veronika Ehrich and Heinz Vater, 26–51. Tübingen: Max Niemeyer Verlag.

Reichl, Susanne. 2000. "Of Lappas and Levis: (Dress-)Code-Switching and the Construction of Cultural Identities in the British Novel of Immigration." *New Literatures Review* 36: 63–75.

Reichl, Susanne. 2002. *Cultures in the Contact Zone: Ethnic Semiosis in Black British Literature*. Trier: Wissenschaftlicher Verlag Trier.

Reitan, Rolf. 2011. "Theorizing Second-Person Narratives: A Backwater Project?" In *Strange Voices in Narrative Fiction*, edited by Per Krogh Hansen, Stefan Iversen, Henrik Skov Nielsen, and Rolf Reitan, 147–174. Berlin and Boston, MA: De Gruyter.

Riach, Alan. 2005. "The Unnatural Scene: The Fiction of Irvine Welsh." In *The Contemporary British Novel since 1980*, edited by James Achson and Sarah C. E. Ross, 35–47. New York, NY and Basingstoke: Palgrave Macmillan.

Richardson, Brian. 1991. "The Poetics and Politics of Second Person Narrative." *Genre* XXIV: 309–330.

Richardson, Brian. 1994. "I etcetera: On the Poetics and Ideology of Multipersoned Narratives." *Style* 28.3: 312–328.

Richardson, Brian. 2002a. "Beyond Story and Discourse: Narrative Time in Postmodern and Nonmimetic Fiction." In *Narrative Dynamics: Essays on Time, Plot, Closure, and Frames*, edited by Brian Richardson, 47–63. Columbus, OH: The Ohio State University Press.

Richardson, Brian. 2002b. "General Introduction." In *Narrative Dynamics: Essays on Time, Plot, Closure, and Frames*, edited by Brian Richardson, 1–7. Columbus, OH: The Ohio State University Press.

Richardson, Brian. 2006. *Unnatural Voices: Extreme Narration in Modern and Contemporary Fiction*. Columbus, OH: The Ohio State University Press.

Richardson, Brian. 2009. "Plural Focalization, Singular Voices: Wandering Perspectives in 'We'-Narration." In *Point of View, Perspective, and Focalization: Modeling Mediation in Narrative*, edited by Peter Hühn, Wolf Schmid, and Jörg Schönert, 143–159. Berlin and New York, NY: De Gruyter.

Richardson, Brian. 2012a. "Antimimetic, Unnatural, and Postmodern Narrative Theory." In *Narrative Theory: Core Concepts and Critical Debates*, edited by David Herman, James Phelan, Peter J. Rabinowitz, Brian Richardson, and Robyn Warhol, 20–25. Columbus, OH: The Ohio State University Press.

Richardson, Brian. 2012b. "Unnatural Narratology: Basic Concepts and Recent Work." *DIEGESIS: Interdisciplinary E-Journal for Narrative Research* 1.1: 95–103. Accessed August 31, 2020. https://nbn-resolving.de/urn:nbn:de:hbz:468-20121113-154559-6.

Richardson, Brian. 2015. *Unnatural Narrative: Theory, History, and Practice*. Columbus, OH: The Ohio State University Press.

Richardson, Brian. 2016. "Unnatural Narrative Theory." *Style* 50.4: 385–405.

Richardson, Brian. 2019. *A Poetics of Plot for the Twenty-First Century: Theorizing Unruly Narratives*. Columbus, OH: The Ohio State University Press.

Richardson, Samuel. 1986 [1753]. "Preface." In *The History of Sir Charles Grandison*, 3–4. Oxford and New York, NY: Oxford University Press.

Ricœur, Paul. 1983. *Temps et récit – Tome I: L'intrigue et le récit historique*. Paris: Éditions de Seuil.

Ricœur, Paul. 1984. *Temps et récit – Tome II: La configuration dans le récit de fiction*. Paris: Éditions de Seuil.

Ricœur, Paul. 1984 [1983]. *Time and Narrative: Volume 1*. Translated by Kathleen McLaughlin and David Pellauer. Chicago, IL and London: The University of Chicago Press.

Ricœur, Paul. 1985. *Temps et récit – Tome III: Le temps raconté*. Paris: Éditions de Seuil.

Ricœur, Paul. 1985 [1984]. *Time and Narrative: Volume 2*. Translated by Kathleen McLaughlin and David Pellauer. Chicago, IL and London: The University of Chicago Press.

Rimmon-Kenan, Shlomith. 2002 [1983]. *Narrative Fiction: Contemporary Poetics*. 2nd ed. London and New York, NY: Routledge.

Roberts, Adam. 2019. "Best Science Fiction and Fantasy Books of 2019." *The Guardian*, November 30. https://www.theguardian.com/books/2019/nov/30/best-science-fiction-and-fantasy-books-of-2019. Accessed August 31, 2020.

Roberts, Laura. 2010. "Philip Pullman and Philip Hensher Criticise Booker Prize for Including Present Tense Novels." *The Telegraph*, September 11. Accessed August 31, 2020. https://www.telegraph.co.uk/culture/books/booknews/7994914/Philip-Pullman-and-Philip-Hensher-criticise-Booker-Prize-for-including-present-tense-novels.html.

Rodríguez Louro, Celeste, and Marie-Eve Ritz. 2014. "Stories Down Under: Tense Variation at the Heart of Australian English Narratives." *Australian Journal of Linguistics* 34.4: 549–565.

Rohde, Christiane. 1993. *Das Präsens in der frühen deutschen Kunstballade*. Marburg: Hitzeroth.
Ronen, Ruth. 1997. "Description, Narrative and Representation." *Narrative* 5.3: 274–286.
Rosa, Hartmut. 2003. "Social Acceleration: Ethical and Political Consequences of a Desynchronized High-Speed Society." *Constellations* 10.1: 3–33.
Rosa, Hartmut. 2010. *Alienation and Acceleration: Towards a Critical Theory of Late-Modern Temporality*. Copenhagen: NSU Press & Nordiskt Sommaruniversitet.
Rosa, Hartmut. 2013 [2005]. *Social Acceleration: A Theory of Modernity*. New York, NY: Columbia University Press.
Rosenberg, Ingrid von. 2017. "A Popular Genre Goes Booker: Hilary Mantel's 'Other' Royal Novels *Wolf Hall* and *Bring Up the Bodies*." In *(Un)Making the Monarchy*, edited by Anette Pankratz and Claus-Ulrich Viol, 151–176. Heidelberg: Universitätsverlag Winter.
Rousselot, Elodie. 2014. "Introduction: Exoticising the Past in Contemporary Neo-Historical Fiction." In *Exoticizing the Past in Contemporary Neo-Historical Fiction*, edited by Elodie Rousselot, 1–16. London: Palgrave Macmillan.
Rubik, Margarete. 2018. "Out of the Dungeon, into the World: Aspects of the Prison Novel in Emma Donoghue's *Room*." In *How to Do Things with Narrative: Cognitive and Diachronic Perspectives*, edited by Jan Alber and Greta Olson, 219–239. Berlin and Boston, MA: De Gruyter.
Rubin, Jay. 2003. *Haruki Murakami and the Music of Words*. London: Harvill Press.
Ruin, Inger. 1983. "Tense Variation in Fiction." In *Papers from the Second Scandinavian Symposium on Syntactic Variation, Stockholm May 15–16, 1982*, edited by Sven Jacobson, 169–176. Stockholm: Almqvist & Wiksell.
Rupp, Jan. 2018. "Fictions of Cultural Memory and Generations: Challenging Englishness in Zadie Smith's *White Teeth* (2000) and Nadeem Aslam's *Maps for Lost Lovers* (2004)." In *The British Novel in the Twenty-First Century: Cultural Concerns – Literary Developments – Model Interpretations*, edited by Vera Nünning and Ansgar Nünning, 103–118. Trier: Wissenschaftlicher Verlag Trier.
Rushkoff, Douglas. 2013. *Present Shock: When Everything Happens Now*. New York, NY: Current.
Ryabkova, Irina, Elena Sirnova, and Elena Sheina. 2017. "Characteristics of Pretend Role Play." In *The Routledge International Handbook of Early Childhood Play*, edited by Tina Bruce, Pentti Hakkarainen, and Milda Bredikyte, 87–96. London and New York, NY: Routledge.
Ryan, Marie-Laure. 1991. *Possible Worlds, Artificial Intelligence, and Narrative Theory*. Bloomington, IN and Indianapolis, IN: Indiana University Press.
Ryan, Marie-Laure. 1993. "Narrative in Real Time: Chronicle, Mimesis and Plot in the Baseball Broadcast." *Narrative* 1.2: 138–155.
Ryan, Marie-Laure. 2003. "Cognitive Maps and the Construction of Narrative Space." In *Narrative Theory and the Cognitive Sciences*, edited by David Herman, 214–242. Stanford, CA: CSLI Publications.
Ryan, Marie-Laure. 2004. "Metaleptic Machines." *Semiotica* 150.1/4: 439–469.
Ryan, Marie-Laure. 2005a. "Logique culturelle de la métalepse, ou la métalepse dans tous ses états." In *Métalepse: Entorses au pacte de la représentation*, edited by John Pier and Jean-Marie Schaeffer, 201–223. Paris: Éditions de l'École des Hautes Études en Sciences Sociales.

Ryan, Marie-Laure. 2005b. "On the Theoretical Foundations of Transmedial Narratology." In *Narratology beyond Literary Criticism: Mediality, Disciplinarity*, edited by Jan Christoph Meister, 1–23. Berlin and New York, NY: De Gruyter.

Ryan, Marie-Laure. 2006. *Avatars of Story*. Minneapolis, MN and London: University of Minnesota Press.

Ryan, Marie-Laure. 2014. "Space." In *Handbook of Narratology: Volume 2*, edited by Peter Hühn, Jan Christoph Meister, John Pier, and Wolf Schmid, 2nd ed., 796–811. Berlin and Boston, MA: De Gruyter.

Ryan, Marie-Laure. 2015 [2001]. *Narrative as Virtual Reality 2: Revisiting Immersion and Interactivity in Literature and Electronic Media*. 2nd ed. Baltimore, MD: Johns Hopkins University Press.

Ryan, Marie-Laure, Kenneth Foote, and Maoz Azaryahu. 2016. *Narrating Space / Spatializing Narrative: Where Narrative Theory and Geography Meet*. Columbus, OH: The Ohio State University Press.

Said, Edward W. 1994 [1978]. *Orientalism*. 25th Anniversary Edition with a New Preface by the Author. New York, NY: Vintage Books.

Saint-Gelais, Richard. 2011. *Fictions transfuges: La transfictionalité et ses enjeux*. Paris: Éditions du Seuil.

Sandberg, Eric. 2017. "Hilary Mantel's *Wolf Hall(s)* and the Circulation of Cultural Prestige." In *Adaptation, Awards Culture, and the Value of Prestige*, edited by Coleen Kennedy-Karpat and Eric Sandberg, 55–73. London et al.: Palgrave Macmillan.

Sargent, Lyman Tower. 1994. "The Three Faces of Utopianism Revisited." *Utopian Studies* 5.1: 1–37.

Scheffel, Michael. 1997. *Formen des selbstreflexiven Erzählens: Eine Typologie und sechs exemplarische Analysen*. Tübingen: Max Niemeyer Verlag.

Schiffrin, Deborah. 1978. *A Quantitative Analysis of the Historical Present Tense in Narrative*. Washington D.C.: ERIC Clearinghouse. Microfilm.

Schiffrin, Deborah. 1981. "Tense Variation in Narrative." *Language* 57.1: 45–62.

Schlenker, Philippe. 2004. "Context of Thought and Context of Utterance: A Note on Free Indirect Discourse and the Historical Present." In *Mind & Language* 19.3: 279–304.

Schneider, Ralf. 2012. "Blending and the Study of Narrative: An Introduction." In *Blending and the Study of Narrative: Approaches and Applications*, edited by Ralf Schneider and Marcus Hartner, 1–30. Berlin and Boston, MA: De Gruyter.

Schofield, Dennis. 1996. "The Second Person: A Point of View?" *Colloquy: Text – Theory – Critique* 1: 67–86.

Scholes, Lucy. 2016. "Book Review: Ian McEwan's *Nutshell* Is a Thriller Narrated by a Foetus." *The National*, September 8. Accessed August 31, 2020. https://www.thenational.ae/arts-culture/book-review-ian-mcewan-s-nutshell-is-a-thriller-narrated-by-a-foetus-1.212363.

Scholes, Robert. 1980. "Language, Narrative, and Anti-Narrative." *Critical Inquiry* 7.1: 204–212.

Scholz, Bernhard F. 1998. "Bakhtin's Concept of 'Chronotope': The Kantian Connection." In *The Contexts of Bakhtin: Philosophy, Authorship, Aesthetics*, edited by David Sheperd, 141–172. Amsterdam: Harwood Academic Publishers.

Schopf, Andreas. 1991. "The Analysis and Reconstruction of the Temporal Structure of Narrative Texts." In *The Function of Tense in Texts*, edited by Jadranka Gvozdanović and Theo A. J. Janssen, 237–253. Amsterdam et al.: Royal Netherlands Academy of Arts and Sciences.

Segal, Erwin M. 1995. "Narrative Comprehension and the Role of Deictic Shift Theory." In *Deixis in Narrative: A Cognitive Science Perspective*, edited by Judith F. Duchan, Gail A. Bruder, and Lynne E. Hewitt, 3–17. Hillsdale, NJ and Hove: Lawrence Erlbaum Associates.

Segal, Erwin M., Gregory Miller, Carol Hosenfeld, Aurora Mendelsohn, William Russel, James Julian, Alyssa Greene, and Joseph Delphonse. 1997. "Person and Tense in Narrative Interpretation." *Discourse Processes* 24: 271–307.

Semino, Elena. 2011. "Deixis and Fictional Minds." *Style* 45.3: 418–440.

Sewell, Kenneth W., and Amy M. Williams. 2002. "Broken Narratives: Trauma, Metaconstructive Gaps, and the Audience of Psychotherapy." *Journal of Constructivist Psychology* 15: 205–218.

Shang, Biwu. 2017. "Ethical Literary Criticism and Ian McEwan's *Nutshell*." *Critique: Studies in Contemporary Fiction* 59.2: 142–153.

Simpson, Paul. 2014. "Just What Is Narrative Urgency?" *Language and Literature* 23.1: 3–22.

Simpson, Philip. 2010. "Noir and the Psycho Thriller." In *A Companion to Crime Fiction*, edited by Charles J. Rzepka and Lee Horsley, 187–197. Malden, MA: Wiley-Blackwell.

Sinding, Michael. 2008 [2005]. "Foregrounding." In *The Routledge Encyclopedia of Narrative Theory*, edited by David Herman, Manfred Jahn, and Marie-Laure Ryan, 2nd ed., 180. London and New York, NY: Routledge.

Singer, Jerome L. 1994. "Imaginative Play and Adaptive Development." In *Toys, Play, and Child Development*, edited by Jeffrey H. Goldstein, 6–26. Cambridge: Cambridge University Press.

Smith, Carlota S. 2008. "Time With and Without Tense." In *Time and Modality*, edited by Jacqueline Guéron and Jacqueline Lecarme, 227–249. Heidelberg and Dordrecht: Springer.

Snyder, Katherine V. 2011. "'Time to Go': The Post-Apocalpytic and the Post-Traumatic in Margaret Atwood's *Oryx and Crake*." *Studies in the Novel* 43.4: 470–489.

Sommer, Roy. 2000. "Funktionsgeschichten: Überlegungen zur Verwendung des Funktionsbegriffs in der Literaturwissenschaft und Anregungen zu seiner terminologischen Differenzierung." *Literaturwissenschaftliches Jahrbuch* 41: 319–341.

Sommer, Roy. 2001. *Fictions of Migration: Ein Beitrag zur Theorie und Gattungstypologie des zeitgenössischen interkulturellen Romans in Großbritannien*. Trier: Wissenschaftlicher Verlag Trier.

Sommer, Roy. 2007. "'Contextualism' Revisited: A Survey (and Defence) of Postcolonial and Intercultural Narratologies." *JLT: Journal of Literary Theory* 1.1: 61–79.

Sommer, Roy. 2010. "Methoden strukturalistischer und narratologischer Ansätze." In *Methoden der literatur- und kulturwissenschaftlichen Textanalyse*, edited by Vera Nünning and Ansgar Nünning, 91–108. Stuttgart and Weimar: J. B. Metzler.

Sommer, Roy. 2012. "The Merger of Classical and Postclassical Narratologies and the Consolidated Future of Narrative Theory." *DIEGESIS: Interdisciplinary E-Journal for Narrative Research* 1.1: 143–157. Accessed August 31, 2020. https://nbn-resolving.de/urn:nbn:de:hbz:468-20121121-124341-0.

Sommer, Roy. 2013. "Other Stories, Other Minds: The Intercultural Potential of Cognitive Approaches to Narrative." In *Stories and Minds: Cognitive Approaches to Literary Narrative*, edited by Lars Bernaerts, Dirk de Geest, Luc Herman, and Bart Vervaeck, 155–174. Lincoln, NE: University of Nebraska Press.

Sommer, Roy. 2017. "The Future of Narratology's Past: A Contribution to Metanarratology." In *Emerging Vectors of Narratology*, edited by Per Krogh Hansen, John Pier, Philippe Roussin, and Wolf Schmid, 593–608. Berlin and Boston, MA: De Gruyter.
Sommer, Roy. 2019. "Brexit as a Cultural Performance: Towards a Narratology of Social Drama." In *Narrative in Culture*, edited by Astrid Erll and Roy Sommer, 297–324. Berlin and Boston, MA: De Gruyter.
Sommer, Roy. 2020a. "Libraries of the Mind: What Happens after Reading." *DIEGESIS: Interdisciplinary E-Journal for Narrative Research* 9.1: 83–99. Accessed August 31, 2020. https://nbn-resolving.de/urn:nbn:de:hbz:468-20200618-091050-9.
Sommer, Roy. 2020b. "'Reading Form': A Narratological Guide to Textual Analysis." In *Methods of Textual Analysis in Literary Studies: Approaches, Basics, Model Interpretations*, edited by Vera Nünning and Ansgar Nünning, 95–112. Trier: Wissenschaftlicher Verlag Trier.
Spengler, Birgit. 2015. *Literary Spinoffs: Rewriting the Classics – Re-Imagining the Community*. Frankfurt a.M. and New York, NY: Campus Verlag.
Stanzel, Franz K. 1955. *Die typischen Erzählsituationen im Roman: Dargestellt an "Tom Jones," "Moby-Dick," "The Ambassadors," "Ulysses," u.a.* Vienna and Stuttgart: Wilhelm Braumüller Universitäts-Verlagsbuchhandlung.
Stanzel, Franz K. 1959. "Episches Praeteritum, erlebte Rede, historisches Präsens." *Deutsche Vierteljahrsschrift für Literatur und Geistesgeschichte* 33.1: 1–12.
Stanzel, Franz K. 1972 [1964]. *Typische Formen des Romans*. 6th ed. Göttingen: Vandenhoeck & Ruprecht.
Stanzel, Franz K. 1981a. "Teller-Characters and Reflector-Characters in Narrative Theory." *Poetics Today* 2.2. 5–15.
Stanzel, Franz K. 1981b. "Wandlungen des narrativen Diskurses in der Moderne." *In Erzählung und Erzählforschung im 20. Jahrhundert: Tagungsbeiträge eines Symposiums der Alexander von Humboldt-Stiftung Bonn-Bad Godesberg veranstaltet vom 9. bis 14. September 1980 in Ludwigsburg*, edited by Rolf Kloepfer and Gisela Janetzke-Dillner, 371–383. Stuttgart et al.: Verlag W. Kohlhammer.
Stanzel, Franz K. 1986 [1979]. *A Theory of Narrative*. Translated by Charlotte Goedsche. Cambridge et al.: Cambridge University Press.
Stanzel, Franz K. 1995 [1979]. *Theorie des Erzählens*. Göttingen: Vandenhoeck & Ruprecht.
Stein, Karen F. 2010. "Problematic Paradice in *Oryx and Crake*." In *Margaret Atwood: "The Robber Bride," "The Blind Assassin," "Oryx and Crake,"* edited by J. Brooks Bouson, 141–155. London and New York, NY: Continuum.
Steinberg, Günter. 1971. *Erlebte Rede: Ihre Eigenart und ihre Formen in neuerer deutscher, französischer und englischer Literatur – Teil I und II*. Göppingen: Verlag Alfred Kümmerle.
Sternberg, Meir. 1981. "Ordering the Unordered: Time, Space, and Descriptive Coherence." *Yale French Studies* 61: 60–88.
Sternberg, Meir. 1982. "Proteus in Quotation-Land: Mimesis and the Forms of Reported Discourse." *Poetics Today* 3.2: 107–156.
Sternberg, Meir. 1990. "Telling in Time (I): Chronology and Narrative Theory." *Poetics Today* 11.4: 901–948.
Sternberg, Meir. 1992. "Telling in Time (II): Chronology, Teleology, Narrativity." *Poetics Today* 13.3: 463–541.
Sternberg, Meir. 2001. "How Narrativity Makes a Difference." *Narrative* 9.2: 115–122.

Stevenson, Randall. 2008 [2005]. "Modernist Narrative." In *The Routledge Encyclopedia of Narrative Theory*, edited by David Herman, Manfred Jahn, and Marie-Laure Ryan, 2nd ed., 316–321. London and New York, NY: Routledge.

Szymański, Wojchiec. 2014. "Aretino's Eyes: Looking at Paintings in Hilary Mantel's *Wolf Hall*." In *The Art of Literature: Art in Literature*, edited by Magdalena Bleinert, Izabela Curyłło-Klag, and Bożena Kucała, 65–75. Cracow: Jagiellonian University Press.

Tang, Ruoxing. 1997. *"Da – horch! Es summt durch Wind und Schlossen...": Das präsentische Erzählen in der deutschen Kunstballade der ersten Hälfte des 19. Jahrhunderts*. Münster: Lit-Verlag.

Tatishvili, Elene. 2011. "Deictic Implications of Tense Forms in Short Narratives." *AUMLA: Journal of the Australasian Universities Language and Literature Association* 116: 1–27.

Tayler, Christopher. 2009. "*Wolf Hall* by Hilary Mantel – Review." *The Guardian*, May 2. Accessed August 31, 2020. https://www.theguardian.com/books/2009/may/02/wolf-hall-hilary-mantel.

Thomas, Bronwen. 2016. *Narrative: The Basics*. London and New York, NY: Routledge.

Tjupa, Valerij. 2014. "Narrative Strategies." In *Handbook of Narratology: Volume 2*, edited by Peter Hühn, Jan Christoph Meister, John Pier, and Wolf Schmid, 2nd ed., 564–574. Berlin and Boston, MA: De Gruyter.

Todorov, Tzvetan. 2008 [1966]. "The Typology of Detective Fiction." In *Modern Criticism and Theory: A Reader*, edited by David Lodge and Nigel Wood, 3rd ed., 226–232. Harlow et al.: Pearson Longman.

Tomashevsky, Boris. 2002 [1965]. "Story, Plot, and Motivation." In *Narrative Dynamics: Essays on Time, Plot, Closure, and Frames*, edited by Brian Richardson, 164–178. Columbus, OH: The Ohio State University Press.

Tomlinson, John. 1999. *Globalization and Culture*. Chicago, IL: University of Chicago Press.

Treuer, David. 2016. "How Does Ian McEwan Pull Off Hamlet Told by a Fetus in *Nutshell*?" *Los Angeles Times*, September 16. Accessed August 31, 2020. https://www.latimes.com/books/la-ca-jc-mcewan-nutshell-20160907-snap-story.html.

Trexler, Adam. 2015. *Anthropocene Fictions: The Novel in a Time of Climate Change*. Charlottesville, VA and London: University of Virginia Press.

Trexler, Adam, and Adeline Johns-Putra. 2011. "Climate Change in Literature and Literary Criticism." *Wires: Climate Change* 2: 185–200.

Upstone, Sara. 2010. *British Asian Fiction: Twenty-First-Century Voices*. Manchester and New York, NY: Manchester University Press.

Van Dyke, Paul. 1904. "Reginald Pole and Thomas Cromwell: An Examination of the Apologia Ad Carolum Quintum." *The American Historical Review* 9.4: 696–724.

Van Peer, Willie. 2007. "Introduction to Foregrounding: A State of the Art." *Language and Literature* 16.2: 99–104.

Van Peer, Willie, Sonia Zyngier, and Jèmeljan Hakemulder. 2007. "Lines on Feeling: Foregrounding, Aesthetics and Meaning." *Language and Literature* 16.2: 197–213.

Vetters, Carl. 1993. "Temps et deixis." In *Le Temps: De la phrase au texte*, edited by Carl Vetters, 85–115. Lille: Presses Universitaires de Lille.

Vetters, Carl. 1996. *Temps, Aspect et Narration*. Amsterdam and Atlanta, GA: Rodopi.

Viola, André. 1988. "The Irony of Tenses in Nadine Gordimer's *The Conversationist*." *ARIEL: A Review of International English Literature* 19.4: 45–54.

Vogt, Jochen. 2014 [2006]. *Aspekte erzählender Prosa: Eine Einführung in Erzähltechnik und Romantheorie*. 11th ed. Munich: Wilhelm Fink Verlag.

Vogt, Robert. 2015. "Combining Possible-Worlds Theory and Cognitive Theory: Towards an Explanatory Model for Ironic-Unreliable Narration, Ironic-Unreliable Focalization, Ambiguous-Unreliable and Alterated-Unreliable Narration in Literary Fiction." In *Unreliable Narration and Trustworthiness: Intermedial and Interdisciplinary Perspectives*, edited by Vera Nünning, 131–153. Berlin and Boston, MA: De Gruyter.
Vogt, Robert. 2018. *Theorie und Typologie narrativer Unzuverlässigkeit am Beispiel englischsprachiger Erzählliteratur*. Berlin and Boston, MA: De Gruyter.
Vuillaume, Marcel. 1990. *Grammaire temporelle des récits*. Paris: Les Éditions de Minuit.
Wagner, Martin. 2018. *The Narratology of Observation: Studies in a Technique of European Literary Realism*. Berlin and Boston, MA: De Gruyter.
Waterman, David. 2010. "Memory and Cultural Identity: Negotiating Modernity in Nadeem Aslam's *Maps for Lost Lovers*." *Pakistaniaat: A Journal of Pakistan Studies* 2.2: 18–35.
Waterman, David. 2015. *Where Worlds Collide: Pakistani Fiction in the New Millenium*. Oxford: Oxford University Press.
Webber, Bonnie Lynn. 1979. *A Formal Approach to Discourse Anaphora*. New York, NY and London: Garland Publishing.
Weber, Dietrich. 1998. *Erzählliteratur: Schriftwerk · Kunstwerk · Erzählwerk*. Göttingen: Vadenhoeck & Ruprecht.
Weedon, Chris. 2012. "Tropes of Diasporic Life in the Work of Nadeem Aslam." In *Metaphor and Diaspora in Contemporary Writing*, edited by Jonathan P. A. Sell, 20–38. Basingstoke and New York, NY: Palgrave Macmillan.
Weik von Mossner, Alexa. 2017. *Affective Ecologies: Empathy, Emotion and Environmental Narrative*. Columbus, OH: The Ohio State University Press.
Weinrich, Harald. 1970. "Tense and Time." *Archivum Linguisticum* 1: 31–41.
Weinrich, Harald. 2001 [1964]. *Tempus: Besprochene und erzählte Welt*. 6th ed. Munich: C. H. Beck.
Weinstein, Cindy. 2015. *Time, Tense, and American Literature: When Is Now?* Cambridge: Cambridge University Press.
Weixler, Antonius. 2012. "Authentisches erzählen – authentisches Erzählen: Über Authentizität als Zuschreibunsgphänomen und Pakt." In *Authentisches Erzählen: Produktion, Narration, Rezeption*, edited by Antonius Weixler, 1–32. Berlin and Boston, MA: De Gruyter.
Wenzel, Peter. 2001. "Spannung in der Literatur: Grundformen, Ebenen, Phasen." In *Spannung: Studien zur englischsprachigen Literatur*, edited by Raimund Borgmeier and Peter Wenzel, 22–35. Trier: Wissenschaftlicher Verlag Trier.
Wessendorf, Markus. 2018. "A Brechtian Reinterpretation of Thomas Cromwell: Hilary Mantel's Novels *Wolf Hall* and *Bring Up the Bodies*." *The Brecht Yearbook* 43: 230–247.
Wharton, David, and Jeremy Grant. 2005. *Teaching Analysis of Film Language*. London: British Film Institute.
White, R. S. 2019. "Horatio: Loyal Friend of *Hamlet* and *Nutshell*." In: *Hamlet and Emotions*, edited by Paul Megna, Bríd Phillips, and R. S. White, 317–333. London: Palgrave Macmillan.
Wilson, Leigh. 2015. "Historical Representations – Reality Effects: The Historical Novel and the Crisis of Fictionality in the First Decade of the Twenty-First Century." In *The 2000s: A Decade of Contemporary British Fiction*, edited by Nick Bentley, Nick Hubble, and Leigh Wilson, 145–171. London et al.: Bloomsbury.
Wittenberg, David. 2018. "Time." In *The Cambridge Companion to Narrative*, edited by Matthew Garrett, 120–131. Cambridge et al.: Cambridge University Press.

Wolf, Werner. 1993. *Ästhetische Illusion und Illusionsdurchbrechung in der Erzählkunst: Theorie und Geschichte mit Schwerpunkt auf englischem illusionsstörenden Erzählen*. Tübingen: Max Niemeyer Verlag.

Wolf, Werner. 2001. "Formen literarischer Selbstreferenz in der Erzählkunst: Versuch einer Typologie und ein Exkurs zur '*mise en cadre*' und '*mise en reflet/série*.'" In *Erzählen und Erzähltheorie im 20. Jahrhundert*, edited by Jörg Helbig, 49–84. Heidelberg: Universitätsverlag Winter.

Wolf, Werner. 2004. "Aesthetic Illusion as an Effect of Fiction." *Style* 38.3: 325–351.

Wolf, Werner. 2007a. "Description as a Transmedial Mode of Representation: General Features and Possibilities of Realization in Painting, Fiction and Music." In *Description in Literature and Other Media*, edited by Werner Wolf and Walter Bernhart, 1–87. Amsterdam and New York, NY: Rodopi.

Wolf, Werner. 2007b. "Metaisierung als transgenerisches und transmediales Phänomen: Ein Systematisierungsversuch metareferentieller Formen und Begriffe in Literatur und anderen Medien." In *Metaisierung in Literatur und anderen Medien: Theoretische Grundlagen – Historische Perspektiven – Metagattungen – Funktionen*, edited by Janine Hauthal, Julijana Nadj, Ansgar Nünning, and Henning Peters, 25–64. Berlin and New York, NY: De Gruyter.

Wolf, Werner. 2009. "Metareference across Media: The Concept, its Transmedial Potentials and Problems, Main Forms and Functions." In *Metareference across Media: Theory and Case Studies*, edited by Werner Wolf, 1–85. Amsterdam and New York, NY: Rodopi.

Wolf, Werner. 2011. "Preface." In *The Metareferential Turn in Contemporary Arts and Media: Forms, Functions, Attempts at Explanation*, edited by Werner Wolf, v–ix. Amsterdam and New York, NY: Rodopi.

Wolf, Werner. 2014. "Illusion (Aesthetic)." In *Handbook of Narratology: Volume 1*, edited by Peter Hühn, Jan Christoph Meister, John Pier, and Wolf Schmid, 2nd ed., 270–287. Berlin and Boston, MA: De Gruyter.

Wolfson, Nessa. 1978. "A Feature of Performed Narrative: The Conversational Historical Present." *Language Society* 7.2: 215–237.

Wolfson, Nessa. 1979. "The Conversational Historical Present Alternation." *Language* 55.1: 168–182.

Wolfson, Nessa. 1981. "Tense-Switching in Narrative." *Language and Style: An International Journal* 14: 226–231.

Wolfson, Nessa. 1982. *CHP: The Conversational Historical Present in American English Narrative*. Dordrecht and Cinnaminson, NJ: Foris Publications.

Worthington, Heather. 2011. *Key Concepts in Crime Fiction*. Basingstoke and New York, NY: Palgrave Macmillan.

Wright, George T. 1974. "The Lyric Present: Simple Present Verbs in English Poems." *PMLA* 89.3: 563–579.

Zabus, Chantal. 1996. "Language, Orality, and Literature." In *New National and Post-Colonial Literatures: An Introduction*, edited by Bruce King, 29–44. Oxford: Clarendon Press.

Zeman, Sonja. 2010. *Tempus und 'Mündlichkeit' im Mittelhochdeutschen. Zur Interdependenz grammatischer Perspektivensetzung und 'Historischer Mündlichkeit' im mittelhochdeutschen Tempussystem*. Berlin and New York, NY: De Gruyter.

Zeman, Sonja. 2018. "Episches Präteritum und Historisches Präsens." In *Grundthemen der Literaturwissenschaft: Erzählen*, edited by Martin Huber and Wolf Schmid, 244–259. Berlin and Boston, MA: De Gruyter.

Zerweck, Bruno. 2019. "The 'Death' of the Unreliable Narrator: Toward a Functional History of Narrative Unreliability." In *Narrative in Culture*, edited by Astrid Erll and Roy Sommer, 215–239. Berlin and Boston, MA: De Gruyter.

Zillmann, Dolf. 1991. "Empathy: Affect from Bearing Witness to the Emotions of Others." In *Responding to the Screen: Reception and Reaction Processes*, edited by Jennings Bryant and Dolf Zillmann, 135–167. Hillsdale, NJ et al.: Larence Erlbaum Associates.

Zint, Nicola. 2001. *Traum und Tempus: Zur Funktion der Textsorte "Traumerzählung" in psychoanalytischen Behandlungsdialogen*. Hamburg: Books on Demand.

Zipfel, Frank. 2001. *Fiktion, Fiktivität, Fiktionalität: Analysen zur Fiktion in der Literatur und zum Fiktionsbegriff in der Literaturwissenschaft*. Berlin: Erich Schmidt Verlag.

Zubin, David A., and Lynne E. Hewitt. 1995. "The Deictic Center: A Theory of Deixis in Narrative." In *Deixis in Narrative: A Cognitive Science Perspective*, edited by Judith F. Duchan, Gail A. Bruder, and Lynne E. Hewitt, 129–155. Hillsdale, NJ and Hove: Lawrence Erlbaum Associates.

Zucchi, Sandro. 2001. "Tense in Fiction." In *Semantic Interfaces: Reference, Anaphora and Aspect*, edited by Carlo Cecchetto, Gennaro Chierchia, and Maria Teresa Guasti, 320–356. Stanford, CA: CSLI Publications.

Zunshine, Lisa. 2006. *Why We Read Fiction: Theory of Mind and the Novel*. Columbus, OH: The Ohio State University Press.

Author Index

Listed here are authors and literary works cited in the text. Pages referenced under the work of an author are not cited again under their name.

Abbott, H. Porter 118n61
Abish, Walter
– *Alphabetical Africa* 71–72
Ardagh, Philip 1
Arias, Rosario 170
Aslam, Nadeem 215, 315
– *Maps for Lost Lovers* 15, 16, 17, 128, 146, 194–217, 280, 302, 303, 304, 305, 315, 318
Assmann, Corinna 205, 208n21
Atwood, Margaret 1, 5
– *Hag-Seed: The Tempest Retold* 146
– *Handmaid's Tale, The* 75–76, 105–106
– *Heart Goes Last, The* 1
– *MaddAddam* 174
– *MaddAddam* trilogy (complete) 174, 180
– *Oryx and Crake* 15, 17, 66n8, 70, 146, 173–193, 200, 302, 303, 317, 318
– *Testaments, The* 5, 6
– *Year of the Flood, The* 174
Augé, Marc 176, 221
Avanessian, Armen, and Anke Hennig 6, 26, 27, 28, 29, 36, 41, 42n36, 43n38, 87n9, 89n11, 105, 111, 112, 120, 171–172, 307

Bakhtin, Mikhail M. 122, 124–125, 127, 304
Bal, Mieke 143
Banfield, Ann 24n6
Barthes, Roland 22n5, 30n15
Beckett, Samuel
– *Unnamable, The* 65
Bekhta, Natalya 306
Bennett, Jane 184
Benveniste, Émile 31–32, 33
Berend, Alice
– *Babette Bomberling's Bridegrooms* 22, 23
Bever, Thomas G. 232
Bode, Christoph 253
Bolt, Robert
– *Man for All Seasons, A* 156, 157n14

Bonheim, Helmut 128–129
Bortolussi, Marisa, and Peter Dixon 56–57
Bourne, Craig, and Emily Caddick Bourne 46–49
Boyle, Danny
– *T2 Trainspotting* 278n4
Bracke, Astrid 176n7
Bradbury, Malcolm
– *History Man, The* 154n7
Brewer, William F., and Edward H. Lichtenstein 237, 238n23
Broich, Ulrich 144n5
Bronzwaer, W. J. M. 24n7
Brook-Rose, Christine
– *Amalgamemnon* 66
Brosch, Renate 156, 157, 162, 163, 170–171
Bühler, Karl 86
Burt, Guy
– *Clock Without Hands, A* 127n78
Butler, Halle
– *New Me, The* 108–109
Butor, Michel 130
Butt, Nadia 216n26

Calvino, Italo
– *If on a Winter's Night a Traveler* 91–92
Caracciolo, Marco 179, 193, 247–248, 258, 259, 260, 261, 266, 270, 272n19
Casparis, Christian Paul 40n32, 50, 68n12, 74n23, 143n4
Chambers, Claire 207–208
Chatman, Seymour 35, 41n34, 100, 114n56, 128–129, 270n17
Childs, Peter 284n12, 285n13
Childs, Peter, and James Green 206n17
Coetzee, J. M. 1, 5
– *Waiting for the Barbarians* 41n34
Cohn, Dorrit 9, 35–36, 38–39, 42n36, 54, 61n15, 66n7, 75n24, 109, 111, 159, 301, 318

https://doi.org/10.1515/9783110708134-016

Collins, Suzanne
- *Catching Fire* 2
- *Hunger Games, The* 2
- 'Hunger Games' series (complete) 5
- *Mockingjay* 2

Culler, Jonathan 73n21, 144n6, 179, 206–207
Currie, Gregory 47n48
Currie, Mark 9, 11, 47n47, 48–50, 238n24

Dalcher, Christina
- *Vox* 1

Damsteegt, Theo 7n14, 42n36
Dangarembga, Tsitsi
- *This Mournable Body* 5, 92n18

Davies, Ben 269, 277
Dawson, Paul 280, 291
De Botton, Alain
- *Course of Love, The* 133

De Groot, Jerome 157n13
Defoe, Daniel
- *Robinson Crusoe* 91

Del Valle Alcalá, Roberto 296
DelConte, Matt 42n35
Dickens, Charles 74n23, 109
- *David Copperfield* 74–75, 100–101, 103

Doležel, Lubomír 276
Donoghue, Emma
- *Room* 3, 15, 17, 44n40, 141, 242n4, 257–275, 302, 303, 305, 314n15, 318

Dore, Margherita 259n4, 261n6, 262n9, 270n16
Doshi, Avni
- *Burnt Sugar* 1, 5

Doyle, Sir Arthur Conan 255
Duras, Marguerite
- *L'Amant* 96n25

Eco, Umberto 85
Ellis, Bret Easton
- *Glamorama* 265n13

Ellmann, Lucy
- *Ducks, Newsburyport* 5

Elton, Geoffrey R. 152
Enright, Anne 1
Epstein, Mikhail 125
Evaristo, Bernadine
- *Girl, Woman, Other* 5, 6, 308

Faulkner, William
- "Rose for Emily, A" 306

Fielding, Henry
- *Shamela* 77–78, 294, 296
- *Tom Jones: The History of a Foundling* 134

Fleischman, Suzanne 9, 33–34, 36, 58, 131, 301, 318
Fludernik, Monika 4n7, 6, 9, 24n7, 27n10, 30n14, 31n17, 32, 39–40, 41, 44, 46, 54–55, 56, 66, 67, 73, 90–91, 92n18, 102–103, 104, 162, 178–179, 229, 244n7, 279n5, 287, 301
Flynn, Gillian
- *Gone Girl* 1

Fowler, Roger 169
Frank, Michael C. 122n69
Freeman, Mark 288
Frey, John R. 24n8
Funk, Wolfgang 163n23

Galgut, Damon
- *In a Strange Room* 3

Gass, William H. 4, 6
Genette, Gérard 8, 10, 35, 37–38, 59, 111, 112, 114, 116, 119, 126n76, 127, 141, 143, 159n17, 161n19, 163, 204, 234n16, 235n17, 255–256, 289n18, 294–295, 304, 305, 306
Gius, Evelyn 310n9
Goethe, Johann Wolfgang von
- *Wilhelm Meister's Apprenticeship* 22

Goetsch, Paul 285n14
Goodman, Nelson 81
Gordimer, Nadine 6n9
Green, Keith 86
Greenblatt, Stephen 155
Gumbrecht, Hans Ulrich 315–317
Gymnich, Marion 151–152, 155n8, 283n10, 285n14, 289–290

Haddon, Mark
- *Curious Incident of the Dog in the Night-Time, The* 60, 133–134, 242n4

Hamburger, Käte 11–12, 21–25, 30, 31, 43, 44n41, 46, 87–88, 171, 229n11
Hanebeck, Julian 256
Haraway, Donna 184

Hawkins, Paula
– *Girl on the Train, The* 5
Healey, Emma
– *Elizabeth Is Missing* 120–121
Heinze, Rüdiger 41n34
Heise, Ursula K. 312n11, 313
Helle, Helle
– *This Should Be Written in the Present Tense* 3, 6
Hensher, Philip 3–4, 6
Herman, David 9–10, 82–83, 85, 93, 96, 106, 107, 123n71, 126, 128–129, 191, 229n10, 301, 304, 309n5
Herman, Luc, and Bart Vervaeck 117
Herrmann, Leonhard 15n24
Hirst, Michael
– *Tudors, The* (television series) 157n14
Hornby, Nick
– *High Fidelity* 103
Horstkotte, Silke 15n24
Howells, Coral Ann 188n23
Huber, Irmtraud 3n2, 6, 7n16, 8, 15n24, 26–27, 29, 39n31, 40–42, 43, 44, 46, 55, 78, 91, 92, 101n31, 102–103, 112, 113, 116n58, 121, 163, 264–266, 307, 310–313, 315
Hühn, Peter 187n21
Hulme, Keri 1
Hyvärinen, Matti, et al. 288

Ishiguro, Kazuo
– *Remains of the Day, The* 166
Ives, Sumner 110n45

Jahn, Manfred 232
James, E. L.
– *Fifty Shades Darker* 1
– *Fifty Shades Freed* 1
– *Fifty Shades of Grey* 1
– *Fifty Shades of Grey* trilogy (complete) 1, 5
James, Erin 177–178, 191–192
James, Marlon
– *Brief History of Seven Killings, A* 110
Jauss, David 7n15, 59n8
Jeffers, Jennifer M. 288n16
Johnston, Andrew James 156n11, 162n22, 171–172

Joyce, James
– *Portrait of the Artist as a Young Man, A* 64, 263–264

Kang, Han
– *Vegetarian, The* 70
Kanwal, Aroosa 194n1
Keen, Suzanne 198, 214n22
Kelly, Aaron 284n12
Kennedy, A. L.
– *Blue Book, The* 92, 96–97
Kepnes, Caroline
– *You* 92
Khan-Cullors, Patrisse, and asha bandele
– *When They Call You a Terrorist: A Black Lives Matter Memoir* 307
Kindt, Tom 196n4
Kindt, Tom, and Hans-Harald Müller 197n5
Koselleck, Reinhart 315
Krauze, Gabriel
– *Who They Was* 5
Kuhn, Roman 245

Lanser, Susan S. 91n17, 280, 289
Lapena, Shari
– *Couple Next Door, The* 141
Le Carré, John
– *Constant Gardener, The* 65n4
Le Guin, Ursula K. 59n8
Le Poidevin, Robin 47n48
Leise, Nina 313
Lemke, Cordula 216
Lively, Penelope 1
Lotman, Jurij M. 183–185, 187

Maček, Dora 282n7
Macrae, Andrea 95n24
Mann, Thomas 4, 12, 17, 318
– *Magic Mountain, The* 1, 2, 318
Mantel, Hilary 6, 152, 155n9, 168
– *Bring Up the Bodies* 3, 7n16, 15, 16, 17, 67, 151–172, 188n22, 222, 302, 304, 305, 318
– *Mirror & the Light, The* 3, 5, 67, 151n1
– "Present Tense, The" 2–3, 6
– Tudor trilogy (complete) 7n16, 67, 151n1

– *Wolf Hall* 3, 7n16, 15, 16, 17, 67, 151–172, 188n22, 222, 302, 304, 305, 318
Margolin, Uri 110n46, 118
Martin, George R.R.
– *A Song of Ice and Fire* series 276
Martínez, Matías 270
Matheson, Richard
– *I Am Legend* 181n13
Maughan, Tim
– *Infinite Detail* 1
Mayer, Sylvia 173–174, 176n7
McAuley, Paul J. 1
McCann, Colum
– *Apeirogon* 5
McCarthy, Cormac
– *Road, The* 181n13
McCarthy, Tom
– *C* 3, 121
McCartney, Paul 1
McDonell, Nick
– *Twelve* 116–117
McEwan, Ian 5, 241n1
– *Nutshell* 15, 17, 141–142, 240–256, 257, 259, 274, 302, 303, 305–306, 314n15, 318
McHale, Brian 153, 175n5, 193, 317
McInerney, Jay
– *Bright Lights, Big City* 92n18
McTaggart, J. Ellis 47, 49
Mehnert, Antonia 176
Meifert-Menhard, Felicitas 254n18
Meisnitzer, Benjamin 27–29, 307
Melville, Herman
– *Moby-Dick; or, The Whale* 88–89
Mendilow, A. A. 49n51
Mengiste, Maaza
– *Shadow King, The* 5
Menhard, Felicitas 231n12
Meretoja, Hanna 72n19
Mesler, Cory
– *Talk: A Novel in Dialogue* 135–136
Meyer, Stephenie
– *Twilight* series 276
Miall, David S., and Don Kuiken 73n22, 215
Middleton, Stanley 6n9
Mildorf, Jarmila 57n6

Mitchell, David
– *Bone Clocks, The* 113–115, 117
Miyahara, Kazunari 1, 154n7
Moggach, Deborah 1
Moody, Rick
– "Grid, The" 41n34
Morgenstern, Naomi 260n5
Morton, Timothy 173n2, 184, 193
Mosher, Harold F. 132, 189–190
Mullan, John 65n4, 74n23
Müller, Günther 114n56
Müller, Wolfgang G. 242n3, 252n15
Murakami, Haruki
– *Hard-Boiled Wonderland and the End of the World* 70, 76

Nabokov, Vladimir
– *Lolita* 60
Nelles, William 126n76
Neumann, Anne Waldron 41n34
Neumann, Birgit, and Ansgar Nünning 99
Nielsen, Henrik Skov 265n13
Norrick, Neal R. 298n26
North, Michael 3n2
Nowotny, Helga 311, 312n11, 316n17
Nünning, Ansgar 59, 85n4, 101, 103n33, 152–155, 165, 166, 174n3, 187–188, 244n8, 246n11, 315
Nünning, Ansgar, and Vera Nünning 287–288
Nünning, Vera 214
Nünning, Vera, and Ansgar Nünning 58n7, 62n16, 140n1, 199n8, 226n6, 230–231, 234n15

O'Connor, Siobhan 160
O'Farrel, Maggie
– *I Am, I Am, I Am: Seventeen Brushes With Death* 307
O'Keeffe, Bernard 285, 288n16
O'Neill, Louise
– *Asking for It* 1
Obioma, Chigozie
– *Orchestra of Minorities, An* 5
Ochs, Elinor, and Lisa Capps 115n57
Ohme, Andreas 66n5

Olson, Greta 269
Ondaatje, Michael 6n9

Parey, Armelle 276–277
Pepper, Andrew 236n21
Pesso-Miquel, Catherine 194n1
Petersen, Jürgen H. 6, 34n23, 42–45, 93n22, 105, 307
Pfister, Manfred 144n5
Pflugmacher, Torsten 131n84
Phelan, James 34n23, 36, 40, 59n10, 122–123, 126, 234n16, 235n17, 257, 259, 264, 266, 270n17
Phelan, James, and Peter J. Rabinowitz 98n28, 227
Pierre, DBC 1
Poe, Edgar Allan 255
Powers, Richard
– *Overstory, The* 2, 131–133
Pratt, Marie-Louise 196
Prince, Gerald 37, 130
Pullman, Philip 3–4, 6

Ramos, Joanne
– *Farm, The* 2
Rauh, Gisa 86–89
Reichl, Susanne 202n12, 203n13
Richardson, Brian 92n18, 184n18, 243n6
Richardson, Samuel 78, 293, 294, 296n24, 304
– *Pamela; or, Virtue Rewarded* 78, 293, 294
Ricœur, Paul 45–46
Rimmon-Kenan, Shlomith 35, 112, 117, 119n62, 159n17, 237n22, 264
Robbe-Grillet, Alain 72n19, 130
– *Jealousy* 44n41, 130–131, 133
Rohde, Christiane 24n8
Rosa, Hartmut 311
Rousselot, Elodie 154n6
Rowling, Joanne K.
– *Harry Potter* series 276
Rubik, Margarete 271n18
Rubin, Jay 70n17
Rushkoff, Douglas 312
Russo, Meredith
– *Birthday: A Love Story Eighteen Years in the Making* 2, 308

Ryan, Marie-Laure 41n34, 94–96, 98, 115n57, 118n61, 192n28, 227, 256

Sacks, Michelle
– *All the Lost Things* 242n4
Saint-Gelais, Richard 277n3
Sargent, Lyman Tower 175
Sarraute, Nathalie 130
Scholes, Robert 35
Segal, Erwin M. 94
Segal, Erwin M., et al. 95n24
Seiffert, Rachel
– *Dark Room, The* 2
Selvon, Samuel
– *Lonely Londoners, The* 110
Shakespeare, William
– *Hamlet* 241
Simon, Claude 130
Simpson, Paul 227
Simpson, Philip 237
Smaill, Anna
– *Chimes, The* 120–121
Small, Judith
– "Body of Work" 56
Smith, Ali
– *Autumn* 1
– *Hotel World* 76–77
– "Seasonal Quartet" (complete) 1
– *Spring* 1
– *Summer* 1
– *Winter* 1
Smith, Zadie
– *NW* 71
– *Swing Time* 69
Sommer, Roy 17n25, 60, 61, 83–85, 127n79, 167, 188n22, 195–198, 217
Stanzel, Franz K. 8, 24, 35, 59, 65n2, 89, 90, 92n19, 106, 120, 158, 200, 202n11, 228, 264, 289n18, 304, 305, 306
Sternberg, Meir 58n7, 132, 238
Sterne, Laurence
– *Life and Opinions of Tristram Shandy, Gentleman, The* 102–103
Swift, Graham 1
– *Light of Day, The* 2, 69

Tang, Ruoxing 24n8
Tatishvili, Elene 91n16, 112n52, 205n15
Thackeray, William Makepeace
– *Vanity Fair: A Novel Without a Hero* 134–135
Todorov, Tzvetan 237, 253n17, 255n20

Tóibín, Colm
– *Testament of Mary, The* 91
Trexler, Adam 173n1
Trexler, Adam, and Adeline Johns-Putra 173n1
Twain, Mark 110
Tyler, Anne
– *Redhead by the Side of the Road* 5

Unsworth, Barry 6n9

Van Dyke, Paul 155n10
Van Peer, Willie 72
Vetters, Carl 31n16, 33n21, 34
Vogt, Jochen 22n5
Vogt, Robert 234–235, 269
Vuillaume, Marcel 41n33, 66n5

Waterman, David 196n3
Watson, S. J.
– *Before I Go to Sleep* 120–121
Weber, Dietrich 112n52
Weinrich, Harald 30–31, 32–33, 34, 42–43, 45
Weinstein, Cindy 126n77
Weixler, Antonius 270
Welsh, Irvine
– *Dead Men's Trousers* 15, 17, 278, 279, 296–299, 302, 304
– *Porno* 278, 279
– *Skagboys* 15, 17, 146, 278–296, 299, 302, 304
– *Trainspotting* 278, 279, 282n7, 284n11, 286n12, 286, 288n16
– 'Trainspotting' novels (complete) 110, 278–279, 280, 298, 299
Whitehead, Colson
– *Zone One* 181n13
Wilde, Oscar
– *Picture of Dorian Gray, The* 65
Wilson, Jacqueline 1
Wilson, Leigh 163n23
Winslow, Don 227n8
– *Border, The* 220n1, 227n8
– *Cartel, The* 220n1, 227n8
– *Cartel* trilogy 220
– *Power of the Dog, The* 15, 16, 17, 128, 215, 218–239, 280, 302, 303, 304, 305, 313–314, 318
– *Savages* 146, 227n8
Wolf, Werner 99, 104n34, 129, 186, 259
Wolfson, Nessa 106
Woolf, Virginia 33
– *Mrs. Dalloway* 22, 65

Zabus, Chantal 203n14
Zarranz, García 262n7
Zeman, Sonja 87n9, 89n12
Zhang, C Pam
– *How Much of These Hills Is Gold* 5
Zillmann, Dolf 215
Zipfel, Frank 112n52, 113n54
Zunshine, Lisa 269n15

Subject Index

Page numbers in italics indicate where technical terms are defined.

absentee narratee 42n35
acceleration 304; ~ in *The Power of the Dog* 220, 225, 226
adeictic tense 44, 90n14
aesthetic illusion 98, *259*, *see also* character-centered illusion, narrative illusion;
~ in *Skagboys* 293
alterations (in Genette's sense) *141*, 235n17
– paralepsis 141n3, *204*
– paralipsis 141n3, *234n16*, 235n17
anachrony *see* analepsis, circumlepsis, hyper-analepsis, hyper-prolepsis, prolepsis, temporal ordering: anachronic presentation of events
analepsis *see* flashback
anisochrony *see* temporal distance between story and narrative discourse
anterior narration *see* prospective narration
Anthropocene fiction *see* climate change fiction
antimimetic narration *see* 'unnatural' narration
aoristic present *see* aspectual present
aporia of synchrony (Avanessian and Hennig) 36, 119
argument (as discourse mode) 128, 129, 130, 133
aspect (as grammatical category) 21n1, 308
aspectual present 27–28
associative storytelling 304; ~ in *Wolf Hall* and *Bring Up the Bodies* 168, 169–171
asynchronous present 111–112; ~ in *Wolf Hall* and *Bring Up the Bodies* 171
authentic narration 121n66, 143; ~ in *Room* 270; ~ in *Wolf Hall* and *Bring Up the Bodies* 163, 172
authorial narrative situation (Stanzel) 65n2, 90n15, 106, 134, 214n23, 289n18, 305; ~ in *Maps for Lost Lovers* 199, 200, 201n9, 202, 216; ~ in *The Power of the Dog* 228, 230, 231

authorial narrator in Lanser's sense *289*;
~ in *Skagboys* 280, 281–282, 289, 290, 291
autobiography 1, 287, 307
autodiegetic narrator 101

ballad 24n8, 33, 68n12
broad present (Gumbrecht) 315–317
broken narrative *287–288*

character-centered illusion *259*;
~ in *Room* 260, 263, 275
character/characterization 176n7, 214n23, *see also* character constellation;
~ in *Nutshell* 241; ~ in *Wolf Hall* and *Bring Up the Bodies* 156–158
– mimetic component of ~ *257n1*; ~ in *Dead Men's Trousers* 298; ~ in *Room* 259, 270
– synthetic component of ~ *257n1*; ~ in *Nutshell* 257, 259
– thematic component of ~ *257n1*
character constellation 195–196; ~ in *Nutshell* 242, 248–250; ~ in *The Power of the Dog* 220; ~ in *Wolf Hall* and *Bring Up the Bodies* 157
character identification 214n23
child narrator 242n4, 247n12;
~ in *Room* 257–275
children's books 5
chronotope
– ~ as a type of narrative progression in the present-tense novel *124–125*, 127, 128, 303, 304; ~ in *The Power of the Dog* 220, 221–228, 230, 236, 239, 313
– ~ in Bakhtin's sense 122, 124, 125, 127, 315, *see also* timespaces
– circumlepsis *127*, 304; ~ in *Maps for Lost Lovers* 216
– comprehensive/timeless ~ *127*
climate change fiction 16, 173–193

cognitive dissonance 17, *258*; ~ in *Room* 258, 259, 261, 273
comment (as discourse mode) 29, 34, 44, 129, 130, 134–135
concurrent narration *see* simultaneous narration
confounding 56–57
consciousness representation *see* free indirect discourse, interior monologue, narrated monologue, psycho-narration, thought report, quoted monologue
contact zone *196*
contextualization (as a means of translation) 203n14
conversational historical present 27n10, 68n12, *106–109*, 136, 286
conversational narrative 17, 27n10, 68n12, 106–109, 136, 145, 286, 291, 296, 298n26, 299
conversational storytelling *see* conversational narrative
coquels *277*, 278, 304
correlations of tense with other narrative strategies and/or phenomena 14–15, 57, 62, 63, 140, *142–148*, 302, 303, 308, *see also* functional interplay; ~ in *Maps for Lost Lovers* 195, 198, 199, 206, 208; ~ in *Oryx and Crake* 180; ~ in *The Power of the Dog* 219; ~ in *Room* 260; ~ in *Skagboys* 286, 291, 296; ~ in *Wolf Hall* and *Bring Up the Bodies* 158, 160, 161, 162, 168, 171
– ancillary strategies 15, *145*, 146, 148, 302; ~ in *Skagboys* 299
– fixed ~ 15, *146*, 147, 148, 302; ~ in *Maps for Lost Lovers* 205; ~ in *Skagboys* 299
– main strategies 15, *145*, 146, 147, 148, 302; ~ in *Dead Men's Trousers* 299
– variable ~ 15, *146–147*, 148, 302
covert narration 60, 97, 133; ~ in *Maps for Lost Lovers* 200, 204; ~ in *Oryx and Crake* 180; ~ in *The Power of the Dog* 220, 228, 229, 230, 236; ~ in *Wolf Hall* and *Bring Up the Bodies* 152, 158, 159
creative writing 7n15, 59n8, 311
crime fiction *see* detective fiction
crisis narrative 174n3

curiosity (as a type of narrative interest) *237*, 238
cushioning 203, *see also* glossing

deceleration 189; ~ in *Maps for Lost Lovers* 215
defamiliarization 248; ~ in *Maps for Lost Lovers* 206, 207, 208n20, 215, 315; ~ in *Nutshell* 248, 252; ~ in *Room* 258, 262
deictic anchoring 48, 90n14, 92
deictic center 22, 86–93
– character as ~ 23, 87, 88, 90; ~ in *The Power of the Dog* 226; ~ in *Wolf Hall* and *Bring Up the Bodies* 162, 165
– – ~ in narrative fiction 86–87
– – ~ in reflector-mode narratives 92
– – ~ in teller-mode narratives 90–92, 264
– narratee as ~ 91–92
– narrator as ~ 23, 87, 88, 90, 192, 264
deictic field *86–87*
– dominant ~ *87*
– embedded ~ *87*
deictic present (Fludernik) *see* deictic use of the fictional present tense
deictic shift 82, *94*, 96, 110n46
– imaginative act of recentering (Ryan) *94*; ~ in *Oryx and Crake* 191, 192
– logical act of recentering (Ryan) *94*
deictic use of the fictional present tense 4n7, 40–41, 46, 55, 66, 67, 89n11, 90, 102–103, 229n11
deixis 21, 39, 48n49, 86, 87, 90n14, 91, 95n24, 304–305, *see also* deictic anchoring, deictic center
– obscure ~ (Brosch); ~ in *Wolf Hall* and *Bring Up the Bodies* 162
description (as discourse mode) 27, 44, 128, 129–133
– dynamic ~ in *Oryx and Crake* 190–193
– filmic ~ 56
descriptized narration (Mosher) 189–190; ~ in *Oryx and Crake* 190
detective fiction 2, 251–256
– hard-boiled detective fiction 236
– police novel 236

Subject Index — 369

– roman noir 236
– whodunit 252, 253n17, 255n20
detemporalization (as a form of tense-switching) 14, 69, *70–71*, 76, 79, 80, 302; ~ in *Maps for Lost Lovers* 201, 202n11; ~ in *Skagboys* 296, 299
dialogue 135–136, 146, 289, *see also* direct speech; ~ in *Maps for Lost Lovers* 202, 206; ~ in *Nutshell* 245, 250; ~ in *Room* 267–268
digitization 313, 315
dimension(s) of fictional present-tense narration 13, 62–63
– formal-structural ~ 13–14, 62, 63, 64–80, 147, 301, 310
– functional ~ 13, 14, 62, 63, 79, 81–139, 268, 301
– syntactic ~ 13, 14–15, 62, 63, 79, *140–148*, 301
direct speech 114, 115, 117; ~ in *Nutshell* 250
discours (Benveniste) 31–32
discourse mode 27, 29, 33, 34, 35, 84, 113, 128–136
discourse vs. story *see* story/discourse distinction
discursive present 43
discursive texts vs. narrative texts (Weinrich) 30, 32, 34, 43
double temporality of narrative 36, 46, 65, 100, 104–105, 120, 131, 238
drama (as genre) 21, 27, 33, 34, 144
dramatic irony 231; ~ in *Nutshell* 252; ~ in *Room* 270–271; lack of ~ in *The Power of the Dog* 231
dubbing *202n12*
duration (Genette) 10, 142, 226, *see also* ellipsis, narrative pause, scene/scenic narration, summary
dystopia *175*
dystopian fiction 1, 175

ecological thought (Morton) 173, 177, 193
ellipsis 10; ~ in *Maps for Lost Lovers* 213
embodiment; ~ in *Oryx and Crake* 182
empathy 16, 17, 198, 258, 303; ~ in *Maps for Lost Lovers* 213–217; ~ in *Room* 270,

271; ~ in *Wolf Hall* and *Bring Up the Bodies* 164
– ambassadorial strategic ~ *198*; ~ in *Maps for Lost Lovers* 198
– bounded strategic ~ *198*
– broadcast strategic ~ *198*
– empathetic circle 198, 199, 205, 216
– strategic narrative ~ (in general) 60, 198
epic present 43
epic preterite 12, *21–22*, 23–25, 26, 30, 43, 46, 87–88, 89, 93n22, 171, 229n11
epistolary fiction 78, 293–296
Erzählzeit vs. *erzählte Zeit see* story time vs. discourse time
essayistic novel 43
eventfulness 187
evocative present 75n24
experiencing vs. narrating self (Stanzel) 69, 89, 91, 92n19, 96, 103, 295, 305;
~ in *Dead Men's Trousers* 298;
~ in *Room* 258, 265, 266, 267;
~ in *Skagboys* 290
experientiality 17, *178–180*; ~ in *Oryx and Crake* 193; ~ in *Wolf Hall* and *Bring Up the Bodies* 162
experimental fiction 5, 15, 16, 65, 154, *see also* New Novel, *nouveau roman*, post-modernist fiction
explanation (as discourse mode) 128, 129, 130, 133–134
exposition 161
– delayed ~ 249
extended present (Nowotny) 311–312, 313, 316n17
extradiegetic communicative level 31n17, 35n24, 199n8, 255–256
extradiegetic narrator 231n12, 289;
~ in *Maps for Lost Lovers* 201
eye-dialect 283

fabula 26, 36n26
factual discourse/factuality 11, 13, 23, 26, 29, 35, 287, *see also* non-fictional discourse
fairy tales 32
fallible narration 269

fictional discourse/fictionality 9, 10, 11, 12–13, 21–25, 26, 27, 29, 30, 32–33, 35, 39, 45–50, 86–87, 94, 99, 106, 129n81, 257, 311

fictional discourse vs. factual/non-fictional discourse (differences) 13, 23–24, 30n11, 32, 33n21, 35, 54, 82, 86–87, 145, 153, 301, 307, 309–310, 318

fictionalizing present 43, 105

figural narrative situation (Stanzel) 65n2, 106, 263, 289n18, 305, see also reflector figure, reflector-mode narrative;
~ in Maps for Lost Lovers 200, 202;
~ in The Power of the Dog 228, 229;
~ in Wolf Hall and Bring Up the Bodies 155n8, 158, 162, 163, 168

film script 144, 227, 304, 313

film-script narration 304; ~ in The Power of the Dog 226, 227

fingierte Mündlichkeit see pseudo-orality

first-person narrative/first-person narrative situation (Stanzel) 7, 22n4, 23, 24, 38–39, 43, 59, 60, 61, 65n2, 69, 70, 71, 74, 78, 86n8, 88–91, 92, 96n25, 101n31, 102, 105, 106, 108, 111, 120, 121, 134, 178, 264, 265n13, 295, 303, 305, 306, see also homodiegetic narration;
~ in Nutshell 141, 240–256, 257, 259, 274, 305–306; ~ in Room 257–275;
~ in Skagboys 280–281, 282–288, 291, 299

flashback 10, 65, 67, 126–127, 235;
~ in Maps for Lost Lovers 200, 205, 209–210, 215–216; ~ in Oryx and Crake 181, 188–189; ~ in Wolf Hall and Bring Up the Bodies 161

flashforward 10, 65, 67, 126, 127, 235;
~ in Wolf Hall and Bring Up the Bodies 160n18

focalization 57, 143–144, 148, 295, 302
– character-focalizer/character-bound focalizer (Bal) 231n12; ~ in Maps for Lost Lovers 204; ~ in Room 266; lack of ~ in Maps for Lost Lovers 201
– external ~ in Genette's sense 125, 143
– external ~ in Bal's and Rimmon-Kenan's sense, identified as zero-~ by Genette 117n60, 143; ~ in Wolf Hall and Bring Up the Bodies 159, 163
– internal ~ 42n36, 92, 96, 117n60, 125, 304;
~ in Maps for Lost Lovers 194, 198, 199, 204, 206, 208, 209; ~ in Oryx and Crake 180, 192; ~ in The Power of the Dog 229, 231; ~ in Skagboys 282; ~ in Wolf Hall and Bring Up the Bodies 152, 155n8, 158, 159, 162, 163, 168, 170
– multiple ~ in The Power of the Dog 226, 227
– narrator-focalizer (Bal) 202

foregrounding of tense 13–14, 72–78, 80
– alternate ~ 14, 73, 74–76, 80; ~ in Oryx and Crake 181, 302
– metanarrative ~ 14, 74, 77–78, 80, 302
– paratextual ~ 14, 74, 76–77, 80, 302, 310
– typographical ~ 14, 73, 76, 80, 302

form-to-function mapping 56, 58, 82, 136, see also function-to-form mapping

free indirect discourse 24n7, 39, 144;
~ in Nutshell 247; ~ in Oryx and Crake 189

frequency (Genette) 10, 143, see also iterative narration, repeating narration, singulative narration

function of fictional tense (textual and cognitive) 14–15, 53, 54, 56, 57–58, 61, 62, 63, 67, 73, 81–139, 141–142, 144, 145, 146, 147, 148, 302, 307, 317
– communicative ~ 14, 83, 106–110, 128, 148, 302; ~ in Skagboys 286
– concept of ~ 83–85
– dominant ~ 14, 141, 147, 148; ~ in Nutshell 274, 302, 303; ~ in Room 264, 274
– immersive ~ 14, 83, 94–98, 109n44, 122, 148, 302; ~ in Oryx and Crake 191;
~ in Room 266, 268, 273, 274;
~ in Skagboys 296; ~ in Wolf Hall and Bring Up the Bodies 168, 170
– metareferential ~ 14, 68, 72, 83, 98–106, 110, 120, 122, 136, 138, 148, 302;
~ in Nutshell 246–247
– non-recurring ~ 14, 141, 147, 148, 302;
~ in Nutshell 243
– recessive ~ 14, 141, 147, 148, 302, 303;
~ in Room 264, 266, 275
– recurring ~ 14, 141, 147, 148, 302

– referential ~ 14, 68, 83, *86–93*, 98, 102n32, 103–104, 109n44, 110, 120, 122, 136, 138, 141, 148, 264, 279, 296, 299, 302; ~ in *Maps for Lost Lovers* 205, 206, 207, 210, 216; ~ in *Nutshell* 240, 246; ~ in *Oryx and Crake* 182; ~ in *The Power of the Dog* 221, 224, 228; ~ in *Room* 266; ~ in *Wolf Hall* and *Bring Up the Bodies* 160, 162, 165, 168
– rhetorical ~ 14, 83, *121–128*, 136, 138, 148, 302; ~ in *Maps for Lost Lovers* 212, 213, 217; ~ in *The Power of the Dog* 227; ~ in *Skagboys* 296
– synchronizing ~ 14, 83, *110–119*, 120, 122, 123, 127, 136, 141, 148, 302, 303, 314n15; ~ in *Dead Men's Trousers* 297, 299; ~ in *Nutshell* 240–241, 246, 249–250, 253–254, 274; ~ in *Room* 266, 267, 268, 272, 274, 275; ~ in *Skagboys* 291, 296
– thematic ~ 14, 70, 83, *119–121*, 122, 127, 136, 148, 302, 303; ~ in *Maps for Lost Lovers* 207, 216; ~ in *Nutshell* 240–241, 246, 249–250, 274; ~ in *Oryx and Crake* 188; ~ in *Room* 263, 264, 274
– transmedial 309
– transmodal ~ 14, 83, *128–136*, 138, 148, 302, 303; ~ in *Maps for Lost Lovers* 205, 216; ~ in *Nutshell* 251; ~ in *Oryx and Crake* 189; ~ in *Room* 266, 273, 274, 275; ~ in *Wolf Hall* and *Bring Up the Bodies* 160, 161
function-to-form mapping 56, 85, *see also* form-to-function mapping
functional interplay (of the fictional present with other narrative strategies and/or phenomena) 14–15, 62, 63, 140, *142–147*, 148, 180, 302, 314n15, 318; ~ in *The Power of the Dog* 221, 225, 236; ~ in *Room* 270; ~ in *Skagboys* and *Dead Men's Trousers* 299
functional matrix of present-tense narration 14, *136–139*, 140, 268, 302, 303, 307, 308, 310, 314n15
future narrative 253, 254n18
fuzzy temporality (Herman) 126, 304

garden-path effect 231–232; ~ in *The Power of the Dog* 232–235
genre fiction 15
genre theory 16, 17, 306
Gleichzeitigkeitsaporie see aporia of synchrony
glossing 203, *see also* cushioning
gnomic present 72, 134; ~ in *Maps for Lost Lovers* 205
'grammatical' fallacy 13, 53, *54*, 111, 301

heterodiegetic narration 59–60, 61, 70, 87, 88, 89, 92, 101, 117, 119, 133, 143, 231n12, 263, 289, *see also* third-person narrative; ~ in *Maps for Lost Lovers* 199, 200; ~ in *Oryx and Crake* 180, 192; ~ in *Skagboys* 280, 282, 287, 289, 290–291, 299; ~ in *Wolf Hall* and *Bring Up the Bodies* 158, 159, 161, 163, 169
histoire (Benveniste) 31–32
historical consciousness (Koselleck) 315–316
historical fiction 2, 5, 15, 16, 17, 67, 144, 151–172
– documentary ~ (Nünning) 153, 168
– historiographic metafiction (Nünning) 153n5
– metahistorical fiction (Nünning) 153n5
– realist ~ (Nünning) 153, 168, 169
– revisionist ~ (Nünning) *152–155*, 157, 165, 166
historical present 4, 12, *23–24*, 27–28, 38–39, 41, 68n12, 70, 72, 74, 96n25, 109, *see also* conversational historical present
historical thought *see* historical consciousness
homodiegetic narration 34n23, 43n39, 59, 61, 69, 70n17, 88, 91n16, 96n25, 101, 103, 114, 115, 117, 119, 120, 143, 231n12, 248, 289, 305, *see also* first-person narrative situation; ~ in *Room* 257; ~ in *Skagboys* 280, 282, 284, 285n13, 286, 289, 290, 299
hybrid genre 307
hyper-analepsis *127*, 304; ~ in *Maps for Lost Lovers* 216

hyper-present (Heise) 312n11
hyper-prolepsis *127*, 304
hypothetical focalization *229*

idiolect 263–264; ~ in *Room* 258–259; 261–262; ~ in *Skagboys* 284–285, 286, 296
I-here-now origo 86, 87, 88, 89, 96, 97
imaginary present 43; ~ in *Nutshell* 141–142
immediacy 28, 40, 56, 57, 114–115, 117, 120, 141, 143, 294, 302, 317; ~ in *Maps for Lost Lovers* 212, 217; ~ in *Oryx and Crake* 175, 192, 193; ~ in *The Power of the Dog* 235; ~ in *Room* 266–267, 272, 273, 274; ~ in *Skagboys* 290, 292, 296, 299; ~ in *Wolf Hall* and *Bring Up the Bodies* 162
immersion 17, 67, *94–95*, 96, 97, 98, 303, see also deictic shift
– emotional ~ in *Room* 268
– spatial ~ 317
– spatiotemporal ~ 60, 177, 178, 317; ~ in *Oryx and Crake* 190–192
– temporal ~ 317; ~ in *The Power of the Dog* 227, 228, 239; ~ in *Wolf Hall* and *Bring Up the Bodies* 171
implied author 123n71
indirect speech, see also free indirect discourse; ~ in *Room* 268; ~ in *Skagboys* 286
instabilities (Phelan) *123*
intercalated narration see interpolated narration
intercultural fiction 16, 110, 194, *195–217*, see also multicultural fiction, transcultural fiction
intercultural mind *197*, 198; ~ in *Maps for Lost Lovers* 217
intercultural understanding 16, 196, 197, see also intercultural mind; ~ in *Maps for Lost Lovers* 198, 205, 216
interior monologue 38–39, 40, 42, 44, 55, 56, 70, 92, 109, 144, 188n24; ~ in *Oryx and Crake* 189; ~ in *The Power of the Dog* 219, 233, 234; ~ in *Room* 264–265
intermediality 145, 148
intermittent use of the present tense 4n7, 5, 12, 74–75

interpolated narration 37, 116n59, 294–295, 296
intertextuality 17, 144, 146, 148, 252n14; ~ in *Nutshell* 241, 251
intradiegetic communicative level 31n17, 35n24, 199n8, 255
intradiegetic narrator 231n12
I-*origo* (Hamburger) 22–23
I-*origines* (Hamburger) 22–23
irony, see also dramatic irony; ~ in *Wolf Hall* and *Bring Up the Bodies* 165n25
isochrony *114*, 146; ~ in *Nutshell* 247; ~ in *The Power of the Dog* 225, 226
iterative narration 10; ~ in *Nutshell* 245
iterative present 245, 262

literary dialect *110*; ~ in *Skagboys* 282–285, 286, 289, 299
literary fiction 5, 15, 176n7, 242

mediacy (Stanzel) 100, 103n33, 135, 235, 242n3
mediality 26, 99, 104
medialization (of the novel) 314
mediating consciousness (Margolin) 118
medieval narrative 27n10, 33, 68n12, 109
– medieval romance 186
memoir 307
mesh (Morton) 184
meta-awareness (Wolf) 104n34, 259
metafiction 68, 153n5
metaization 104
metalepsis (Genette) 143, *256*
– discourse ~ see rhetorical ~
– figurative ~ 143
– immersive ~ *256*
– narratorial ~ see immersive ~
– ontological ~ 143
– rhetorical ~ *256*
metanarration 3, 67–68, 77–78, *99*, 102, 103n33, 104, 143, 148, 302; ~ in *Nutshell* 242, 246–248, 257
metareference 98–99
– fictio-~ *99*, 143
– fictum-~ *99*, 143
mimesis (Ricœur) 45

mimesis of narration 59n12, 101, 102, 106, 120, 121, 143; ~ in *Nutshell* 244
mimetic dimension of narrative (Phelan) 98; ~ in *Maps for Lost Lovers* 211; ~ in *Wolf Hall* and *Bring Up the Bodies* 162
mind-reading 269n15; ~ in *Room* 269
mind-style 169, 304; ~ in *Wolf Hall* and *Bring Up the Bodies* 169–170
model *for* the world (McHale) 175, 317
model *of* the world (McHale) 175n5
model reader 85
modernist fiction 26, 33, 126
multicultural fiction *197*
'multifunctionality argument' 54–55, 58
multifunctionality of fictional tense usage 140–142, 145, 147, 148, 264n11, 303, 314n15, *see also* functional matrix of present-tense narration; ~ in *Maps for Lost Lovers* 199, 217; ~ in *Nutshell* 241; ~ in *Room* 274, 275
multimodal novel 309
multiperspectivity 62n16, 140n1, 144, 148, 302; ~ in *Maps for Lost Lovers* 199; ~ in *The Power of the Dog* 220, 221, 225, 236, 239; ~ in *Skagboys* 282, 288
– multiperspective focalization 144, 199n8; ~ in *The Power of the Dog* 226; ~ in *Skagboys* 280
– multiperspective narration 144, 199n8, 226n6; ~ in *The Power of the Dog* 231; ~ in *Skagboys* 280, 288, 314
– multiperspective structure 144, 226n6

narrated monologue 44, 265; ~ in *Oryx and Crake* 189; ~ in *Wolf Hall* and *Bring Up the Bodies* 159
– self-~ 109
narrating time vs. narrated time *see* story time vs. discourse time
narration vs. focalization 24n7, 113, 118, 204 229, *see also* teller-mode narrative vs. reflector-mode narrative
narrative analysis 279
narrative as discourse mode 29, 34, 43, 53, 128, 129
narrative authority 17, 144, 231n12, 302, 308; ~ in *Skagboys* 279, 289–292, 299

narrative design 2, 8, 59, 60n14, 61, 63, 83, 147, 197, 307; ~ of *Oryx and Crake* 180; ~ of *The Power of the Dog* 221; ~ of *Room* 260, 274
narrative distance 142–143, 302, *see also* temporal distance; ~ in *The Power of the Dog* 225; ~ in *Wolf Hall* and *Bring Up the Bodies* 169
narrative dynamics 122–123, *see also* readerly dynamics, textual dynamics; ~ of *Maps for Lost Lovers* 199; ~ of *Oryx and Crake* 184, 187; ~ of *The Power of the Dog* 220n1
– chronotopic ~ *see* chronotope as a type of narrative progression in the present-tense novel
– topochronic ~ *see* topochrone
narrative illusion (in Nünning's sense) 59, *101*, 102, 106, 143, 264, 302, *see also* mimesis of narration; ~ in *Nutshell* 241, 244; ~ in *Skagboys* 286
narrative interest 107, 227n9, 239, *see also* curiosity, narrative intrigue, suspense, surprise
narrative intrigue 237, 238
narrative levels 31n17, 35, 36, 37, 39, 42, 65n2, 67, 143, *see also* story/discourse distinction, metalepsis
narrative norm (Fleischman) 33, *36*, 318
narrative pause 10, 102, 115, 131, 133
narrative planes *see* narrative levels
narrative progression 122, 123n71, 124, 125, 126, 238, 304, 313, *see also* narrative dynamics; ~ in *Dead Men's Trousers* 298; ~ in *The Power of the Dog* 220–221, 236
narrative setting 60n14, 70, 76, 94, 97, 101, 124, 125, 128, 131, 142, 160, 168, 175, 176, 192n29, 213; ~ of *Maps for Lost Lovers* 205, 206, 209, 210, 216; ~ of *Nutshell* 246; ~ of *Oryx and Crake* 182, 190, 192; ~ of *The Power of the Dog* 221, 222, 223, 227, 313; ~ of *Room* 260, 271
narrative situation (Stanzel) 41, 42, 59–60, 65n2, 89n12, 113, 117, 143, 263, 305, 306, 311, *see also* authorial narrative situation, figural narrative situation,

first-person narrative situation; ~ in *Nutshell* 247; ~ in *The Power of the Dog* 220, 228, 230, 231
narrative urgency 16, 56, 57, 302, 317; ~ in *The Power of the Dog* 227, 239
narrativity 9, 26, 34, 58, 128, 178, 179
narrativization (Fludernik) 73, 85n5, 166, 178–179, 187–188
narratized description 132
narratology
– classical ~ 8, 85n4, 131n84, see also structuralist ~
– cognitive ~ 8, 81
– context-oriented ~ 85
– contextualist ~ 17, 306, 308, see also context-oriented ~
– cultural ~ 318
– diachronic ~ 306, 307
– discourse-oriented ~ 59
– eco-~ 177–178
– feminist ~ 308
– formal ~ 17
– historical ~ see diachronic ~
– intercultural ~ 196–197
– linguistic ~ 8, 279
– postclassical ~ 8, 17n25
– psycho-~ 56–57
– rhetorical ~ 8, 122; ~ in *Maps for Lost Lovers* 205
– story-oriented ~ 59n9
– structuralist ~ 8, see also classical ~
– text-centered ~ 85
– transmedial ~ 17, 85n4, 306
narratorial comment 39, 91, 92, 104, 106, 246n11; ~ in *Maps for Lost Lovers* 203–205; ~ in *Nutshell* 253; ~ in *The Power of the Dog* 229; ~ in *Wolf Hall* and *Bring Up the Bodies* 159, 160, 162
'natural' narrative (Fludernik) 178, 244, 287, see also conversational narrative
naturalization 72, 73, 85n5, 178, 193; ~ in *Nutshell* 245–247; ~ in *Skagboys* 296
natureculture (Haraway) 184
new media (including social media) 313–315
New Novel see *nouveau roman*

non-fictional discourse 12, 24n7, 27, 30n11, 32, 33n21, 35, 53, 61n15, 115n57, 129n81
'non-place' (in Augé's sense) *176*, 221
nouveau roman 5, 24n8, 33, 44, 130
novel expansion *276–279*

omnipresence, narratorial; ~ in *The Power of the Dog* 230; ~ in *Wolf Hall* and *Bring Up the Bodies* 160
omniscience, narratorial; ~ in *Maps for Lost Lovers* 201n9; ~ in *The Power of the Dog* 220, 230, 236, 239; ~ in *Skagboys* 280, 291; ~ in *Wolf Hall* and *Bring Up the Bodies* 160
oral narrative/orature 33, 56, 68n12, 106n37, 145, 285
orality 108, 110, 302; ~ in *Skagboys* 279, 299
orality vs. literacy/oral vs. written narrative 145, 285n14; ~ in *Dead Men's Trousers* 300; ~ in *Skagboys* 289–292, 299
order (Genette) 142, see also analepsis, prolepsis, temporal ordering
orientation (for the reader)
– spatial ~ 304; ~ in *The Power of the Dog* 225, 227; ~ in *Wolf Hall* and *Bring Up the Bodies* 169
– spatiotemporal ~ 93, 94, 304; ~ in *Maps for Lost Lovers* 200
– temporal ~ 89n12; ~ in *Nutshell* 140
overt narration 59, 60n13, 65, 101, 106, 118, 119, 121, 134, 169, 187, 192, 305; ~ in *The Power of the Dog* 229, 230; ~ in *Wolf Hall* and *Bring Up the Bodies* 158, 159, 161

pace 57, 84, 115, 125, 133, 142, 215, see also acceleration, deceleration; ~ in *Maps for Lost Lovers* 210, 214–215; ~ in *The Power of the Dog* 221, 225, 227, 238, 314
past-tense vs. present-tense narration see present-tense vs. past-tense narration
person (as narratological category) 7, 24n7, 31, 55, 59–60, 61, 143n4, 306
perspectival present 28
perspective see external focalization, internal focalization

perspective structure 230–231
perspective taking 258n3; ~ in *Maps for Lost Lovers* 213; ~ in *Room* 266–275
picaresque novel 186
place, sense of 125n75, 142
plot 70, 71, 91, 95, 100, 124n72, 128, 130, 160, 178, 186, 192n29, 237, 253n17; ~ of *Maps for Lost Lovers* 210; ~ of *Nutshell* 241, 242, 245, 247, 248, 250–251, 252, 254, 256; ~ of *Oryx and Crake* 185–187, 190; ~ of *The Power of the Dog* 220, 223, 224, 227, 232, 234, 313; ~ of *Room* 271; ~ of *Skagboys* and *Dead Men's Trousers* 279; ~ of *Wolf Hall* and *Bring Up the Bodies* 161, 163
– ~ in Lotman's sense *184–185*
– (in)consistency of ~ in *Maps for Lost Lovers* 211–213
poetic language 315; ~ in *Maps for Lost Lovers* 199, 206–208, 214, 215
poetry 21, 27, 34, 144, 206–207
post-apocalyptic fiction 173–193
posterior narration *see* retrospective narration
posthuman space 180; ~ in *Oryx and Crake* 182–183, 184, 193
postmodernist fiction 27, 71, 153, 265, 276, 311, 313
prequel *277–278*, 304
present shock (Rushkoff) 312, 313
present-tense vs. past-tense narration (differences) 8, 12, 15, 54, 58–59, 61, 95, 98, 123, 124, 154n7, 258–259, 268, 301, 302, 306
principle of minimal departure *95–96*, 97, 193
prior narration *see* prospective narration
prison novel 271n18
projective locations *191*
prolepsis *see* flashforward
prospective narration 37, 100, 110n47, 112, 113, 116n59, 143, 152, 304, 318; ~ in *Wolf Hall* and *Bring Up the Bodies* 165
pseudo-description 132
pseudo-orality *285n14*
psychological fiction 271
psycho-narration 44, 265

qualia *180*; ~ in *Oryx and Crake* 182
quoted monologue 109; ~ in *Oryx and Crake* 189; ~ in *The Power of the Dog* 222

reader/readership
– flesh-and-blood ~ 85, 97, 107, 125n75, 202, 233
– implied ~ 92n18, 96, 97, 255n20
– in-group ~ 198; ~ of *Maps for Lost Lovers* 199–205
– intended ~ 197; ~ of *Maps for Lost Lovers* 202
– out-group ~ 198
readerly dynamics *227*, 238
reader's address 92, 96, 106
realist writing 27, 38–39, 109, 110, 130
real-time reporting 9, 115n57, 301
refamiliarization 248
reflector figure (Stanzel) 264; ~ in *The Power of the Dog* 229, 230; ~ in *Wolf Hall* and *Bring Up the Bodies* 158, 163, 199n8
reflector-mode narrative 90n14, 92, 96, 116, 117n60, 119, 120, 265; ~ in *Maps for Lost Lovers* 200; ~ in *Oryx and Crake* 190
reflexive present *see* discursive present
repeating narration 10
report (as discourse mode) 129
reportability *see* tellability
retrospective narration 17–18, 29, 35, 37, 39n31, 40–41, 42, 55, 91, 95, 100, 111–112, 113, 115, 116n59, 118n61, 121, 143, 152, 230, 258, 264, 294, 304, 305n2, 312, 318; ~ in *Oryx and Crake* 189–190; ~ in *The Power of the Dog* 221; ~ in *Wolf Hall* and *Bring Up the Bodies* 165, 171
risk narrative *173–174*
– narrative of anticipation *173–174*
– narrative of catastrophe *173–174*, 175–177
romance 5
route perspective *191*

scene/scenic narration 10, 114–115, 117, *see also* isochrony; ~ in *Nutshell* 247, 250; ~ in *The Power of the Dog* 226
science fiction 1, 175n5
second-person narrative 7, 55, 92, 96, 106, 143, 306

self-reference 99n29, *see also* self-reflection
self-reflection 99n29, 154
semantics of space (Lotman) 183, *184–185*, 187
sequels *276–277*, 278, 279, 304
short story 2, 41n34, 56, 140n2
simultaneity (between narrative events and narrative mediation) 27, 42, 95, 111, 117, 119, 146, 235, 263, 272, *see also* real-time reporting, simultaneous focalization, simultaneous narration, simultaneous presentation, synchronicity
simultaneous focalization 116–117, *118–119*, 189, 266, 303–304
simultaneous narration 9, 10, 13, 36, 37–40, 55, 56, 95, 110–116, *118–119*, 143, 146, 265–266, 294, 301, 303, 304, 305, 312, 314, 318, *see also* real-time reporting; ~ in *Maps for Lost Lovers* 213; ~ in *Nutshell* 240–241; ~ in *The Power of the Dog* 227, 230, 239; ~ in *Room* 260, 264–265, 267, 268, 270, 273, 274; ~ in *Skagboys* 296
simultaneous presentation *118–119*, 188, 189, 236, 265–266, 303, 304, *see also* simultaneous focalization, simultaneous narration
singulative narration 10
situatedness (Herman) *106*
small stories *288*; ~ in *Skagboys* 288, 291
social acceleration (Rosa) 311, 312, 313, 314, 315
space, representation of 57, 84, 124–125, 142, 148, 302, *see also* topochrone, spatial non-contextualization
spatial non-contextualization 304; ~ in *The Power of the Dog* 222, 224; ~ in *Wolf Hall* and *Bring Up the Bodies* 168–169, 171
speculative fiction 1, 175n5, 317
speech (as discourse mode) 30n15, 129, 130, 135, 136
speech report 247, 268
speed *see* narrative pace
story/discourse distinction 31n17, 35, 39, 41n33, 65, 100, 101, 144, 238, 255–256, 266, 268, 306; ~ in *Maps for Lost Lovers* 201
story-driven experience (Caracciolo) 179–180, 193
story time vs. discourse time 114, 115, 213, 226
storyworld (Herman) 10, 15, 16, 43, 48, 49, 55, 60, 61, 71, *81–82*, 85, 89, 91, 93, 94, 95n24, 96, 97, 98, 100, 104, 105, 110, 116, 117, 120, 122, 124, 126, 127, 129, 132, 138, 142, 171, 173, 179, 277, 279, 303, 304, 305; ~ of *Maps for Lost Lovers* 199, 200, 201, 205, 213, 215, 315; ~ of *Nutshell* 241, 242, 244, 245, 246; ~ of *Oryx and Crake* 176, 177, 180, 181, 182–183, 184, 186, 187, 189, 191, 192; ~ of *The Power of the Dog* 222, 224, 227, 235, 236; ~ of *Room* 259, 262, 270, 274; ~ of *Skagboys* and *Dead Men's Trousers* 299; ~ of *Wolf Hall* and *Bring Up the Bodies* 160n18, 162, 166, 168
structuralist taxonomy (Genette) 305
style 21, 30n15, 60n14, 76, 78, 81, 84, 110, 126, 154, 214n23, 227n8, 285n14, 293n21, 294, 304; ~ in *Maps for Lost Lovers* 195, 198, 206, 212; ~ in *The Power of the Dog* 226, 314; ~ in *Room* 260
subsequent narration *see* retrospective narration
sujet 26
summary (as a category of duration) 10, 133; ~ in *Nutshell* 247
surprise (as a type of narrative interest) 17, *237–238*, 302, 303; ~ in *Dead Men's Trousers* 298; ~ in *The Power of the Dog* 221, 238–239, 313
suspense 16, 17, 236, *237*, 238, 302, 303; ~ in *The Power of the Dog* 221, 238–239, 313; ~ in *Room* 271
– what ~ 227n9
synchronic focalization 117
synchronicity (between story time and discourse time) 9, 41n34, 56, 95, 110, 113, 115, 120, 123, 127, 146, 189, 238, 250, 252, 265–266, 305n2, *see also* simultaneous focalization, simultaneous

narration, simultaneous presentation, simultaneity; ~ in *Maps for Lost Lovers* 212, 217; ~ in *Nutshell* 249–250; ~ in *Oryx and Crake* 187; ~ in *The Power of the Dog* 219; ~ in *Room* 258, 268, 270
synthetic dimension of narrative 98

teleology 40, 41n34, 187; ~ in *Skagboys* 291, 299; ~ in *Wolf Hall* and *Bring Up the Bodies* 170; lack of ~ in *Oryx and Crake* 186–187; lack of ~ in *The Power of the Dog* 235
tellability 106–108, 109, 187n22, 286, 287, 296
– dark boundary of ~ 298
teller-mode narrative 90, 101, 116, 118, 120, 121, 134, 264, 265
teller/reflector dichotomy 90, 96, 106
'telling to the moment' 304, see also 'writing to the moment'; ~ in *Dead Men's Trousers* 279, 296–298, 299, 300
telling vs. showing 125; ~ in *The Power of the Dog* 225, 227
temporal distance between story and narrative discourse 28, 29, 36, 41, 55, 66, 69, 100, 101n31, 102, 103, 110, 112, 115, 116, 117, 118, 124, 143, 165, 255, 305; ~ in *Maps for Lost Lovers* 213; ~ in *Nutshell* 247; ~ in *Skagboys* 290; ~ in *Wolf Hall* and *Bring Up the Bodies* 170; lack of ~ in *Nutshell* 255; lack of ~ in *Room* 265, 267; lack of ~ in *Skagboys* 290
temporal ordering
– anachronic/non-chronological presentation of events 65, 66, 126, 142, 277, 278
– chronological presentation of events 65, 100, 133, 142, 235n18, 277; ~ in *Nutshell* 254n18; ~ in *Oryx and Crake* 186, 189; ~ in *The Power of the Dog* 225; ~ in *Room* 269
temporal relation between narrative events and narrative mediation 8, 10, 13, 29, 37, 43, 48, 54, 58, 61, 66n5, 101, 113, 116, 142
temporal structure of narrative 29, 38n30, 46–50, 65, 78, 91n16, 165, 252, 277, see

also double temporality of narrative; ~ in *Wolf Hall* and *Bring Up the Bodies* 166
temporalization (as a form of tense-switching) 14–15, 69, 93, 122n68, 302; ~ in *Maps for Lost Lovers* 199, 200, 201, 209; ~ in *Oryx and Crake* 181
tense
– definition of fictional ~ 61
– definition of grammatical ~ 61
– grammatical tense vs. fictional tense 13, 266, 301, 310
tense alternation 13–14, 32, 68–72, 74, 76, 79, 80, 88–89, 93, 101, 102, 103, 303, 310, see also tense-mixing, tense-switching; ~ in *Maps for Lost Lovers* 199–205, 209; ~ in *Room* 274–275; ~ in *Skagboys* 295, 299; ~ in *Wolf Hall* and *Bring Up the Bodies* 160
tense-mixing 13, 71–72, 74, 76, 79, 80, 302
tense shift see tense alternation
tense structure of narrative (Currie) 11, 318, see also temporal structure of narrative; ~ in *Nutshell* 253; ~ in *Room* 274
tense-switching 13, 69–71, 74, 76, 79, 80, 93, 302, see also conversational historical present, detemporalization, historical present, temporalization
tense usage, formal aspects of 13, 64–68
– central ~ 13, 67, 79, 80, 302
– global ~ 13, 66, 67, 79, 80, 83, 134, 302, 303; ~ in *Maps for Lost Lovers* 216; ~ in *Nutshell* 242, 274; ~ in *Oryx and Crake* 191, 193; ~ in *Room* 270; ~ in *Skagboys* 291; ~ in *Wolf Hall* and *Bring Up the Bodies* 154
– heterogeneous ~ 13, 64, 65–66, 79, 80, 101, 302, 310; ~ in *Maps for Lost Lovers* 212; ~ in *Oryx and Crake* 180–182; ~ in *Skagboys* 292, 293
– homogeneous ~ 13, 64–65, 79, 80, 301
– local ~ 13, 66–67, 79, 80, 302
– peripheral ~ 13, 67–68, 79, 80, 302
tensed understanding of time (A-theory) 46–50
tenseless understanding of time (B-theory) 12, 46–50, 309

tensions (Phelan) *123*
text type 30, 32, 34, 43, 45, 128, 129n81, 252n14
textual dynamics *227*, 238
thematic dimension of narrative 98n28
third-person narrative/narrator 7, 22, 24, 32, 38n30, 39, 42, 59, 60, 61, 88, 90, 91n17, 106, 109, 120, 121, 306, *see also* heterodiegetic narration; ~ in *Oryx and Crake* 188n24; ~ in *The Power of the Dog* 228; ~ in *Skagboys* 299
thought report 222
thriller 1, 5, 15, 16, 144, 219–239, 270, 271, 313
– psychological ~ 271
timespaces 89, 92, 94, 97, 122, 124, 277, 278, 303, 308; ~ in *Maps for Lost Lovers* 199, 206, 208, 209, 210, 315
topochrone 124, *125*–127, 128, 303, 304, *see also* circumlepsis, hyper-analepsis, hyper-prolepsis; ~ in *Maps for Lost Lovers* 199, 200, 205–213, 216, 217, 315
tour strategy *see* route perspective
tour structure 186
traditional narratological paradigm (e.g. Genette and Stanzel) 8–9, 11, 13, 35, 37–40, 44, 46, 54, 59, 65n3, 304–306
transcultural fiction *197*
turning point 17, *166*, 174n3, 188n23; ~ in *Wolf Hall* and *Bring Up the Bodies* 166–167
typological circle (Stanzel) 106, 228, 264n10, 305
– authorial-figural continuum 228

ulterior narration *see* retrospective narration
underreporting 234
'unnatural' narration 17, 119, 121, 144, 148; ~ in *Nutshell* 243–248, 257
unreliability *see* unreliable narration

unreliable narration 17, 40, 60, 144, 148, 231n12, 302, 308, *see also* fallible narration, underreporting; ~ in *Room* 260, 270
– altered ~ in *The Power of the Dog* 234–235
– ironic-~ in *Room* 269
untrustworthiness *see* unreliable narration

vibrant matter (Bennett) 184
voice (as narratological category) 29, 37, 57, 59, 61, 106, 114, 116n59, 129, 133, 143, 148, 160, 302, 305, 306; ~ in *Maps for Lost Lovers* 199; ~ in *Nutshell* 243, 248; ~ in *Oryx and Crake* 187; ~ in *The Power of the Dog* 229; ~ in *Room* 257, 260, 263, 272; ~ in *Skagboys* and *Dead Men's Trousers* 280, 289, 290, 291; ~ in *Wolf Hall* and *Bring Up the Bodies* 159, 161

we (first-person pronoun plural) 55; ~ in *Nutshell* 244n9; ~ in *Wolf Hall* and *Bring Up the Bodies* 171
'we'-narrative 55, 90, 106, 143, 244n9, 306
world building 10n21, 15, 122, 137, *see also* worldmaking
worldmaking 9–11, 14, 15, 54, 81–85, 93, 94, 122, 136–139, 175, 301, 308, 309, *see also* world building; ~ in *Nutshell* 240–256; ~ in *Oryx and Crake* 182, 183
– expansive ~ 277, 304, *see also* novel expansion
'writing to the moment' (Richardson) 78, *293*–296, 304
written narrative 292–296, 299

you (second-person pronoun) 55; ~ in *Oryx and Crake* 191–192
young adult fiction 5

zero point (deixis) *see* deictic center

www.ingramcontent.com/pod-product-compliance
Lightning Source LLC
Chambersburg PA
CBHW031751220426
43662CB00007B/356